SOC

INEQUALITY

& THE POLITICS
OF REPRESENTATION

SOCIAL INEQUALITY

& THE POLITICS OF REPRESENTATION

A Global Landscape

Celine-Marie Pascale

American University, Washington DC

Editor

Los Angeles | London | New Delhi
Singapore | Washington DC

Los Angeles | London | New Delhi
Singapore | Washington DC

FOR INFORMATION:

SAGE Publications, Inc.
2455 Teller Road
Thousand Oaks, California 91320
E-mail: order@sagepub.com

SAGE Publications Ltd.
1 Oliver's Yard
55 City Road
London EC1Y 1SP
United Kingdom

SAGE Publications India Pvt. Ltd.
B 1/I 1 Mohan Cooperative Industrial Area
Mathura Road, New Delhi 110 044
India

SAGE Publications Asia-Pacific Pte. Ltd.
3 Church Street
#10-04 Samsung Hub
Singapore 049483

Acquisitions Editor: David Repetto
Editorial Assistant: Lauren Johnson
Production Editor: Eric Garner
Copy Editor: Janet Ford
Typesetter: C&M Digitals (P) Ltd.
Proofreader: Joyce Li
Cover Designer: Scott Van Atta
Marketing Manager: Erica DeLuca
Permissions Editor: Karen Ehrmann

Copyright © 2013 by SAGE Publications, Inc.

Printed in the United States of America

Library of Congress Cataloging-in-Publication Data

Social inequality & the politics of representation : a global landscape / [edited by] Celine-Marie Pascale.

p. cm.
Includes bibliographical references.

ISBN 978-1-4129-9221-3 (pbk.)

1. Equality. 2. Social stratification. I. Pascale, Celine-Marie, 1956- II. Title: Social inequality and the politics of representation.

HM821.S645 2013
305—dc23   2012031488

This book is printed on acid-free paper.

SUSTAINABLE FORESTRY INITIATIVE
Certified Chain of Custody
Promoting Sustainable Forestry
www.sfiprogram.org
SFI-01268
SFI label applies to text stock

12 13 14 15 16 10 9 8 7 6 5 4 3 2

BRIEF CONTENTS

ANNOTATED TABLE OF CONTENTS

Section 2: Race

Section 3: Sexuality

destabilize cultural and political landscapes. She illustrates how these soap operas simultaneously produce competing discourses of nostalgia for the past relationships between Turkey and Bulgaria and xenophobia with respect to their current relationship.

18. Weizhun Mao. *Tiny Netizens Mocking the Great Firewall: Discourse, Power, and the Politics of Representation in China, 2005 to 2010*

Weizhun Mao uses discourse analysis to examine a variety of Internet sites, including chatrooms, bulletin boards, blogs, microblogs, and social networking services to highlight the online struggle between government censors and Internet users in China. Mao demonstrates how Internet users, known as netizens, employ a variety of strategies, including the formation of a new language that generates a sense of identity and community, as they subvert censorship.

19. Roberta Villalón. *Framing Extreme Violence: The Collective Memory-Making of Argentina's Dirty War*

One of the bloodiest phases of Argentinean history began 35 years ago. Known commonly as the Dirty War, tens of thousands of people were disappeared, tortured, and killed. Roberta Villalón uses Goffman's frame analysis to examine two testimonial accounts of this period in time—one official and one unofficial—in order to understand public efforts to shape collective memory. Villalón powerfully demonstrates that collective memory is a political struggle for the future.

20. Margarita Astoyants. *The Changing Dynamics of Political Discourse About Orphans in Soviet and Post-Soviet Periods*

Orphanages in Russia first appeared in the 17th century and continue to this day. Margarita Astoyants examines the discursive construction of what it means to be an orphan during three key historical moments in Russian history: the October Revolution and Civil War (1920–1926); the Great Patriotic War (1941–1945); and Perestroika (2002–2005; 2008–2009). Using poststructural discourse analysis of newspapers and radio programs from the State Archive of the Rostov Region, she skillfully illustrates how public discourse about the meaning and presence of orphans shapes public reaction.

INTRODUCTION

As globalization continues to transform social and economic processes in ways that profoundly affect daily lives, it is important that scholars and students have access to research that offers both insights and tools for understanding the (re)production of inequalities in a global landscape. In a global landscape it is necessary to understand the practices of representation through which inequalities gain meaning—both within and across national boundaries.

As an international collection of critical scholarship, *Social Inequality & The Politics of Representation: A Global Landscape* takes a fresh look at inequalities in 20 countries on 5 continents. It offers both rich insight and cultural critique—yet it does not offer a universal paradigm, nor is it concerned with debates about scholarship from "the center" or "the periphery." The collection answers the call advanced by scholars such as Patel (2010) and Connell (2007) who advocate a de-centering of North American/European sociology by placing scholarship from countries around the globe on equal footing.

The authors in this book examine representational practices that make inequalities meaningful in specific ways at particular times and places. This style of analysis enables readers to make connections across national boundaries and across categories of nationality, race, class, gender, and sexuality. For example, readers are able to consider how the strategies of power evident in the gendering practices of "civilizing" Kurdish women in Turkey have resonance with the strategies of power used to marginalize indigenous peoples and languages in Mexico—as well as perceive a similar outline of power deployed strategically by transgendered men in Malaysia who construct their own language to resist oppression. In these chapters, readers are introduced to the ways language can be mobilized to marginalize and oppress groups of people as well how it can be mobilized as a form of resistance.

Throughout, readers will find that national discourses variously marginalize and privilege groups of people within the nation-state and that these discourses have key commonalities and differences. Consequently, readers will find new insights into how power, privilege, and inequality gain meaning and legitimacy across a range of cultures. *Social Inequality & The Politics of Representation* takes up timely issues around the globe, including: analyses of media debates in Austria regarding the right of Muslim women to wear veils; the cultural policing of sexuality in Nigeria; strategic subversion of Internet censorship in China; and political asylum cases for lesbian women and gay men in Italy. Each chapter provides a general overview of relevant cultural and historical contexts for an international audience as well as a brief introduction to relevant methodological and theoretical frameworks. Consequently, it is a richly diverse and accessible collection.

Social Inequality & The Politics of Representation makes important and unique contributions to literature on inequalities by analyzing how inequalities are constructed in traditional media, new media, and personal interaction. For example, research in this book includes analyses of television in Bulgaria and Turkey, newspaper articles in Brazil, South Korea, Serbia, and Ireland, talk radio shows in South Africa, interviews in Mexico, planning policies in the United States, historical documents in Russia, photographs in Austria, international media in Uganda, conversations in Mexico and Malaysia, new media in China, and artwork in Germany.

Authors in this book define language broadly as that which communicates meaning. As such "language" includes all systems of representation—all processes of signification. As a consequence, readers will find a variety of analytical styles, including frame analysis, semiotics, poststructural discourse analysis, critical discourse studies, and conversation analysis. Chapters animate these analytical frameworks in ways that do not require prior expertise—thus making the book useful to graduate methods and theory courses that take up issues of language and society, as well as to substantive undergraduate courses on inequalities.

As a collection of international scholarship, *Social Inequality & The Politics of Representation* examines a variety of practices and contexts used to construct privilege and inequality. In essence, the chapters explore relationships between practices of accumulation, dispossession, and political power (Gray, 2010, p. 17) as they emerge around the globe today. The book examines how particular kinds of social subjects are constructed in public imagination and draws out relationships between knowledge and power. In the process, *Social Inequality & The Politics of Representation: A Global Landscape* provides a conceptual vocabulary for understanding the production of inequality and privilege that travels beyond the North American framework of intersectionality.

LANGUAGE AND REPRESENTATION

The book begins with the premise that everything we know about the social world comes to us through language. Everything gains meaning, importance, and relevance through systems of language—even our inner most thoughts are constructed through language. Consider the material reality of a stand of trees. It exists, one could point to it. Yet, one person may see the trees as cubits of lumber, another may see them as a sacred grove, another may see them as a place to camp, and a fourth may see them as obstacles to clear for development. Even while the physical presence of the trees is the same for everyone, the *meaning* of them may not be. Meaning cannot be separated from context or from the language used to make sense of both the context and the trees. The analyses in this book do not juxtapose false and true knowledge, but rather explore the practices through which knowledge comes to appear objective and social life meaningful.

In daily life, we often believe that we simply recognize the world around us. However, it is impossible to perceive anything just by looking. Consider the example of money—the meaning of money must "already be there" before we look at it, in order for us to understand what it is and how to use it. To the extent that we can recognize money when we see it, we are seeing through a cultural eye. This is true when we think about the trees, and even when we think about ourselves. These fairly simple examples become quite complicated when we also consider how language, as a system of representation, (re)produces relations of power.

Knowledge is created through language; knowledge is also legitimized or marginalized through language. At both national and global levels we can see this in discussion of issues such as global warming and population growth. Further, knowledge is always a cultural enterprise—not an individual one. Even cognition and perception are cultural as well as individual processes. Consequently, many scholars in this book adopt Michele Foucault's expression of knowledge/power to indicate that all knowledge is an expression of power and all power is an expression of knowledge—they cannot meaningfully be separated from each other. Consequently, the creation of knowledge is always a political act—one that naturalizes and rationalizes particular relations of power. Even the gross power of physical violence begins with some form of dehumanizing language. In the 21st century, this may have become most evident in debates that frame one person's "freedom fighter" as another person's "terrorist." How we each learn to name ourselves and the world around us is an expression of knowledge/power. Social identities are not an essence but a positioning constructed through systems of representation (including memory, myth, news, and science) all of which are implicated in networks of power.

Language is always fraught with conscious and unconscious motivations, competing investments, political perspectives, and economic interests. As a signifying practice, language produces both knowledge/power and tangible material consequences. Consequently, *Social Inequality & The Politics of Representation* examines the "politics of representation"—the cultural struggles over how events, processes, people, institutions, and countries are to be understood. In this sense, the book examines language as a point of articulation between social structures and social life, as well as between social imagination and social being. Studies of language/representation offer sociologists a particularly productive site of investigation because they regard individual agency, social constraint, and the cultural organization of knowledge/power. Bertrand Russell (1938, p. 10) once said that the fundamental concept in the social science is power—in the same sense in which energy is the fundamental concept in physics. Sociological studies of language offer an effective tool for making visible the ways that power operates in everyday practices.

Language is a cultural system par excellence. "Without language there is no social interaction; without social interaction there is no social structure, no culture" (Pascale, 2011, p. 162). Sociological analyses of language and representation push the formal boundaries between social theory and empirical analyses as they bring new insights into the (re)production of culture, knowledge, and power. The chapters in this book exemplify some of the best work in studies of language and society.

The authors in this collection write in a time when debates regarding the nature of relationships between secular and religious communities abound—as do debates about technology, globalization, and global media. The chapters offer insight as well as opportunities for discussion and debate on how inequalities experienced locally are (re)produced globally, as well as what it means to produce authoritative knowledge about social life. In this sense, the chapters work at getting at the liminal, or in between, spaces where new ways to understand ourselves and others emerge.

The 21st century challenges the familiar juxtaposition between local and global contexts. It has become increasingly important to think of local contexts as much more than an immediate context. To a significant extent, locality is a dynamic integrative environment—both spatially and historically (Pennycook, 2010). From this perspective, language and representation are more than local practices—they are practices through which locality is created. Language and representation are not activities that take place within contexts, but practices that create, shape, and define contexts. In this sense, language and representation are constitutive practices—they are the primary way in which social life is organized and made meaningful.

As a collection of perspectives on language, society, and inequality, the book's overarching contribution to the field of sociology draws from vibrant international and diverse transdisciplinary scholarship that includes cultural studies, communication, media studies, anthropology, and socio-linguistics. Across and within all fields that study language/representation, the word "discourse" is used frequently. Even within a single discipline and within a single country, this word can refer to a broad range of things. So it is all the more reason that the word "discourse" warrants some discussion. Each chapter provides a definition of "discourse" as it is used in that particular analysis as well as an overview of key analytic strategies. For now, suffice it to say that the word "discourse" can be used to refer to: conversation or discussion; a lecture, speech, or treatise; language-in-use (spoken or written words); a specialized form of knowledge/jargon (legal discourse); as schema that organize ways of thinking; and as a system of representation that produces objects of knowledge. In some fields, such as Critical Discourse Analysis, the word discourse may be used to mean all of these things in a single article—leaving readers to parse the particular meaning of the word through context and usage.

Given this range and variation regarding the word "discourse," there are a few important things that can be said about five of its six variations: Discursive practices produce characteristic ways of seeing by drawing boundaries that define what we see and fail to see, what we accept and contest. Consequently, discursive practices distinguish characteristic ways of speaking and writing as well as ways of interpreting events. The exception to these statements is the understanding of "discourse" as a synonym for "conversation." Technically speaking, this particular usage is not part of any specific analytic framework but expresses an overlap between vernacular and scholarly language.

Just as every text is intertextual (drawing from and contributing to other texts), it is also true that every text is polysemic—meaning it can be read in more than one way. The polysemic nature of texts makes the work of textual analysis both important and challenging. At a minimum, the authors in this book share a common goal, which is to demonstrate the kinds of logic that make everyday practices meaningful.

This collection includes 10 different frameworks for analyzing language: Conversation Analysis, Critical Discourse Analysis, Cultural Studies, Discourse Analysis, Frame Analysis, Semiotics, Socio-linguistics, Poststructural Discourse Analysis, Textual Analysis, and blended strategies that incorporate several of these approaches. It also includes a range of empirical analyses of texts, theoretical studies of language and blended analyses. The analytical frameworks in this collection take up different levels of analysis. Conversation analysis and sociolinguists

focus on conversation in a very narrow context while semiotics and poststructural discourse analysis focus more broadly on cultural issues and signifying practices. Frame analysis, textual analysis, critical discourse, and cultural studies offer insights gained from blending levels of analysis—each in slightly different ways. Overall, the breadth of analytical frameworks showcases the richness of theories and methods for producing sociological studies of language and their usefulness for understanding inequalities in a global landscape.

INEQUALITIES IN A GLOBAL LANDSCAPE

Studies of inequality are at the core of Sociology and many other social sciences. But what is inequality? To whom do we seek to be equal? On the one hand, the concept of equality expresses an ideal that all people are treated fairly and have access to the same social and economic opportunities. In this sense, everyone would belong to the nation-state as a full citizen—not only in a formal sense of documentation but also a daily sense of belonging. So what does it mean to treat people "fairly"? Is it fair to treat everyone the same or does fairness demand taking into account the ways that groups of people have been systematically disadvantaged? What constitutes "the same social and economic resources"? In the United States, for example, there is an often tacit understanding that the resources and cultural citizenship available to middle-class white men tend to be the standard against which inequalities are measured. On closer consideration, we would find this group to be narrowed even more by (dis)ability, heterosexuality, and religion. In the United States, tacit knowledge would lead us to expect that everyone should have access to the same forms of education, housing, employment, income, health care, legal protection, and quality of life that is considered to be "ordinary" for this group. In reality this "ordinary" standard of living is dependent on inequality. It is impossible for everyone to achieve anything like this quality of life. As is true in many countries, the United States depends on people who have little education to labor for low wages in jobs such as picking crops, cleaning offices, caring for children, and washing dishes. People who hold these jobs often live in substandard housing; their children generally have access to poor educations and their families have little health care. For low-wage workers, life is marked by uncertainty and insecurity. Imagine all of the forms of low-wage work that exist. Now imagine the cost of services if people doing this work were paid a living wage that made health care, education, and good housing possible.

Privilege is a system of social structures and dynamics that organize and distribute resources along particular lines. Privilege is secured when marginality and dispossession are naturalized. Consequently, people who benefit from low-wage work learn to believe that "unskilled" workers—like those who labor in the fields—deserve to be paid little. The current system of agriculture demands a large body of unskilled workers to harvest our food—their life chances are not an accident. So, if we are going to advocate equality, we need to be willing to rethink the nature of privilege.

On a global scale, North America and Europe might be considered the standard against which material inequality is measured. Yet as early as 1998, the United Nations Human Development Report documented that only 20% of the world's population lived in the wealthiest countries and yet they consumed 86% of all goods and services. In this context, what does "equality" mean? As world consumption expands at an unprecedented rate, the United Nations reports that 2.6 billion people lack basic sanitation, 1.3 billion have no access to clean water, 1.1 billion lack adequate housing. There are not enough resources in the world to create anything like "equality" unless many of us are willing to live with considerably less.

How committed are you to resolving inequality now? What changes would you be willing to make in your standard of living so that others could have access to clean water and sanitation? Keep in mind that access to water and sanitation is just a starting point—it's probably not how

anyone reading this book thinks about equality. To solve the problems of inequality, we need to solve the problems of privilege. Sociological studies of representational practices through which the presence and meaning of inequalities and privilege are constructed can help us to address material disparities.

Social Inequality & *The Politics of Representation* challenges outmoded binary thinking about the symbolic and material, structural and interactional, as well as the local and global. It helps readers to develop insights into the suffering of others and also into the ordinary ways that we each participate in perpetuating that suffering. By linking symbolic practices to their material consequences, social structures to individual actions, and local perspectives to global politics, we can see more clearly how good people perpetuate bad systems. Importantly, through studies of language we come to see the ways in which we are implicated in our own oppression and in the oppression of others. This insight provides tremendous opportunities and resources for change. There are many ways to be involved in changing the world. Studies of language give us one way to reconsider how we can change our own relationships to inequalities.

While human slavery and forms of military domination are on the rise, it is also true that for many people around the globe, systems of inequality are maintained not by physical force but through the complicity of ordinary people. Antonio Gramsci referred to this form of cultural domination as hegemony. Hegemony is established through social processes that persuade ordinary people that the interests and needs of the dominant group are in fact their own. People are dominated not by weapons but by the imposition and elaboration of ideas and habits. In hegemony, the sense of antagonistic domination disappears (Baudrillard, 2010, p. 33). People come to participate in their own oppression by internalizing the social system that subordinates them. For example, in many societies dominated by men, women (most especially heterosexual women) learn to see high-heeled shoes as beautiful and choose to wear them even though they severely limit or disable their basic abilities. High-heeled shoes make walking and standing for extended periods painful and make it impossible to run quickly. The value of high-heeled shoes is not comfort or utility, but the belief that they increase women's sex appeal for men. Similarly class hegemony succeeds when working-class and poor people come to adopt the political views and affiliations of the wealthy. Consider, for example, that every metropolitan newspaper in the United States has a business section but none has a workers section—and no one seems to think this is remarkable. This would seem to be possible only if the interests of business are believed to be the same as the interests of workers—or if the interests of the workers were irrelevant. In a white racial hegemony, people of color adopt the values of white people—such as hairstyles, standards of beauty, ways of speaking, and behaving. Since hegemony literally rewards people for being complicit with their own subordination, people of African descent often succeed more easily if they have white-identified hairstyles.

Although inequalities might once have been created through formal laws, for the most part they continue today as ordinary practices—indeed they so often appear to be ordinary that they come to seem insignificant in the landscape of our days. This is how hegemony works. Yet hegemony is never secured once and for all; it is constantly challenged and renegotiated. Consequently, it becomes very important to examine the relationship between discursive and material realities. By encouraging readers to think deeply about the ways that we reproduce inequalities, this book offers readers the opportunity to think through the ways that we can each interrupt hegemonic systems and begin to make them less sustainable by making them less ordinary.

ABOUT THIS BOOK

Social Inequality & The Politics of Representation: A Global Landscape encourages readers to think in a complicated way about the relationships

between the symbolic, the social, and the material—hence it can be said to articulate the predominant challenge faced by cultural theory. The annotated table of contents provides a familiar organization of chapters by topics of race, class, gender, sexuality, and nationality. This organization has strategic usefulness for classrooms; however, in this section I want to provide a more conceptual framing that offers a dynamic, global perspective on privilege and inequality. This section links together broad issues of language/representation and inequality to demonstrate both the global aspect of these processes and the (re)production of power/knowledge.

In the cultural theory paradigm that juxtaposes local and global contexts, scholars often write about hybridity as a layering of identities. Just as scholars in this collection challenge the juxtaposition of local and global contexts, they challenge the concept of hybridity. Consider that in language use—expressions, images—do not occur for the first time. Every image, every expression is part of an expression that has been repeated before and will be repeated again. This is not to say there is no originality, but that originality is the creative repurposing of the familiar. This can be understood as relocalization of others' expressions (Pennycook, 2010, p. 34). The concept of relocalization leads us to focus on similarity, difference, and repetition.

In this collection, Hong Kong scholar Jackie Jia Lou's critical semiotic reading of "Chinatown" architecture in the capital of the United States is a good example of relocalization. Although people of Chinese ancestry left this community a long time ago, the appearance of a "Chinatown" is maintained through the relocalization of Chinese architecture, language, and art. Lou demonstrates that even planning policy cultivates this relocalization by requiring that business and streets must be in Chinese as well as English. Yet, the benefits of this relocationization of Chinese culture do not accrue to Chinese residents but instead toward largely non-Chinese business owners.

Studies of language examine what is said, how it is said, and what is not said in particular contexts. This is a particularly useful way for understanding how regimes of power/knowledge circulate both over time and place. In English, there is an old adage that the more things change the more they stay the same. Indeed relationships of inequality have changed dramatically in the last decade, yet inequalities continue to increase. Change doesn't always mean things are getting better. Kevin Whitehead's analysis of radio talk shows in post-apartheid South Africa demonstrates some of the ways that white people perpetuate a racialized system while avoiding explicit talk about race. In particular, his study illustrates how white callers made references to wealth and poverty in ways that are clearly meant to indicate race.

The discursive and material linkages between race and class are not unique to South Africa. Roland Terborg and Laura García Landa argue that a narrow focus on economic inequality overlooks the many ways that linguistic racism shapes economic life in profoundly meaningful ways. Indigenous peoples continue to experience the impact of colonial discourses that threaten their own languages and undermine life chances, particularly with regard to education and employment. Terborg and Landa demonstrate that the failure of economies cannot always be measured in numbers—and that economic well-being is not always tethered to purely economic elements. Language is fundamental to identity and to cultural survival—it embodies a way of seeing the world and a way of being in the world.

The power of colonial histories maintains a forward momentum around the globe despite the collapse of colonial empires. Social categories of race, class, gender, sexuality, and nation have all been imagined by, or in dialogue with, colonial classifications. The integrity of these categories is often challenged by contemporary scholarship. For example, scholars have debunked the fiction that everyone has one and only one place in each of the categories of race, ethnicity, class, gender, sexuality, and nationality. However, the added challenge for international and transnational scholarship is to imagine the meanings of difference globally.

Since meaning and imagination are inseparable aspects of processes of signification, Arjun Appadurai's powerful argument for imagination as social practice is particularly relevant to thinking about the production and meaning of difference globally. In the 21st century, a sense of self is conditioned by the experience of globality—rather than by a single cultural logic. By globality, I do not mean an inclusive and integrating global landscape but rather one permeated by what Appadurai refers to as global flows of people, media, finances, technology, and ideas.

In this collection, Nadezhda Georgieva-Stankova demonstrates how the flow of commercial soap operas between Turkey and Bulgaria contributes to shaping both personal identities and cultural politics. Through the transnational flow of soap operas, the histories of Turkey and Bulgaria are drawn into a newly reimagined present that is fraught with power struggles that cultivate both xenophobia and nostalgia. Georgieva-Stankova's engaging analysis of blogs demonstrates how the purportedly simple pleasure of soap opera can destabilize cultural and political landscapes.

The presence of undocumented immigrants in the United States—part of the global flow of migration—is contributing to a new public discourse of race-baiting. While a cultural history of white people in the United States quickly shows that whites have always believed racism to be a thing of the past, public discourse on racism has taken a new turn. By analyzing a conservative television talk show, Shiao-Yun Chiang illustrates that not only are expressions of racism openly sanctioned, so are claims of racism. This interesting account demonstrates how political conservatives will tempt opponents to make claims of racism and then publicly reprimanded them for those views. It is an intricate but common rhetorical move in U.S. public media that relegates the presence of racial inequality to the past by making it nearly impossible to raise the issue in the present.

Scholars in this book take up the identities of race, class gender, and nationality as strategic or tactical identities while rethinking the location of agency and the meanings of difference. Hemant

Shah explores the complicated experiences of belonging and alienation that emerge for generations of Indian-identified residents living in post-Amin, Uganda. Drawing from cultural studies, Shah demonstrates that in a diasporic context transnational media have helped to produce very strategic notions of identity and belonging.

Martin Power, Amanda Haynes, and Eoin Devereux explore the presence and meaning of poverty in Ireland within the broader context of the importance of the myth of classlessness in Ireland's public imaginary. Power, Haynes, and Devereux explode the myth of classlessness by examining media coverage of a marginalized housing estate, Moyross, in Limerick in the Southwest of Ireland. They argue that media are complicit with class warfare "from above" that produces the appearance of classlessness by stigmatizing people who are poor.

Similarly, Viviane de Melo Resende and Vivian Tamalho demonstrate how media in Brazil naturalize the presence of extreme poverty. They argue that journalism (re)produces a discourse that naturalizes homelessness, reifies poverty as a permanent feature of society, and ignores social inequality. Resende and Tamalho explore the power of metaphors used for understanding poverty and how these become part of everyday practices that reinforce the marginalization of people who are homeless.

Scholars in this collection forge new ways of understanding and deconstructing signifying practices that have sustained national and global flows of people, media, finances, technology, and ideas. Yet, "flow" does not accurately capture the violence that often accompanies this movement. Ebru Sungun analyzes the ways that the project of nation building in Turkey targeted women and young girls. The Turkish government paired new social, educational, and economic opportunities for girls with a cultural indoctrination aimed at eradicating Kurdish language and culture. The meanings of Turkish and Kurdish identities were (re)presented through mandatory education.

Sungun's analysis of linguistic genocide will remind readers of the chapter by Terborg and Landa on Indigenous languages and poverty. While nation-states are generally represented as coherent entities, as global citizens we must consistently distinguish between the state—as a legal, political, and economic power—and nations that are composed of people who often hold competing collective identities, despite the commonalities of a shared state. This point is underscored by much of the scholarship in this book. Swedish scholar, Kjerstin Andersson interviews young men about their own use of violence in racialized "fight stories" that construct mirroring positions of immigrant and Swedish forms of masculinity. In her analysis of talk about violence, it is impossible to disentangle youth and masculinity from the discourses of nationalism and racism.

While Andersson considers violence within the changing racial landscape created by immigration, Nataša Simeunović Bajić offers readers a critical analysis of violence against the Roma minority in Serbia—a group of people who have been legal citizens for generations. Bajić illustrates some of the ways that representations of "otherness" maintain cultural alienation. She also places these practices within an important and extensive cultural history of dispossession that brings into question the culpability of individuals, institutions, and the state.

Consistently, readers are reminded that the everyday actions of ordinary people express both agency and constraint. Without question, individuals choose their own words and actions yet these are always also shaped by broader cultural practices. The relationship between the agency and constraint come into sharp focus as Margarita Astoyants examines the representational practices through which the meaning and social value of orphans in Russia has changed over the last century. Astoyants traces how the state at times has honored and at times scorned orphans. She connects government discourses to everyday practices and the tangible consequences for orphaned children.

While Gramsci is perhaps most remembered for his work on the oppressive force of hegemony, he argued that hegemony takes two forms—from above, which is oppressive, and from below (the process through which subaltern views become hegemonic), which is liberating. Language is a powerful force for enacting and resisting oppression; readers will see this in the way that public discourse shapes public belief, in the destruction of Indigenous languages and in the creation of new languages. Weizhun Mao examines language practices that create and sustain a socially sanctioned community of "netizens." Mao explores how Internet users in China employ a variety of linguistic strategies to evade government censors in a multiplicity of online spaces. He demonstrates how process has generated creative practices and at times what appears to be a new form of language that produces a sense of community among users.

Similarly, in Malaysia, *maknyah* (male-to-female transgendered people) have developed their own language to resist oppressive discrimination. Caesar DeAlwis, Maya Khemlani David, and Francisco Perlas Dumanig examine how transgendered women cope with the pressures of living under Islamic law. The creation of a creative and private language not only enables discrete communication, it establishes a sense of community. Intimacy is a potent source of vulnerability around the world for sexual and gender minorities. In a global landscape, intimate vulnerabilities also arise in relationship to immigration.

Valentina Pagliai offers key insights into media and political discourses used to construct political asylum cases for lesbians and gay men. Pagliai closely follows two prominent asylum cases that engaged much of Europe—one for an Iranian lesbian seeking asylum in Britain, and another of an Albanian gay man seeking asylum in Italy. She illustrates how these asylum cases were quickly used in ways that constructed Iran and Albania as lacking modern civilization and thus reinforcing racist positions.

Sexuality and gender are articulated through long histories. Sanya Osha both challenges and rewards readers with a complex analyses of the colonial, Christian, and Islamic discourses that took root in different regions of Nigeria. Osha argues that as a consequence, the construction of the body and of heterosexuality in Nigeria has

developed in very different ways. He offers key insights into the "crisis of manhood" and how these discursive regimes maintain a phallocratic system that oppresses women.

Just as the rise of Islam within countries such as Nigeria and Malaysia transformed established relations of power, the entry of Islam into global, political, and social spheres has troubled dominant ways of thinking. Ricarda Drüeke, Susanne Kirchhoff, and Elisabeth Klaus take up media representations of religious veiling by Muslim women in Austria. Drüeke, Kirchhoff, and Klaus deconstruct nationalist discourses that circulate in photographic images of veiled Muslim women in press photography. On one hand, veiling transgresses spatial and gendered boundaries and confronts the meaning of public space in Western cultures. On the other hand, the practice of veiling offers a complicated politic since Western women's liberation movements have been premised on the right of women to control their own bodies. The practice of veiling challenges prevailing notions of feminism; veiling can both make visible and subsume women's identities. In this sense, the practice of veiling in Europe creates a liminal space, an in-between-ness that produces both proximity and alterity. Importantly, Drüeke, Kirchhoff, and Klaus argue that the presence of Islam in Europe challenges the binaries of public/private life by making religious practice (represented here by veiling) that is generally confined to private realms part of daily public space. The authors level a strong critique challenging the notion of public space as equally available to all people. To large extent, Antke Engel shares this critique as she challenges the self-proclaimed liberal and pluralist discourses of Western nations. In a very thoughtful theoretical essay, Engel explores the paradoxes of inclusive discourses in Germany with respect to queer sexualities. Her analysis deftly shows how the very construction of pluralism depends on a cultural imagination and a set of cultural practices that create disparate publics.

Most broadly, cultural or sociological studies of language analyze the material consequences of social imaginaries. In this sense, they analyze the cultural processes through which we learn to think of ourselves and each other. Hae Yeon Choo and Myra Marx Ferree take up the issue of imagined communities and the politics of belonging with respect to lesbian and gay youth in South Korea. Choo and Ferree analyze newspaper articles about teenage homosexuality and demonstrate how the presence and meaning of lesbian and gay teenagers is constructed and contested in media. To some extent, this analysis returns readers to the notion of global flows since personal intimacies can be attacked as an influence of outside and unwelcome cultural influences that threaten national identity. Choo and Ferree illustrate the various ways that citizenship is always contingent and partial for lesbian and gay youth in South Korea.

Roberta Villalón also advances a critique of social imaginaries through an analysis of cultural memory. She examines public records that document Argentina's "Dirty War" in which tens of thousands of people were "disappeared," tortured, and killed. She argues that in order for the horrors of the "Dirty War" to serve a purpose, they must be remembered both by Argentineans and others—yet historical memory is always political, intertextual, and as much about the present as the past. By examining two accounts of this period—one official and one not—Villalón powerfully demonstrates that collective memory is a political struggle for the future.

In a global landscape it quickly becomes apparent that the ability to control language is one of the most fundamental forms of power. Through language we come to know the world, to value ourselves and others and to find meaning in difference. Through language we come to know our pasts and to imagine our futures. Chapters in this book explore the classificatory power of the state, the representational power of media, as well as the everyday practices of oppression and resistance among average people.

As part of an emergence of a transnational public space, *Social Inequality & The Politics of Representation: A Global Landscape* comes replete with cleavages, contradictions, and overlaps. On the one hand, it displaces Western European scholarship yet on another, it privileges the analytic framework of race, class, gender, sexuality, and nation developed in those countries. Sociology will only truly decenter Western scholarship when it reconstructs its core categories of analysis. Yet at its best, the book maps a sociological imaginary that may help readers to find both a constant displacement of political and intellectual frontiers and new paths to equality.

REFERENCES

Baudrillard, J. (2010). *The agony of power* (A. Hodges, Trans.). Los Angeles, CA: Semiotext(e).

Connell, R. (2007). *Southern theory.* Cambridge, UK: Polity.

Gray, H. (2010). Culture, masculinity and the time after race. In H. Gray & M. Gómez-Barris (Eds.), *Toward a sociology of the trace* (pp. 87–108). Minneapolis: University of Minnesota Press.

Pascale, C. M. (2011). *Cartographies of knowledge: Exploring qualitative epistemologies.* Thousand Oaks, CA: Sage.

Patel, S. (2010). *The ISA handbook of diverse sociological traditions.* London, UK: Sage.

Pennycook, A. (2010). *Language as a local practice.* New York, NY: Routledge.

Russell, B. (1938). *Power: A New Social Analysis.* London, UK: Allen & Unwin.

ACKNOWLEDGMENTS

This book would have been unthinkable without the networks, insights, and inspiration provided by the International Sociology Association (ISA). Over the years, I have been sustained in equal measure by inspirations and opportunities provided by the ISA. I am grateful to all of my colleagues at the ISA, and most especially to those in the Research Committee on Language and Society, for helping to deepen my own thinking and for enriching my scholarship. In addition, I want to acknowledge the International Institute of Sociology (IIS) and the International Congress of Qualitative Inquiry (ICQI) and to thank my colleagues in each association for all they have contributed to this collection. I also thank the administration of American University for supporting international conference travel that has made my participation in these organizations possible.

Universities increasingly recognize the importance of global studies—both at undergraduate and graduate levels—yet scholarship that is truly international remains quite limited. In the spirit of Sujata Patel's *The ISA Handbook of Diverse Sociological Traditions* and Raewyn Connell's *Southern Theory,* this collection attempts to de-center Western perspectives on issues of inequality and to broaden disciplinary perspectives on language and society.

I owe enormous thanks to all of the scholars whose work is included here. Over the last several years, we have worked not only across disciplines and cultures, but also in second, third, or fourth languages. My appreciation for their patience and generosity cannot be overstated.

I thank the editorial staff at Sage, in particular Dave Repetto for signing this book. I also thank the reviewers for their insightful comments and suggestions that have guided this work. I owe special thanks to Elizabeth Luzzi and Karen Ehrman for their patient work on permissions and art. They could not have been more kind—especially when it became clear that I really had no idea what I was doing! I thank Eric Garner for his skill with production management and most especially to Janet Ford for her diligence, patience, and expertise as an editor.

I offer my heartfelt thanks to my spouse Mercedes Santos and to the friends and family who sweeten our lives—making the hard bits manageable and the good bits even better—and, as always, to Juniper for being all that can't be put into words.

SECTION 1

CLASS

1

CLASS INVISIBILITY AND STIGMATIZATION

Irish Media Coverage of a Public Housing Estate in Limerick

MARTIN J. POWER, EOIN DEVEREUX, AND AMANDA HAYNES

INTRODUCTION

In this chapter, we unveil some of the daily realities of a class-based society through a case study of a highly stigmatized public housing estate, Moyross, in Limerick in the southwest of Ireland. We examine how print and broadcast media produce and circulate classed representations and pathologizing/stigmatizing discourses[1] about poor people and the places where they live.

Through media, Ireland's "Third City," Limerick, has acquired an intensely negative reputation over time. It is generally agreed that Limerick had reached a new low in the 1980s when some media referred to it as "Stab City." The blanket media representation of the city as a place of crime, social disorder, poverty, and social exclusion further increased in recent years, and focused almost exclusively on the extremely violent disputes of rival drug gangs in Limerick's local authority

estates, including Moyross. Our analyses focus on how the mass media contributed to the stigmatization of this socially distant estate; how these characterizations contributed to the marginalization of Moyross and its residents; and then we contrast media depictions with alternative (primary and academic) sources of information of the residents.

We begin by establishing and exploding the myth of a classless Ireland—a self-imagining that is central to understanding the significance of media representations of extreme disadvantage manifesting in estates such as Moyross, without reference to the structural roots of poverty. We argue that the media participates in rendering invisible the relationship between middle-class advantage and the social exclusion of the working class/underclass[2] by painting the problems experienced by the latter as a product of their own personal shortfalls. In doing so, we argue that media constructions contribute to maintaining the existing class structure.

things wrong with Limerick

2

THE CLASS STRUCTURE IN IRELAND AND MYTHS OF A CLASSLESS IRELAND

Irish society is often self-imagined as a classless society and class-based discourses have historically been frowned on in the public arena. There is a shared acceptance of neoliberal principles and those ideological differences that do exist between the two main center-right political parties (Fianna Fáil and Fine Gael) are framed as Civil War Politics (and therefore competing versions of Nationalist ideologies that have traditionally shaped public discourse) rather than as class-based allegiances (Coakley, 1999). Indeed, all mainstream Irish political parties practice a *clientelist* politics (Gallagher & Komito, 1999), which individualizes problems rather than seeing them in class terms. The result has been to "retard the political development and consciousness of the economically dominated classes" (Hazelkorn, 1986, p. 339, as cited in Gallagher & Komito, 1999).

Despite the prevalence of commonsense understandings of a classless society, class inequality has been and remains a significant element of Irish society (Tovey, Share, & Corcoran, 2007, p. 171). The myth of a classless Ireland was perpetuated most strongly during the "Celtic Tiger" economic boom.[3] Populist economic commentators such as David McWilliams argued that

> the nation is blurring and the most significant aspect of this is in class. Ireland is becoming the most middle-class, suburban nation in Europe and the most startling development [...] has been the rapid social mobility the country is experiencing [....] We are now a middle-class nation (2005, p. 15).

To support his proposition, McWilliams (2005, p. 25) highlighted the research compiled by Amárach consultants in 2005, which found that over 50% of Irish people self-reported as middle class while less than 30% reported as working class, "reflecting the massive switch to white collar jobs over a short period of time."

The McWilliams data may have been accurate but it most certainly should not be seen as evidence of the "death of class" in Irish society. It is true that since the 1970s, Ireland's occupational structure transitioned to one based on industry and service provision—a transformation that allowed considerable mobility to the professional and managerial classes. However, it is also important to recognize that having a job is not in and of itself a solution to poverty. Indeed, Ireland saw the percentage of working poor increase from 3.2% in 1994 to 7.4% in 2000 and to 9.8% in 2004 (CSO, 2005, cited in Murphy, 2007, p. 119). This was more than a threefold increase in poverty that occurred throughout the height of the economic boom. Indeed, just under half of those at risk of poverty in 2008 lived in a household where at least one person was employed (Daly, 2010, p. 4).

Moreover, there is strong evidence that the relative advantages enjoyed by more affluent socioeconomic groups were largely maintained in spite of the social mobility that McWilliams (2005) addressed. For example, this is a society in which educational credentials became ever more important to labor market position and thus affected social mobility rates. The empirical data show that while rising participation rates in third-level education in Ireland assisted all socioeconomic groups, the working class has not gained any great advantage in relative terms (cf. O'Connell, Clancy, & McCoy, 2006). Indeed, Whelan & Layte (2007) found that while absolute mobility increased during the 1990s and early 2000s, "relative mobility and equality of opportunity stayed stable over time." Tellingly, they reported that disparities in opportunities between those at either end of the socioeconomic ladder were "greater in Ireland than in other European countries" (Tovey, Share, & Corcoran, 2007, p. 171).

Allen (as cited in Tovey et al., 2007, p. 171) argues that inequality such as described above "... is ideologically articulated by key opinion forming groups as a feature of life that only applies to the socially excluded." He is referring to inequalities in terms of disparities between the classes with those at the lower end of the social spectrum deemed responsible for their existence and that is why they experience such inequalities. For example, McWilliams (2005, p. 19) was perturbed that "the gap between the very rich and the very poor is reported again and again," however, he argued that "focusing on individual tragedies [. . .] overlooks the great opportunities seized by the majority." In essence, such views effectively place the blame for social and economic exclusion at the feet of those that experience it. Allen (1999, p.39) quite correctly argues that such hegemonic discourses function to maintain the existing class structure and is the preserve of "a contented majority" in that it fails to recognize the relationship between middle-class advantage and the social exclusion of others in our society.

Indeed, the reality is that despite the perception that economic growth would "trickle down" to benefit the poor or less advantaged (Callan & Nolan, 1994, p. 3), the rising tide of the "Celtic Tiger" boom did not lift all boats, as some of those vessels had already been leaking below the waterline.

Ireland's most recent social partnership agreement,[4] known as Towards 2016, "recognizes the importance of measures to build an inclusive society [. . .] and the social partners are committed to the achievement of a participatory society and economy with a strong commitment to social justice" (Cousins, 2007, pp. 2–3). Yet social partnership, which was supposed to be negotiated for the social good, coincided with changes that caused the ratio of social security spending to GDP to fall considerably, while there was a corresponding upward transfer of wealth (Allen, 2003, p. 68; Lynch, 2007). The policy direction pursued by the current (and previous) Irish government has been essentially an "*ad hoc* slash and burn approach to cutting public spending" (Dobbins, 2010 cited in Daly, 2010, p. 3), which in essence most severely affects those who are the most vulnerable in society.

While there have certainly have been improvements in absolute conditions over the past 20 years, these have been accompanied by a simultaneous growth in relative inequality. Welfare benefits in real terms rose from 1987 up until 2009 (when they were cut back); however, it is crucial to note that even when benefits were increasing, they did not rise at a similar rate to the gross average industrial wage. This resulted in a greater gap between welfare benefits and average earnings throughout this period (Turner & Haynes 2006, p. 93; McCashin, 2004; Kirby, 2002). Tellingly, even during the country's economic boom, Irelands' risk of poverty rate was "1.25 times the European Union (EU) average and one of the highest of all member states." The primary explanation for Ireland's high poverty rate was the poor performance of the Irish welfare system in addressing the risk of poverty after social transfers (Walsh, 2007, pp. 45–46). Social transfers are all social security benefits either in cash payments or in kind—a transfer of social services from the state to the citizen. Ireland still has a comparatively "high degree of economic inequality" in spite of our economic boom, and significant sections of the Irish population continue to "experience deprivation and exclusion as a result of inadequate financial resources" [. . .] and this is clearly linked to social class (Tovey et al., 2007, pp.178–180). Such evidence unravels the myth of a classless Ireland. In reality, the Irish class structure[5] is much the same as that in other countries in which neoliberal policies have come to dominate producing, as a result, a highly skewed distribution of wealth.

THE IMPORTANCE OF CLASS REPRESENTATIONS

The academic debate regarding whether or not the late 20th century was marked by the "death of class" (Pakulski & Waters, 1996) occurred in conjunction with the emergence of a political rhetoric of inclusion, meritocracy, and social mobility. Terms like social exclusion and underclass quickly replaced discussions that had centered on the working class and the existence of a class structure (Skeggs, 2005, p. 47 as cited in

Tyler, 2008, p. 20). Within this context, Morris (1994, p. 80) identified two broad ideological positions. The *cultural* position sees the source of social exclusion as lying in the attitudes and behavior of the underclass itself. By contrast, the *structural* position sees the source of social exclusion as rooted to the structural inequalities—both in the labor market and state actions—that disadvantage particular groups in society. It is apparent that most discourse and public policy regarding people who are socioeconomically marginalized is of the cultural variety, which attributes the presence of poverty to personal deficits (Byrne, 1999, p.128). If anything, we would hold that these processes have intensified in the last 15 years or so. In the current neoliberal era, one hears about "the marginalized" and the "socially excluded," but there is little discussion on who is excluding or marginalizing them (Allen, 2000, p. 37). This process obstructs class consciousness and is reinforced as neoliberal, individualistic ideologies injecting myths into public discourse that are constructed as *fact*. These myths stigmatize the working/underclass (Lens, 2002, p.144), consequently absolving the state and the system of stratification resulting from global capitalism of any responsibility for their circumstances (Edelman, 1998, p. 134). The dominant ideology is successfully communicated through key words, which act as cognitive prompts in the general public, to facilitate and strengthen previously held beliefs about the causes of poverty and social exclusion, as well as beliefs about those who experience them (Edelman, 1998, cited in Lens, 2002, p.144).

Previous research on media coverage of social class, poverty, inequality and social exclusion revealed that these interconnected issues often were either largely invisible in a mass media setting or were the subject of sensationalist and ill-informed coverage (cf. Bullock, Fraser Wyche, & Williams, 2001; Clawson & Trice, 2000; Devereux, 1998, 2007b). Besides ignoring the very existence of a class structure, media content was shown to obfuscate realities of structural inequalities whether they were based on class, ethnicity, or gender (or a combination of all three). Where social class is concerned, this ideological work was achieved in a variety of ways. In the 1980s, media scholars argued that when the working or blue-collar classes were visible, they were likely to be portrayed as the *happy* or *deserving* poor (Gould, Stern, & Dow Adams, 1981; Thomas & Callanan, 1982; Butsch, 1992). Representations of these classes significantly underplayed the realities of hardships and the likelihood of class conflict. Moreover, according to Williams (1988), prime time television in the United States served to exoticize and "other," the lives of the poor for middle-class viewers.

THE SUBALTERN

A key feature of the current political debate in Ireland is the Moral Underclass Discourse (MUD) that stresses moral and cultural sources of poverty and exclusion (Levitas, 2000, p. 360). It also reaffirms long-held cultural beliefs about the working class as being a *dangerous* threat to the moral and social order (see Skeggs, 1997; Wood & Skeggs, 2008). In this context, researchers have focused in particular on media representations of those who are dependent on state welfare (see, for example, Lens, 2002; Golding & Middleton, 1982). Welfare recipients are regularly pathologized and vilified in media. Although it has to be conceded that some media content (e.g., *Shameless USA* and its original United Kingdom version) powerfully suggests that the underclass can triumph in the face of adversity, specific subgroups within the working and underclass have been shown to be the targets of media driven moral panics. White women who are single parents—often called "Chavs" in the United Kingdom and "Trailer Trash" in North America—have been the subject of significant levels of negative media representation. In the early 2000s, the British print and broadcast media, for example, began to focus more and more on the emergence of a chav culture. The term *chav* came to signify membership of the white underclass. Unlike older examples of the dishonest or undeserving poor, chavs were defined in terms of their excessive (judged to be tasteless) consumption and feckless lives (Hayward & Yar, 2006).

In the context of fluctuating understandings of class, we argue that the denigration of the underclass is best understood as an indicator of middle-class aspirations to redefine class confines (Tyler, 2008, p.18). Middle-class representations of the underclass serve to negatively stereotype them as reprehensible, shameful, and disgusting (Law, 2006, p. 28), in the process producing approval for middle-class values, and maintaining the "symbolic order" (Skeggs, 2005, p. 970). In no small way, such "class disgust" (Tyler, 2008) contributed toward legitimizing both welfare cutbacks by the state and the furtherance of hegemonic ideologies about the poor underclass (see Lens, 2002; Skeggs, 2005: Lawlor, 2005; Golding & Middleton, 1982).

Media producers could decide to confront hegemonic beliefs about poverty, but most often they do not. Instead they typically reinforce hegemonic believes by controlling the type of information that reaches the general public in ways that shape and/or limit both our social knowledge and our understanding of the social world (McCullagh, 2002, p. 22). In the United States for example, when poverty is analyzed, the poor are rarely asked for their views and the media instead rely on so-called expert opinions to interpret what poverty entails (Adair & Dahlberg, 2005, p. 5). The net result is that hegemonic ideologies and discourses about social class, poverty, and inequality that stigmatize and pathologize are rarely challenged. While we acknowledge that audiences have agency in decoding media messages (Hall, 1999), it's crucial to note that audiences are limited in their capacity to assess the accuracy of the representations they consume without direct personal experience or alternative information on a given issue (Bullock et al., 2001, pp. 229–230).

The media thus operates as a very powerful institution for the dissemination of ideologies and discourses that shape national consciousness (Adair, 2001, p. 454) and construct the underclass as *devils* or *undeserving poor* (Devereux, 1998; Golding & Middleton, 1982; Lens, 2002, p.144; Bullock et al., 2001, pp. 229–230; Hayward & Yar, 2006, pp. 11–12). Examining media representations of social class and "poor places" is important because if public attitudes are informed by inaccurate, ideological, and stigmatizing representations of poor people and the places where they live (see Adair & Dahlberg, 2003, for a U.S. context), then policies preferred by the public (and political elites) are likely to reflect these inaccuracies and unlikely to seek to tackle the structural causes of inequality (Clawson & Trice, 2000, p. 61). Such constructions therefore contribute to the reproduction of privilege and disadvantage labels from one generation to the next.

THEY LIVE WHERE YOU WOULDN'T DARE TO DRIVE: STIGMATIZING PLACES

In addition to studying the stigmatizing and "othering" of specific groups (usually members of the underclass or poor), researchers also have examined how the *places* in which marginalized groups live are stigmatized (Greer & Jewkes, 2005; Bauder, 2002; Blokland, 2008; Hastings, 2004). Goffman's (1963) classic sociological work on stigma as a "spoiled identity," has influenced an important body of scholarship that examines how mass media and other social forces contribute to negative stereotypes that damage the reputations of the places in which poor people reside. The literature demonstrates convincingly that the negative reputations of such places can, in themselves, have a profound effect on the life chances and self-image of those who live in neighborhoods that carry a stigma (Permentier, Ham, & Bolt, 2007; Permentier et al., 2008; Permentier et al., 2009). Stigmatization processes therefore affect both the perspectives of those inside and outside such places.

Studies that attempt to explain how specific neighborhoods come to be stigmatized (cf. Gourlay, 2007; Wassenberg, 2004a) consistently refer to negative and sensationalist media coverage of poor neighborhoods. Citing the Dean and Hastings (2000) work, Palmer et al. (2004, p. 411) argue that poor neighborhoods are constructed in a media setting (and in many people's minds) as "problem places" for "problem people." In examining the Australian context, for example, Palmer, Ziersch, Arthurson, and Baum contend that

> the media, in particular, but by no means exclusively, contributes to the stigmatisation of certain suburbs and those who live in them, by promoting images and reputations of suburbs overrun by drugs, crime, mental health issues, youth disorder and the perennial favourite—'single mothers' (2004, p. 411).

Given the pervasiveness of such powerful negative constructions in the mainstream media, can they ever be properly overcome or challenged? A small number of research studies take a more hopeful and less deterministic view by arguing that it is possible for residents in stigmatized neighborhoods to repair their damaged reputations. For example, the reclamation of a damaged reputation may to some degree, be possible, through the use of alternative or community-based media (cf. Howley, 2010). However, while researchers working in a variety of cross-national locations have produced evidence that some residents have challenged stigmatizing hegemonic discourses about their neighborhoods, we would not wish to overstate the effectiveness of these strategies in altering a neighborhoods stigmatized identity (cf. Palmer et al., (2004) (Australia); Conway, Cahill, & Corcoran (2009) (Dublin); and Dean & Hastings (2000) (Glasgow)). While connotations about places can and do sometimes change— for example through gentrification processes— changing shared (negative) perceptions about places is difficult to achieve. As Wassenberg notes

> improving the image of an area is a long-lasting process. In problematic areas, image promotion always needs to be combined with (a range of) other measures. Even where the actual situation is improving, a stigma can last for many years, maybe even a lifetime (2004b, p. 229). (See also Dean & Hastings, 2000.)

What is more powerfully demonstrated in the literature is the degree to which a neighborhood's pathologized identity can negatively affect the residents' self-image and life chances. Bauder (2002, p. 88) for example noted that "some employers do not advertise in newspapers that circulate in inner-city neighborhoods." Internationally, a body of work continues to demonstrate how stigmatization can lead to a neighborhood being "redlined" by potential investors, resulting in fewer or scarce employment opportunities, and also negatively affecting the service provision for residents (cf. Musterd & Andersson, 2006; Aalbers, 2005; Dujardin et al., 2008; and Rospabe & Selod 2006). Writing in a Dutch context, Permentier et al. (2007, 2008, 2009) adopt a neighborhood effects approach. They show how the residents of neighborhoods with damaged reputations are not only stigmatized but also suffer in material and psychological terms from the stigma. They cite as concrete examples of some of the effects of stigmatization: low levels of social participation, poor or nonexistent job prospects, difficulties in getting mortgages from banks, and poor self-esteem among residents.

METHODS

The data that inform our analysis in this chapter were generated as part of a larger study that seeks to understand mass media representations of Moyross. Following the approach developed by the Glasgow University Media Group, this research was carried out using a tripartite methodology (Philo, 1990). The strategy of triangulation is employed to enhance the credibility of our interpretation (Lincoln & Guba, 1985). Specifically, we triangulate the findings of our analysis of media content with those generated from research with residents of Moyross and with media professionals.

We began our analysis by presenting the findings of a qualitative content analysis of a complete sample of 420 articles drawn from four newspapers, which were chosen for their diversity of audiences and styles. Specifically, we selected our sample from a national broadsheet, two national tabloids, and a local imprint that were published between January 1, 2006 and December 31, 2007. We also analyzed a local licensed radio station's documentary, broadcast in November of 2006. The documentary was based on a composite of radio broadcasts covering a major national media story about an arson attack in Moyross on two resident children.[6] Our analysis of content also included television broadcasts, which we selected from the national public television station's, Radio Telifis Éireann's (RTÉ) prime time news programs (*Six One News* and *9 O'Clock News*) broadcast between September 1, 2006 and December 31, 2006. We located and retrieved content by using keyword searches of RTE's proprietary news archive. In instances where the same report was broadcast by both programs, only one was included in our sample. The content analysis was based on a close critical reading of all selected print and broadcast texts. Our interest in how media discourses contribute to and reproduce hegemony is influenced by both Neo-Marxist and Foucauldian approaches (see Van Dijk, 1998). In practice, we follow Smith and Bell's understanding of discourse analysis that they see as involving

> . . . a close examination of text, including visual imagery and sound as well as spoken language. It is concerned with both the form of the text and its use in a social context, its construction, distribution and reception. It aims to understand and elucidate the meanings and social significance of the text (2007, p.78).

Apart from coding for rudimentary features such as word length, author, and sources our main focus was on the lexical devices used to construct media reports about the estate. This analysis revealed how the structures of everyday power relationships concerning class can be embedded within media texts. Having established the nature of the media content across newspaper, radio, and television formats, we proceeded to gather primary data from both journalists and audience members.

We conducted semistructured interviews with five journalists who work in the print and broadcast media sectors. All but one of the journalists held a broad job description with regard to covering events in the Limerick region. One of our interviewees works as a reporter with a provincial newspaper, which publishes four separate titles. That interviewee's work was primarily as a crime and court reporter, but with a secondary broader assignment base. The second interviewee worked for national broadcast media. The third interviewee worked in the local broadcast media. The fourth interviewee was a regional reporter for a broadsheet newspaper and also has reported on Moyross for a provincial title. The final interviewee worked as a freelance journalist, supplying copy to tabloid and broadsheets as well as occasionally reporting for national radio on Limerick issues. To complete our tripartite methodology, we conducted two focus groups in Moyross following preliminary analysis of the print and broadcast media content. Each involved six participants, five of whom were residents of Moyross. Participants were sourced through the Moyross Community Forum and as such, many of the residents we interviewed were active in their community. In each focus group, one nonresident community activist also participated. The adoption of a tripartite approach facilitated a more holistic understanding of the processes that shape journalists' decision making with regard to the construction of media content.

MOYROSS: THE "POLITICS OF REPRESENTATION"

This chapter is situated in the context of a wider sociological debate about the ways that mass media can contribute toward stigmatizing both the people who are socially excluded and the places where they live. As previously discussed, many poor places around the globe suffer material inequalities and "poor reputations that are reinforced though stigmatizing assumptions that portray their residents negatively" (Palmer et al., 2004, p. 411). We live at a time where there is an "unhealthy fascination" with crime; a time when "narratives of 'individual' causes of 'social decline' are endlessly and cyclically reproduced in the media" (Greer & Jewkes, 2005, p. 20).

Moyross is an area on the northside of Limerick City, consisting of 12 separate parks[7] and over 1,000 households, which were built between 1973 and 1987 (see Figure 1). The area is commonly known as the Moyross estate. Housing is generally of a high standard with 69% of the housing stock rented from the Limerick City Council. The remaining 31% of houses are either owner-occupied or on tenant purchase (Moyross. ie, 2011a). The area is one of the most deprived, not only in the city of Limerick, but on the island of Ireland. Using census data from 2006, the electoral division, which encompasses most of Moyross, can be categorized as "extremely disadvantaged" according to Haase and Pratschke's (2005) index of absolute and relative disadvantage (Haase & Pratschke, 2008).

In the context of this chapter, the residents of Moyross are classified as a mixture of working class and what has been termed the *underclass*. Sixty-four percent of families residing in Moyross are headed by single parents (Paul Partnership, 2008, p.10). Levels of unemployment and school dropout rates are high compared to city and national averages. The male unemployment rate was 28.8%, in contrast with 8.8% at the national level (Fahey, Norris, McCafferty, & Humphreys, 2011, p. 39). The 2006 census (cited in Moyross. ie, 2011a) showed that 29% of the population of Moyross left school at or before the age of 15. Moreover, only 6% of the population had completed third-level education compared with 30.5% of the national population (Fahey, Norris, McCafferty, & Humphreys, 2011, p. 39). Additionally, community and social facilities have been undeveloped in Moyross for many years (Humphreys & Dineen, 2006, p. 4). Indeed, Moyross Community Enterprise Centre is the biggest employer in the community while Speedline Engineering is the only significant commercial employer in Moyross (Moyross.ie, 2011a; see also Community Development Network Moyross, 2008).

In recent years, Moyross has gained infamy through the media as a site of violence perpetrated by criminal gangs and general social disorder (Fitzgerald, 2007, p. 7). Yet such generalizations overlook the lived realities of the majority of residents and the differences in the physical and social conditions within and across the 12 distinct parks of Moyross. In most of the estate there are very strong community ties and levels of social capital (see Humphries, 2011). However, "as a consequence of the spatial clustering" (see Fahey, 1999; Norris, & O' Connell, 2002; O' Connell, 2007 as cited in Hourigan, 2011a, p. 42) of the most "disadvantaged of the disadvantaged" (Hourigan, 2011b), a small minority of individuals in certain parts of some of the 12 parks perpetuate community violence, antisocial behavior, organized crime, and intimidation. Fahey et al. (2011, p. 52) noted the impact of such social order problems on the fortunes of a residential area, which 10 years previously had appeared to be improving. "Demand for housing in Moyross (as in certain other estates) fell off, and there was virtually no market for the housing that previously had been bought out by tenants" (Fahey et al., 2011, p. 51). However, for the vast majority of residents the Moyross estate remains the site of an active and vibrant community that is involved in education, job creation, sports, community media, and religious initiatives—all aspects of Moyross life[8] rarely communicated to outsiders.

We argue that for the most part, media coverage of this locality highlights the very real challenges that the area faces with regard to crime and social order, but at the expense of any significant engagement with the positive characteristics of the locale or its residents. The "stigmatized other" in such estates attracts "the scrutiny and criticism of the media" merely by failing to "conform to cultural and economic norms" (Greer & Jewkes, 2005, p. 29). Repeatedly, the "truly powerless rather than the truly evil" are "demonized and stigmatized" by the mass media (Greer & Jewkes, 2005, p. 29). In seeking a balanced media account of true life experiences of Moyross, we hold that the media's pathologizing negatively impacts on residents, on external perceptions of the people and the place, and on the potential for a future regeneration of the area.

Figure 1.1 Aerial photograph showing the 12 parks of Moyross

Source: Limerick Regeneration Agency/Peter Barroa.

CONSTRUCTING A (MIS)REPRESENTATION OF MOYROSS

Of the 420 articles in our print media sample, 70% were about crime. The period of our study incorporates a particularly heinous and infamous arson attack on two resident children, Gavin and Millie Murray; however, this does not negate the overwhelming predominance of crime-related articles in our sample. The majority of these articles detail specific incidents of violent crime, such as murders, shootings, armed robbery, and arson attacks on homes. A smaller number of articles focused on the availability of drugs and drug seizures. A huge proportion of the television news stories that we examined (22 out of 24) had crime as their primary theme and all the reports were episodic rather than thematic in orientation—in other words they focused on a precipitating event

rather than examining an underlying issue such as social exclusion or marginalization. We argue that, in particular, the constant association between the area and murder contributes to its severe stigmatization.

After crime, the urban regeneration project in Limerick was the next and most common primary theme of the articles in our sample, representing 10% of all articles. Media professionals interviewed shared an understanding of Moyross that focused on the structural causes of the exclusion experienced there. One media professional interviewee stated "There's a massive social divide in Limerick more than any other city in this country . . . actually it's massive." Yet, we found that out of the 44 articles we had categorized as focusing primarily on regeneration, only three can be regarded as engaging in any meaningful way with the causes of Moyross's problems.

The Limerick Leader, Moyross's local newspaper, acknowledges (uncritically) the ignominious image of the estate, citing the target areas of Limerick's regeneration project, ". . . the deprived estates whose names are synonymous with crime, antisocial behavior and neglect." A national newspaper, the *Mirror* (Nov 8, 2007) acknowledged that "The decent people of troubled Moyross [. . .] must be sick to the back teeth of their estate being constantly dragged through the mud," and goes on to discuss the impact of what they regard as a pathological minority to the "blackening of a city's name." The author of an article in the *Irish Independent* (August 26, 2007) specifically states that "The stigma of having [. . .] Moyross as an address is also a cause of discrimination by employers. . . ." Despite these acknowledgments, there is a dearth of critical commentary on the estate's stigmatized image, with the exception of the *Limerick Leader* editorial on September 21, 2006, in which the editor wrote: "Moyross is not a jungle or an estate people should be ashamed to say they are from."

A number of the regeneration article headlines stand out as particular examples of the role of subeditors in the stigmatization of an area. For example, headlines of the national newspapers refer to Moyross as a "troubled city suburb" (*Irish Independent*, October 25, 2006), "crime ridden housing estate" (*Irish Independent*, March 31, 2007), and a "gangland" estate (*Irish News*, September 11, 2007). In fact, 38 articles, across the entire sample, characterized Moyross as "troubled," sometimes grouping Moyross with other disadvantaged public housing estates. Notably, the term *troubled* is one employed routinely by journalists and subeditors rather than by their sources. In our sample of television news stories aired from September to December 2006, we found the convention of constructing Moyross as a *troubled estate* extends beyond the reporting styles of individual reporters. The epithet is used by newscasters in introducing reports about Moyross and even as a descriptor within RTÉ's news archive itself. Within television news, the underlying causal reasons

for Moyross's marginalized status are largely invisible. The makers of television news might argue that in a 90-second report there is no room to refer to the background reasons for poverty and exclusion, yet there does not seem to be a problem in finding the space for assertions that pathologize areas like Moyross.

Aside from geographical qualifiers such as estate, the most common descriptor for Moyross was *notorious*, and a number of articles employ the metaphor of a war zone to describe the estate. Indeed, one of our media professional interviewees spoke of being introduced on radio as "We now have [. . .] from the Gaza Strip," echoing the war zone discourses evident in our content analysis.

A major complaint of our resident participants was that the media fail to differentiate between areas within the expansive Moyross estate. The estate consists of 12 distinct parks and residents noted that criminality and antisocial behavior are largely concentrated in a much smaller number of locales within the overall estate. However, the media professionals we interviewed agreed that Moyross and "the troubled estate of Moyross" are used as a form of shorthand in communicating with audiences. While accepting the implications of writing about Moyross (as if it were a single entity), the journalist we interviewed suggested that to distinguish among the parks would provide too great a level of detail—that national audiences could not relate to the parks and had no interest in this level of coverage. One of our media professional interviewees asserted:

> . . . everybody is tainted with the one brush . . . if you say Pine View Gardens Moyross, people hear Moyross. If you are from Sarsfield Gardens . . . it's still Sarsfield Gardens Moyross, so people will still know.

It is important to note that our analysis demonstrated that the use of pathologizing epithets in reference to Moyross is not inevitable. In stark contrast to the stigmatizing discourses evident within much of the print media coverage, the local radio station's documentary sensitively narrates the story of the September 2006 arson attack on Millie and Gavin Murray, and its aftermath. Based on an amalgamation of archive news coverage and interviews, what emerges in this human interest documentary is a consciously balanced account. Unusually, normalizing discourses are up front and immediate. Moyross is portrayed as being no different than the rest of the nation. It emerges as a place united in its anger and grief. There are no references at all to the troubled estate of Moyross. There is one further striking difference in how the story is told; (the radio station's own news service specifically located the arson attack as happening in Pineview Gardens (one of the 12 parks), while the nationally syndicated INN news talks of the Moyross estate in its report) This radio documentary is exemplary in that it seeks to balance the viewpoints of those most affected by this horrific attack with the perspectives of community and national leaders. Crucially, (it narrates a catastrophic story without ever once pathologizing Moyross or its residents) It is noteworthy that this most consistently balanced coverage emanated from a media organization that made a conscious decision to eschew the repetition of stereotypes of Moyross:

> We've made a conscious decision to do that . . . we are conscious of an imbalance over the years and we at some point maybe in the last five years made a decision and said, okay, let's try where possible to give an overall picture on an ongoing basis so that when crime happens—and we must cover it—it is within the context of saying but there's another story here and there are lots of people and events taking place that are worth covering. . . . We sat down and thought about it and said, is there an imbalance? Yes. Have we perhaps contributed to that imbalance in the large sweep of things? Perhaps we have. So, let's try to make sure that we don't and let's try at least (Local Radio spokesperson).

VISUAL REPRESENTATIONS

At a visual level, the imagery used within the television news reports on Moyross convey a strong message about a place that is completely beyond the pale, out of control, and in the grip of lawlessness and criminality. There is a sense that media organizations tend to view the audience as socially distant and located outside of Moyross, and consequently see themselves as providing a (safe) window into this place. As well as crime scenes, audiences repeatedly witness images of boarded up and burned-out houses, wandering horses, and hooded youths.[9] Given the focus on crime in the reports on Moyross, we also see a preponderance of images concerned with policing, surveillance, and the courts. In spite of the homogenizing tendencies of this media coverage, it is interesting to note that specific places in Moyross—such as the entrances to particular parks (for example, Pineview Gardens or Delmege Park[10])—are used numerous times. We argue that this is done in order to (connote a place that is cut off from mainstream society. In essence, it is depicted as a place that the imagined viewer cannot, will not, or should not go.)

Our examination of television news coverage also found a dependency on the use of archival footage in reporting on Moyross. This included the aforementioned burned-out and boarded-up houses, and the burned-out patch of ground resulting from the September, 2006 arson attack on Millie and Gavin Murray. There may be practical (and economic) reasons for repeatedly using the same images of Moyross but their repetition is, we argue, likely to affect audience perceptions and misunderstandings. Indeed, in recognizing the professional codes (see Hall, 1974) used by some media professionals, one of our focus group residents felt that she could recite the likely footage to be used at will:

> If the camera comes in here in the morning [. . .] you'll see the school—a quick shot—and the church, and it just goes up the hill and then you'll have the burned-out houses. Then it goes down over Hartigan's Hill and you have the burned-out houses down there.

She holds that media professionals choose not to film "better" parks.[11] The media professionals whom we interviewed agreed that the use of archive footage by broadcast and print media was potentially problematic. They variously attributed the use of archive footage or stock photographs to the routinization of media work, lack of understanding of the local context, as well as cost. Some of the resident participants in our focus groups indicated that this practice can also lead to inaccuracies, with images from elsewhere on occasion portrayed as being from Moyross:

> There are certain things shown on TV that do not exist in Moyross. There was a hill there and I know for a fact it wasn't Moyross.

In the print media articles, pathologizing discourses often focused on the visual appearance of Moyross.[12] Some are balanced in their depiction of the physical conditions in the estate. For example, an article by David Hurley accompanies reference to the existence of burned-out houses in Moyross with a quote from a senior official within Limerick City Council who emphasized the selectivity of a focus solely on damaged housing stock (*Limerick Leader*, June 2, 2007). However, more articles make exclusive reference to burned-out and otherwise damaged housing. One article describes "hundreds of derelict and badly damaged houses" (*Irish News*, Sept 12, 2007) while another article in the *Irish Independent* describes Moyross as follows

> (Graffiti, including slogans such as 'scum' and 'rats out,' adorns the shattered homes and burned waste scars the roads. Hooded teenagers roam the streets, suspiciously eyeing strangers, even driving alongside cars so they can check out the occupants for their bosses. Anyone who has opposed the gangs has been forced out. Toward the rear of Moyross, the scene is apocalyptic. Delmege Park is a wasteland, its houses destroyed and completely uninhabitable.)

CONTEXTUALIZING POSITIVE STORIES TO REPRODUCE STIGMA

We find that even positive stories about Moyross are contextualized by reference to the stigmatized image of the locality (see Dean & Hastings, 2000, p. 21). For example, a good news story about a production of the Nativity story in Moyross,[13] was preceded by the information that this area was "ONE of the country's most socially deprived areas, which has suffered extensively from feuding criminal gangs, antisocial behavior and drug dealing . . . " (*Irish Independent*, December 15, 2007). We would argue that for media, (the newsworthiness of these stories was derived not from the event being reported, but rather from the juxtaposition of that positive event with the dominant representation or stigmatized image of the estate) Media professional interviewees were in agreement with our assessment. One stated:

> I think Moyross definitely does have that appeal [criminality] unfortunately that's a negative appeal and I know from even my own point of view if something positive happens and I try to push it to our News Editor I'd have a way better chance if there was some major crime out there, about that making it to the front page.

Our journalist participants acknowledged the news value of negative stories. There was general agreement that bad news is perceived as commercially viable and that as such, negative stories are more likely to be published and to receive prominent coverage:

> When it bleeds it leads. If something negative happens in Moyross it's on the nationals . . . if it's a negative story it is closer to getting to the front page than a happy clappy story in relation to Moyross . . . . but I think that's across the board in the local media (Journalist interviewee).

In the context of such practices, it can be more difficult to develop an alternative to the dominant interpretation of events.

Commercial considerations are key to undermining the perceived value of positive news. Newspaper journalists, both local and national, spoke of their media organizations' coverage of positive events in terms of profit motivation as well as responsibility to their readership. It was their perception that local media give more space to positive events in Moyross in publications that are seen to have a bigger market in the area as ". . . they are also looking at audience and readers and loyalty. . . ."

THE USE OF INTERNAL AND EXTERNAL SOURCES

The articles in our sample evidenced a strong reliance on official sources (in particular, political figures, clergy, police, and legal professionals). Relations and friends of crime victims were also employed as sources. The articles used a significant number of anonymous sources, particularly anonymous police sources. We found that our broadcast sample used community activists as sources; however they relied predominately on national and local politicians to comment on events in the estate. The low usage of Moyross residents or community representatives evidences a reliance on external sources to give their version or representation of life in the estate. This practice also limited the opportunities for residents to challenge misrepresentations. While residents who were used as sources did not always present positive depictions of living in Moyross, particularly in anonymous comments, one of the participants in our focus groups suggested that residents are more likely to be used as sources where their comments are negative.

> They don't want to listen to the people like us that's willing to say the positive side of Moyross. If I can say something bad I'll have a reporter down to me and I'm great and I'll be on the television, I'll be on the radio and everything. And if they go to Mary and she has something good to say, well you're not going to put Mary on you're going to put me on, because I am the one that's running the place down. . . .

Changes in the production context, both local and national, are creating additional obstacles to active engagement with the local context for all journalists. While bigger stories attract journalists to the locality, many stories are now researched remotely by phone and e-mail. Of course, the dangers of this increasingly ubiquitous news practice are a greater reliance on sources rather than first hand observation, on official sources (who are more readily identifiable and contactable) and, according to one of our journalist-interviewees, on a smaller number of sources.

IMPACT ON RESIDENTS

Wassenberg (2004a and 2004b) clarifies that the media's impact is on external images. Residents we interviewed were highly conscious of "outsiders" perceptions of their estate. As a result, one resident argued that people living beyond Moyross misperceive it as a "total disgrace" and a "no-go estate." The residents felt strongly that there are very positive aspects to Moyross, which are seriously neglected in media coverage and impact on external perceptions of the area.

> They haven't seen what we have [. . .] There's such beautiful places out here [. . .] they're never shown like that [. . . .] But if there is a shooting or a mugging or a robbery—Moyross, Moyross, Moyross.

Residents cited specific examples of how their locale's stigmatized identity translates into prejudice and differential treatment in relation to obtaining mortgages, insurance, and the refusal of full service from delivery companies, particularly taxi services:

> One lady in particular she was in her seventies and she ordered a taxi from town with her groceries and she said Moyross. That man pulled up outside Watchhouse Cross [on the outskirts]. That lady was living up in the very top of Moyross. She had to walk with six bags.

Additionally, residents cited examples of others who have succumbed to pressure to change or hide signifiers of their identity as Moyross residents:

I know people who have changed their accents and you probably do too, from Moyross [. . .] one girl [. . . she said] that's how I felt when I was a teenager if I was to get ahead I'm going to have to change my accent.

This process of disidentification is highly significant. One of the chief signifiers of class is identified as a person's accent. Particularly in Limerick, the stereotypical Limerick city accent is perceived as a primary identifier and plays a significant role in how people are identified and subsequently judged (see Power, 2009). In this instance, the girl is aware of this reality and made a conscious decision to alter her accent as it links her to Moyross and a stigmatized or devalued identity. Her stigmatized identity is configured through an "improvement discourse" in which she perceives that, in order to better herself, she must disidentify and differentiate herself from those who have been pathologized (Skeggs, 1997). This can be viewed as a direct result of the pathologization of the working class and underclass (and by extension the estates in which they live) by middle-class groups (in this instance, journalists).

CONCLUSIONS

Our shared commitment to the political economy perspective leads us to conclude that the content produced by journalists rarely challenges existing power structures and, in fact, tends to serve to reproduce the hegemonic order governing a class-based society. Our chapter clearly demonstrates that journalism obscures the experiences of class as it continues to recycle classed discourses—the result is a lasting stigmatization of people and places. Such stigmatization processes have tangible impacts on the current living conditions and future possibilities of the residents of places like Moyross.

The role of the mass media in demonizing the excluded and the places in which they live is neither new nor surprising (see, for example, Skeggs, 2005; Wassenberg, 2004a; Dean &

Hastings, 2000). Eschewing any notion of journalistic neutrality or objectivity, we need to ask exactly *whose* interests are best served by this type of coverage. Framing the issues of social exclusion and poverty as individual problems (Lens, 2002, pp. 137–144) facilitates an "abdication from acknowledging class relations" (Skeggs, 2005, p. 54), causing the identification of class discrimination, and the specificity of class cultures, identities, and struggles to be suppressed (Tyler, 2008, p. 20). Despite the fact that communal class identities are fragile, our personal identities continue to involve "relational comparisons" with those from other classes signifying "the reforming of class cultures around individualized axes" (Savage, 2000, p. xii cited in Bottero, 2004, p. 989). In other words, this position recognizes that while class (and class identification) has changed, as social subjects identify themselves in more complex (individualized) ways, class remains an important aspect of our "relational comparisons" with each other.

For us, class continues to be an important unit of analysis. In this chapter, we have shown how media-based discourses on the working class and underclass, and the places that they live, continue to be pathologizing and ultimately contribute to maintaining the existing class structure. Our case material is not unique. These processes are replicated across the globe and contribute in no small way to the perpetuation of the hegemonic neoliberal ideology that continues to impose a "class war from above" (Harvey, 2005) on the poor of the world.

NOTES

1. At its simplest the term *discourse* means a form of knowledge. We use the term predominantly in a Foucauldian sense where a discourse is "at once singularly authoritative and employed in the interests of existing structures of authority and power" (Deacon et al., 1999, p.147).

2. In an Irish context, the term *working class* refers to those who are largely employed as (skilled or

non-skilled) manual labor. The underclass would be understood as those, such as single parents and the long-term unemployed, who are exclusively dependant on the state to provide for their welfare. While both *classes* are susceptible to poverty and social exclusion, the main difference between the two groups in this context is in relation to "blame" attributed to that poverty and exclusion. While the working class are likely to be viewed as the "deserving poor," the underclass are almost always viewed as choosing that way of life—the so-called culture of poverty syndrome.

3. The "Celtic Tiger" boom refers to a period from 1994 to 2008 when the Irish economy underwent a period of unprecedented and rapid economic growth. The ensuing rise in employment and prosperity caused many to reflect that Ireland had become completely capitalist in outlook. During this time period the level of employment rose from 51.7% in 1993 to 68.1% in 2006. Simultaneously, unemployment fell from 15.6% to 4.3% (CSO, 2006a, as cited in Kirby, 2008, p. 13).

4. Social Partnership is a corporatist arrangement whereby the government, business sector, unions, and the voluntary and community organizations come together for the "good of the country" to concur on national wage agreements, and so forth.

5. We have a small elite upper class, with the 300 richest people in Ireland now worth almost €57bn. Indeed, almost €6.7bn was added to their combined wealth over the last year, despite Ireland going through an unprecedented economic crisis (Webb, 2011). We have a relatively large middle class, though this is likely considerably smaller as a result of the economic crisis, which has seen huge increases in unemployment, and negative equity in relation to property, as an example. The remainder of the population is split between the working class/underclass. The size of the underclass is also likely to have increased quite substantially as a result of the huge loss of manual jobs over the last number of years and the massive rise in unemployment since 2009.

6. On September 10, 2006, Millie Murray and her 5-year-old brother Gavin were severely burned in an arson attack on their mother's car in Pineview Gardens, one of the 12 (see footnote 7) of Moyross. Three teenagers from Moyross received prison sentences for their role in the attack. This arson attack was the final catalyst for state intervention in Moyross and resulted in the establishment of the Limerick Regeneration Project.

7. There are essentially 12 distinct neighborhoods (Pineview Gardens, Delmege Park, Castlepark, Sarsfield Gardens, Craeval Park, Dalgaish Park, Cosgrave Park, Cliona Park, Hartigan Villas, College Avenue, Whitecross Gardens, and Ballygrennan Close) which are all referred to as *parks*.

8. For example, there are two residents' associations in Moyross, the Moyross Residents Forum and the Moyross Residents Alliance (see http://mralimerick.com). Additionally, the last 6 years have seen the window box project "encourage residents to display window boxes and hanging baskets, to add colour to the Parks, lift the spirit of the community, and promote and improve the image of Moyross. In 2011, the committee filled 970 window boxes and hanging baskets" (Moyross.ie, 2011b). For an overview of the extensive range of activities that this vibrant community is involved in, go to http://www.moyross.ie/Estate.html.

9. These are still the first images you find if you "Google" Moyross. The fascination with horses in the media may well be connected to their association with Irish Travellers, a minority group who also have a very stigmatized identity (for a discussion, see Hayes, 2006). Interestingly, the Moyross estate was almost entirely absent from Google Street View until September, 2011. The images of the estate up until that date were taken from a middle-class estate to the west of Moyross and from a road running along the northeast perimeter of the estate. No images from anywhere within the 12 parks of Moyross were available. The limited number of photographic images in Street View displayed some derelict houses that no longer existed, desolate spaces, graffitied walls and streets that were relatively deserted (see Neville, Power, Devereux, Haynes, & Barnes, 2011 for a detailed discussion of how new media are also stigmatizing this location).

10. These two parks are probably the most well-known (nationally) in the Moyross estate.

11. In essence the parks where the "advantaged of the disadvantaged" reside (Hourigan, 2011b, pp. 60–73).

12. Although an article by *The Mirror* (November 8, 2007) incorporates reference to the perceived intergenerational transmission of deviant values and norms from a criminal minority to the children of Moyross and Southill. "These scum are passing on their poison to a new generation. Impressionable kids they may be and bravado they may spout but in a few years they could carry through their threats."

13. August 2007 saw the Franciscan Friars of the Renewal officially open a friary in Delmege Park, Moyross. In December 2007, the monks held a live Nativity play with the residents of Moyross playing various parts in the play. It was a resounding success and generated great pride among the residents. Father O'Dea, parish priest in Moyross at that time, spoke of the monks' impact on the estate. "There was an image that Moyross was a disaster. Three or four years ago they were leaving the parish, waiting to get a new house someplace else. Now people are staying and people are wondering can they come back into the parish again" (RTÉ, 2008).

REFERENCES

Aalbers, M. (2005). Place-based social exclusion: Redlining in the Netherlands. *Area*, *37*(1), 100–109.

Adair, V. (2001). Branded with infamy: Inscriptions of poverty and class in the United States. *Signs: Journal of Women in Culture and Society*, *27*(2), 451–471.

Adair, V., & Dahlberg, S. (Eds.). (2003). *Reclaiming class: Women, poverty and the promise of higher education in America*. Philadelphia, PA: Temple University Press.

Allen, K. (1999). The Celtic Tiger, inequality and social partnership. *Administration*, *47*(2), 31–55.

Allen, K. (2000). *The Celtic Tiger: The myth of social partnership in Ireland*. Manchester, UK: Manchester University Press.

Allen, K. (2003). Neither Boston nor Berlin: Class polarisation and neo-liberalism in the Irish Republic. In C. Coulter & S. Coleman (Eds.), *The end of Irish history? Critical reflections on the Celtic Tiger* (pp. 56–73). Manchester, UK: Manchester University Press.

Bauder, H. (2002). Neighbourhood effects and cultural exclusion. *Urban Studies*, *39* (1), 85–93.

Blokland, T. (2008). "You got to remember you live in public housing": Place-making in an American housing project. *Housing, Theory and Society*, *25*, 31–46.

Bottero, W. (2004). Class identities and the identity of class. *Sociology*, *38*(5), 985–1003.

Bullock, H., Fraser Wyche, K., & Williams, W. (2001). Media images of the poor. *Journal of Social Issues*, *57*(2), 229–246.

Butsch, R. (1992). Class and gender in four decades of television situation comedies—Plus ça change, *Critical Studies in Mass Communication*, *9*(4), 387–399.

Byrne, D. (1999). *Social exclusion*. Buckingham, UK: Open University Press.

Callan, T., & Nolan, B. (1994). *Poverty and policy in Ireland*. Dublin, IE: Gill and Macmillan.

Clawson, R., & Trice, R. (2000). Poverty as we know it: Media portrayals of the poor. *Public Opinion Quarterly*, *64*, 53–64.

Coakley, J. (1999). Society and political culture. In J. Coakley & M. Gallagher (Eds.), *Politics in the Republic of Ireland* (3rd ed.) (pp. 37–71). Dublin, IE: Routledge.

Community Development Network Moyross. (2008). *Annual report 2008*. Limerick, IE: Community Enterprise Centre, Moyross.

Conway B., Cahill, L., & Corcoran, M. (2009). The "miracle" of Fatima: Media framing and the regeneration of a Dublin housing estate (*NIRSA Working Papers*, No. 47 March). Maynooth, IE: NUI/NIRSA. Retrieved July 3, 2011, from http://eprints.nuim.ie/1521.

Cousins, M. (2007). *Welfare policy and poverty*. Dublin, IE: Institute of Public Administration and Combat Poverty Agency.

Daly, M. (2010). *Ireland: In-work poverty and labor market segmentation. A study of national policies*, Belfast, UK: Queens University Press. Retrieved July 3, 2011, from www.peer-review-social-inclusion.eu.

Deacon, D., Murdoch, G., Golding, P., & Pickering, M. (1999). *Researching communications*. London, UK: Hodder Arnold.

Dean, J., & Hastings, A. (2000). *Challenging images: Housing estates, stigma and regeneration*. Bristol, UK: Polity Press/Joseph Rowntree.

Devereux, E. (1998). *Devils and angels: Television, ideology and the coverage of poverty*. Luton, UK: University of Luton Press.

Devereux, E. (Ed.). (2007). *Media studies: Key issues and debates*. London, UK: Sage.

Devereux, E. (2007). *Understanding the media* (2nd ed.). London, UK: Sage.

Dujardin, C., Selod, H., & Thomas, I. (2008). Residential segregation and unemployment: The case of Brussels. *Urban Studies*, *45*(1), 89–113.

Edelman, M. (1998). Language, myths and rhetoric. *Society*, *35*(2), 131–139.

Fahey, T., Norris, M., McCafferty, D., & Humphreys, E. (2011). *Combating social disadvantage in social housing estates: The policy implications of a ten-year follow-up study.* Combat Poverty Agency/ Department of Social Protection Working Paper Series, Dublin, Ireland. Retrieved July 2, 2011, from http://www.lenus.ie/hse/bitstream/10147/132723/1/CombatingSocialDisadvInSocialHousing Estates.pdf.

Fitzgerald, J. (2007). *Addressing issues of social exclusion in Moyross and other disadvantaged areas in Limerick city.* Report to the Cabinet Committee on Social Inclusion. Limerick, IE: Limerick City Council.

Gallagher, M., & Komito, L. (1999). The constituency role of TDs. In J. Coakley & M. Gallagher (Eds.), *Politics in the Republic of Ireland* (3rd ed.). Dublin, IE: Routledge.

Goffman, E. (1963). *Stigma.* London, UK: Penguin.

Golding, P., & Middleton, S. (1982). *Images of welfare: Press and public attitudes to poverty.* Oxford, UK: Martin Robertson.

Gould, C., Stern, D., & Dow Adams, T. (1981). Television's distorted vision of poverty. *Communication Quarterly, 29*(24), 309–14.

Gourlay, G. (2007, September 12–14). *It's got a bad name and it sticks. . . . Approaching stigma as a distinct focus of neighbourhood regeneration initiatives.* Paper presented at the EURA Conference, The Vital City, Glasgow, UK.

Greer, C., & Jewkes, Y. (2005). Extremes of otherness: Media images of social exclusion. *Social Justice, 32*(1), 20–31.

Haase, T., & Pratschke, J. (2005). *New measures of deprivation for the Republic of Ireland.* Dublin, IE: Pobal.

Haase, T., & Pratschke, J. (2008). *An inter-temporal and spatial analysis of data from the Census of Population, 1991, 1996, 2002 and 2006.* Retrieved July 2, 2011, from https://www.pobal.ie/WhatWeDo/Deprivation/Pages/Informationfor Beneficiaries.aspx.

Hall, S. (1974). The television discourse: Encoding and decoding. *Education and Culture, 25,* 8–14.

Hall, S. (1999). Encoding, decoding. In S. During (Ed.), *The cultural studies reader* (2nd ed.) (pp. 507–517). New York, NY: Routledge.

Harvey, D. (2005). *A brief history of neoliberalism.* Oxford, UK: Oxford University Press.

Hastings, A. (2004). Stigma and social housing estates: Beyond pathological explanations. *Journal of Housing and Built Environment, 19,* 233–254.

Hayes, M. (2006). *Irish travellers: Representations and realities.* Dublin, IE: The Liffey Press.

Hayward, K., & Yar, M. (2006). The "chav" phenomenon: Consumption, media and the construction of a new underclass. *Crime Media Culture, 2*(1), 9–28.

Hourigan, N. (2011a). A history of social exclusion in Limerick. In N. Hourigan (Ed.), *Understanding Limerick: social exclusion and change* (pp. 44–59). Cork, IE: Cork University Press.

Hourigan, N. (2011b). Divided communities: Mapping the social structure of disadvantaged neighbourhoods in Limerick. In N. Hourigan (Ed.), *Understanding Limerick: Social exclusion and change* (pp. 60–73). Cork, IE: Cork University Press.

Howley, K. (Ed.). (2010). *Community media.* London, UK: Sage.

Humphreys, E., & Dineen, D. (2006). *Evaluation of social capital in Limerick City and environs,* Report to the HSE Mid-West Area and the Limerick City Development Board. Limerick, IE: University of Limerick.

Humphries, E. (2011). Social capital, health and inequality: What's the problem in the neighbourhoods?. In N. Hourigan (Ed.), *Understanding Limerick: Social exclusion and change* (pp. 185–210). Cork, IE: Cork University Press.

Kirby, P. (2002). *The Celtic Tiger in distress: Growth with inequality in Ireland.* Basingstoke, UK: Palgrave.

Kirby, P. (2008). *Explaining Ireland's development: Economic growth with weakening welfare.* Social Policy and Development Programme Paper No. 37, United Nations Institute for Social Development. Geneva, Switzerland.

Krippendorf, K. (2004). *Content analysis: An introduction to its methodology* (2nd ed.). Thousand Oaks, CA: Sage.

Law, A. (2006). Hatred and respect: The class shame of Ned "humour." *Variant, 25,* 28–30.

Lawlor, S. (2005). Disgusted subjects: The making of middle-class identities. *The Sociological Review,* 429–446.

Lens, V. (2002). Public voices and public policy: Changing the societal discourse on welfare. *Journal of Sociology and Social Welfare, 29*(1), 137–154.

Levitas, R. (2000). What is social exclusion?. In D. Gordon & P. Townsend (Eds.), *Breadline Europe* (pp. 357–364). Bristol, UK: The Policy Press.

Lincoln, Y., & Guba, E. (1985). *Naturalistic inquiry.* Thousand Oaks, CA: Sage.

Lynch, K. (2007). *How much inequality is there in Ireland and who cares?.* Paper accepted for Pobal Conference, Realising Equality and Inclusion: Building Better Policy and Practice. November 22· 2007. Dublin Croke Park Conference Centre, Dublin, Ireland.

McCashin, A. (2004). *Social security in Ireland.* Dublin, IE: Gill and Macmillan.

McCullagh, C. (2002). *Media power: A sociological introduction.* New York, NY: Palgrave.

McWilliams, D. (2005). *The Pope's children: Ireland's new elite.* Dublin, IE: Gill & Macmillan.

Morris, L. (1994). *Dangerous classes: The underclass and social citizenship.* London, UK: Routledge.

Moyross.ie (2011a). *A history of the Moyross estate.* Retrieved July 3, 2011, from http://www.moyross.ie/Estate.html.

Moyross.ie (2011b). *Moyross is blooming great summer project 2011.* Retrieved July 3, 2011, from http://cdnmoyross.blogspot.com/2011/04/moyross-is-blooming-great-summer.html.

Murphy, M. (2007). Working-aged people and welfare policy. In Combat Poverty Agency (Ed.), *Welfare policy and poverty* (pp. 101–138). Dublin, IE: Institute of Public Administration and Combat Poverty Agency.

Musterd S., & Andersson, R. (2006). Employment, social mobility and neighbourhood effects: The case of Sweden, *International Journal of Urban and Regional Research, 30*(1), 120–140.

Neville, P., Power, M., Devereux, E., Haynes, A., & Barnes, C. (2011, September 8). *Why bother seeing the world for real: The visual politics of Google Street View and the representation of Moyross, Limerick, Ireland.* Framing the City: The Centre for Research on Socio-Cultural Change Annual Conference, University of Manchester, UK.

O'Connell, P., Clancy, D., & McCoy, S. (2006). *Who went to college in 2004? A national survey of entrants to higher education.* Dublin, IE: Higher Education Authority.

Pakulski, J., & Waters, M. (1996). *The death of class,* London, UK: Sage.

Palmer, C., Ziersch, A., Arthurson, K., & Baum, F. (2004). Challenging the stigma of public housing: Preliminary findings from a qualitative study in South Australia. *Urban Policy and Research, 22*(4), 411–426.

Permentier, M., van Ham, M., & Bolt, G. (2007). Behavioural responses to neighbourhood reputations. *Journal of Housing and the Built Environment, 22,* 199–213.

Permentier, M., van Ham, M., & Bolt, G. (2008). Same neighbourhood…different views? A confrontation of internal and external neighbourhood reputations. *Housing Studies, 23*(6), 833–855.

Permentier, M., van Ham, M., & Bolt, G. (2009). Neighbourhood reputation and the intention to leave the neighbourhood. *Environment and Planning, 41,* 2162–2180.

Paul Partnership. (2008). *Meeting the needs of one parent families in Limerick City.* Dublin, IE: POBAIL.

Philo, G. (1990). *Seeing and believing.* London, UK: Routledge.

Power, M. (2009). Outwitting the gatekeepers of the purse: The impact of micro-level interactions in determining access to the Back to Education Allowance Welfare to Education Programme. *International Review of Modern Sociology, 35*(1), 25–42.

Rospabe, S., & Selod, H. (2006). Does city structure cause unemployment? The case of Cape Town. In H. Bhorat & R. Kanbur (Eds), *Poverty and policy in post-apartheid South Africa* (pp. 262–287). Cape Town, ZA: HSCR Press.

RTÉ. (2008, November 2). *Would you believe: Monks of Moyross.* RTÉ1 [Television broadcast] Retrieved July 3, 2011, from http://www.rte.ie/tv/wouldyoubelieve/monksofmoyross.html.

Skeggs, B. (1997). *Formations of class and gender: Becoming respectable.* London, UK: Sage.

Skeggs, B. (2005). The making of class and gender through visual moral subject formation. *Sociology, 39*(5), 965–982.

Smith, P., & Bell, A. (2007). Unravelling the web of discourse analysis. In E. Devereux (Ed.), *Media studies: Key issues and debates.* London, UK: Sage.

Thomas, S., & Callanan, B. (1982). Allocating happiness: TV families and social class. *Journal of Communication, 32*(3), 184–190.

Tovey, H., Share, P., & Corcoran, M. (2007). *A sociology of Ireland.* Dublin, IE: Gill & Macmillan.

Turner, T., & Haynes, A. (2006). Welfare provision in boom times: Strengthening social equity in Ireland? *Irish Journal of Sociology, 15*(2), 86–100.

Tyler, I. (2008). Chav mum chav scum: Class disgust in contemporary Britain. *Feminist Media Studies, 8*(1), 17–34.

Van Dijk, T. (1998). *Ideology: A multidisciplinary approach*. London, UK: Sage.

Walsh, J. (2007). Monitoring poverty and welfare policy 1987–2007, In Combat Poverty Agency (Ed.), *Welfare Policy and Poverty* (pp. 13–58). Dublin, IE: Institute of Public Administration and Combat Poverty.

Wassenberg, F. (2004a). Renewing stigmatised estates in the Netherlands: A framework for image renewal strategies. *Journal of Housing and the Built Environment, 19*, 271–292.

Wassenberg, F. (2004b). Large social housing estates: From stigma to demolition? *Journal of Housing and the Built Environment, 19*, 223–232.

Webb, N. (2011, March 13). The rich just got richer—top 300 now have €57 bn, *The Sunday Independent*. Retrieved July 3, 2011, from http://www.inde pendent.ie/business/.

Whelan, C., & Layte, R. (2007). Opportunities for all in the new Ireland. In T. Fahey, H. Russell, & C. Whelan (Eds.), *The best of times? The social impact of the Celtic Tiger*. Dublin, IE: Institute of Public Administration.

Williams, B. (1988). *Upscaling downtown: Stalled gentrification in Washington D.C.* Ithaca, NY: Cornell University Press.

Wood H., & Skeggs, B. (2008). Spectacular morality: Reality television, individualisation and the re-making of the working class. In D. Hesmondhalgh & J. Toynbee (Eds.), *The media and social theory* (pp. 177–193). London, UK: Routledge.

2

INEQUALITY AND REPRESENTATION

Critical Discourse Analysis of News Coverage About Homelessness

VIVIANE DE MELO RESENDE AND VIVIANE RAMALHO

INTRODUCTION

This chapter analyzes identity-building processes in the news article, "Ivan the Homeless Gardener Builds Garden in 307 South" (*Ivan, o andarilho...*) ... *gram-* ... wspaper *Correio Braziliense* in April 20... article narrates the story of a 57-year-old homeless man ... examine ho... employs ... discourse resources ... particu- ... omeless ... reader...

... sis, lan- ... , "texts ... social, structural, cognitive ... al, and ... rclough, ... tions of ... people ... this par- ... sustain beliefs, attitudes ... social values that natural- ize the problem of social inequality in Brazil.

[handwritten annotations: Method of anal. — critical discourse analysis, linguistic — discursive resources; genetic struct. anal. of; meta com; eval + ident + rel; text]

This news article is particularly interesting because it was published in the *Correio Braziliense*, the most traditional newspaper in Brasília, Brazil's capital. Consequently, it contains many examples of ideological discourse from economically privileged social classes, which have partially contributed both to obscuring and naturalizing extreme poverty in Brazil.

Through a generic structural analysis, we show how rhetorical movements contribute to a romantic narrative that legitimizes dominant relations of power. For example, this romantic narrative legitimates the idea that Ivan is only living in the streets because he is mentally ill and wishes to do so. Our analysis draws from critical discourse analysis (cf. Chouliaraki & Fairclough, 1999; Resende & Ramalho, 2006; and Ramalho & Resende, 2011) as well as analyses of rhetoric, evaluative comments, identity and metaphors. Our goal is to understand how processes of identification in the text construct the positive value of what otherwise would be deemed undesirable actions. In short, we examine how this news article reifies homelessness as a permanent, natural, and even admirable condition (see Fairclough, 2003; Resende, 2009a; Lakoff & Johnson, 2002). This analysis is further examined and broadened in Ramalho and Resende (2011).

This chapter is divided into six sections. The first section reviews key components of critical discourse analysis (CDA) that are relevant to this study. The next section provides a social context to help readers understand the problem of extreme poverty in Brazil. The third section examines the structure of the selected news article, illustrates specific rhetorical movements and considers their effects. The forth section presents our analysis of evaluative instances, and in the fifth and sixth sections we present, respectively, analyses of relational identity building and the use of metaphors in the text. Finally, we summarize the above-mentioned analyses.

It is important to clarify that research in CDA does not come only from academic interest or from reflections centered in the field's meta-linguistics.[1] Rather, CDA investigations embody a critical framework concerned with language use in relationship to power in situated contexts; the motivation of CDA is to "investigate critically social inequality as expressed, signaled, constituted, legitimized and so on by language use (or in discourse)" (Wodak, 2004, p. 225). Language has been shown to be a resource both for establishing and supporting domination, and also for disputing and overcoming these conditions.

Premised on a dialectal relationship between language and society, our analysis allows us to explore the social function of language—in particular, how it promotes hegemonic representations of extreme poverty. In addition we consider the potential effects of these hegemonic representations for the reproduction and/or transformation of social inequality in Brazil.

CRITICAL DISCOURSE ANALYSIS AND IDENTITY PROCESSES IN TEXTS

Critical discourse analysis is used to develop a situated study of the functioning of language in society. According to Fairclough (2003) and Chouliaraki and Fairclough (1999), CDA belongs to the critical tradition of social sciences, devoted to offering scientific support for tackling social problems related to power and justice.[2] In CDA, language manifests itself as *discourse* in social practices (Fairclough, 2003). Discourse is an irreducible part of how we act and interact, as well as how we represent and identify ourselves, others, and aspects of the world by means of language. The term *discourse* also can refer more concretely to "particular ways of representing part of the world," and is tied to specific interests (Fairclough, 2003, p. 26). For example, we can analyze a neoliberal discourse in newspapers that is generally associated with the middle class. In order to address discourse in the second sense— ways of representing the world—we refer to a particular discourse, or to 'discourses' in plural (Ramalho & Resende, 2011, p. 17).

For critical discourse analysts, language is an irreducible part of social life; language and society share an internal and dialectical relationship in which "social matters are partly matters of discourse" and vice versa (Chouliaraki & Fairclough, 1999, p. 7). Besides being a means of representing the world and (inter)acting on it, discourse is also a way to identify oneself and others. It contributes to the construction of "particular conducts," and contributes to the formation of social or personal identities. According to Chouliaraki and Fairclough (1999, p. 63), we can say that the "type of language used by a particular category of people and related to his/her identity" somehow expresses how this category of people identify themselves and how they identify other people. This is not, however, a simple, one-dimensional matter.

Drawing from a transformational perspective of society building propounded by critical realists (cf., Bhaskar, 1998), we understand that individual action and social structure are mutually constituted. Social actors, in this sense, are neither completely free nor completely constrained by social structure. People are not just prepositioned in the way they participate in social events and texts but are, rather, social actors who *take action* in the world. Thus, Fairclough (2003) argues that identity is not merely a textual process, since it does not only boil down to discursive construction alone. In this ontological perspective of the social functioning of language, there are other social practice moments that also have implications over identity construction, and discourse is conceived as one integrating and irreducible moment of social practices in articulation with other moments: action and interaction, social relationships, people (with beliefs, values, attitudes, stories, etc.) and the material world (Fairclough, 2003). The irreducibility principle means that we cannot understand identity only in discursive terms.

Even though, it is true that identity is partially a process of meaning, and according to Castells (2001), is based on cultural interrelated attributes that prevail over other sources of meaning. However, identity involves nondiscursive aspects and it may suffer interference from dominant institutions, but only *when* and *if* the actors internalize them and build the meaning of their own identities on this basis. In other words, social actors may assume or internalize certain hegemonic meanings as constituting their identities in a disciplinary manner, or react to these meanings associated with dominant institutions; for instance, the legitimizing identity of "homeless by choice" opposed to the resisting identity of a "person who is homeless and knows and claims his rights." Thus, one must consider the effects of social consensus and constraints as well as the individual, reproductive, or transforming agents involved in self-identity building.

Consider for example, Canclini (2006) observes a current identity displacement from citizen to consumer and argues that the identity transformations caused by advanced capitalism do not represent merely a homogenization process, but, rather, the reordering of differences and inequalities, without suppressing them.[3] In this process, questions of citizenship have come to be defined "more by individual consumption of goods and means of communication than by abstract rules of democracy or by participation in political organizations" (Canclini, 2006, pp. 14, 29). Modern identities based on place are giving way

to identities configured by consumption (based on what you possess, or on what can be possessed); this process results in new identities, which include the long-term unemployed; informal, unstable workers; migrants propelled by poverty; the destitute, lacking fundamental human rights (Campione, 2003 p. 60). In this context of questionable "freedoms of choice" and "individual freedoms," the celebrated "identity flexibility" is less a means of emancipation, as states the hegemonic discourse, than a nefarious instrument of freedom redistribution, since "the more choices the rich seem to have, the less bearable to all is a life without choosing" (Bauman, 2001, pp. 104–106). Yet it is also clear that most of the world population today does not have access to the goods and services offered for this *consumer-based, identity-building* existence. As we know, the world's richest 20% currently own 82.7% of all the wealth, while 6% is shared among two-thirds of the poorest (Dowbor, 2009). These are alarming data; however, they are not referred to in various texts regarding consumer-based identity building. Champagne (1997, p. 78) claims that "the gap between consumer desires and available income that tends to be instilled in young people has never been as wide as today." Clearly, this shortage and discrepancy, in contrast with the model of society, which identifies itself by what it consumes, are also raw materials for identity-building tied to social exclusion.

Before moving on to analyze the text, we wish to emphasize that critical discourse analyses about homelessness and its representation have been employed in an integrated manner by *Red Latinoamericana de Análisis Crítico del Discurso de la Pobreza Extrema*. This investigation network, which gathers researchers from Argentina, Brazil, Chile, and Colombia plays a crucial role in stimulating deep and integrated understanding of sociodiscursive problems involved in homelessness in Latin America (see, among other works, Pardo, 2008; Pardo Abril, 2008; Quiroz, 2008; Silva, 2008; Montecino, 2010; Resende, 2010; Silva & Pardo Abril, 2010).

POVERTY AND REPRESENTATION OF POVERTY IN BRAZIL

In recent years, Brazil has invested in programs designed to eradicate poverty, which have proved successful according to the Institute of Applied Economic Research (Instituto de Pesquisa Econômica Aplicada) (IPEA, 2010, p. 8): "Between 2003 and 2008, the annual average decrease in national absolute poverty rate (up to half minimum wage per capita) was −3.1%, while the national extreme poverty rate (up to one-quarter minimum wage per capita) was −2.1%." Yet, there are still 16.2 million people living in extreme poverty, which corresponds to 8.5% of the population. Most Brazilians found in this category are black or multiracial,[4] and are concentrated in the north and northeast of Brazil, which are also the regions with less industrialization and lowest Human Development Index. A recent research study conducted at the University of Brasília concluded that there are 2,500 homeless people in the nation's capital, but the National Homeless People Movement (Movimento Nacional da População de Rua, MNPR) has questioned these data, claiming that the homeless population in the Federal District is underestimated in the study.

From time to time, the Brazilian government feels the need to "justify" to the privileged few the need to join efforts to combat poverty. What is clear to some is alternatively seen by the economically favored classes as "welfarist practices," which reallocate money from the rich to alleged "bums who do not want to work." A study of the following text in a newspaper targeting middle-class and upper-class readers in Brasília seeks to illustrate, based on the analysis of some linguistic-discursive categories, representations of the homeless situation, and therefore extreme poverty. As mentioned in the beginning of the chapter, the news article is particularly interesting because it was published in the *Correio Braziliense*, the most traditional newspaper in Brazil's capital, and reveals many examples of ideological discourses from the economically privileged classes.[5] In our analysis, we seek to map connections between what is discursive and what is nondiscursive. In addition, we consider social effects such as social changes that favor those who have least benefitted from capitalism or the consequences of reproducing power asymmetries, including economic disparity in Brazil.

"IVAN, THE HOMELESS GARDENER . . . ": GENERIC STRUCTURE AND RHETORICAL MOVEMENTS

The text analyzed in this chapter was published in the section "City Chronicles" in *Correio Braziliense*, the main newspaper of Brazil's capital. [See Appendix at end of chapter for complete article.] In general, the news articles in this section are dedicated to "personalities" living in town. The selected text tells the story of a 57-year-old man who was homeless for at least five years in Brasília. In this analysis, we discuss which aspects of this story are being privileged, which are reduced in importance, and which are excluded. We also see how, by means of linguistic-discursive resources employed in the text, a particular representation of reality and particular identities are constructed for the actors involved. Moreover, we consider how the text imprints the world and its readers. From this section, we analyze the text, noting that all critical discourse analysis is necessarily incomplete, biased and open to revision. The level of depth we bestow the category description is just enough for the particular text. For a more complete discussion, we recommend consulting the sources cited in the article.

Since it is anchored in the journalistic practice, the text that we analyze in this chapter is produced through and mediated by relationships between editors, journalists, readers of the capital city's main newspaper, the large-scale printing technology, and the Internet. Thompson (2002a, p. 79) calls this type of mediation "mediated quasi-interaction," due to the low degree of interpersonal reciprocity and the widespread articulation of social practices in different times and spaces. Fairclough (2003) points out that predominately one-sided communication flow and information availability lead to a significant increase in the capacity to transmit potentially ideological messages on a wide scale.

As modes of interaction, discourse genres imply specific activities tied to individual practices. In Bakhtin's terms, each social activity possesses specific purposes, or "intentional scopes" (1997, p. 291). Therefore, it is appropriate, according to Fairclough (2003, p. 70), to question "what are people doing discoursally," and to what effect. However, any analysis of "purposes of the activity," that is the purported ends or the functions of social policy, must be a cautious one for different purposes may be implicit, hierarchically combined, or merged so that the boundaries can be somewhat unclear. For instance, news articles that are meant to inform—at least in principle—may include strategic purposes, or be guided toward "selling" either a product, an idea, certain values, or a particular world view. These purposes materialize in texts in what is denominated "generic structure," specifically referencing the structural organization, the format of the text, or a textual aspect molded by discursive genres. This structure may be more homogenous in certain genres (such as a rental agreement) with rigidly fixed textual stages and elements that are predictable, ordained, and easily identified. In other genres which are freer, heterogeneous, plastic, unstable (such as a journalistic chronicle), it may not be possible to verify such a structure. Therefore, it may not be enough to approach certain genres in terms of generic structure.

In our analysis we apply a flexible concept of genre organization by asking: Is the text a news article? A journalistic chronicle? A literary chronicle? Or all of the above? Does it contain any elements of news reporting: headlines (with a process in the present tense "construct"), lead, news facts, photographs, or testimonies? We have found elements of a chronicle, a hybrid genre, which merges literature and journalism—such as descriptive sequences (physical descriptions of

Ivan) and narratives (narrations of Ivan's actions), as well as the *problem-solution* macro organization narrative. The aim of this section is therefore to investigate discursive hybridism that may indicate possible changes in journalistic practices and that allow for the circulation of potentially ideological meanings in texts that merge information and entertainment.

The text starts by introducing Ivan as someone who chose to become a "street dweller." It proceeds to narrate Ivan's story, with the initial problematization and typically literal narrative turnarounds, which romanticize Ivan's situation, as seen in this excerpt: [6]

(1) "Está tudo muito verde. Está faltando cor. Isso aqui estava sem graça." Ivan *trouxe então* a policromia . . .

"It's all very green. The colors are missing. This here looked boring." Ivan *then brought* polychromia . . . [7]

In this example, Ivan's voice is reproduced, supposedly using his exact words. In the beginning of the text (see Appendix), Ivan's romanticized character starts to be built with a typically literary structure. The last part of the text is dedicated to finding a "solution" for Ivan's life: counting on the help of a "solidary community" for getting scraps of food ("half a roast chicken" and "a bottle of strawberry yogurt") and other "gifts."

We can see that, in addition to disguising a critical case of neglect toward Ivan and reifying it as an "option in life," the generic structure, or rhetorical movement, contribute to legitimate dominance relations by means of a romanticized narrativization (Thompson, 2002b) where Ivan is the hero, but he exists only because of the alleged kindness of the neighborhood. Narrativization also serves to legitimate the idea that Ivan is only living in the streets because he is mentally ill and wishes to do so:

(2) *Esta não é a primeira vez* que Ivan constrói jardins na 307 Sul. *Há cinco anos*, ele esteve por lá, *conta o motorista de táxi José Mendonça*, 71 anos, 37 de praça, 26 no mesmo ponto.

"Fez um jardim, só que, coitado, era época de seca, mas mesmo assim ele fez. Agora voltou e do mesmo jeitinho, não ficou nem um pouquinho mais velho." *Da vez anterior, Ivan não falava do vovô ilustre.*

Mas contava que Deus estava "umbicando o planeta." (Nem o Houaiss nem o Aurélio registram o verbo "umbicar." O que mais se aproxima, foneticamente, é "imbicar," dar rumo certo, dirigir).

This is not the first time Ivan built gardens at 307 South. *Five years ago*, he was around that neighborhood, *says the taxi driver José Mendonça*, 71 years old, 37 years at the job and 26 on the same corner. "He made a garden but, poor thing, it was during the dry season, but he did it anyway. Now he came back exactly the same, he didn't get any older." *Last time, Ivan did not talk about his renowned grandfather.*

But he would say that God was "umbicating the planet." (Neither Houaiss nor Aurélio dictionaries record the verb "umbicar."[8] The closest word, phonetically, is "imbicar," which means head to the right direction, drive.)

In the *journalistic chronicle*, the narration creates Ivan's "insanity"—contrasting discourses of sanity and authority, as is the case when quoting the "dictionary," which legitimate Ivan's situation as a personal choice, and not as a shortcoming of society and the state. This is reinforced at the end of the text through Ivan's own voice:

(3) " . . . esse progresso todo, carro, moto, micro-ondas, amaciante de roupa, não serve para nada. *A responsabilidade é pessoal.* Ninguém é julgado pela cabeça de ninguém."

" . . . all this progress, cars, motorcycles, microwaves, fabric softeners, are all for nothing. *Responsibility is personal.* Nobody is judged by anyone's mind."

In the following sections, we broadened the analysis on identity processes within the text, focusing on the categories of evaluation, relational identity, and metaphor, respectively.

EVALUATION IN THE TEXT "IVAN, THE HOMELESS GARDENER . . . "

In discourse analysis, evaluation is a category referring to the perspectives of the speaker, more or less explicit, regarding what he or she considers to be good or bad, or what he or she does or does not desire, and so forth (Fairclough, 2003). Evaluations, as a particular way of positioning oneself before the world, are always biased, subjective, and consequently, tied to individual identity processes. If these processes involve ideological standpoints, they may act in favor of dominance projects.

In the text we highlight some of the linguistic-discursive forms of evaluative statements, such as affective evaluations, and value assumptions.[9] In *evaluation statements*, the evaluative element can be explicit, such as with an attribute, a verb, an adverb, or an exclamation point. Or it can also be less explicit or merely assumed. *Affective evaluations* are statements that involve psychological events, such as reflections, feelings, and perceptions (Halliday, 1985, p. 106). Finally, *value assumptions* include the most implicit evaluation, with no transparent markers, such as the example (4) given below:

(4) Ivan agradece e comenta . . .: "Comer não é problema. Recebo a *solidariedade* dos moradores dos edifícios. Já fiz muitas *amizades*. Se as pessoas estão gostando de mim, isso é muito *bom*."

Ivan thanks her and comments . . .: "Food is not a problem. I accept the *solidarity* of the community. I made many *friends*. If people like me, that's really *good*."

Here we have a value assumption, where the word "solidarity" constitutes an evaluative element with a latent positive connotation. This allows us to verify that Ivan is represented in the text as someone who positively assesses his relationship with the community, also seen in the classification of these people as his "friends" and in the explicit evaluative statement "that's really good," emphasized by the adverb "really."

Another case of value assumption appears in example (5):

(5) Tem por ferramenta apenas uma pá de pedreiro, *presente* de um motorista de táxi do ponto ao lado.

His only tool is a mason shovel, a *gift* from a taxi driver from the corner.

In this example, the word "gift" has a positive connotation, which again represents the relationship as positive between Ivan and the middle-class people who surround him, thus emphasizing an alleged "kindness" manifested by those who see Ivan living in the streets.

There are other relevant evaluations, such as:

(6) Ana Luiza Rodrigues diz que ela e o marido se *encantaram* quando, num passeio de fim de tarde pela quadra, viram o *cuidado* com que Ivan põe tampinhas coloridas de garrafas sobre as pedras que delimitam um dos jardins. "*Que capricho! Que delicadeza a dele*", ela diz. "Ele é muito *carinhoso*. Fica na chuva cuidando das plantas."

Ana Luiza Rodrigues says that she and her husband were *delighted* when, during an afternoon stroll around the block, they saw how *carefully* Ivan placed colorful bottle caps on the stones that delimit one of the gardens. "*How meticulous! How delicate he is,*" she says. "He is a very *caring* person. He stays in the rain tending to the plants."

Here there are explicit evaluative statements with the affective mental process "delighted," which expresses positive perception; with the attribute "caring"; with exclamations ("How meticulous! How delicate he is"), as well as another positive value assumption, "carefully," which has an eminently positive, desirable meaning.

All these positive evaluations, repeated, and in italics in the text are very questionable because they dissimulate, by means of euphemisms, the not-so-positive or not-so-desirable situation of a citizen who has been virtually abandoned by the state, reaching the point where

"delightful" is the word expressed to identify the condition of a human being who "stays in the rain tending to the plants."

The evaluations help us to notice that the speaker's discourse, from a social, cultural, and historical perspective, belongs to someone who is favorably positioned toward Ivan's destitute situation. Thus the text is acting ideologically evidencing the service of dominance relations implied in the social problem, since homelessness is so naturalized that it becomes positively evaluated. The upper middle-class community is identified as kind-hearted people who help the "homeless gardener." Ivan, in turn, is presented as someone who is grateful for this "help."

RELATIONAL IDENTITY IN THE TEXT "IVAN, THE HOMELESS GARDENER . . . "

Relational identification concerns the identity of social actors in texts in terms of personal, family, or work relationships. This type of identification is *relational* in the sense that it depends on established social relations and the positions held by the social actors (Resende, 2009a). Ivan's identity is built in two ways in the text: (1) as a lunatic, delirious, crazy; and (2) as a charity beneficiary. In the first case, specific vocabulary is used from science that "classifies" and defines what is "madness," for instance ("delirious," "erratic," "wanderer," "fantasy"), and speech representation using Ivan's direct speech. This form of identity-building predominates in the first part of the text. In the second case, when Ivan is identified as a charity/solidarity beneficiary, we say identification is relational because building Ivan's *image* as a beneficiary depends on the representation of established social relations, denoting continuity between relational and identificational aspects in the text. This can be seen in the examples below:

(7) Tem por ferramenta apenas uma pá de pedreiro, *presente* de um motorista de táxi do ponto ao lado.

His only tool is a mason shovel, a *gift* from a taxi driver from the corner.

(8) "Fez um jardim, só que, *coitado*, era época de seca, mas mesmo assim ele fez." [Voz do taxista]

"He made a garden but, *poor thing*, it was during the dry season, but he did it anyway." [Taxi driver's voice]

(9) Passava pouco das 11h, quando uma moradora da quadra *trouxe para Ivan, na volta do supermercado, dois sacos plásticos: um com metade de um frango assado e outro com uma garrafa de iogurte de morango.*

It was shortly past 11 a.m. when a neighbor, *on the way back from the supermarket, brought Ivan two plastic bags: one with half a roast chicken and another with a bottle of strawberry yogurt.*

(10) Outra moradora . . . *traz um saco plástico com pães.* Conta que todos os dias passa por ali e *leva algo para Ivan comer.*

Another neighbor . . . *brings a plastic bag full of bread.* She says that she stops by every day and *brings Ivan something to eat.*

(11) Ivan agradece e comenta . . .: "Comer não é problema. *Recebo a solidariedade dos moradores dos edifícios.*"

Ivan thanks her and comments . . .: "Food is not a problem. *I accept the solidarity of the community.*"

Thus Ivan is represented as a lucky beneficiary of charity and warmth from "solidary neighbors" and a friendly taxi driver, as seen in examples 7, 9, and 10. In excerpt 11, even Ivan identifies himself this way in the representation of his speech, and according to the journalist, states that "he made many friends." The text does not question, however, if this type of relationship can really be classified as *friendship*. Should one expect from a friend a lunch invitation or plastic bags full of food? Should one expect fulfillment of immediate needs or support for solving the problems that generate these unfulfilled needs? Do these "solidary neighbors" and the journalist know that Ivan is by law entitled to his rights? According to Article 6 of the Brazilian Constitution (1988), "Education, health, work, leisure, security, social security, protection of motherhood and childhood, and assistance to the destitute, are social rights, as set forth by this Constitution." However, this is not what occurs in real life, especially regarding the homeless population.

There is a fine line in the relationship between homeless people and the *included* society, rarely surpassing piety[10] (see how Ivan is identified as "poor thing" in example 8) and charity ("food is not a problem"). Without clearly stating it, the text implies that there are no ears to hear Ivan's *delirious* voice: "He repeats the same story many times *to whoever wishes to listen.*"[11]

Metaphor in the Text "Ivan, the Homeless Gardener . . . "

The essence of metaphor consists in "understanding and experiencing one kind of thing in terms of another" (Lakoff & Johnson, 2002). Our conceptual system is by nature metaphorical that is, we always comprehend the world according to our own physical and cultural experience, and in terms of other aspects with established correlations. The metaphorical concepts that structure our thoughts, also structure our perceptions, our behavior, our relationships, our personal and social identity. By selecting particular metaphors within a universe of other possibilities, a speaker understands his or her reality and identifies it in a particular manner, albeit guided by cultural aspects. What ensues, Fairclough (2001, p. 241) observes is that "all types of metaphor necessarily highlight or enshroud certain aspects of what is represented."

Lakoff and Johnson (2002, p. 50) discuss three types of metaphors. The *conceptual metaphors,* where we understand aspects of concepts in terms of another (see excerpt 12, below); *orientational metaphors,* where we organize concepts in relation to a spatial organization (excerpts 13 and 14), and, finally, *ontological metaphors*, where we understand our experiences in terms of entities, objects and substances (excerpts 15 and 16).

(12) É para *driblar* a ansiedade que Ivan da Cunha, carioca, 57 anos, *quixotescamente* magro e inquieto . . .

In order to *dribble*[12] (circumvent) anxiety, Ivan da Cunha, born in Rio de Janeiro, 57 years old, *quixotically* thin and restless . . .

(13) Ivan continua crente que Nosso Senhor está umbicando a Terra, o que significa "*levando para baixo* tudo o que não presta, ladrão, traficante, assaltante."

Ivan continues to believe that the Lord is "umbicating"[13] the Earth, which means "*taking down* everything that is no good: thieves, drug dealers, muggers."

(14) Avisa que, depois que Deus umbicou o mundo, "*só vai cair* quem estiver com perfume podre por dentro."

He warns that, after God "umbicated" the world, "only those who have rotten perfume within *will go down.*"

(15) . . . constrói um jardim de plantas naturais, enfeitadas com peças de plástico, de metal, de papel, que *o lixo lhe oferece* em sua vida de morador de rua.

. . . builds a garden of natural plants ornamented with scraps of plastic, metal and paper that *the garbage offers him* in his life as a street dweller.

(16) Em alguns momentos, conta *pedaços de sua vida* que parecem estar conectados com a realidade.

Sometimes, he tells *pieces of his life* that seem to be connected to reality.

In excerpt 12, in addition to the metaphor that conceives Ivan's hardships in life in terms of a *game* ("dribble"[14]), there is the use of one of the main metaphors responsible for building not only the journalistic-literary style of the chronicle, but also Ivan's and the journalist's identification. By means of metaphor (quixotically), the speaker shows his understanding of Ivan's situation, drawing a comparison with Cervantes' character Don Quixote, the roaming knight, whose deeds oscillate between fantasy and reality, just as Ivan is represented in the text: as the "wanderer-gardener"

hero. The excerpts below reinforce this *romantic* interpretation (17 and 18), using the words *heroic* (19 and 21), and *visionary* (17, 18, and 20) to describe Ivan's dramatic condition, which is further corroborated by other passages in the text:

(17) Ivan entremeia natureza e objetos, *realidade e delírio no seu errático viver.*

Ivan intertwines nature with objects, *reality* with *delusion*, in his erratic lifestyle.

(18) O sotaque carioca é a prova de que Ivan *não vive apenas na imensidão da fantasia.*

His carioca accent is proof that Ivan *does not only live within the realm of fantasy.*

(19) "Agora voltou e do mesmo jeitinho, *não ficou nem um pouquinho mais velho.*" [Voz do taxista]

"Now he came back exactly the same, *he didn't get any older.*" [Voice of the taxi driver]

(20) Ivan divide o mundo entre o bem e o mal . . .

Ivan divides the world into good and evil . . .

(21) O jardineiro das flores de tampa de garrafa . . .

The gardener of bottle-cap flowers . . .

For the reader familiar with the classic Don Quixote, it is not hard to notice the suggestive association between "the Knight of the Sad Countenance" and the "the gardener of bottle-cap flowers" (excerpt 21). This particular way of identifying Ivan dissimulates dominance relations, concealing and masking the serious problem of social inequality because it recognizes Ivan's incessant battle to survive as a done deed.

In the above excerpts, there are appreciations selected by the journalist about what Ivan would consider bad (excerpts 13 and 14), in the form of orientational metaphors that point "down," since, according to Lakoff and Johnson (2002), in Western culture generally what is bad is understood by spacing down. There are also ontological metaphors, through which the speaker understands Ivan's life in terms of an object ("pieces," excerpt 16) whose existence is assured by "garbage," which, unlike Ivan's life, is personified.

FINAL CONSIDERATIONS

Our analysis shows that the text "Ivan the Homeless Gardener Builds Garden in 307 South" materializes discourses that naturalize the homeless situation, first by ignoring very serious issues regarding social inequality, and then by reifying the homeless situation when representing it as permanent. The invisibility of the homeless population and the degree in which contemporary societies are inured to extreme poverty are partially discursive problems, tied to the naturalization of discourse about social insecurity and dissimulation of dire social matters (Resende, 2009c; Ramalho & Resende, 2011).

In our section on genre analysis, the narration builds on Ivan's *insanity*, and in contrast to discourses of sanity and authority, legitimizes Ivan's situation as an individual choice and not a shortcoming of society and the state. The rhetorical movements contribute to legitimate dominance relations by means of narrativization in a romanticized story with Ivan as the hero. Narrativization also serves to legitimate the idea that Ivan is only living in the streets because he is mentally ill and so wishes.

Positive evaluations, repeated and underlined in the text, are extremely questionable due to the fact that they conceal the less positive or desirable aspects of the situation in which a citizen has been abandoned by the state. Ivan is represented as someone who views his relationship with the community in a positive light, and the street situation is so naturalized that it is viewed as positive.

Ivan's identification is built in two ways in the text: as a lunatic, a delirious madman; and as a beneficiary of charity. In the first case, specific vocabulary is used and speech representation evinced through Ivan's direct speech. In the second case, Ivan's *image* as a beneficiary depends on the representation of established social relations, denoting continuity between relational and identificational aspects in the text. The articulation of disciplinary discourses with Ivan's voice is notable and, in the text, it represents the "internal coherence in Ivan's delirium."

Based on Thompson (2002b), an analysis of Ivan's identification and the representation of his situation reveal at least two *modi operandi* of ideology. The first mode, dissimulation, obscures dominant relations of power by the use of euphemisms, which consist in positive value-building of undesirable actions and relations. The second mode is reification, in which a transitory situation is represented as permanent and natural by means of naturalization, which represents Ivan's condemnable and reversible situation, not as a result of capitalist exploitation, but rather as something natural and even admirable.

NOTES

1. According to Quiroz (2008, p.79), discourse analysis is a means, more than an end in itself, designed to explore the systematic manner in which social actors or groups legitimate world views, or how they oppose them by offering alternatives to hegemonic forms of constructing social reality.

2. The interdisciplinary traits of this body of work can be explained by the "breakdown of epistemological boundaries" regarding social theories, which aims to both subsidize its own sociodiscursive approach and offer support so that social research may also contemplate discursive aspects (Resende & Ramalho, 2006, p. 14). CDA also offers theoretical-methodological frameworks for analyzing a broad range of social science data, including ethnographic data.

3. These tendencies point toward a process in which identities are increasingly less organized around national symbols and begin to inspire themselves in what is suggested by means of communication (Canclini, 2006), which shows the global-local dialectics (rendered viable by communication technology) in the constitution of identification processes of identities.

4. The word in Portuguese is *pardo*, a comprehensive skin color category, including people of Amerindian and/or African descent.

5. It is worth remembering that the relationship between discourse meanings—action, representation, identification—is dialectical, such that each one internalizes traits of another, without being reduced to one. This implies, for instance, that a *particular discourse* (representation) can be legitimized in specific *genres* (action/relation) and inculcated in *styles* projected in the construction of identities and identifications.

Therefore, discourses, genres, and styles occur in semantic, grammatical, and lexical traces of texts. This implies that relatively stable forms of employing language in order to represent, interact, identify, and be identified in social practices are materialized in texts. Although the relationship between discourses, genres, and styles is dialectical, specific traits (vocabulary, semantic, and grammatical relationships) are, in principle, associated with specific genres, discourses, and styles. Genres occur in meanings and forms of action in texts. Discourses are associated with meanings and representational forms. Styles, in turn, are meanings and forms of identification (Fairclough, 2003, p. 67). When speaking here of "analytical categories" (rhetorical movements; evaluation; relational identity; metaphor), we are therefore referring to textual forms and meanings associated with specific ways of representing, interacting, identifying and being identified in situated social practices (Ramalho & Resende, 2011).

6. In all examples, the highlights are ours and indicate the element being analyzed. For all the excerpts of the analyzed text, we kept the original in Portuguese, followed by the translation. The entire newspaper article is reproduced in the Appendix.

7. We comment on this aspect of the text again further on; for now, we are only interested in discussing rhetorical macrostructure.

8. *Houaiss* and *Aurélio* are the most important Portuguese language dictionaries in Brazil.

9. Evaluation statements are statements about what is considered desirable or undesirable, relevant or irrelevant. Evaluation is subject to an intensity scale—for instance, evaluative adjectives and adverbs are grouped into semantic sets of terms that vary from low to high intensity, such as in the continuum good to great to excellent. In the case of affective evaluations, evaluations are said to be "affective" because they are generally marked subjectively. In other words, they explicitly mark the statement as being the author's, in structures such as "I *hate* this," "I *like* this," "I *adore* this." As examples suggest, these cases also observe gradation between low and high affinity. Value assumptions are cases in which evaluation is not triggered by relatively transparent evaluation markers, where values are deeply inserted into the text.

10. See Resende (2009b) for more information on the subject.

11. According to the reporter, the story that Ivan "repeats . . . *to whomever wishes to listen,*" concerns Ivan's "deliriums" (that he is the former President Fernando Henrique Cardoso's grandson and brother of world-famous celebrities of the music industry (Celine Dion), fashion industry (Gisele Bündchen) and Brazilian soap star (Juliana Paes). These "deliriums" are employed in the text to construct his romanticized story. Ivan's madness in not directly stated, but it is made clear by means of references to these distorted stories.

12. This is a soccer term that refers to movements that a player makes with the ball to deter an opposing player from taking the ball—"dribbling" anxiety, therefore, is avoiding anxiety.

13. The word *umbicate* does not exist in the Portuguese language, and therefore cannot be translated. This is, as suggested by the text in its reference to the dictionary—see example 2—a word invented by Ivan in his "delirium." The closest meaning for this excerpt is, "the Lord is guiding, orienting the Earth."

14. See note 7.

REFERENCES

Bakhtin, Mikhail. (1997). *Estética da criação verbal* (Maria E. Galvão G. Pereira, Trans.). São Paulo, BR: Martins Fontes. (Original work published 1953).

Bauman, Zygmunt. (2001). *Modernidade líquida* (Plínio Dentzien, Trans.). Rio de Janeiro, BR: Jorge Zahar.

Bhaskar, Roy. (1998). Philosophy and scientific realism. In M. Archer, R. Bhaskar, A. Collier, T. Lawson, & A. Norrie (Eds.), *Critical realism: Essential readings* (pp. 16–47). London, UK: Routledge.

Brasil. (1998). *Constituição da República Federativa do Brasil*. Retrieved from http://www.planalto.gov.br/ccivil_03/constituicao/constitui%C3%A7ao.htm.

Campione, Daniel. (2003). Hegemonia e contra-hegemonia na América Latina. In C. N. Coutinho, & A. P. Teixeira (Eds.), *Ler Gramsci, entender a realidade* (pp. 51–66). Rio de Janeiro, BR: Civilização Brasileira.

Canclini, Nestor García. (2006). *Consumidores e cidadãos: Conflitos multiculturais da globalização* (Maurício Santana Dias, Trans.). Rio de Janeiro, BR: UFRJ.

Castells, Manuel. (2001). *O poder da identidade.* (Klauss B. Gerhardt, Trans.). São Paulo, BR: Paz e Terra.

Champagne, Patrick. (1997). A visão mediática. In P. Bourdieu (Ed.), *A miséria do mundo* (pp. 63–79) (Mateus S. Soares de Azevedo, Trans.). Petrópolis, BR: Vozes.

Chouliaraki, Lilie, & Fairclough, Norman. (1999). *Discourse in late modernity: Rethinking critical discourse analysis*. Edinburgh, UK: Edinburgh University Press.

Dowbor, Ladislau. (2009). *A crise financeira sem mistérios: Convergência dos dramas econômicos, sociais e ambientais*. Retrieved from http://www.cartamaior.com.br.

Fairclough, Norman. (2001). *Discurso e mudança social* (Izabel Magalhães, Trans.). Brasília, BR: Universidade de Brasília.

Fairclough, Norman. (2003). *Analysing discourse: Textual analysis for social research*. London, UK: Routledge.

Halliday, Michael A. K. (1985). *Introduction to functional grammar*. London, UK: Edward Arnold.

Instituto de Pesquisa Econômica Aplicada (IPEA). (2010). Pobreza, desigualdade e políticas públicas. *Comunicados da Presidência, 38*. Retrieved from http://www.ipea.gov.br/sites/000/2/comunicado_presidencia/100112Comunicado38.pdf.

Lakoff, George, & Johnson, Mark. (2002). *Metáforas da vida cotidiana* (Mara Sophia Zanotto, Trans.). São Paulo, BR: Mercado de Letras, Educ.

Miller, Carolyn. (1994). Rhetorical community: The cultural basis of genre. In A. Freedman & P. Medway (Eds.), *Genre and the new rhetoric* (pp. 67–78). London, UK: Taylor & Francis.

Montecino, Lésmer. (2010). Historias de vida de personas en situación de calle de Santiago de Chile: Descriptión de una prática discursiva. In L. Montecino (Ed.), *Discurso, pobreza y exclusión en América Latina* (pp. 245–272). Santiago, CL: Cuarto Propio.

Pardo Abril, Neyla. (2008). *¿Que nos dicen? ¿Que vemos? ¿Que és. . . pobreza?* Bogotá: Universidad Nacional de Colombia.

Pardo, María Laura. (2008). Una metodología para la investigación lingüística del discurso. In M. L. Pardo (Ed.), *El discurso sobre la pobreza en América Latina* (pp. 55–78). Santiago, CL: Frasis.

Quiroz, Beatriz. (2008). La identidad vinculada a la calle en el discurso de personas sin techo. In M. L. Pardo (Ed.), *El discurso sobre la pobreza en América Latina* (pp. 79–97). Santiago, CL: Frasis.

Ramalho, Viviane, & Resende, Viviane M. (2011). *Análise de discurso (para a) crítica: O texto como material de pesquisa*. São Paulo, BR: Pontes.

Resende, Viviane M. (2009a). *Análise de discurso crítica e realismo crítico. Implicações interdisciplinares*. São Paulo, BR: Pontes.

Resende, Viviane M. (2009b). "It's not a matter of inhumanity": A critical discourse analysis of an apartment building circular on 'homeless people.'" *Discourse & Society, 20*, 363–379.

Resende, Viviane M. (2010). A crise do movimento nacional de meninos e meninas de rua no Brasil e o protagonismo juvenil: Uma crítica explanatória com base em análise discursiva. In L. Montecino (Ed.), *Discurso, pobreza e exclusión en América Latina* (pp. 349–364). Santiago, CL: Cuarto Propio.

Resende, Viviane M., & Ramalho, Viviane. (2006). *Análise de discurso crítica*. São Paulo, BR: Contexto.

Silva, Denize Elena G. (2008). A pobreza no contexto brasileiro: Da exclusão econômica e social à ruptura familiar. *Discurso & Sociedad, 2*, 265–296.

Silva, Denize Elena G., & Pardo, Neyla G. (2010, April). Miradas cruzadas hacia la pobreza desde una perspectiva crítica transdiciplinaria. *Cadernos de Linguagem e Sociedade, 11*(1), 66–90.

Swales, John M. (1990). *Genre analysis: English in academic and research settings*. Cambridge, UK: Cambridge University Press.

Thompson, John B. (2002a). *Ideologia e cultura moderna: Teoria social crítica na era dos meios de comunicação de massa* (Pedrinho A. Guareschi, Trans.). Petrópolis, BR: Vozes.

Thompson, John B. (2002b). *A mídia e a modernidade: Uma teoria social da mídia* (Wagner de Oliveira Brandão, Trans.). Petrópolis, BR: Vozes.

Wodak, Ruth. (2004). Do que trata a ACD—Um resumo de sua história, conceitos importantes e seus desenvolvimentos. *Linguagem em (Dis)curso, 4*, 223–243.

APPENDIX 2.1

Ivan the Homeless Gardener Builds Garden in 307 South

He tells delirious stories, but plants real bushes and flowers. He then hangs colorful objects on them. All this to control anxiety and "humanize stupidity." In order to dribble from anxiety, Ivan da Cunha, born in Rio de Janeiro, 57 years old, quixotically thin and restless, builds a garden of natural plants ornamented with scraps of plastic, metal and paper that the garbage offers in his life as a street dweller. Ivan intersperses nature with objects, reality with delirium, in his erratic lifestyle.

The homeless gardener began creating his garden shortly more than a month ago, beside Block K and in front of Block J at SQS 307. His only tool is a mason shovel, a gift from a taxi driver from the corner. He squats on the grass and removes garbage and rubble ("this was looking too ugly") and digs little pits with his long and bony fingers.

He removes seedlings from abandoned gardens nearby and builds his own green paradise. The green monotony intrigues him. "It's all very green. The colors are missing. This here looked boring." Ivan then brought polychromia: he picked colorful plastic bottle caps and made flowers out of them. Empty bottles of fabric softener, for instance, transform into flowers hanging from the tip of a tree branch. "Color livens the mood, humanizes stupidity," he says with surprising fluency in vocabulary.

"I do this to kill time, so I don't get too anxious, while I wait for [former president] Fernando Henrique Cardoso, my grandpa, to come for me. He will come with my sisters Gisele Bündchen, Celine Dion, and Juliana Paes. We will head to Toronto, in Canada, Celine has property there. They will bring me a nice pair of sneakers, clean clothes, but before I will have to take a soap bath."

Pieces of Life

There is internal coherence in Ivan's delirium. He repeats the same story many times to whoever wishes to listen. Sometimes, he tells pieces of his life that seem to be connected to reality. He says he was born in Rio de Janeiro when it was still called Estado da Guanabara, that he lived in Laranjeiras. His carioca accent is proof that Ivan does not only live within the realm of fantasy. He says he had a mother, but not a "human dad." That he has two sisters "in flesh and blood," Rosinha and Teresinha, "plus the three others I did not know (Gisele, Celine, and Juliana), the celebrities." That he has been a machine operator, a mason's helper, and a watchman. That he came from Vilhena, Rondonia, "two thousand kilometers away," that he has been to Central America ("Nicaragua, Guatemala, Costa Rica, Panama, El Salvador"). He says he did not go to Mexico because "immigration did not allow it," but that he will now go to the Federal Police to provide a passport "with a five-by-seven photograph." After Toronto he will head to Tokyo and Baghdad—he, his grandpa, and his three sisters.

This is not the first time Ivan builds gardens at 307 South. Five years ago, he was around that neighborhood, says the taxi driver José Mendonça, 71 years old, 37 years at the job and 26 years

33

on the same corner. "He made a garden but, poor thing, it was during the dry season, but he did it anyway. Now he came back exactly the same, he didn't get any older." Last time, Ivan did not talk about his renowned grandfather.

But he would say that God was "umbicating the planet." (Neither *Houaiss* nor *Aurélio* include the verb "umbicar." The closest word, phonetically, is "imbicar," which means head to the right direction, drive). Ivan continues to believe that the Lord is umbicating the Earth, which means "taking down everything that is no good: thieves, drug dealers, muggers." He says that, the other day, a teenager sat next to him on the garden bench, and asked him if he "had any drugs to sell." Ivan remembers the episode with considerable indignation. He says the only things he does wrong are smoking ("straw cigarette because it has no nicotine") and drinking coffee. He drank beer before, but today he will not touch it.

Solidary Neighbors

It was shortly past 11 a.m. when a neighbor, on her way back from the supermarket, brought Ivan two plastic bags: one with half a roast chicken and another with a bottle of strawberry yogurt. Ana Luiza Rodrigues says that she and her husband were delighted when, during an afternoon stroll around the block, they saw how carefully Ivan placed colorful bottle caps on the stones that delimit one of the gardens. "How meticulous! How delicate he is," she says. "He is a very caring person. He stays under the rain tending to the plants." Another neighbor, Walkyria Oliveira, 81 years old, living in Brasília for 47 years on the same block brings a plastic bag full of bread. She says that she stops by every day and brings Ivan something to eat. "He feeds the birds." Ivan thanks her and comments, after Ms. Oliveira leaves: "Food is not a problem. I accept the solidarity of the community." I made many friends. If people like me, that's really good."

Ivan divides the world into good and evil, God and "that one" (Ivan pronounces the name Lucifer only once and with an expression showing repulsion). The gardener of bottle-cap flowers says that when the Lord umbicated the world, he separated the good from the evil, because "all this progress, cars, motorcycles, microwaves, fabric softeners, are all for nothing. Responsibility is personal. Nobody is judged by anyone's mind." He warns that, after God umbicates the world, "only those who have rotten perfume within will go down."

The "Horned One" prevented him from having children in flesh and blood. "He was stealing from me, but the Lord paid me back. He gave me a beautiful wife and five kids, three girls and two boys"—all in another realm, the immaterial one. And he smiles a fulfilled smile. At this time, if it is not late at night, Ivan is planting real and fake flowers in his garden.

Source: Correio Braziliense. "Ivan, o andarilho-jardineiro, constrói jardim em gramado da 307 Sul." Published on April 3, 2009.

3

LINGUISTIC DISCRIMINATION, POVERTY, AND THE OTOMÍ IN MEXICO

ROLAND TERBORG AND LAURA GARCÍA LANDA

INTRODUCTION

According to the standard measurement of the poverty line (cf. Rowntree, 1902; Orshansky, 1965), poverty in Mexico is generally associated with income and a person's access to food, clothing, housing, and health. We hold a wider view and see poverty as a failure in the capacity to meet a person's needs, according to the kind of life he or she pursues in a given context, and considering interpersonal variables (Sen, 1981, 1984, 1992; Rodríguez Campos, 2009). In this chapter, we use sociolinguistics to examine poverty among indigenous people in Mexico. In particular, we rely on the concept of conversational inference, which Gumperz (1991) characterizes as referring to processes that evoke a cultural background and which enable us to interpret speech.

Our aim is to show that people who speak indigenous languages face discriminating discourses that result in tangible forms of poverty that are not always captured by the poverty line. Using indigenous language excludes people from participating in external activities with other communities, and even in most of the domains within their communities. In contrast, when people use Spanish they gain access to food, clothing, housing, health, and education. Our research was conducted in a village where both the indigenous language of Otomí and Spanish are spoken. We found that speaking Otomí is strongly correlated with living in poverty—even when speakers speak Spanish, but with an accent that reveals their native language is Otomí. Our previous research showed that people who speak Spanish with such an accent are considered less qualified for better paying jobs (Terborg & Velázquez, 2008a). In this chapter, we build on our earlier research and demonstrate some of the ways in which speaking Otomí places people at greater risk of poverty. In short, we find that rates of poverty may differ according to the language one speaks.

POVERTY IN MEXICO

Of course there are multiple and complex causes of poverty in Mexico. Consider for example, that the economic crises and natural disasters of the 1990s strongly and negatively affected the national economy. In addition, over the years economic difficulties have been exacerbated by a comparative trade disadvantage, which generates an unequal interchange of merchandise and leads to underdevelopment. In 2003, economic conditions worsened in Mexico as a consequence of the combined effects of fluctuations in the international economy and badly directed government efforts within Mexico. For example, the neoliberal practice of cutting government support to agricultural production combined with international competition forced Mexican agronomy to compete in unequal conditions. Further, political instability and dishonest power groups contributed to deepening poverty (Torres Medina, Juárez Sánchez, Ramirez Valverde, & Ramirez Valverde, 2007). Even the impact of technology has intensified existing economic inequalities.

Of the 120 million people living in Mexico, 44% live under the poverty line (Bureau of Western Hemisphere Affairs, 2010). The official poverty line in Mexico is set at an income of $1.08 per a day. This is the level at which an individual does not have enough resources to buy food; however, this figure has not been updated as the cost of food has changed. As a result, the official poverty line constantly spirals downward and worsens the living conditions of the poor (Hunter, 2004; Rodriguez Campos, 2009). Beyond this simplistic notion of poverty as the cost of food, more complex notions of poverty address a relative social standard approach. In a relative standards approach, poverty is the inability to participate fully in social life due to insufficient resources. It is the impossibility of living a normal life in a given society, as perceived by the community itself. In this sense, poverty has to do with social needs not just material goods. In short, in this framework poverty is related to citizenship. Participation as

a citizen means participating in the economic, civil, cultural, and political realms of a society. In this framework, "poverty inhibits participation and leads to a second class citizenship" (Lister, 2004, p. 165). From this perspective, poverty shapes the kinds of opportunities that are opened and foreclosed to individuals regarding daily aspects of life such as food, housing, clothing, health, travel, community participation and social inclusion. Consequently, when determining poverty, individual differences, interpersonal variables, welfare, and social exclusion are all important. But how do we measure this notion of poverty?

The methods to measure poverty in Mexico have varied over the last decades (Damián & Boltvinik, 2003). The most common approaches use either the poverty line method (LP) or the method of integrated poverty measure (MMIP), which combines the poverty line, unsatisfied basic needs (NBI) and the length of time in poverty. Some critics point out that the samples for these measures are not representative, based on the fact that neither the poorest homes (generally in the indigenous regions where Spanish is not spoken) nor the richest ones are considered in the surveys. One consequence of this limitation is that it causes distortion both in the calculation of poverty and of income growth. The most widely used method for measuring poverty in Mexico is the poverty line (LP). However, this is an indirect measure. For example, based only on income and the cost of food, one can determine if a person *should* be able to meet his or her basic needs— but there is no way to verify if the person is *actually* able to do so. One of the main limitations of this method is that it presupposes that the satisfaction of basic needs depends only on current income; it does not take into account other sources of well-being. As a consequence, an individual can have a certain number of basic needs unsatisfied (education, health, and housing) and yet not be considered poor if his or her income is above the poverty line (Damián & Boltvinik, 2003). In addition, these statistics are generally expressed per capita; consequently poverty is conceptualized by regions.

An alternative way of measuring poverty in Mexico is based on the cost of groceries in rural and urban areas. In 1979, Comisión Ecónmica para América Latina (CEPAL), known as CCNA in Mexico, developed a list of foods and quantities that are needed to satisfy basic caloric requirements—and the costs of these items are used to establish the poverty line. However given the outdated costs and the fact that the proportion of food is not a constant in time, this measure also underestimates poverty (Damián & Boltvinik, 2003).

A third method to measure poverty was developed for the first official study on the evolution of poverty in Mexico (1984–1992). In this study, the Instituto National de Estadística y Geografía (INEGI) and CEPAL included other factors in addition to food to calculate the poverty line. Yet, one of the pitfalls of this method is its ability to reconcile different poverty lines for rural and urban regions.

The limitations of existing methods led to the development of an integrated measure of poverty (MMIP) that includes income, unsatisfied basic needs, and the evaluation of well-being at home, including factors such as time available for domestic work, education, and recreation (Damián & Boltvinik, 2003). Yet in more recent years, the Consejo Nacional de Evaluación de la Política de Desarrollo Social (National Council of Social Development Policies Evaluation) proposed a multidimensional measure for poverty in Mexico. The Ley General de Desarrollo Social (LGDS) known as the General Law of Social Development set out

to guarantee the full exercise of the social rights set forth in the Political Constitution of Mexico, ensuring access to social development to the population as a whole. The law establishes as goals of the Política Nacional de Desarrollo Social (National Policy for Social Development), the promotion of conditions that allow enjoyment of social rights—both individual and collective—as well as the promotion of economic development with a social perspective aimed to raise population income and to reduce economic and social inequality. Freedom, distributive justice, solidarity, social participation and respect for diversity, transparency and

people's free will are the basic principles on which social policy should rest, according to the law (CONEVAL, 2010, p. 9).

The General Law of Social Development serves two functions. On the one hand, it created a public institution (with procedural and managerial autonomy) Consejo Nacional de Evaluación de la Política de Desarrollo Social (CONEVAL), to develop guiding principles and criteria for the characterization, detection, and measurement of poverty as well as to organize, evaluate, and legalize social development policies and programs. At the same time, the General Law of Social Development set forth legal definitions of social rights. For example, Article 6 of the General Law of Social Development defines social rights as having to do with nondiscrimination, education, health care, food, housing, enjoyment of a healthy environment, work, and social security. While, Article 36 of the same law stipulates that CONEVAL include at least the following eight indicators in measures of poverty:

- Current per capita income.
- Average educational gap in the household.
- Access to health services.
- Access to social security.
- Quality and spaces of the dwelling.
- Access to basic services in the dwelling.
- Access to food.
- Degree of social cohesion (CONEVAL, 2010, p. 9).

Within this framework, "A person is considered to be multidimensional poor when the exercise of at least one of her social rights is not guaranteed and if she also has an income that is insufficient to buy the goods and services required to fully satisfy her needs" (CONEVAL, 2010, p. 28).

After establishing an income and social deprivation index, any person can be categorized in one, and only one, of the following groups:

1. *Multidimensional poor.* People with an income below the well-being threshold and with one or more social deprivations.

2. *Vulnerable due to social deprivation.* Socially deprived people with an income higher than the well-being threshold.

3. *Vulnerable due to income.* Population with no social deprivations and with an income below the well-being threshold.

4. *Not multidimensional poor and not vulnerable.* Population with an income higher than the well-being threshold and with no social deprivations (CONEVAL, 2010, p. 32).

Among the multidimensional poor, it is also possible to identify populations in extreme multidimensional poverty. Among the 13 indicators of extreme multidimensional poverty are income below the well-being threshold, deprivation caused by an education gap; lack of access to health care, social security, food, housing, and basic housing services (CONEVAL, 2010, pp. 33–34).

In addition, the General Law of Social Development incorporated social cohesion among the indicators of poverty. In this way, it acknowledges the relevance of these contextual aspects measured at a territorial scale. Indicators of social cohesion include

the degree of social polarization of every state and municipality; the income ratio of the population living in extreme multidimensional poverty relative to the population that is not living in multidimensional poverty and that is not vulnerable; and, social networks (CONEVAL, 2010, p. 52).

Given this broader understanding of poverty in Mexico, we examine how discrimination by Mexican speakers against indigenous people and their languages contributes significantly to poverty. In particular, we assert that in history the dominant Mexican discourse has produced the association of indigenous peoples and their languages with poverty, ignorance, and disregard—despite the fact that indigenous people and their languages have a very honorable place throughout history.

The history of poverty in indigenous regions highlights the discrimination that Indians have suffered both during the Conquest period and after the Bourbon dynasty, which confined the use of indigenous languages to the most intimate domains. However, some languages such as Nahuatl served legislative purposes at certain points in history and speakers of that language were valued for their knowledge of the language (Barriga & Martin Butragueño, 2010). By contrast, today indigenous language speakers, since they speak little or no Spanish, are not even considered in the surveys regarding poverty (Damián & Boltvinik, 2003). Thus, we presume that Otomí speakers must be facing poverty, since a limited command of Spanish leads to limited access to education, to badly paid jobs, and to limited access to governmental health and legal services. As a consequence of rural economic conditions, many indigenous people migrated to urban environments in the hopes of raising their standard of living. However, in many cases their inclusion in a different set of work activities has led to a reconstruction of their lives and identities, as we will see in subsequent sections.

THE LINGUISTIC CONTEXT

As defined by the Instituto Nacional de Lenguas Indígenas, there are 68 linguistic groups in Mexico. In some way, the concept of linguistic group may be equivalent to the fuzzy concept of language (INALI, 2009). Most of these languages are in danger of extinction because of the dominant shift to the Spanish language. This affects languages with very few speakers, like Tlahuica, Matlazinca, Cochimí, Cucapá, Kikapú, Paipai, or Lacandon (Bartolomé, 1997, p. 31), as well as some villages with languages with a larger number of speakers. In the last decades, there has been a great decrease of speakers of the languages belonging to the family of Otomangue. In the State of Mexico, in the areas surrounding Mexico City, to the east, north, and west, if Spanish is excluded, Otomí and Mazahua are the most spoken languages. Its local capital,

Toluca is on the border between Mazahua and Otomí about 60 kilometers west of Mexico City. The Otomí language is spoken in the area east of Toluca and there are many villages in the State of Mexico were this language is threatened (González Ortiz, 2005).

Fishman (1991, pp. 87–110) defined eight stages of language shift associated with decline. According to this classification, Lastra describes several villages in Mexico that have reached the sixth and seventh stage (Lastra, 2001). The many causes for language shift are complex and intertwined. The most important are material backgrounds, public education, and the negative language attitudes of the over-arching culture that threaten local identities (Zimmermann, 1992). In an advanced stage of language shift, language attitudes are crucial (Crystal, 2000, p. 81). If most members of the speech community speak both languages, the minority language may be supported by positive attitudes. But negative attitudes in the community probably are the most critical in propelling shifts language in language use.

In our research we analyzed language shifts in the use of Otomí in San Cristóbal Huichochitlán. This is a village of approximately 2,000 residents about 4 kilometers north of Toluca. Our research consisted of questionnaires regarding language knowledge and language use. We separated and analyzed the subjects in our data by age groups. We found that the transmission of Otomí in the last 20 years has largely decreased. It is probable that during the next years or decades, Otomí will no longer be passed down to the next generation (see Terborg, García Landa, & Moore, 2006).

We also analyzed negative attitudes toward speakers of the Otomí language, since these attitudes play such a crucial role in language shift. It is important to stress the degree to which these negative attitudes are shared by speakers of Otomí and how much that internalized view also contributes to an acceleration of language shift. In this chapter, we present the results of a survey to illustrate the phenomenon of language shift in the mentioned village. Then, we illustrate the special problem of negative language attitudes in the context of Mexican history and present examples of different types of words or sentences that represent different kinds of values or ideologies. Finally, we present an analysis of interview fragments from local speakers of Otomí and compare them with the different discourse types from the past and present. Thus, we pay special attention to those persons who are representing ideologies of the past.

THE VILLAGE OF SAN CRISTÓBAL HUICHOCHITLÁN

Relying on the results of a 2001 to 2002 survey, we began our research with the knowledge that Otomí use has been considerably weakened in the village of San Cristóbal Huichochitlán (see also Lastra, 2001). To gain a better understanding of what was happening to Otomí speakers, we divided speakers in the village into three age groups: Group *A* from 5 to 20 years, Group *B* from 21 to 40 years, and Group *C* over 40 years. As is true in the census, we did not take into account children under 5. The age distribution of these groups provided overall balance to our study. For example, although Group *A* only covered an age span of 15 years, this was the largest group of Otomí speakers, whereas the smallest number of speakers was in group *C*. This distribution reflects both the high birth rates and the low life expectancy among the indigenous people in Mexico, who suffer from the worst forms of poverty.

We divided reported language skills into basic categories. Since people commonly say that they still understand a language that they do not actually speak (this is true for indigenous languages and for Spanish), we created four categories. In Category 1, the person speaks the language very well; in Category 2, the person speaks the language but not well; in Category 3, the person only understands the language, but does not speak it; and in Category 4, the person does not speak or understand the language.

Table 3.1 Language Skills by Age Group

Age group	Well	Little	Only understands	Any
A. 5–20 years	3%	12%	72%	13%
B. 21–40 years	77%	5%	13%	5%
C. over 40 years	100%	0%	0%	0%

The results demonstrated that members of Group *C* all had a good knowledge of Otomí, but 85% of the members of age Group *A* could barely transmit Otomí to their children. This is congruent with Lastra's data regarding language use in the State of Mexico, although her report does not include specific information about San Cristóbal Huichochitlán (Lastra, 2001, p. 156). Therefore, using Fishman's previously mentioned 8–point scale for tracking the stages of language decline, we determined that the process of language shift away from Otomí usage is in the late stages calculated at between 6 and 7 on the scale. At this point, popular attitudes become very important for the future of this indigenous language (see also Crystal, 2000, p. 81). Next, we discuss poverty and its role in some of these popular attitudes.

LANGUAGE ATTITUDES TOWARD INDIGENOUS LANGUAGES

Discrimination toward minority languages is well-known worldwide and appears in different ways. Cases of discriminatory comments are relatively common and are not limited to those who speak Otomí. Here we pay special attention to attitudes and values with regard to Otomí speakers. Often this is a deliberate act of discrimination. Other kind of attitudes may be more unconscious and are related to paternalistic behaviors. The person who is expressing discrimination does this in a well-meaning way thinking that indigenous people behave like children.

These kinds of attitudes have a long tradition and are related to characterizations like "indio"— a word that has a negative connotation, often reinforced by the adjective "pobre" (poor). This becomes particularly evident in expressions like "gente de costumbre" (people of traditions) and "gente de razón" (people of reason), which cannot be literally translated and have to be understood in the context of Mexican history. What are now considered discriminating discourses, decades ago used to be the common discourse. The first may be related to "ordinary people." Bartolomé defines these expressions as "paradox identities." Although belonging together, they express something negative, such as the oppositives: *policeman-thief*, *virgin-whore*, and *white man-indian* (indio).

En relación con lo anterior debemos apuntar que en la mayor parte de las áreas de relación interétnica de México sobreviven las bárbaras calificaciones coloniales que designan a los indios como *gente de costumbre* confrontada con la *gente de razón* que serían los mestizos y blancos (Bartolomé, 1997, p. 46).

So *gente de razón* refers to people who are able to speak Spanish and *gente de costumbre* is specific to people who speak an indigenous language. Accordingly, gente de razón may refer to people who are civilized, well educated, and more likely to be wealthy while the *others* still have to be civilized, educated, and brought out of poverty (Terborg & Velázquez, 2008b). In this sense, *gente de razón* is associated with Spanish speakers and *gente de costumbre* with the Otomí and by deduction, uncivilized, noneducated, and poor people.

After the Mexican Revolution, which ended around 1920, there was an attempt to assimilate the indigenous populations into the national culture. As a consequence, a new identity emerged that Bartolomé called "Construction of Indianness" (*construcción de la indianidad*). This gave rise to a new discourse emphasizing a more inclusive society; for example, it is now accepted that a fellow citizen acknowledge his or her identity as an indigenous person and as a speaker of an indigenous language. Open discrimination and the discourse demanding the civilization of the indigenous population are no longer accepted. This attitude is also true among most citizens who do not belong to any ethnic minority. "Indianness" became part of the national identity.

> El maestro bilingüe tzeltal que ahora habla del valor de la identidad y cultura de su pueblo, está utilizando un lenguaje institucionalmente legitimizado, así como antes lo era la castellanización y la integración (Bartolomé, 1997, p. 66).

People who highlight their indigenous identity and culture are using a discourse that is now institutionally justified. Yet discourses on indignity started with a colonial discourse that did not include any integration of the indigenous population, since they were constructed as being inferior. At the beginning of the last century, the Mexican Revolution (which included the involvement of indigenous peoples) gave rise to an integrative discourse and a corresponding integrative ideology. The new discourse mirrored a broader emancipatory ideology, which is still valid today. However, despite the discursive emphasis on integration and emancipation, speakers of indigenous languages were still considered underdeveloped. In the past *indios* were identified as such by their language and, on this basis were considered culturally and intellectually underdeveloped by Spanish speakers. While

attitudes are changing, speakers of indigenous languages (who do not speak Spanish with the proficiency of a native speaker), continue to be considered culturally and intellectually inferior. Today, the colonial discourse and the integrative discourse cannot always be clearly separated. However, today's official discourse, which Bartolomé calls "institutionally legitimized language," can easily be distinguished from both of the previous discourses.

The current modern discourse clearly rejects discrimination and racism toward indigenous people. It also rejects the two earlier stigmatizing discourses of colonialism and integration regarding indigenous identity. While it is still possible to hear utterances that may reflect these early discourses, any person who makes such an utterance risks being called racist or being publicly exposed for this behavior. Anyone who uses the word "indio" or who says that indigenous people have to be civilized can be rebuked. However, this last fact is unimportant to Otomí speakers in San Cristóbal Huichochitlán who face such disregard that it creates obstacles for their ability to meet their most basic needs: food, housing, housing services, health, education, among others.

Indigenous people can earn about 40 constant pesos a day for working someone else's lands, but since such work is only available for six months of the year, emigration to larger cities to look for jobs becomes a necessary reality. Migration to the cities compels indigenous people to learn Spanish in order to get a job; however, once employers perceive their rural and indigenous origin, they offer only the lowest salaries. As a result indigenous people soon find that although they are employed in the cities, their salaries are even lower and their living expenses much higher. So while saying the word *indio* to an indigenous person is no longer acceptable, discrimination toward indigenous language speakers is a common practice. It is a practice that risks the basic rights of indigenous peoples as Mexican citizens and confines them to cyclical poverty.

The analysis

As noted earlier, our analysis relies on the sociolinguistic concept of conversational inference, which refers to those mental processes that enable us to interpret speech by evoking relevant cultural background information (Gumperz, 1991). Conversational inference is related more broadly to "contextualization," a term Gumperz refers to

> . . . speakers' and listeners' use of verbal and non-verbal signs to relate what is said at any one time and in any one place to knowledge acquired through past experience, in order to retrieve the presuppositions they must rely on to maintain conversational involvement and assess what is intended. In this sense, contextualization should be understood as a theory of interpretation in which situated interpretations, inferences and assumptions build on knowledge of the world (Gumperz, 1991, p. 230).

Contextualization cues, per Gumperz, "function relationally and cannot be assigned context-independent, stable, core lexical meanings" (1991, p. 232).

We analyzed interviews with six residents in San Cristóbal Huichochitlán and situated these within the context of Mexican history in its wider sense; that is the interpretation of "gente de razón" or "gente de costumbre" in association with indigenous languages and the construction of poverty. All the interviewees were speakers of Otomí and Spanish. All were native speakers of Otomí. Two people, Ana and Jovita, were native speakers of Spanish; Santiago, grew up with Otomí, but spoke with a native's fluency of Spanish. The other three residents, Ernesto, Juana, and Guillermina spoke Spanish as a second language.[1] When they spoke Spanish, it was evident to us that they aquired a fluency after learning Otomí.

All interviews were transcribed while using normal orthographically writing conventions, but some features of conversation in a second language were considered. In the same way, emphasis was highlighted with capitals. Unintelligible passages are marked by brackets with ellipses. As we mentioned before, the offical discourse rejects any open expression of negative attitudes toward indigenous peoples or their languages. Thus, Ana (Group 1) reported that some time ago the former director of the local school disqualified speakers of Otomí.

> Oh yes . . . this has happened . . . But, yeah . . . not at Toluca . . . also here in the secondary school. When the director came . . . and when . . . he first came . . . this man started to say . . . No . . . these indios . . . these who knows.[2]

Ana does not relate exactly what the new director did, but that the parents in an assembly at school rebelled against him.

> He said that the more he had the opportunity to stamp on the indios, even better for him.[3]

Table 3.2 Interviewed Speakers of Otomí

Group 1 Spanish native fluency	Group 2 Spanish second language
• Ana (25 years old—nine school years, daughter of Juana and Ernesto) • Santiago (41 years old—eight school years) • Jovita (27 years old—nine school years)	• Ernesto (56 years old—six school years, married to Juana) • Juana (56 years old—three school years, married to Ernesto) • Guillermina (38 years old—one school year)

If we observe the use of the word *indios* and the image of "stamping on the indios," we perceive the school authority's attitude toward people who appear to be Indian and toward Otomí speakers. Based on daily experiences of this nature, we can infer the conditions prevalent in that community regarding education access for the indigenous people. The comments of a single person have to be understood in the context of the research as a whole. The comments of our subjects correspond to the general behavior we observed in the village. Some indigenous students might leave school, as some of the interviewees did. Or, students might persist in school, perhaps with the hope of better job opportunities, but knowing they have to resist the negative attitudes. This was the case of those interviewees who attained 6 to 9 years of education. In fact, if we compare the interviewees' years of education with their age, we notice that they either stopped their education early or started school late. In both situations even those who attained higher levels of education did not continue studying. As with Ernesto, Juana and their daughter Ana, who only have a few years of education (from 1 to 9), the kind of jobs obtainable are not high quality—thus lower salaried—which again impacts the educational possibilities for their children. Ana went further in school than her parents, but she still remains behind other youngsters at her age, who have at least three more years of education. In this specific context, the examples relate to the discussion of degrees of poverty and underscore the inability to achieve satisfaction with educational needs because of social deprivation.

> Santiago also mentioned some common expressions that seem to be synonymous for "indio."
> YEA!! . . . all these eaters of nopals . . . these dirty people.[4]

Santiago explained that people who generally converse in Otomí, change to Spanish when they are in Toluca. When we asked how people in the city of Toluca react to hearing Otomí, Santiago replied that these kinds of expressions (nopaludos, mugrosos) are common reactions from the inhabitants of Toluca. That is why Otomí speakers self-censor. Even though she is considered a native speaker of Spanish, Jovita also had negative experiences when speaking Otomí outside of San Cristóbal Huichochitlán. Nevertheless, she is very confident and says with a dismissive gesture that someone who is laughing at her can only be an ignorant person.

> Well . . . sometimes [they refer to us as] . . . well, the Indian women and something like that . . . [but I think] poor people . . . they descend from the same race too. It does not mean that as they are from Toluca, the city, they may believe . . . they are GRINGOS,[5] or something like that. Well, all of us who are living here descend from the indios. Don't we?[6]

And she adds that surely all who live in the vicinity descended from the indios. We found this kind of self-confidence particular with Jovita, Ana, and Santiago in Group 1. Therefore, they all predominantly use the "legitimate institutional discourse" (Bartolomé, 1997, p. 66), which doesn't tolerate any open discrimination. This discourse—as we discuss shortly—justifies indigenous cultures. Jovita, Ana and Santiago used this type of discourse, but this is not true for everyone.

Jovita and Santiago also support the preservation of Otomí, notwithstanding the fact that neither of them transmits Otomí to their children. Jovita said that she would like her children to have a good command of understanding and speaking both languages, Spanish and Otomí. Santiago would like all the children of San Cristobal Huichochitlán to be able to speak in Otomí.

> Even the smallest children [. . .] well [. . .] are already starting to speak in Spanish . . . But, well, I think it is even a matter of . . . of [intention] sometimes, yes sometimes, that's what we were talking about some minutes ago [. . .] Because I think we have to teach Otomí to the little boys because that's it . . . they are starting to speak in Spanish and we do not give them the opportunity to learn Otomí.[7]

Santiago also recognizes his generation's responsibility for not having transmitted Otomí to the children. In his own family, the oldest children speak Otomí, but not the two youngest ones. He regrets not paying more attention to the acquisition of Otomí in his children; and Jovita justifies her behavior by asserting that she does not have the patience to translate everything and it is easier for her to switch into Spanish.

As we see, all individuals in Group 1 defend the local culture and their language. Their discourse draws from the official discourse that rejects discrimination and racism toward indigenous people; this was true throughout the interviews. Although their discourses are not always congruent with their actions (i.e. teaching their children Otomí), they know by the standards of the dominant discourse in Mexico what is "correct" today.

This was not the case with Juana, who expressed satisfaction about the fact that Otomí is spoken less and less.

> it was all going on . . . in Otomí, but by now, finally . . . thank   God . . . everything   has changed . . . and no more, they do not speak in Otomí anymore.[8]

Juana's utterance stands in stark contrast to the previous interviews with Santiago, Jovita, and Ana and in contrast to the official state discourse.

Many members of the village claim to know only Spanish. Santiago and Jovita, as well as other informants confirmed that there are many cases of self-censorship among speakers of Otomí. People just deny being speakers of Otomí. For example, Jovita reported cases where other Otomí speakers deny being able to speak Otomí—even to her as a speaker of Otomí. Yet it is clear that they are Otomí speakers when they are going to participate in a conversation in Otomí.

> Sometimes "I do" and sometimes—"I DON'T UNDERSTAND"—but she understands. We realize it, because we say anything . . . and then . . . they come back . . . so . . . they try to participate in our conversation.[9]

In this excerpt, when Jovita says, "I do," she is repeating a common answer from other people who speak Otomí. Sometimes people tell you that they know Otomí but sometimes they say "I DON'T UNDERSTAND" when they really do understand. Their facility with Otomí becomes clear later when they participate in the conversation.

In the last examples, we can see negative attitudes among the Otomís toward their own language. So it seems surprising that Juana, whose Spanish is not seen as perfect by native speakers, does not worry whether or not all speakers of Otomí will shift into Spanish. Juana sees the language shift as something positive. In contrast, those Otomí who speak Spanish rather well are worried that Otomí may disappear in the community. Ernesto, and Guillermina, also from Group 2, made comments similar to those of Juana. For example, Ernesto said the following:

> OUR PEOPLE ARE GRADUALLY CIVILIZING because . . . because of the schools . . . because of our own education . . . now, of course, they have enough . . . yes, well . . . they are getting educated, becoming better educated . . . isn't it? . . . and so . . . I was one of the lucky among them.[10]

As we have shown, historically only speakers of Spanish were considered to be civilized. This was the distinction between "gente de razón" and "gente de costumbre." Notably, Ernesto emphasizes the importance of school and that he was one of the lucky fellows who had the opportunity to attend school and participate in the process of becoming civilized. Probably, he was one of "the first civilized people" in the village. He succeeded in rising from the abyss and became a civilized person. Ernesto, as well as his wife, still equates Otomí and the indigenous culture with poverty and lack of education. The same discourse comes from Guillermina.

> So, that's why . . . well . . . it is the same why . . . well . . . young people from here . . . WELL—THEY FEEL THAT WE ARE ALREADY A LITTLE HALF CIVILIZED because now we are speaking in SPANISH.[11]

We highlighted the pitch with capitals where Guillermina emphasizes that they are going to be civilized. "To be civilized" is something that marks the discourses of people of Group 2. When an Otomí speaker is discriminated against, participants in Group 2 characterize the discrimination as being one's own fault because he or she is not civilized. To become civilized is everyone's personal task. During the interview, Guillermina had difficulty explaining the significance that "being civilized" held for her, and so we repeatedly asked what it meant to be civilized or not civilized. She responded:

> Well, we are now going to be more civilized because before we were using other kinds of clothes.[12]

> Oh . . . in the past we were of very, um, very poor.[13]

> Well, our parents were . . . how can I tell you? . . . very low, very poor . . . although working very hard . . . well no . . . we could not live as today. We only had an adobe house.[14]

So for Guillermina, poor people aren't civilized. Being poor is associated with the local culture, specifically wearing typically indigenous clothing, such as the traditional wide skirt called "*chincuete*" that is worn by women. Although she starts to reflect and concludes that the *chincuete* is more expensive than a common skirt, she nonetheless associates this skirt with poverty. In the same way, Guillermina associates the past with poverty as she reflects on her parents who, although hardworking, never became wealthy and lived in an adobe house. Since her parents could not participate fully in social life due to insufficient resources, she seems to associate all of her culture with poverty and the impossibility of living a "normal" life as it is perceived by the dominant culture in her community. Guillermina shares the widespread values of good living that are part of the wider Mexican community; in this discourse, a good life includes access to certain good and services, as well as participation in the economic, civil, cultural, and political spheres of their society. As an individual who pursues a

"good life," Guillermina understands that speaking Otomí is a hindrance to attaining her goals, so she easily displaces it with Spanish.

It is very likely that the persons of Group 2, particularly when they are in Toluca, face even more discrimination because of the imperfect Spanish that they speak; however, they did not mention this in interviews (unlike the speakers of Group 1). It almost appears that the participants in Group 2 accepted the mistreatment as something appropriate for the uncivilized and therefore an inherent part of second-class citizenship (Lister, 2004). None of the speakers of Group 2 regretted the fact that Otomí is losing vitality. As we have seen before, Juana even welcomed the shift from Otomí to Spanish because, for her, this meant the end of poverty and ignorance.

Unlike the interviews with people in Group 1, the people in Group 2 did not use any institutionalized official discourse. What is particularly surprising, however, was that speakers in Group 2, used discriminatory terms such as those which had been used in integrative discourses and perhaps partly colonial discourses. Consequently, the impression emerges that discourses that discriminate against the Otomí are cultivated by speakers of Otomí, particularly by speakers as defined in Group 2. This explains their interest in favoring Spanish, for they aspire to attain first-class citizenship.

CONCLUSION

According to our present findings, the language shift from Otomí to Spanish in San Cristóbal Huichochitlán is a fact, and it would be difficult to stop this process. This finding is consistent with the results of our research from 2001 to 2002 (see also Terborg, García Landa, & Moore, 2006; Terborg, Velázquez, & Trujillo, 2007; Terborg & Velázquez, 2008a, 2008b). As always, the causes are diverse and complex. Clearly, the negative attitudes of the dominant speakers of Spanish toward the speakers of Otomí contributes to this trend. Also as we expected, the attitudes of speakers of Otomí toward their own language often are negative. These negative attitudes did not become evident in Group 1 in our interview because the speakers are very proud of their culture; however, the fact that they prefer Spanish to Otomí during conversation with their children is striking. At the same time, this is understandable given that speakers of Otomí are always exposed to discrimination and second-class citizenship. We see this reported by Santiago and Jovita. Nevertheless, both Santiago and Jovita approve in some way of the use and maintenance of Otomí and admit that they have neglected Otomí in the education of their children. However, those speakers whose Spanish is distinctive and whose accent reveals them as residents of the country or speakers of a language other than Spanish (Group 2), do not exhibit any self-confidence or appreciation regarding their own culture and language.

Unlike the speakers in Group 1, their discourse cannot be found in this open and discriminative form by speakers whose first language is Spanish and who are members of the dominant Spanish-speaking culture. Particularly striking in our data, is the repeated utterance that now the Otomí are going to become *civilized citizens*. Although the members of Group 2—because of the way they speak—are likely to be objects of discrimination more often than members of Group 1, there are very few references to discrimination in their interviews. It seems that members of Group 2 view the experienced mistreatment as self-inflicted. For example, Guillermina stresses the fact she does not speak Spanish very well and that she is *only half civilized*, which might imply limited participation as a Mexican citizen.

We found Gumperz's observation of the failure of mutual understanding between two English speakers in a conversation with different ethnic backgrounds to be relevant to our data. Gumperz wrote:

> . . . they differ significantly in their notions of what types of activities constitute this event, how these activities are reflected in contextualization conventions, and what can and cannot be said.

Such differences are not rare and not confined to interethnic situations (Gumperz 1991, p. 246). There is a notion of context "that deals with the cognitive processes through which cultural and other types of background knowledge are brought into the interpretative processes" (Gumperz 1991, p. 247).

In our examples we do not have a conflict between different speakers. However, we do find different contextualization conventions between the cases of Groups 1 and 2. Poverty is not only a material phenomenon but also a socially constructed one for those speakers who feel less fluent in Spanish. This kind of construction still relies on the old paternal discourses from the beginning of the 20th century.

We consider that the maintenance of an indigenous language is guaranteed by the pressure of those who speak it as their first language. But as we have seen, these speakers do not exert much pressure for the use of their own language. Thus, we may verify this practice as one of the source causes for the rapid language loss of Otomí over the last three decades in San Cristóbal Huichochitlán, and validate that this practice is gaining in importance during this last stage of language shift.

Finally, if life satisfaction depends on the quality of a person's life, then noneconomic goods such as love, emotional support, friendship, feeling reciprocity, good relationships with neighbors and colleagues all have an important impact on people experiencing well-being (Rojas, 2010). From this perspective, we clearly see that when people from San Cristóbal Huichochitlán speak Otomí, as defined by Lister (2004), they are participating as "second-class citizens." This is due to the fact that the state only recognizes those social organizations that serve the state's interests and disregards organizations that search for justice and respect for their own rights. Consequently, when indigenous organizations in the poorest communities appropriate the use of their own languages, they are marginalized and excluded. As we pointed out before, we cannot talk about full citizenship when human rights are constantly infringed and when the most basic rights are annulled (Mota, 2002, pp. 199–202). Together material poverty and constructed poverty are destroying local cultures—validating that destruction of local identity and cohesion may lead to even more problems related to poverty.

NOTES

1. All the names used in this research are pseudonyms.

2. Ah SÍ -Sí ha habido - Pero sí - no en Toluca -también incluso aquí con la escuela secundaria. - Llegó el señor director - y cuando . . . empezó a llegar - entonces él - este señor ya empezó a decir - No - que estos indios - que estos quién sabe qué.

3. Pues dijo que - que mientras más tuviera la oportunidad de - de pisotear a los INDIOS - que mejor.

4. ¡SÍ! . . . esos nopaludos - esos mugrosos -

5. This is a term used to represent North Americans from the United States.

6. Pues - a veces - o que las indias y que no sé qué. - Pero pobrecitos - porque ellos también descienden de allí mismo. - No porque sean de Toluca - de ciudad - crean que - pues - son GRINGOS - o algo así. - Pues - todos los que somos de aquí provenimos de los indios ¿no?

7. Inclusive ya los más chiquitos - este ya- ya están empezando a hablar el español . . . Pero - Bueno, fíjese que yo creo hasta es cuestión de . . . de (intención) a veces - A veces - Hace ratito que estábamos platicando - Digo hay que enseñarle el otomí a los chamacos porque realmente . . . están empezando a hablar el español y no les vamos a dar chance para que aprendan el otomí.

8. Porque . . . iba a seguir todo - en otomí - Pero ahora ya - ya - gracias a dios - ya han cambiado todo - y ya no - ya no hablan en otomí.

9. Muchas veces sí, y muchas veces - NO ENTIENDO - pero sí entiende. Nosotras nos damos cuenta - y porque decimos cualquier cosa - y allí - y ya vuelven a - ay - o sea - ellos se meten a la plática.

10. SE VA CIVILIZANDO NUESTRA GENTE - por . . . las escuelas, . . . por nuestra propia educación - Ora - desde luego allí - es que tienen que le alcanza - Va - este . . . - Se va preparando - Va sobresaliendo ¿no? - Y entonces . . . yo tuve la dicha también . . . de ser uno de ELLOS.

11. Entonces - por eso - este - pues por lo mismo - este - ya casi los jóvenes de aquí - YA - BUENO - SIENTEN QUE NOSOTROS YA ESTAMOS UN POQUITO SEMI CIVILIZADOS porque estamos hablando en ESPAÑOL.

12. Pos de que se está civilizando un poquito - porque antes usábamos ropa de otra forma.

13. Ah - porque antes éramos muy - muy este - muy de bajo recurso.

14. O sea - nuestros padres eran muy -¿cómo le diré? - muy bajitos de bajo recurso pues - Por más que trabajaban - pos no - No - no vivíamos pues así. - Teníamos puro casa de adobe.

REFERENCES

Barriga, Rebeca, & Martin Butragueño, Pedro (Eds.). (2010). *Historia sociolingüística de México*. Vol. 1. México, DF: El Colegio de México.

Bartolomé, Miguel Alberto (1997). *Gente de costumbre y gente de razón. Las identidades étnicas en México*. México, DF: Instituto Nacional Indigenista, Siglo Veintiuno Editores.

Bureau of Western Hemisphere Affairs (2010). Retrieved March 20, 2011 from http://www .state.gov/r/pa/ei/bgn/35749.htm.

Consejo Nacional de Evaluación de la Política de Desarrollo Social (CONEVAL). (2010). *Metodología para la medición multidimensional de la pobreza en México*. México, DF: CONEVAL.

Crystal, David (2000). *Language death*. Cambridge, UK: Cambridge University Press.

Damián, Araceli and Boltvinik, Julio (2003). Evolución y características de pobreza en México. *Comercio Exterior*, *53*(6), 519–531.

Fishman, Joshua A. (1991). *Reversing languagesShift. Theoretical and empirical foundations of assistance to threatened languages*. Clevedon, UK: Multilingual Matters.

González Ortiz, Felipe (2005). *Estudio sociodemográfico de los pueblos y comunidades indígenas del Estado de México*. Toluca, MX: El Colegio Mexiquense.

Gumperz, John J. (1991). Contextualization and understanding. In Alessandro Duranti, & Charles Goodwin (Eds.), *Rethinking context. language as an interactive phenomenon* (pp. 229–252). Cambridge, UK: Cambridge University Press.

Hunter Wade, Robert (2004). Is globalization reducing poverty and inequality? *World Development* *32*(4), 567–589.

INALI (2009). *Catálogo de las lenguas indígenas nacionales*. Mexico City, MX: Instituto Nacional de Lenguas Indígenas.

Lastra, Yolanda (2001). Otomí language shift and some recent efforts to reverse it. In J. A. Fishman (Ed.), *Can threatened languages be saved? Reversing language shift, revisited: A 21st century perspective* (pp. 142–165). Clevedon, UK: Multilingual Matters.

Lister, Ruth (2004). *Poverty*. Cambridge, UK: Polity Press.

Mota Díaz, Laura (2002, Apr.–Jun.). Globalización y pobreza: Dicotomía del desarrollo en América Latina y México. *Espacio Abierto, 2*(2), Asociación Venezolana de Sociología Venezuela, 189–204.

Orshansky, Mollie (1965). Counting the poor: Another look at the poverty profile. *Social Security Bulletin, 28*, 3–29.

Rojas, Mariano (2010, Jan.–Jun.). Mejorando los programas de combate a la pobreza en México: Del ingreso al bienestar. *Perfiles Latinoamericanos, 35*, 35–59.

Rodríguez Campos, Katya (2009). La política contra la pobreza en México. Ventajas y desventajas de la línea oficial a la luz de experiencias internacionales, *Gestión y Política Pública, 8*(1), 107–148.

Rowntree, Seebhom (1902). *Poverty: A study of town life*. London, UK: Macmillan.

Sen, Amartya (1981). *Poverty and famines: An essay on entitlement and deprivation*. Oxford, UK: Clarendon Press.

Sen, Amartya (1984). Poor relatively speaking, *Resources, Values and Development*. Oxford, UK: Basil Blackwell.

Sen, Amartya (1992). *Inequality re-examined*. Cambridge, MA: Harvard University Press.

Terborg, Roland, García Landa, Laura, & Moore, Pauline (2006). Language planning in Mexico. In R. B. Baldauf & R. B. Kaplan (Eds.), *Language planning & policy. Latin America, Vol. 1. Ecuador, Mexico and Paraguay* (pp. 115–217). Clevedon, UK: Multilingual Matters.

Terborg, Roland, Velázquez, Virna, Trujillo Tamez, & Alma Isela (2007). La vitalidad de las lenguas indígenas en México: El caso de las lenguas otomí, matlazinca, atzinca y mixe. In M. Kniffki-Schrader & Garcia L. Morgenthaler (Eds.), *Romania en interacción: Entre historia, contacto y política. Ensayos en homenaje a Klaus Zimmermann* (pp. 607-625). Frankfurt am Main, DE: Iberamericana Vervuert Verlag.

Terborg, Roland, & Velázquez, Virna (2008a). La muerte de lenguas y la desventaja de ser nativo hablante del otomí en México, *UniverSOS, Revista de Lenguas Indígenas y Universos Culturales, 5*, 129–143.

Terborg, Roland, & Velázquez, Virna (2008b). Sprachverdrängung von indianersprachen in Mexiko. Eine analyse der negativen spracheinstellungen zum Otomí. In B. Ahrenholz et al. (Eds.), *Empirische forschung und theoriebildung. Beiträge aus soziolinguistik, gesprochenesprache-und zweitspracherwerbsforschung. Festschrift für Norbert Dittmar zum 65. geburtstag* (pp. 105–113). Frankfurt am Main, DE: Peter Lang.

Torres Medina, Alejandro Ramón, Juárez Sánchez, José Pedro, Ramírez Valverde, Benito, & Ramírez Valverde, Gustavo (2007, Sept.–Dec.). Pobreza en territorios indígenas de México. El caso del Municipio de Xochitlán de Vicente Suárez en la Sierra Nor-Oriente de Puebla. *Ra Ximhai, Revista de Sociedad, Cultura y Desarrollo Sustentable, 3*(3), 781–803.

Zimmermann, Klaus (1992). *Sprachkontakt, ethnische identität und identitätsbeschädigung. Aspekte der assimilation der Otomí-Indianer an die hispanophone Mexikanische kultur*. Frankfurt am Main, DE: Iberamericana Vervuert Verlag.

4

RACE-CLASS INTERSECTIONS AS INTERACTIONAL RESOURCES IN POST-APARTHEID SOUTH AFRICA

KEVIN WHITEHEAD

INTRODUCTION

Since the term was first coined by Crenshaw (1989), intersectionality has been an influential concept in social scientific theory and research (Davis, 2008; McCall, 2005). The central focus of intersectionality is "the interaction between gender, race, and other categories of difference in individual lives, social practices, institutional arrangements, and cultural ideologies and the outcomes of these interactions in terms of power" (Davis, 2008, p. 68). One prominent line of research within the paradigm of intersectionality examines how relationships of inequality among social groups are changing over time and across contexts (McCall, 2005). South Africa represents an important site for investigating such relationships; the collapse of the apartheid[1] system gave rise to a dynamic period of change with respect to the country's previous rigidly racialized class structure. This period of change is reflected in a substantial body of post-apartheid research that has investigated post-apartheid race-class

intersections as they are conceptualized in official policies and realized in aggregate societal patterns. However, everyday understandings of these phenomena, and the ways in which ordinary people engage with them in interactional contexts, have been underexamined (cf. Winant, 2001).

In this chapter, I examine how South Africa's complex post-apartheid, race-class intersections are displayed and mobilized in ordinary interaction by analyzing commonsense knowledge—that is, taken-for-granted, "socially sanctioned grounds of inference and action that people use in everyday life, and which they assume that other members of the group use in the same way" (Garfinkel, 1956, p.185). I begin by providing a brief overview of the historical origins and current patterns of race-class intersections and describe some ways in which they can be seen as both legacies of, and departures from, those of the apartheid system. I then present some findings from an ethnomethodologically informed, conversation analytic investigation of audio-recorded data drawn from South African radio talk show broadcasts (cf. West and Fenstermaker's, 1995 ethnomethodological approach to intersections between race, class, and gender). In the first part of my analysis, I demonstrate some ways in which taken-for-granted, common-sense knowledge about race-class intersections can be produced and resisted in interactions. I then examine some ways in which speakers actively draw on these common-sense understandings and deploy them to *do* things in the course of everyday interactions. This analysis reveals some of the ways in which commonsense knowledge of race and class reflects and reproduces continuities and discontinuities (between the apartheid and post-apartheid periods) at the level of everyday interactions.

RACE-CLASS INTERSECTIONS IN POST-APARTHEID SOUTH AFRICA

Under the apartheid system, race and class in South Africa almost completely overlapped with one another.[2] This was a result of the efforts of the architects of apartheid to establish a rigid and totalizing system that affected every aspect of people's lives and prevented any form of interracial interaction under potentially egalitarian circumstances (Clark & Worger, 2004; Frederickson, 1981; Posel, 2001). This system was implemented through the passage of literally hundreds of laws, which were enforced by state-sanctioned violence on a broad scale. These laws included those designed to implement "grand apartheid" policies such as "separate development," "Bantu Education," and "job reservation," which ensured that whites[3] had privileged access to the most desirable land, educational qualifications, and professions, while reducing blacks to a ready supply of cheap semiskilled and unskilled labor (Clark & Worger, 2004). In addition, a range of "petty apartheid" laws were designed to institutionalize racial segregation and privilege in informal everyday settings by mandating superior "whites only" amenities, including buses, railway cars,

ambulances, libraries, swimming pools, and beaches (Guelke, 2005).

This white supremacist system was interrupted when, following decades of resistance from both within and outside of South Africa, the apartheid government agreed to enter into negotiations with opposition movements, led by the African Nation Congress (ANC) to bring an end to apartheid. At the time of these negotiations, the ANC had long avowed a socialist program (outlined in the 1954 Freedom Charter) based on redistribution of wealth from those who had gained it illegitimately under apartheid to those who had been oppressed by the system. However, it soon became clear that they would have to make substantial compromises if they were to achieve their primary aim of political rights for all South Africans without significant conflict (Adam & Moodley, 1993; Winant, 2001). While some opponents of a negotiated settlement were mobilizing for the eventuality of a civil war, the possibility of a mass exodus of skilled professionals due to white emigration presented a concern for the ANC, even in the absence of an armed conflict (Louw, 2004). In addition, local and global capitalist interests had a significant stake in South Africa's economy, and (after belatedly abandoning white supremacy) were among the most effective advocates for ending apartheid in order to stabilize South Africa's capitalist economy (Louw, 2004). This made it difficult to repudiate the demands of capital without risking the economic collapse that threatened to result from the adoption of a primarily socialist and redistributive system (Winant, 2001).

The most significant outcome of these opposing pressures for the negotiated transition to democracy was that whites and capitalist interests were assured of retaining their property rights and the wealth they accumulated during apartheid, while the ANC achieved their aim of securing political and civil rights for all South Africans, and won political control of the country in the 1994 elections (Louw, 2004; Winant, 2001). As a consequence, post-apartheid South Africa has been characterized as a country with an economic system largely controlled by a white capitalist elite, and a political system controlled by a black nationalist elite (Louw, 2004).

Following their election, the ANC government made high-profile attempts to alleviate white fears, and largely acceded to the demands of capitalist interests, taking on a corporatist and neoliberal economic approach involving compromises with the largely white business sector, and privatizing formerly state-owned industries (see, e.g., Bond, 2000; Louw, 2004). With respect to the demands of the majority of its constituents for the delivery of a better life, the government has made significant achievements, providing running water, electricity, housing, land, education and medical care to millions who were denied these basic rights under apartheid (Clark & Worger, 2004). However, the neoliberal economic approach has also resulted in millions of people losing their newly acquired access to services such as running water and electricity as a result of their inability to pay the fees charged by privatized service providers (Desai, 2002). Moreover, as a result of choosing to adopt a pro-business approach rather than risk a more radical redistribution of wealth, the government lacks the resources to adequately compensate blacks for the 350 years of oppression they have suffered, to the extent required to bring them as a group to the same economic level as whites (Frederickson, 2002). This has resulted in the government's attempts to alleviate poverty and unemployment being viewed as too slow and not effective enough, and South Africa remaining starkly racially stratified in numerous respects (Louw, 2004; Seekings & Nattrass, 2005).

The South African economy still relies heavily on exploiting undereducated, cheap, and predominantly black labor (Clark & Worger, 2004; Winant, 2001). Unemployment poses a massive challenge, with an overall rate estimated at 25% (as of early 2011), but the estimated rates for different racial groups—29% of Africans, 22.6% of Coloureds, 11.7% of Indians, and only 5.9% of whites—demonstrate the strong racial dimension of the problem (Statistics South Africa, 2011). Poor black families have generally lacked the

economic resources to move into the more desirable (formerly white) residential areas, resulting in continuing *de facto* urban segregation, with predominantly white suburbs surrounded by all-black townships and shack settlements located on the edges of cities (Christopher, 2001).

Although it has extended South Africa's social welfare system considerably, a primary feature of the ANC government's approach to reducing racial inequality was the adoption of market-based policies designed to facilitate the entry of blacks into the middle and wealthy classes. Affirmative action hiring, particularly in public service, and the program of Black Economic Empowerment (BEE) have been centerpieces of this approach (Bond, 2000; Franchi, 2003). These policies have had a substantial impact on inequality between blacks and whites by contributing to the emergence of black wealthy and middle classes (which now comprise approximately 10 million people; close to 20% of the population), and thus to the rapid deracialization of the wealthier sectors of the population (Louw, 2004; Seekings & Nattrass, 2005). However, the primary beneficiaries of these policies have generally been those people who were already in a position to take advantage of them; approximately 70% of the population, almost all black, remain systematically exploited and excluded in much the same way as they were under apartheid (Seekings & Nattrass, 2005; Terreblanche, 2003). As a result, inequality among blacks (and in particular Africans) has increased dramatically, while whites (although their share of wealth has been reduced somewhat) remain predominantly in the top 30% of the population in terms of wealth, and continue to disproportionately own and manage the economy (Bhorat & Kanbur, 2007; Terreblanche, 2003).

There is thus both substantial post-apartheid continuity and discontinuity of the racial economic order that operated under apartheid. Significant changes have occurred with respect to the substantial emerging black middle class; however, poverty, wealth, and inequality remain significantly racialized. This led Louw (2004, p. 178) to refer to the post-apartheid economic system as one of "blurred racial capitalism" (as opposed to the racial capitalism of apartheid). That is to say the apartheid-era racial cleavage is now somewhat obscured or blurred, but in many respects remains largely intact.

In the following sections, I turn to an examination of how people in South Africa reproduce and use these complex race-class dynamics in ordinary interactions. I turn first to an examination of the *content* of commonsense connections between race and class, and the ways in which speakers in my data recurrently, and often collaboratively, treat these connections as taken for granted. I then explore in more detail some ways in which these commonsense connections can be deployed as *interactional resources* that speakers use in the course of producing ordinary actions-in-interaction (cf., for e.g., Hansen, 2005; Kitzinger, 2005; Whitehead & Lerner, 2009).[4] First, however, I provide a brief description of the data and method used in the analysis that follows.

DATA

The data set consists of approximately 115 hours of interactional radio shows broadcast on three different South African radio stations. This includes several hours of pilot data that were recorded in May 2006, and May to June 2007, in order to assess the feasibility of using radio broadcasts as a data source, with the remainder of the data recorded over a three-month period from March to June 2008. The data collection was designed to include 1) broadcasts with a high degree of interactivity (for example, interviews with guests and calls from listeners), 2) both government-operated and independent radio stations, 3) radio stations that broadcast to a wide audience, either through conventional radio or streaming online, and 4) shows broadcast at various times throughout the day. On this basis, and on the basis of geographical and other self-identifications provided by callers in the data, the radio shows that make up the data

corpus were available to people from a broad cross-section of South African society. However, the data corpus is not intended or claimed to constitute a random or nationally representative sample, either of South African speakers or of interactions in post-apartheid South Africa. The data were analyzed using conversation analytic techniques (cf. Sacks, 1995; Sacks, Schegloff, & Jefferson, 1974; Schegloff, 2007), informed by ethnomethodological perspectives (cf. Garfinkel, 1967; Sacks, 1995), and aided by detailed transcripts[5] (see Whitehead, 2011a, for further discussion of the data and methodological approach used in this study).

THE POST-APARTHEID RACIAL COMMON SENSE OF WEALTH AND POVERTY

Race and class were recurrently linked together in the data in three broad respects. These related to commonsense connections between 1) the racial category "black" and poverty or lack of wealth, 2) the racial category "white" and wealth or class privilege, and 3) the racial category "black" and wealth, particularly the newly emerging (post-apartheid) wealth.[6] In the discussion that follows, I examine some illustrative cases in which these race-class intersections were produced as taken-for-granted realities in contemporary South Africa.

Excerpt 1 shows an instance of speakers orienting to tacitly shared knowledge and, in collaboration with recipients,[7] reproducing commonsense links between blackness and poverty. In this case a caller, in the course of criticizing people, whom he claims have not been vocal enough in complaining about an "electricity crisis,"[8] moves smoothly between using a racial category ("black") and a class category ("poor") to refer to those he is criticizing. In doing so, and with the collaboration of his recipient (the host of the show), the caller treats as taken for granted an association between the categories "black" and "poor," such that they can be used as proxies for one another.

```
Excerpt 1:
[172 - SAfm 4-28-08]

 1   C:   .hhh I was disappointed not to hear from- from- from our
 2        black friends h um: about the electricity crisis, uh- I-
 3        I- I: think they suffer the most and it was just white
 4        people phoning in to your station, .hh[h
 5   H:                                         [I'll tell you
 6        why:, uh=well sorry no le- I'm interrupting, sorry.
 7        (.)
 8   C:   No I- I would just encourage them to share: (.) to share
 9        the crisis that they have cause I think .hhh we all suffer
10        but I think the poor people in: in the- in the- in the
11        outlying areas who can't afford other forms of- of- of-
12        of- of- of electricity, .hh they suffering the most an-
13        and- an' we need a mouth for them when- someone needs to
14        s- to: speak on [their behalf we need to (hear from them.)
15   H:                   [Ja.
```

The caller begins by expressing his disappointment that "our black friends"[9] have failed to call in to the radio station during a discussion of the "electricity crisis" to share their experiences, claiming that "they suffer the most," but that "it was just white people phoning in to your station" (see lines 1–4). This raises a potential puzzle regarding the basis for the caller's claim that black people "suffer" more than white people as a result of the discussed events. Following a foreclosed response from the host (which I return to shortly), the caller explicitly reveals the basis of this claim by referring to the same group of people he had previously formulated racially, as "our black friends," but this time using a class category, "poor people" (line 10). In doing so, he treats "black friends" as effectively synonymous and interchangeable with "poor people." Moreover, the connection between these two formulations of the same group of people is further strengthened by the caller's repetition of the word "suffer(ing)" shortly following both formulations (see lines 3, 9, and 12). In addition, his use of the term "outlying areas" (line 11) invokes

the spatial arrangements legislated by the apartheid regime (see Christopher, 1997), thereby further reinforcing the race-class intersections the caller has produced, and implicitly linking them to the apartheid era.

The host's responses to the caller demonstrate his collaboration with the commonsense race-class links the caller has produced. He initially begins to respond in line 5 (even though the caller has projected, by taking a long in-breath in line 4, that he is going to continue), but then cuts himself off and apologizes for interrupting, thereby tacitly inviting the caller to continue (lines 5–6). Although he does not at this time complete the response he began, it is noteworthy that before cutting himself off he was projectably headed toward producing an account for why the people referred to by the caller have not called the radio station to complain ("I'll tell you why:," lines 5–6). It is thus apparent that the host was not about to treat the caller's claim as a puzzle, instead showing his understanding of the caller's claims to the degree that he was prepared to address the matter of why the "black friends" mentioned by the caller were not inclined to share their experiences on-air. Furthermore, in his next response (see line 15), the host displays agreement with the caller (line 15), thereby tacitly aligning (cf. Sacks, 1995; Schegloff, 1992a) with the caller's commonsense equation of "black" with "poor." Commonsense links between race and class (specifically blackness and poverty) are thus treated as unproblematic, and collaboratively produced as taken for granted, by both the caller and host.

Excerpt 2 shows another instance of the taken-for-granted association between blackness and poverty, as well as the converse links between whiteness and wealth or privilege. Prior to this excerpt, a caller raised the issue of the high rates of violent crime in South Africa, and questioned why government officials are not more outraged or willing to talk about the issue. In response, the host constructs a narrative of "hypocrisy" in South Africa's justice system, mobilizing these commonsense links between race and class while arguing that some criminals are treated differently than others as a result of poverty being largely a legacy of apartheid.

```
Excerpt 2:
[156 - Safm 4-25-08]
1    H:   You know what it is?
2         (.)
3    H:   We are in that conundrum, (0.2) where there's a bit of
4         hypocrisy >you see?< .hh We have a lot of poor people in
5         this country, .h[h
6    C:                  [Unfortunate[ly (it's still there.)
7    H:                              [Ja- we- eh uh lu- le- hear me
8         out here. .h[h They're poor, .h and that poverty came
9    C:               [Mm.
10   H:   supposedly, .h or definitely:, (.) m- for most of us, .hh
11        from this apartheid thing, you see? [.hhh
12   C:                                       [Which was evil,
13   H:   Okay, which was wrong, .hh and then (.) now we've got (.)
14        crime. (.) Now guess what? .hh White people (.) are getting
15        hurt, right? .hh So, the hypocrisy says .hh "well, it's a
16        poor guy:, .h and that's a white guy, .h you know, .h just
17        don't (.) be too hard about it." [.hh That's where the
18   C:                                    [(.hh)
19   H:   problem is. .hh The integrity should say (0.2) "I do not
20        care.
21   C:   (Yeah.)
22   H:   How you became poor, where you got poor, .hh as a country,
23        (0.2) it is not allowed for you to steal. (.) Okay? .h[h
24   C:                                                         [No.
```

```
25   H:    That's what we've got in our constitution. .hh Let alone
26         murder somebody. .h So we gonna klap you.' (("klap" is an
27         Afrikaans word meaning "hit" that is frequently employed in
28         colloquial South African English.))
```

Of particular significance in the host's account is his production of an asymmetrical reference (see Whitehead & Lerner, 2009), constructing a contrast between "a poor guy" and "a white guy" (line 16). This reference is asymmetrical in that it involves contrastive references to members of categories from two distinct collections, namely class ("poor") and race ("white"). By producing a reference in this form, the host implicitly connects the two collections of categories, thereby tacitly racializing the category "poor" and tacitly treating the category "white" as class-relevant (Whitehead & Lerner, 2009). In this way, the host orients to and reproduces commonsense connections between black poverty and white wealth, using these taken-for-granted connections as resources to produce his response to the caller.

The host also mobilizes, in the course of his account, other commonsense connections between race and class. The first of these appears in the connection he draws between the current prevalence of poverty in South Africa and the previous system of apartheid (see lines 4–5, 8, and 10–11). By suggesting that contemporary poverty is a direct result of apartheid, the host implicitly racializes those experiencing poverty, invoking the apartheid system's privileging of white South Africans at the expense of their black counterparts. A second apparent link between race and class is evident in the host's suggestion that "white people (.) are getting hurt" (lines 14–15). In making this claim, the host appears to be producing a narrative of white people becoming crime victims at the hands of poor (black) people as a result of being perceived as beneficiaries of the privileged class status conferred on them under the apartheid system.

Despite the complex nature of the commonsense linkages the host appears to be deploying,

and despite the fact that a lot of his apparent reasoning remains taken for granted and unspoken, his recipient (the caller) shows no evidence of having difficulty in understanding his account. On the contrary, she displays agreement or understanding in several places throughout the host's account (see lines 6, 9, 12, 21, 24). As in the case of Excerpt 1, this attests to both the collaborative treatment of the race-class intersections as known-in-common, and to the collaborative process of their reproduction as such in interactions like this (cf. Garfinkel, 1967; Heritage, 1984b).

Excerpt 3 illustrates the third aspect of commonsense links between race and class mentioned above, namely speakers' orientations to an association between blackness and (newly-emerging) wealth—in contrast to the links between black poverty and the apartheid system shown in the previous excerpts. This excerpt is drawn from an interview with a guest who works as a guide for a range of outdoor and adventure sports and activities. In responding to a question from the host about the cost of these activities (line 1), the guest describes the increasing numbers of people who are coming to see them as representing good value for money, using as an illustrative example his observations of a recent increase in the number of "black people doing caravanning" (lines 16–17). This use of black people as an illustrative example appears to be designed to dispel the commonsense view that activities such as these are the domain of white people—a view that the host and guest previously discussed in the interview. However, it also rests on the unspoken assumption that substantial numbers of black South Africans are not only developing an interest in participating in these activities, but also have the material resources required to do so.

```
Excerpt 3:
[132 - SAfm 4-23-08]
1   H:  Is it quite expensive, Jeff?
2   G:  Um, (.) I think more and more people- (.) in- in the
3       beginning people found it to be: ex- expensive especially:
4       u:m our local tourists, South African tourists. .h[hh
5   H:                                                    [(°Ja.°)
6   G:  U:m, but increasingly people are finding that it's- .hh
7       (0.2) it's (.) it's more (.) exciting and mor- and- and-
8       and fun .hh to spend that amount of money, an- (.) something
9       that you really (0.6) enjoy, .hh instead of spending: .hh
10      six to seven hundred rand just (n-) (.) sitting: hh next to
11      a pool at a- at a- at a .hh (.) fairly mediocre hotel. hh
12      .h[h So:
13  H:    [0- or drinking it away [at some uh cocktail bar I guess.
14  G:                            [Or drinking it away you know. .hh
15      So: (0.2) more and more people are- are: I mean I've seen
16      now, over the last year, an increase in: for example .hh u:m
17      (.) uh: black people doing caravanning for example you know
18      because .hh it is becoming: (0.2) a better option: (.) for-
19      for holidaying you know where .hh you really: where you
20      really feel (.) .hh the country around you. h So: .h[h
21  H:                                                      [0- If
22      I want to get uh: some of this adrenaline rushes you're
23      talking about how do I go about it, who do I call?
24      ((interview continues))
```

The temporal formulations the guest uses in his response to the host's questions contribute to the treatment of black wealth as being newly-emerging. That is, the guest initially formulates a period ("in the beginning," lines 2–3) during which "South African tourists" found these types of activities "expensive." He then contrasts this with a more recent period ("now, over the last year," line 16) when "black people" are participating in increasing numbers. In light of his apparent use of common-sense race-class links in constructing this example, this temporal contrast appears to allude to the relatively recent

emergence of the middle-class black people now engaging in the activities being discussed. In this way, black wealth, and newly emerging black wealth in particular, serves as an unspoken backdrop underpinning the guest's claims.

Unlike the previous two excerpts, the recipient does not actively collaborate in the speaker's production of these race-class links by showing agreement or understanding. However, following the guest's possible completion of his response at line 20, the host produces his next question (lines 21–23). In doing so, he treats the guest's prior answer as adequate, thereby indicating no difficulties in understanding or accepting the answer and the commonsense knowledge underpinning it, and contributing to the production of this commonsense knowledge as unspoken but unproblematic (cf. Heritage, 1984; Schegloff, 1992a).

USING RACE-CLASS COMMON SENSE

While I have thus far focused primarily on the commonsense race-class connections collaboratively produced by speakers, it is clear that this common sense is not produced independently of particular contexts of action, but instead is *used to do things* in interactions. In Excerpt 1, the caller uses it in the course of producing a complaint; in Excerpt 2, the host uses it in the course of accounting for the behavior of government officials, as observed by a caller; and in Excerpt 3, the guest uses it to answer a question and, more specifically, to illustrate his claim in favor of the activities through which he earns his livelihood. In this section, I discuss in more detail

these features of speakers' use of common-sense race-class intersections, examining additional data that further illustrate their mobilization as interactional resources.

In Excerpt 4, which is from later in the same call shown in Excerpt 1, the host responds to the caller's complaint by challenging his claim that poor black people "suffer the most" when electricity supplies are interrupted. Although the host disagrees with the caller, he deploys the same commonsense race-class linkages that the caller produced in his complaint. Specifically, the host uses taken-for-granted assumptions about race and poverty as resources in accounting for why the people the caller has complained about are not more vocal about the "electricity crisis."

In his account, the host claims that, in contrast to the caller's claims, those whose silence the caller complained about are actually affected the least by the power cuts. In doing so, he resists the logic of the caller's assumptions regarding which types of people "suffer the most," while leaving intact the commonsense category of "poor black" that the caller implicitly constructed. Moreover, the host

```
Excerpt 4:
[172 - SAfm 4-28-08]
 1    H:   But the- you know what the joke is Dwayne? .hh When your
 2         you- you (.) have electricity (.) .hh coming to your house,
 3         but [you constantly get cut off because you can't afford
 4    C:       [(Ja, I know.)
 5    H:   to pay for it, .hh because the economy is not really working
 6         with you. .hh [When you come to power cuts, you are more
 7    C:                 [Ja (but look the-)
 8    H:   used to it than the guy in Sandton, .hh who's got the
 9         generator going a lot of food [in the fridge, .hh da da
10    C:                                 [(            )
11    H:   da, .h that's gonna rot, if it's- it's not gonna happen.
12         .hh So you will get that tho:se who are hit the most .h are
13         the ones who are gonna complain the most.
```

reinforces the race-class common sense the caller produced, describing what he treats as typical experiences of the "black friends"/"poor people" the caller identified as the targets of his criticism (lines 1–3 and 5–6), and using this description as a resource for claiming that such people are "used to" (line 8) living without electricity.

The host also draws a contrast between the type of people the caller complained about and a "guy in Sandton" who he suggests would be more affected by power cuts, and would therefore be more vocal about the situation (see lines 8–9 and 11–13). This serves to further reinforce race-class common sense by allusively (particularly through his reference to Sandton, an affluent Johannesburg suburb that was reserved for white people under apartheid) setting up a hypothetical wealthy white person in contrast to the poor black people he and the caller have been discussing (see Whitehead's 2007, 2009 analyses of allusions to race, and geographical locations as proxies for race in particular).

A more explicit use of white wealth as an interactional resource is shown in Excerpt 5, where the host uses it as a resource for joking. Prior to the stretch of interaction shown in the excerpt, the host and caller discussed a study that reported substantial racial inequalities in income levels in South Africa. Following this discussion, in lines 2 and 3, the caller questions how such inequalities can "after fourteen years of democracy, still exist." In the host's response, he uses commonsense knowledge of white wealth as a basis for a joking suggestion that the caller's "short term solution . . . is to find a white girlfriend" (lines 9 and 11).

```
Excerpt 5:
[606 - 702 Talk Radio 5-9-08]
 1   C:   Ja so now I- I need somebody that is clued up hheh .hh with
 2        eh the labor laws as to: .hh how can that .hh st- still
 3        after fourteen years of democracy, still e[xist, (and-)
 4   H:                                             [.hhh This is the
 5        issue, this is the issue, and this is why we talk about
 6        affirmative action and all the rest of it because if you
 7        look at the reality if you look at where the money is, and
 8        who's got the power, obviously that need to change, or it
 9        needs to be leveled out at least, .hh but I th[ink your
10   C:                                                 [Mm.
11   H:   short term solution Zakele, .hh is to find a white
12        girlfriend. ((smile voice))
13        (0.7)
14   H:   hh hu[h huh huh
15   C:        [Sorry?
16   H:   I said you[r heh heh your solution is [to find a white
17   C:             [hhh hhuh huh huh             [.hhh
18   H:   g[irlfriend. ((smile voice))
19   C:    [Mm. Mm. ((smile voice))
```

The host's response initially acknowledges the importance of the issue, and its relationship to affirmative action policies (lines 4–6), before linking the issue to the overall distribution of money and power (lines 7–9). Although he does not mention race explicitly, it is clear (in the context of the foregoing discussion of racial inequalities in income) that these distributional claims are references to racialized patterns of wealth and status. These implicitly produced race-class intersections then serve as the basis for the host to joke that finding a "white girl-friend" is a favorable "short-term solution" available to the caller in the face of such patterns of inequality. That is, the host jokingly suggests that the caller could be understood as being in a disadvantaged class position by virtue of being black, and that he could improve his position by sharing in the taken-for-granted wealth of a hypothetical white partner.[10]

In response, the caller first initiates "repair" (see, for example, Schegloff, 1992b) in line 15, and then (just after the host has begun to repeat the joke), displays his appreciation of the joke, and his understanding of the commonsense knowledge it was based on, by laughing along with the host (lines 16–17). Therefore, consistent with the excerpts examined above, the caller collaborates with the host in producing the race-class link underpinning the joke as known-in-common.

A final case, shown in Excerpt 6, illustrates a caller's use of taken-for-granted black wealth as a resource for complaining about racial quotas (a particularly controversial aspect of post-apartheid affirmative action policies) in elite sports teams. In his complaint, the caller argues that the quota system focuses solely on race at the expense of recognizing the importance of class, and that as a result it unfairly advantages black athletes from wealthy backgrounds over less wealthy white athletes.

```
Excerpt 6:
[401 - 702 Talk Radio 3-26-08]
 1   C:  I- I just think we need to distinguish subtly between .hh
 2       development of young players and the quota system.
 3   H:  Okay.
 4   C:  Um:: (.) I'm looking specifically let's say .h my son is
 5       in uh (.) standard six at a government school, .h born in
 6       nineteen ninety four, the new South Africa, (0.2) .hh I mean
 7       (in) four years' time he'(ll) be the same age as: Francois
 8       Steyn wa[s when he was selected for Springboks or super
 9   H:          [Mm.
10   C:  fourteen.
11   H:  Ja.
12   C:  Now they- under the quota system a black guy who went to
13       Michaelhouse, or (.) Hilton, or one of those schools, .hh
14       will get preference (0.2) then the su- my son who's been at
15       a government school or other white kids who've been at
16       government school[s.
17   H:                    [Mm.
```

(Continued)

(Continued)

```
18       (0.7)
19   C:  So I think (i- i-) you know the difference needs to
20       be on development of the under com- u- (.) the under
21       privileged communities.
22   H:  Yes. I [agree with you.
23   C:        [Ra-
24   C:  Rather than (0.5) putting a- a- a- a- a person of
25       color into a side just because he's (a/of) color
26       irrespective of whe[ther he's got a degree, and
27   H:                     [Ja.
28   C:  .h[h how rich his parents are. (E-) [Cause nobody's
29   H:    [Sure.                              [Mm.
30   C:  looking at the richness of the parents they're
31       j[ust looking at the color of the skin.
32   H:    [Sure.
```

The caller produces his complaint by contrasting a hypothetical "black guy who went to Michaelhouse, or (.) Hilton" (both exclusive and highly resourced private high schools) with "my son who's been at a government school or other white kids who've been at government schools" (lines 12–16). He thus invokes commonsense knowledge of the disparities in resources between private and government high schools, and the accompanying advantages for young athletes resulting from attending private schools. This in turn is based on the taken-for-granted assumption that there are significant numbers of black families with sufficient wealth to pay the fees required for their children to attend schools like these, and that a policy that fails to take into account their existence could be seen as unfair. The caller thus treats the quota system as assuming taken-for-granted black poverty, and challenges it by mobilizing taken-for-granted black wealth. The caller concludes his complaint by making this assumption more explicit, suggesting that the quota system erroneously treats race as a proxy for class, "looking at the color of the skin" (line 13) at the expense of considering "the richness of the parents" (line 12).

Once again (as in many of the previous cases), the recipient (the host) collaborates with the speaker's use of commonsense, race-class intersections by agreeing with the caller on several occasions (lines 4, 9, 11, and 14). He thereby displays his recognition of, and alignment with, the same commonsense knowledge the caller has used in formulating his argument.

CONCLUSIONS

The data I have presented offer evidence of continuities and discontinuities between the apartheid and post-apartheid periods with respect to commonsense knowledge about race-class intersections in South Africa. The content of this commonsense knowledge points to the enduring nature of the legacies of apartheid, not just in the material structures of the society described in the introduction, but also in the ways that ordinary people observe and make sense of the patterns of wealth, poverty, and inequality around them. However, in contrast with the taken-for-granted assumptions of black poverty and white privilege resulting from apartheid policies and their legacy, there is also emerging a body of commonsense knowledge about race and wealth not always overlapping. This demonstrates some ways in which the post-apartheid changes in the relative material conditions of people of different racial categories are observable in everyday interactions. These findings suggest that the category systems of race and class that were centrally important during apartheid have retained their significance in the post-apartheid period, but at the same time, the content of the commonsense knowledge associated with racial and class categories, and the relationships between them, appears to be more malleable (cf. Tilly, 1998; Whitehead & Lerner, 2009). In this sense, the findings provide evidence of the observable impacts of social changes, such as those that have occurred in South Africa, at the level of everyday interactional practices.

This analysis also points to a mechanism through which commonsense associations between race and class are produced and reproduced. That is, each time a person orients to or deploys such commonsense knowledge, and particularly when this occurs collaboratively, the knowledge is reinforced as being relevant or consequential. Moreover, as the data demonstrate, the utility of this commonsense knowledge as a resource for the production of ordinary actions (such as complaining, accounting, answering, disagreeing, joking, and so on) provides a basis for its ongoing production and reproduction in the course of everyday interactions. In this regard, it is worth emphasizing that, although matters of both race and class are topicalized in various ways in the interactions I have examined, the commonsense links between them are not explicitly interrogated, but instead remain largely taken for granted even when used interactionally. Thus, the use of this commonsense knowledge by speakers and recipients recurrently remains tacit, with its relevance treated as self-evident rather than specifying or questioning

why or *how* it is relevant. That this does not recurrently (if ever) result in difficulties in understanding among coparticipants points to the interactional accomplishments involved in producing this type of knowledge as an unproblematic backdrop to the topics being discussed.

Finally, and in light of the above points, these findings demonstrate the significance of everyday talk-in-interaction as a site at which social structures (for example, those related to race and class) are both reflected and reproduced. Thus, on the one hand, commonsense knowledge about South Africa's race and class structures (both historical and contemporary), and the ongoing links between them, is mobilized as an interpretive resource whenever speakers mention or orient to race-class intersections in the course of their exchanges. At the same time, everyday interactions provide an ever present place where race-class commonsense can become relevant, and thereby get renewed and reproduced, but can also be resisted and challenged.

NOTES

1. This Afrikaans term, meaning "separateness," is commonly used to describe the white supremacist racial system implemented in South Africa by the National Party from 1948 to 1994. See, for example, Clark and Worger (2004), Guelke (2005), and Louw (2004), for historical overviews of the apartheid system.

2. A debate over the question of whether apartheid was primarily a system of class exploitation or one of racial domination was prominent in the social scientific literature of the time (see Wolpe, 1990). This debate, however, is largely beyond the scope of this chapter.

3. A note on terminology: Following the convention established in the South African liberation struggle, I use the term "black" synonymously with "people of color," to inclusively refer to all groups not defined as "white" by apartheid legislation. However, on occasions when it is relevant to differentiate between the groups codified by apartheid legislation, I use the distinct terms "African" (those classified as "Native," "Bantu," or "black" under apartheid), "Indian" (a term that generally included all individuals of Asian descent), and "Coloured" (individuals, usually of

mixed race, who were not classified as members of any of the other official race groups). Of course, like all racial categories, these categories are historically contingent social constructions, and I use them for the purposes of addressing their significance as "social facts," rather than to suggest that race is an essential, natural or intrinsically consequential human characteristic.

4. It is important to note that, while I separate these two aspects of race-class commonsense (their content and their use as interactional resources) for analytic purposes, in practice they are inextricably bound together in the ways in which they are mobilized in interactional episodes.

5. A list of the transcription symbols utilized is provided by Jefferson (2004), and can be accessed at http://www.liso.ucsb.edu/Jefferson/Transcript.pdf. In addition, a "Transcription Module" on Conversation Analytic transcription (which includes links to sound files exemplifying the features of speech production that the various transcription symbols are used to represent) can be accessed at http://www.sscnet.ucla.edu/soc/faculty/schegloff/TranscriptionProject/index.html.

6. It is worth noting that, while white poverty has been treated as an issue of concern for well over 100 years in South Africa (Terreblanche, 2003), I have yet to locate any instances of white poverty being treated as a taken-for-granted, commonsense reality. Instead, poor white people, on the rare occasions when they are mentioned, tend to be treated either as a historical problem or a contemporary anomaly.

7. The term "recipient(s)" is used by conversation analysts to refer to "the particular other(s) who are the co-participants" (Sacks et al, 1974, p. 727) in an interaction in which an utterance of interest is produced. Recipients are thus those who receive an utterance, and who may subsequently respond to it.

8. The caller is apparently referring to a period during which demands for electricity in South Africa were exceeding supply capacity, resulting in regular interruptions of electricity supply to substantial numbers of households.

9. This reference to "our black friends" is an instance of an affiliative racial categorization that appears to be designed to manage the potential delicacy of complaining about "racial others" (i.e., members of racial categories other than that of the speaker). See Whitehead (2010, 2011b) for further analysis of this practice. It is also worth noting the caller's apparent assumption that he can accurately racially identify other callers based on the on-air voice samples they

provide during their calls. I examine both of these phenomena in more detail in forthcoming reports.

10. Two other features of the commonsense knowledge deployed by the host in this joke are worth noting. First, he treats racial identification of the caller as an unproblematic matter, even though the caller has not explicitly racially self-identified (cf. Excerpt 1 above). Second, he is apparently oriented to normative heterosexuality by virtue of suggesting that a potential partner for the caller would necessarily be female (cf. Kitzinger, 2005b).

REFERENCES

Adam, H., & Moodley, K. (1993). Comparing South Africa: Nonracialism versus ethnonationalist revival. *Third World Quarterly, 14*(2), 339–350.

Bhorat, H., & Kanbur, R. (2007). *Poverty and policy in post-apartheid South Africa.* Cape Town, ZA: HSRC Press.

Bond, P. (2000). *The elite transition: From apartheid to neoliberalism in South Africa.* London, UK: Pluto Press.

Christopher, A. J. (1997). Racial land zoning in urban South Africa. *Land Use Policy, 14*(4), 311–323.

Christopher, A. J. (2001). Urban segregation in post-apartheid South Africa. *Urban Studies, 38*(3), 449–466.

Clark, N. L., & Worger, W. H. (2004). *South Africa: The rise and fall of apartheid.* Harlow, UK: Pearson Education.

Crenshaw, K. (1989). Demarginalizing the intersection of race and sex: A black feminist critique of antidiscrimination doctrine, feminist theory, and antiracist politics. *University of Chicago Legal Forum, 14*, 538–554.

Davis, K. (2008). Intersectionality as buzzword: A sociology of science perspective on what makes a feminist theory successful. *Feminist Theory, 9*(1), 67–85.

Desai, A. (2002). *We are the poors: Community struggles in post-apartheid South Africa.* New York, NY: Monthly Review Press.

Franchi, V. (2003). The racialization of affirmative action in organizational discourses: A case study of symbolic racism in post-apartheid South Africa. *International Journal of Intercultural Relations, 27*, 157–187.

Frederickson, G. M. (1981). *White supremacy: A comparative study in American and South African history.* New York, NY: Oxford University Press.

Frederickson, G. M. (2002). *Racism: A short history.* Princeton, NJ: Princeton University Press.

Garfinkel, H. (1956). Some sociological concepts and methods for psychiatrists. *Psychiatric Research Reports, 6,* 181–195.

Garfinkel, H. (1967). *Studies in ethnomethodology.* Engelwood Cliffs, NJ: Prentice-Hall.

Guelke, A. (2005). *Rethinking the rise and fall of apartheid.* New York, NY: Palgrave Macmillan.

Hansen, A. D. (2005). A practical task: Ethnicity as a resource in social interaction. *Research on Language and Social Interaction, 38*(1), 63–104.

Heritage, J. (1984). *Garfinkel and ethnomethodology.* Cambridge, UK: Polity.

Jefferson, G. (2004). Glossary of transcript symbols with an introduction. In G. H. Lerner, (Ed.), *Conversation analysis: Studies from the first generation* (pp. 13–23). Philadelphia, PA: John Benjamins.

Kitzinger, C. (2005a). Heteronormativity in action: Reproducing the heterosexual nuclear family in after hours medical calls. *Social Problems, 52*(4), 477–498.

Kitzinger, C. (2005b). "Speaking as a heterosexual": (How) does sexuality matter for talk-in-interaction? *Research on Language and Social Interaction, 38*(3), 221–265.

Louw, P. E. (2004). *The rise, fall and legacy of apartheid.* Westport, CT: Praeger.

McCall, L. (2005). The complexity of intersectionality. *Signs: Journal of Women in Culture and Society, 30*(3), 1771–1800.

Posel, D. (2001). Race as common sense: Racial classification in twentieth-century South Africa. *African Studies Review, 44*(2), 87–133.

Sacks, H. (1995). *Lectures on conversation* (Vols. 1, 2). Oxford, UK: Blackwell.

Sacks, H., Schegloff, E. A., & Jefferson, G. (1974). A simplest systematics for the organization of turn taking in conversation. *Language, 50,* 696–735.

Schegloff, E. A. (1992a). Repair after next turn: The last structurally provided defense of intersubjectivity in conversation. *American Journal of Sociology, 97*(5), 1295–1345.

Schegloff, E. A. (1992b). In another context. In A. Duranti, & C. Goodwin (Eds.), *Rethinking context: Language as an interactive phenomenon.* Cambridge, UK: Cambridge University Press.

Schegloff, E. A. (2007). *Sequence organization in interaction: A primer in conversation analysis* (Vol. 1). Cambridge, UK: Cambridge University Press.

Seekings, J., & Nattrass, N. (2005). *Class, race and inequality in South Africa.* New Haven, CT: Yale University Press.

Statistics South Africa (2011). *Quarterly labour force survey, quarter 1, 2011.* Pretoria: Statistics South Africa. Retrieved from http://www.statssa.gov.za/publications/P0211/P02111stQuarter2011.pdf.

Terreblanche, S. (2003). *A history of inequality in South Africa: 1652–2002.* Pietermaritzburg, ZA: University of Natal Press.

Tilly, C. (1998). *Durable inequality.* Berkeley: University of California Press.

West, C., & Fenstermaker, S. (1995). Doing difference. *Gender & Society, 9*(1), 8–37.

Whitehead, K. A. (2007). *Managing racial common sense in interaction: The use of allusions to race.* Paper presented at the 78th Annual Conference of the Pacific Sociological Association (PSA), Oakland, CA.

Whitehead, K. A. (2009). "Categorizing the categorizer": The management of racial common sense in interaction. *Social Psychology Quarterly, 72*(4), 325–342.

Whitehead, K. A. (2010). *Racial categories in the social life of post-apartheid South Africa.* Ph.D. Dissertation, Department of Sociology, University of California, Santa Barbara.

Whitehead, K. A. (2011a). An ethnomethodological, conversation analytic approach to investigating race in South Africa. *South African Review of Sociology, 42*(3), 1–22.

Whitehead, K. A. (2011b). *Self-deprecating racial self-identifications in complaint sequences.* Paper presented at the International Institute for Ethnomethodology and Conversation Analysis (IIEMCA) Conference, Fribourg, Switzerland.

Whitehead, K. A., & Lerner, G. H. (2009). When are persons "white"? On some practical asymmetries of racial reference in talk-in-interaction. *Discourse and Society, 20*(5), 613–641.

Winant, H. (2001). *The world is a ghetto: Race and democracy since World War II.* New York, NY: Basic Books.

Wolpe, H. (1990). *Race, class and the apartheid state.* Trenton, NJ: Africa World Press.

SECTION 2

RACE

5

THE REPRESENTATION OF ETHNIC-CULTURAL "OTHERNESS"

The Roma Minority in Serbian Press

Nataša Simeunović Bajić

INTRODUCTION

Society in any aspect of study cannot be regarded as a homogeneous and stable structure. Most modern societies are multicultural, which necessarily implies the existence of a majority and various minorities. A common focus of analysis in the social sciences and one of the most important criteria for evaluating the democratization of a society is the status of ethnic minorities. The study of ethnic minorities is particularly relevant to Serbia and its transition to a modern democratic society, which began in 2000 after the collapse of the Milošević regime. The status of an ethnic minority cannot be separated from its representation in the media. Mass media are one of the most important institutions for the social representation of any experience. Media messages directly shape the understanding and perceptions of minority ethnic groups. The public's perceptions toward minorities rely heavily on the media reporting.

In Serbia, what most members of society know about the Roma is not as a consequence of any direct contact, but rather the end result of a complex process of media production of meaning. Since the public opinion and media discourse are of great importance to interracial and intercultural communication, this chapter examines the ways that the Roma are represented in the Serbian press. The goal of this research is to examine media messages about this ethnic minority and to identify general trends in the reporting of "Roma otherness."

THE HISTORY OF ROMA OTHERNESS

Roma do not have a written history. Written documents about the Roma that exist today were produced by people who had direct contact with them; as a result, many aspects of Roma history remain unidentified.[1] What Roma nomads know about their history, while moving from place to place and from country to country, is included in their oral storytelling. The Roma have never formed a common national consciousness or exhibited statehood tendencies, as such. Today they remain a very diverse ethnic group. However, homogeneity can be recognized in many parts of their folklore heritage. For a long time, the origins of the Roma were a matter of mere speculation. Thanks to linguists and their research—especially to the German linguist, Jakob Karl Christof Ridiger—we now understand the connection between the Roma language and Indian languages and have traced the origins of the Roma to India (Clebert, 1967; Hancock, 2002). The Roma language belongs to the Indo-Aryan language group, a subgroup of Indo-Iranian language (Indo-European family of languages) mainly represented by Sanskrit. Indeed, the Roma language retains some basic features from Sanskrit (Marjanović, 2006). There is still no answer to explain why the Roma abandoned their homeland. Many studies show that the Roma left India somewhere between AD 800 and 950. There are several theories about their directions of travel and migration. According to Ludwig (1995), the Roma set out from Punjab where they initially had settled. Yet, there are hypotheses that in addition to Punjab, they settled in other parts of Pakistan, including Rajasthan and Gujarat (Đurić, 2006). Another theory attributes the homeland of Roma to Kabul (Vukanović, 1983). The latest theory by Marcel Courthiade asserts that the Roma originated in Kannauj, India (Bašić, 2003). What is known for certain is that the entry of the Roma into Europe was subtle and not offensive (Vukanović, 1983). One record of the Persian poet Abu'l-Qāsim Mansour, better known as Ferdowsi, in the book *Shāhnāmeh*, describes the migration of Roma as beginning sometime in the 5th century, after the invasion of the Huns:

> Persian shah Bahram Gur, asked the Indian king Shangul to send him 10,000 players who with their music would put in the good mood Persian people.

The Indian ruler had sent the best of the best, Luri musicians. They then refused to leave Persia until a shah ordered them to leave and then they began to wander (Clebert, 1967; Mitić, 2006).

Today there are several theories about how the Roma settled the European continent. The most popular one describes the Roma as coming to Europe from two directions: from Turkey across the Bosphorus, and from Africa over Gibraltar. According to Byzantine chronicles, in the 9th century the Roma lived in Byzantine Empire (Vukanović, 1983). They came to be known by the defamatory name, Cigani (Gypsies), which originates from the Greek word ατσίγγανοι translated *atsinganoi* or "don't touch" (Hancock, 2002). It was an etymon (root) of later forms for the name, for example, in Turkish, *Cingene*; in Hungarian, *Czigany*; in Romanian, *Tigany*; in Italian, *Zingari*; in French, *Tsiganes*; in German, *Zigeuner*; in Polish, *Cyganie*. There are different interpretations about the history of Roma: some connect their name to their legendary Egyptian origins while others associated their name with the craft of forging, which gypsies commonly practiced. However, the centuries-long attitudes among European nations toward the Roma and the constant use of defamatory names demonstrate that the term Ατσίγγανοι is derived from the word Αθίγγανοι. Indeed, this was a name for the heretical sect in the 8th and 9th century AD, who were skilled in magic and dealt with predicting the future (Kenrick, 2007; Vukanović, 1983). Some Roma groups in Europe, Asia, and Africa practiced these crafts. Therefore, it is assumed that many nations where the Roma had lived started to call them by this name. The first mention of the word *Gypsies* dates from the year 1068 and was found in a hagiography made by an abbot of the Iviron monastery on Mt. Athos, Greece. The officially accepted term, Roma (Romi in Serbian) originates from the Roma word *Rrom*, which means a *man* or *people*.

By the 15th century, the Roma were mentioned in chronicles, annals, acts, edicts, adjudications, and publications in many European countries. Mitić (2006) points out the repressions toward the Roma:

> In that time began the first repressions toward them. The Roma were accused of and hanged for robbery, riot, and witchcraft. They were persecuted across borders, and at best case they were restricted to colonies that were intended also for the Jews and other people from the margins [. . .] Probably the first document, directly aimed against Roma, the act from 1471, enacted in Lucerne, forbade them to enter to the soil of Switzerland (p. 26).

Since that period, the Roma have carried the burden of stigma and persecution. In Romania and Hungary, the Roma were enslaved (Clebert, 1967), and a German chronicle in the 17th century identified them as animals: "A nice deer was shot, also five doe, three goodly wild boars, nine smaller wild boars, two Roma men, one Roma woman and one Roma child" (Mirga & Mruz, 1997, p. 49). By the beginning of the 19th century, Germany had a popular sport known as "Gypsy hunts" or "Heidenjachten" (Timeline of Romani History).

In the period 1500 to 1800, Germany published approximately 150 laws against the Roma. Joachim Hohmann in his *History of the Roma Persecution in Germany* (Geschichte der Zigeunerverfolgung in Deutschland), first published in 1981, documented the Roma banishment beginning with banishment from Meissen in 1416, from Frankfurt in 1449, from Bamberg 1463, and so forth. In 1596, authorities in Cologne, Germany, ordered the extermination of the Roma (see Đurić, 2006). In Italy, England, France, Denmark, Czech Republic, Poland, Romania, Spain and, in general, in almost all of the European countries, the Roma faced cruel and oppressive actions that included the seizure of property, fines, haircuts, castigation, branding, cutting off ears, blinding, hanging, and being cut into quarters and placed on a wheel. During the reign of Maria Theresa of the Habsburg Empire, Vienna pursued an aggressive policy of Roma assimilation that included government seizure of Roma children who were

then brought up in state hospices. Adult Roma were legally forced to marry other non-Roma people and adapt to the life of other citizens (Ludwig, 2001, p. 76). At that time, they were still forbidden to trade horses, to elect their tribal elders, to live in tents and to speak in their language (Clebert, 1967).

The experience of the Roma in what had been the Ottoman Empire was quite different. Researchers assert that Roma started to come to Europe during the conquests of the Turks. The first Turkish census, which noted Roma in a territory of the Ottoman Empire, was dated 1491 (Zirojević, 1976). Clebert used his study about Roma to note that the Southeast part of Europe was the only territory where they were not subjected to repression (1967). Byzantine and Serbian chronicles mention that the first groups of the Roma arrived in Serbian territory during the medieval reign of Stefan Uroš of Dečanski (King of Serbia from 1322 to 1331). It may be that the first group of Roma to come to Serbia were part of a circus. In Belgrade, the Roma are mentioned for the first time in documents that were written in 1536 (Zirojević, 1976), however it is unclear if the Roma had been there even earlier.

In the 16th century, in Serbia and other South Slavic countries that were part of the Ottoman Empire, Roma had free expression and the right to their ethnicity. Turkish authorities did not interfere with their lifestyle and customs, rather their rights and duties were governed by religion and class affiliation (Vukanović, 1983). In The First Serbian Uprising (1804–1813), Roma had their own duke who came to Parliament on equal terms with other dukes. At the beginning of the 20th century, the first Serbian scientific papers about the Roma were published (Bašić, 2005)—many of these were written by Tihomir Đorđević. Unlike the suffering of the Jews, which was known among the wider international public, little is known about the persecution of the Roma, generally or specifically, during the Holocaust. Indeed, there are very few studies on the Roma. Detailed descriptions of the suffering of Roma in the Holocaust are given by Christian Bernadac in the book, *The Forgotten Holocaust*, in which he proved that the most horrific Nazi experiments were carried out on the Roma people by Dr. Josef Mengele, who conducted experiments with twins and dwarfs:

> Two Gypsy children, barefoot are squatting on a cement floor of a square cell with meter and a half long walls, without windows. They had no reflexes at all. . . . These poor children, snatched from their parents, still have a chance to survive because they are twins. Their lives depend on the mania of a Doctor Mengele who has been dedicated to them because of genetic experiments [. . . .] For instance, an injection of some chemical substances would be given to one of the twins and then the reaction was expected if someone does not forget about it in the meantime. . . . I remember Mengele very well: children called him, Uncle Mengele. Every time he came in the Gypsy camp, children went out to meet him because he often brought chocolates. . . Mengele reassured them and made them enter into his car so he can drive them to the crematorium. Children started to cry again after arrival. He shot them by himself (Bernadac, 1981, p. 210).

We also know that during the Nazi regime from 1933 to 1945, the Roma were subjected to alarming forms of torture. In addition, there were large numbers of Nazi proclamations, demands, commands, and prohibitions that referred to the Roma. For example, four months before Kristallnacht (Crystal Night), between June 12 and June 18, 1938, the Nazi's conducted what was called the Gypsy cleanup week (Zigeuneraufraumungswoche). Thousands of the Roma were arrested, beaten, and deported to concentration camps. And, it is little known that in January 1940, the gas (Zyklon-B crystals) that was later used in the camp gas chambers was first tested on 250 Roma children (Hancock, 1997). The Nazi's built special camps and Marzahn, a suburb of Berlin, was the first internment camp for the Roma. Cynically, it was called the Resting Place (Rastplatz). On December 16, 1942, Himmler ordered that Roma all across Europe be deported to Auschwitz-Birkenau. Many children held in the camp died as the result of cruel medical experiments performed by Dr. Mengele (U.S. Holocaust Museum, *Sinti*

and Roma: Victims of the Nazi era). In Croatia, a concentration camp known as Jasenovac was well known for killing Roma along with Serbs and Jews (Bruchfeld & Levine, 1998). The exact number of the Roma killed in the Nazi persecution may never be determined, but the number is estimated at between 500,000 and one and a half million (Hancock, 1997). Leh Mruz, a Polish ethnologist and Romanologist, believes that the Roma have not healed from their losses during the war; their tradition and culture were permanently destroyed. This brutal and comprehensive destruction of group and ancestry relations irrevocably damaged the system of internal cultural cohesion for the Roma (Đorđević & Balić, 2004).

Although the Roma were victims of Nazi genocide, after World War II their persecution continued—particularly at the institutional level. For example in Wuerttemberg in 1950, a minister of West Germany said that the Roma were not persecuted because of their race, but because of their antisocial behavior (Porajmos, n.d.). A post-Nazi government claimed that all legitimate official measures that had been taken against the Roma were enacted before the institution of state policies of 1943 and as a consequence the Roma did not qualify for restitution (U.S. Holocaust Museum, Genocide of European Roma (Gypsies), 1939–1945). This blatant rejection of responsibility for atrocities committed against the Roma is characteristic of postwar collective action. This attitude extended the marginalized position of the Roma. For several decades, there was a trend to minimize the Holocaust of the Roma. Indeed, it was not until the 1980s that German officials formally recognized the genocide of the Roma.

In communist countries (especially Yugoslavia), the Roma were offered social integration by virtue of state employment programs, that included for example a workers' self-management and health care system. "In addition, the government did not allow any racist excesses, which the Roma today, unfortunately, are exposed to in almost all parts of Eastern Europe" (Ludwig, 2001, p. 78). However, under the rubric of integration, assimilation was gradually enforced through legal bans of the Roma's nomadic way of life. In Yugoslavia, the Roma assimilated as qualified and high skilled workers (Vukanović, 1983). It was very important for the improvement of their life standard, but it also caused the loss of many of their traditional crafts and customs.[2]

The fall of communist regimes during the 1990s, the transitions in Southeastern Europe, a global economic crisis, and the disintegration of the "welfare states" in Western Europe, generated numerous racist attacks on the Roma and led to the demand for their expulsion from European countries, with no right to asylum (Cahn & Guild, 2010). By the 1970s, Roma leaders, organizations, and movements were directing much of their energy toward gaining formal recognition of the political status of the Roma. The International Roma Congress (RIC) held its first conference in London in 1971.

> International Roma Union (RIU) paved the way to lobby formation and negotiations on the Roma issues with the international community and within it. The concept of the Roma nation emerged in the RIU complete with the introduction of basic symbols, such as a national hymn and flag" (Mirga & Georgi, 2004, p. 12).

A United Nations (UN) Sub-Commission on Prevention of Discrimination and Protection of Minorities accepted a resolution in 1977, which was the first of its kind to mention the Roma as a minority. Since then, the United Nations, Council of Europe, Organization for Security and Co-operation in Europe (OEBS) and the European Union have accepted several resolutions and recommendations that generally relate or specifically relate to the Roma. In 1992, the UN Human Rights Commission approved Resolution 65 for the Roma`s protection. That same year, the European Charter for Regional and Minority Languages recognized the Roma language as a nonterritorial language. In Serbia, the Roma have been listed as a national minority since 2002.

THEORETICAL FRAMEWORK

Mass media have a role as a very important social institution and have often been viewed as presenting an unbiased reflection of social reality (conforming with the concept of media as a mirror of reality). Today, that concept has been replaced by an understanding of media representation as a means of constructing reality through various forms of interpretation. Media are not reflections of reality, rather they invoke and reconstruct various aspects of reality by attempting to stabilize or reify symbolic meanings as fixed.

> But, there is no one, true meaning. Meaning 'floats.' It cannot be finally fixed. However, attempting to fix it is the work of representational practice, which intervenes in the many potential meanings of an image in an attempt to privilege one (Hall, 1997).

One of the inevitable consequences of media is the establishment and distribution of power. The maintenance of public order is produced through media representations that create a spontaneous cultural consent to dominant relations of power.

> Discrimination is a consequence of this domination and different groups may be discriminated in many ways. But the repercussions of that variety are always the same—minorities are excluded from the mainstream and their experiences go unheard (Milivojević, 2003, p. 17).

The groups who are discriminated against become complicit in their domination in that they learn to consent to the version of reality reflected in media. Through dominant media they learn to accept the economic, cultural, and political values of the dominant groups. This is the goal of the dominant social groups—they strive to maintain existing social relations. As a result of media inequality, the scope of equality in social life narrows in contemporary democratic societies. Public demands for equality affect the existing social order, which is why dominant groups strive to minimize this presence in media.

Foucault defines discourse as "general domain of all statements" and "regulated practice that accounts for a number of statement" (1972, p. 80). This aforementioned discourse, in its specific practice or form, does not depend on the subject, in its construction or cancellation. Discourse and power are inseparable categories. Discourse is the way that knowledge is articulated in a certain society and institutions and in which power is regulated and defined. Foucault argues "that since we can only have a knowledge of things if they have a meaning, it is discourse—not the things-in-themselves—which produces knowledge" (Hall, 2001, p. 73). However, discourse is not based on the conventional difference between thinking and action. Discourse creates knowledge through language and discursive practice is the practice of interpretation. According to Van Dijk (1988, p. 8) discourse is a "communicative event or communicative act." He argues that discourse can be analyzed at both the mycrostructural and macrostructural levels. A microstructure analysis concerns the linguistic aspects of a text, while a macrostructure analysis concerns the thematic and organizational structure of the text. Differences between traditional linguistic analysis and analysis of discourse is that discourse analysis is not limited to the semantic study of sentences; rather it is the study of language usage in everyday interaction between people. Fairclough (1995) gives a further explanation of discourse analysis by discussing the three different modes of communication—text, discourse, and socialization. He also relies on intertextual analysis, which is wider than the concept of linguistic analysis. Unlike linguistic analysis, Fairclough's critical discourse analysis focuses on the discursive character of power. That is why it is an excellent tool for understanding how ethnic minorities, as such, are socially constructed and defined in and by discourse. Using critical analysis discourse, I point out the ideological effects of a discourse, whose consequences are the inequality and otherness of the Roma people.

METHOD AND METHODOLOGY

My preliminary research design surveyed Internet editions of the most important Serbian newspapers that were published between 2002 and 2007 (*Blic, Kurir, Glas javnosti,* and *Danas Dailies*)[3]. Why did I select these exact periods of time and online editions? At the end of the 20th century and at the beginning of the 21st century, Serbia went through enormous changes—the dissolution of Yugoslavia, wars, the breakup of socialism, all of which caused inevitable conflicts in the social systems and engendered numerous consequences. A presumption was made that after the downfall of Milošević's regime enough time had elapsed for a democratic society to develop. It was also presumed that the attitudes of the majority regarding minorities, especially the Roma people, were changed as well. The fact that the Roma people were recognized as a national minority in 2002 by the "Law on the protection of rights and freedoms of national minorities" (Official journal of the *Federal Republic of Yugoslavia*, No.11, 2002) was a major reason for that assumption.

After the downfall of Milošević's regime, the Serbian transformation from an industrial society to an information society progressed more slowly than in the developed countries. The primary causes of this slow transformation can be found in bad economics, a flawed legal framework, and a weak infrastructure. But, in spite of these factors, the development of an information society was deemed to be of utmost importance. The Informatics and Internet Development Agency was founded by the Government of the Republic of Serbia in 2000. Over the next few years (specifically the period covered by the survey), there was a significant growth of Internet users, predominantly due to an improved and more affordable quality of access to the Internet. A survey conducted by the Centre for Research of Information Technologies (CePIT) showed that 56% of the participants started using the Internet in the three previous years; in addition, it indicated that the number of users increased during that time period because there was access to information about the Internet (Petrović et al., 2005).

The advantages of the Internet instantly became clear to the owners of media, and as a result, the vast majority of print editions of newspapers became available on the Internet by 2002. Consequently, the daily newspapers that I have chosen to analyze (*Blic, Kurir, Glas javnosti,* and *Danas Dailies*) were already accessible online before the period of the survey. In addition, there are several key reasons for selecting these newspapers specifically. First, they were all started at the end of the 20th century or at the beginning of the 21st century, when the capital structure of the media was changing. Second, there are differences in their editorial positions, representing a wide and comprehensive market demographic: *Danas Daily* is a very influential daily newspaper with a small circulation, which is read primarily by educated readers; *Blic* is a daily newspaper, with a high circulation, combining both a serious and a tabloid approach to journalism with a middle-class audience; *Glas javnosti* is a semi-tabloid whose circulation began to decrease due to the initiation of *Kurir*, a very influential, inexpensive tabloid with the highest circulation. Third, the websites of these newspapers had the highest website traffic. Ranking of website traffic, which was published in December 2004, showed that the most visited media websites in Serbia were *Blic, Glas javnosti, Danas,* and *Kurir.* Among various websites in Serbia, *Blic* holds second position (Najposećeniji sajtovi, 2011). Fourth, the numbers of people who read the Internet editions of printed daily newspapers has been continually increasing, as they become more widely available, and free of charge.

According to predictions by the vast majority of social scientists, all media are going to be incorporated into the Internet. By comparing newspaper circulation to daily website traffic (the best way to compare circulation), one can easily predict that websites are read more often than the printed daily newspapers with the largest circulation.[4] Fifth, the archives of print media are not organized and completely available to researchers. There is no institution where print media content can be systematically researched.

A search of the archived online editions of the selected daily newspapers from 2002 to 2007 revealed that there were no articles on Roma people. Any mention of the Roma people was so rare that for a study it was inadequate to use quantitative content analysis or a Statistical Package for the Social Sciences (SPSS). There were simply not enough articles to use this method of analysis. During the research period, a total of 96 articles were found. In this chapter, I analyze 10 of those articles that best demonstrate how the Roma are "othered."

Since the total lack of articles on the Roma people indicates that topics on them are marginalized, I decided to use critical analysis in order to determine the manner of presentation of the Roma people in various newspaper articles. The selections were chosen based on the following assumptions:

1. The news media frequently refer to the Roma minority as "Others" using a discourse of "us" versus "them."

2. The most common stereotype encountered was the description of the Roma people as filthy criminals, and that they are to blame for their own bad lives.

3. The articles support the reinforcement of the existing economic, political, and social balances of power.

The goal of my research is to report the ways the Roma people are presented in various newspaper articles by using detailed critical discourse analysis. The scientific contribution of this chapter is particularly significant because this topic has not yet been systematically researched by domestic experts in Serbia.

HOW AN "IMPASSIONED TRAVELER" BECOMES A "PAPER COLLECTOR"?

The Roma are the poorest ethnic and social community in Serbia, and according to many indicators, in the whole of Europe. The Roma in Serbia look for an escape out of poverty in various and often unusual ways. The heart of the problem for Roma is their exclusion from society (often institutionally), especially in areas of employment, education, and health care. Despite these institutional obstacles, the Roma are often blamed for their own hardships and accused of lacking a sense of personal responsibility. Of course, this is a reformulation of age-old stereotypes—the Roma cannot get out of material and cultural poverty simply through a collective anthropological and sociopsychological predisposition.

At one time, the Roma were referred to by their occupation: for example, bear tamers, rackers, coppersmiths, feather collectors, scrap metal collectors, musicians, and so forth. Due to technological developments, many of those professions have disappeared, but the Roma are still working with the low-end and unpleasant businesses. On the streets daily, it is the Roma who play and sing in the buses, who wash and clean streets and car glass, and who collect paper.

The underground economy in Serbian society, where the Roma often traditionally operate, is now a widespread arena for the so-called "survival strategy" that emerged as a consequence of the war in the former Yugoslavia. We see it every day on the streets, markets, and flea markets. Roma communities often struggle to afford basic necessities, such as food and housing. Once the Roma were nomadic and moved about from place to place under the "gypsy tent." They move about today, but less often, and instead remain and exist in unsanitary enclaves, especially at the edges of the cities. It is estimated that there are about 600 illegal Roma settlements in Serbia with approximately 150 of these colonies in Belgrade (Renzi, 2010).

GARBAGE, MUD, AND DUST: ROMA AS EXOTIC OUTSIDERS

When the authors of news reports try to describe places where the Roma live, they mostly start with the syntagm (a sequence of words in a particular syntactic relationship to one another) "cardboard boxes," referring to the basic material they use to build their improvised homes. Thus an article titled, "The battle for the alley where children are fishing for the snakes" describes a Roma settlement in Zemun:

> Most of the "shacks" are made out of cardboard, wood, and rusty tin, in an environment filled with garbage and various sorts of waste. There is no sewer and water in the improvised houses, which for many are just an abstract noun, while lamps sporadically reveal the contours of the place (Božić, 2003).

Further description indicates almost a forbidden dark zone where you do not want to approach other people:

> The dangers of life in this slum "alley" are personified by the fact that recently a taxi driver was killed and his body dropped there. Characteristic of each household is a high fence, which often exceeds the height of the hut. Even a small hole in the fence is barricaded, so that any view of the interior of the courtyard is almost impossible (Božić, 2003).

The subject of the article was opposition to the construction of a new Roma settlement. At the

Figure 5.1 *Roma men preparing to collect scrap paper.*

Source: Belgrade, Serbia, author, Nataša Simeunović Bajić.

end of the article, the author cites the opinion of some native Roma who are against immigration of the new Roma, "because they believe there will be less work for them" (Božić, 2003). The message seems to be clear: the old and the new Roma fight for existence in an area where the children fish for snakes. The article's presentation leaves their readers with an image that causes fear, resistance, and disfavor.

Similarly, an article titled "We will throw the children under the dredgers" (Medenica, 2002), reports on the threat to others that is posed by the demolition of an illegal Roma settlement near the IMT tractor factory in Belgrade. Again, the sensational headline broadcasts the inhumanity of the Roma, by portraying the Roma children as undernourished. This description reproduces the stereotype that the Roma do not care about their children, but rather reproduce just to exploit or sell their offspring. The article quotes one Roma man who gives us information about their primary work: "We are honest and hardworking people, we live collecting and selling cardboard and paper, explains Enver Dibrani, the representative of the native" (Medenica, 2002). It is important to note that there is a grammatical error made by the author in this quotation. It is correct in the genitive plural form to use the term "natives." Readers need to be aware that using this word correctly is, in itself, a sign of showing respect, on the other hand, writing this word incorrectly, as is true here, is a sign of a lack of respect and discrimination.

Consider as well, an article from the column *Black Chronicle* beginning with the sensational and emotional title: "Dead newborn child found on a garbage dump" (I. C., 2005). The facts in this story are that some Roma who collect papers at the garbage dump found a dead baby. First, the author of the text did not have to specify the ethnicity of the people who found the baby. Because of this identification, she brings the recognition of two stereotypes into play: one that all Roma dig around in landfills and the other that Roma are associated with the poor treatment of children. Second, as this was a short news story, it does not usually require a photograph—yet the

story is accompanied by a photograph of the people who found the body. The content of this photography is discriminatory in itself because the people are not only recognizable as part of the Roma ethnic minority, they also look like people in a scene from a horror film. In addition, a weapon carried by one of the men is visible. The visual content entirely shifted the semantic field of the story away from a dead infant and toward a particular construction of the Roma.

The consistency of sensationalism is also apparent in the article "The hill of the junkyard" (R. P., 2007), which describes the difficulties of workers from a communal cleaning company whose job it is to remove large piles of trash. The article emphasizes that the Roma drag piles of trash "from other landfills, as well as from the container." The author of the article presented it in a very picturesque manner: "The fact that free climbing is not just an aspect of extreme sports, is proven by employees from communal utilities cleaning the mountain of garbage" (R. P., 2007). Even the routine subject of removing garbage is approached from an emotional and sensational angle. The article does not quote employees, but rather creates an image of the Roma that fits with existing stereotypes that emphasize the dirtiness, negligence, and laziness of all members of this ethnic minority. In addition, the author quotes a Roma woman who lives in this mountain of garbage in Radnička`s street:

> It is not true that we just throw out garbage, all that who hates to get down the side to the container, throw down trash from their home and it fall, wherever it fall. Although I collect old things, anything that I do not use, I return it into the container - says Jasmine (R. P., 2007).

It is naive to think that the image of the Roma will be tempered by Jasmina`s statement. Immediately thereafter, and at the end of the article, the author quotes a non-Roma man, Milorad Nikolić:

> I do not know how they can talk [about] how they do not throw trash when I watch them every day doing that. Jasmina threw away a wheelchair that

she had received from one organization after she broke her arm and leg in a car accident. She could take them back so that someone else can use them. I do not know how they can live that way (R. P., 2007).

So a report about the job of removing waste, which should be routine, significantly ends in this discriminative note.

In an article titled "The state helps only when we burn" (Petrović, 2005), the narrative is flavored with numerous quotations that serve to highlight stereotypes associated with the Roma: distorted grammatical forms, a lack of education, bad manners and lack of information. For example,

My son marr'd in Šabac, daughter-in-law no want to see me, so I came here. Have two days I do not eat bread. Today I cooked for lunch - nothing. I have nervousness on the nerves of all, says Radmila. -When was Tito, you could sleep and in parks. And how to sleep now in parks, when these criminals will kill. You see what happens night. But sleep here in the cards. And you can burn. Like these children which burnt out, we heard on TV. This now state is helping, only when we burn, and come to sweep us—yesterday talked a group of the Roma, with dirty hands (Petrović, 2005).

Four photos were even added to this text. The visuals offer a strong sense of the collective representation of the Roma as an ethnic group that is part of a lower level of culture and civilization. Within the present process of tabloidization of media, everything can become an opportunity for sensationalism and discrimination. The online editions of print media do not really care why the Roma collect paper, how they can live on such meager earnings, or whether the construction material of the shacks is really cardboard. The media interest in people who collect papers is sporadic. Paper collectors are mentioned only if the image is needed to contribute to the stereotypical image of the Roma as naturally associated with garbage, mud, and dust. In the media, the Roma are represented as exotic outsiders. Or, as one study noted: "Media reporting on Romani people seems to follow a rule which is sometimes given to students of journalism: A train that arrives on time is not news, but a train which derails is" (Waringo, 2005).

CAN WE BLAME ROMA FOR THEIR FATE?

The fact that the Roma do not have a democratic home country should not be crucial to their social and political status. The Roma are the poorest and most socially marginalized ethnic group in Serbia. A large number of Roma still have not resolved the basic issues of citizenship and health insurance. Every day, the Roma face mild to severe forms of discrimination. At the core of the discrimination is the widespread and rigorous stereotype that the Roma are themselves to blame for everything that happens to them. In everyday life, people find clear guidelines about social structure, roles in a society and acceptable behavior. People usually accept these guides as a product of common sense and the natural order of things. Therefore, the Roma, as a marginalized group, have very little chance to reinvestigate their image. Compounding the problem and adding to the stereotype is the fact that the Roma live in separate enclaves with more or less visible physical boundaries to their environment.

Efforts to improve the situation of the Roma require very precise information. But members of the majority are often skeptical toward accepting minorities and fear that the rights of the majority would be reduced or jeopardized if members of minorities exercise their rights. The mass media are one indication of society's acceptance of social differences of all kinds—including ethnic differences. Most media representations address the needs, wishes, and tendencies of the majority. The print media that I analyzed created a negative image of the Roma's capacity for introspection and integration.

Figure 5.2 *Roma musicians.*

Source: Šabac, Serbia, author, Nataša Simeunović Bajić.

Consider, for example, an article titled "The secret that no one will ever reveal" (Jovanović, 2004). This interview with actress Milena Ražnatović concerns her leading performance in the film "Gypsies Go to Heaven." Ražnatović is quoted talking about the Roma:

> I really tried to inform as many as possible about that people and how I managed to see, they have been wandering across the world from the fourteenth, fifteenth century. I think they will wander forever. Now, is it that way because they do not fit into our civilization, or because we do not fit into theirs, I do not know? In recent years, a lot was spoken about the Roma culture, there are some shows about the Roma, but my impression is that they are not too much interested. Those are people who have their own criteria that we can hardly understand. They do not leave written records about themselves, their history and stories about the Gypsies, we wrote and all stories about them are our vision of their life. I think that no one from the "outside" will ever succeed to reveal that essence (Jovanović, 2004).

In this quote, I see stereotypical prejudices against the Roma firmly rooted in the media, and the cultural and public discourse. These statements assume that Roma are people who like to wander and that they have chosen such a path.

Further, that they are not interested in their own culture, which implies that the Roma are to blame for the lack of knowledge about the Romani held by non-Roma. In addition, they seem have their own values, which allude to their otherness and to the fact no one will ever understand them. There are several problems in this narrative. First of all, Ražnatović builds her opinion about the Roma based on well-known stereotypes. Second, the author of the text chose this particular quote for publication, and thus contributed to the stereotyping. Third and most important, the positive associations related to Roma culture have been replaced here with the attitudes and prejudices that are very common in everyday life and public discourse. Neither the author nor the actress attempted to reexamine generally accepted ideas about the Roma; they just accepted the common sense order of things where the Roma remain labeled as the "other," and remain responsible for whatever happens to them. The title of the article, "The secret that no one will ever reveal" describes a particularly common framing by the majority of the Roma: How will we ever live with them if we cannot understand them?

Another stereotype about the Roma emerges in an article titled "They steal from those who feed them" (Trifunović, 2007). The article is about the Serbian Center for Social Work in Bor, which was the target of thieves. The head of the institution is quoted as identifying the thieves as Roma: "The worst of all is that we have been robbed and let down by those who turn to our help with social security, such as the Roma who came from all sides" (Trifunović, 2007). If the Roma turn to social services for help, and yet also steal from us, then the conclusion is that they are to blame for their fate and do not want to come out of the "enchanted circle of poverty." Is it really like that? Why even in this text the author did not consult anyone from the Roma society? Where are the testimonies of the police? If this characterization is true, why didn't the journalist asked: Why this is happening? Why are the Roma not satisfied? How much assistance do they receive? None of these aspects are dealt with in this article. Instead, the article headline deeply imprints and reinforces the common dominant beliefs about the Roma. Similar stereotypical beliefs are also explicitly affirmed in these titles: "Gipsy business" (Petrović, 2007); "'Collateral damage' on the outskirts of life" (Badžaku, 2005); "Life in a garbage" (Vranešević, 2006); "We Gypsies also have a right to live!" (V. V., 2006).

The mass media are social institutions that mediate information to a large public of heterogeneous audiences. Mass media use stereotypes to shape the understanding and view of the world. Yet what do they offer us? The treatment of Roma regarding issues of introspection and responsibility are superficial. There is a clear lack of information and an apparent lack of interest among journalists. In this sense, the media reflect the distribution of sociopolitical power in society. Thus, Roma, who have very little sociopolitical power, are represented through the distorted and ideologically controlled media landscape. The articles are consistently sensationalist in their approach. The conclusion is that these articles create an even greater marginalization and social isolationism for the Roma.

CONCLUSION

While the long history of the Roma with Serbs in the Balkans contains happy and unhappy moments, the period during the 1990s was especially hard. During this time, Serbia was totally isolated from the rest of the world in the social, political, and economic arenas. After the fall of Slobodan Milošević`s regime, the mass media in Serbia underwent—with great difficulty—a conversion to a state-operated system in order to act as a public service and to professionalize the media and reduce hate speech. However, it is important to retain a critical attitude toward the Serbian media because the development of the Serbian civil society is far below the degree that exists in Western countries. The deficient democratic dimension of the media is clearly evident in the way that the Roma are represented in the daily press—yet this treatment of the Roma passes

largely unnoticed. In the print media I studied, there is no tendency to decrease the ethnic intolerance toward the Roma. Rather, public attention is redirected toward the Roma and away from other issues such the problems of bad public companies, issues of privatizations and the common political instability of Serbia. This is a key reason why the tendency toward sensationalism and political utilization of newspaper articles about Roma continues to be one of the key problems of the Serbian press.

In the sensationally slanted news reports, the Roma threaten the socioeconomic order and cultural capital of Serbian society. Their media appearance is sidelined—they have very little participation in the formation of the media agenda. For the most part, Roma people are described as a group. They are collectively labeled as an ethnic-cultural otherness; the Roma community is shown as inferior, which is a direct consequence of the secondhand nature of the reporting about the Roma people.

The media representation of the Roma people has a negative impact on their position in society. For a very long time, the Roma people have been portrayed as "other" and labeled as unacceptable, and as this study shows, in many cases this portrayal is written by a journalist, whose job it is to report and interview people in a credible, unbiased manner. In reality, journalists continue to succumb to stereotypes and reproduce a well-known negative picture of the Roma people, which in turn maintains the status quo. From time to time, serious articles with unbiased reporting have been published, but it is very rare and not enough to improve the mass media image of the Roma. In most media representations, the Roma still remain presented as dirty, uncultured, uneducated, criminals and beggars who are responsible for their bad social position.

In any country, a media agenda can be said to express a social agenda. Media make and perpetuate cultural values that express the dominant ideology. Mainstream media in Serbia repeat the dominant negative images of the Roma through exclusion, generalization, labeling, highlighting the negative characteristics of Roma behavior, invoking the past to suggest ingrained features of Roma culture and nullifying any positive romantic attributes associated with the Roma. These are the most popular persuasive media techniques (Simeunović, 2009). News coverage of the Roma, consistently involves the same themes, actors, stories, and conflict situations. What one can conclude from this treatment of the Roma people by mainstream media is that the media in Serbia have only minimally improved their professionalism since democratic changes were instituted. The laws and inherent rules of media reporting are not implemented enough and therefore, the end result is a continuing, chaotic media sphere in Serbia.

NOTES

1. One of the reasons for the Roma's lack of written history is the centuries old resistance by the Roma to different social norms—including literacy. Also, the Roma were often banished from societies and subjected to many forms of isolation.

2. Several important studies on the life and traditions of Roma were published in the former Yugoslavia. More important was the 1980 publication of the first book on the grammar of the Roma language in Skopje (former Yugoslav republic of Macedonia) by two authors, Krume Kepeski and Šaip Jusuf.

3. Texts are also published in print editions in their unchanged form. It can be checked in Ebart Media Documentation.

4. The predictions were based on previous quantitative research and are those expressed in Varagić, D. (2007, December 15). Tiraži štampe polako gube trku od najposećenijih sajtova [The printed media are becoming less read than the most visited websites]. Retrieved from http://www.draganvaragic.com/weblog/index.php/386/tirazi-stampe-polako-gube-trku-od-najposecenijih-sajtova/.

REFERENCES

Badžaku, G. (2005, November 17). "Kolateralna šteta" na periferiji života. ["Collateral damage" on the outskirts of life] *Danas [Newspaper]*. Retrieved January 6, 2008, from http://www.danas.co.yu.

Bašić, G. (2003). *Upitnosti jedinstvenog romskog identiteta [Questions about unique Roma identity]*. Niš, RS: Sven.

Bašić, G. (2005). The origin and identity of the Roma in Serbia. In B. Jakšić & G. Bašić (Eds.), *Umetnost preživljavanja [The art of survival]*. Belgrade, RS: Institut za filozofiju i društvenu teoriju.

Bernadac, C. (1981). *Zaboravljeni holokaust: pokolj Cigana [The forgotten Holocaust: The massacre of the Gypsies]*, Zagreb, HR: ČGP Delo.

Božić, M. (2003, February 19). Bitka za sokak gde deca pecaju zmije. [The Battle for the alley where children fishing for the snakes]. *Danas [Newspaper]*. Retrieved January 3, 2010, from http://www.danas.rs/danasrs/naslovna.1.html.

Cahn, C., & Guild, E. (2010). *Recent migration of Roma in Europe*. A study for the Commissioner for Human Rights for the Organization for Security and Co-operation in Europe. Retrieved January 3, 2011, from http://www.osce.org/hcnm/78034.

Clebert, J. P. (1967). *Cigani [Gypsies]*. Zagreb, HR: Stvarnost.

Đorđević, D., & Balić, O. (2004). Romi, od zaboravljene do manjine u usponu [The Roma, from forgotten to minority on the rise]. In D. Đorđević (Ed.), *Romi, od zaboravljene do manjine u usponu [The Roma, from forgotten to minority on the rise]* (pp. 41–69). Niš, RS: Odbor za građansku inicijativu.

Đurić, R. (2006). *Istorija Roma [Roma history]*, Belgrade, RS: Politika.

Fairclough, N. (1995). *Critical discourse analysis: The critical study of language*. London, UK: Longman.

Foucault, M. (1972). *The archaeology of knowledge* (A. M. Sheridan Smith, Trans.). New York, NY: Pantheon Books.

Hall, S. (1997).The Spectacle of the Other. In S. Hall (Ed.), *Representation: Cultural representations and signifying practices* (pp. 225–279). London, UK: Sage in association with The Open University.

Hall, S. (2001). Foucault: Power, knowledge and discourse. In M. Wetherell, S. Taylor, & S. J. Yates (Eds.), *Discourse theory and practice: A reader* (pp. 72–81). London, UK: Sage.

Hancock, I. (1997). Genocide of the Roma in the holocaust. Excerpted from I. E. Charney (Ed.), *Encyclopedia of genocide*. Retrieved January 3, 2011, from http://www.reocities.com/~patrin/genocide.htm.

Hancock, I. (2002). *We are the romani People: Ame Sam e Rromane Džene*. Hatfield, UK: Hertfordshire University Press.

Hohmann, J. (1981). *History of the Roma persecution in Germany* (Geschichte der Zigeunerverfolgung in Deutschland). Frankfurt am Main, DE: Campus.

I. C. (2005, December 9). Mrtvo novorođenče pronađeno na deponiji [Dead newborn child found on a garbage dump]. *Kurir.[Newspaper]*. Retrieved January 3, 2011, from http://arhiva.kurir-info.rs/Arhiva/2005/decembar/09/H-03-09122005.shtml.

Jovanović, Z. (2004, April 27). Tajna koju niko nikad neće otkriti [The secret that no one will ever reveal]. *Blic [Newspaper]*. Retrieved January 3, 2011, from http://www.blic.rs/stara_arhiva/.

Kenrick, D. (2007). *Historical dictionary of the Gypsies (Romanies)* (2nd ed.). Lanham, MD: The Scarecrow Press.

Law on protection of rights and freedoms of national minorities (2002). *Official Journal of the Federal Republic of Yugoslavia, No.11/2002*.

Ludwig, K. (2001). *Leksikon etničkih manjina u Europi* [*Lexicon of ethnic minorities in Europe*]. Political Publications. Pan liber, HR: Osijek-Zagreb-Split.

Marjanović, M. (2006). Romski jezik [Roma language]. In R. Mustafić (Ed.), *Ciganeska: uvod u romsku istoriju, jezik i kulturu* [*Ciganeska : Introduction in Roma history, language, and culture*]. Nš, RS: Punta.

Medenica, M. (2002, October 5). Bacićemo decu pod bagere. [We will throw children under dredgers]. *Glas javnosti [Newspaper]*. Retrieved January 3, 2011, from http://arhiva.glas-javnosti.rs/arhiva/2002/10/05/srpski/BG02100404.shtml.

Milivojević, S. (2003). *Media monitoring manual*. London, UK: Media Diversity Institute.

Mirga, A., & Georgi, N. (2004). Romi u dvadeset prvom veku [The Roma in the twenty-first century]. In D. Đorđević (Ed.), *Romi, od zaboravljene do manjine u usponu* [*The Roma, from forgotten to minority on the rise*] (pp. 12–40). Niš, RS: Odbor za građansku inicijativu.

Mirga, A., & Mruz, L. (1997). *Romi-razlike i netolerancija* [*Roma-Differences and intolerance*]. Belgrade, RS: Akapit.

Mitić, I. (2006). Romska istorija [Roma history]. In R. Mustafić (Ed.), *Ciganeska : Uvod u romsku istoriju, jezik i kulturu* [*Ciganeska: Introduction in Roma history, language, and culture*]. Niš, RS: Punta.

Najposećeniji sajtovi Srbije i Crne Gore [The most visited sites in Serbia and Montenegro]. Retrieved January 3, 2011, from http://info.krstarica.com/l/mediji/najposeceniji-sajtovi-srbije-i-crne-core/.

Petrović, D. (2005, February 3). Država pomaže tek kad izgorimo. [The state helps only when we burn]. *Glas javnosti [Newspaper]*. Retrieved January 3, 2011, from http://arhiva.glas-javnosti.rs/arhiva/.

Petrović, D. (2007, September 30). Ciganjska posla. [Gypsy's business]. *Kurir [Newspaper]*. Retrieved on January 3, 2011, from http://arhiva.kurir-info.rs/Arhiva/2007/Septembar/30/V-07-30092007.shtml.

Petrović, M., Golčevski, N., & Milovanović, G. (2005). Korisnici i nekorisnici interneta: sociodemografska slika, odlike i struktura upotrebe interneta. [Users and non-Internet users: Socio-demographic picture, feature, and the structure of the use of Internet]. In G. Milovanović, M. Sitarski, M. Petrović, N. Golčevski, S. Barišić, & T. Milovanović (Eds.), *Mreža u razvoju* [*Development of Internet*]. Belgrade, RS: Boš.

Porajmos (n.d.). Retrieved January 3, 2011, from http://en.wikipedia.org/wiki/Porajmos#cite_note-15.

R. P. (2007, February 16). Brdo otpada. [The hill of the junkyard]. *Kurir [Newspaper]*. Retrieved January 3, 2011, from http://arhiva.kurir-info.rs/Arhiva/.

Renzi, L. (2010). *Roma people in Europe: A long history of discrimination*. European Social Watch report 2010, Retrieved January 3, 2011, from http://www.socialwatch.eu/wcm/documents/Roma_a_long_history of discrimination.pdf.

Simeunović, N. (2009). Tretman Roma u štampanim medijima u Srbiji [Treatment of Roma minority in Serbian print media]. *CM: Communication Management Quarterly,10*(4), 71–92. Novi Sad, RS: Protocol; Belgrade, RS: Fakultet političkih nauka.

Timeline of Romani history (n.d.). *Patrin Web Journal*. Retrieved January 3, 2011, from http://www.reocities.com/Paris/5121/timeline.htm.

Trifunović, S. (2007, October 3). Kradu od onih koji ih hrane [They steal from those who feed them]. *Blic* [Newspaper]. Retrieved January 3, 2011, from http://www.blic.rs/Vesti/Srbija/14926/Kradu-od-onih-koji- ih-hrane.

United States Holocaust Memorial Museum (1933–1945). Washington, D.C. *Genocide of European Roma (Gypsies), 1939–1945*. Retrieved

January 3, 2011, from http://www.ushmm.org/education/resource/roma/RomaSBklt.pdf.

United States Holocaust Memorial Museum (1933–1945). Washington, D.C. *Sinti and Roma: Victims of the Nazi era*. Retrieved January 3, 2011, from http://www.ushmm.org/education/resource/roma/RomaSBklt.pdf.

Van Dijk, T. (1988). *News analysis: Case studies of international and national news in the press*. Hillsdale, NJ: Erlbaum.

Varagić, D. (2007, December 15). *Tiraži štampe polako gube trku od najposećenijih sajtova [The printed media have been becoming less read than most visited websites]*. Retrieved January 3, 2011, from http://www.draganvaragic.com/weblog/index.php/386/tirazi-stampe-polako-gube-trkuodnajpose cenijihsajtova/?utm_source=feedburner&utm_ medium=feed&utm_campaign=Feed%3A+DVWe bLog+%28Dragan+Varagic+Web+Log%29.

Vranešević, I. (2006, August 4). Život na đubrištu [Life in a garbage]. *Glas javnosti [Newspaper]*. Retrieved January 6, 2008, from http://arhiva.glas-javnosti.co.yu/arhiva/.

Vukanović, T. (1983). *Romi (Cigani) u Jugoslaviji [Roma (Gypsy) in Yugoslavia]*. Vranje, RS: Nova Jugoslavija.

V. V. (2006, April 8). I mi Cigani moramo da živimo [We Gypsies also have a right to live!] *Glas javnosti [Newspaper]*. Retrieved January 3, 2010, from http://arhiva.glas-javnosti.rs/arhiva/.

Waringo, K. (2005). *Gypsies, tramps and thieves: A portrait of Romani people in the media*. Retrieved January 3, 2011, from http://www.ezaf.org/down/IIIAZK23.pdf.

Zirojević, O. (1976). Cigani u Srbiji od dolaska Turaka do kraja XVI veka [Gypsies in Serbia from arrival of Turks to the end of 16th century]. *Jugoslovenski istorijski časopis*, *1*(2), 67–77.

6

"YOU ARE TRYING TO MAKE IT A RACIAL ISSUE!"

Race-Baiting and Social Categorization in Recent U.S. Immigration Debates

SHIAO-YUN CHIANG

INTRODUCTION

In the United States there has been a highly charged national debate on immigration reform since a strict immigration control bill—The Border Protection, Anti-terrorism, and Illegal Immigration Control Act—was passed by the U.S. House of Representatives in 2005. In 2006, millions of people across the country marched against this legislation (see *Chicago Tribune*, March 11, 2006), and since then, massive rallies have occurred in response to any new immigration bill introduced either federally (e.g., The Comprehensive Immigration Reform Act of 2007) or at the state level (e.g., Arizona SB 1070 in 2010). In the media, representatives of pro-immigrant and anti-immigrant groups repeatedly debate against each other in favor of their own group interests. Opposing groups utilize different rhetorical strategies to positively present their position and negatively portray the opposing stance.

One of the common strategies used in these immigration debates is the allegation and refutation of race-baiting. While the charge of race-baiting can be leveled for different purposes, in the U.S. sociopolitical discourse[1] race-baiting is perceived as a problematic, ill-intended practice for personal or group gains at the sacrifice of national unity. To accuse a public figure of race-baiting is to position her or him negatively in public discourse. One of the earliest charges of race-baiting regarded a notorious campaign advertisement in 1988 for then-Republican presidential candidate, George H.W. Bush. The ad used images of Willie Horton (an African American man who received an early prison release) to attack the Democratic presidential candidate, Michael Dukakis for being soft on crime "via a clearly racialized image" (Massey, 2002, p. 23). This commercial was considered by many to be "the most disgraceful practice" for a short-term political gain because "it tapped deep into the

81

fear system" through a "deliberate use of racial-ized images" (Massey, 2002, p. 23).

More recently, in U.S. sociopolitical dis-course, conservatives have used charges of "race-baiting" to refer to what they perceive to be groundless accusations of racism—essentially the equivalent of "playing the race card." For example, President Obama made the following remarks on the 2010 Arizona SB 1070.

One of the things that the law says is local officials are allowed to ask somebody who they have a sus-picion might be an illegal immigrant for their papers. But you can imagine, if you are a Hispanic American in Arizona—your great-grandparents may have been there before Arizona was even a state. But now, suddenly, if you don't have your papers and you took your kid out to get ice cream, you're going to be harassed (*The Washington Times*, May 3, 2010).

The headline for that article was "Obama's Race-baiting," and the editorial on May 3, 2010, vehemently accused President Obama of "fanning the flames of ethnic discord." Appar-ently the President's critics viewed those remarks as "race-baiting"—a tactic of raising concerns about racism when purportedly none exists. For example, Rep. Steve King, as reported by ABC on May 14, 2010, assailed President Obama's effort to "make race the issue" with Arizona State immigration law "when it is law enforcement that is the problem"(Tapper, May 14, 2010).[2]

This redefinition of the term *"race-baiting"* is evidenced in many conservative articles. *Human Events*, the leading conservative magazine, pub-lishes commentaries in which the two phrases "race-baiting" and "play the race card" are inter-changeably used. In another example during a discussion of the Henry Louis Gates case, Gary Bauer, former presidential candidate and now a leading conservative commentator, did not seem to make any distinction when he accused Obama of "initiating a new era of race-baiting" (Bauer, July 18, 2010) and "gratuitously playing the race card" (Bauer, March 7, 2011). The present study does not intend to define the term "race-baiting"

or argue what it should be. Rather, the goal of this article is to examine the discourse of race-baiting that involves the accusation and refuta-tion of racial remarks. In particular, this chapter examines some of the most recent debates on U.S. immigration reform, in an attempt to expli-cate how group representatives make an effort both to position themselves positively and to position others negatively in confrontations (Augoustinos & Every, 2007; Chiang, 2010). The matter of analytic interest here is the specific procedures of how the issue of race is brought into play with the issue of immigration legisla-tion. Additionally, how the use of racial remarks can become consequential on social actors' posi-tive presentation of self in relation to their con-flicting group goals.

RACE AND SOCIAL CATEGORIZATION

Categorization is generally considered as essen-tial and fundamental to human systematic inquiry "because it satisfies a basic human need for cog-nitive parsimony" (Hogg & Abrams, 1988, p. 72). The process of social categorization is based on identification and classification of individuals in the social world, which results in group forma-tion (Tajfel, 1981). Social identification evokes similarities and differences in social interactions, from which social identities are developed (see Turner, 1985). When individuals subjectively classify themselves and others into different social groups, intergroup bias can be produced (Billig & Tajfel, 1973). A basic intergroup behav-ior is that individuals tend to favor in-group members in comparison with out-group mem-bers due to the need for positive self-esteem (Tajfel & Turner, 1986). Hence, social categori-zation, while central to human epistemology, provides the bedrock for prejudice and discrimi-nation (Billig, 1985).

Race is a type of social categorization in the Western world. From the 17th century to the early 20th century, racial categorizations referred to what was believed to be the biologically diver-gent human populations. The current use of race in social sciences has been reconceptualized as a social construction that has tangible material consequences (López, 1994). In this view, race has little to do with genetics or biology (Bonilla-Silva, 1997); indeed, a large body of studies demonstrate how race is constructed in a variety of social discourses (Augoustinos & Every, 2007; Bonilla-Silva & Forman, 2000; Buttny, 1999; Pascale, 2008; Van Dijk, 1992; Verkuyten, 2001; West & Fenstermaker, 1999). In light of social constructionism, discursive psychology, and ethnomethodology, race is not seen as a self-evident category, but a process in which individuals get defined in race-related terms.

When racial differences became ideological and largely institutional, racism might emerge, or as Memmi said, "Racism only begins with an interpretation of differences" (1999, p. 29). Racism refers to the general belief that one race is destined to be inferior due to certain inherent characteristics while another race is congenitally superior (Benedict, 1945; Schaefer, 1990). While it is debatable whether racist practices are as old as human society or as recent as the rise of capitalism in the West, the ideological formation of racism is mostly regarded as a modern development. For sociopolitical, economic, and cultural reasons, racism thrived in 18th- and 19th-century Europe and the United States, and evolved into a radical ideology in the early 20th century to legitimate some institutional practices, such as the genocide of Semites and the segregation of African Americans (Fredrickson, 2002).

Despite the long history of racism, it was not until the 1960s that the civil rights movement in the United States put an end to legal racial segregation.[3] During this time, policies (e.g., the Civil Rights Act and affirmative action) were enacted to ensure equalities for minorities, and later new immigrants. However, these measures for ending racist practices were met with a backlash from white Americans who viewed such policies as "reverse racism"—or a form of discrimination against whites (cf. Bonilla-Silva & Lewis, 1999). The voices of people who were against affirmative action in the media (Holmes, 1998), as well as the testimonies of those who experienced so-called "color-blind racism" in the academia (Bonilla-Silva, Lewis, & Embrick, 2004) reflect a deep-seated concern by white racial groups for the preservation of their own racial privilege (cf. Feagin, 2000).

Interactions among racial groups in the West have become increasingly subtle because of governmental regulations and ideological influences. To present a desirable social image, racial groups must avoid displaying any racial and ethnic bias as they strive to represent their group interests and fulfill their goals. Thus, the communication of racial issues has become more and more strategically implicit in sociopolitical discourses (see also Billig, 1991; Van Dijk, 1987, 1992). In the United States, the First Amendment of the U.S. Constitution protects freedom of expression, even racist speech (Downing, 1999). However, public figures of any social group still would be negatively positioned and perceived if they were charged with either perpetuating racism or making accusations of racism (i.e., playing the race card) for personal and group benefit (Chiang, 2010).

RACE AND IMMIGRATION DEBATE

Public discourse on immigration is infused with issues such as race, ethnicity, discrimination, and xenophobia. A common pattern in the public debates on immigrations in Western societies is the discursive opposition between "us" and "them" (Billig, 2006). As noted by Van Dijk (2000), immigration in Western media is usually described as a threat, and immigrants (including asylum seekers and refugees) are negatively presented as a dehumanized category of aliens. For example, as seen in these cited works from seven different countries, immigrants, refugees, and asylum seekers are generally depicted as abnormal, socially disruptive, threatening, and unable to assimilate (United Kingdom, KhosraviNik, 2009 and Lynn & Lea, 2003; Australia, Every & Augoustinos, 2007; France, Van Der Valk, 2003; Belgium, Blommaert, 2001; Netherlands, Verkuyten, 2001; Spain, Del-Teso-Craviotto, 2009; and Austria, Van Leeuwen & Wodak, 1999).

Every U.S. public school teaches that the United States is a nation of immigrants. However, since the new colonies were established, it has been a normal practice in U.S. history for former immigrants to try to keep out newcomers (Espenshade & Hempstead, 1996). U.S. immigration policies have varied over time based on the socioeconomic needs of the United States. In the period from the 1980s to date, American attitudes toward immigration have been hardening (Espenshade & Hempstead, 1996). The epitome of this trend might be California's Proposition 187, which was passed in 1994. This was the first time that a state took on the work of the federal government and passed immigration legislation. This Proposition excluded undocumented immigrants from receiving public education and health care facilities. Its basic rationale was to deter unauthorized immigrants from entering the United States by denying public services to those who had entered the country illegally (Mailman, 1995).

The passage of Proposition 187 might be attributed to the discursive fabrication of undocumented immigrants living in the state of California as "enemies" or "invaders" taking jobs and abusing public services (Martin, 1995; Mehan, 1997). The media and the state, with all their rhetorical might, successfully shifted the burden of California's economic uncertainties and other alleged problems onto undocumented residents by framing them as the negative "other," and won the support of local voters by appealing to their self-interest (Hasian & Delgado, 1998). For example, elite media and vernacular discussions framed the issue of undocumented immigrants with metaphors such as "dangerous waters," "army," and "animals to be lured, pitted or baited" (Santa Ana, 1999, p. 200). For pro-immigrant groups, the passage of California Proposition 187 was more indicative of a racist basis than an economic concern (cf. Ono & Sloop, 2002).

Public debates on immigration have continued into the early 21st century in the United States as pro-immigrant groups provide initiatives for immigration reform while anti-immigrant groups endeavor to increase immigration restrictions. Since 2005, national debates have been centered on the various proposals for Comprehensive Immigration Reform (CIR) in both Houses of Congress and in the Arizona State legislation, SB 1070. While CIR claims to balance different group interests, its proposal for legalizing illegal immigrants in the United States has received the strongest opposition from anti-immigrant groups (Hiroshi, 2010). Indeed Arizona's SB 1070 is deemed as the most stringent anti-immigration legislation in recent U.S. history and the bill is accused of causing extreme racial profiling (cf. Archibold, 2010). This state legislation became a national controversy and sparked rallies in over 70 U.S. cities (CBC News, May 1, 2011). Existing studies are informative regarding the structures and strategies of the legal and political discourses on the recent U.S. immigration legislations. For example, Chacon (2007) examined the current immigration control legislations and found that they are all packaged in the national security rhetoric which describes immigrants as a threat to national security. Fryberg and her associates (2011) examined both conservative and liberal articles from five national and two local newspapers about Arizona SB 1070 and they demonstrate how media locations and political ideologies affect the framing of arguments on this anti-immigration bill. However, existing studies primarily focus on the textual structure and rhetorical strategies of documents and news articles. Very few looked into the actual interactions between two opposing groups in public debates on immigration legislations.

AIMS OF THE PRESENT STUDY

This chapter examines two CNN interview debates conducted by Lou Dobbs: one with U.S. Rep. Luis Gutierrez of Illinois and another with Arizona State Rep. Steve Gallardo. Lou Dobbs, the former CNN anchor, is wellknown for debating immigration issues with the representatives of different interest groups on his program *Lou Dobbs Tonight*. Unlike reporters, Dobbs does not hold his own point of view in check. His hard-line opinions and inflammatory remarks on illegal immigrants (see Haskell, 2009) and particularly his denouncement of Mexican immigrants as an army of invaders appeals to some segments of American society, but infuriates others (see Hart, 2010). Luis Gutierrez is the U.S. Representative for Illinois and most recognized as the national leader on comprehensive immigration reform. Steve Gallardo is an Arizona state Senator and former state Representative. Both Gutierrez and Gallardo are Democrats and are considered to be two of the leading figures of pro-immigration groups; both are Hispanic/Latino Americans. Drawing on these debates, this study aims to find out 1) how the issue of race is involved with the issue of immigration legislation, and 2) how public figures strive to represent their different group interests.

"Oh, is it racist now?"

Lou Dobbs's interview/debate with Rep. Luis Gutierrez went live on CNN on November 28, 2007. The purported goal of this interview was to learn about the Comprehensive Immigration Reform bill proposed by Rep. Luis Gutierrez and Rep. Jeff Flake in the House of Representatives. The bill was titled "Security Through Regularized Immigration and a Vibrant Economy Act of 2007" (STRIVE Act), but it did not pass in Congress. Proponents claimed that the STRIVE Act increased border security, strengthened interior enforcement, and provided a program for illegal immigrants and new immigrant workers to obtain legal citizenship (cf. National Immigration Forum, 2011). In

contrast, opponents argued that the STRIVE Act would not stop illegal immigration or serve to tighten border security, but that it merely provided amnesty to millions of illegal immigrants who were living in the United States (cf. DeWeese, 2008).

Lou Dobbs prefaced the interview with his own view that this legislation "would put millions of illegal aliens on a path to citizenship." So, although the interview officially started with Lou Dobbs making a brief inquiry about the legislation that Luis Gutierrez and Jeff Flake had proposed, it quickly turned into a fiery confrontation. It did not take long for viewers to realize that Dobbs didn't want answers from Rep. Gutierrez, but rather wanted to argue about the legislation. The respective goals of each side became obvious by the manner of their accusations and refutations. Lou Dobbs's goal was to expose to the "American people" that the so-called Comprehensive Immigration Reform bill was nothing but an amnesty for illegal immigrants in the United States; whereas, Gutierrez's goal was to emphasize that his legislation aimed to offer a comprehensive solution to illegal immigration by securing borders and finding a pathway for undocumented residents to attain legal citizenship.

Dobbs initially staked out his position in his preface to the interview and after a brief inquiry about the legislation, reasserted his own views. At his second turn, Dobbs categorized all the Democratic leaders in Congress as "a pack of fools" who failed to represent the will of the American people. Semantically, Dobbs's choice of words displayed his ridicule at the proponents of CIR. Pragmatically, Dobbs's questions appear to be reproaches rather than requests for information.

DOBBS:	Let's start with your legislation, along with Congressman Flake. You've got, what, 79 sponsors right now in the house. Do you believe it's going to see the light of day? Is it going to be passed?
GUTIERREZ:	I think it's necessary that the democratic congress, this democratically controlled congress take up the legislation to show the courage and to show the fortitude that it should on such a vital and important issue as comprehensive immigration reform. I don't know if they're going to show that kind of courage. I mean, we ran saying we would bring about comprehensive immigration reform. We are the majority. We shouldn't wait for the minority. We should act.

DOBBS:	The democratic leadership, let's be honest, in both the house and senate absolutely looked like a pack of fools. They haven't done anything. Your poll ratings in both the house and the senate are devastatingly low, historic low levels. It's just a little over a year ago that that leadership was voted in by the people. It's got to be of great concern to you guys to see the democratic leadership on the senate immigration reform, twice in a row, to lose that vote with a republican president pushing it. What's the point? At what point does the Democratic Party in this country understand the American people won't stand for amnesty?
GUTIERREZ:	Here's what I think. I think that in the senate, they have attempted it twice. One time it did pass. The house failed to act when the republicans . . .

While Dobbs's first question contained a downtoner ("you've got, what, 79 sponsors") and a disbelief ("see the light of the day"), Gutierrez did not give a simple yes or no response, instead he highlighted the determination of the Democrats to pass this bill in Congress. Dobbs's categorization of the Democratic leadership (including Rep. Gutierrez himself) as "a pack of fools" clearly showed his personal disapproval reflecting what he described as the common will of the American people. In spite of Dobbs's derisive grouping and labeling, Gutierrez took his rhetorical question as a sincere request for a reason, and he offered a lengthy explanation (not included here) about what happened to the Senate bill and the House bill in the previous and the current year. While Dobbs tried to create an intergroup opposition by attributing the failures of the previous legislations to the American people's will, Gutierrez suggested that they did not pass because the two Houses did not coordinate well.

Dobbs continued to strengthen his characterization of the Democratic leaders as standing in opposition to the American people. He asked a series of rhetorical questions which again reproached the Democratic leaders for ignoring the will of the American people. In spite of Dobbs's provocative tone, Gutierrez did not emotionally react, but offered another lengthy explanation (not included here) proving that the American people's perception of CIR was not exactly what Dobbs claimed it to be.

DOBBS:	What about the will of the majority in this country, Congressman? Why is it the democratic leadership, these democratic presidential candidates, every one of them, pushing comprehensive immigration reform, which is amnesty, which your own congressional office said would be a disaster? You continue to push for it as if the American people don't mean a damn thing to you. What happened to the idea of the majority rules in this country?
GUTIERREZ:	I think that if you look at poll after poll, when the American people have spoken, they believe in comprehensive immigration reform . . .

As evident from the excerpt above, Dobbs's primary strategy for achieving his goal was to create an intergroup opposition through contrastive categorizations. While grouping consistently all the Democratic leaders in contrast to the American people, Dobbs also created a juxtaposition of his opponent as a representative of an interest group against American people ("You continue to push for it as if the American people don't mean a damn thing to you"). While Dobbs's questions took on the linguistic forms for seeking explanations, they produced a double interactional effect as indicated in Gutierrez's response. First, those questions could cast doubt on Gutierrez's claims that the Democratic majority represented the will of the American people. Second, they obviously put Gutierrez on the defense pressuring him for a justification in order to avoid being excluded from Dobbs's category of American people.

Besides accusing all of the Democratic leaders of ignoring the will of the people, Dobbs also appealed to national security and American interests. His questioning revealed his understanding of what proponents of CIR wanted and what he claimed the American people wanted. That is, border security and immigration reform should be tackled as two separate steps. While Gutierrez did say that his bill had a large portion on security issues, he made another justification below.

DOBBS:	why will you not secure our borders and our ports as a condition precedent to immigration reform law?
GUTIERREZ:	Because it will fail if that's all you do.
DOBBS:	Ah . . .
GUTIERREZ:	Because Lou, you will still have 12 million people in this country, we don't know where they live, we don't know where they bank, and we don't have any vital information on them. You have 12 million people walking around this country and you feel secure without knowing who they are? [. . .] And it's also . . . we know if you deported 12 million people tomorrow and they vanished from the United States of America, it would cripple certain sectors of our economy.
DOBBS:	Name one.
GUTIERREZ:	Agriculture.
DOBBS:	It would not. It won't even begin to.
GUTIERREZ:	60% of our agricultural workers, according to our own Department of Agriculture, our own Department of Labor, are undocumented workers in this country, that is a fact –
DOBBS:	Wouldn't even begin to.

Dobbs made a shift here from his broad accusation that all Democratic leaders ignored the people's will to an explicit charge against Gutierrez for failing to put national security first. When Dobbs asked a loaded question ("why will you not secure our borders . . .") which could cast doubt on his opponent's reasons for proposing this legislation, Gutierrez provided two reasons without trying to clarify his intention.

In response to Dobbs's juggling between national security and immigration reform, Gutierrez continued his explanation of why these two issues must be dealt with simultaneously. To turn away from Gutierrez's elaboration and viewpoint, Dobbs started to zero in on his own views of where the real problems originate, namely, the Mexican border. It was at this point of the interview that Mexican immigrants became the focus of attention.

DOBBS:	Congressman is, you're over complicating a straightforward issue. Secure our borders, secure our ports.
GUTIERREZ:	we want to do that . . .
DOBBS:	Just for the following reasons, because that southern border is the principal source of meth – methamphetamines, cocaine, heroin, and marijuana into this country. It would be a major step toward ending the war on drugs.
GUTIERREZ:	and, and if . . .
DOBBS:	And number two, to stop illegal immigration. Number three, we're now six years past September 11th and no one in this congress and administration can possibly stand before the American people and rationalize the fact that 95% of the cargo entering this country is not inspected, that we still have a border in which millions of people are crossing that border.

> GUTIERREZ: And we have—and the issue is that half of the undocumented workers in the United States of America did not cross that border.

Instead of asking questions as interviewers are supposed to do, Dobbs started to debate with Gutierrez by directly stating his position. Gutierrez became aware where Dobbs was leading the interview when he started his rebuttal by pointing out that "half of the undocumented workers in the United States of America did not cross that border." Dobbs's highlight of the Mexican border and Mexican immigrants shifted the focus of attention from general illegal immigrations specifically to an Hispanic group, which Gutierrez represents. At this turning point, Gutierrez got emotional and made a confrontation ("you always talk about Mexican border").

GUTIERREZ:	Can I, So, but you want to focus simply on the border. So if we secure the border –
DOBBS:	I said ports.
GUTIERREZ:	You said ports and borders.
DOBBS:	I said ports and borders.
GUTIERREZ:	You said ports and borders, Yea, if we did everything . . .
DOBBS:	Borders, borders.
GUTIERREZ:	No, no, you always talk about Mexican border.
DOBBS:	No. . .
GUTIERREZ:	You never speak about the Canadian border. You haven't spoken about the Canadian border during this conversation.
DOBBS:	I said ports and borders
GUTIERREZ:	It's always Mexico and drugs!
DOBBS:	Oh, is it racist, is it racist? Come on . . .
GUTIERREZ:	I didn't say that. I didn't say that. You are the one who mentioned . . .
DOBBS:	use it, use it . . .
GUTIERREZ:	I didn't, I didn't . . .
DOBBS:	Come on. Get in the game.
GUTIERREZ:	No, I won't. I won't
DOBBS:	Come on. Your friend Josh Hoyt, you said all the [inaudible]
GUTIERREZ:	I won't.
DOBBS:	Come on.
GUTIERREZ:	I won't.
DOBBS:	Just give me one shot.
GUTIERREZ:	This is too serious an issue for the American people, for me, to use the racial issue . . .

The issue of race began to surface when the focus of the debate shifted to the U.S.-Mexican border. Although Dobbs did say ports and borders, his repeated reference to the Mexican border ("borders, borders") made Gutierrez self-conscious ("you always talk about Mexican border" and "you never speak about the Canadian border"). While Gutierrez did not exactly accuse Dobbs of making racist remarks, his emotionally charged utterance ("It's always Mexico and drugs!") was certainly not a description, but an accusation that Dobbs is stereotyping Mexicans. Dobbs did not actually deny the accusation, but sarcastically urged Gutierrez to start introducing racism. In spite of Dobbs's repeated provocations, Gutierrez resolutely refused to go in that direction, which would've excluded him and his ethnic group from Dobbs' categorization of "American people."

Notwithstanding repeated urging by Dobbs, Gutierrez refrained from accusing Dobbs of racism, but that did not stop Dobbs from indirectly accusing Gutierrez of playing the race card ("Forget your socioethnocentric nonsense") and race-baiting ("And you find that racist"). In response to Dobbs's angry accusation, Gutierrez retaliated in self-defense ("You are the one who keeps mentioning Mexico" . . .). The issue of race was thus brought out into the open when the two parties started to accuse and deny.

DOBBS:	Let's get serious, let's get serious, Forget your socioethnocentric nonsense and let's get to the American people.
GUTIERREZ:	See, here you go once again, you called me socioethnocentric . . .
DOBBS:	Absolutely! Absolutely! You know it.
GUTIERREZ:	I am not known to be socioethnocentric
DOBBS:	Of course you are
GUTIERREZ:	You're the one who keeps mentioning Mexico, and drugs, and criminalizing the . . .
DOBBS:	Yea, it's over 60 . . .
GUTIERREZ:	. . . the undocumented workers who come here to this country
DOBBS:	Can I ask you a question? Let me ask you a question. May I ask you a question?
GUTIERREZ:	You're the one that does it
DOBBS:	Let me ask you a question
GUTIERREZ:	You admitted here on this program that 40% of the undocumented workers did not cross that border. Yet you never emphasize what we need to do in order to control them. I do have that in my legislation.
DOBBS:	Ok, Here we go.
GUTIERREZ:	Yes
DOBBS:	The reason I focus on Mexico is more than 60% of the illegal aliens in this country are from Mexico. The reason I focus on the border with Mexico is because it is the principal source of methamphetamines, heroin, cocaine, and marijuana into this country.
GUTIERREZ:	Yes
DOBBS:	And you find that racist—
GUTIERREZ:	No, I find it –
DOBBS:	I find it amazing that you could possibly ignore it.
GUTIERREZ:	I ask the American people, I hope you "Tivo" (record) this, because I never raised the issue of race here whatsoever.

DOBBS:	No, I'm asking you –
GUTIERREZ:	I never called him . . . he self-accused himself. I didn't do it here. Nor will I ever.
DOBBS:	You're very kind.
GUTIERREZ:	Thank you.

Even though Gutierrez did not make an explicit allegation, Dobbs accused him of raising the issue of race (which used to be the definition of playing the race card, and now is the redefinition of race-baiting by the conservatives). Ironically, TV viewers actually referred to Dobbs as a race-baiter in this debate. For example, *Chicago Sun-Times* (April 6, 2006) made this observation in a column article: "CNN anchor Lou Dobbs, leading a strident crusade against illegal immigration, dangled bait in front of Rep. Luis Gutierrez (D-Ill.) but he did not bite." As evident in the above, Dobbs failed to entice Gutierrez into a race talk after repeated provocations.

In response to Dobbs's accusation, Gutierrez kept repudiating two things: 1) he was not being socioethnocentric but was just as concerned as Dobbs (if not more) about national security; and 2) he never raised the issue of race, rather, it was Dobbs that kept singling out and then stereotyping Mexican immigrants. However, Dobbs emphasized that he focused on Mexican borders because that was the "principal" source of illegal immigration and drugs. He then rebuked Gutierrez for ignoring all these problems and raising the racial issue,

"And you are trying to make it a racial issue!"

Lou Dobbs hosted an interview/debate with Arizona State Rep. Steve Gallardo on September 6, 2007. They were joined by Arizona State Rep. Russell Pearce, author of the controversial Arizona bill, SB 1070, which requires Arizona State enforcement officers to determine an individual's immigration status during a lawful stop or detention. The purported intent of this bill and all its provisions was "to make attrition [of immigration] through enforcement" "to discourage and deter the unlawful entry and presence of aliens" in the United States (Arizona SB 1070, 2010, P. 2). Opponents, including President Obama, said that the law was "misguided," "unconstitutional," and "racist," and that it would encourage "racial profiling" and in particular "discrimination against Hispanics" (Archibold, 2010). By contrast, proponents of the bill asserted that "the law would prohibit the use of race or nationality as the sole basis for an immigration check" (Cooper, 2010).

In this interview, Dobbs brought together the author of this legislation and its major opponent. Since Dobbs supported the legislation (Fox news, 2010) and sided with Russell Pearce, the interview quickly turned into an intense confrontation with Steve Gallardo, an opponent of the legislation. Dobbs started his interview with a seeming request for clarification about a charge made by the American Civil Liberties Union (ACLU) that this legislation violated constitutional due process. Gallardo explained that this law failed to deal with discrimination issues but the word "discrimination" prompted Dobbs to ask what the discriminatory aspect was.

DOBBS:	My question is this, sir. What in this bill denies due process?
GALLARDO:	There is nothing in this particular bill that deals with the discrimination aspect of this—of the legislation.
DOBBS:	What is discriminatory about . . .
GALLARDO:	There's nothing in there that would . . .

DOBBS:	Then I will change it—then I will change the question. What is discriminatory?
GALLARDO:	There is nothing in this particular bill that would prevent any employer from turning down an applicant for employment because of their fear of this person being perceived as undocumented. Someone who looks like me, someone who may be perceived to be from Mexico, could be denied employment because of this bill. If we were serious about this bill, let's have a discriminatory aspect to this bill. Let's have some language that deals with the discrimination part of this particular bill.
DOBBS:	What is the discriminatory aspect of it?
GALLARDO:	Someone who's qualified . . .
DOBBS:	It punishes people for hiring illegal aliens once they're . . .
GALLARDO:	Not at all. Not at all. Not at all. What it does, it forces employers to keep records and to keep applicants to a higher standard. It forces employers to really think twice of—in regards to hiring anyone . . .
DOBBS:	Well, why in the world . . .
GALLARDO:	. . . who is perceived to be (INAUDIBLE) . . .
DOBBS:	. . . shouldn't they think twice about hiring an illegal alien, for crying out loud?
GALLARDO:	So, Mr. Dobbs, you don't think that—that if there's anything wrong with me being held to a higher standard in applying for a job because of the color of my skin, is that what you're telling me?
DOBBS:	Oh, you know . . .
GALLARDO:	(INAUDIBLE) set the standards . . .
DOBBS:	. . . Mr. Gallardo you were doing really good until right then. And you know that's a . . .
GALLARDO:	No. No . . .
DOBBS:	. . . nonsensical, absurd question.

While Gallardo explained the discrimination aspect, Dobbs did not seem satisfied as he asked the question three times. The formulation of Dobbs' question "What is discriminatory?" sounded like a sincere request for explanations, and therefore Gallardo provided his point of view as an answer. When Dobbs changed his tone and questioned "Why in the world shouldn't they think twice . . .," Gallardo appeared to interpret that question to mean more than what was said ("Is that what you're telling me?"). Then they became emotionally engaged, starting their accusations and refutations, as seen below.

DOBBS:	So let me answer it for you . . .
GALLARDO:	That's exactly what you said.
DOBBS:	. . . as straightforwardly as I can.
GALLARDO:	That's exactly what you said.
DOBBS:	No, it's not exactly what I said. And if your intellect doesn't carry you farther than that, we're going to have a very short conversation, aren't we?
GALLARDO:	Hey, you're asking the questions. I'm (INAUDIBLE) . . .
DOBBS:	Yes, I am. But I did not ask anything approximating what you're suggesting.

GALLARDO:	You're asking . . .
DOBBS:	What I'm asking you is straightforward. Why should the employers not have a heavy burden and a responsibility to follow the law and not hire illegal aliens of any color?
GALLARDO:	I agree with you. I agree with you. I agree with (INAUDIBLE) . . .
DOBBS:	Well, thank you. That's all we're trying to get to. And you're trying to make it a racial issue . . .
GALLARDO:	No. No. That was—that was not (INAUDIBLE) . . .
DOBBS:	. . . Mr. Gallardo. And that is beneath you . . .
GALLARDO:	That was not the question.
DOBBS:	. . . and it's beneath contempt. And it has no place . . .
GALLARDO:	No.
DOBBS:	. . . in this discussion or this debate.

Evidently, Dobbs understood Gallardo's interpretation of his question to be racially biased, and he made a fierce refutation and a derogative remark (i.e., "if your intellect doesn't carry you farther than that . . ."). Before Gallardo tried to reaffirm his interpretation (i.e., "You're asking . . ."), Dobbs reformulated his question with an emphasis (i.e., "illegal aliens of any color"). Then Gallardo was about to turn away from race, but Dobbs did not give up the chance to make a counteraccusation (i.e., "you're trying to make it a racial issue"). At Gallardo's rebuttal attempt, Dobbs followed up his accusation with a reproach (i.e., "that is beneath you").

INTERGROUP IDEOLOGIES AND IMMIGRATION DISCOURSE

Immigration discourse is permeated with intergroup ideologies that promote a collective sense of "us" and project a demonical image of "them" (see Mehan, 1997). The two interactions above evidence some of the basic intergroup dynamics in immigration debates. Anti-immigration representatives classify themselves as a group of citizens who are concerned about their national security and their fellow citizens' interest whereas describing pro-immigration representatives as concerned only about their own group without considering any external threats to their nation. In contrast, pro-immigration representatives make an

effort to justify their actions as fulfilling some national needs and protecting a wronged community while criticizing opponents for demonizing immigrants. To achieve their respective objectives, the two opposing parties may appeal to race as leverage in their immigration debates.

The issue of race could be raised when one immigrant group was singled out and negatively positioned. Gutierrez answered all the questions Dobbs asked about his immigration bill and about undocumented immigrants in general (even though his formulations were provocative or derisive). However, he reacted emotionally when Dobbs shifted the focus of attention to Mexican immigrants and described them as a threat to the national security. According to social identity theory (Tajfel & Turner, 1986), a basic need for positive group image leads individual members to defend the whole group. As a representative of the Hispanic community, Gutierrez (and probably anyone) would certainly stand up for his group ("It's always Mexico and drugs!") because of the basic need for a positive group image. The same is also true of the second case in which Gallardo interpreted Dobbs's provocative question as racially biased. In other words, what alternatives are left to these representatives when they feel that their socioethnic group is wronged?

Appealing to race (either explicitly or implicitly) can bring consequences to a public figures' image. On the one hand, a public figure's positive image certainly is threatened if they are accused of any racist practice (Van Dijk, 1992). As shown above, Dobbs's reactions were either fanatical or sarcastic when there were any attempts to accuse him of a racist practice. On the other hand, the positive image of a public figure is also jeopardized if they are accused of charging someone else of racism or of raising issues of race in general. As shown above, Gutierrez and Gallardo almost made equally enthusiastic refutations when Dobbs sarcastically invited the former to accuse him of racism and vehemently lashed out at the latter for appealing to race. In other words, the issue of race has become a sort of dilemma in American society. Public figures must raise racial concerns—without using the word "race"—in order to maintain a positive public image.

The procedures used in the above conversations demonstrate how a public figures' national identity can be juxtaposed with their group identity. A common strategy that anti-immigration groups use to gather support and lambaste their opponents is to appeal to national security (see Chacón, 2007). As shown above, Dobbs's primary strategy was to characterize himself as a representative of the "American people" who ardently do not want amnesty for illegal immigrants. Hence, those who supported CIR and opposed Arizona SB 1070 were categorized as "them": from Dobbs's perspective, this included the whole democratic leadership who did not "give a damn" about national security or the will of the American people. This reframing does exert a check on pro-immigration representatives such as Gutierrez who said, "it is too serious an issue for the American people, for me, to use the racial issue."

CONCLUSION

Race as a type of social categorization exists as part of the collective consciousness of U.S. society. This chapter provides examples of how public figures in U.S. immigration debates raise and refute charges of race-baiting in order to position themselves positively and others negatively. The two interactions showed how the issue of race was interactionally called for and how it became contextually consequential. More specifically, the racial issue

was raised implicitly by Gutierrez and explicitly by Gallardo because they were interactionally boxed into those specific responses by Lou Dobbs. That may provide a plausible reason why the media referred to Lou Dobbs as a race-baiter while Gutierrez and Gallardo were described as playing the race card. Thus, the specific procedures of raising the issue of race analyzed in the interactions here may shed some light on our understanding of the process and meaning of race-baiting.

NOTES

1. Discourse here refers broadly to the use of language in social context.
2. Race-baiting as used in this context does not seem to reflect the Merriam-Webster dictionary definition: "the making of verbal [malicious] attacks against members of a racial group."
3. In the 1960s, the United Nations also started an initiative for ending racist practices.

REFERENCES

A show of strength. (2006, March 11). *Chicago Tribune*. Retrieved October 31, 2011 from http://articles.chicagotribune.com/2006-03-11/news/0603110130_1_immigration-debate-pro-immigrant-illegal-immigrants.

Archibold, Randal C. (2010, April 24). U.S.'s toughest immigration law is signed in Arizona. *The New York Times*. Retrieved October 15, 2010 from http://www.nytimes.com/.

Arizona immigration law sparks huge rallies. (2010, May 01). *CBC News*. Retrieved November 6, 2011 from http://www.cbc.ca/news/world/story/2010/05/01/arizona-immigration-law-protests.html.

Arizona SB 1070 (2011). Retrieved September 11, 2010 from http://www.azleg.gov/legtext/49leg/2r/bills/sb1070s.pdf.

Augoustinos, M., & Every, D. (2007). The language of "race" and prejudice: A discourse of denial, reason, and liberal-practical politics. *Journal of Language and Social Psychology, 26*(2), 123–141.

Bauer, G. (2010, July 18). Liberals still acting stupidly on race. *Human Events*. Retrieved November 16, 2011 from http://www.humanevents.com/2010/07/18/liberals-still-acting-stupidly-on-race.

Bauer, G. (2011, March 07). The 10 most shameless race card plays. *Human Events*. Retrieved November 16, 2011 from http://www.humanevents.com/2011/03/07/the-10-most-shameless-race-card-plays.

Benedict, Ruth F. (1945). *Race and racism*. London, UK: Routledge and Kegan Paul.

Billig, M. (1985). Prejudice, categorization and particularization: From a perceptual to a rhetorical approach. *European Journal of Social Psychology, 15*, 79–103.

Billig, M. (1991). *Ideology and Opinions.* London, UK: Sage.

Billig, M. (2006). Political rhetoric of discrimination. *Elsevier Encyclopaedia for Language and Linguistics.* Oxford, UK: Elsevier.

Billig, M., & Tajfel, H. (1973). Social categorization and similarity in intergroup behavior. *European Journal of Social Psychology, 3*(1), 27–52.

Blommaert, J. (2001). Investigating narrative inequality: African asylum seekers' stories in Belgium. *Discourse & Society, 12*, 413–449.

Bonilla-Silva, E. (1997). Rethinking racism: Toward a structural interpretation. *American Sociological Review, 62*(3), 465–480.

Bonilla-Silva, E., & Forman, T. A. (2000). I'm not a racist, but. . . : Mapping white college students' racial ideology in the U.S.A. *Discourse & Society, 11*(1), 50–85.

Bonilla-Silva, E., & Lewis, A. (1999). The new racism: Racial structure in the United States, 1960s–1990s. In Paul Wong (Ed.), *Race, ethnicity, and nationality in the United States: Toward the twenty-first century* (pp. 55–101). Boulder, CO: Westview Press.

Bonilla-Silva, E., Lewis, A., & Embrick, D. G. (2004). I did not get that job because of a black man. . . : The story lines and testimonies of color-blind racism. *Sociological Forum, 19*(4), 555–581.

Buttny, R. (1999). Discursive constructions of racial boundaries and self-segregation on campus. *Journal of Language and Social Psychology, 18*, 247–261.

Chacón, J. M. (2007). Unsecured bordered: Immigration restrictions, crime control, and national security. *Connecticut Law Review, 39*(5), 1827–1890.

Chiang, S.Y. (2010). Well, I'm a lot of things, but I'm sure not a bigot: Positive self-presentation in confrontational discourse on racism. *Discourse & Society, 21*(3), 273–294.

Cooper, J. (2010, April 26). Ariz. immigration law target of protest. *Associated Press. MSNBC.* Retrieved October 15, 2010 from http://www.msnbc.msn.com/.

Del-Teso-Craviotto, M. (2009). Racism and xenophobia in immigrants' discourse: The case of Argentines in Spain. *Discourse & Society, 20*, 571–592.

DeWeese, T. (2008). The STRIVE Act of 2007 sells America and Americans into bondage of the NAU!. Retrieved October 15, 2010 from http://www.p2fe.com/deWeese1-23-08.html.

Downing, J. D. H. (1999). Hate speech and first amendment absolutism discourses in the U.S. *Discourse & Society, 10*(2), 175–89.

Espenshade, T. J., & Hempstead, K. (1996). Contemporary American attitudes toward U.S. immigration. *International Migration Review, 30*(2), 535–570.

Every, D., & Augoustinos, M. (2007). Constructions of racism in the Australian parliamentary debates on asylum seekers. *Discourse & Society, 18*, 411–436.

Feagin, J. R. (2000). *Racist America: Roots, current realities, and future reparations*. New York, NY: Routledge.

Fox news (2010, May, 11). *Lou Dobbs on Arizona immigration law*. Retrieved October 15, 2010 from http://www.foxnews.com/on-air/oreilly/2010/05/11/lou-dobbs-arizona-immigration-law.

Fredrickson, G. M. (2002). *Racism: A short history*. Princeton, NJ: Princeton University Press.

Fryberg, S. A., Stephens, N. M., Covarrubias, R., Markus, H. R., Carter, E. D., Laiduc, G. A., & Salido, A. J. (2011). How the media frames the immigration debate: The critical role of location and politics. *Analyses of Social Issues and Public Policy, 11*(1), 1–17.

Hart, P. (2010, January). Hasta la vista, Lou Dobbs. *FAIR (Fairness and Accuracy in Reporting)*. Retrieved from http://www.fair.org/index.php?page=4032.

Hasian, M. J., & Delgado, F. (1998). The trials and tribulations of racialized critical rhetorical theory: Understanding the rhetorical ambiguities of Proposition 187. *Communication Theory, 8*(3), 245–270.

Haskell, R. E. (2009). Unconscious linguistic referents to race: Analysis and methodological frameworks. *Discourse & Society, 20*(1), 59–84.

Hiroshi, M. (2010). What is "Comprehensive Immigration Reform"? Taking the long view. *Arkansas Law Review, 63*, 225–241.

Hogg, M. A., & Abrams, D. (1988). *Social identifications: A social psychology of intergroup relations and group processes*. London, UK: Routledge.

Holmes, S. A. (1998, April 5). The nation: Re-rethinking Affirmative Action. *The New York Times*. Retrieved from http://www.nytimes.com/1998/04/05.

KhosraviNik, M. (2009). The representation of refugees, asylum seekers and immigrants in British newspapers during the Balkan conflict (1999) and the British general election (2005). *Discourse & Society, 20*, 477–498.

Lopez, I. F. H. (1994). The social construction of race: Some observations on illusion, fabrication and choice. *Harvard Civil Rights-Civil Liberties Law Review, 29*(1), 1–62.

Luis vs. Lou: Rep. Luis Gutierrez (D-Ill.) does not take CNN's Lou Dobbs bait. (2006, April 6). *Chicago Sun Times*. Retrieved November 06, 2011 from http://blogs.suntimes.com/sweet/2006/04/post_8.html.

Lynn, N., & Lea, S. (2003). "A phantom menace and the new Apartheid": The social construction of asylum-seekers in the United Kingdom. *Discourse & Society, 14*, 425–452.

Mailman, S. (1995, January 3). California's Proposition 187 and its lessons. *New York Law Journal, 3*, col.1.

Martin, P. (1995). Proposition 187 in California. *International Migration Review, 29*(1), 255–263.

Massey, D. S. (2002). A brief history of human society: The origin and role of emotion in social life. *American Sociological Review, 67*(1), 1–29.

Mehan, H. (1997). The discourse of the illegal immigration debate: A case study in the politics of representation. *Discourse & Society, 8*, 249–269.

Memmi, A. (1999). *Racism* (Steve Martinot, Trans.). Twin Cities, MN: University of Minnesota Press.

National Immigration Forum (2011). Comprehensive immigration reform in the 110th Congress. Retrieved August 30, 2011 from http://www.immigrationforum.org/policy/legislation/comprehensive-immigration-reform-in-the-110th-congress.

Obama's race-baiting. (2010, May 3). [Editorial]. *Washington Times*. Retrieved August 30, 2011 from http://www.washingtontimes.com/news/2010/may/3/.

Ono, K. A., & Sloop, J. M. (2002). *Shifting borders: Rhetoric, immigration, and California's Proposition 187 (mapping racisms)*. Philadelphia, PA: Temple University Press.

Pascale, C. M. (2008). Talking about race: Shifting the analytical paradigm. *Qualitative Inquiry, 14*(5), 723–741.

Santa Anna, O. (1999). "Like an animal I was treated": Anti-immigrant metaphor in U.S. public discourse. *Discourse & Society, 10*, 191–224.

Schaefer, R.T. (1990). *Racial and Ethnic Groups* (4th ed.). Glenview, IL: Scott Foresman.

Tajfel, H. (1981). *Human groups and social categories*. Cambridge, UK: Cambridge University Press.

Tajfel, H., & Turner, J. C. (1986). The social identity theory of intergroup behavior. In S. Worchel & W. G. Austin (Eds.), *Psychology of intergroup relations* (2nd ed.) (pp. 7–24). Chicago, IL: Nelson-Hall.

Tapper, J. (2010, May 14). GOP Congressman: President Obama playing "race bait games" with Arizona immigration law. *ABC News*. Retrieved February 19, 2011 from http://abcnews.go.com/blogs/politics/2010/05/gop-congressman-president-obama-playing-race-bait-games-with-arizona-immigration-law/.

Turner, J. C. (1985). Social categorization and the self-concept: A social-cognitive theory of group behaviour. In E. J. Lawler (Ed.), *Advances in group processes* (Vol. 2, pp. 77–122). Greenwich, CT: JAI Press.

Van Der Valk, I. (2003). Right-wing parliamentary discourse on immigration in France. *Discourse & Society, 14*, 309–348.

Van Dijk, T. A. (1987). *Communicating racism: Ethnic prejudice in thought and talk*. Thousand Oaks, CA: Sage.

Van Dijk, T. A. (1992). Discourse and the denial of racism. *Discourse & Society, 3*(1), 87–118.

Van Dijk, T. A. (2000). New(s) racism: A discourse analytical approach. In S. Cottle (Ed.), *Ethnic minorities and the media* (pp. 33–49). Buckingham, UK: Open University Press.

Van Leeuwen, T., & Wodak, R. (1999). Legitimizing immigration control: A discourse-historical analysis. *Discourse Studies, 1*, 83–118.

Verkuyten, M. (2001). "Abnormalization" of ethnic minorities in conversation. *British Journal of Social Psychology, 40*, 257–278.

West, C., & Fenstermaker, S. (1999). Accountability in action: The accomplishment of gender, race, and class in a meeting of the University of California Board of Regents. *Discourse & Society, 13*(4), 537–563.

Wetherell, M., & Potter, J. (1992). *Mapping the language of racism: Discourse and the legitimation of exploitation*. New York, NY: Columbia University Press.

7

GLOBAL MEDIA AND CULTURAL IDENTITIES

The Case of Indians in Post-Amin Uganda

HEMANT SHAH

INTRODUCTION

The global movements of people and the spread of electronic media (and its cultural products) are among the most distinctive features of the current epoch. The unprecedented scale and scope of this global movement has had profound consequences for the cognitive and social processes that are at the root of the formations and transformations of cultural identities. Identity is linked to space in the sense that location and culture are linked historically, mythically, and psychologically. Not long ago, it was quite common to think about identity as linked strongly to a single place and to view "home" as constituting and circumscribing our consciousness, values, and the limits of imagination. "Who we are" was determined by "where we are from" (see reviews in Mitra, 2005; Karim, 2003). However, the intensification of the global circulation of people and media images tremendously complicates this matter (Appadurai, 1996; Cunningham & Sinclair, 2001).

On the one hand, in the context of globalization struggles over cultural identity are interwoven more than ever before with questions of community and nation(alism) and are fraught with economic and political tensions. On the other hand, the struggles of cultural identities are signs of the modulating strength of ties between place, community, and culture, which may generate desires for rethinking and practicing new kinds of transnational cultural identifications and identities. Clifford (1992) famously wrote that instead of viewing cultural identities as connected to "roots," we must think of them as linked to "routes." Clifford's notion of culture as travel is particularly relevant in the context of diasporic communities, in which viewing *one* location and *one* "home" as central to formation of cultural identity is no longer a convincing theoretical or practical position.

In an age of globalization, one of the important sites for struggles over cultural identities is transnational media. The process of identity formation is a contested one in which media represent both resources and constraints for the construction of "imagined selves and imagined worlds" (Appadurai, 1996, p. 3). Global circulation of media products has reduced, in an important sense, the distances between global migrants and their countries of origin. Sharing media images from "home" may create a sense of transnational bonding, but as Aksoy and Robins (2003) have noted these images may also undermine the images of "home" held by migrants and create new bases for transforming cultural identities. This chapter examines how a diasporic community of Indians in Uganda negotiates questions of cultural identity. Of central concern are the roles transnational media assume—both as institutions and cultural texts—in the community's cultural identity formation and transformation. This essay argues that Indians in Uganda construct, refashion, and assert elements of identity, even those stereotypical elements that may have been imposed by others, in strategic ways in order to forward their social or economic interests in the new environment. In connection to these strategic assertions of identity, Indians make differing claims about their connectedness to their old and new "homes." Access to and uses of the cultural products of global Indian media are sometimes centrally connected to these processes.

INDIANS IN UGANDA

Indians were central to Uganda's economic, political, and cultural history from the late 1800s onward. The Indian community rapidly became an indispensable part of the country's manufacturing base and agricultural production. Indians held positions of political leadership at local and national levels. Schools for Indian children and Hindu temples for Indian worshippers were a common sight throughout Uganda.[1] But Indian success and insularity came to be resented by native black Ugandans. Twice—in 1945 and in 1949—Ugandans engaged in anti-Indian rioting

(see Mutibwa, 1992). In May 1970, President Milton Obote proposed nationalizing Indian-dominated industries. Many Indian business owners said they would close shop and leave the country. Fearful of economic collapse, Obote offered immediate citizenship to the 35,000 non-citizens among the country's 80,000 Indians. But Obote's actions contributed to even more widespread discontent.

Eventually, in January 1971, Idi Amin overthrew Obote and in the months following, anti-Indian rhetoric reached a crescendo. In December 1971, Amin summoned Indian leaders to Kampala and accused them of being "saboteurs" who were trying to undermine the economy (Marrett, 1987, p. 8). In January 1972, Amin told a gathering of Indian businessmen "Uganda is not an Indian colony." Amin also accused Indians of "economic malpractice" and of failing to integrate into the African community (Mamdani, 1984; Mamdani, 1999, p. 305; Yadav, 1998). Finally, in November 1972, Amin expelled Indians from the country and confiscated their homes, businesses, schools, and places of worship (Adams & Bristow, 1978, 1979).

All but a few dozen families, who managed in one way or another to remain in the country, were forced to vacate on short notice. Twenty years later, in 1992, Yoweri Museveni, who came to power following a civil war, invited Indians to return to Uganda, enticing some with an offer to reclaim their lost properties and others with incentives to establish new business enterprises in the country (Abidi, 1996; Tukahebwa, 1998). By 2005, about 15,000 Indians had settled in Uganda (Sachedina, 2007) I have listed this newer source and have adjusted the number of Indians in Uganda in the text.

As one might guess, the process of property reclamation was fraught with tension and controversy of every kind imaginable, as some Indians returned to reclaim properties while others entered Uganda for the first time. Some of the most intense debates were those over words such as "home," "Indian," and "Ugandan" because their meanings had consequences for the property reclamation process. In many ways, the struggle over property reclamation, which continued well into the 2000s, was a struggle over identity itself: Could one be Indian *and* Ugandan? What did "home" mean for first-time arrivals *versus* for those returning to ancestral soil?

A changing media landscape complicated the question of cultural identities. Museveni had agreed to allow competition in the broadcasting sector by permitting private radio and television firms to operate in the country. Almost over-night, several private FM radio stations and a handful of private television stations began broadcasting. However, on the whole, Indians had a limited presence in the over-the-air broad-cast sector. A second consequence of the liberal-ization of the media sector was the establishment of cable television and direct broadcast systems. Together, these television and broadcast systems constitute what has been called *narrowcasting* to migrant communities via transnational television (Naficy, 2003). Firms moved quickly to establish cable television systems that downlinked a diverse bouquet of multilingual programming choices from India and delivered it into Indian homes throughout the country.

In 1997, Indian entrepreneur Subash Chandra, owner of the India-based Zee Group, established Kampala Siti Cable, which distributes Indian programs obtained from India via the satellite. For about $30 per month subscribers can receive several channels, such as Sony, MTV, Zee, Chan-nel [V], EenaduTV, Sahara, and several channels of Doordarshan (India's national television net-work). The Doordarshan offerings include one sports channel in Hindi and English, one Hindi news channel, one national news channel in Eng-lish, one international news channel in English, one channel of Gujarati-language programming, and one channel of news and entertainment pro-gramming in the Punjabi language.

With continuous access to news and enter-tainment from "home" can Indian identity be grounded in Uganda? Does an electronic signal jam-packed with voice and data that is bounced off a satellite in geosynchronous orbit, have any-thing at all to do with how Indians in Uganda

identify themselves? Uganda in the early 2000s came to represent a geopolitical space where two important aspects of globalization—movement of people and transnational electronic media—were relatively nascent forces and provided a fresh case to examine questions about cultural identity within a "diasporic communication space" (Sreberny, 2001).

CULTURAL IDENTITIES AND DIASPORAS

In Cornell and Hartmann's book, *Ethnicity and race: Making identities in a changing world* (1998), the process of identity formation and transformation revolves around the functions of assignment and assertion. Cultural struggles over identity are an interaction between "the passive experience of being 'made' by external forces" and "the active process by which the group 'makes' itself" (p. 80). People, institutions or groups may assign others to certain categories of identity but those others also assert their own claims by rejecting, building on, or refining the assigned identities. The assigned identities may then be revised in response. Thus, cultural iden-tity formation is a continuous process.

In the literature on cultural identities and dias-pora, Stuart Hall's writing about migrations, media, and identity has framed much of the dis-cussion. Hall (1990) tells us that cultural identity is both fixed and unstable, a constant engage-ment with assignments and assertions of identi-ties tempered by vectors of continuity and rupture. Even though individuals at different times and places may inhabit many "selves," cultural iden-tity reflects common experiences and cultural codes that provide stable and continuous frames of reference and meaning. These selves can be retrieved and nurtured to create a potent mixture of blind faith in the past (a discourse of "who we *were*") and boundless passion to assert that identity in the here and now (a discourse of "who we *are*"). A discourse is simply a "particular way of representing" (Hall, 1996, p. 201).

However, a discourse is not simply a single or general utterance. A discourse is a group of coherent statements, symbols, or texts that work together to convey a particular type of knowledge or understanding—both by asserting a particular understanding and by limiting alternative ways of understanding. For example, a discourse of "who we are" may comprise nationalistic symbols, patriotic songs, pledges of allegiance, public declarations of exceptionalism, and so on. Together, these expressions may work to promote ideas about national or cultural superiority while at the same time delegitimizing or marginalizing ideas that suggest otherwise. Discourse, then, is key to the production of social meaning and action. Therefore, as Hall (1990) reminds us, we should not underestimate or neglect the power of discursively constructed, suddenly salient, cultural identities to inspire collective expression, action, and movements.

Despite the importance of common experience and cultural codes, cultural identities are also affected by ruptures and discontinuities, which often reside alongside with, or even within, the discourses of "who we were" or "who we are." As a result, Hall formulates the understanding of cultural identity as something constantly evolving:

> Cultural identity is a matter of becoming as well as of being. It belongs to the future as well as to the past…. Far from being grounded in a mere rediscovery of the past, which is waiting to be found, and which, when found, will secure our sense of ourselves into eternity, identities are the names we give to the different ways we are positioned by, and position ourselves within, the narratives of the past (Hall, 1990, p. 225).

By emphasizing the notion of "positioning," Hall highlights the fact that, for migrant communities especially, there is always a politics of identity— that identity formation and transformation is always contested through the interactions of assignment and assertion, always a combination of continuity (with the past, with languages, with narratives, and so on) and rupture (created, for example, by slavery, expulsion, conquest, etc.).

In the context of global migrations, Sreberny (2001) and Vertovec (1999), among others, suggest that international networks, modes of consciousness, and cultural products are key to understanding how members of diasporic communities assert cultural identities. In addition, media systems function to multiply and link communities in local, multilocal, or transnational configurations that have important consequences for exclusion and inclusion.

William Safran (1991) provides the classic definition of diaspora in reference to the Jewish history of displacements. His definition posits a homeland from which an original community has dispersed but to which the community believes they will return; a belief that the host community will never fully accept the newcomers; a determined effort to develop autonomous mechanisms to satisfy cultural and social needs; and a community commitment to maintain support for the homeland. Safran has been criticized for reifying the "homeland" and for suggesting that migrant communities are inevitably marginalized by the host society (Tsagarousianou, 2004).

Cohen (1997) expanded Safran's definition and added the possibility of voluntary migration, thus recognizing the possibilities for new forms of collective identities and emphasizing creative formulations of cultural production within diasporas. But Cohen's conceptualization of diaspora has been criticized for too strongly retaining the "links to the past" as well as for retaining a checklist approach to identifying a diasporic community. As Tsagarousianou (2004) notes, Cohen's effort to demarcate the contours of diaspora studies may, in fact, lead to freezing complex and ongoing processes.

Given these limitations of more-or-less "traditional" approaches to diaspora, Dudrah (2002) suggests the idea may best be understood as a heuristic concept, which evokes a number of processes linked to the social conditions and cultural identities brought into play by transnational migrations. In contrast, diaspora as a descriptive concept simply lists "frozen" dimensions of the phenomenon such as homeland, extent of marginalization, and the role of the past. Dudrah's suggestion is in line with Clifford's recommendation that "rather than locating essential features [of diaspora] we might focus in dispora's borders" because "the relational positioning at issue here is not a process of absolute othering, but rather of entangled tension" (Clifford, 1994, p. 307).

Similarly, Aksoy and Robins (2003, pp. 90–91) are concerned that diaspora studies have reified the "drama of separation and the pathos of distance from the homeland" to an extent that feelings of alienation, discomfort, and anxiety have become master narratives for diasporic identities and consequently are thought to be inevitable experiences for migrants. Aksoy and Robins point out that many contemporary migrant communities live, as it were, multiple lives—multilingual, multicultural, and socially competent in a variety of settings. As a result, a nation-based imagined community may be irrelevant for migrants involved in a transnational mobility.

Brah (1996) argues that the complexity of migration patterns of people who originate from the same place cannot be captured by a singular notion of diaporic community. Instead, Brah suggests, multiple journeys must be understood as a "confluence of narratives" within which communities are "differently imagined under different historical circumstances" (1996, p. 183). Thus, the identity of a diasporic community is "far from fixed or pre-given" and each migrant journey must be understood within "the crucible of the materiality of everyday life" in new locations (p. 183). Diaspora signifies, from this perspective, not a checklist of characteristics but "an interpretive frame referencing the economic, political, and cultural dimensions of contemporary forms of migrancy" (Brah, 1996, p. 186). As a frame for understanding migrant communities, the concept of diaspora itself may be viewed as discourse—defining into existence particular configurations of peoples, technologies, finances, and ideas in specific places.

Clifford (1994) notes that diaspora is a condition in which people who are displaced manage to form connections with *homes*—both the old and the new. But it is not simply a matter of forging connections. A distinction must be made in terms of the strength of ties to both the old and new places. Tsagarousianou (2004) demonstrated in her studies of Greek Cypriots in London that there is a difference between *feeling at home versus having a stake in the place*. The idea of "having a stake in the place" is not a simple linear progression from not having a stake, to having a stake. The process may proceed at a different pace in different realms for different parts of the community.

The ways that members of diasporic communities negotiate the tensions of feeling at home versus feeling that they have a stake in the place, are of course, varied and complex. In many cases, these social and cultural negotiations involve a self-conscious manipulation of cultural identities. I use the phrase *"flexible essentialism,"* a deliberate fusion of Ong's "flexible citizenship" (Ong, 1999) and Spivak's "strategic essentialism," (Spivak, 1996, p. 216) to capture certain forms of self-representation involved in the identity politics of positioning.[2]

Essentialism is the belief that individuals embody real essences that exist independently of any social construction. These essences may be physical, biological, linguistic, or cultural. Dominant groups in a given social formation often assign essential identities to the less powerful. Strategic essentialism is a process in which the less powerful knowingly, willingly, and temporarily claim an essential identity (but without commitment to the essence) for gains and benefit of various kinds.[3] Thus, flexible essentialism (1) recognizes that assigned identities can be essential but also have multiple dimensions (i.e., economic, political, cultural, etc.); and (2) mobilizes and asserts specific dimensions of assigned essential identity in strategic ways depending on the context (see Lee, 2006, p. 222; Ong, 1999, pp. 129, 132–33; Tsagarousianou, 2004, p. 58). A person engaging in flexible essentialism has not accepted the assigned essential identity as true, but is claiming to embody and is asserting one or more of its various dimensions for personal gain.

Aihwa Ong tells a story about Michael Woo, a Los Angeles politician who argues that Asians are skilled at money making, deal making, sizing up people, and so forth, therefore the Asians that move about the Pacific Rim should serve as ideal liaisons between Western and Asian entrepreneurs (Ong, 1999, pp. 131–136). Woo's invocation of long-standing stereotypes of Asians' "essential" qualities is an example of strategic essentialism by flexible citizens. It is this ability to self-consciously shift and slip from one assigned essential subject position to another that I'm calling flexible essentialism.

By contrast, flexible citizenship refers to strategies used by transnational migrants to "both circumvent and benefit from nation state regimes by selecting different sites for investments, work, and family relocation" (Ong, 1999, p. 112). Flexible citizens are characterized by their ability to respond "fluidly and opportunistically to changing political-economic conditions" (Ong, 1999, p. 6). Ong's flexible citizens are wealthy capital accumulators but even average, everyday migrants can become flexible citizens. For example, Inda (2000, p. 93) notes that flexibility is an ontological condition in which migrants of all kinds (laborers, farm workers, high-tech experts, etc.), maneuver within, respond to, engage with, and manipulate "transnational circuits and postnational zones" daily as a matter of fundamental routine, and as naturally as breathing.

METHOD

This chapter explores how Indians in Uganda deal with feelings of home and flexible essentialism in relation to their assertions of cultural identity as members of a transnational diaspora. The study is based on archival research; in-depth interviews with Indian community leaders, business owners, and workers; and participant observation with two Indian community groups. This research was done in Kampala, Uganda's capital city, in May–June 2000 and in March 2003. Two archives in Kampala provided fairly comprehensive documentary evidence on the cultural, social, economic, and political position of Indians in Uganda. The holdings of the Makerere

University Institute for Social Research included historical and statistical information on the number of Indians, their role in the Ugandan economy, and the extent of the Indian community's political activity in Uganda. At the Center for Basic Research, a privately funded think tank, I pieced together the recent history of Indians in Uganda from a comprehensive, well-indexed newspaper archive. In addition, the Center published a number of occasional papers on various topics, including media and interethnic relations in Uganda. I made contacts with my interview subjects through two main informants in the Indian community, a professor of library science at Makerere University and an independent entrepreneur who also was a member of the Kampala city government. Through these individuals, I endeavored to meet and interview members of the Indian community from various social and economic backgrounds.

In total, I interviewed 22 community members: five small-shop owners (e.g., money exchange, gas station, pharmacy), six professionals (educators, lawyers, etc.), six business owners (banks, travel agency, hotel, real estate, foreign exchange, etc.), and five workers (clerks, messengers, janitors). Interviews were conducted in public places such as restaurants, offices, or in private homes. Thirty-minute interviews were typical; the range was from 20 minutes to 90 minutes, and a handful of people were interviewed more than once. The shorter interviews were with the "workers" who were either reluctant to chat during business hours, even during lulls, or refused to talk outside business hours. No women outside of the "professional" category agreed to be interviewed. In fact, I managed to talk about my research interest to only two women: a personal interview with a professor at Makerere University and a short phone conversation with a lawyer. Thus, the results and patterns described here refer almost exclusively to male experiences. The extent to which the Indian diaspora in Uganda is discursively constructed and understood by members of the community as a masculine space is an issue that needs further study.

I also attended one public meeting of the India Association of Uganda and one prayer meeting and dinner at the local Hindu temple. At the IAU meeting, about 100 people attended and I watched as they went through the agenda and discussed and voted on issues, and later talked with perhaps a dozen attendees about their experiences and connections to Uganda. At the Hindu temple, I also talked to as many people as possible during the post-prayer meal. All respondents are identified by their initials only.

DIASPORA AND INDIAN IDENTITIES IN UGANDA

Within diasporic communities of Indians scattered around the world there is, of course, a large range of narratives of "becoming," that involve mobility, money, and media. But one common cultural code among these diasporic communities is the *idea* of "India," though it operates in different ways in the migrant imagination (cf. Dudrah, 2002; Durham, 2004; Mallapragada, 2000; Manuel, 2000; Ray, 2001). Though highly dependent on time and space, "India" represents a number of things for various migrant communities. "India" is a physical place, but also a value, an anchor for family ties, a safe haven for children, a guardian of culture, a transit point, a retirement home, a bank, a temple/mosque/gurudwara/church, and a TV signal. Thus, despite the undoubtedly diverse narratives of movement among the various migrant communities of the Indian diaspora, an important dimension of community consciousness is oriented to "India" in one way or another, and to one extent or another. From this perspective, "India" does not function strictly or even fundamentally as "homeland," as suggested by Safran (1991). And "Indian-ness," following Hall (1990), is a matter of discursive positioning, not simply a matter of essential cultural traits (see also Ray, 2001). Ties to "India" and orientations toward "Indian-ness" are the vectors that help shape how Indians in Uganda negotiated matters of "feeling at home

versus a stake in the place" and the process of "flexible essentialism."

Feeling at Home Versus a "Stake in the Place"

Indians in Uganda are involved in dispersed diaspora networks spanning India, Bangladesh, Sri Lanka, Great Britain, Canada, United States, Kenya, South Africa, and Tanzania, among other countries. Even the handful of families who had managed to remain in Uganda after 1972 are now linked through relatives, friends, and business associates to places outside Uganda. Some Indians in Uganda have invested heavily in the country. However, most have not been active in Ugandan politics or culture. Few Indians take part in political campaigns or party politics. Fewer still participate in Ugandan cultural activities or consume local media and popular culture. Yet, many Indians in Uganda belong to the Indian Association of Uganda (IAU) and publicly identify themselves as members. For some members, "Uganda" in this association name is a geopolitical empty space when it comes to investing or putting in time. It is merely a space to move through on the way to somewhere else. Similarly for this group, "India" in the name of the association refers to what Hall (1990, p. 225) calls the discourses of "who we were" *and* "who we are." Yet for other immigrants, the meanings of Uganda and India are more complicated. At one IAU meeting I attended, members enthusiastically sang the Indian national anthem, recited Hindu and Muslim prayers and welcomed into the "Indian" family a mixed-race Indian-Ugandan woman and her children who were lifelong residents of Uganda. The anthem signaled perhaps a profound nostalgia for home—even though many of the singers may have left the geopolitical space of India behind for good. Beyond nostalgia, however, there was an assertion of cultural identity as Indians, for both Hindus and Muslims. But perhaps most important of all was the ceremony for the mixed-race mother and her children. The woman literally embodied the integration of cultures and the idea of assim- ilation. The ceremony was itself a discursive construction of "who we are" in Uganda. It was a performance of inclusion and inclusiveness, which publicly stated that "home" is Uganda- India. At the same time, it embodied tensions that represent a dilemma experienced by migrants of all kinds: feeling at home versus having a stake in the place.

For example, there are clear differences in terms of "a stake in the place" between Indians with a pre-1972 history in Uganda and those who arrived for the first time during the Museveni era. The pre-1972 community members and their descendants seem to have a much stronger stake in the place. Many of the returning Indians turned their attention to reclaiming properties, which they had been forced to abandon in 1972. According to Indian-community leaders, perhaps 5,000 properties have been reclaimed all over Uganda—mainly private residences and busi- nesses, but also schools and places of worship.

Although several Indian schools had been functioning in Kampala at the time of the expul- sion, the schools re-established by members of the pre-1972 community, made a point of admit- ting Ugandans, ostensibly as a sign of their com- mitment to the country. The head of the Indian Association of Uganda said that Indians are "committed to investing in Uganda's future as a way to give back to the community" (S. P., 2003). These schools do not have any specific "Indian" curricular content or any extra-curricular activities that are particularly "Indian."[4]

From the perspective of the returning Indians, reclaiming properties that formerly were Hindu temples and schools for Indian children was an important part of the reclamation process. The established Indian community sought to ensure continuity and connection with "Indian values and traditions," if not India itself; re-establishing temples was a key strategy (T.P., 2000). The importance of the temple as a nostalgic marker of values, traditions, and community solidarity— of who we are—for the pre-1972 groups was emphasized by one of those who managed to stay in Uganda:

After Amin told everyone to leave, there was just a few of us in Kampala. Some were Hindus, some were Muslim; there was two Sikh families also. So we looked out for each other. We are all Indians. One month we would all meet at the *mandir* [Hindu temple], the next time at the mosque. Then we would see, who is there, who is not there. And we checked to see if all were all safe. Did they need anything? (P. S., 2003).

Now at least two Hindu temples are fully opera- tional again in Kampala and while they cater to the entire Hindu community, it is the new arriv- als, many of them young men working as custo- dians, drivers, and clerks who view themselves as on the way to Europe or the United States, who meet regularly for prayer meetings, meals, and a connection to "home." These young men seek comfort within a communal space that is familiar and rewards them, in a sense, for expressing who they were (that is, Indian and Hindu). Yet, the men see the temple as a transi- tory space, a way station on their route to the West. For these young workers who had little stake in the place, the temples provided a feeling of "home," of "India," while for the pre-1972 Indian community for whom Uganda *is* home, the temples represent not a place of nostalgia but of rooted cultural practice.

As for politics, most Museveni-era Indians are interested only to the extent that it can enhance their economic position. A professor at Makerere University in Kampala said:

The new [Indian] immigrants are not interested in local issues or politics except to the extent that it affects their ability to do business. *Their ties are to India. They stay here only as long as the can make money.* If their profits stop, they will leave (S. A., 2003, emphasis added).

Many other interviewees confirmed this account. The "new immigrants" seem to have little or no stake in the place beyond viewing it as a source of profit. At best, the new arrivals have a "leg in two places" (R. P., 2003). This analysis echoes Rad- hakrishnan's reflection on "ethnicity in the age of diaspora" (2003, p. 125): While Museveni-era

Indians may have financial investment in Uganda, their emotional investment is in "India."

Among the Indians with ties to pre-1972 Uganda, a few actively take part in political campaigns, party politics, and elections. Two Indians were elected to positions at the Local Council III level, which is similar to an alderperson representing a district of an American city. One of them represents a district of predominantly poor and working class Ugandans while the other represents a district more evenly mixed between Indians and Ugandans. In addition, the latter also has been particularly active in petitioning the Constitutional Committee of Uganda to include Indians as an indigenous population of Uganda. By legal definition, all ethnic groups living in Uganda in 1927, the year the country's borders were officially surveyed by the British colonial government, are considered Uganda's indigenous populations. This Local Council III representative has argued that since Indians were living in Uganda in 1927, they ought to be considered one of Uganda's 85 or so indigenous groups (P. K., 2003). Being designated indigenous would give many Indians a true "stake in the place." However, P. K. also insists that being designated an indigenous Ugandan would not make him any less an Indian.

> I am of Ugandan soil. But I am Indian. My great-grandfather came from Kutch [a region in India bordering Pakistan]. We still speak Kutchi[5] in the house. My wife only watches Indian serials. Yes, Indians must interact with Ugandans but we also should retain our culture and the institutions that can keep it alive (P. K., 2003).

P. K. makes clear that for some in the diaspora, having a stake in the place of long-time residence does not necessarily diminish a connection to "home," which for P. K. was symbolized by ancestry, language, and even popular culture. P. K. represents one way that Indians in Uganda embody assimilation or integration. Home, for P. K., may be best described as multi-local but with one location (India) being most salient only in the nostalgic imagination, which is kept alive through "home" language and media.

Media liberalization provided an opportunity to invest in radio and television but investing in local media was limited and programming dedicated to Indian communities scarce. However, the opportunity to create cable television networks for the Indian community was attractive to Indian businessmen. For example, though most Indians moved tentatively, if at all, into the media sector, two Indian businessmen whose families were among those that remained in Kampala after 1972 invested quickly in FM radio stations. They already had a stake in the place and their stations catered to local interests and tastes in music and information with only minimal programming targeted toward Indians.

In contrast, those Indians who were recent arrivals took advantage of a business opportunity to establish cable and satellite television systems. While almost every Indian family in Kampala has a subscription to one of the cable systems (B. B., 2003), it is the transient young Indian men who seem particularly tied to these programs. In a sense, the Indian programming is their anchor, which recreates a feeling of home in Kampala. I ran into a group of these men as they were leaving their shared flat near the grounds of the university and we conversed about their experiences in Kampala. In terms of their media use and their orientation to Uganda, one of them said:

> We work and we watch Indian serials. *We don't watch the other [local] shows because we don't know the language and we don't care about the [local] news.* We don't go out, we don't have friends outside; we cook only at the flat. ... We want to go to London or America. There we will make more money and live a better life than here (A. A., 2003, emphasis added).

A. A. and his friends have no stake in the place but the Indian cable system, like the Hindu temples in the city, helps them to feel at home. However, home means familiar themes, stories and film stars, but it is not something that must be returned to immediately, if ever.

Will Indians other than the pre-1972 community ever have a stake in the place? Perhaps, but it may take a generation or more. P. K.'s son, for example, attends school with Ugandan children and moves easily between English at school, Luganda with his Ugandan friends, and Kutchi at home. Many of the schools that were reclaimed by Indians have Indian and Ugandan staff and students who seem to mix easily and comfortably. As I observed in several Indian homes, young people watch a variety of *local* indigenous language programming along with Indian satellite television programs.

Flexible essentialism

Some Ugandans told me (in a sincere attempt to compliment me—I am of Indian heritage) that Indians and Jews are the world's best business people. This ages-old stereotype was in play when Museveni invited Indians to return to Uganda. He said he wanted their business acumen and their abilities to negotiate global markets on behalf of Ugandan industries (Herculean Task of Winning Back Asian Indians, 1997). Indians in Uganda have at times embraced this stereotype by claiming that they do, indeed, possess business skills no other group has and arguing that their presence can invigorate the Ugandan economy. Indians have asserted this essentialized cultural quality to justify investments in Uganda, demand favorable financial terms from the government, and maintain hiring practices that often exclude Ugandans.

In terms of activities within the media sector, Indian involvement reinforces the perception that Indians are business savvy, an idea that Indian entrepreneurs embrace as they negotiate the local business world. For example, unlike the two long-time Indian businessmen who invested immediately in FM radio, the newly arrived Indian businessmen resisted investing in that sector. P. K., the Indian businessman and community leader, told me:

The [domestic] media sector is weak. The whole sector is severely underdeveloped. Indians are, by nature, risk averse, so Indians do not invest there [in the media sector] because it's hard to make any money (P. K., 2003).

Thus, local Indian entrepreneurs calculated that there was only a small market for Indian-oriented programs and the stations in which Indians ultimately invested were targeted toward listeners with much broader, pan-ethnic tastes (N. K., 2003; J. O., 2003).

Another example of Indian community embracing and asserting their business-acumen identity is evidenced in the negotiations between the Indian Association of Uganda and Radio Uganda. The association had asked for one hour of time per week to broadcast a show devoted to news, music, and business concerns for Uganda's Indian community. Radio Uganda wanted payment for access to its studios and airtime. The association argued, however, that the time ought to be free of cost since Radio Uganda is a government service for all Ugandans. One of the negotiators for the Association, R. T. said (only half in jest, I suspect):

They are not asking anyone else for payment, only us. But in any case, what kind of businessman would I be if we agreed to their terms. We need to get a good deal (R. T., 2003).

R. T. revealed here how the association's negotiating position is justified, in part, by asserting the supposedly essential identity of the Indian as a shrewd businessman.

Though Indians, at times, showcase their businessman identity, one business owner said that Indians actually prefer to be "invisible" regarding their actual business activities

because when we are seen in our shops [or in our] cars, that is taken by them [Ugandans] automatically as success and that creates resentment. In reality, the shop owners, so many of the businessmen are not so successful (S. P., 2003).

The strategic nature of asserting identity as expert entrepreneurs is highlighted by the fact that Indians do not want to be perceived by the general public as successful. They only want to reveal that element when it suits their purpose. Indians have played up their business acumen as reason enough to expect acceptance by Ugandans.

Another aspect of Indian identity that is occasionally and strategically asserted by the Ugandan Indian community (as well as by Indian migrant communities the world over; see Thompson [2002]; Lal [1999]) is what could be called their perceived cultural superiority around Hinduism. Some Indians in Uganda take a great deal of pride in one particular story about community resistance to Amin's security officers. The tale supposedly highlights extreme devotion to their religion. A third-generation banker recalled how his father and two friends, all who had remained in Kampala after the expulsion order, refused the demands of the Kampala City Council to hand over the deed and keys to the Hindu temple just off the main marketplace in Kampala.

> They [the council] sent police and still they [the three Indians] refused and finally the police beat them up. My father was taken to State House [a detention center] and beaten again. He was released later but KCC didn't get the temple (S. T., 2003).

He said his father "put himself at risk for *our* traditional values" (S. T., 2003, emphasis added). Others told similar tales of protecting the temple and, therefore, Hinduism, in various ways. This assertion of past piety not only was used to claim current religious distinction vis-à-vis black Ugandans, but also was used as part of an argument for reclaiming properties such as offices or houses formerly linked to the temple. For example, community leaders insisted that Indian children must have the opportunity to attend "culture classes" at or near a temple and managed to secure a space adjacent to the largest Hindu temple in Kampala (P. P., 2003).

However, the Hindu identity in Uganda is an exclusive construction in the sense that it is articulated with community property ownership (of temples, schools, and businesses) and middle class status. Thus, publicly asserted Hindu identity in Uganda often excludes not only black Ugandans but also certain Indians such as the transient workers and Muslims. Thus, on the one hand, flexible essentialism helps the Indian community at large assert an identity (as unparalleled business people and devout Hindus) that justifies their presence in Uganda. On the other hand, flexible essentialism contributes to an internal fragmentation of the community in which a self-defined elite assigns inferior status to low-wage, transient Indian workers and to non-Hindus.

CONCLUSION

In a historical study of Indians in the United States, Vijay Prashad (2000) pointed out that Indian labor was desired, but their culture was not—except in the most exoticized and demeaning forms. For the approximately 20 million Indians in the diaspora today, this situation is still true in many ways. In an ironic inversion of this formulation, many Indians in Uganda desire the country as an opportunity for realizing wealth and profit but generally they do not want to participate in Ugandan culture. Instead, they desire selective participation and a culturally distinct community.

But what is the nature of the community? What is its identity? Indian cultural identity in Uganda is signaled, in part, by the efforts to strategically assert "Indian" essential characteristics and culture in Uganda; efforts such as reclaiming Hindu temples and schools, performing Indian culture at public meetings, and establishing a cable television system that downlinks programming specifically for the Indians. The understanding of community is based, at least in part, on a discourse about "home" that emphasizes narrow notions of "Indian-ness," which, in turn, most highly privileges middle-class, business-and-property-owning Hindus, even though the number of Indians occupying all these categories simultaneously is relatively small and the actual demographics of the Indian community are more complicated. Mamdani (1995, p. 89) notes that this narrowly constructed community—particularly its class dimension—was emphasized in international news reporting of the return of

Indians to Uganda. Perhaps the formation of an Indian community identity around the axes of religion, class, and capital accumulation is not so surprising given that Hindu fundamentalism, with a vision of global commercial reach, has emerged as a core feature of Indian ethnic consciousness and community mobilization among certain Indian immigrants and their descendants all over the world (Gillespie, 1995; Lal, 1999).

What is the role of media in this process of binding a diasporic community together? Who is included in the community of Ugandan Indians? And what are the consequences of this configuration? It seems that there may be a mutually reinforcing relationship in which asserted Indian distinctiveness in Uganda, aided by highly selective participation in the domestic media industry and the establishment of a parallel cable television system carrying transnational media content and catering to Indian tastes and preferences, may help to preserve an *imagined* unity of Indian community identity in Uganda with "Indianness" at its core and an *imagined* seamless transnational connection to the idea of "India." The emphasis on the imagination is not meant to suggest that Ugandans are steeped in false consciousness or that they have been somehow duped into embracing community unity and transnational connections. Instead, the emphasis is meant to convey the centrality of the work of the imagination to the discursive formation of "home" and to the assertions of cultural identities in diasporic communities. The ways in which Indians participate strategically within the economic, political, and cultural arenas of Ugandan life has some resonance with Chakravartty's analysis (2000) of South Indian flexible citizenship in the United States. In addition, some Indians in Uganda mobilize certain elements of cultural identities assigned to them—in a process of flexible essentialism—in order to rationalize their selective participation in Ugandan life.

Lal (1999) and Prashad (2000) remind us that segments of diasporic communities are not only the most fervent and enthusiastic supporters of what they perceive to be the hallowed traditions

of "home," but they can also be committed to the most retrograde versions of those traditions. This kind of Indian identity that is constructed through a process of an "imaginative rediscovery" of a past, is part of the identity formation process discussed by Hall (1990, p. 224). It is the kind of identity that communities who feel somehow vulnerable or insecure (like some diasporic communities, for example), may try to establish by harkening back to a glorious history and cultural characteristics, full of time-proven traditions, values, skills, and faith. But lurking below this rhetorically singular identity are a number of discontinuities and instabilities that have been created by the actual diversity of the community. This diversity is captured both by the dilemma of feeling at home vs. having a stake in the place and the activation of flexible essentialism.

INTERVIEWS

S. A. (March, 2003). Professor of Library Sciences, Makerere University, Kampala.

A. A. (March 17, 2003). Worker in Indian-owned Kampala dry-goods store.

B. B. (March 19, 2003). Manager, Siti Cable, Kampala.

P. K. (March 18, 2003). Local Council III, Kampala Central District.

N. K. (March 20, 2003). General Manager, Sanyu 2000 FM radio.

J. O. (March 20, 2003). Marketing Manager, Dembe FM radio.

T. P. (May 31, 2000). Head, Gujarati Samaj. Former Chairman, India Association of Uganda.

P. P. (March 25, 2003). Member, Gujarati Samaj, Indian cultural organization.

R. P. (March 20, 2003). Head, Uganda-India Friendship Society.

S. P. (March 24, 2003). Chairman, India Association of Uganda.

P. S. (March 18, 2003). Owner, Shell Petrol Station.

S. T. (March 19, 2003). Owner, S.T. Forex Bureau, banking and foreign exchange company.

R. T. (May 24, 2000). Chairman, India Association of Uganda; business owner.

R. T. (March 17, 2003). Past Chairman, Indian Association of Uganda; business owner.

NOTES

1. A vast majority of Indians in Uganda, then and now, are Hindus. In much smaller numbers are Sikhs and Ismaili Muslims.

2. Paul Gilroy has used this exact phrase previously but for a different purpose. In a discussion about the "idea of the black racial family" and its various connections to the cultural and the pastoral, to kinship and bio-politics, and to the ideal and the imaginary, he wrote that despite the reality of the "unashamedly hybrid character of black Atlantic cultures," black neonationalist political and academic discourses strategically invoke one or the other versions of the "essential" black family to promote political or theoretical agendas. This appeal to different versions of the "black family," Gilroy wrote, "is best understood as flexible essentialism" (1993, p. 99).

3. Similarly, there is a strategic dimension to the concept of flexible citizenship: There are "moments and motivations behind the shifts and slippages from one [essential] subject position to another" (Lee, 2006, p. 214). Lee's point is important because in recognizing "shifts and slippages" among subject positions, she highlights something that is often overlooked: that even essential identities might have multiple dimensions.

4. Initials have been used throughout to identify the interviewees while ensuring their anonymity.

5. Kutchi is the indigenous language of the Kutch region of western India.

REFERENCES

Abidi, S. (1996). The return of Asians to Uganda. *African Quarterly, 36,* 45–58.

Adams, B., & Bristow, M. (1978). The politico-economic position of Ugandan Asians in the colonial and independence eras. *Journal of Asian and African Studies, 13,* 151–166.

Adams, D., & Bristow, M. (1979). Ugandan Asian expulsion experiences: Rumour and reality. *Journal of Asian and African Studies, 14,* 191–203.

Aksoy, A., & Robins, K. (2003). Banal transnationalism: The difference that television makes. In K. Karim (Ed.), *The media of diaspora* (pp. 89–104). London, UK: Routledge.

Appadurai, A. (1996). *Modernity at large: Cultural dimensions of globalization.* Minneapolis: University of Minnesota Press.

Brah, A. (1996). *Cartographies of diaspora: Contesting identities.* London, UK: Routledge.

Chakravartty, P. (2000). *The emigration of high-skilled workers to the United States: Flexible citizenship and India's information economy.* Working paper. Center for Comparative Immigration Studies. University of California, San Diego.

Clifford, J. (1992). Traveling cultures. In L. Grossberg, C. Nelson, & P. Treicher (Eds.), *Cultural studies* (pp. 96–116). New York, NY: Routledge.

Clifford, J. (1994). Diasporas. *Cultural Anthropology, 9*(3), 302–338.

Cohen, R. (1997). *Global diasporas: An introduction.* London, UK: UCL Press.

Cornell, S., & Hartmann, D. (1998). *Ethnicity and race: Making identities in a changing world.* Thousand Oaks, CA: Pine Forge Press.

Cunningham, S., & Sinclair, J. (Eds.). (2001). *Floating lives: The media and Asian diaspora.* Lanham, MD: Rowman and Littlefield.

Dudrah, R. K. (2002). Zee TV-Europe and the construction of a pan-European South Asian identity. *Contemporary South Asia, 11*(2), 163–181.

Durham, M. (2004). Constructing the "new ethnicities": Media, sexuality, and diaspora identity in the lives of South Asian immigrant girls. *Critical Studies in Media Communication, 21*(2), 140–161.

Gillespie, M. (1995). *Television, ethnicity and cultural change.* London, UK: Routledge.

Gilroy, P. (1993). *Black Atlantic: Modernity and double consciousness.* Cambridge, MA: Harvard University Press.

Hall, S. (1990). Cultural identity and diaspora. In J. Rutherford (Ed.), *Identity, community, culture, difference* (pp. 237–247). London, UK: Lawrence and Wishart.

Hall, S. (1996). The West and the rest: Discourse and power. In S. Hall, D. Held, D. Hubert, & K. Thompson (Eds.), *Modernity: An introduction to modern societies* (pp. 184–227). Cambridge, MA: Blackwell.

Herculean Task of Winning Back Asian Investors. (1997, November 10). *New Vision,* 1.

Inda, J. X. (2000). A flexible world: Capitalism, citizenship and postnational zones. *PoLAR, Political and Legal Anthropology Review, 23,* 86–102.

Karim, K. (2003). *The media of diaspora.* London, UK: Routledge.

Lall, V. (1999). The politics of history on the Internet: Cyber-diasporic Hinduism and the North American Hindu diaspora. *Diaspora, 8,* 137–172.

Lee, R. (2006). "Flexible citizenship": Strategic Chinese identities in Asian Australian literature. *Journal of Intercultural Studies, 27,* 213–227.

Mallapragada, M. (2000). The Indian diaspora in the U.S.A. and around the web. In D. Gauntlett (Ed.), *Web studies: Rewriting media studies for the digital age* (pp. 179–185). London, UK: Arnold.

Mamdani, M. (1984). *Imperialism and fascism in Uganda.* Kampala, UG: Fountain.

Mamdani, M. (1995). *And fire does not always beget ash: Critical reflections on the NRM.* Kampala, UG: Monitor.

Mamdani, M. (1999). *Politics and class formation in Uganda.* Kampala, UG: Fountain.

Manuel, P. (2000). *East Indian music in the West Indies: Tan-singing, chutney, and the making of Indo-Caribbean culture.* Philadelphia, PA: Temple University Press.

Marrett, V. (1987). *Immigrants settling in the city.* Leicester, UK: Leicester University Press.

Mitra, A. (2005). Creating immigrant identities in cybernetic space: Examples from a non-resident Indian website. *Media, Culture & Society, 27,* 371–390.

Mutibwa, P. (1992). *Uganda since independence.* Trenton, NJ: Africa Press.

Naficy, H. (2003). Narrowcasting in diaspora: Middle Eastern television in Los Angeles. In K. Karim (Ed.), *The media of diaspora* (pp. 51–62). London, UK: Routledge.

Ong, A. (1999). *Flexible citizenship: The cultural logic of transnationality.* Durham, NC: Duke University Press.

Prashad, V. (2000). *The karma of brown folk.* Minneapolis: University of Minnesota Press.

Radhakrishnan, R. (2003). Ethnicity in the age of diaspora. In J. E. Braziel & A. Mannur (Eds.), *Theorizing diaspora* (pp. 119–131). Cambridge, MA: Blackwell.

Ray, M. (2001). Bollywood down under: Fiji Indian cultural history and popular assertion. In S. Cunningham & J. Sinclair (Eds.), *Floating lives: The media and Asian diasporas* (pp. 136–184). Lanham, MD: Rowman & Littlefield.

Sachedina, O. (2007). Uganda: The return; Asians back in Africa. *Frontline/World: Rough Cut* [Television News]. Retrieved June 6, 2007 from http://www.pbs.org/frontlineworld/rough/2007/05/uganda_the_retu.html.

Safran, W. (1991). Diasporas in modern societies. Myths of homeland and return. *Diaspora, 1,* 83–99.

Spivak, G. (1996). Subaltern studies: Deconstructing historiography. In D. Landry and G. MacLean (Eds.), *The Spivak reader* (pp. 203–235). London, UK: Routledge.

Sreberny, A. (2001). *The gaze of the media: Community, exile, and diaspora among the Ilil'.* Paper presented at the conference Rethinking Public Media in a Transnational Era, New York University.

Thompson, K. (2002). Border crossings and diasporic identities: Media use and leisure practices of an ethnic minority. *Qualitative Sociology, 25*(3), 409–418.

Tsagarousianou, T. (2004). Rethinking the concept of diaspora: Mobility, connectivity, and communication in a globalized world. *Westminster Papers in Communication and Culture, 1*(1), 52–66.

Tukahebwa, G. (1998). Privatization as a development strategy. In H. B. Hansen & M. Twaddle (Eds.), *Developing Uganda* (pp. 59–97). Kampala, UG: Fountain.

Vertovec, S. (1999). Three meanings of "diaspora," exemplified by South Asian religions. *Diaspora, 6*(3), 277–300.

Yadav, S. N. (1998). The return of Indians to Uganda. *Indian Journal of African Studies, 9,* 79–107.

8

REPRESENTING AND RECONSTRUCTING CHINATOWN

A Social Semiotic Analysis of Place Names in Urban Planning Policies of Washington, D.C.

JACKIE JIA LOU

INTRODUCTION

Chinatowns exist throughout the world. Like most Chinatowns in North America, the Chinatown in Washington, D.C. is located in the urban center. Originally formed along Pennsylvania Avenue after the first Chinese resident of the District settled there in 1851, it was relocated to the current site to make space for the Federal Triangle development project in 1927. It then slowly expanded from the block of H Street NW between 6th and 7th Streets (Chow, 1996; Hathaway & Ho, 2003). Eighty-five years later, it is still a small Chinatown, geographically and demographically, in comparison with its counterparts in larger North American cities, such as New York, San Francisco, or Toronto.

Its tiny frame, however, embodies a rather unique visual appearance. At the crossroads of H and 7th Streets stands the world's largest single-span traditional Chinese-style archway, glittering in the sun with gold shingles. Beyond the archway, the shop signs on most stores in the vicinity, whether or not they are Chinese-owned carry bilingual signs in Chinese and English. This consistently bilingual linguistic landscape is the result of a series of efforts by the local Chinese community in the 1980s to preserve the neighborhood by requiring all businesses in the area to have Chinese signage as an incorporated part of the District's urban planning policies (Pang & Rath, 2007). More recently, this particular visual representation of the neighborhood has been criticized by academics, journalists, as well as pedestrians. Most academic analyses of Chinatown's curious linguistic landscape phenomenon regard it as a commercial strategy to symbolically commodify the neighborhood and to turn it into a cultural tourism destination (cf., Pang & Rath, 2007; Lou, 2007; Leeman & Modan, 2009).

Local papers have attacked this landscape as "fake" (Gillette, 2003), or described it more poetically as "varnish" on a "vanishing neighborhood" (Moore, 2005). Although I concur with this interpretation to some extent, I also wonder whether or not the impression of inauthenticity can be blamed on the "varnish" alone. Is it not the stark contrast between representation and practice that makes the neighborhood look "fake"? While the Chinese community is held largely responsible for this policy regarding signage, who is responsible for the "vanishing neighborhood"? And why have so many non-Chinese owned stores that are also part of (trans-)national chains, such as Starbucks and Urban Outfitters, moved into the neighborhood in recent years?

All of these questions call for a careful examination of relevant urban planning policies. I began with a larger ethnographic, sociolinguistic study of the neighborhood (Lou, 2009), in which I observed several major changes regarding Chinatown. First, since 1980 the boundary of Chinatown had grown smaller. Second, the government's stance toward the preservation of the neighborhood had shifted. Third, new place names had emerged and gained importance in the area around Chinatown. Consequently, using the case of Washington, D.C.'s Chinatown, this chapter illustrates how discursive representations of places, such as toponyms or place names, are motivated by and have repercussions for their material constructions.

URBAN PLANNING POLICY AS DISCOURSE[1]

The images of postindustrial American cities are deeply intertwined with their economic development. As Sharon Zukin (1995) eloquently argued,

> culture is more and more the business of cities—the basis of their tourist attractions and their unique, competitive edge. The growth of cultural consumption (of art, food, fashion, music, tourism) and the industries that cater to that consumption fuel the city's symbolic economy, its visible ability to produce both symbols and space (p. 2).

Further, because of its central significance in urban economy, the cultural representation of a city is rarely a democratic process. Zukin observes, "[p]eople with economic and political power have the greatest opportunity to shape public culture by controlling the building of the city's public spaces in stone and concrete" (p. 11).

The nature of inequality and power inherent in representation and its material ramifications have caused many scholars to reclaim the central role of language and discourse in urban planning. Imploring geographers to pay attention to the role of language in place-making in general, human geographer Yi-Fu Tuan (1991) points out, "without speech, humans cannot even begin to formulate ideas, discuss them, and translate them into action that culminates in a built place" (p. 684). The power of words is even more apparent in the commodification of urban space in the name of culture—an entirely new public discourse has to be constructed before the actual place can be built. In his research on the urban development of Times Square, for example, Reichl (1999) observed that the final approval of Times Square's redevelopment was dependent on a political discourse that "drew on cultural images of Times Square past, present, and future" (p. 3). Jensen (2007) goes even further to claim that "when the issue is urban planning and intervention, no plan is made without a narrative element" (p. 217).

The growing interest in language and discourse in urban planning and geography runs parallel to the renewed interest among linguists in re-examining the relationship between language, space, and place. In traditional variationist sociolinguistics, place is conceived of in purely objective, physical terms (Johnstone, 2004, p. 65). But for others who study language, including sociologists and anthropologists, physical places are always to some extent constructed through discourse (Schegloff, 1972). In this sense, language becomes one of the main semiotic means by which place, as "social construction *par excellence*" comes into existence (Boas, 1934 quoted in Basso, 1988, p. 101).

Narrative analysis is among the most often studied forms of language in connection with this experiential view of place. Like place, narrative is a phenomenological concept; it is the chief means through which human beings recapitulate, organize, and construct experiences, and thereby learn about the world around us (Schiffrin, 1994; Berger, 1997). Researchers often turn to public discourses to illustrate the constructive power of narrative in place-making. For example, Johnstone (1990) examined a corpus of local newspaper stories about the flood in the U.S. city of Fort Wayne, Indiana, in 1982 and found that the city was increasingly portrayed as an animate heroic figure who "saved itself" (1990, pp. 109–125). Finnegan's 1998 study of Milton Keynes, a new city in southern-central England, found that urban planning documents portrayed the city as organically growing into an ideal place for people to live and work—a stark contrast to the story circulated in the mass media that represented the city as a "concrete jungle," and "an artificial and unnatural settlement" (p. 41). It is in these public stories that the ability of narrative in constructing place becomes most evident.

However to date, the linguists' contributions in this area seem to have been limited to representation alone. Few studies have examined the urban planning policies as discourses (with the exception of two urban scholars, Richardson & Jensen, 2003), and little is known regarding how exactly language contributes to the material construction of place. As Richardson and Jensen (2003) emphasize, urban planning policies are not only discourse constructions, they must "be understood in relation to their 'spatial object'"(p. 20). Consequently, this chapter examines the concrete connections between discourse and the place that it represents. Specifically, the analysis examines the semiotic properties of place names and suggests that indexicality[2] might be the key to understanding these connections.

PLACE NAMES AND SEMIOTICS

Place names have been studied in sociolinguistics and linguistic anthropology as a window into the spatial organization of cultural identities and social structures. In his study of language and landscape among the Western Apache, Basso (1988) observed that place names not only describe the geographic features but also evoke people and events. For example, in the Appalacian mountains, Blu (1996) noticed that three racial communities (White, Black, and Lumbee Indians) in the United States refer to the same place with different names. Even in mundane face-to-face interactions of focus group discussions, Myers (2006) found that participants frequently used place names as resources for identity management. Further, urban and political geographers have examined place names as discursive representations that frame and control spaces. Consider, for instance, that three new territories captured by the State of Israel were inscribed with Hebrew place names to reinforce the connection between the people and the land and to extend an Israeli nationalist ideology (Cohen & Kliot, 1992). In Osaka, Japan, an area formerly known as "Kamagasaki" was renamed as "Yoseba" to erase the stigma associated with the old place name (especially after riots occurred there in the 1960s) and to create a new policy area where day laborers are segregated from their neighbors (Haraguchi, 2003).

Many studies of place names treat them as textual representations—as names that simply designate a particular place. As Rose-Redwood (2008) notes, "few studies of place-naming, however, have explicitly examined the performative dimensions of toponymic inscription" (p. 881). Rose-Redwood's case study of New York City is theoretically grounded by the linguistic philosopher, J. L. Austin's 1975 seminal work, *How To Do Things with Words*. For Austin and for Rose-Redwood, to the extent that words can create the things they are said to describe—they are performative. Rose-Redwood argues that the renaming of Sixth Avenue in New York as Avenue of the America's produces "a space of political utterances," in which the new street name was rendered ineffective by ordinary New Yorkers' persistence in calling the street "Sixth Avenue." In this chapter, I would like to suggest another theoretical framework, specifically C. S. Peirce's writings on semiotics, which I believe offer a complementary, if not superior, approach to study the materiality of place names.

In classic Peircian semiotics (Peirce, 1991 [1873]), a sign is related to the object that it represents in three different ways, which I briefly define and illustrate by using "Hong Kong," the name of the author's current place of residence, as an example. First, a sign is an *icon*, when it resembles the object, such as a realist painting or an onomatopoeia. "Hong Kong" can be considered *iconic* in that it literally means "fragrant harbor" (also the title of a novel by John Lanchester), thus describing its geographic feature. Second, a sign is a *symbol*, when it is arbitrarily related to the object, that is, purely through cultural conventions. For example, the object "tree" is represented in different languages by different words. "Hong Kong," then, can be symbolically represented for some as a "shopping paradise," for others as a "culture desert," or as "Asia's World City," by a government orchestrated publicity campaign (Flowerdew, 2004). Third, a sign is an *index*, when it simply points to the object of the represented, for instance, the exit sign. "Hong Kong" is thus an index in the utterance "Welcome to Hong Kong," as it points to the location of the speaker.

It is not difficult to see that place names are more often used as index than icon or symbol. However, perhaps because the indexical property of place names is so obvious, it has been rarely examined. At the same time, among the three types of semiotic relationships, *indexicality* has garnered most attention in the field of linguistic anthropology. In the words of Duranti (1997), the concept highlights the fact that "communication is not only the use of symbols that 'stand for' beliefs, feelings, identities, events, it is also a way of pointing to, presupposing or bringing into the present context beliefs, feelings, identities, events" (p. 36). Thus, in light of the preceding discussion, I suggest that, in order to fully understand how the discursive representation of

place shapes the physical environment, it is essential to investigate how place names function as an *index* in addition to functioning as a *symbol* or *icon*.

DATA AND METHODS

This case study traces the occurrences of the place name Chinatown in the urban planning policies of Washington, D.C. Does each occurrence function primarily as an icon, symbol, or index? How does the discourse surrounding the occurrence represent Chinatown? How have these representations shifted over time? And what are the material motivations and consequences of such shifts in the semiotic representations of the neighborhood?

To answer these questions, I examine three urban planning documents that directly concern the Chinatown neighborhood: (1) District of Columbia Municipal Regulations, which includes Section 1705 ("Chinatown"), Chapter 17 "Downtown Development Overlay District") and Title 11 ("Zoning") first published in 1991 (Office of Zoning of the District of Columbia, 1991);[3] (2) The Downtown Action Agenda, published in 2000 (Office of Planning of the District of Columbia, 2000); and (3) Chapter 9 ("Urban Design") and Chapter 16 ("Central Washington Element") of the Comprehensive Plan of Washington, D.C., revised in 2006 (Office of Planning of the District of Columbia, 2006). Close discourse and semiotic analyses of these texts reveal several shifts in the official representations of Chinatown over the years and offer an explanation for the difficulties faced by the local Chinese community to preserve the neighborhood. These three policy documents were chosen for the analysis because they are the only urban planning policies that explicitly refer to the design of Chinatown.

Although the District of Columbia Municipal Regulations on zoning still carries more legal authority than the other two texts, it is anticipated that these "softer" documents will inform future "harder" policies in the policymaking cycle.

Analysis

The three policy documents used for this study demonstrate the growing emphasis on the development of the downtown area of Washington, D.C. An overlay district[4] was created in the 1991 Zoning Regulation to apply special development policies. The priority of this area was again accentuated in the 2000 Downtown Action Agenda. Its importance was reiterated and to some extent even augmented in the 2006 Comprehensive Plan, in which a new policy area called "Central Washington" was created to include more areas beyond the traditional downtown. As stated in the 2000 Downtown Action Agenda, "the last economic boom left in its wake a strong office environment, but not a dynamic downtown" (Office of Planning of the District of Columbia, 2000, p. 1). The overarching goal of these evolving policies has been to turn the area into a place where people will come not only to work during the day but also to live, to shop, and to attend events and activities both day and night. The ramifications of this vision of a "living downtown" affect both Chinatown and the various other neighborhoods encompassed in the area. Therefore, any changes in the representations of the neighborhood must be considered against the backdrop of the shifts of urban planning priorities in Washington, D.C. on a larger spatial scale.

Although this is not a quantitative analysis, it is important to mention as an overview, that the place name, Chinatown, occurs a total of 41 times in the three policy documents examined (nine times in the 1991 Zoning Regulation, seven times in the 2002 Downtown Action Agenda, and 25 times in the much longer 2006 D.C. Comprehensive Plan). Table 8.1 provides an overview. In the first two documents, Chinatown primarily functions as an index, pointing to the physical area of Chinatown: 8 out of 9 times in the Zoning Regulations and 6 out of 7 times in the Downtown Action Agenda. Its function in the Comprehensive Plan is more varied: 10 out of 25 times as a symbol, defining the significance of Chinatown, 10/25 as an index, pointing to the area, and 5/25 as an icon, depicting what it looks like. The

difference can be, to a certain extent, explained by the different genres of these texts. The District Regulation and the Action Agenda are policy documents that focus on the actions that can or cannot be carried out in the indexed areas. On the other hand, the main objective of the Comprehensive Plan is to provide reasons for these actions, hence the emphasis on the symbolic descriptions of these areas.

It is also important to note the temporal sequence in which these documents were published. The temporal order of these texts highlights the anticipatory orientation of policy discourse (Scollon, 2008) and its critical role in mediating between representation in discourses and changes in the material world. The Zoning Regulation and the Downtown Action Agenda preceded the development of the 2006 Comprehensive Plan and were very likely informed by an earlier version of a Comprehensive Plan, which unfortunately is no longer available. At the same time, it is reasonable to expect that the 2006 Comprehensive Plan could provide justifications for actions sanctioned by future zoning regulations or other regulatory texts.

In the following analysis, I discuss each semiotic function of the place name Chinatown in these documents in turn. After showing how the iconic and symbolic representations of Chinatown have changed over the years, I link these changes with the shifts in the indexical definitions of the neighborhood, which pave the road for the material reconstruction of Chinatown.

"Chinatown" as an Icon

Like most dictionaries, the *Oxford English Dictionary* defines Chinatown as "a section of a large town, especially a seaport, in which Chinese live as a colony and to a great extent follow their own customs." Its etymological history shows that the place name originated in late 1880s and was associated with descriptive terms such as "wild with joy" (1857), mounting "noise" (1892) and "filth and wretchedness" (1902). To the extent that they describe the geographic and social features of the neighborhood, these previous identifications

Table 8.1 Overview of the Occurrences of Chinatown

	"Chinatown" as Icon	*"Chinatown" as Symbol*	*"Chinatown" as Index*	*Total Number of Occurrences*
1991 Zoning Regulation	0	1	8	9
2000 Downtown Action Agenda	0	1	6	7
2006 Comprehensive Plan (Chapter 9 and 16)	5	10	10	25
Total	5	12	24	41

can be considered as iconic representations of Chinatown, such as those more often found in literary genres such as travel writing and biographies. In the three urban policy documents examined, Chinatown appears as an icon only in the 2006 Comprehensive Plan. Among these five occurrences, textual descriptions of the visual features of the neighbourhood are juxtaposed with photographic representations.

The first occurrence of Chinatown as an icon is found in the second sentence of the excerpt below.

> Chinatown presents an interesting case. *While on the one hand, preserving Chinatown's authenticity has to be about more than just preserving facades or using Chinese characters on street signs, on the other hand, there has been a marked reduction in the number of Chinese businesses.* It remains to be seen if Chinatown can maintain an authentic role as the center of a dispersed Asian community. Historic preservation should be strongly promoted [sic] Downtown where the historic fabric is still largely intact, but contemporary architecture also should flourish in places where new construction is appropriate (Office of Planning of the District of Columbia, 2006, p.10, emphasis added by the researcher).

The highlighted sentence captures two contradictory images of Chinatown: "preserving facades or using Chinese characters on street signs" and "marked reduction in the number of Chinese businesses." An undated photograph captioned as "H Street NW, Chinatown" is shown to illustrate the mentioned façade and signs with Chinese characters (Figure 8.1). Ironically, the supermarket shown in the picture actually also illustrates the second sentence, as it was closed in 2005.

Each side of this paradox is then further elaborated in a special Chinatown section of the same document (pp. 30–32).

> The distinctive "Friendship Arch" at the intersection of 7th and H Streets NW is the centre of Washington's Chinatown. Decorative metal lattice work and railings, Chinese signs, and Chinese façade and roof details greet visitors to the blocks of H Street between 5th Street and 8th Street NW (Figure 2, para. 1613.1).

First, Chinatown is iconically represented by the "Friendship Arch," supported by an illustrative photograph of the arch to the left of the paragraph on the same page (Figure 8.2). Then, Chinatown is verbally described in terms of "decorative metal lattice work and railings, Chinese signs, and Chinese façade and roof details," visual features that visitors could expect to use to identify the neighborhood. Following this iconic description of the neighborhood is an indexical definition of its boundary as composed of three blocks of H Street, which I examine later as an index.

Figure 8.1 A photographic representation of Chinatown in the Washington, D.C. 2006 Comprehensive Plan

H Street NW, Chinatown

Source: Office of Planning of the District of Columbia. (2006). *Comprehensive Plan.* Washington, DC: Office of Planning.

Figure 8.3 A photo of Chinese traditional dance in the 2006 Comprehensive Plan with original caption

Today Chinatown is struggling to retain its identity as the area around it booms with new retail, office, entertainment, and housing development.

Source: Office of Planning of the District of Columbia. (2006). Comprehensive Plan. Washington, DC: Office of Planning.

Figure 8.2 Photograph of Friendship Archway as an iconic photo of Chinatown in the 2006 Comprehensive Plan

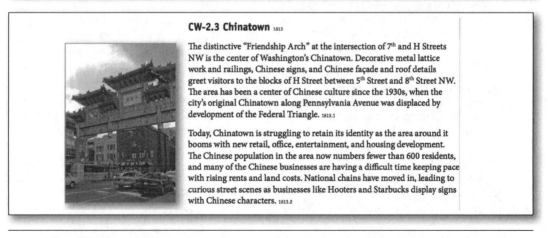

CW-2.3 Chinatown 1613

The distinctive "Friendship Arch" at the intersection of 7th and H Streets NW is the center of Washington's Chinatown. Decorative metal lattice work and railings, Chinese signs, and Chinese façade and roof details greet visitors to the blocks of H Street between 5th Street and 8th Street NW. The area has been a center of Chinese culture since the 1930s, when the city's original Chinatown along Pennsylvania Avenue was displaced by development of the Federal Triangle. 1613.1

Today, Chinatown is struggling to retain its identity as the area around it booms with new retail, office, entertainment, and housing development. The Chinese population in the area now numbers fewer than 600 residents, and many of the Chinese businesses are having a difficult time keeping pace with rising rents and land costs. National chains have moved in, leading to curious street scenes as businesses like Hooters and Starbucks display signs with Chinese characters. 1613.2

Source: Office of Planning of the District of Columbia. (2006). Comprehensive Plan. Washington, DC: Office of Planning.

In the next paragraph of Figure 8.2, the visual landscape of Chinatown is immediately contrasted with its changing social landscape. Along with the dwindling Chinese population, the Chinese characters on the shop signs of non-Chinese-owned national chains are identified as a problem.

Curiously, a photograph of a traditional Chinese dance performance (Figure 8.3)—rather than the earlier iconic representation of a Chinatown street scene—carries a caption referring to Chinatown as "struggling to retain its identity." Through the caption, the photograph of traditional dance moves away from an icon toward becoming a symbol, a sign that has no resemblance to or physical connection with its referent. The next section of the analysis examines the more symbolic representations of Chinatown.

"Chinatown" as a Symbol

The common dictionary definition of Chinatown that was noted in the previous section also functions as a symbol loaded with cultural meanings, albeit often negative ones. As shown in the entry, Chinatown has been associated with words such as "wretchedness" and "sinister repute." These are subjective, affective values attached to the sign, which have over time become conventionalized perception. How is Chinatown then discursively constructed as a symbol in the policy documents?

The 1991 Zoning Regulation states the main objective of the listed policies is to

(a) Protect and enhance Chinatown as Downtown's only ethnic cultural area (Office of Zoning of the District of Columbia, 1991, p. 1).

This statement not only defines Chinatown as an "ethnic cultural area," but the quantifier "only" also suggests the area's potential to symbolically represent the ethnic cultural diversity of the entire Downtown area. Grammatically, Chinatown in this clause is the object, hence the receiver of the actions of "protecting and enhancing." The government, on the other hand, is the agent who performs the actions. The imperative clause also indicates that said actions will happen.

Yet, the zoning mandate for Chinatown is weakened in several ways by a similar statement in the 2000 Downtown Action Agenda:

Just north of Gallery Place, Chinatown should be preserved and enhanced as one of Downtown's most unique districts—offering special cultural and retail experiences.

In the Action Agenda, Chinatown's identity is less specifically defined as "one of Downtown's most unique districts," The participial phrase "offering special cultural and retail experiences" refines the area description slightly with the additional information explaining what is meant by "unique." The Action Agenda replaces the "ethnic" aspect of Chinatown found in the Zoning Regulation with "retail experiences." Second, in the grammatical structure of the sentence, Chinatown as the subject of a passive clause, is still the receiver of the actions of preservation and enhancement. However, it is now unclear who should carry out said actions of preservation or enhancement. Finally, the modal verb "should" conveys a weaker sense of certitude than the imperative clause. Thus, while in 1991, the actions are to be carried out without negotiations, in 2000, they are considered to be essential.

Chinatown's status as an ethnic and cultural area in downtown becomes even more uncertain in the 2006 Comprehensive Plan. Most occurrences of the place name arise in connection with discourses that bring the identity of Chinatown into question, as in the following excerpt:

Chinatown presents an interesting case. While on the one hand, preserving Chinatown's authenticity has to be about more than just preserving facades or using Chinese characters on street signs, on the other hand there has been a marked reduction in the number of Chinese businesses. It remains to be seen if Chinatown can maintain an authentic role as the centre of a dispersed Asian community.

Following the iconic description of the paradoxical image of Chinatown in the second sentence (discussed earlier), the last sentence of the paragraph acknowledges Chinatown's role "as the center of a dispersed Asian community." However, this is a reference to the past, as it adopts a highly agnostic stance toward the future through the hedging clause "it remains to be seen," the "if" conditional clause, and the modal verb "can." Furthermore, in the grammatical structure of the text, Chinatown changed from an object, the receiver of protection and preservation in the previous symbolic definitions, into a subject in the subordinate clause. Thus, Chinatown now appears to be taking responsibility for its own destiny.

The analysis so far has examined the shifts from iconic to symbolic representations of Chinatown in Washington, D.C. planning documents. What then are the material effects of these changes in the discourse? The next section takes up an analysis of the representation of the place name as an index.

"Chinatown" as an Index

C. S. Peirce defined indexes as signs that have "some kind of external relation with what they refer to" (Duranti, 1997, p.17). The external referent of a place name is obviously the physical space—in this case study, it is the neighborhood of Chinatown in Washington, D.C. But where exactly does it start and end? How is its boundary defined in the policies? In urban planning policies, how boundaries are defined determines whether or not a certain area is subject to specific rules and regulations. The analysis presented in this section first focuses on how definitions of Chinatown establish the indexical links between the place name and the geographic area to which it refers. The second part of the analysis then turns to look at how the definitions of other place names compete indexically with Chinatown for the geographic area.

The Chinatown section in the 1991 Zoning Regulation first outlines four policies to be applied to the area (Figure 8.4).

Among these protective measures, the first item (a) also includes a symbolic definition in the prepositional phrase "Chinatown as Downtown's only ethnic cultural area," which we discussed in the previous section. Then, it gives the indexical definition of the area in Item 1705.2:

> This section applies to properties in the following squares: 428, 452, 453, 485, and 486, and those portions of squares 429 and 454 that are north of a line extending the midpoint of G Place eastward from 9th Street to 6th Street.

Here, the area is defined in terms of numbered squares and portions of them, but it is not immediately clear what the referents of the numbered squares are. There is no figure below the paragraph or in the document appendix. Since "G Place," "9th Street," and "6th Street" could be indexing either the actual streets or the representations of them on a map, I located the Zoning Map, available as a separate document on the website of the Office of Planning. The Zoning Map is a set of 35 PDF files. Map 6 contains the Chinatown area. Figure 8.5 shows what the Map looks like when first opened.

Apart from several prominent geographic features such as Rock Creek meandering across the center-left of the city and the perfect round shape of the Naval Observatory to the west, few other places are easily identified. The map is covered in pale yellow shades (indicating buildings), ragged black lines (boundaries of overlay districts), and dotted or patterned red squares (Planned Unit Developments). Several times of zooming in later, familiar place names and street names are visible in light gray. As a result, it took several hours to finally locate the squares that constitute Chinatown as mentioned in Item 1705.2 of the Zoning Regulation (shown in Figure 8.6; boundary traced and highlighted in red by the researcher). In summary, the indexical connection between the place name "Chinatown" and the geographic area is established in three stages across two documents. First, the place name is textually defined in the Zoning Regulations in terms of numbered squares, which then index visual squares on the Zoning Map, which further index corresponding physical areas externally. The first indexical connection between the Zoning Regulations and the Map is also not clearly stated or perhaps assumed to be common knowledge shared by urban planners.

In comparison, the indexical definition of Chinatown in the 2000 Downtown Action Agenda was much easier to locate. It is circled on a somewhat simplified map, embedded as a figure in the document. The place name "Chinatown" is also printed directly over the physical area that it indexes. However, the shape of its

Figure 8.4 First two items of Title 11 of the 1991 D.C. Zoning Regulations

1705   CHINATOWN

1705.1   The principal policies and objectives from the Comprehensive Plan for the Chinatown area are to:

  (a) Protect and enhance Chinatown as Downtown's only ethnic cultural area;

  (b) Maintain and expand the existing concentration of retail uses emphasizing Chinese and Asian merchandise and related wholesale operations serving residents, visitors, tourists, and business travelers;

  (c) Reinforce the area's economic viability by encouraging mixed use development, including substantial housing, cultural and community facilities, offices, retail and wholesale businesses, and hotels; and

  (d) Protect existing housing and the most important historic buildings with suitable preservation controls, residential and commercial zones, and economic incentives.

1705.2   This section applies to properties in the following squares: 428, 452, 453, 485, and 486, and those portions of squares 429 and 454 that are north of a line extending the midpoint of G Place eastward from 9th Street to 6th Street.

Figure 8.5 The first glance at the Zoning Map

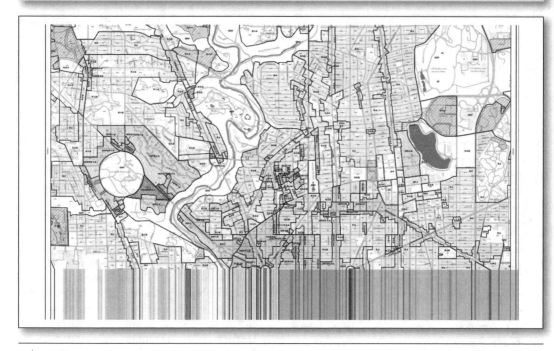

Source: Office of Zoning of the District of Columbia. (2000). *Zoning Regulations of the District of Columbia.* Washington, DC: Office of Documents and Administrative Issuances.

Figure 8.6 Chinatown indexed in the Zoning Map (1991)

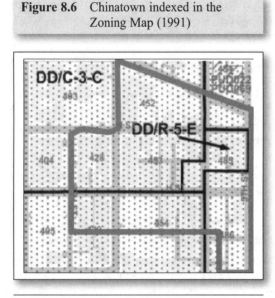

Source: Office of Zoning of the District of Columbia. (2000). *Zoning Regulations of the District of Columbia.* Washington, DC: Office of Documents and Administrative Issuances.

boundary has changed from the irregular polygon as shown above in Figure 8.6 to a much smaller rectangle with rounded corners (Figure 8.7). According to the map legend, the medium purple lines also indicate the neighborhood as an area in transition, which verges on a symbolic definition. So, the borderlines on the map do not simply define the physical boundaries of each area but also their changing significance in the context of urban transformation.

It also did not take too much effort to locate Chinatown in the 2006 Comprehensive Plan. It is highlighted in green with black borderlines and numbered 2.3, which according to the map legend on the same page, indexes Chinatown (Figure 8.8). Again, we can see that the area has morphed into a rectangular shape and is much smaller than that in the 1991 Zoning regulation.

This shrunken Chinatown, however, would be congruent with a general perception of the size of the neighborhood. Many people are not

aware of the reduction of its size over time in urban planning maps and policies. The size of Chinatown is not the only thing that has changed from 1991 to 2006. The modality of its visual representation on the map shifted over time as well.[5] In addition "Chinatown" is now faced with competition from other place names, notably "Gallery Place" and "Penn Quarter." While for the most part, these two places remain, on the surface, subareas of downtown, the space indexed by them has expanded and overlaps significantly with the area originally indexed as Chinatown.

The 1991 Zoning Regulation created a Downtown Development (DD) Overlay District, including various subareas (see 1700.1)

> The Downtown Development (DD) Overlay District is applied to the core of the Downtown area, including subareas identified in the Comprehensive Plan as the Downtown Shopping District (Retail Core), the Arts District, *Gallery Place, Chinatown, Pennsylvania Quarter*, Convention Center, and Mount Vernon Square, and areas designated for historical preservation and housing mixed use, which areas overlap geographically with the subareas (Emphasis added by the researcher).

Not only is Chinatown listed here as an equal subarea with Gallery Place and Pennsylvania Quarter, it also seems to enjoy a higher status. As shown in the table of contents of this section, the subsection 1705 is dedicated to the neighborhood, placing it in the same league with downtown Shopping District (1703) and Downtown Arts District (1704). The area indexed by Chinatown is also defined in this document (although as previously discussed, the definition is somewhat convoluted), whereas "Gallery Place" and "Pennsylvania Quarter" are left undefined.

Ten years later, the 2000 Downtown Action Agenda symbolically defines "the Gallery Place" as "the primary destination for regional and one-of-a-kind retail, entertainment, and cultural uses in Downtown" (p. 11). Indexically, it defines the area as "centered at the intersection of the

Figure 8.7 Chinatown indexed in 2000 Downtown Action Agenda

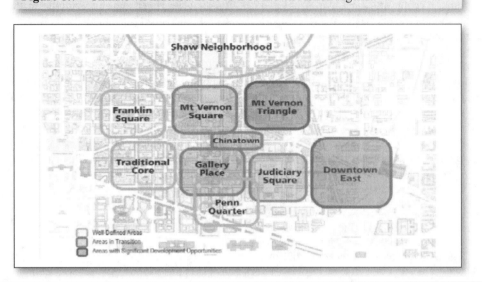

Source: Office of Planning of the District of Columbia. (2000). *Downtown Action Agenda*. Retrieved from http://planning.dc
.gov/DC/Planning/In+Your+Neighborhood/Wards/Ward+2/Small+Area+Plans+&+Studies/Downtown+Action+Agenda

Figure 8.8 Chinatown indexed in the 2006 Comprehensive Plan

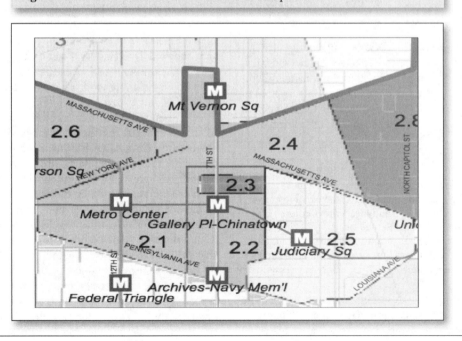

Source: Office of Planning of the District of Columbia. (2006). Comprehensive Plan. Washington, DC: Office of Planning.

F Street and 7th Street corridors," two blocks away from the center of Chinatown. At the same time, the boundary of "Gallery Place" is left undefined and thus open-ended. In fact, one of its projected "anchors"—the Gallery Place retail, entertainment, and residential complex—is located in Square 454, which falls partially within the borders of Chinatown as defined by the 1990 Zoning Regulation. The 2000 Downtown Action Agenda reads:

> Strategy One: Establish Gallery Place and 7th Street as a Center for Entertainment and Retail.
>
> Approximately 1 million square feet of new retail space should be strategically clustered at specific Downtown locations. The Gallery Place area, centered at the intersection of the F Street and 7th Street corridors, should be the primary destination for regional and one-of-a-kind retail, entertainment, and cultural uses in Downtown. The Gallery Place project on Square 454 will serve as one anchor for the area. It will offer 356,000 total square feet of retail and entertainment, with a 25-screen movie theater, numerous large entertainment restaurants and retailers, 160 residential units, and five levels of structured parking (p. 11).

The encroachment of Gallery Place into the Chinatown area is also reflected in the indexical definition, which is by the place names themselves. Three times out of 14 total occurrences of the place name "Gallery Place" in the Downtown Action Agenda, the name is conjoined with "Chinatown" with a slash mark, as in the following example.

> Parking Structures—New municipal parking garages at Judiciary Square, the existing convention center site, and near **the Gallery Place/Chinatown area** may be necessary to implement the "park once" program for visitors and downtown commuters (Office of Planning of the District of Columbia, 2000, p. 33, emphasis added).

In contrast to the conjunction mark "&," the slash indicates "Gallery Place" and "Chinatown" are alternative names for the same area (also note the singular form of "area" in the example).

This trend of merging Gallery Place with Chinatown, however, did not continue in the 2006 Comprehensive Plan. Out of 19 total occurrences of "Gallery Place" in this document, it only appears once with "Chinatown," listed conjoined with "and," as separate areas, and another time hyphenated with "Chinatown," as in the official name of the subway station. On the other hand, "Gallery Place" coexists instead with the place name "Penn Quarter," 10 out of 19 times, conjoined by the slash mark indicating alternatives. Together they constitute a "Policy Focus Area," indexically defined as:

> This Policy Focus area is located east of Metro center and the Retail Core. It is roughly bounded by 9th Street NW on the west, 5th street NW on the east, Pennsylvania Avenue NW on the south, and I Street NW on the north. The area includes the Gallery Place-Chinatown Metrorail station and the Archives-Navy Memorial Metrorail station. Its character is more diverse than the Metro Center area, with a large number of housing units, galleries, theaters, museums, and hospitality uses as well as offices and retail shops (2006 Comprehensive Plan, chap. 16, p. 28).

As we can see on the map in Figure 8.8, the 2006 area indexed by "Gallery Place/Penn Quarter" now circles around and overlaps the shrunken Chinatown neighborhood, as it was defined in the 1990 Zoning Regulation.

Analysis in this section has shown two ways in which the size of the area indexed by the place name Chinatown has been reduced over the years. First, in the 2000 Downtown Action Agenda and the 2006 Comprehensive Plan, a smaller Chinatown area on the map is easier to locate for someone who is not a specialist in urban planning in contrast to the 1991 Zoning Regulation. Without comparison, the public is largely unaware of the reduction. Second, parts of the area originally indexed by Chinatown have been reassigned to other place names, especially "Gallery Place." In the 2000 Downtown Action Agenda, "Gallery Place" indexes an area that has a center but has no boundary and the name also blatantly merges with Chinatown."

The strategy becomes more subtle in the 2006 Comprehensive Plan, where "Gallery Place" is combined with another place name "Penn Quarter." On the surface, it appears that they are separate subareas from Chinatown, but the area that they index overlaps considerably with the latter.

CONCLUSION

Place Naming as Political Action

To summarize, the analysis in this chapter has shown that, in the urban planning policies of Washington, D.C., Chinatown has been represented as a contradictory icon and a problematic symbol. In addition to the government's increasingly agnostic stance toward the neighborhood's preservation, through semiotics its indexable area has been reshaped and reduced. These reductions are further obscured by the increased numbers of maps that designate a smaller geographic area for Chinatown. In other words, the transformation of the neighborhood from icon to symbol is associated with the indexical change.

What are the material motivations and benefits behind this reconfiguration? The answer is, not too surprisingly, money. As mentioned earlier, Chinatown is located in the heart of the Downtown Business Improvement District, which generates more than 11% of local tax revenue for the D.C. government. Compared with small Chinese businesses or senior Chinese residents living on welfare, newly built luxury condominiums in Gallery Place and Penn Quarter bring in more property tax from real estate developers as well as more local income tax from the condominium residents, who are mostly young professionals. Reassigning some parts of the area indexed by "Chinatown" to "Gallery Place" and "Penn Quarter" discreetly expands the spatial scope of policies for the newer neighborhoods while simultaneously reducing the effective area that is supposed to maintain and preserve Chinatown's

ethnic characteristics. These findings demonstrate indexicality as "an important aspect of how power relations and power dynamics are played out in institutional encounters where a minority group is confronted with a new set of indexes" (Duranti, 1997, p. 19). The shift in the indexable area is much less noticeable and thus much less likely to provoke public outcry against the government and the developers in the defense of ethnic diversity in urban neighborhoods than, say, changing the name of the neighborhood, as portended in the merge of "Chinatown" and "Gallery Place" in the 2000 Downtown Action Agenda. At the same time as the indexical change, zoning regulations still require that streets and stores in Chinatown have Chinese signage, so on the surface, ordinary citizens can hardly notice any change in the size of the neighborhood.

In this chapter, I have suggested "indexicality" as a particularly fruitful aspect of discourse to examine the linkages between semiotic representation and material reconstruction. As Duranti (1991) points out, it is through indexicality that language gains the power of making things happen.

> To say that words are indexically related to some "object" or aspect of the world out there means to recognize that words carry with them a power that goes beyond the description and identification of people, objects, properties, and events. It means to work at identifying *how* language becomes a tool through which our social and cultural world is constantly described, evaluated, and reproduced (p.19, emphasis added)

This chapter has further demonstrated that the power of indexicality lies not only in the signifier of, but also in the signified (or, the "indexable," per Scollon & Scollon, 2003). It is hoped that through this deepened understanding of how language works (even in a small example of a place name), we can be more aware and even anticipate material consequences of semiotic representations.

NOTES

1. In this chapter, I follow Fairclough's definition of discourse as "language use, whether speech or writing, seen as a type of social practice," which is "shaped by relations of power, and invested with ideologies" (Fairclough, 1992).

2. Following Scollon and Scollon (2003), indexicality is defined as the property of signs to point to other things.

3. The 2000 update did not make any amendment to the 1991 Zoning Regulations.

4. An overlay district makes it possible for special urban planning policy to appy to this area.

5. According to Kress and van Leeuwen (1996), highly technological visual images such as maps usually correspond to decreased visual content. A map, unlike a photograph, does not usually depict the background, assume an alternate perspective, or use millions of colors. And as is apparent in the 1991 zoning map of Chinatown, in planning maps the technological modality is even higher with areas indicated by numbered squares. The 2000 Downtown Action Agenda map is arguably of a lower technological modality, using three shades of purple to indicate approximately the boundary of each neighborhood. The map drawing in the 2006 Comprehensive Plan is more precise and thus of a higher technological modality than the 2000 map but still of a lower modality than the 1991 map. The 2006 map does not label all the side streets or number squares within a block. However, this medium technological modality actually makes the 2006 map more appropriate and accessible to the non-specialist audience, with colourfully shaded blocks and clearly numbered neighborhoods. So, we can see that a smaller area is indexed by the same place name Chinatown in the more accessible and readable policy document.

REFERENCES

Austin, J. L. (1975). *How to do things with words.* Cambridge, MA: Harvard University Press.

Basso, K. H. (1988). "Speaking with names": Language and landscape among the Western Apache. *Cultural Anthropology, 3*(2), 99–130.

Berger, A. A. (1997). *Narrative inquiries in popular culture, media, and everyday life.* Thousand Oaks, CA: Sage.

Blu, K. I. (1996). "Where do you stay at?": Homeplace and community among the Lumbee. In *Senses of Place* (pp. 197–227). Santa Fe, NM: School of American Research Press.

Chow, E. N.-ling. (1996). From Pennsylvania Avenue to H Street, NW: The transformation of Washington's Chinatown. In *Urban odyssey: A multicultural history of Washington, D.C.* (pp. 190–207). Washington, DC: Smithsonian Institute Press.

Cohen, Saul B., & Kliot, N. (1992). Place-names in Israel's ideological struggle over the administered territories. *Annals of the Association of American Geographers, 82*(4), 653–680.

Duranti, A. (1997). *Linguistic anthropology.* Cambridge, UK: Cambridge University Press.

Fairclough, N. (1992). *Discourse and social change.* Cambridge, UK: Polity Press.

Finnegan, R. (1998). *Tales of the city: A study of narrative and urban life.* Cambridge, UK: Cambridge University Press.

Flowerdew, J. (2004). The discursive construction of a world-class city. *Discourse & Society, 15*(5), 579–605.

Gillette, F. (2003). Year of the hooter: The district's Chinese character gets lost in the translation. *Washington City Paper The Fake Issue—Keepin' It Unreal, 22* (52).

Haraguchi, T. (2003). Construction of place and institutional practice in the process of the "production" of Yoseba: The case of Kamagasaki, Osaka City. 人文地理 (*Human Geography), 55*(2), 121–143.

Hathaway, D., & Ho, S. (2003). Small but resilient: Washington's Chinatown over the years. *Washington History, 15*(1), 43–61.

Hutton, C. (2009). *Language, meaning and the law.* Edinburgh, UK: Edinburgh University Press.

Jensen, O. B. (2007). Culture stories: Understanding cultural urban branding. *Planning Theory, 6*(3), 211–236.

Johnstone, B. (1990). *Stories, community, and place: Narratives from middle America.* Bloomington: Indiana University Press.

Johnstone, B. (2004). Place, globalization, and linguistic variation. In C. Fought (Ed.), *Sociolinguistic variation: Critical reflections* (pp. 65–83). Oxford, UK: Oxford University Press.

Kress, G., & van Leeuwen, T. (1996). *Reading images: The grammar of visual design.* London, UK: Routledge.

Leeman, J., & Modan, G. (2009). Commodified language in Chinatown: A contextualized approach to linguistic landscape. *Journal of Sociolinguistics*, *13*(3), 332–362.

Lou, J. (2007). Revitalizing Chinatown into a heterotopia: A geosemiotic analysis of shop signs in Washington, D.C.'s Chinatown. *Space and Culture*, *10*(2), 145–169.

Lou, J. (2009). *Situating linguistic landscape in time and space: A multidimensional study of the linguistic construction of Washington, D.C. Chinatown.* (PhD. Dissertation). Georgetown University, Washington, DC.

Moore, J. (2005). *Beyond the archway: D.C. Chinatown debate: Vanish vs. varnish.* Washington Asia Press.

Myers, G. (2006). "Where are you from?": Identifying place. *Journal of Sociolinguistics*, *10*(3), 320–343.

Office of Planning of the District of Columbia. (2000). *Downtown Action Agenda.* Retrieved from http://planning.dc.gov/DC/Planning/In+Your+Neighborhood/Wards/Ward+2/Small+Area+Plans+&+Studies/Downtown+Action+Agenda.

Office of Planning of the District of Columbia. (2006). *Comprehensive Plan.* Retrieved from http://planning.dc.gov/DC/Planning/Across+the+City/Comprehensive+Plan/2006+Comprehensive+Plan.

Office of Zoning of the District of Columbia. (1991). *Zoning Regulations of the District of Columbia.* Retrieved from http://dcoz.dc.gov/info/reg.shtm.

Pang, C. L., & Rath, J. (2007). The force of regulation in the land of the free: The persistence of Chinatown, Washington DC as a symbolic ethnic enclave. In M. Ruef & M. Lounsbury (Eds.), *The sociology of entrepreneurship, research in the sociology of organizations* (Vol. 25, pp. 195–220). New York, NY: Elsevier.

Peirce, C. S. (1991 [1873]). On the nature of signs. In J. Hoopes (Ed.), *Peirce on signs: Writings on semiotic by Charles Sanders Peirce* (pp. 141–143). Chapel Hill: The University of North Carolina Press.

Reichl, A. J. (1999). *Reconstructing Times Square: Politics and culture in urban development.* Lawrence: University Press of Kansas.

Richardson, T., & Jensen, O. B. (2003). Linking discourse and space: Toward a cultural sociology of space in analysing spatial policy discourses. *Urban Studies*, *40*(1), 7–22.

Rose-Redwood, R. S. (2008). "Sixth Avenue is now a memory": Regimes of spatial inscription and the performative limits of the official city-text. *Political Geography*, *27*, 875–894.

Schegloff, E. A. (1972). Notes on a conversational practice: Formulating place. In D. N. Sudnow (Ed.), *Studies in social interaction* (pp. 75–119). New York, NY: Free Press.

Schiffrin, D. (1994). *Approaches to discourse.* Oxford, UK: Blackwell.

Scollon, R. (2001). *Mediated discourse: The nexus of practice.* London, UK: Routledge.

Scollon, R. (2008). *Analyzing public discourse: Discourse analysis in the making of public policy.* London, UK: Routledge.

Scollon, R., & Scollon, S. (2003). *Discourses in place: Language in the material world.* London, UK: Routledge.

Tuan, Y.-F. (1991). Language and the making of place: A narrative-descriptive approach. *Annals of the Association of American Geographers*, *81*(4), 684–696.

Zukin, S. (1995). *The cultures of cities.* Cambridge, MA: Blackwell.

SECTION 3

SEXUALITY

9

SEXUAL CITIZENSHIP AND SUFFERING SUBJECTS

Media Discourse About Teenage Homosexuality in South Korea

HAE YEON CHOO AND MYRA MARX FERREE

INTRODUCTION

In the early 1990s, South Korean newspapers began to draw attention to teenage homosexuality, using it as the fulcrum of a debate between those who lamented sexual liberalization as a moral crisis and those who perceived it as a mark of recognition for gay and lesbian human rights. Public concern intensified in 2001, with the Youth Protection Act, which prohibited access by teenagers to materials with homosexual content, and in 2003, when the National Human Rights Commission in South Korea recommended the repeal of this Youth Act. In this debate, conservatives presented homosexuality among teenagers as a sign of immorality and as a foreign import. Gay and lesbian activists, on the other hand, framed homosexuality as a human rights issue, and argued that South Korea as a modern nation-state must accept homosexual teenagers as members of the national

community and provide them protection from discrimination. This public contention over the meaning of teenage homosexuality revealed concerns over South Korean nationhood and citizenship, as it deeply engaged with the questions of who belongs within the imagined national boundary, what are their entitled rights, and what values and practices must they embody in order to show that they are worthy citizens.

This chapter analyzes how media reporting discursively constructed sexual citizenship for South Korean youth. In the tradition of critical discourse analysis, we understand discourses to be specific sets of diverse and contradictory claims that assert the social meaning of persons, relationships, and behaviors (Lombardo, Maier, & Verloo, 2009). We use newspaper articles about teenage homosexuality from 1900 to 2005 to consider how larger concerns about globalization and nationalism in South Korea become significant in constituting the rights and responsibilities (citizenship) that are expressed or limited through one's individual sexuality. However, this chapter seeks to move beyond its examination of sexual citizenship for homosexual teenagers to throw light on how sexual citizenship in any nation becomes constituted discursively, especially in and through mass media. In other countries such as India, the United States, Britain, and France, legal and social debates around homosexuality have been focused on different issues, including antisodomy laws and same-sex marriage or partnerships. During the period of our research, these issues had not yet arisen politically in South Korea. Yet across all these countries, the media have provided the public with a discourse that puts homosexuality at the heart of debates about individual membership in the nation itself and also about the nation's position in a global community of nation-states.

This transnational discourse raises issues of sexual citizenship that is inclusion and exclusion in a national community based on the social meaning of sexual practices of individuals. In the case of South Korea, not only homosexuals and homosexuality but also teenagers and teen sexuality became the objects of discursive contention. Media controversy surfaced in debates about the Youth Protection Act, which banned teenagers from Internet access to materials about homosexuality. That the sexuality of teenagers would be a focus of special concern is not unique to South Korea, as controlling all teenage sexuality has been Integral to the biopolitics of modern states (Foucault 2008). Teens are at the center of debates in many countries about national identity and citizenship, both because they embody the future of the nation and because their bodies are easier targets of regulation than those of adults (Cheng, 2005; Espiritu, 2001; Jackson, 2005). But national debates over teenage homosexuality became an especially crucial media forum for defining the nation and sexual citizenship in South Korea, highlighting this country's heightened anxiety about change in an age of globalization.

In this chapter, we examine the various configurations of sexual citizenship in South Korean media discourses that surfaced in debating teenage homosexuality. After discussing the literature on the media and sexual citizenship and laying out the South Korean political context, we show how the issue of teenage homosexuality is discursively contested by two sets of actors with different media relationships: conservative-moralists and human rights advocates. We then discuss the convergence of the tropes used by these two sides into a common discourse in which teenage homosexuals are portrayed as suffering subjects, thus calling forth the rhetoric of protection. We argue that this discourse of a suffering subject constructs a specific type of partial citizenship for homosexual youth. Despite efforts to reconceptualize sexual citizenship, the discourses of suffering and victimhood deny homosexual youth a public presence, pleasure, and desire. Teenage homosexuals are offered only partial citizenship, in which their silence becomes the price of their inclusion.

CITIZENSHIP, MEDIA, AND DISCOURSE

As "imagined communities," nation-states produce citizens by constructing commonalities among their members—that is, through the active physical and symbolic exclusion of others (Alexander, 1994; Anderson, 1983; Calhoun, 1993). Citizenship, in this sense, is "a powerful instrument of social closure and profoundly illiberal determinant of life chances" (Brubaker, 1996, p. 230). We approach citizenship not as a legal category imposed top-down on individuals by a nation-state, but rather as a continuum of rights, belonging, and participation in the polity that is negotiated on the ground. The concept of "partial citizenship," developed by Rhacel Parrenas (2001) in her study of Filipina migrant domestic workers in diaspora, helps clarify the ambiguous nature of this social closure. By calling the migrants' citizenship "partial," Parrenas refers to their incomplete integration in their receiving nation-states and the exclusion and limitation of rights they experience, despite the crucial work of reproduction they perform for the receiver country.

Yet, one does not have to leave one's home to experience partial citizenship. Gender and sexuality remain central to reproducing nationhood, and in a global context, the lives of non-normative sexual subjects are rendered deviant and unworthy of belonging to the nation (Grewal and Kaplan, 2001; Kim-Puri, 2005). We take sexual citizenship to mean how one's sexuality is used to define a complex mix of legal rights and public recognition as equal and full members of a community. The term "partial citizenship" meanwhile, can be considered more useful than the concept of "second-class citizenship" because it draws attention to the various configurations of limitation and exclusion that can apply in different contexts. Partial sexual citizenship is constituted in various ways in the intersections of sexuality with age and gender, as certain rights and forms of recognition are offered or denied in such configurations.

The media plays an important role in shaping and reflecting public discourses and in constructing social problems and social inclusion (Bacchi, 1999). Policy discourses in particular are those that define the relationships among states and their citizens. They appear in and across specific texts (from constitutions to policy proposals to party platforms) but are made most accessible to publics via various types of media reporting. Yet, far from being a neutral lens into policy discourses, news reports are highly mediated by social structures of journalism and produce discourses in their own right (Brown & Ferree, 2005). Such media discourses do not merely reflect public opinion (Gamson & Modigliani, 1989), policy-makers' agendas (Bacchi, 1999), or the actual weight of a social problem (Stone, 1988), but actively frame certain issues as significant and worthy of public concern (Boero, 2007; Brown & Ferree, 2005; Misra, Moller, & Karides, 2003).

With the media providing the arena in which public debates and contentions become visible (Gamson & Modigliani, 1989), it is important to scrutinize media work in giving a discursive conflict its particular shape. Media constitute a discursive domain where they "do not just transmit messages, they translate and transform them for the media audience" (Best, 1990, p. 19). As a result, the media not only serve as a visible site of debates, but also construct particular discourses: the media take certain ideas, repetitively present them, and turn them into "common sense" about some people, relationships, or behaviors (de Goede, 1996). A media discourse on a subject (such as abortion or immigration) makes the "sides" of a debate self-evident, excludes some speakers and gives standing to others, and establishes certain frames as shared "common sense" for both sides (Ferree, Gamson, Gerhards, & Rucht, 2002). Analyzing media discourse thus becomes an important window into understanding how teenage homosexuality enters into public awareness, becomes defined as debatable in certain terms and not others, and is constructed as an aspect of South Korean citizenship.

Aware of the significance of media discourses, the gay and lesbian movement has made media activism (especially in terms of the issue of representation) an important part of its agenda (Fejes & Petrich 1993). The issues of visibility and recognition have moved to the foreground, especially in the relation between the transnational gay and lesbian movement and the media. Against the systematic exclusion and negative stereotyping of gay and lesbian subjects in media, gay and lesbian media activists demanded positive portrayals, arguing that "affirmative images of lesbians and gays in the mainstream media...can be empowering for those of us who have lived most of our lives with no validation at all from the dominant culture" (Hennessy, 1994–5, pp. 31–32). Visibility and public recognition are powerful means to affirm the lives of marginalized subjects and for the movement organized to achieve them (Butler, 2004; Gamson, 1998).

Despite the powerful appeal of visibility, however, not all forms of publicity bring equally positive consequences. Clarke (2000, pp. 30–31) cautions scholars and activists against confusing "commercial publicity" with "democratic political representation." The presence of gays and lesbians in the corporate advertisements, for instance, does not directly translate into the extension of rights for sexual minorities. Scholars of media and sexuality have called for a careful analysis of the dynamics of visibility. Upon close examination, even a supposedly "positive" portrayal of gays and lesbians can reinforce heterosexism (Hantzis & Lehr 1994), with the "everyday" representation of sexual nonconformists in daytime talk shows, for instance, intensifying animosities and separating bad sexualities from good ones (Gamson, 1998).

Since the media are an important arena for (re)producing debates on citizenship, the dilemmas posed by issues of publicity and recognition in the media also invokes the meanings attached to sexual citizenship. Scholars of sexual citizenship demonstrate how a heteronormative model of citizenship has been imposed on non-normative sexual subjects, and how the quest for sexual citizenship on the part of gay men and lesbians imposes the dilemma of asking for rights and inclusion from the state and the citizen-body, on the one hand, and critiquing how this national body has been defined against their existence, on the other (Bell & Binnie, 2000; Phelan, 2001; Richardson, 2000; Weeks, 1998). Sexuality and gender are often seen as crucial axes along which nationhood is imagined and constituted, both physically and discursively (Gal & Kligman, 2000; Yuval-Davis, 1997). Homosexuality is considered in many postcolonial nation-states to be either a "foreign" product or the effect of Western influence, and thus antithetical to "authentic" national culture and belonging (Alexander, 1994; Bacchetta, 1999; Cheng, 2005; Puar, 2001). In this context, the quest for sexual citizenship challenges the state's exclusion of sexual subalterns—an exclusion that denies gays and lesbians recognition as citizens both on material and symbolic levels.

Moreover, citizenship requires "more than the assumption of rights and duties; more importantly, it also requires the performance and contestation

of the behavior, ideas, and images of the proper citizen" (Manalansan, 2003, p.14). What is at stake in sexual citizenship is thus an analysis of the terms of recognition and inclusion, not just in terms of formal rights, but also in terms of the "behavior, ideas, and images" of being a proper sexual citizen-subject. When framed narrowly within a language of rights, the gay and lesbian struggles for sexual citizenship can lead to a model of citizenship where homosexual subjects are privatized and de-eroticized (Cossman, 2002; Warner, 1999). While sexuality is "simultaneously a domain of restriction, repression, and danger as well as a domain of exploration, pleasure, and agency (Vance, 1984, p.1), the language of rights has not always been successful in addressing the pleasure aspects. In fact, in the conflict between the Christian Right and human rights claims in the political discourse in the United States (Stein, 2002; Moon, 2004), liberal gay rights supporters tend to emphasize the fixed nature of sexual identity (i.e., "homosexuals are born that way") along with the "pain" of being gay and lesbian (Lee, 2006; Moon, 2005) while the Christian Right presents homosexuality as a universal but immoral desire that, in giving pleasure, needs to be controlled by law and social morals (Stein, 2002). Meanwhile, the use of the gay and lesbian rights language in non-Western countries runs the risk of reproducing Western hegemony by denouncing a non-Western country's intolerance toward gays and lesbians as proof of its "backwardness," while celebrating the West as a site of modernity and progressive rights (Grewal & Kaplan, 2001; Massad, 2002; Wilson, 2006).

The South Korean case contributes to this literature on sexual citizenship by offering a concrete analysis of the discursive struggles shaping sexual citizenship as a nation-state enters the era of globalization. Using the concept of "partial citizenship" (Parrenas, 2001), we attempt to go beyond a dichotomous understanding of sexual citizenship, where gay and lesbian rights activists advocate for full sexual citizenship while conservatives try to deny them altogether. Additionally, by focusing on teen homosexuality and attending to the different constructions of gay men and lesbians, we show how the discourse of sexual citizenship is intersectional and offer a more nuanced examination of a particular configuration of partial inclusion.

GLOBALIZATION AND SEXUALITY IN CONTEMPORARY SOUTH KOREA

As a postwar nation-state, South Korea's modern history is filled with many transformations, including a shift to democratic governance and an advanced capitalist global economy. After democratization in 1987, the South Korean state initiated various globalization efforts such as implementing neoliberal economic policies in global trade and finance, joining organizations of global governance such as the United Nations (1991), and lifting the ban against foreign cultural goods from Japan, a former colonial power (1998). As political democratization progressed, cultural emphasis shifted from understanding the patriarchal family as a central social unit—a Confucian notion institutionalized by its authoritarian regimes—to the notion of individual rights.

Despite these changes, same-sex desire, intimacy, and sexual relationships among teenagers were not new phenomena brought about by globalization in the 1990s. In South Korea, the nonnormative embodiment of gender existed before the collective mobilization of sexual identity groups in the 1990s. For example, a group of women in the 1970s called themselves *bajissi* (trousers), dressed in masculine outfits, and dated feminine women, and a homoerotic subculture among gay men formed in the 1970s in certain geographic areas like Chongno in Seoul (Kwon-Kim & Cho, 2011). Such subcultures had limited visibility and were known among only a small group of people, but homoerotic desires and intimacy among teenage girls were broadly known and tolerated. With a high percentage of gender-segregated middle and high schools, girls' same-sex relations were treated as a less harmful substitute for heterosexual contact

during adolescence. This subtle form of acceptance, however, began to change with the growing visibility of homosexual subjects in the 1990s.

Inspired by Korean diasporic gay activists and gay and lesbian foreigners' meetings in South Korea, gay and lesbian activism began in the mid-1990s. It started with the founding of the gay men's organization, Chingusai in 1994, the lesbian organization, Kirikiri in 1994, a few campus organizations in the capital city of Seoul in 1995, and the Homosexual Rights Coalition in 1997 (Kwon-Kim & Cho, 2011; Seo, 2001). On the one hand, this activism heightened consciousness about homosexuality and stirred anxiety. For instance, in the 2000s, girls' schools in Korea became a target of moral surveillance, and *iban*[1] girls who performed and sang in drag on the streets as part of an urban homoerotic subculture faced increased regulation from their peers and teachers (Lee, 2006). On the other hand, the gay and lesbian community started to grow, particularly in on-line sites where access to information has become possible while remaining anonymous. These rapid changes created national anxiety about sexual morality and culture, which became crystallized in the issue of teenage homosexuality.

Media discourse on teenage homosexuality was particularly spurred by the Youth Protection Act. Enacted in 2001 by the National Information-Communication Ethics Committee and the Youth Protection Committee, the law prevented teenagers under 18 from searching for homosexuality-related terms on the Internet. For instance, a high-school student would need a national social security number proving that he was over 18 in order to search the term "gay" on the Internet. Under the guise of protecting youth from immorality, this law, which associated homosexuality with incest and bestiality, made all homosexuality-related websites inaccessible to anyone below 18 years of age. Against this legal backdrop, various actors took the opportunity to speak about both the positive and negative consequences of repeal.

The gay and lesbian organizations in Korea brought the language of human rights to the fore by filing a petition with the National Human Rights Commission against the Youth Protection Act. In 2003, the Human Rights Commission found it to be discriminatory against gays and lesbians and recommended its repeal. The Youth Protection Committee accepted their recommendation. This legal decision caused a backlash in 2003, particularly among Christian organizations with major church organizations formally condemning homosexuality. The response of Christian organizations, in turn, was construed as leading to the suicide of a young gay man, Yugudang, a gay activist and devout Christian, who expressed his frustration with Christian antigay sentiment in his suicide note. These two events made 2003 a particularly charged moment in the media discussions of teenage homosexuality, where two contending discourses, those of conservative moralists and human rights activists, had standing in the media and framed the issue for the public.

METHODS

Newspaper articles about teenage homosexuality offer a domain of discourse in which both the transformation of public discourse over time and the contestation of different discursive frames can be seen. Using keyword searches in a Korean newspaper database (www.kinds.or.kr), we found 208 articles in six national daily newspapers from 1990 to 2005 that directly discuss the issue of teenage homosexuality. The time frame of 1990 to 2005 was selected because the database only began in 1990, and because this time period is one that is characterized by the swift transformation of values and attitudes accompanying the Korean state's push toward globalization.

From the ten national newspapers in the database, we chose the two mainstream newspapers with the highest circulation (*Chosun* and *Donga*), two progressive newspapers (*Hankyore* and *Kyunghyang*), and two religion-based newspapers (*Segye* and *Kookmin*).[2] This sampling reflected our theoretical understanding of newspapers as

active participants in shaping public debate. By selecting newspapers that were identified with different public constituencies, we could capture the relative standing that each paper gave to certain types of speakers as well as the frames that characterized their discourse. Moreover, by including newspapers with targeted readerships and also those with the broadest, most inclusive circulation, we can see the extent to which the discourse around teenage homosexuality shifted over time between and within contending groups and their mainstream audiences. Both of the religious newspapers are largely Christian, *Kookmin* is mainline Protestant while *Segye* is published by the Unification Church (i.e., the "Moonies"). Christianity is the second major religion in South Korea, accounting for 20 to 25% of the religious population, and has been an influential agent in antihomosexuality debates. "Progressiveness" refers to the stance of advocating for political, economic, and social rights (i.e., propagating human rights in South Korea); the two progressive papers selected here are advocates for such causes and are aligned with democratization movements and activists.

To identify the domain of discourse defined as being about "teenage homosexuality," we first searched the database using the combination of keywords, "adolescent (*Chongsonyon*)," "teenage (*sipdae*)," and "homosexuality (*Dongsongae*, *Dongsongyonae*, Gay, Lesbian, *iban*)." Among the 578 articles that came up within this search, we deleted articles that were either duplicates or mentioned "homosexuality" and "teenager" in one article but did not relate them in any way. Our final sample of 208 articles discussed homosexuality in a variety of ways from discussing the oppression of homosexual teenagers to the detrimental influence of homosexuality on teenagers. This chapter focuses on our qualitative analysis of this media discourse, one in which two contending frames were employed by conservative moralists and human rights advocates. We pay particular attention analytically to how the contending frames relate to the nation-state, the discursive common sense produced across frames, and the implications of these frames for different configurations of partial sexual citizenship.

RE-IMAGINING THE KOREAN NATION UNDER GLOBALIZATION

In this South Korean media discourse, teenage homosexuality appears as an issue that is closely tied to understandings of the South Korean nation-state and how it should respond to the changes brought about by globalization. Given the choice of papers that represent two sets of significant actors, it is not surprising to find the discourse on homosexuality divided between two main frames, conservative-moralist and human rights, which run through both sets of newspapers. The conservative-moralist discourse condemns homosexuality as a foreign threat external to the Korean nation and argues for the need to protect innocent teenagers from immorality. A human rights discourse calls for the inclusion of homosexuals as citizens in order to constitute South Korea as a modern nation-state that meets global standards. The discourse as a whole— defined by what is contentious as well as shared in talking about teenage homosexuality—invokes the ideas of "foreign"/"global" to frame the position of the state in a transnational world, and uses ideas of "morality"/"modernity" to frame how the South Korean nation should understand itself and understand worthy sexual citizenship.[3]

Homosexuality as a Threat from Outside

The conservative-moralist position frames homosexuality as a foreign import with a negative influence on teenagers' morality, thus harming the nation's future. In this discourse, the idea of homosexuality as being exported to Asia from the West, which Ara Wilson (2006) terms "an import-export logic," is salient. In this discourse, the nation is re-imagined as hetero-normative, but vulnerable to threats of homosexuality from the outside (Alexander, 1994; Bacchetta, 1999; Cheng, 2005; Puar, 2001). Newspaper stories that include this frame, regardless of which newspaper they appear in, typically blame Japanese homoerotic comic books, American "obscene" movies with sexual content, and Internet pornography in general, all of which are considered "foreign." A common thread in many of the newspaper articles, regardless of whether they were progressive, religious, or mainstream was a message of warning against the many social evils brought about by the Internet and foreign cultural goods. Along with other obscene sexual behavior, homosexuality is framed as a vice with the potential to harm teenagers.

Consider the following report about the arrest of smugglers who illegally distributed "violent and immoral Japanese comic books." Subtitled "Shocking Murder and Homosexual Scene: the Cause of Teenagers' Immoral Crimes," the article describes various scenes in the comic books, emphasizing those seen as detrimental to Korean teenagers: "[Among these comic books] 'Crying Freeman' has a shocking scene where a person is stabbed with a hook and two women fondle each other; 'Myunto' has a scene where a son murders his mother when she tries to stop him from killing himself" (*Chosun*, Sept. 1, 1994). Here, the image of "two women fondling each other" is juxtaposed with images of extreme violence, making it unnecessary to explain how and why they are connected and harmful ideas.

The conservative media deploys the idea of homosexuality as a sign of excessive and deviant sexuality rather than as a sign of a sexual partnership choice (i.e., same or other gender). This discourse blames foreign-made cultural goods and portrays the Korean nation as being in potential danger of being contaminated by such global influences. For example, an article on the suicide of a schoolboy who killed himself in remorse after being found watching pornography, accuses immoral sexual culture, including homosexuality, of causing this tragic incident: "The seriousness of the problem lies in the fact that teenagers can access pornography very easily [. . . .] Teenagers first enjoy [pornography] out of curiosity but then become addicted. They then get involved in homosexuality, go to bars, and even become prostitutes" (*Kookmin*, Aug. 30, 1995).

The fact that most pornography is heterosexual rather than homosexual is irrelevant to this news article. In this story, the divide between homosexuality and heterosexuality remains weak, as homosexuality is framed as just another immoral sexual behavior symptomatic of abnormal hypersexuality that includes going to bars and prostitution. This anxiety about teenagers' sexuality is heightened by the easy access teenagers are seen to have to "immoral" sexual cultural goods through the Internet or imported videotapes and publications. In this globalized culture, the South Korean state is framed as needing to protect teenagers from powerful foreign threats.

In addition to "the West," Japan is frequently identified as a source of excess sexuality, which reflects Korea's particularly strong nationalist sentiment toward its former colonial power. In an article titled "Adolescent Violence, Homosexuality, Underage Prostitution: the Harms of Japanese Comic Books are Already Widespread," a journalist describes two schoolgirls "in a relationship":

> Kim (15), a third-year in B Girls' Middle School is in a 'special relationship' with her classmate. Whereas Kim uses harsh language and wears sporty pants in school, her friend is pretty and feminine. They sit on each other's laps, hug and kiss each other in the classroom regardless of who's looking [. . .] Such homosexual-like relationship spreading among some teenagers is greatly influenced by Japanese comic books (*Hankyore*, Oct. 22, 1998).

The article does not explain why these two girls' relationship is because of the "harmful" effects of Japanese comic books; rather, it assumes that connection to be self-evident to readers. In this article, foreign cultural goods are described as posing a danger to both the sexual order and gender order—notice the "masculinized" behavior of Kim. Ironically, while the article criticizes these girls' behavior as an effect of foreign influence, the description of their behavior reveals the extent to which same sex desires are freely expressed in public ("regardless of who's looking") in South Korean girls' schools. Actively erasing local histories of same-sex eroticism, conservative-moralists urge readers not to confuse friendship among girls with homosexuality: "This problem seems to come from interpreting our culture of same-sex intimacy with the Western concept of homosexuality" (*Segye*, July 28, 2003). These statements erase the sexuality from "our culture of intimacy," dismiss homoeroticism as being foreign to the nation, and once again, render South Korean citizenship as heteronormative.

Homosexuality as Global Human Rights

Whereas the morality of the nation is the preferred frame for conservative-moralists, the human rights frame is connected to a more positive view of South Korea's integration in global relations. Framing South Korea as joining the ranks of global-modern, nation-states, the National Human Rights Commission, as an indicator of the nation's modernity, used the voices of gay and lesbian rights activists to support extending human rights. Other developed countries serve as a positive reference point for change. Human rights language was most evident within the debate when the Youth Protection Act was reviewed and ultimately rejected by the National Human Rights Commission. Consider this statement by the National Human Rights Commission, reported in every newspaper in April, 2003:

> There is a global tendency to recognize homosexuality as a normal sexual orientation, and social consciousness is growing in South Korea that we should protect the human rights of homosexuals. The Youth Protection Committee's inclusion of homosexuality as an abnormal sexual expression in developing its criteria for harmful media violates the constitutional rights of homosexuals, including their right to pursuit of happiness, right to equality, and freedom of expression (*Donga*, Apr. 3, 2003).

This statement by a state agency acknowledges "homosexuals" as a distinctive group who are entitled to citizenship rights and protection from the state. In constituting this new homosexual citizen, the reliance on "a global tendency" for its justification inevitably invokes global standards for making its case.[4]

The invocation of global standards and how they are constituted is more salient in the progressive newspaper, as seen in this interview with Tae-Hoon Im, a gay rights activist who filed a petition against the Ministry of Education for the homophobic content of its textbooks:

> He is a homosexual. And he is the representative of the 'Homosexual Rights Coalition.' He says, "Homosexuality is just another form of sexual orientation like heterosexuality. Homosexuality is not disease that spreads AIDS or sexual perversion." The WHO and the American Psychological Association do not view homosexuality as a disease or sexual perversion to be cured. Norway and Denmark legalized same-sex marriage and the European Community (sic) prohibits discrimination against homosexuals (*Hankyore*, Sept. 1, 1999).

After introducing the activist's viewpoint that homosexuality is neither a disease nor a sexual perversion, the article introduces transnational and global authorities to support this viewpoint. Relying on the authority of global organizations such as WHO (World Health Organization) and the various legal rights granted homosexuals by advanced capitalist countries such as Norway and the European Union, the article urges the South Korean state to follow their example in order to join the ranks of "developed" countries.

Local gay activism is also reframed by the human rights side of the debate in relation to gay and lesbian activism in more developed countries, using them as the standard by which South Korean society is measured. Consider the following interview with a gay rights activist:

> There is a youth who dreams of Stonewall in this land, in a shabby publisher's office rather than in a gay bar, with a pen rather than stones. He is Jiyong Yang (24), a homosexual. He is the president of Homosexual Rights Coalition and an editor of Yiyeon Munhwa, a press specialized in homosexual publications (*Kyunghyang*, May 13, 1999).

The article introduces an ambitious youth, a homosexual, and gives him a space to speak. By invoking Stonewall, the icon of American and increasingly transnational gay activism, the article makes a discursive connection between the local Korean gay activism in which Yang is involved and global gay rights activism. After speaking of the young man's difficult years of struggling with his sexual identity during his youth and his dream to end oppression for homosexuals, the article laments: "It doesn't seem like his dream will come true in the near future, because our society has no culture of tolerance for minorities, treating homosexuals just as they were in feudal times" (*Kyunghyang*, May 13, 1999).

The analogy between "our society" and "feudal times" creates a close link to the developmental narrative, where the poor treatment of homosexuals ("no culture of tolerance") is equated with national "backwardness." By closely tying local gay rights to global gay activism, modernity and global practices, the human rights frame makes it imperative for the South Korean state to extend citizenship rights and protection to homosexuals.

CONSTRUCTION OF PARTIAL SEXUAL CITIZENSHIP

Although the two sides of this debate employ different frames about homosexuality and about the nation, the conservative-moralist and human rights arguments also share tropes that place them in the same discourse about sexual citizenship. Despite their oppositional stances on the issue of how the South Korean state and society need to respond to teenage homosexuality and its relation to intensifying globalization, their rhetoric converges in the way they portray teenage homosexuals as suffering subjects and in need of protection. We argue that this framing constructs teenage homosexuals as only partial sexual citizens. Different configurations of partial sexual citizenship emerge from this discourse for teenage boys and girls, and different tropes are used to keep their own voices out of public discourse. Whereas conservative-moralists deny gays and lesbians public presence and visibility, the human rights activists downplay the political activism and eroticism of homosexual citizens. Both therefore construct a teenage sexual citizen who is silent and largely invisible, and who needs and is offered protection by the state without having the right to sexual pleasure and desire.

The Vulnerable Boy-Victim

In the conservative media, teenage boys are portrayed as needing protection from their own hypersexual urges, framed as their "curiosity." The following article describes a boy, an innocent victim who is recruited to prostitute himself in a gay bar:

> Even though this is an extreme case, some teenagers, after visiting homo-bars, even work there, prostituting themselves to homosexuals. Sung (17), a high school drop-out, was caught by police working at H homo-bar early last February in Hongik-dong, Sungdong-gu. He saw an ad in a local newspaper "WANTED: Male waiters around 20 years old—room and board provided." Although he was not homosexual, he had been working at the bar for more than a month. At first he cleaned the bar and served drinks and food, but soon he began to sit with customers and later perform strip dances on the stage. Later, he even began to prostitute himself in the back room. Sung says, "I tried to quit when I first found out it was a homo-bar, but *I was curious.* Also, it paid good money, so I continued working." (*Kookmin*, June 7, 1995, emphasis added)

This article shows how teenage boys can easily fall into homosexuality because of their sexual "curiosity," making even boys who are "not homosexual" into male prostitutes. The power of this curiosity is enhanced by the fact that Sung enters prostitution neither by force nor dire economic need—the monetary temptation and his own curiosity are strong enough. In the conservative-moralist discourse, the boundary between homosexuality and heterosexuality remains fluid and permeable, making everyone vulnerable to the danger of homosexuality. In this article, the boy Sung becomes a prime example of the immorality of teenagers, with Sung's own words, which do not seem to take the matter seriously, paradoxically accentuating his ignorance about the gravity of his own situation. Without giving the teenager Sung an opportunity to speak his own experiences of working as a hustler in a gay bar, the journalist makes this judgment for the audience, defining his situation as "an extreme example."

The links between homosexuality, masculine sexual arousal, and the AIDS epidemic are explicit in the conservative media, and central to framing the boy as a victim. This framing of AIDS is supported by mainstream media coverage, which reports the number of teenagers who are infected with AIDS through homosexual acts, all male. As a warning to society, an article reports the testimony of an HIV-positive youth, Kim:

> Kim found out that he was infected when he was a senior in high school in May 1992. He started having homosexual sex *out of curiosity* when he was studying with a friend late at night in his junior year for an exam. He says, "I thought I'd rather die. A moment's pleasure led to an irreversible doom" (*Kyunghyang*, May 20, 1995, emphasis added).

Offering a first-person testimony of a "victim of AIDS," the article emphasizes the "irreversible" harm that can result from a momentary "curiosity" with homosexuality. By omitting any information about the friend that Kim had sex with and whether he was HIV positive, the article gives an impression that it is any homosexual sex that causes AIDS. It also portrays Kim as a hardworking and innocent boy, who falls into misery worse than death in failing to avoid the temptation of "a moment's pleasure."

Constructing the image of vulnerable youth, the conservative-moralist frame argues for the necessity of the Youth Protection Act. After the National Human Rights Commission recommended repealing the Youth Protection Act, an article in a mainstream paper quotes the head of a teacher's organization:

> It is true that the Human Rights Commission's decision has some positive aspects in terms of protecting the human rights of homosexuals, but we are concerned that it might stimulate a wrong kind of curiosity among teenagers, and make them view homosexuality as an acceptable thing to which they can easily have access (*Chosun*, Apr. 3, 2003).

This speaker frames the partial citizenship offered to homosexuals in the conservative-moralist frame. He acknowledges that homosexuals have "human rights" and that the state needs to protect their rights, although what these rights are is not clear from the quote. What is clear is that their rights do not include the rights to public presence and visibility, which would lead them into contact with teenagers, which "might stimulate a wrong kind of curiosity." The speaker does not feel the need to elaborate why teenagers should not view homosexuality as an acceptable way of life or have access to homoeroticism; rather, it is taken for granted that teenagers are ignorant and vulnerable and that they can be harmed by making homosexuality an "acceptable thing." Using the rhetoric of protection for the vulnerable boy-victim, and largely ignoring girls, conservative media frame sexual citizenship as partial by limiting homosexuals' access to public space.

The Suffering Homosexual Teenager

Media presentation of the human rights frame relies heavily on the voices of gay and lesbian activists. Arguing for the repeal of the Youth Protection Act, the human rights speakers

invoked an image of a suffering homosexual teenager, who is confused and isolated and in need of information and support from the gay and lesbian community. Quoting a gay activist who manages a website for homosexuals, a progressive paper reports:

> Many homosexuals are going through lots of confusion during adolescence when they begin acknowledging their own sexual identity, and even attempt suicide. If we stop these communities from helping them to live their lives with dignity and confidence, where would teenage homosexuals gain support?" (*Hankyore*, Jan. 25, 2002)

In this discourse, the negative influence of social discrimination and oppression on the lives of teenage homosexuals becomes the central issue. Teenage homosexuals are portrayed as a particularly high-risk group for mental health problems, and the suicide of the young gay man Yugudang in 2003 intensified this concern. For instance, consider this reporting on Yugudang's funeral: "Homosexuals say 'there is probably no homosexual who has never put a knife to their wrist'" (*Kyunghyang*, May 7, 2003). Even though this statement is put in quotation marks, in fact, it is not a direct quote from anyone specifically at the funeral. Rather, the article presents it as a general sentiment among "homosexuals," accentuating suffering as the overarching experience of the gay and lesbian community.

By framing the gay and lesbian community as experienced in suffering, the media's embrace of human rights assigns adult gay and lesbian activists a special, limited social role as protectors of teenage homosexuals. The gay and lesbian activists are portrayed as sharing the same personal histories of difficulty, and thus capable of taking care of the troubled teenagers. A lesbian activist, Ms. Kim, said that coming out—the act of telling people that she is a lesbian—comes with a lot of risk. "Identity confusion, crimes targeting lesbians, there are so many difficulties that face us. Many lesbians are suffering from depression." She also had years of confusion. She realized that she was a lesbian at the age of 17 when she had a crush on her female classmate. "A lot of women suffer, not being certain whether they are really lesbians or not." Kim said, "I suffered two years from self-remorse. I will comfort the pain of sexual minorities from my own experience" (*Chosun*, May 23, 2005). In this framing, the suffering of teenage homosexuals is emphasized with the terms "self-remorse," "confusion," and "pain." Also noteworthy is the use of the English phrase, "coming out," along with a Korean definition of its meaning, making it a part of the public vocabulary. This rhetorical act not only imports a descriptive term but also the script of coming out, which includes the premise of a "closeted" stage of being isolated, suffering, and self-doubting (Seidman, Meeks, & Traschen, 1999).

In media discourse, gay and lesbian activists are framed as serving society by protecting and nurturing teenagers, using their own experiences to "help" and "comfort the pain of sexual minorities." The lesbian activist's teenage years, the two years she described as suffering from self-remorse, are now turned into resources for helping other sexual minorities, especially adolescent ones in pain. This media portrayal of the activists hides the other aspects of their politics, including their active struggles against the state, such as organizing protests and filing petitions for legal reforms. Constructing gay and lesbian activism only as a site of comfort and support for needy people obscures the political content of their activism.

By accentuating the pain and suffering of gays and lesbians, the pleasure of same-sex desire is also silenced in this discursive construction of gay and lesbian human rights. Consider the following article, which takes a sympathetic attitude toward the difficulties of gays and lesbians. Myoung-Woo Kim, the owner of Lesbos, a lesbian café/bar in Seoul, is described as a motherly figure for suffering teenage lesbians.

> Now Ms. Kim is looking for a person who can carry on her role. Someone should take care of adolescent *iban* (homosexuals) who come to Lesbos during

the day, and answer numerous phone calls from young girls who are worried and confused. Someone should stand at the very front and represent lesbians. We all know this is not an easy task— coming out takes more than mere courage. Kim does not regret her life so far. She says, "it [being lesbian] was painful and difficult, but I couldn't do anything about it because it was something I was born with, something I couldn't choose. I hoped the world would become a less difficult place for those of us who are just a little 'different' (*Donga*, Feb. 18, 2004).

This article is unusual in emphasizing the importance of representation and public visibility for gays and lesbians, issues central to democratic governance and citizenship, and also states both the necessity and difficulty of "coming out." Despite the fact that visibility for gays and lesbians is still a contentious issue in South Korea, as the debates around the Youth Protection Act show, the article brings this claim to the level of common sense by addressing readers as "we"—that is, members of a common discursive community—and using the rhetoric of "we all know." Despite these clearly progressive elements, it is noteworthy that this article still depicts Lesbos, a lesbian café/bar, almost as a teenage lesbian drop-in center or a hotline for counseling. The fact that lesbians, adult and teenage alike, go to Lesbos for fun and pleasure, to drink, hang out, dance, and cruise, is made invisible. Instead, Ms. Kim, a successful business owner, is portrayed as having had a "painful and difficult" life and is now taking care of young lesbian girls who suffer from worries and confusion, and need help. In this framing, the core quality that links these teenage homosexuals to Ms. Kim, other activists, and the broader gay and lesbian community is their suffering rather than either the activists' shared political goals or the pleasure and bonding felt in sharing homoerotic spaces and culture.

The sexual citizenship constructed in the media by even human rights advocates thus remains partial. Whereas the partial citizenship offered by conservative-moralist media framing allows gays and lesbians unspecified basic rights yet denies them public presence and visibility, the media discourse presented by human rights advocates gives these subjects representation and visibility. In this discourse, where nurturance features prominently, lesbians are also very visible. Yet the trope of the suffering teenager found even in progressive papers discursively constructs another partial configuration of sexual citizenship, one that downplays the political activism and eroticism of homosexual citizens and so restricts their voices.

CONCLUSION

In South Korean media discourse, teenage homosexuality is a charged issue and is linked to larger questions about rearticulating nationhood and citizenship in an increasingly globalized world. Both conservative-moralists and human rights advocates participate in a discourse that debates the nation's responses to globalization in the domain of sexuality. The former claims to make the Korean nation "moral" by protecting teenagers from foreign threats; the latter wants to make it "modern" by protecting the rights of homosexuals. Both sides are involved in a common discourse about nationalism but also share a similar construction of the homosexual teenager as suffering, although with different gendered emphases on sexual curiosity and nurturance. This discourse is nominally about teenagers but has implications for sexual citizenship in general. Each of the contending frames makes the sexual citizenship of gays and lesbians in South Korea only partial, but in different ways: one denies homosexual subjects a public presence and visibility; the other limits the political activism and eroticism of homosexual citizens.

Despite its importance for reflecting and shaping public discourse, media discourse does not represent all positions. The media tend to create a dichotomy between contending positions rather than presenting the existing heterogeneity of discourse in the public itself. For instance, there are significant differences among gay and lesbian

activists in how they conceptualize the human rights of homosexuals and in the way they approach legal issues and cultural activism, but these positions are not articulated in the media. Variation in framing also exists on the right, between those who rely more on the language of Christianity and those who use a more nationalist, traditional Korean argument about sexual morality. The range of positions that we found cannot be attributed only to the existence of differentiated media constituencies for the progressive and Christian newspapers, since the same narrowing to a two-sided debate is evident in the mainstream papers as well. These heterogeneities, although obscured in the media's dichotomous construction of the discourse as a debate between pro-gay and anti-gay positions, offer a productive direction for future research. Such exploration could fruitfully use a more ethnographic study of a wider arena of political discourse, including the various actors involved in the struggle to define sexual citizenship in South Korea.

NOTES

1. The literal translation of the Korean term *iban* is "different class," and is used to refer to nonheterosexuals as an umbrella term, mostly gays and lesbians, but also includes bisexuals and transsexuals. Used originally as a slang term within gay and lesbian communities in the 1990s, it is now popularized by gay and lesbian activism and widely used colloquially among adults and teenagers. South Koreans commonly use the English transliterated terms including gay, lesbian, queer, and transgender, as well as Korean terms including homosexuals, bisexuals, and sexual minorities. We use the term homosexual and gay and lesbian in this chapter since they are the most commonly used terms during the period under examination, when bisexual, transgender, and queer activism had not yet fully emerged in the public sphere.

2. According to the recent statistics from the Korean Press Foundation, the circulation numbers in 2005 for the two mainstream papers, *Chosun* and *Donga*, are 2.37 million and 2.05 million, respectively. The circulation information for other papers is not available to the public.

3. Until the late 1990s, both mainstream and progressive papers were not very different from religious newspapers in terms of their thematic content. Religious newspapers, however, tended to be much more detailed in their accounts of homosexuality and passionate about their opposition to it. Beginning in the late 1990s, progressive newspapers increasingly began to differentiate themselves from the mainstream by discussing the issue of teenage homosexuality in terms of human rights and by incorporating the voices of gay and lesbian activists.

4. For a similar invocation of global norms in the cases of migrant workers' human rights, see Gurowitz (1999) and Kim (2009).

References

Alexander, M. Jacqui. (1994). Not just (any) body can be a citizen: The politics of law, sexuality and postcoloniality in Trinidad and Tobago and the Bahamas. *Feminist Review*, 5–23.

Anderson, Benedict. (1983). *Imagined communities.* London, UK: Verso.

Bacchetta, Paola. (1999). When the (Hindu) nation exiles its queers. *Social Text*, 141–166.

Bacchi, Carol. (1999). *Women, politics and policies. The construction of policy problems.* Thousand Oaks, CA: Sage.

Bell, David & Binnie, John. (2000). *The sexual citizen: Queer politics and beyond.* Cambridge, UK: Polity.

Best, Joel. (1990). *Threatened children.* Chicago, IL: University of Chicago Press.

Boero, Natalie. (2007). All the news that's fat to print: The American "obesity epidemic" and the media. *Qualitative Sociology*, *30*, 41–60.

Brown, Jessica A. and Myra M. Ferree. (2005). Close your eyes and think of England: Pronatalism in the British print media. *Gender & Society, 19*(1), 5–24.

Brubaker, Roger. (1996). *Nationalism reframed: Nationhood and the national question in the new Europe.* Cambridge, UK: Cambridge University Press.

Butler, Judith. (2004). *Undoing gender.* New York, NY: Routledge.

Calhoun, Craig. (1993). Nationalism and ethnicity. *Annual Review of Sociology, 19*(1), 211–239.

Cha, Joonchul. (1995, May 20). Bookuroun gwago balhimnida AIDS isipde sookyonhan gobek (I share my shameful past, a solemn confession from an AIDS patient in his 20s). *Kyunghyang,* p. 23.

Cheng, Sea-ling. (2005). Popularizing purity: Gender, sexuality, and nationalism in HIV/AIDS prevention in South Korean youths. *Asia Pacific Viewpoint, 46*, 7–20.

Choi, Sunhyun. (2003, Apr. 3). Dongsungae saite yuhaemaeche anida chungsonyunbohobup johang kookga inkwonwi sakje kwonko (Homosexual websites are not harmful—The National Human Rights Commission recommends the repeal of the Youth Protection Law). *Chosun,* p. 16.

Clarke, Eric. O. (2000). *Virtuous vice: Homoeroticism and the public sphere.* Durham, NC: Duke University Press.

Computer umranmule ppajyodununde kommeng bumodel nomu morunda (Computer-illiterate parents are ignorant as their children fall into lewd materials on-line). (1995, June 7). *Kookmin,* p. 5.

Cossman, Brenda. (2002). Sexing citizenship, privatizing sex. *Citizenship Studies, 6*, 483–506.

de Goede, Marieka. (1996). Ideology in the U.S. welfare debate. *Discourse & Society, 7*, 317–357.

Espiritu, Yen L. (2001). 'We don't sleep around like white girls do': Family, culture, and gender in Filipina American lives. *Signs, 26*, 415–440.

Fejes, Fred & Petrich, Kevin. (1993). Invisibility, homophobia, and heterosexism: Lesbians, gays and the media. *Critical Studies in Mass Communication, 10*(4), 396–416.

Ferree, Myra Marx, Gamson, William A., Gerhards, Jürgen, & Rucht, Dieter. (2002). *Shaping abortion discourse: Democracy and the public sphere in Germany and the United States.* Cambridge, UK: Cambridge University Press.

Foucault, Michel. (2008). *The birth of biopolitics: Lectures at the College de France, 1978–1979.* London, UK: Palgrave Macmillan.

Gal, Susan & Kligman, Gail. 2000. *The politics of gender after socialism.* Princeton, NJ: Princeton University Press.

Gamson, Joshua. (1998). Publicity traps: Television talk shows and lesbian, gay, bisexual, and transgender visibility. *Sexualities, 1*(1), 11–41.

Gamson, William A., & Modigliani, Andre. (1989). Media discourse and public opinion on nuclear power: A constructionist approach. *American Journal of Sociology, 95*, 1–37.

Grewal, Inderpal & Kaplan, Caren. (2001). Global Identities. *GLQ, A Journal of Lesbian and Gay Studies, 7*, 663–679.

Gurowitz, Amy. (1999). Mobilizing international norms: Domestic actors, immigrants, and the Japanese state. *World Politics*, *51*(3), 413–445.

Han, Minsu. (1995, Aug. 30). Une Junghaksengu Jasarel sengakhanda (Thinking about a suicide of a middle school student). *Kookmin*, p. 23.

Hantzis, Darlene & Lehr, Valerie. (1994). Whose desire? Lesbian (non)sexuality and television's perpetuation of heterosexism. In Jeffrey Ringer (Ed.), *Queer words, queer images: The communication and (re)construction of homosexuality*. New York: New York University Press.

Hennessy, Rosemary. (1994–5). Queer visibility in commodity culture. *Cultural Critique*, *29*, 31–76.

Hong, Jinsoo. (2004, Feb. 18). Chungsonyun yuhaemul gijunse dongsungae sakje (Deleting homosexuality from the list of harmful materials for adolescents). *Donga*, p. 7.

Huh, Yoonhee. (2005, Apr. 23). Gotongbatnun yosong dongsungaejaduli suilgosun? (Where can suffering female homosexuals rest?).*Chosun*, p. 9.

Hwang, Sangchol & Jung, Sera. (1998, Oct. 22). Chongsonyun pokryuk dongsungae wonjo gyoje ilbon manhwa heak imi pojye (Adolescent violence, homosexuality, underage prostitution: The harms of Japanese comic books are already widespread). *Hankyore*, p. 27.

Ilbon pokryok manhwa bokje choltoe (Crackdown on illegal copies of Japanese violent comics). (1994, Sept. 1). *Chosun*, p. 31.

Jackson, Sue. (2005). 'Dear Girlfriend. . .': Constructions of sexual health problems and sexual identities in letters to a teenage magazine. *Sexualities*, *8*, 282–305.

Kim, Kwangho. (1999, May 13). Dongsunae Suho chonsa Yangjiyong (Jiyong Yang, guardian for homosexuality). *Kyunghyang*, p. 19.

Kim, Nora H. J., (2009). Framing multiple others and international norms: The migrant worker advocacy movement and Korean national identity reconstruction. *Nations and Nationalism*, *15*(4), 678–695.

Kim-Puri, H. J., (2005). Conceptualizing gender-sexuality-state-nation: An introduction. *Gender & Society*, *19*, 137–159.

Kwon-bak, Hyowon. (2003, May 7). Sahoe chabyul jukemuro hanguhan chungsonyun chumo (Mourning a teenager's death who protested societal discrimination with death). *Kyunghyang*, p. 8.

Kwon-Kim, Hyun-young & Cho, John. (2011). The Korean gay and lesbian movement 1993–2008: From 'identity' and 'community' to 'human rights.' In Gi-Wook Shin & Paul Chang (Eds.), *South Korean social movements: From democracy to civil society*. New York, NY: Routledge.

Lee, Jesoon. (1999, Sept. 1). Dongsungaenun Sungjok Jihyangil Ppun gyogwaso pyongyon gochedala (Homosexuality is only sexual orientation; Demanding the prejudice in textbooks). *Hankyore*, p. 19.

Lee, Ji-eun. (2006). Beyond pain and protection: Politics of identity and *Iban* girls in Korea. *Lesbian Studies*, *10*(3/4), 49–67.

Lee, Youngsun. (2003, Jul. 28). Ujongkwa dongsungae (Friendship and homosexuality). *Segye*, p. 34.

Lombardo, Emanuela, Meier, Petra, & Verloo, Mieke (Eds.). (2009). *The discursive politics of gender equality: Stretching, bending and policy-making*. London, UK: Routledge.

Manalansan, Martin F. (2003). *Global divas: Filipino gay men in the diaspora*. Durham, NC: Duke University Press.

Massad, Joseph. (2002). Re-orienting desire: The gay international and the Arab world. *Public Culture*, *14*, 361–385.

Misra, Joya, Moller, Stephanie, & Karides, Marina. (2003). Envisioning dependency: Changing media depictions of welfare in the 20th century. *Social Problems*, *30*(4), 482–504.

Moon, Dawne. (2004). *God, sex, and politics: Homosexuality and everyday theologies*. Chicago, IL: University of Chicago Press.

Moon, Dawne. (2005). Emotion language and social power: Homosexuality and narratives of pain in church. *Qualitative Sociology*, *28*(4), 327–349.

Parrenas, Rhacel. (2001). Transgressing the nation-State: The partial citizenship and "imagined (global) community" of migrant Filipina domestic workers. *Signs*, *26*(4), 1129–1154.

Phelan, Shane. (2001). *Sexual strangers: Gays, lesbians and dilemmas of citizenship*. Philadelphia, PA: Temple University Press.

Puar, Jasbir K. (2001). Global circuits: Transnational sexualities and Trinidad. *Signs*. *26*, 1039–1065.

Richardson, Diane. (2000). Claiming citizenship? Sexuality, citizenship and lesbian/feminist theory. *Sexualities*, *3*, 255–272.

Seidman, Steven, Meeks, Chet & Traschen, Francie. (1999). Beyond the closet? The changing social meaning of homosexuality in the United States." *Sexualities*, *2*, 9–34.

Seo, Dong-Jin. (2001). Mapping the vicissitudes of homosexual identities in South Korea. *Journal of Homosexuality*, *40*, 65–79.

Son, Hyorim. (2003, Apr. 3). Inkwonwi dongsungae injong nonran (Controversy over the Human Rights Commission's recognition of homosexuality). *Donga*, p. 31.

Stein, Arlene. (2002). *The stranger next door: The story of a small community's battle over sex, faith, and civil rights.* Boston, MA: Beacon Press.

Stone, Deborah. (1988). *Policy paradox: The art of political decision making.* New York, NY: Norton.

Vance, Carole S. (1984). *Pleasure and danger: Exploring female sexuality.* New York, NY: Routledge.

Warner, Michael. (1999). *The trouble with normal.* Cambridge, MA: Harvard University Press.

Weeks, Jeffrey. (1998). The sexual citizen. *Theory, Culture & Society, 15*(3-4), 35–52.

Wilson, Ara. (2006). Queering Asia. *Intersections: Gender, History and Culture in the Asian Context, 14.* Retrieved from http://wwwsshe.murdoch.edu.au/intersections/issue14/wilson.html.

Yukyung, Une dongsungaejau internet dungkepje ssaum (A struggle of one homosexual with the Internet censorship). (2002, Jan. 25). *Hankyore,* p. 9.

Yuval-Davis, Nira. (1997). *Gender and nation.* London, UK: Sage.

10

HIDDEN SEXUALITIES

Behind the Veil and in the Swamps

SANYA OSHA

INTRODUCTION

Nigeria is the largest black nation in the world. It is also one of the most complex societies in existence and its complexity is largely as a result of possessing several ethnic groups who speak a multiplicity of languages. Political scientists claim that Nigeria has over 250 ethnicities, while linguists assert that the country probably has more than 500 languages and dialects. Religion also plays a prominent role in identity formation and the sort of life choices people make. In this regard, Islam, Christianity, and traditional religion (or what some term animism), are all practiced in Nigeria. Consequently, any discussions about sexuality within the Nigerian context are better served if this complexity is taken into consideration. For instance, the perceptions of the body and sexuality can become and often do become volatile issues when marginal or opposing sexual identities make an appearance in the larger public domain. This chapter examines sexuality as expressed as heterosexuality and not homosexuality because the Same Sex Marriage Prohibition Act of 2006 in Nigeria criminalizes homosexuality—which makes the open interrogation of same-sex relations quite problematic, if not hazardous.

In the Beginning God Created...

In postcolonial contexts, readings of the various types of sexuality can be exceedingly productive. In such contexts, the conflation, mutual reinforcement, and at times, nullification of precolonial and postcolonial cosmologies and paradigms in turn create scenarios that Western models and concepts fail to sufficiently explain. The continuities and discontinuities between tradition and modernity, precolonial and postcolonial taxonomies, and Western and non-Western practices within postcolonial contexts produce conditions of highly hybridized possibility and modes of social practice, which necessarily require alternative analyses. This essay addresses the hybridization of the social space that characterizes a postcolonial milieu in relation to sexuality.

In adopting this approach, I intend to point out the crisis of phallocratic systems in relation to processes of contemporary globalization. In other words, I discuss the crisis of manhood, the overturning of a prevailing sexual order, and some specific discursive regimes that reproduce and reinforce the phallocentric matrixes on the one hand, and those that subvert them on the other. I hope to show that in this discursive matrix, the sex(ed) subject can be seen as a prey to different technologies of power and their various mechanisms of production and legitimation. Because of their largely antidemocratic nature, these forms of power (in some instances, a fundamental *state of modern unfreedom*) usually fail to liberate the postcolonial subject within the entire field of sexuality. True, the discourse of sexuality is in large part a function of power (Foucault, 1978, 1985, 1986).[1] And as power undergoes complex and numerous processes of decentralization and democratization, it can be argued—and in this chapter I support the argument—that the expressions of human sexuality become more varied and complex. On the other hand, there is a thesis that authoritarian regimes of power in the postcolonial context of Africa tend to promote sexual orders that limit the manifestation of multiple and highly developed forms of sexuality because of their essentially repressive nature. This is not to say that the repression thesis does not operate in other contexts or that it does not have different configurations and meanings according to different sociocultural and historical conditions. Indeed, the point would be to highlight the various trajectories and features assumed by the repression thesis from one context to another (Foucault, 1978, pp. 4–6).[2]

To understand a particular regime of sexuality, we have to know the precise mechanisms of power involved and the particular interests they serve. For our purposes, this chapter examines (1) the sexual order that prevails in the northern part of Nigeria, which is largely Islamic; (2) the intrusion of colonialism into a part of southern Nigeria and its impact on the nature of sexual politics therein; (3) the effects of new modes of production on the organization of sexuality; (4) the postcolonial origins of commercial sex work in midwestern Nigeria and its transformation as a site of sexuality within the current wave of globalization; (5) the correlation between certain kinds of authoritarian structures of power and sexuality in northern and midwestern Nigeria; (6) and finally, the crisis of masculinity in postcolonial contexts and the resulting new technologies of domination.

It is important to note that the British mode of colonial infiltration in northern and southern Nigeria differed. In the north, the British left the traditional rulers to act as intermediaries for the colonial administrators and often those traditional authorities were left intact. Here, the British practiced what is known as indirect rule. The colonialists practiced what is known as direct rule in southern Nigeria and hence the need to examine the coupling of colonialism and sexuality. In southern Nigeria, the effects of modernization were more keenly perceived as both Western education and capitalist modes of production were introduced. In addition, Christian missionaries played a prominent part in converting indigenes in the south to Western forms of social life. These key differences make colonialism in northern and southern Nigeria quite distinct in relation to one another—and particularly so with regard to sexuality.

The north of Nigeria is largely Islamic and so a distinct mode of sociopolitical regulation prevails there. This is not to say that this mode of sociopolitical regulation is entirely uniform. It is not, and significant pockets of Christian modes of worship and secularism exist. However, it is safe to indicate the prominent role Islam plays in defining social life for the majority of the population. In the Midwest, the other site of investigation, the majority of the population subscribes to Christianity. Accordingly, in the two geographic areas the manner in which both Christians and Muslims engage with, and react to, the dynamics of globalization are usually not the same. And understandably, the ways in which the global politics of culture and sexuality affect these regions are also different and diverse. For instance, the spread of political Islam as a form anti-West ideology can be found in the north and understandably this development affects not only the wider political context of the region but also issues at the level of micropolitics. In addition, the presence of a political Islam affects local conceptions of global cultural politics and provides a dichotomizing logic that marks everyday life as a struggle between Islamic and Western sentiments (Mamdani, 2004).

The exploration of these various discursive trajectories reveals that in addition to the repression caused by state power, violence in a thoroughly deinstitutionalized aspect or nonstatist form is also a major determinant of quite a number of different sexual configurations. In this regard, notions of pleasure are relegated to the background and oftentimes, sex is associated with random postcolonial violence. More importantly, within any given postcolonial context, many regimes of sexuality contest for dominance and these regimes are in turn inflected by factors of religion, culture, region, ethnicity, power, and by their relationships to new regimes of globality. Thus, an examination of an order of sexuality in a particular region necessarily invites a conceptual approach that ought to be different from one that applies to another region.

This essay suggests that the degree of complexity involved in tracking various regimes and discourses of sexuality within a given nation-space can be quite enormous. The organization of the discourses and regimes of sexuality in northern Nigeria is markedly different from those of southern Nigeria but both regions, no matter how fragile they might appear to be sometimes, are conjoined in many ways by the imperatives of nationality, constitutionality, and history. The point of this essay is not to find similarities in the regimes of sexuality in these two regions but to demonstrate the diversity that exists within each region in terms of their different conceptions of power and sexuality. The essay also suggests that contexts of inadequate or poor institutional structures may go a long way in shaping a more general order of sexuality.

Sex and the Veil

Hijab is not only covering face and body by a woman, it also means purdah or staying of woman in their matrimonial houses. They do not mix up with men, save as allowed by the Sharia. This is evident in Quaran 33:33, which says: And stay in your houses and do not display yourselves like that of the times of ignorance . . . .(Je'adayibe, 2004, p. 16).

Generally, in Islamic communities of northern Nigeria the discussion of sex is taboo (Slaheddine, 1999, pp. 48–51). However, in the West the desacralization of the discursive production of sexuality actually led to its transformation into a social and institutional epistemology or more precisely, a science (Foucault, 1978). The Holy Prophet urges all Muslims to procreate and since the injunction is a strictly religious one, its desacralization and eventual secularization has not been quite possible. The religious injunction to procreate might also account for the phenomenal demographic growth of Muslim populations all over the world and the subsequent transnationalization of the Islamic ethos (Huntington, 1996). For instance, Islamic scholars in Nigeria usually draw inferences from countries such as Tunisia, Pakistan, the Sudan, and Indonesia (Babaji, 2004). In relation to sexual politics, this obviously has a number of consequences. First, it means the continual reinforcement of a patriarchal system of social relations. Second, it also means the spread of political Islam as a political economy (Mamdani, 2004). It could also be argued that these factors may lead to the suppression of sexual difference and the various discursive domains in which the politics of difference and representation are articulated and mobilized.

All of these factors undoubtedly strengthen the system of compulsory heterosexuality in such communities. And because of the fundamental traditionalism (perhaps also communalism) of such cultures, the rise of oppositional subcultures and counter-discourses to the hegemonic order has proven to be problematic. Further, the field of sexuality is a terrain where the Islamic ideology can wage an effective struggle against its ideological opposites since the politics of sexuality is very often articulated on fervently ideological grounds.

Within the Islamic context, the separation between the state and religion, between the private and the public spheres is if anything, less evident than what exists in the West. Consequently, the private realm where sexual difference is usually mobilized and articulated is not exactly distinguishable from the public sphere, which rigorously polices the collective sexual conduct. Thus oppositional sexual subcultures are liable to be suppressed at the very point of gestation by the patriarchate that enforces a decidedly heterosexual orientation. It is this generalized conflation of the public and the private realms within Islamic contexts that discourages the development of countercultural formations and multiple discourses of sexuality. Also within the context of the *Sharia* legal code as interpreted by its advocates, there is no conflict between jurisprudence and religion. This unity of conceptuality further constrains the possibilities for the articulation of a politics of difference. In addition, the defenders of the sexual and religious status quo are sometimes articulate and well educated and can be quite vehement in defending the old order:

> Many people in the world today have either refused to understand and appreciate the true status of women under Sharia law, or they have understood it, but for selfish and biased reasons and/or interests have continued to challenge and degrade the position of Sharia law with respect to women (Babaji, 2004, p. 3).

The author of these words, which represent a dominant view of sexual politics in northern Nigeria, once again, does not factor the politics of gender and representation into this stance. Having sharply ignored these variables, the author goes on to mention that the *Sharia* legal code deals with all exigencies concerning marriage, inheritance, employment and/or occupation, the private and the public domains, education, politics, and

the economy. The *Sharia* legal code, we are reminded, is derived from *Allah*. As such, the injunctions of the legal code are "immutable and unchallengeable" (ibid.). The author goes on to assert that "Sharia law seeks to establish justice, equity and fairness to all human beings without discrimination on the basis of sex" (ibid.). The legal code, we are informed, is, in fact, guided by universal welfarist values:

> One of the chief important purposes of Sharia law is to secure and provide to all mankind, both women and men, individually and collectively. It seeks to establish rule of law, to maintain peace and security and to promote the welfare of all people (Babaji, 2004, p. 3).

The author concludes that discourse and the politics of difference are not possible beyond the strictures of the Quran:

> Sharia law to a Muslim is seen as a divine law based on the Holy Quran and the Sunnah of the Holy Prophet. The injunctions of the Sharia in these two primary sources affecting human (including women's) rights, are therefore divine and immutable and no one (including the United Nations or the Constitution of a particular nation) has the power or right to abrogate, suspend and/or amend them for the promotion of what human beings perceive and conceptualize as 'fundamental human rights' for being human beings (Babaji, 2004, p. 7).

However, the unity of conceptuality that this kind of discourse assumes is undermined when it borrows from a global human rights discourse without problematizing the history and status of the discourse. Babaji finds no contradiction in pointing out that "some of the basic rights of women as human beings under Sharia include the rights to life, to justice, to equality of human beings and freedom from discriminations" (Babaji, 2004, p. 8). Babaji claims a discourse of universalism for the legal code but it is not one that is derived from Islamism. Rather, the discourse of universalism is borrowed from the global resources of secularism. A contradiction lies in the espousal of the discourse of universalism on the one hand, and the projection of an assumed unity of conceptuality within the *Sharia* legal code, on the other. Babaji does not seem to notice this contradiction let alone problematize it.

At this juncture, it ought to be pointed out that the introduction of the *Sharia* legal code in most parts of northern Nigeria can be linked to a broader struggle for power at the national level. The first president of the republic in the fourth democratic dispensation, Olusegun Obasanjo is Christian and his emergence as president was as a result of an intricate balancing of various political, ethnic, and religious interests and forces. Obasanjo is a Christian southerner who was not completely accepted by the muslim north, where federal political power is widely thought to reside. The political opposition between northern and southern Nigeria is not only based on region but also religion, cultural and social outlooks. Some of Obasanjo's acts during his first term as president further tilted this already fragile balance of interests with the significant northern political forces. Thus within this context, the introduction of the *Sharia* legal code can be construed to register northern disapproval of the Obasanjo administration and an indication by northern Nigerian to embark on a quest for greater religious and political autonomy. However, the resulting implications of this political strategy have a tremendous impact on the general economy of gender and sexuality in the region.

Let us now examine some examples within the specificity of Nigeria. In examining these examples, we shall observe how the hegemonic sexual order is not only supportive of compulsory heterosexuality but is also repressive toward countercultural postures regarding gender. In other words, the development of a vibrant discourse on feminism outside the confines of academia may not be achieved in the immediate future.

We might as well recall that several parts of northern Nigeria have adopted the *Sharia* Islamic code as a way of life, as well as a mode of political organization that seeks to transform Nigeria into a theocracy. The immediate consequence of this development is an increased policing of the general sexual conduct of individuals in those areas.[3] During the beginning of the introduction of the legal code, the segregation of the sexes was more rigorously observed and infringements on accepted norms of sexual behavior were severely punished.[4] This further reinforces the claim that the *"private"* is not private within the context of the *Sharia* legal code and also that the public (hence the collective) supersedes and precedes the private. The most radical consequence of this sequence is that the private does not exist within the orbit of the *Sharia* legal code. But since the system of compulsory heterosexuality promotes the dominance of men over women in northern Nigeria (at least it is not oppressive to men in the same way as it is to women), let us dwell for a moment on the condition of the female sex within that milieu.

Several of the factors that have been identified that work against women in northern Nigeria include genital mutilation, forced child marriages and economic dependence, urban overcrowding, domestic violence, homelessness, forced prostitution and trafficking in women, ethnic and religious violence, and finally, discriminatory inheritance and property rights (Olawale, 1996).

Genital mutilation or female circumcision is a customary practice, which restricts the expression of female sexuality but also the natural ability of the female subject to enjoy carnal relations. This pervasive devaluation of the vagina by the patriarchy has been termed *"dictature des couilles"* by a trenchant feminist.[5] Later in this essay, we shall see how tropes of femininity, feminization and devaluation are conjoined within a signifying economy of the phallogocentric order.

A major health hazard in northern Nigeria is the problem of *vesicovaginal fistulae* (VVF). Indeed, VVF is rampant in communities that encourage child marriages. It occurs when a girl is not anatomically prepared for sexual intercourse and childbearing and does injury to the girl's birth canals, urinary bladder, rectum, and nerves. The condition is thus explained:

> The VVF gynecological complications manifest as uncontrollable discharge of urine and feces from the girl's genitals. She is therefore constantly wet and smelly. VVF patients are highly susceptible to kidney and nerve infections, physical deformity, or even death (Olawale, 1996, p. 59).

This sort of violence is legitimated within the culture and the discursive production of sexuality is shrouded by a pronounced anthropomorphism that discourages a countercultural discourse of sexuality within the matrix of the phallogocentric signifying economy. Furthermore, because the institutional mechanisms of power that legitimize this structure of sexual relations also effectively mask their fundamental ideological operations, a substantial number of women continue to support the hegemonic order. Hegemony, however predominant, is always vulnerable to forces of subversion (Comaroff & Comaroff, 1991).[6] Nonetheless the so-called forces of subversion will have experienced a major drawback as a result of the institution of the *Sharia* code.

Also noteworthy is the fact that the *purdah* system has been strengthened in northern Nigeria. This means women are kept in doors and away from gainful employment. This form of economic disempowerment prevents the development of a truly revolutionary feminist movement and also an alternative discourse on sexuality and gender prerogatives. However, perhaps there is an opportunity for a radical questioning of the existing order, but paradoxically by the agents and beneficiaries of the order itself.

It can be argued that processes of feudalization exist within the postcolonial Islamic matrix. These processes refer to a precoloniality that is not quite amenable to forms of modern government and techniques of surveillance. Since established lines of social stratification exist, the sex(ed) subject can be found in the margins of society where formalized power doesn't always

reach. Cultural mechanisms of power protect the most powerful from public scrutiny and generate a shroud of secrecy that contribute to the feudalistic climate. Indeed, these conditions of secrecy where the powerful violate accepted sociomoral injunctions are potentially subversive of the hegemonic order. The conditions of feudalist secrecy constitute the margins whereby the consciousness and activity of the sex(ed) subject, together with alternative discourses of sexuality, can be articulated and (dis)articulated outside the regimes of the existing order. Those secretive unpoliced margins, in other words, are where the unnameable is named, *the–not–done* attempted, and the sex(ed) subject is dislodged from its conventional locus and sent on more adventurous errands. Away from the prying eyes of formal institutions, it is possible to practice whatever sexuality one chooses. The feudalism in this sort of context, acts as both a source of repression and of liberation. It acts as a source of repression because it supports a status quo that maintains unequal relations of gender and discourages a public articulation of alternative discourses of sexuality. But it can also act as a basis for an emancipatory politics because of the rather porous forms of modern governance that exist within this sort of postcolonial milieu. Since feudalism is constantly being challenged and eroded by the march of modernity, there are severe limits as to the determination and organization of sexuality.

So far, I have highlighted the contours of the northern Nigerian regime of sexuality, which as we shall see differs markedly from what exists in the south or in what (in old political terms) used to be called the Midwest.

Sex and the Swamps: A New Mode of Production

What used to be called the Midwest is presently known as Edo-Benin, a culturally rich region in the southern part of Nigeria where colonialism and Christianity made significant inroads. This section examines how discourses of sexuality change when new modes of production are set in motion. In precise terms, it attempts to unravel the discursive knot within, and at the same time accentuate the link between colonialism and sexuality. In addition, it demonstrates how patterns of sexual behavior are liable to change when a new mode of production emerges (Comaroff & Comaroff, 1997). The Edo society of Nigeria is a particularly useful site for analyzing the specific connection between sexuality and new modes of production. In this region, the nexus among money, power, and sex(uality) is quite interesting. In recent times, there has been a fervent outcry about the unprecedented spread of commercial sex work among girls of Edo origin. Hundreds of Edo girls leave the shores of Nigeria every year for cities in Europe to engage in commercial sex work. Some simply relocate to other states of the Nigerian federation to ply the sex trade. This alarming development has led to efforts to determine the historical origins of prostitution among Edo girls (Usuanlele, 1999).

Before the advent of colonization, traditional Edo Society existed as a system of compulsory heterosexuality in which the trope of masculinity predominated. The family, in spite of established forms of polygamy and extended family connections, was a central unit of social life. Women were confined to the domestic sphere and their sexuality both within and outside that sphere was strictly regulated by the patriarchate. The patriarchate achieved this regulation through the imposition of taboos together with a series of restrictions. Girls were betrothed to suitors at an early age. Widows got remarried to their in-laws. A woman's sexual violations or misconduct was believed to bring bad luck, disease, and even death to her husband, her children and to herself. This stable cosmological framework provided the basis for a communalism in which the individual was subject to the will and regulatory mechanisms of the collective. By extension, this implied that the price of belonging to the community meant the abrogation of social "difference." Difference that was not mediated by

convention was usually the route to social death, exclusion, or even madness. Within the relatively stable conditions of this *habitus* (Bourdieu, 1977),[7] an entrenched form of patriarchy predominated in which all subjects performed according to a recognizable set of social, moral, and cultural codes.

If we agree that the body is a site of incorporated history, as Pierre Bourdieu avers, then it is logical to expect a disruption of that history when an alien set of historical imperatives enters into a given social field. The beginning of colonization meant a rupture in the mode of social relations that existed in traditional Edo society.[8] In fact, this rupture of the domestic space also created a series of dichotomies within the old social structure.

British colonization brought about new relations between labor and capital and led to the emergence of new technologies of domination. The colonial economy established by Britain divested the traditional society of its institutions, mechanisms, and practices of social control and regulation. Under these circumstances, the colonial subject—whether male or female—faced a series of challenges that made life more difficult. For instance, how were they to operate within the dynamics of an entirely new mode of production? The monetarization of the domestic economy disempowered many people and created new forms of social stratification. Young men took to wage labor in order to cater to new private needs that were hardly ever fulfilled. This form of monetarization and marketization overturned the traditional codes of trade by barter and in so doing, created new kinds of social dispossession.

As men became bound to wage labor, this profoundly affected the domestic space where the combined effects of colonialism and capitalism were fast transforming the homestead. In pursuing a means of livelihood, men renounced a space in which they had previously been invested with unquestioned authority. Sexist discrimination ensured that men secured most of the jobs provided by the colonial economy while women remained even more economically vulnerable.

Women, vulnerable even in the best of conditions, were forced to leave the domestic sphere in order to survive within the new economy as it had very few opportunities open to them.

For women, survival usually entailed the ascription of a different kind of history to her body. This history drew its raison d'être from monetized sex trafficking. The mines and plantations attracted a pool of labor that was, in turns, distracted and pacified by women who sold sex for a living. In this way, the female body came to assume a different kind of history. The unattached female body was marked as an object of sale by the emergent colonial economy. The onslaught of the colonial economy not only disrupted the stability of the traditional homestead but threw up a new system of values and mode of conduct that for a time left many confused. I am not denying women's agency—agency is never completely destroyed, but merely highlighting the profundities of the rupture in the traditional precolonial society. These discontinuities in the domestic space transformed the dispositions of the postcolonial subject (both men and women) to correspond with the demands of the colonial economy.

True, even before the colonial encounter, a system of compulsory heterosexuality existed in the precolonial paradigm and the interests that created this historical conjuncture were decidedly masculinist.[9] But the intrusion of the colonial enterprise into the domestic space destabilized the precolonial order of things in a rather profound way. The colonized subject could no longer remain completely stable within its customary space. The logic of capital (even in its rudimentary form) necessitated that subjects of the precolonial paradigm had to transgress the domestic space according to its disruptive logic. Quite frequently, the unities of families were undermined as men went far afield to work. However, that rupture was relatively minimal when compared to the discontinuities caused by Bretton Woods institutions, which induced structural adjustment programs, and the processes of contemporary globalization (Comaroff & Comaroff, 2000a). The Bretton Woods policies further undermined

the economic viability of many homes some of which simply disintegrated under the weight of unfavorable economic circumstances.

GLOBAL UNCERTAINTIES

To be sure, in Nigeria, structural adjustment programs of the postcolonial period and subsequent processes of contemporary globalization have inflicted even greater degrees of economic disempowerment. This struggle for survival caused further rupturing not only of the constitution of the domestic space, but in this specific instance mobilizing bodies well beyond the national space. Under contemporary globalization, the national economy has been reduced to a comatose state and productive sectors are experiencing far-reaching processes of deformalization where the powers and legitimacy of the state are being severely tested. The welfarist pretensions of the state were renounced under contemporary globalization as social services such as education, housing, health care, and transport were severely undermined. In addition, the collapse of public infrastructure and utilities during the present postcolonial era meant that the subject-citizen had to use alternative forms of institutional support that were, in many cases, the very products of processes of informalization. As a result of these processes of informalization and deinstitutionalization, a blurring of the demarcation between the legitimate and illegitimate, between the boundaries of nation-states and between various regions and organizations of commerce has occurred. Years of military misrule (in the 1960s, 1970s, 1980s, up until 1999) had eroded formal institutions of modern governance in most of Nigeria. Governmental corruption became even more rampant as the quality of life among the general citizenry worsened.

This new political economy in which the nation-states of Africa now play a greatly diminished role in the existence of the subject-citizen means that everyone has to negotiate a welter of informal arrangements, associations, practices, and regions in order to survive.

These informal arrangements include the provision of personal security such as vigilantes in place of bona fide law enforcement agencies, the patronage of ruthless loan sharks, and organization of sanitary disposal systems. These developments have further created more tensions and placed heavier burdens on the domestic space. As the national economy of Nigeria declined, it became attractive for Edo indigenes to travel to Europe and the Americas in search of economic opportunities. Oftentimes, these opportunities were to be found in the informal sectors of foreign economies doing illegal work. For women, more often than not, sex work provided the only option after the collapse of the formal economy. Men on their part usually engaged in credit card fraud.

For the women of Edo, the Nigerian national space became a sort of cipher that had little to offer. The shores of Europe became far more attractive—despite their postindustrial capital, digitalized social stratification, and numerous dangers to the alien and unwanted body. For those at home, the disaporic Edo women doing sex work in Europe were no longer thought to be at the margins; they had become the very engine of a productive economy that brought back the glamour and seductions of Western wealth to the postcolony. The fact that sex work is a culturally and historically devalued mode of production is often downplayed. In other words, there has been a significant transformation of the consciousness of sexuality related to the moral reevaluation of commercial sex work. The powerful images of abundance that postindustrial society projected seem to be more appealing than the images and intimations of its underside of pornographic excess.

Nonetheless, there have been official schemes by government to discourage the institutionalization of sex work as a site of production.[10] But these schemes appear more to be an exercise in moralism without an enabling framework. The formal economic sector remains exceedingly weak, unemployment among both the educated and uneducated remains high and the provision of social services is not forthcoming.

In this section, I have tried to trace the development of commercial sex work to the advent of the colonial encounter, which brought about a new form of relations of exchange and a rupturing of the precolonial domestic space. However, this rupture was largely confined to the Edo region and its environs. On the other hand, processes of contemporary globalization not only denuded the Edo domestic space of its relative stability but went on to transgress the traditional concept of territoriality. The Nigerian national space ceased to be a site of primary attraction due to its serious economic crises. In the same vein, the unprotected and socially devalued margins of Europe became infinitely more attractive.

A General Economy of Postcolonial Sexuality

There is also a lot to be said about discourses of sexuality as they relate to both institutionalized and deinstitutionalized forms of power. Nigeria, similar to other parts of the African postcolony, is a site marked by the most startling kinds of hybridity; the sex(ed) subject/object is constructed accordingly with the same degree of difference, variation, and violence. One way to note this peculiar kind of hybridity is to observe how the Western concept of marriage operates in the postcolonial context.

Michel Foucault describes how the modern concept of marriage was informed by the Malthusian principle in which the dominant order sought to regulate and police the population. According to Foucault,

at the heart of this economic and political problem of population was sex: it was necessary to analyze the birth rate, the age of marriage, the legitimate and illegitimate births, the precocity and frequency of sexual relations, the ways of making them fertile or sterile, the effects of unmarried life or of the prohibitions, the impact of contraceptive practices—of those notorious "deadly secrets," which demographers on the eve of Revolution knew were already familiar to the inhabitants of the countryside (1978, pp. 25–26).

By instituting mechanisms of regulation, an entire spectrum of discursive industries, value systems, practices, and establishments were empowered. In other words, there was a deliberate complication of the social space in which the sex(ed) subject was not only normalized and named but also in which the development of the very discourse of sexuality itself was institutionalized through a series of well-developed mechanisms. In the domestic site, the organization of space had familial sexuality as its central focus. The same can be said of the work place, the educational institutions, barracks, and so on.

But in the postcolony, it can be argued that the policing of the social space is not as systematic due to the tradition of extended family structures that undermine the Western model of the nuclear family (Simone, 2004). For example, polygamy is still a widespread practice that further hybridizes the social space even within the frame and practice of a modern economy. The phenomenon of overcrowding (Mbembe, 2001) in most African urban centers can also be ascribed to the unsystematic policing of the social space, which undoubtedly defeats the Malthusian principle.

Thus the African postcolonial social body as a whole is often marked by multiple binarisms; precolonial/postcolonial, premodern/modern, polygamy/monogamy, formal/informal, male/female. However crude these binarisms may appear in delineating the nature of the social space, they do serve a functional purpose. But more specifically, consider the way in which institutionalized forms of power discursively produce sexuality. For example, a striking analogy is provided by the death of the late Nigerian dictator General Sani Abacha who succeeded in turning the nation into "the sick man of Africa." It is often claimed that Abacha "overdosed on Viagra, taken to fortify his body from the strain of his notorious sexual appetite" (Maier, 2000, p. 4). Even more spectacularly, he expired in the arms of a pair of Indian prostitutes who had been flown into the country on the presidential jet without travel documents. Abacha's demise in this manner had a powerful hold on the popular imagination. This homology between power and

sexuality is beginning to receive adequate academic attention. The ultimate ruler in the postcolony must live up to the societal expectation of "pumping grease and rust into the backsides of young girls" (Tansi as cited by Mbembe, 2001, p. 110). In other words,

> The male ruler's pride in possessing an active penis has to be dramatized through sexual rights over subordinates, the keeping of concubines, and so on. The unconditional subordination of women to the principle of male pleasure remains one pillar upholding the reproduction of the phallocratic system (ibid.).

This sexual economy is maintained by state violence. The criminalization of the state in the African postcolony and the steady erosion of the bases of its legitimacy and authority have led to an almost compulsive dramatization of its remaining relics. The state must not only possess but act on the ability to dispense random and often deinstitutionalized violence otherwise, it is deemed worthless. Some of the means by which it does this involve staging lavish parades and ceremonies to elicit the awe of its subjects and ensure the continued subjugation of a politically and economically disempowered populace. This lack of *actually existing rights* within the populace on the one hand, and the centralization of the means of violence (although this is not always the case in strife torn regions of the African continent) on the other, reproduce a sexual economy in which the democratic interaction between the sexes becomes difficult if not impossible in periods of extreme conflict. This sexual economy not only reproduces the subjugation of the female subject (in some cases in the most degrading manner) but also simultaneously fetishizes the phallus as a symbol of power, domination, and violence. These tropes of domination and devaluation undoubtedly mark the collective unconscious and therefore continue to reinforce the sexual status quo. The status quo promotes the view that the possession of the female subject goes hand in hand with the acquisition of some form of power: either in terms of wealth, or control, or of a means of violence. But there are even more productive ways of highlighting the correlation between sex and violence. Indeed there are many similarities between the sexual economies of both precolonial and postcolonial Nigeria.

This particular form of violence has also entered into the general economy of sexuality (Mbembe, 2001). From Liberia, to Sierra Leone, to Rwanda and Burundi the story is the same. As a result, gang rape is now considered a common feature within such a context.[11] To accentuate even further the centrality of this form of violence within the sexual economy, it is instructive to note that in Nigeria, the rampant cases of armed robbery especially in the urban centers have a sizeable component of gang rape (Udegbe & Omolola, 1994). These cases often go unreported but the phenomenon pervades the collective unconscious.

The combination of the gun and phallus in the construction of the general economy of sexuality is thus very powerful even when not voiced as a rigorous and systematic discourse of the public. It is often argued that the state in the postcolony promotes and sustains an economy of violence. The specificities of this destructive economy are in turn appropriated by the larger society and distilled into the domestic space. To construct an alternative discourse of sexuality, the disempowering conjuncture between sex/ power/violence has to be ruptured. The phallus as a symbol of domination has to be demystified, and the vagina as a mere receptacle of violence must be deconstructed.

In this section, I further examine how the general economy of sexuality in the postcolony has been affected by adverse processes of contemporary globalization. How, for instance, have new degrees of economic disempowerment ruptured the sexual positionalities within the domestic space and what are the most significant effects of this rupturing? In answering this question, we observe that new tropes of sexualization and genderization are entering into the sexual field. But these tropes are also linked with struggles for power (often times in its crude manifestations).

In Nigeria, some groups are advancing arguments that the figure of the *father* in its previous mode of patriarchy is under siege (Ashforth, 1999). This is consistent with what is happening, in many postcolonial contexts, where there exists what has been termed "the crisis of masculinity" (Comaroff & Comaroff, 2000a). Under conditions of contemporary global capitalism, the utopian dreams generated by the collapse of communism on the one hand, and the dismantling of the apartheid system on the other, have been dispelled. The workplace, industry, and "regular" blue-collar jobs are under siege as a result of a spectral mobility of capital (Friedman, 1999). In the same vein, "the end of work" has been proclaimed (Forrester, 1996).

Indeed neoliberalism is exploding many of the dearly held myths and historically constituted categories such as "the family," "parenthood," "the labor force," "youth," and so on. For instance, it has been argued that "the family" in the African postcolony (and elsewhere) is being deconstructed (Comaroff & Comaroff, 2000b). From Soweto to Lagos and Yaounde, the same crisis of masculinity exists in conditions where old jobs are fast disappearing and new ones are not forthcoming. This creates unbearable tensions within the domestic space where patriarchal forms of domination exist. In its present formation, post-Fordist capitalism is destroying many stable traditional social orders without replacing them with credible alternatives in areas still grappling with building modern institutions. However, old habits and dispositions die hard. The myth of the all powerful *father* as the head of family still holds its allure even to youth who evidently are going to be permanently dispossessed and who are witnessing genuine processes of demasculinization. These conditions assault their very sense of maleness (masculinity) with all its previous challenges, rights, and privileges. The most significant outcome of this trope of demasculinization can be seen not only within the domestic sphere but also at work. For instance, it has been noted that the labor force is increasingly being feminized to further strengthen profits and the capacities for accumulation. Capital seeks vulnerable groups—the poorly educated, women with no social and economic capital, and illegal immigrants—who are less capable of voicing opposition to its modes of exploitation.

The way that the violence of capitalism is played out in the domestic sphere further disempowers men and increases their sense of frustration. Within a sexist and outmoded understanding of the family, it means a lot for men to be able to provide for all. Clearly, under neoliberal conditions this can no longer be so. Without a job, men are put at risk as the perceived harmony of the domestic space is jeopardized. In postcolonial societies where forms of patriarchy are still hegemonic, those tensions are bound to be even more pronounced as old constructions of self, status, and power are rapidly undermined. Paradoxically, in such a context, as processes of demasculinization gain momentum, men continue to attempt to police and define female sexuality that is, in terms of legitimating discourses of sexuality pertaining strictly to women.

This attempt to define female sexuality assumes many forms. Men try to prescribe what type of clothes women wear, where they can go and cannot go, what they can do and cannot do and their general repertoire of responses in periods of courtship. Men still attempt to uphold all these jaded formulas. In other words, in spite of their diminishing powers and influence under the forces of global capitalism, men still insist on exerting the old forms of social control and regulation. Perhaps more than anything else, these forces are what will finally dissolve the long held mythologies of the phallocratic system.

CONCLUSION:
THE HOME WITHOUT A FATHER

In the African postcolony, several factors are working to change the traditional ordering of the domestic space, most importantly, the conditions created by neoliberalism. Perhaps for the first time, the figure of the *father* is undergoing real and radical demythification (read disempowerment). However, anthropomorphic forms of patriarchy still exist especially in regions where the Islamic religion prevails. But those forms themselves are not free from the disruptive effects of global capitalism and the radical reordering of the domestic space that it brings in its wake. In the postcolony, the categories of "the family," "male," and "female" have to be rethought in terms of the ruptures, discontinuities, and reconstitutions that not only undermine the conventional conceptions of those categories but also seek to recontextualize the very notion of the nation-state itself. Indeed traditional forms of patriarchy will continue to attempt to prevail thereby compounding the problem of domestic violence but the instabilities caused by this dynamic nexus of tensions are where the struggles to recreate our enfeebled social and domestic categories must be waged.

In other words, these crucial moments of destabilization obviously indicate that our previous forms, discourses, and dispositions of sexuality are no longer generally applicable. And these uncertain moments perhaps provide the vital openings by which we can be liberated from the matrixes constructed by outmoded discourses of sexuality (Trend, 1996).[12] However, the processes of contemporary globalization continue to undermine the cohesion of both conventional territoriality and the domestic space. These processes bring in their wake times of great uncertainty as evidenced in several quarters where the old orders are fighting back, reinforcing unfashionable ideological regimes because no alternate process has been created to provide the hope and succor those old orders once supplied. The reaffirmation of the *Sharia* legal code in most parts of northern Nigeria corroborates this view. What does this state of postcolonial existential flux imply for analyses of sexuality? Obviously, it means our conceptual mechanisms for reading the contours and transformations of sexuality must acquire even greater mobility and flexibility.

The sites analyzed for this essay, northern Nigeria and the region that used to be called midwestern Nigeria (now politically called the south) cannot be more different with regards to the conceptual terrain on which the politics of sexuality is articulated. In the north, a conflation of the public and the private realms exists; also, the injunctions of the *Sharia* legal code extend beyond the sphere of religion as it informs the operations of the organs of state as well as the questions and preoccupations of jurisprudence. Here, the female subject is largely silent, confined as it were, to a religiously enforced domesticity. In this ideological terrain, the male subject, backed by the academy and the law enforces this order even in moments when his acts sometimes undermine it. In many ways, the introduction of the *Sharia* legal code was not a ploy to simply keep women subjugated. Indeed, at the national level it should also be construed as a broader political struggle between men. The adoption of the legal code in most parts of the north constitutes a questioning of the federal power structure and a willingness to undermine its legitimacy in constitutional terms. But in carrying out this great political maneuver, significant shifts also occurred in the politics of gender and sexuality within the broad spectrum of the region. Thus a political strategy that was intended to transform the political equation at the national level in fact did more to change the nature of northern regional politics and consequently, the politics of gender and sexuality.

On the other hand, in the Edo-speaking region of Nigeria ideologues of religion exert no such influence. Rather, the subjectification of women and the configuration of the domestic space were ruptured by two major modes of production—the colonial economy and contemporary processes of globalization. The logic and exertions of the colonial economy disrupted the stability of the domestic space. Both men and women were forced out of the traditional spaces of domesticity and were compelled to enter into new regions and activities of commerce. The entry into these new regions of commerce led to a transformation of the politics of sexuality within the confines of the region and to some extent, the nation-space. However, processes of contemporary globalization led to an even greater disruption of the stability of the domestic space as well as the economic devaluation of the nation-space itself. This compelled women within the Edo-speaking region to seek their economic fortunes beyond the shores of Nigeria and this usually entailed a transformation of the politics of sexuality. In essence, popular myths about the prevalence of commercial sex work among Edo girls can only make sense against the background of an awareness of these disruptive shifts in local and global modes of production.

The regimes of sexuality in northern Nigeria and the Edo-Benin region of the country are quite obviously dissimilar. This basic difference also reflects the dissimilarity existing in the political field between the two regions. This, in turn, can be traced to the colonial encounter that upheld distinct modes of colonial penetration and administration. As such, even the ongoing conversation with modernity in the two regions is marked by their specific histories of colonialism and modes of religious worship among other factors.

Notes

1. See Michel Foucault, *The history of sexuality* Vol. 1, translated by Robert Hurley (London: Penguin Books, 1978); *The history of sexuality* Vol. 2, translated by Robert Hurley (London: Penguin Books, 1985); and the *The history of sexuality* Vol. 3, translated by Robert Hurley (London: Penguin Books, 1986).

2. One is aware that Foucault explores a different dimension to the repression thesis. Foucault ascribes the spread of the repression thesis to the growth of capitalism in which sexuality was repressed to aid the development of a work ethic. See his *history of sexuality:* Vol. 1: 4–6.

3. The *Sharia* police, locally known as the *Hisba* are quite active in the *Sharia*-administered states.

4. The trials of Amina Lawal and Safiya Hassanini for fornication created a lot of controversy within Nigeria and drew the attention of the global media.

5. Calyxthe Beyala, the Cameroonian novelist and public intellectual has written copiously and stridently about the phenomenon of "the dictatorship of the balls."

6. See John L. Comaroff and Jean Comaroff, *Of revelation and revolution: Christianity, colonialism and consciousness in South Africa* (Chicago: University of Chicago Press, 1991). In the beginning of this volume, they argue that hegemony is never a stable construct. For other arguments, see Judith Butler, Enesto Laclau, and Slavoj Zizek, *Contingency, hegemony, universality* (London: Verso, 2000).

7. I employ this concept as advanced by Pierre Bourdieu, *Outline of a theory of practice* translated by Richard Nice (New York: Cambridge University Press, 1977).

8. For an account of how previously stable relations are severely disrupted by new modes of production, see Dani W. Nabudere, *Africa's First World War: Mineral Wealth, Conflicts and War in the Great Lakes Region.* Pretoria: AAPS Occasional Paper Series, *8*(1), (2004).

9. Read Judith Butler, *Gender trouble: Feminism and the subversion of identity* (New York and London: Routledge, 1990) and Even Kosofsky Sedgwick, *Epistemology of the Closet*, (Berkeley and Los Angeles: University of California Press, 1990). For non-Western and postcolonial discussions of sexuality, see Tshikala K. Biaya's Eroticism and Sexuality in Africa: Directions and Illusions, *CODESRIA Bulletin*, Numbers 3/4, (1999); S. Murray and R. Will (Eds.), *Boy—Wives and Female Husbands: Studies* in *African Homosexualities* (New York: St. Martin's Press, 1998); M. Eppredit, The unsaying of Indigenous homosexualities in Zimbabwe: Mapping a blind spot in an African masculinity, *Journal of South African Studies 24*(4), (1998); and Francoise Verges, Sex, milk and death: The enigma of sexuality, *CODESRIA Bulletin, 3/4,* (1999).

10. Eki Igbinedion, the wife of the former Edo State governor launched the Idia Renaissance to combat the popular view that Benin City is the "Sex capital of Nigeria." Relatedly, Charles Idahosa, a supporter of the Edo State governor and member of the board of the Nigerian Television Authority said in an interview, "Hardly any family exists in Benin which has no daughter in Italy," *The Guardian Sunday*, April 7, 2002.

11. The prevalence of many kinds of full-scale conflict in the African postcolony has led to the widespread phenomenon of child-soldiers who now play a very prominent role in the perpetration of violence.

12. See David Trend (Ed.), *Radical democracy: Identity, citizenship and the state* (New York and London: Routledge, 1996). In this volume, one often comes across the view that there is a correlation between the broadening and intensification of democracy and the multiplication of discourses of sexuality.

REFERENCES

Albert, Olawale. (1996). *Women and urban violence in Kano, Nigeria.* Ibadan, NG: Spectrum Books.

Ashforth, Adam. (1999). Weighing manhood in Soweto. *Council for the Development of Economic and Social Research in Africa, CODESRIA Bulletin, 3–4.*

Babaji, B. (2004). *Equity for women under Sharia Law in Nigeria,* Lagos, NG: Gender and Development Action.

Biaya, Tshikala K. (1999). Eroticism and sexuality in Africa: Directions and illusions. *CODESRIA Bulletin, 3–4.*

Bourdieu, Pierre. (1977). *Outline of a theory of practice* (Richard Nice, Trans.). New York, NY: Cambridge University Press.

Butler, Judith. (1990). *Gender trouble: Feminism and the subversion of identity.* New York, NY: Routledge.

Butler, Judith, Laclau, Enesto, & Zizek, Slavoj. (2000). *Contingency, hegemony, universality.* London, UK: Verso.

Comaroff, John L., & Comaroff, Jean. (1991). *Of revelation and revolution: Christianity, colonialism and consciousness in South Africa.* Chicago, IL: University of Chicago Press.

Comaroff, John L., & Comaroff, Jean. (1997). *Of revelation and revolution: The diatectics of modernity on a South African frontier* (Vol. 2). Chicago, IL: University of Chicago Press.

Comaroff, John L., & Comaroff, Jean. (2000a, Spring). Millennial capitalism: First thoughts on a Second Coming. *Public Culture, 12*(2).

Comaroff, John L., & Comaroff, Jean. (2000b). Naturing the nation: Aliens, apocalypse, and the postcolonial state. *HAGAR: International Social Science Review, 1*(1).

Eppredit. M. (1998). The "unsaying" of indigenous homosexualities in Zimbabwe: Mapping a blind spot in an African masculinity. *Journal of South African Studies, 24*(4).

Forrester, Viviane. (1996). *The economic horror* (Sheila Molovancy–Chevallier, Trans.). Cambridge, UK: Polity Press.

Foucault, Michel. (1978). *The history of sexuality* (Vol. 1). (Robert Hurley, Trans.). London, UK: Penguin Books.

Foucault, Michel. (1985). *The history of sexuality* (Vol. 2). (Robert Hurley, Trans.). London, UK: Penguin Books.

Foucault, Michel. (1986). *The history of sexuality* (Vol. 3). (Robert Hurley, Trans.). London, UK: Penguin Books.

Friedman, Thomas. (1999). *The Lexus and the olive tree*. New York, NY: Farrar Straus and Giroux.

Huntington, Samuel P. (1996). *The clash of civilizations and the remaking of world order*. New York, NY: Touchstone.

Je'adayibe, Gwamna Dogara. (2004). *Sharia, gender and rights of non-Muslims in northern Nigeria*. Lagos, NG: Gender and Development Action, 16.

Maier, Karl. (2000). *This house has fallen: Midnight in Nigeria*. New York, NY: Karl Maier Public Affairs.

Mamdani, Mahmood. (2004). *Good muslim, bad muslim*. New York, NY: Pantheon Books.

Mbembe, Achille. (2001). *On the postcolony*. Berkeley: University of California Press.

Murray, S., & Will, R. (Eds.). (1998). *Boy—wives and female husbands: Studies in African homosexualities*. New York, NY: St. Martin's Press.

Nabudere, Dani W. (2004). Africa's first world war: Mineral wealth, conflict and war in the Great Lakes region. Pretoria: *Association of African Political Science (AAPS)* Occasional Paper Series, *8*(1).

Sedgwick, Kosofsky. (1990). *Epistemology of the closet*. Berkeley: University of California Press.

Simone, Abdou Maliq. (2004). *For the city yet to come: Changing life in four African cities*. Durham, NC: Duke University Press.

Slaheddine, Ben Fradj. (1999). Faith and pleasure in Islam: The case of Tunisia. *CODESRIA Bulletin,3–4*.

Trend, David (Ed.). (1996). *Radical democracy: Identity, citizenship and the state,* New York, NY: Routledge.

Udegbe, B. I., & Omolola, O. O. (1994). Adolescence and sexual violence in a Nigerian urban environment. In I. O. Albert, J. Adisa, T. Agboola, & G. Herault (Eds.), *Urban management and urban violence in Africa* (Vol. 1). Ibadan, NG: IFRA.

Usuanlele, Uyilawa. (1999). Colonialism and the origin of female prostitution among the Benins of Edo State. *Benin Studies Newsletter, 4*(3).

Verges, Francoise. (1999). Sex, milk and death: The enigma of sexuality. *CODESRIA Bulletin, 3–4*.

11

THE BAD AND THE GOOD (QUEER) IMMIGRANT IN ITALIAN MASS MEDIA

VALENTINA PAGLIAI

INTRODUCTION

This chapter[1] examines the Italian media response to the first case where refugee status was granted to a gay man (pseudonym of Arben) on the basis of sexual discrimination in his country of origin (Albania), and compares it to a similar case in Britain involving a lesbian woman from Iran named Pegah. I consider these two cases within the larger fields of racist and sexist discourse, and the political field of the construction of "otherness" and nation-state boundaries. I examine how media and political parties deploy discourses on sexuality and human rights to construct a "lack of civilization" of the home societies of immigrants, thus reinforcing racist positions against them. In particular, I examine how these two cases of Queer[2] asylum seekers were used to build representations of the immigrants' home countries as premodern and "savage" in order to position the Italian national self as modern, western European, and morally superior.

First, I compare the conservative press and parties' positive support for granting refugee status to Arben and Pegah to their general homophobic stances. Second, I argue that such a contradiction must be understood in terms of the negative racialized and gendered images of immigrants in general, and Muslim immigrants in particular, that are continuously constructed by the Italian mass media. I consider how support for Arben's refugee case both racialized and gendered Albanians as a whole, constructing them as morally inferior (male) Others from whom the "feminized" gay man had to be protected. Here, the projection of homophobia onto the non-European Other allows the concurrent erasure from view of homophobic discrimination in Italy.

The reasons that allow such co-optation of Queerness must be carefully considered. Acceptance of sexual minorities in Italy is connected to processes of imagination of the Italian nation-state as "modern" and as European. Such acceptance can also be part of nation-building efforts, as noted by William Leap in his analysis of post-apartheid South Africa (2004, p. 136). This also creates the so-called new, modern, neoliberal citizen, as tolerant of "differences." But these same national formations also necessitate racist ideologies that can naturalize the boundary between the citizens and the foreigners. As Tom Boellstorff and Leap note, sexuality becomes part of "international interchanges" (2004, p. 2). Race and gender are entangled in the articulation of political transactions that have deep resonance on the life of immigrants, Queers, and nonqueers.

In showing the articulation of racist discourse with discourse about sexuality and homophobia, my work locates itself in the field of Critical Discourse Analysis (CDA). As Deborah Cameron (2001) notes, discourse analysis is actually an umbrella term with several meanings, partially due to the fact that different disciplines and currents of thought define "discourse" in very different ways, from simply language beyond the sentence, to language use in social context, to a more Foucaultian view of discourse as "practices which systematically form the objects of which they speak" (Foucault, 1972, p. 49). This last definition, in particular, is closer to Critical Discourse Analysis' call for a study of how discourse, as Ruth Wodak notes, "constitutes situations, objects of knowledge, and the social identities of and relationships between people and groups of people" (1996a, p. 15). This definition for critical discourse analysis is also the definition I adopted in my research.

In critical discourse analysis, there has been a continuing interest in the study of mass media discourse (van Dijk, 1991; Fowler, 1991; Fairclough, 1995; Maneri, 2009) and political discourse (Wodak, 1989, 1996b; Wetherell & Potter, 1992; Fairclough, 2000). As Wodak writes, discourse practices can "help produce and reproduce unequal power relations [. . .] through the ways they represent things and position people" (1996a, p. 15). Particular attention is given to the consequences of language use in the mass media on everyday understanding of truth and reality and the way elites may reinforce their power through mass media. Teun Van Dijk (1987, 1991) in

particular has looked at the hegemonic use of mass media in his analysis of British and Dutch press. In analyzing the answers that the mass media—and political groups through them—presented in Arben and Pegah's cases, my analysis contributes to this field of CDA. To this end, my research generally considers a wide range of discourse practices, from those found in everyday conversations to those emerging in political discourse. In this chapter, I focus in particular on the second form of discourse.

ARBEN'S CASE

In 2006, the Antidiscrimination Center (ADC) of the Province of Pistoia in Tuscany,[3] and the Arcigay[4] (one of the major lesbian, gay, bisexual, transgender (LGBT) associations in Italy) brought a case to court to obtain refugee status for an illegal immigrant based on his sexual identity as a gay man. Arben was a young immigrant from Albania, who self-identified as gay. He had legally entered Italy in 2004 to study at the University of Florence. However, when his parents in Albania found out that he was gay, they cut off his funds and asked him to return to Albania and marry immediately. Arben refused and started to work but was unable to earn enough money to pay the university fees, thus he had to drop out of school. No longer at the university, he could not renew his visa, which expired after a year. This made him an illegal immigrant and he lived in fear of being arrested and sent back to Albania.

Eventually, his case came to the attention of the Arcigay and the ADC; the agencies decided to collaborate on his case. However on the basis of the Geneva Convention, Italy only grants refugee status when a person can be sent to prison or condemned to death in their original country, for belonging to a certain group. Since Albania repealed the laws that punished homosexuality with prison terms in 1995, Arben did not qualify for refugee status. Moreover, at the time, the Italian law regarding refugees did not expressly include sexual minorities among those groups that could obtain refuge. Therefore, a case had to be built to show personal danger based uniquely on the presence of clear and demonstrable *discrimination* against the person, as a member of a social group, and by appealing directly to statements in the Italian Constitution. However, discrimination—as anybody encountering it probably knows—is hard to demonstrate.[5]

Gathering the documentation that could establish the presence of discrimination against homosexuals and sexual minorities in Albania took the ADC almost a year.[6] In the meantime, in 2006, the representative of the Green Party in the European parliament, Giampaolo Silvestri,[7] added an amendment to a package of laws passed to adapt Italian laws to the European Union (EU) norms. This amendment, which included sexual minorities among those eligible to request refugee status, was approved with the passage of Law N.13 on February 6, 2007.

The ADC was now ready to go to court with Arben's case. But, suddenly Arben was arrested by the police and deported to a CPT (Centro di Permanenza Temporanea—Temporary Permanence Center) in Southern Italy. The CPTs, notwithstanding their innocuous name, are in effect concentration camps where immigrants may spend months at a time, in worse than prison conditions, waiting to be sent back to their countries of origin or to obtain a permit to stay. Facing the possibility of immediate repatriation, the ADC requested and obtained faster processing of the case. Of those last days, I remember everybody in the ADC being in a frenzy, literally people working on the case were skipping meals and sleep, and some were driving back and forth across Italy to make sure Arben was kept safe while in custody. Just before repatriation became effective, the ADC was able to obtain refugee status. Arben is now back living in Tuscany, in an undisclosed location due to possible threats to his safety, and is back studying at the university.

The ADC was able to successfully argue that refugee status had to be granted, as the person would otherwise face serious personal, clear and demonstrable discrimination in his country of origin. This was the first case of this kind in Italy

and set a precedent, opening the door to other cases.[8] Indeed, even in Europe, only one similar case in Sweden had been brought to court.[9] Arben's case brought the issue of civil and personal rights of sexual minorities to the fore in Italy and reaffirmed the Italian state's duty to protect sexual minorities independently of citizenship.

IMMIGRATION IN ITALY AND THE MEDIA ANSWER

In pursuing this case, the Antidiscrimination Center struggled against a growing perception of immigrants as an undesirable presence. Traditionally an immigrant-exporting society, Italy has seen the immigrant presence grow fourfold in the past two decades to more than 4.2 million by 2009 or 6.9% of the resident population (ISTAT, 2009).[10] The majority of immigrants coming to Italy today are from the ex-communist countries of Eastern Europe (more than 2.1 million by 2009; data ISTAT, 2009) and secondarily, from Muslim countries of the circum-Mediterranean area and Pakistan (about 745,000 by 2009; data ISTAT, 2009). In terms of receiving structures, laws, educational systems, and so forth, Italy has been totally unprepared for this influx. Immigration legislation was practically absent until 1987, and today is still in a flux that keeps many immigrants in a legal limbo (Macioti & Pugliese, 2003).

The majority of immigrants are legal and hold work permits and/or residency. The number of illegal immigrants is relatively low, probably around 10% of the total number of legal immigrants (see Blangiardo, 2004, p. 41). However, the media have fostered an association of immigrants with illegality and with criminality, leading the general population to see them as an unstoppable flood that risks overcoming the native Italians. The racist rhetoric against immigrants, coming both from the mass media and from the government,[11] has been similarly increasing over the past two decades. The mass media have often been biased against immigrants and depict them in demeaning ways or as dangerous. Sibhatu (2004) in her work on mass media and racism in Italy has shown "the distorting and instrumental role of the media" (2004, p. 260) in Italy and their "centrality in guiding public opinion" (2004, p. 270; my translation). Gardner (2004) shows that while only a small fraction of immigrant women are prostitutes, the media give them disproportionate attention. In addition, the prostitutes are portrayed as slaves of other immigrants thus the problem is seen as internal to the immigrant group itself, which serves to further demonize them (2004, p. 256). Gardner points out that the mass media create a fear of the immigrants by portraying them as criminals and talking about them as an invasion that will smother a zero-growth Italian population (2004, p. 250). Foot (2001) in his study of immigrants in Turin, also shows how the media contribute to create an image of the immigrants as dangerous and criminals, leading to their harassment by the police.

The climate of hostility is growing and has recently led to racist violence by extremist groups. The governmental coalition, headed by Berlusconi, added to the fire by blaming immigration for all kinds of evils and promising (at election time) to stop it. Witness the series of laws enacted to restrict immigration and to "control" criminality—that links the image of the criminal with the image of the *clandestine* (undocumented) immigrant and other minorities (such as the Roma). The latest example is the passing of the *leggi sulla sicurezza* (security laws) in July 2009. This package of laws, viewed by many immigration attorneys as contrary to the Italian Constitution, is one of the harshest anti-immigrant directives in the world. Among other aspects, it criminalizes the very status of "clandestinity" not simply the act of illegal entry. It legalizes the *ronde*, namely private citizens' vigilantes, to patrol public spaces such as post offices, banks, and bus stops. It stipulates a significant fine and prison term for anyone providing services to illegal immigrants. In sum, the image of immigrants that people in Italy find in the media, and often mirror in everyday discourses, is one of illegality, illness, prostitution, criminality, danger, and flood (see also Pagliai, 2009, 2010). Arben's case immediately

caught the attention of the media. However, in the flurry of articles following the official news of the court's decision, their answer to this case was notably positive. With a few exceptions, most mass media maintained a neutral, mildly favorable, or favorable position on Arben's case.[12] *L'Unità*, a left-wing newspaper remarked on "The importance and the absolute novelty of his [Arben's] case," noticing that "Before today only the extremely laic and civil Sweden had been able to do something like this" (Semmola article, May 5, 2007, p. 11, my translation). Even a conservative newspaper such as *Il Giornale*, in an article with an ambiguous title ("Political Asylum to an Albanian Only because He Is Homosexual"), clearly took the side of Arben. In it, journalist Maria Sorbi writes: "Arben might not have risked death in Albania, but his life would have been ruined, certainly, by needing to fake what he is not" (May 5, 2007, pp. 1, 18, my translation).

PEGAH'S CASE

Pegah Emambakhsh is an Iranian lesbian woman who escaped to England in 2005, seeking refuge after her partner in Iran was arrested and sentenced to death by stoning. She was first refused asylum and threatened with deportation in 2007, and again in 2008. On August 13, 2007, she was arrested in Britain and put in the Yarls Wood prison. The motive for the refusal was that she could not give proof of being lesbian. She finally received asylum in England on February 11, 2009 after pressure from human rights groups and a campaign that attracted international attention in Europe.

In contrast to the relative silence over the case in Britain (see Hooper, *The Guardian*, August 24, 2007) the case received enormous attention in Italy. Italian politicians, through the mass media, gave their strongest support to Pegah's case even proposing that if England should refuse her, Italy would be ready to welcome her. Surprisingly, these favorable statements came not only from the left, which has generally fostered LGBT and immigrant rights (i.e., Franco Grillini, then an elected representative for the Democratic Left, and Barbara Pollastrini, Minister of Rights and Equal Opportunities), but also from the Italian Right and Catholic Conservatives, who have been otherwise stern in their denial of equal rights to sexual minorities (and against immigration).

In Italy and more broadly in Europe the majority of the voices raised to protect Pegah's right to receive asylum were those of the gay associations; however, the presence of voices from politicians that would not usually favor LGBT rights was notable. For example, Clemente Mastella, then Italian Minister of Justice who in August 2007 stated: "We must do everything possible so that the Iranian Pegah may come here to us, with asylum rights, according to what is provided for by our Constitution. As for what regards us we have full availability/willingness" (*La Sala*, August 25, 2007, my translation). Mastella was one of the creators of the aforementioned "security laws" package, later passed by the Berlusconi government, that criminalizes immigration and denies many human rights to immigrants.[13] The political party Forza Italia also opposed any attempt to legalize same-sex marriage or to allow LGBT couples to adopt. It's leader, Silvio Berlusconi, then Italy's Prime Minister, affirmed, when interrogated about his affairs with much younger women "well, it's better to be passionate about beautiful women than to be gay" (*Corriere della Sera*, November 2, 2010, my translation).

Clemente Mastella was not alone. Other leaders of Forza Italia followed suit, including Franco Frattini, then vice-president of the European Commission on Justice, who insisted that Britain had the duty to protect and give asylum "if there should be even just a reasonable suspect that this person is homosexual" (Quotidiano.net,[14] August 28, 2007; my translation). Frattini, in recent years has favored attempts to censor the Internet in Italy, spoken against multiculturalism, been reprimanded by the European Parliament for racist comments against Romani, and requested monetary help from the European Union to patrol the Italian coasts against "illegal" immigrants arriving by boat (*Notizie.it*, February 13, 2011).

The mass media echoed the voices of the politicians in generally asking for the protection of Pegah. Why were the mass media and politicians so favorable to these particular immigrants? To answer this question, I believe, we must look at the way in which immigrants, and in particular Albanian and Muslim immigrants, are represented in Italy, and the particular forms that racism takes in this context.

THE RACIALIZATION AND GENDERING OF ALBANIANS

Hostility against Albanians in Italy has strong racialized and gendered overtones. To understand the how it is racialized, we must abandon a model of race as based purely on the attribution of biological differences, and consider how racialization can be based on the naturalization of cultural differences. According to Etienne Balibar (1988), a *new racism* is emerging in Europe where cultural differences have become naturalized as racial differences (see also Barker, 1982; van Dijk, 2000). As Paul Gilroy notices (2004, p. xii), cultural racism has now been substituted for what was previously biologically based racism. Racist claims are hidden under assertions of "civilizational differences" (2004, p. xiii) so that "the convenient argument that some cultural differences are so profound that they cannot be bridged has become commonplace" (2004, p. xv). As Gerd Baumann (1996) argues, "culture" itself has been naturalized in dominant discourse. "This reification" writes Bauman, "is the very cornerstone that holds the dominant discourse together across all political divides" (1996, p. 11). This discourse has been used by the new conservative right to argue, as Nora Räthzel notes, "that in order to preserve the variety of cultures, people from different cultures need to stay in their respective places" (2002, p. 7).

In Italy, immigrants from Albania are a strongly racialized group. Arriving in large numbers after the fall of their communist government, they constitute Italy's second largest group of immigrants according to ISTAT statistics: in

2009, 466,684 or about half a million, which is up from 168,963 in 2003 (Papavero, 2004, p. 356). By comparison, in 1990 only 424 Albanians were present (ISTAT, 2001). The rapidity of this change makes Albanian immigrants particularly socially evident, which partially explains why Albanians are today seen as the prototypical immigrant. They are depicted as the "new barbaric horde" in Italy. They are even more evident in those regions that have absorbed a large flux of immigrants, such as Tuscany where 9% of the residents at the end of 2009 were immigrants; of these, 66,042 were Albanians. More than half of these immigrants lived in the Florence-Prato-Pistoia Metropolitan area where I was doing my study (ISTAT, 2009). In Italy in general, and in Tuscany in particular, racializing discourses against the Albanians are common as are discriminatory acts.

In Pistoia, where the ADC is located, more than half of the immigrants are of Albanian origin. This means that they are the most visible immigrant group and the recipients of a great deal of racist discourse. The Tuscans I interviewed often described Albanian immigrants as "innately violent" and prone to crime, such as "selling their sisters and daughters into prostitution" and working as pimps. Clearly, this racialization is at the same time gendered: Albania is generally portrayed as a patriarchal and macho society where women have few rights and where there is an old-fashioned view of masculinity as honor bound and in some way "primitive" and violent. The Albanian "other" is a (sexually dangerous) patriarchal male.[15]

In building the case for Arben to achieve the refugee status concession, the ADC at times used similar racialized and gendered discourses to depict Albania as a fundamentally homogenous and fixed society, and invoked "Albanian culture" as the problematic element that leads to the discrimination of the sexual minorities. This argument was used by the ADC to demonstrate the danger of discrimination and possible physical harm if Arben had been repatriated. For example, in the attached synthesis in the dossier prepared for the court case, we read: "The so called *outing* is very little diffused, due to the prejudices that are still today dominant in Albanian culture."[16] The documentation was also presented in a way that negated the existence of the same discriminations in Italy.

The reification of culture in cultural racism shows that, as Unni Wikan had previously noted, culture is an "inherently dangerous" concept (2002, p. 76), especially when understood as fixed traditions, or in deterministic senses. For one, the concept tends to underscore a homogeneity in social groups and therefore can be deployed as an ideological tool of domination. As Wikan points out, it is important to keep in mind that "culture is a concept, not a thing; it has no autonomous or material existence" (2002, p. 87). As a pure analytic concept, Wikan continues, culture does not "have any power—beyond what people attribute to it [. . . .] Culture is often portrayed as if it possessed uncontestable and uncontested authority, whereas authority actually rests with those who hold power" (2002, p. 87). Any analysis that attributes agency to culture must, therefore, be critically scrutinized.

It is important to examine the strategic functions of the ADC appeals to "culture" in their report on Arben's case. The ADC was indirectly compelling the Italian authorities to disassociate themselves from that same kind of discrimination, but situating them already in a "higher moral ground" where such discrimination should not and could not happen. In a sense, their appeals to culture were intended to coax the Italian authorities into granting asylum, by implying that nothing less is expected of a "more civil" country. They circuitously told Italian courts and lawmakers that: "Italians are civilized, therefore we do not do these things— and if you should do them, then you would be as prejudiced as the Albanians are."[17] However, the main thrust of the ADC dossier reports on Arben was to denounce the action of Albanian police (and in particular Tirana's Station No. 1 was mentioned several times) and hence identify a clear agent connected to the Albanian power structure rather than a more amorphous notion of "culture." The ADC assembled a list of testimonials from other cases of sexual minorities who had suffered discrimination at the hands of the police in Albania. They reported unwarranted searches, arrests, beatings, and tortures. Many of the documents included were created for the purpose of raising international awareness of the oppression of sexual minorities in Albania—such as reports from international commissions and non-governmental organizations (NGOs) and also by Albanian associations—and to reveal the harsh treatment and police violence (namely state violence).

Thus, while the ADC case did include a reification of Albanian culture, it mostly pointed at a structural problem in the formulation and application of the law there. Yet state violence and police brutality against sexual minorities in Albania were generally ignored and disappeared in the mass media reaction to this case. Instead, "Albanian culture" was invoked (and given agency) as the problematic element that led to the discrimination. The mass media also focused on the Albanian "family structure"—in particular Arben's family.

The newspapers followed a similar storyline that pursued the novelty of the case and included excerpts from an interview with Arben describing the treatment of gay people in Albania and the violence he faced from his family. Then, the newspaper mentions Arben's "Italian friends," stating (or having Arben state) that he is happy and comfortable among them. The conservative *Il Giornale*, for example, contrasts Arben's family, who has "threatened him heavily. Even death threats" (Sorbi, May 5, 2007, p.18) to the Italian friends that "encouraged him." The articles often include statements from the ADC or people involved in the case, who often describe the legal side in some detail. Arben's arrival in Italy (or his stay) is generally followed by a statement underlining that he is "able to live his own life" (Fatucchi, May 5, 2007, p. 7)—a passage pictured from constraints and danger to freedom and acceptance. *Il Giornale* also inserted a report in the same May 5th issue detailing the countries (70 at the time) where homosexuality was considered a crime. The same discourse is present

across the political divide (as predicted by Gerd Bauman). In the leftist daily, *L'Unità*, we read that although in Albania homosexuality is no longer a crime "this is not true at the level of people's culture" (Semmola, May 5, 2007, p. 11).

At the same time, the mass media presented an image that allowed Italians to see themselves as fundamentally more enlightened and on a superior moral ground. The newspapers, for example, continuously contrasted the situation of oppression in Albania to the "freedom" of Italy. In Italy, the story told was that Arben would no longer be discriminated against based on his sexuality. For example, *La Nazione* wrote about the obtaining of refugee status: "An existence finally free, in 'a country—he says—where my condition has never represented an handicap'" (Trinci, May 5, 2007, my translation).[18]

In many subtle ways, the mass media were thus picking up and amplifying the mentioned indirect discourse in the ADC court case presentation: we are civilized, therefore we tolerate difference. Here in Italy is freedom; here is order. There (in Albania) is chaos. Here is the protective masculinity; there is the violent offending one. This is a duality in the construction of masculinity in many ways similar to the one noted by Nicholas De Genova and Ana Ramos-Zayas (2003) in their analysis of Puerto Rican and Mexican relationships in Chicago. On one side, a backward, "implicitly 'barbaric' or 'uncivilized' masculinity, best understood as the routine behavior of deficiently modern, 'Third World' men, an atavistic behavior that had merely been transplanted through migration to the United States and was fundamentally out of place" (2003, p. 110). Against this was positioned a masculinity "informed by absolute moral strictures that demanded self-control and demonstrated self-discipline" (2003, p. 110). Thus the mass media, even while portraying Arben in a positive light, were constructing a negatively racialized and gendered image of Albanians. They depicted Arben's case as one in which the Italians had successfully stepped in, to protect the "feminized" male from the other males. How can we avoid being reminded, here, of the colonialist trope of the white West protecting third-world women from third-world men—amply critiqued by postcolonial and feminist scholarship (Said, 1979; McClintock, 1995; Mohanty, 1997; see also Ghosh, 2008). Lacking in the mass media was an analysis of the presence of discrimination against sexual minorities in Italy, or of police violence in Albania. In sum, the process of obtaining due rights for a minority person passed through a homogenization of the Albanian other, against which the individual sexual minority was made to stand as oppressed, and in which the oppression of sexual minorities in Italy was simultaneously erased from view.

THE CONSTRUCTION OF THE SAVAGE HOMOPHOBIC MUSLIM

In the details of Pegah's case we see a similar process of representation happening; except in this case, the "Other" constructed is Arab/Muslim (the two terms are practically never distinguished in Italian mass media and popular culture). After September 11th, in European newspapers the continuous pairing of images of terrorism with images of Arabs or Muslims grew exponentially and has strengthened to the point that, in my research, I found people in everyday conversations using the term "terrorist" and "Arab" interchangeably (see also Pagliai, 2009). In Italy, this image is paired with two other images—that of the veiled/oppressed Muslim woman and that of the "religious fanatic" Muslim who wants to negate Italian religious freedom. The image of the "religious fanatic" is often reinforced, both in everyday conversation and media discourse, by two stories: the invading Muslim who wants to build mosques, and the Muslim who is trying to force the removal of the Catholic crucifix from Italian schools. It is with this context in the background that we view the reaction to Pegah's case, where the three discourses overlap.

Violation of human rights in general and LGBT rights in particular are undoubtedly rampant in Iran today. "Sodomy" is punished with the death penalty, being lesbian is punished with a hundred lashes or even with death by stoning. Shortly before Pegah's case, a young gay man, Makwan Moloudzadeh, had been put to death. Following the lead of gay rights associations and movements, such as EveryOne and the Arcigay, the Italian mass media reinforced these facts, But added to these much-needed denunciations of human rights violations, the mass media also interwove two other discourses: one of savagery and one that generalized from Iran to "all Muslim/Arabs" as connected to religious intolerance and sexist oppression. For example, Fabrizio Cicchitto, vice-coordinator of Forza Italia and congressman,[19] with a strongly anti-immigrant position, affirmed his agreement with Italy "giving asylum in Italy to Pegah Emambakhsh, whom the barbaric Iranian government wants to stone to death, because she is lesbian" (De Giovannangeli, August 25, 2007, p. 13). And if there was any doubt about Cicchitto's concern for asylum seekers, note that the Forza Italia party, during its government term created agreements with Libya to repatriate undocumented people seeking asylum. Immigrants arriving to Italy across the Mediterranean, no matter the country of origin, were sent to Libya where they "disappeared" in desert prisons. Refusal to allow for the human rights of people seeking asylum and human trafficking were widespread and unchecked in Libya, where documentation has shown cases of people abandoned to die in the desert between Libya, Sudan, or Chad.[20]

Il Quotidiano.net published the news regarding Pegah (August 27, 2007) under the heading "Religious Intolerance" and sandwiched between an article entitled "Moroccan Woman Rebels to the Husband Owner," and one entitled "[He] Does not Tolerate the Madonna and Bricks It Up." This second about a Moroccan immigrant who tries to destroy an ancient shrine to the Virgin, and its statuette, outside of the house where he lives.

In the daily center-left journal *La Repubblica*, in an article titled "Let's Save Pegah from Stoning," the author starts the article with a graphic description of a stoning. And he concludes writing that Great Britain:

> has been and remains a refuge for many Muslims that profess openly to hate [Great Britain], partially exactly because of its liberal opinions on homosexuality, and for its laws on human rights. Some Muslims, accused of instigating terrorism, have been deported, but not the larger majority. Still [. . .] to deport Pegah Emambakhsh would be not only unjust: it would be unworthy of a civil/civilized State (Lloyd, August 23, 2007, my translation).

Thus the author has constructed an indexical field that weaves together Iran, homophobia, and asylum seekers with Muslim "terrorists." Note the ambiguity in the statement that some "have been deported" but not the majority. In the sentence the word "majority" could ambiguously refer both to the terrorists, or to Muslims in general, who thus become what Paul Silverstein and Chantal Tetreault have dubbed "suspect citizens" (2006). In addition, the whole story is couched between the opening spectacle of savagery in the stoning, and the final statement regarding the responsibility of a "civil/civilized" State to protect the possible victim, Pegah. In this vision, Iran becomes the focal metaphor for "all Arabs/ Muslims." Also, note the irony of proposing that Britain has a duty to protect Muslims (Pegah) against themselves: we welcome them, and they hate us, because we protect (their) human rights.

In discussing the representation of immigrants as the "abnormal" compared to the "normality" of the citizen self, Jan Blommaert and Jef Verschueren write that "migrants are our Indians, no longer a Plinian race, but at least 'pagans' (of the expansionistic and fanatical Islamic type) and 'savages' (barbarians who chop off hands, imprison their circumcised wives, and allow polygamy). In contrast to the Indians of old, they not only *symbolize* the intra-European enemy. They *are* the enemy. They seem to have penetrated in our midst, abusing our openness. They seem to form a threat to our society, which risks destruction as a result of its own tolerance if we remain unopposed to their abnormalities" (1998, p. 21). Yet, what is also

striking in the cases of both Pegah and Arben is that the abnormality is homophobia—an interesting twist from a country (Britain) that, until a few decades ago, refused entry to LGBT people, who were seen as "perverts." The Queer, instead, is normalized—not quite part of the self, but a "weak" Other who must be protected.

These representations become even clearer in the readers' commentaries on the articles, or in blogs commenting on the events. Notable among these commentaries is the extreme-right fascist and xenophobic blog "Libere Risonanze" (Free Resonances). This blog advocates the reinstatement of the death penalty (in Italy) and conducts virulent campaigns against immigrants, including sustaining the vigilante's right to "self-defense," and is highly critical of Amnesty International and human rights' campaigns. When it comes to Pegah's case, the authors' response becomes suddenly mild and enlightened. In their blog of August 27, 2007 they write:

> Pegah Emambakhsh is an Iranian citizen, her story is like those of many women and men who live, even in our country, a sexual condition different from the majority of us: Pegah in fact is lesbian. In a civil country these people make their own choice, live their preferences in a private manner, without exhibiting, without overshowing,[21] as it is required, after all, from any hetero couple as well. A civil country must be able to protect the freedom of each of us but be vigilant that this freedom not go overboard[22] in bad taste and in the imposition, at times naïve, of obscene acts. [. . .] In regard with Pegah, I warmly hope that the European Union will accept the asylum request: we serenely/calmly import the worst scum from any country of the world and then we turn our nose[23] when it comes to saving the life of an innocent.

The "civil/civilized" country is represented as allowing freedom (as long as it is exercised in private) but depicted as maybe too naïve in its importing of the "worst scum." LBGT rights are acceptable as long as normalized and kept private—along neoliberal lines—while their stance against immigration is clear—and yet, the appeal is to offer Pegah asylum in Italy.

Cases such as Pegah's are thus deployed by the conservative parties and by the extreme right alike to construct a portrait of Arab/Muslims as uncivilized savages, which coincides with the terrorist portrayal. These type of cases are also deployed by the Right and by the Left to propose an image of the Self as progressive, civilized, and modern.

Homophobia reinforces sexism in this portrait. Just as in colonialist tropes, already noted in Arben's case, we encounter the exotic female *other* who has to be protected from her own men. Pegah is a perfect symbol: she is discriminated against as woman and as lesbian, and as such needs protection. She comes to be imagined as the quintessential feminine: the woman that is completely untouched by males. This image may have in fact an origin in the popularization of the feminist-lesbian view of lesbianism of the seventies and eighties. Arlene Stein (1997) noted that in the seventies, as part of the emergence of feminist lesbian movements, the older idea of lesbians as "inverted" and thus masculine females was substituted with an image of lesbianism as "woman-identified" behavior (1997, p. 381; see also Sara Hoagland & Julia Penelope, 1988; Rich, 1980). As Eve Sedgwick writes: "Thus women who loved women were seen as more female [. . .] than those whose desire crossed boundaries of gender. The axis of sexuality, in this view, was not only highly coextensive with the axis of gender but expressive of its most heightened essence" (1990, p. 36). This conceptualization was also present in Italian feminism. This image was, after all, as Stein points out, already present in older visions of lesbians as "passionate friends" of Victorian memory (Stein, 1997, p. 382).

The image of the "barbarous Arab," is even older in Europe, as old as Europe itself, in fact. For thousands of years, the Mediterranean has been the theater of wars between armies coming from Northern Europe and from Africa. In folklore, the depiction of the Arab has consistently been as "ferocious" or barbarous savages. As Inmaculata Garcia Sanchez notes (2010; see also Flesler, 2008) in her discussion of anti-immigrant politics in Spain, it is through a recurrence of "discursive and semiotic mechanisms" that the trope of the invading "moor" is used to imagine present North African immigrants (2010, p. 4). In a sense, history is collapsed between these two focal points.

Of course, Pegah did need and deserve political asylum and protection. And she is not the only one who does. In fact, it was the restrictive and racist laws in Europe that created the need for the whole humanitarian effort in her defense in the first place. It was the European refusal that created the danger of repatriation and imprisonment for Pegah.

THE "TRENDINESS" OF BEING GAY AND THE UNFASHIONABLE IMMIGRANTS

But is it really true that discrimination against sexual minorities does not exist in Italy? Not quite. The attitudes are various, and are also changing fast, but homophobia does exist. While Tuscany is characterized by a long-standing tradition of tolerance toward sexual minorities,[24] this is paired with an unstated "don't ask don't tell" rule. Queer persons who do come out are subject to ridicule and/or discrimination. LGTB rights are limited under Italian state laws, as LGBT couples cannot marry or adopt children. Homosexuality and transsexuality are still medicalized and episodes of hate crimes, aggression, and violence against Queer persons happen almost daily (see Arcigay's Lotta Violenza reports for continuous coverage of these events). The Northern League's politician Calderoli, spokesperson for the party, went so far as to declare in a public speech that the concession of refugee status to sexual minorities would transform Italy into "the heaven of all the world's fags" (*Quotidiano.Net*, "Immigrati," September 21, 2006) proposing a delirious dream of "homosexual invasion." More recently, the Northern League has opposed LGBT adoption rights with openly homophobic arguments (such as equating being gay with pedophilia).[25]

However, in recent times the trend has been toward accepting LGBT sexualities, even when out of the closet. The expression "coming out," absent in Italian, has been borrowed from English in the form "outing" and it is used, interestingly, as a noun after the verb "to do": *fare outing*—"to do outing," meaning "to come out of the closet." This mirrors similar trends throughout Europe. A battle to obtain equal rights for marriage and adoption is in full swing, and sexual minorities have been elected as representatives in the Italian government. Apart from the already mentioned Silvestri, Vladimir Luxuria was the first male-to-female transsexual elected to the parliament (for the *Partito per la Rifondazione Comunista*); Titti De Simone, who is lesbian, was elected as a representative in the parliament for the PRC; and Franco Grillini, a gay man, was elected as representative in the parliament for the Democratic Left Party. Finally, Nichi Vendola, a gay man, the president of the Apulia Region and past representative in the parliament for PRC, today is an upcoming leader of the Italian Left.

The overall picture is one of contradictions, and undoubtedly contradictions are present in Albania and in the Muslim world as well. Albania, for example, as part of a continuing attempt to be seen as "European" has recently passed anti-homophobia legislation (Adnkronos/Dpa, July 30, 2009), which is still missing in Italy. While there is no excuse for the persecution against gays and lesbians in Iran, it must be noted that the same country does not prosecute transsexuals because, due to a fatwa by Ayatollah Ruhollah Khomeini, transsexuality is seen as a curable illness. The Iranian state funds surgery and hormone therapy and today, Iran has the second highest number of sex-change operations (Tait, *The Guardian*, September 26, 2007). But, such contradictions often disappear in mass media representations.

Laura Maragnini, in her article "Il mondo gay è morto" ("The gay world is dead," Panorama, October 5, 2006) decries the "normalization" of being gay. She quotes personalities of the cinema and politics in Italy who are out-of-the-closet sexual minorities. She notices how the Italian TV has grabbed on to the gay trend to produce an increasing number of gay-oriented programs. Being gay, she argues, has lost its oppositional power with respect to society. She quotes from an interview with Daniel Casagrande, director of the *Giornate di Cinema Omosessuale* at the Venice Film Festival, where he says: "The cinema is adapting to it, [. . .] a touch of LGBT is almost in every movie, from the lesbian couple in the *Caimano* to the one in *La Bestia del Cuore*" (Panorama, October 5, 2006; my translation). In the same article, Rep. Franco Grillini is quoted saying that "gays are trendy" (Panorama, October 5, 2006; my translation). And it may be true that to be openly against gay is simply "uncool" right now in Italy. To be openly against immigrants, instead, is acceptable and even considered as a "natural" answer to "invasions." A perception exists then, that being gay in Italy today is acceptable and even fashionable.

There is more to this "trendiness" than simple fashion of the time, though. A representation of the Self as modern is constructed here against the background of the representation of the "barbaric" racial Other. Representing the Italian society as modern also means upholding the manifest destiny of the last one hundred and fifty years of nation building on the peninsula: a history that created Italy as a European, colonialist, and neocolonialist power. The moral superiority of the citizen of the nation-state, founded in progressive, positivistic thinking is reaffirmed today in the moment when the deep changes introduced in the society—including by transnational fluxes—risk undermining its privilege. Here then, the modern civil subjects—and their privatized sexuality—are opposed to the premodern immigrants who belong to "barbaric" immoral/submoral nation-states that contain and control sex, women, and gays through violence.

At least with respect to Italy, I think there is also a bit of self-uncertainty: Italy has always been betwixt and between, as much a racialized "other" to Northern Europe as a part of it. This can be perceived in the comparisons that the politicians and newspapers draw between themselves and other European countries. In Arben's case, for example, a comparison with Sweden is brought up by the ADC and then by many other newspapers' articles. The tone is generally self-congratulatory as reported in the *L'Unità* newspaper on May 5, 2007: since only Sweden had a similar case in the past, Italy can now be compared to that state and be described as "very laic and highly civil/civilized" (Semmola, May 5, 2007, p. 11). In Pegah's case, note the words of Aurelio Mancuso, president of the Arcigay, who, in condemning homophobic remarks by Luca Volontè (Catholic politician of the UDC), says that "the real problem is that in our country so many homophobic racists are given voice, [. . .] who in *occidental political societies* are rarely taken into consideration" (Arcigay, August 28, 2007, emphasis added). In this case, Mancuso implies a distinction between "occidental" societies where there is little tolerance for racist and homophobic discourse, and a "non-occidental" society where this discourse is present and where Italy risks association, *if* the country gives a "voice" to people like Volontè.

Hadley Z. Renkin, in his analysis of homophobia in Hungary, notes that LGBT people have come to be seen as "a kind of "indicator species" for the production of democracy, civil society, and a truly "European" civilization, or the triumph of tolerant, liberal transnationalism over illiberal nationalism" (2009, p. 32). He also notes that "critically, this kind of Othering also functions to obscure the 'West's' homophobia, directing attention from hegemonic intolerance there" (2009, p. 25). In a sense, the homosexual is not just a product of modernity—as Foucault has noted (1978)—but also can produce modernity, or even more, be symbolically deployed in discourses about modernity.

CONCLUSIONS

Part of the strength and resilience of racist ideologies is their ability to be flexible, to co-opt and deploy diverse and opposing discourses, and to be productive of new categorizations of humanity. In a homophobic world, one that denies rights to sexual minorities as well as other

minorities, our gaze and critical analysis must orient not only to homophobic discourse but also, unfortunately, to "gay friendly" discourse. As Eithne Luibhéid notes, analysis of Queer immigration must be careful of the possible appropriation "to serve foreign policy objectives" (2005, p. xxv).

As Blommaert and Verschueren note, democracy and human rights are often presented together as indissoluble in the discourses that Europeans present about the self (1998, p. 107) and that construction is pitted against the representation of the "undemocratic" other—the Eastern European excommunist, or the Islamic other. Blommaert and Verschueren argue that this discourse is "culturalized" and "presented as part of a European *cultural heritage*. Europeans are thus depicted [. . .] as *democratic* by *nature*, and respect for human rights becomes an essential feature of their cultural identity" (1998, p. 107; original italics). Thus the representation of the immigrant other, including the Queer immigrant other, can be used to further this sense of moral, cultural—and in the end racial—superiority.

NGOs and groups like the ADC that work at protecting minority rights must be particularly vigilant against the circulation of racist discourses. By obtaining refugee status for Arben, the Antidiscrimination Center of the Province of Pistoia obtained a wider victory of great consequence. It redefined sexual choices as "normal" before the law that were otherwise still seen as "abnormal" in Italy, and thus obtained recognition of sexual minorities as subjects before the law. At the same time, they obtained to redefine as abnormal, and possibly punishable, discrimination against people on the basis of sexual choices. Yet, they could not avoid the co-optation of their arguments by the mass media, enabled by the reification and essentialization of culture in racializing and racist terms.

It was clear to me in my work that the people at the ADC were well aware of this co-optation; they recognized the limits to their agency even as they acted through the cracks of power to protect individuals. Ultimately, the system of state laws regarding immigration creates discrimination.

Beyond a simple dynamic of acquiescence and resistance, there is the irony, of a proimmigrant stance drawing on and feeding into racist politics of representations of the very immigrant group being protected. This irony is couched in the almost schizophrenic state of individuals inside a system working actively against it as they try to change it. As they exploit whatever opportunities they can, they also become part of the system's contradictions.

Nor should we forget the primary reason why Arben and the ADC had to go through the whole court proceeding, and the reason why a campaign was needed to assure Pegah's safety: it was Italy that had refused Arben, it was Europe that had refused Pegah. It was the Italian state structure that had rendered it impossible for Arben to remain in Italy, to study and work in the first place. It was the climate of suspicion and the racist and homophobic regimenting attitudes toward immigrant bodies that led the British authorities to question Pegah's "sincerity" in declaring herself lesbian.

In conclusion, I want to underline that the moment of obtaining refugee status is often presented as a final resolution to the plight of LGBT immigrants (see also Luibhéid, 2005). And yet, it is only the beginning of new struggles against discrimination. In the aftermath of obtaining asylum, Arben's identity must be hidden; he disappeared from view in order to remain safe. Of his new life, nothing is said. Now he is just another Queer, just another immigrant. Facing enduring homophobia and racism in an Italy that hates Albanians, his struggle has just begun.

NOTES

1. The research for this article was made possible by grants from the Wenner Gren Foundation for Anthropological Research, the National Science Foundation, Oberlin College, and by a fellowship from the Remarque Institute. I am indebted to Susan Frekko, Erika Hoffman-Dilloway, Rafael Lainez, and Chantal Tetreault for their suggestions on previous versions.

2. I use the word *Queer* here as an umbrella term to include all LGBT identified persons as well as other sexual minorities, such as pansexuals, polyamourous persons, etc. This is in line with the recent adoption of the term in the name of the Association for Queer Anthropology (AQA). The word *Queer*, once an insult, has undergone a decades-long process of reappropriation, during which it has come to acquire a political meaning as well. As Michael Warner notes, the term *Queer* "rejects a minoritizing logic of toleration or simple political interest representation in favor of a more thorough resistance to regimes of the normal" (1993, p. xxvi).

3. My fieldwork was carried out under the sponsorship of the ADC and also the Social Observatory of the Province of Pistoia and the Social Observatory of the Province of Prato. Between 2005 and 2009, I conducted observations on participants at the ADC and in the Tuscan Metropolitan Area in general. I video recorded everyday conversations, interviewed local persons and members of the local government, antiracist associations, conducted focus group interviews with members of recreational clubs, and media-watch.

4. The Arcigay is a branch of the ARCI, the *Associazione Ricreativa Culturale Italiana* (Italian Recreational and Cultural Association).

5. The ADC is particularly interested in cases where there may be multiple forms of discrimination operating, putting the individual in a situation of "fragility" in the system. That was the case with Arben who was discriminated because of his status as an immigrant, as an Albanian, and as a gay person, all at the same time. As Barbara Beneforti, one of the workers there, put it: "When there are multiple discriminations, then the intervention of the Center is even more valid, since [in this case] it is difficult to protect the person, not just in a sector, but in more than one" (personal communication). Namely, no single rights-protecting organization can answer separately to a systemic discrimination, The ADC instead, in these cases, acts as a "coordinating net" bringing together different associations or NGOs to protect particular rights. To structural discrimination, thus, the ADC opposes a systemic answer.

6. This lengthy collection process was due to the inherent difficulty of gathering evidence in Albania, where sexual minorities are afraid to denounce discrimination against them.

7. Silvestri is also the first openly gay Italian senator and one of the founders of the Arcigay.

8. The second case, brought to court by the ADC in 2007, was a request of asylum for a transgender person from Morocco. The ADC again won the case.

9. Information from the ADC Dossier. Laws regarding LGBT asylum are different in different European countries. As a comparison, in the United States, Queer immigrants escaping from violence and discrimination in their home countries have been able to ask for asylum since 1993, although continuing social and legal barriers remain (see Randazzo, 2005, p. 34). Unfortunately, the PATRIOT Act and successive restrictions to U.S. immigration have made matters worse in recent years (Randazzo, 2005, p. 52).

10. By comparison, the number of people with a permit to reside in Italy in 1992 was 648,935 (Macioti & Pugliese, 2003, p. 37; Zincone, 2001).

11. The two are actually doubly connected in Italy since Prime Minister Silvio Berlusconi, also head of the governmental coalition, controls the main Italian mass media (TV and newspapers) through the Fininvest group. This fact, along with an increasing censorship over the media, has been reducing freedom of speech in Italy over the last decade.

12. The exceptions were a few cases of politicians, such as Roberto Calderoli and newspapers connected to the Northern league. I will return to this later.

13. Mastella, as of the time of this writing, is the leader of the Popular Union of Democrats for Europe for the South (*UDEUR Popolari per il Sud*), a conservative Christian party. Since 2008, Mastella has been under investigation for possible connections to the mafia.

14. This is an online archive that gathers the articles of three Italian dailies: *Il Giorno, La Nazione,* and *Il Resto del Carlino.* They three are connected and they generally express a center-right political point of view.

15. Ironically, these are similar to stereotypes often heard about Italians and Italian Americans in the United States.

16. Unpublished ADC dossier created for the court case.

17. Unpublished ADC dossier created for the court case.

18. Notice also the use of the term "condition" to refer to homosexuality (as if a euphemism was needed) and its connection to being a "handicap." The quote should not be assumed to be word-for-word or from a recording.

19. Fabrizio Cicchitto is also under court inquiry since 2009 accused of money laundering.

20. For further information, see the current campaigns of EveryOne (EveryOne, 2010). As I write,

after the recent civil war in Libya, these agreements between Italy and Libya have been suspended. In fact, in the last period of his government, Berlusconi did a quick about-face and went from demonstrations of friendship with Gaddafi to hostility toward his old ally.

21. In the original Italian, "ostentare" has a subtle meaning of displaying and make a show of something as if it was something to be proud of, even when not.

22. The Italian word "dilaghi" litt "over-lake-ing" implies a sense of flooding.

23. An expression meaning not wanting to partake with something that is perceived as "dirty," and smelly (such as the "scum" previously mentioned) as well as feeling superior.

24. Florence, in particular, has traditionally been a haven for sexual minorities, including those escaping from persecution in other countries, and the city was home to many famous intellectuals and artists who were also sexual minorities, such as Michelangelo and Machiavelli.

25. See also their manifesto that intimates LGBT people should "get your hands off from our family" (Lega Nord Brescia website).

REFERENCES

Albania: Berisha, discriminare i gay e' inaccettabile. Tirana vuole legalizzare I matrimoni tra omosessuali. (2009, July 30). *Adnkronos/Dpa* [Multimedia news agency]. Retrieved from http://www.adn kronos.com/IGN/News/. Also reported on Di'Gay project GDP, from http://www.digayproject.org/Home/albania_berisha.php?c=2403&m=9&l=it.

Balduzzi, Erica. (2010, November 27). Se non pagate morirete qui. I ricatti dei trafficanti dopo gli accordi Italia-Libia. *EveryOne 2010* [Group for International Cooperation on Human Rights Culture]. Retrieved from http://www.everyone group.com/it/EveryOne/MainPage/Entries/2010/11/27_Se_non_pagate_morirete_qui._I_ricatti_dei_trafficanti_dopo_gli_accordi_Italia-Libia.html.

Balibar, É. (1988). Y a-t-il un neo-racisme? In E. Balibar & I. Wallerstein (Eds.), *Race, nation, class* (pp. 17–36). Paris, FR: La Decouverte.

Barker, M. (1982). *The new racism: Conservatives and the ideology of the tribe.* Frederick, MD: Aletheia Books.

Baumann, G. (1996). *Contesting culture: Discourses of identity in multi-ethnic London*. Cambridge, UK: Cambridge University Press.

Blangiardo, G. C. (2004). La presenza straniera in Italia. Primo bilancio dopo la regolarizzazione del 2002. In Fondazione ISMU (Ed.), *Nono rapporto sulle migrazioni 2003* (pp. 41–53). Milan, IT: Franco Angeli.

Blommaert, J., & Verschueren J. (1998). *Debating diversity: Analyzing the discourse of tolerance*. London, UK: Routledge.

Boellstorff, T., & Leap, W. L. (2004). Introduction: Globalization and "new" articulations of same-sex desire. In W. L. Leap & T. Boellstorff (Eds.), *Speaking in Queer tongues: Globalization and gay language* (pp. 1–21). Urbana: University of Illinois Press.

Cameron, D. (2001). *Working with spoken discourse*. London, UK: SAGE.

Comunicato stampa [Press release]. (2007, August 28). *Arcigay* [Non-profit national Italian gay rights organization]. Retrieved from http://www.arcigay.it/governo-ufficializzi-sua-disponibilit%C3%A0-alla.

De Genova, N., & Ramos-Zayas, A. Y. (2003). *Latino crossings: Mexicans, Puerto Ricans and the politics of race and citizenship*. New York, NY: Routledge.

De Giovannangeli, U. (2007, August 25). Disposti all'estradizione della donna in Italia. L'ipotesi emerge durante un incontro tra funzionari dell'ambasciata britannica a Roma con l'associazione EveryOne. *L'Unità* [Newspaper], p. 13.

EveryOne 2010 (2010, November 27). Se non pagate morirete qui. I ricatti dei trafficanti dopo gli accordi Italia-Libia. Retrieved from http://www.everyonegroup.com/it/EveryOne/MainPage/Entries/2010/11/27_Se_non_pagate_morirete_qui._I_ricatti_dei_trafficanti_dopo_gli_accordi_Italia-Libia.html.

Fairclough, N. (1995). *Media discourse*. London, UK: Arnold.

Fairclough, N. (2000). *New labor, New language?* London, UK: Routlegde.

Fatucchi, M. (2007, May 5). Minacciato di morte perché gay, è rifugiato. *La Repubblica* [Newspaper], pp. 1, 7.

Flesler, D. (2008). *The return of the Moor: Spanish responses to contemporary Moroccan immigration*. West Lafayette, IN: Purdue University Press.

Foot, J. (2001). San Salvario, Turin: The creation of a dangerous place, 1990–99. In R. King (Ed.), *The Mediterranean passage: Migration and new cultural encounters in Southern Europe* (pp. 206–230). Liverpool, UK: Liverpool University Press.

Foucault, M. (1972). *The archaeology of knowledge and the discourse on language*. New York, NY: Pantheon.

Foucault, M. (1978). *The history of sexuality. Volume I: An introduction*. New York, NY: Random House.

Fowler, R. (1991). *Language in the news: Discourse and ideology in the British press*. London, UK: Routledge.

Frattini, Contro Immigrati Pattugliamenti e Respingimenti. (2011, February 13). *Notizie.it*. http://www.notizie.it/frattini-contro-immigrati-pattugliamenti-e-respingimenti/.

Garcia-Sanchez, I. G. (2010). The return of the Moor: Building a mosque in the Spanish heartland. (Unpublished paper). Presented at the American Anthropological Association Conference.

Gardner, P. (2004). Make capital out of their sympathy: Rhetoric and reality of U.S. slavery and Italian immigrant prostitution along the color line from the nineteenth to the twenty-first century. In H. Raphael-Hernandez (Ed.), *Blackening Europe: The African American presence* (pp. 249–261). New York, NY: Routledge.

Ghosh, D. (2008). *Sex and the family in colonial India: The making of empire*. New York, NY: Cornell University Press.

Gilroy, P. (2004). Foreword: Migrancy, culture, and a new map of Europe. In H. Raphael-Hernandez (Ed.), *Blackening Europe: The African American presence* (pp. xi–xxii). New York, NY: Routledge.

Hoagland, S. L., & Penelope, J. (1988). Radical lesbians, "The women-identified woman." In S. L. Hoagland & J. Penelope (Eds.), *For lesbians only: A separatist anthology* (pp. 17–22). London, UK: Only Woman Press.

Hooper, J. (2007, August 24). Italy asks Britain not to deport Iranian lesbian. *The Guardian*. Retrieved from http://www.guardian.co.uk/uk/2007/aug/24/iran.italy.

Immigrati. (2006, September 21). *Quotidiano.Net* [Italian news website]. Retrieved from http://qn.quotidiano.net/2006/09/21/5436939-IMMMI-GRATI.shtml.

ISTAT. (2001). Istituto Nazionale di Statistica Italiano. Retrieved from http://www.demo.istat.it/.

ISTAT (2009). Istituto Nazionale di Statistica Italiano. Retrieved from http://www.demo.istat.it/.

La Sala, F. (2007, August 25). Salvare Pegah. Cara "Londra" . . . Un'immane cecità e una vergogna llanetaria. . . . Lunedì pomeriggio sit-in a Roma. *L'Unità*. Retrieved from http://www.lavocedi fiore.org/SPIP/article.php3?id_article=2496.

Leap, W. L. (2004). Language, belonging, and (homo) sexual citizenship in Cape Town, South Africa. In W. L. Leap & T. Boellstorff (Eds.), *Speaking in Queer tongues: Globalization and gay language* (pp. 134–162). Urbana: University of Illinois Press.

Lega Nord Brescia. *Manifesti*. Retrieved from http://www.caparini.com/propaganda/manifesti.htm.

Lloyd, J. (2007, August 23). Salviamo Pegah dalla lapidazione. *La Repubblica*. Retrieved from http://www.repubblica.it/2007/08/sezioni/esteri/gb-iran-pegah/gb-iran-pegah/gb-iran-pegah.html.

Lotta Violenza. (n.d.). *Arcigay*. [Non-profit national Italian gay rights organization]. Retrieved from http://www.arcigay.it/?s=lotta+violenza.

Luibhéid, E. (2005). Introduction: Queering migration and citizenship. In E. Luibhéid & L. Cantú Jr. (Eds.), *Queer migrations: Sexuality, U.S. citizenship, and border crossings* (pp. 9–46). Minneapolis: University of Minnesota Press.

Macioti, M. I., & Pugliese, E. (2003). *L'esperienza migratoria: Immigrati e rifugiati in Italia.* Rome, IT: Laterza.

Maneri, M. (2009). I media e la guerra alle migrazioni. In S. Palidda (Ed.), *Razzismo democratico: La persecuzione degli stranieri in Europa* (pp. 66–86). Milan, IT: Agenzia X.

Maragnani, L. (2006, October 5). Il mondo gay è morto. *Panorama.it.* [Italian news website]. Republished in *Gay News* (2010, December 2). Retrieved from http://www.gaynews.it/view.php?ID=70388.

Mastella: "Accogliamo Pegah in Italia." (2007, August 27). *Quotidiano.Net.* [Italian news website]. Retrieved from http://qn.quotidiano.net/2007/08/27/32656-mastella_accogliamo_pagah_italia.shtml.

McClintock, A. (1995). *Imperial leather: Race, gender, and sexuality in the colonial contest.* New York, NY: Routledge.

"Meglio le belle ragazze che essere gay" Le battute del cavaliere: "Ruby è un problemino, dove posso sistemarla?". (2010, February 11). *Corriere della Sera.it.* [Online news agency]. Retrieved from http://www.corriere.it/politica/10_novembre _02/berlusconi-salone-motociclo-milano_d0a03188-e66c-11df-a903-00144f02aabc.shtml.

Mohanty, C. T. (1997). Under Western eyes: Feminist scholarship and colonial discourses. In A. McClintock, A. Mufti, & E. Shohat (Eds.), *Dangerous liaisons: Gender, nation, & postcolonial perspectives* (pp. 255–277). Minneapolis: University of Minnesota Press.

Omosessualità e legge. (2007, May 5). *Il Giornale, 34*(106), 18.

Omossessualità e shariafobia. (2007, August 27). *Libere Risonanze* [Web log post] Retrieved from http://libererisonanze.blogspot.com/2007_08_01_archive.html.

Pagliai, V. (2009). Conversational agreement and racial formation processes. *Language in Society, 38*, 549–579.

Pagliai, V. (2010). Nowadays it is OK to be racist (even if you are Leftist): Building the normality of racism in media discourse in Italy. (Unpublished paper). Presented at the Council for European Studies conference, Montreal, Canada.

Papavero, G. (2004). Allegato statistico: L'immigrazione in cifre. In Fondazione ISMU (Ed.), *Nono rapporto sulle migrazioni 2003* (pp. 355–376). Milan, IT: Franco Angeli.

Pegah chiede asilo politico, Frattini: "Valutare rischi" (2007, August 28). *Quotidiano.Net.* Retrieved from http://qn.quotidiano.net/2007/08/28/32883-pegah_chiede_asilo_politico_frattini_valutare_rischi.shtml.

Randazzo, T. J. (2005). Social and legal barriers: Sexual orientation and asylum in the United States. In E. Luibhéid & L. Cantú Jr. (Eds.), *Queer migrations: Sexuality, U.S. citizenship, and border crossings* (pp. 30–60). Minneapolis: University of Minnesota Press.

Räthzel, N. (2002). Developments in theories of racism. In The Events Foundation (Ed.), *Europe's new racism? Causes, manifestations, and solutions* (pp. 3–26). New York: Berghahn Books.

Renkin, H. Z. (2009). Homophobia and Queer belonging in Hungary. *Focaal—European Journal of Anthropology, 53*, 20–37.

Rich, A. (1980). Compulsory heterosexuality and lesbian existence. *Signs, 5*, 631–660.

Said, E. (1979). *Orientalism*. New York, NY: Vintage Books.

Sedgwick, E, (1990). *Epistemology of the closet.* Berkeley: University of California Press.

Semmola, E. (2007, May 5). Gay e perseguitato: L'Italia lo accoglie come rifugiato politico. *L'Unità*, p. 11.

Sibhatu, R. (2004). *Il cittadino che non c'é: L'immigrazione nei media Italiani*. Rome, IT: EDUP.

Silverstein, P., & Tetreault C. (2006). Postcolonial urban apartheid. *Quarterly for the Social Science Research Council, 5*, 8–15. An earlier version was published at http://riotsfrance.ssrc.org/Silverstein_Tetreault/.

Sorbi, M. (2007, May 5). Asilo politico a un Albanese solo perché è omosessuale. *Il Giornale, 34*(106), 1, 18.

Status di rifugiato perché è gay. (2007, May 5). *La Nazione (Firenze), 149*(122), 2.

Stein, A. (1997). Sisters and Queers: The decentering of lesbian feminism. In R. N. Lancaster & M. Di Leonardo (Eds.), *The gender sexuality reader: Culture, history, political economy* (pp. 378–391). New York, NY: Routledge.

Tait, R. (2007, September 26). Sex change funding undermines no gays claim. *The Guardian*. Retrieved from http://www.guardian.co.uk/world/2007/sep/26/iran.gender.

Trinci, S. (2007, May 5). Asilo al gay minacciato di morte. *La Nazione (Pistoia), 149*(122), 1, 6.

van Dijk, T. A. (1987). *Communicating racism: Ethnic prejudice in thought and talk*. Newbury Park, CA: Sage.

van Dijk, T. A. (1991). *Racism and the press*. London, UK: Routledge.

van Dijk, T. A. (2000). New(s) racism: A discourse analytical approach. In S. Cottle (Ed.), *Ethnic minorities and the media* (pp. 33–49). Buckingham, UK: Open University Press.

Warner, M. (1993). Introduction. In M. Warner (Ed.), *Fear of a Queer planet: Queer politics and social theory* (pp. 7–31). Minneapolis: University of Minnesota Press.

Wetherell, M., & Potter, J. (1992). *Mapping the language of racism: Discourse and the legitimation of exploitation*. New York, NY: Harvester Wheatsheaf.

Wikan, U. (2002). *Generous betrayal: Politics of culture in the new Europe*. Chicago, IL: University of Chicago Press.

Wodak, R. (Ed.). (1989). *Language, power and ideology*. Amsterdam, NL: Benjamins.

Wodak, R. (1996a). *Disorders of discourse*. London, UK: Longman.

Wodak, R. (1996b). The genesis of racist discourse in Austria since 1989. In C. R. Caldas-Coulthard & M. Courthard (Eds.), *Readings in critical discourse analysis* (pp. 107–128). London, UK: Routledge.

Zincone, G. (Ed.). (2001). *Commissione per le politiche di integrazione degli immigrati, secondo rapporto sull'integrazione degli immigrati in Italia*. Bologna, IT: Il Mulino.

12

THE SURPLUS OF PARADOXES

Queering Images of Sexuality and Economy

ANTKE ENGEL

INTRODUCTION

Self-proclaimed liberal and pluralist Western[1] states happily turn to gender and sexual politics in order to demonstrate their presumed progressiveness. Cultural imagery of diverse sexualities, nonnormative desires, and ambiguous genders become tokens that stand in for tolerance and integrative capacities that are mostly lacking in the fields of migration and asylum politics, and in relation toward so-called ethnic minorities. This lack of integration is in fact supported by another mode of gender and sexual politics: Racist constructions of a dichotomy between "Western superiority" and "Southern backwardness" evolve from pointing out sexual violence (coined as honor crimes, female genital mutilation, enforced marriage, corrective rape) in "the Other," while simultaneously claiming to provide legal measures and counseling institutions for overcoming what are marked as "archaic reminiscences." However, this kind of occidentalist[2] self-assurance is based on ignorance at multiple levels: ignorance toward dominant Western cultures'

own involvement in hate crimes, homo- and transphobia, and sexual violence as a constitutive moment of gender socialization, ignorance concerning knowledge and research, and ignorance of the social and legal measures available or developing in various contexts of the global South in order to judge, delegitimize, persecute, repair, and reconcile sexual violence. This is how I would characterize the socio-historical background of German mainstream culture in the first decade of the 21st century.

My analysis is a counterpoint to this background of ignorance and searches for perspectives in queer politics that discredit occidentalist premises.[3] I examine queer cultural politics in order to figure out possibilities for undermining the occidentalist claim to superiority. In particular, I acknowledge the complex and contradictory entanglement of LGBTI (lesbian, gay, bisexual, transgender/transsexual, intersex) constituencies in these power/knowledge regimes and in the modern processes of neoliberal governance. My thesis is that queer perspectives turn out to be particularly helpful for understanding late modern forms of governance and domination, in so far as they are built on paradoxical figurations of pleasure and pain, freedom and coercion, agency and submission, repression and normalization that are also characteristic for certain neoliberal transformations (Engel, 2002, 2007b, 2009a).

This chapter contains central ideas from my book *Bilder von Sexualität and Ökonomie. Queere kulurelle Politiken im Neoliberalismus* (Images of Sexuality and Economy. Queer Cultural Politics in Neoliberalism), published in Germany in 2009. The chapter, like the book, is motivated by a certain skepticism concerning diversity discourses and tolerance pluralism as well as by the optimism that there will always be articulations of difference or dissidence that are not appropriable by the given socio-symbolic order. Instead of subscribing to a narrative of progress, I argue that diversity discourses and tolerance pluralism, even if they go along with sexual liberalization and the pluralizing of sexed and gendered ways of existence, produce new social divisions, normative normalizations and hierarchizations, both locally and globally. Diversity is the motto offered by a neoliberal economy as an organizing principle that promises economic growth.[4] It is taken up by political actors and institutions that equate market integration with political integration or, more specifically, market freedom with sexual freedom. Difference becomes a promise, yet neoliberal affirmations of sexual plurality and ambiguity have to be considered against the background of developments of upward redistribution of wealth and resources and the substitution of differentiated forms of integration and exclusion for ideals of equality (Hennessy, 2000; Duggan, 2003; Engel, 2007b).

Nevertheless, what is now coded as diversity politics can also be understood as the outcome of political activism in Western societies in the 80s and 90s: for example, feminist and LGBTI activism, migrant and antiracist activism as well as people with disabilities claiming rights and recognition. In these struggles, claims for freedom and self-determination have been combined with those for social justice and equality. No matter whether one was lacking resources and recognition, sexual politics in the decades around the turn of the century consisted in shamelessly claiming public space for living a lesbian, gay, bisexual, or transgender life. In German metropoles, as well as in Vienna, Austria's capital, where I experienced my coming out and queerly coming to age, one did not escape experiences of sexism, heterosexism, homo- and transphobia, However, these were countered by politicized communities and subcultures, which provided remedies, recognition, and space for socio-sexual experimentation. Frictions and fractions were constitutive moments of these activist politics (Engel, 2007a). Acknowledging conflicts, the effects of heterosexism, racism, antisemitism, classism, and ableism, and the complexity of social identities has meant integrating heterogeneity and political dissent into political practices—or splitting up into presumably homogenized groups. Internal conflicts over power and domination have affected deadlocks, yet have also inspired reconfigurations of political projects. They have provided the ground for queer theory's questioning of the normative effects and exclusions that go along with identity constructions. Accordingly, I understand queer politics of representation to be organized around polysemy, ambiguity, and strategies of equivocation or un-disambiguation (*VerUneindeutigung*)[5] rather than striving for the visibility of presumably prediscursive identities (Engel, 2002, 2006). In societies where the regulation of sexuality takes place, not so much in the form of rigid normativity and exclusion as in the form of flexible normalization and differentiated integration, new forms of understanding domination and violence are needed (Duggan, 2003). While open physical violence or repression may decline, psychic pressure may still structure individual life, and symbolic as well as structural violence defines who is "normal" and who may live a valued life (Butler, 2004). Questions of representation and cultural politics become more vibrant when violence is transmitted as a normalizing effect through visual and textual media. However, the other side of the coin is that queer politics of representation or cultural and artistic production carry potentials as forms of political intervention.

In *Bilder von Sexulität und Ökonomie*, I argue that in late modern Western societies neoliberal versions of pluralism not only make use of cultural politics, but particularly depend on image production and imagination as means of creating hegemonic alliances between disparate constituencies.[6] The thesis is that these alliances take place through a process of dealing with social differences that I call "projective integration." As a characteristic moment of neoliberal governance, projective integration fosters individualization and distinctiveness in order to motivate people to actively work themselves into the established socioeconomic relations. Rather than assimilating difference into the norm or creating multicultural niches next to the norm, projective integration aims at turning difference into cultural capital. It does so through providing cultural imagery that invites people to identify with precarity as a form of individual freedom— the freedom to offer one's Asperger's Syndrome to the computer industry, the freedom to function as the alibi Black working class graduate of an elite university, the freedom of being pushed into the glorious exemption position when speaking as a Muslim lesbian. Differences are not simply affirmed, but images function as screens of projection, interpellating its readers to dwell on the threshold of "difference as promise" and "difference as threat."[7]

This chapter aims at undermining occidentalist superiority by cooperating with an artwork that sets in motion discourses of neoliberal economy, late modern racism, and queer sexual politics. The center of attention is the cover image of my book, a collage by contemporary Austrian artist, Ines Doujak. Doujak works in photography and installation, creating vivid and voluptuous scenarios inspired by sexual fantasies that do not submit to normative gender expectations, binary sex differentiation or heteronormalized bodies and desires. For Doujak, embodiments, movements, and unexpected constellations of bodies and objects are the sites where violent legacies and traces of economic exploitation and political oppression are contained—and transformed. Concrete historical or geopolitical struggles, particularly concerning the conquest, colonization, and postcolonial exploitation of Latin America and the myriad ways of subversion and resistance— ambiguous and contradictory rather than pure and straightforward—inspire Doujak's work.[8]

QUEER CULTURAL POLITICS IN NEOLIBERALISM

In late modern Western societies, images of dissident sexualities and gender ambiguity can be found in art, media, and sexual subcultures as well as in commercial advertising. With their themes of sexual diversity and the multiplicity of desires, these images are sites of a discursive overlap between queer perspectives in commercial discourses and neoliberal perspectives in queer discourses. This discursive overlap is the terrain of cultural politics. According to New York–based queer theorist Lisa Duggan (2003), neoliberal hegemony depends to a large degree on cultural politics and the way certain sections of marginalized groups have been invited into an alliance with hegemonic forces. Or, to put it another way, by refraining from cultural politics, the traditional left misses opportunities to oppose neoliberal transformations through interventions in the production of knowledge and the cultural imaginary. How can one use cultural politics to develop a radical critique of the complex and intertwined relations of domination? Taking up Duggan's critique, I point toward, and indeed strengthen, tendencies in queer theory and politics that make use of their own entanglements with the very discourses they want to oppose. In this chapter, I analyze artwork by Viennese artist Ines Doujak to demonstrate how cultural politics may evolve from the overlaps of queer and neoliberal discourses and provide an analysis of what I call the "queer politics of paradox" (Engel, 2009a, 2011).

The concepts of individuality and diversity are sites of struggle in cultural politics. Do political claims that call on individuality and diversity support freedom and social recognition, or do they simply have the effect of complicating the production of social hierarchies? Neoliberal discourses claim that market freedom and sexual freedom are a perfect couple—sexual difference itself is constructed as cultural capital. Here the process of projective integration is useful for understanding the way neoliberal socioeconomic order rules society and regulates subjectivity through an affirmative investment in difference. I understand this process as a characteristic feature of late modern governmentality.[9]

Since projective integration depends on the production and circulation of images, it is promising to analyze how visual cultural representations are activated by, or connect to, processes of projective integration. For instance, one must ask if the processes of projective integration enabled Ines Doujak's work, which was produced with the backdrop of queer discourses and politics, to be exhibited at the international art exhibition *documenta XII* in Kassel? And if so, does it therefore become a product of neoliberal politics and a sign of the appropriation of queer culture? Or, does it push projective integration somewhere else and subvert the neoliberal imaginary and symbolic order?

DRAG FEEDING

In this chapter, I examine Ines Doujak's untitled collage from the series *Victory Gardens* (2007) under the headline *Drag Feeding*. It is an image that both presents the practice of feeding in drag and shows drag being fed. The collage displays two figures in an orientalist setting, one of whom pours a copious amount of rice from a big bronze bowl into the open mouth of the other. Given the parallel angles of their bent bodies, the figures appear to be in a harmonious constellation. However, significantly, this "harmony" depends

Figure 12.1 Ines Doujak: untitled, from the series *Victory Gardens* (2007), photography on historical design, 70x40 cm.

Source: Reproduced courtesy of the artist.

on the fact that the receiving figure must overstretch backward and tilt its head in order to be "pleased" by the rice—given over to the other. Nevertheless, this subordination does not hinder the figure from having its eyelids devotionally lowered when taking in the overabundance. On Doujak's canvas, pleasure and pain, lust and coercion seem indistinguishable. In this way, the constellation could be read as a sadomasochism or SM-scenario—although the colorful, campy representation of bodies and location confounds this kind of sexualization by not feeding into clichéd expectations of rubber, leather, and chains.

Other ambiguities and undecidabilities supplement the paradox of pleasure and pain in this image. The work activates various oppositions—such as those between North and South and male and female—but instead of simply inverting their traditional hierarchies, it challenges them, creating a more intricate hermeneutic field. Against established cultural expectations, it is the figure coded as "Latina," particularly through visual reference to media images of the actress Carmen Miranda, who subdues and controls the figure coded as "white." But in the work, the price of control is giving away resources to "the North" that might be needed in "the South." Maybe, for the Miranda figure, it is worth the price, because the ironic assumption of control over the food supply effects a radical decentering of the North? Maybe it is a form of Southern self-empowerment to represent the oversupply of the North as an effect of the sadistic cruelty of the South? Maybe the figures are, as their fashion design suggests, both members of the metropolitan middle classes who simply do not care about global inequalities? Since all three of these readings are supported by the image, the reader must grapple with the question of whether a reworking of racialized relations of power and domination takes place or not.[10]

Concerning gender relations, it is more obvious that traditional hierarchies and clichés are thwarted—though this does not mean that there is less polysemy. The reader is confronted with ambiguous gender constellations, which allow for all kinds of desire. While the gender of the figure who combines bald head, long, mascarablackened eye lashes and formal shirt remains undecidable, the dress and makeup of the other figure signals femininity, though this might be trans-femininity. Thanks to their hyperbolic, iridescent style, both figures can also be understood as being in drag. Thus, the relationship between the two figures can be decoded as a heterosexual, lesbian, gay and/or transgender constellation. A heterosexual version encounters a female figure having the resources to control a male. A lesbian version sees an instance of feeding and caring represented as a scenario of sexualized power—thus challenging the cliché of desexualized, nonaggressive lesbian sexuality, and also parodying the ongoing global malnourishment of girls and women. Finally, reading the figures in drag means perceiving care relations as camp performance, which accentuates how

gendered, racialized, and classed social relations are constituted through sexualized power, control, and submission.

It is notable that even though Doujak plays with ambiguity and confusion, the image decisively refers to social relations of power and domination. None of the constellations mentioned above can be decoded as ambiguous without reference to (post)colonial, racist, classist, and (hetero)sexist regimes. Interestingly, all of these constellations invite one to read the piece as thematizing the asymmetries of the global food supply— all the while insisting that these are gendered and sexualized social relationships. Thus, I read *Drag Feeding* as connecting to an understanding of queer theory and politics that does not reduce sexuality and gender to moments of subjectivity or intimate social relationships, but instead asks how they become organizing principles of society and its institutions, including its legal, political and economic systems, and questions how they intersect with other processes of social differentiation and hierarchization. The term "heteronormativity" provides an analytical tool for these purposes. It indicates how heterosexuality and homosexuality depend on a rigid binary gender order and how the normative, hierarchized gender order is sustained by heterosexual desire. However, it also allows one to investigate how notions of identity and difference are built on a "gendered" logic of A/non-A (also called phallogocentrism) that perceives difference as always in a subordinated relation to the defining centre and which creates a "heterosexualized," complementary relation between identity and difference. As such, the term heteronormativity may ground a perspective that understands queer theory as a critique of identity logic in general, and of any system of subordination, homogenization, and hierarchization.[11]

THE QUEER STRATEGY OF EQUIVOCATION

Doujak's collage, with its complex references to various systems of domination and its systematic subversion of identity closures, supports the above mentioned understanding of queer theory. Moreover, in the way the artwork manifests queer politics, it seems to fit nicely into what I call the "queer strategy of equivocation" (*VerUneindeutigung*) (Engel, 2002; 2006). Where a clear-cut identity, meaning, or norm is installed, naturalized, or made unquestionable, the strategy of equivocation renders it ambiguous.[12] A queer strategy of equivocation is proposed as an alternative to queer strategies of proliferating genders or to strategies of abolishing gender altogether, both of which seem to be problematic ways of breaking the heteronormative, androcentric logic. The proliferation of identities or social categories neither prevents their normative function of excluding otherness nor undermines hierarchization. Similarly, abolishing genders liquidates the analytical terms that enable one to criticize relations of power and domination and simultaneously effects a universalization that overwrites difference. In contrast to these troubled options, a queer strategy of equivocation focuses on the norms and normative imaginaries that are at work in (gender or any other) identity categories. Equivocation is a procedural measure that does not pursue a specific ideal way of organizing relations of gender, sexuality, and desire. Instead it aims to disrupt concrete and historically changing norms[13] in a flexible and context-specific way. Equivocation employs representations and practices that resist being pinned down to a single meaning but that construct realities and conditions of power at work in these processes.

The strategy of equivocation finds its limits, however, when relations of domination make use of ambiguity itself and thus produce cultural iterations that cannot be challenged by rendering them ambiguous. What to do with the fact that images of gender ambiguity, iridescent desires, polymorphous bodies, and diverse sexualities have become part of mainstream cultural imagery and are deployed in commercial media and advertising? Does Doujak's collage fit neatly into this corpus of images? But then, how can one explain that the image, though making use of ambiguity, does not become relativistic, but

provides decisive interventions into various relations of power and domination? In order to work on these questions, I take two steps. First, I take a closer look at the mechanism of projective integration and the possibilities of visual cultural politics. Second, I return to Doujak's piece in order to find out how the strategy of equivocation could be radicalized.

In focusing on ambiguity, providing space for multiplicity and polysemy, and claiming the impossibility of fixing meaning, the strategy of equivocation loses sight of agonistic or antagonistic modes of politics.[14] Sometimes ambiguity is not the product of un-disambiguating a norm but of de-thematizing a contradiction. For example, if somebody, in order to be employable for a certain job, needs to adopt a Western name yet does not identify when being called that name. In such a case, it might be necessary to point out the relations of domination effective in and constitutive of the ambiguous relation. Yet, are these relations of domination to be understood as contradictions—contradictions that rely on a simple either/or logic which ultimately reify exclusionary identities and systems of power and domination? Or would radical queer politics want to translate such traditional left-wing political logics into a perspective that keeps up the anti-identity impetus of ambiguity? My thesis is that the figure of the paradox is the pivotal point for critical practices because it provides for non-exclusionary, complex, and dynamic conceptualizations of agonistic and antagonistic relationships. The concept of paradox uses the way projective integration blurs the boundaries between queer and neoliberal discourses as an entrance point for agonistically inciting the ambiguity, thereby turning it into a "queer politics of paradox."

Projective Integration

Projective integration provides a late-modern alternative to assimilatory and multicultural modes of integration; the three together defining the current hegemonic situation. While the latter depend on and reproduce the marking of individuals and social groups as different, deviant, or other, projective integration effects a reworking of subjectivity, which now has to integrate difference into itself. Projective integration is specific in that it consists of an affirmative investment in difference—an investment that simultaneously challenges the norm and blurs the boundary between normality and deviance. In processes of assimilation or tolerance, the "norm" is stabilized as a reference point for regulating difference as the problematic "other." In contrast, projective integration celebrates difference as cultural capital and individualizes responsibility for social recognition and economic success /survival.

Under the operations of projective integration, difference is coded as socially constructed. As such, it is not fated, but calls for amelioration and refinement. Rather than socioeconomic conditions, it is the individual's capacities and resources that are seen as responsible for one's social positioning. Lack of success is your own personal problem. Thus, the individual is asked to develop a "virtuous management of difference," dwelling on the precarious threshold of difference as a promise and difference as holding the threat of turning into stigma or effecting discrimination. Cultural images provide the blueprint for self-technologies that navigate this threshold. Images are a central component in the current processes of the social regulation of difference. In being projected onto the self, cultural images support a form of subjectivity that is ready to acknowledge difference, also as part of oneself rather than to uphold a rigid differentiation between self and other. The term "projective" refers to the role of images in projective integration, employing the multiple meanings of optical, psychic, and social processes, which all consist of images being cast on a surface—a body standing in for identity/difference. Projection is predominantly understood as a process of repudiating difference; it might, however, also be a process of idealization—projecting onto the other what one does not dare, or care, to live out oneself. Both moments are combined in the social process of projective integration, which

may succeed in activating the individual to skillfully manage the threatening threshold between images of stigma and images as cultural capital.

I propose to understand images as "agents of governmentality" that may support hegemonic transformations, but also counterhegemonic and queer politics, and I concentrate on images of nonnormative or dissident sexualities and genders in order to support this understanding. "Image," here, is purposely meant to be a complex, polysemic term, which consists of a simultaneity of the image as *material object* endowed with certain characteristics; of imaginations implied by the *cultural imaginary* (the historical archive of available images, including principles and techniques of representation); and of *phantasies*, personal digestions of cultural and biographical images turned into individual designs that transport desire (Engel, 2009b). This complexity becomes relevant in and organizes any process of perception so that, on this level, one can draw similarities between artistic production, commercial advertising, or political imagery (even though it might be useful to distinguish them, if one wishes to consider conditions of production, circulation, and reception of images). If one wants to understand how images function as agents of governmentality or as means of production in the social field, constituting subjectivities, social relations, and resistance, it is necessary to consider the complexity and polysemy of the image. It is exactly because formal (discursive and aesthetic) elements, cultural imaginary and personal phantasies become activated simultaneously (without necessarily producing coherent or congruent meanings) that beholders are called on to make sense of the ruptures, displacements, and deferrals between these dimensions and thus become actively and affectively involved with the image.

Projective integration is a mechanism of hegemonic domination and a late modern form of governmentality, which aims at convincing the individuals to work themselves into the given socioeconomic relations. It explicitly does not rely on a clear-cut opposition of social forces but instead employs entanglements and overlaps of social forces and discourses. But why is it specifically images of sexuality—and particularly representations of exceptional, but harmless sexuality—that instruct the process of projective integration and support the constitution of neoliberal subjectivities? Images of dissident sexualities and gender ambiguities play a particular role in the processes of projective integration because sexuality stands in for distinctiveness, indicating the specificity or even singularity of an individual, and functions as the code of highly valued difference. In these images, a cultural imaginary is activated that presents sexuality as something that people value as a personal good and are ready to defend against external interference. Correspondingly, references to sexuality support people's willingness to take up the management of differences as their own personal business. If gays and lesbians turn into celebrated figures of late modern media and culture, this is less because they are seen as indispensable consumers, ideal employees, or embodiments of an especially desired life-style, and more because they stand in for the virtuous management of difference.

If we now return to the reading of Doujak's artwork, could one can argue that her employment of sexual imagery invites her smoothly into the late modern, neoliberal process of projective integration? And moreover, that her use of ambiguities and paradoxes merely marks the overlaps between queer and neoliberal discourses rather than proposing a distinctively queer critique or resistance? In discourses on sexuality, paradoxes are well established and valued phenomena. According to a patriarchal and racist "division of labor," there is a certain tradition of splitting up paradoxical moments in order to create coherent, hierarchized, socio-sexual roles, for example when women, or Asian gays are stereotypically depicted as passive, thus securing the position of activeness and control to masculinity and/or whiteness. Yet, one also finds that sexuality is affirmatively taken on as something paradoxical in itself, creating sexual positions that combine self-assertion and self-loss, recognition and subordination, singularity and objectification, and lust and coercion (Holzhey,

2001). Thus, references to sexuality in cultural discourse and imagery may very well mark paradoxes as something pleasurable.

This is most interesting since paradoxes are equally appealing figures in both queer politics and neoliberal cultural politics and, indeed, become the hinge between the two fields. The paradox seems to be the ideal candidate for queer politics because it disrupts rigid gender identities and normative desires. The paradox becomes even more fascinating because it also enjoys high status in neoliberal cultural politics in which paradoxical appellations—for example, to be exceptional but strictly normal, or to live out personal autonomy but simultaneously take responsibility in privatized care relations—aim at activating the individual's capacities to make impossible ends meet. At the same time, the paradox depoliticizes these contradictions into fate or fact. Neoliberal cultural politics make use of paradoxes in order to call people into responsibility for tasks that might otherwise be understood as communal obligations, as an example, if individual consumer desires or distinctive family values are activated in order to legitimize that a formerly public health care gets privatized. The double deployment in queer and neoliberal discourses means that the paradox can point toward those areas where these discourses and imageries overlap and where one can ask: How can queer politics develop out of their entanglement in late modern, neoliberal relations of domination? In answer to this question, I argue that *Drag Feeding* parasitically inhabits the process of projective integration.

From the Strategy of Equivocation to the Politics of Paradox

If *Drag Feeding* not only points out but also reworks the asymmetries of global food supply, it does so by relying on a political strategy that does not create clear-cut oppositions but instead creates juxtapositions that carry subtle tensions. The image shirks conventional oppositions of rich versus poor or male versus female, choosing instead to offer up discordant notes of tropical vegetation combined with bourgeois tapestry or drag meeting trans. Further, by representing political contradictions as ambivalent, polysemic, and paradoxical rather than following an either/or logic, the image shifts attention from images of the South as victim versus the North as advocate or benefactor to the North's oversupply, stressing the dependencies of the dominant position. The relationships become more complex, polysemic, and in need of interpretation.

The image employs the rhetorical figure of the paradox when it suggests that there is pleasure in pain or that control depends on giving away, or even sacrificing, one's own means of survival. By quoting the Christian myths that pleasure results from pain and that suffering finally turns into happiness, the image provides a restaging of the colonial mission, but inverts it in a carnivalesque way through appropriating the role of the oppressor/benefactor. Simultaneously, the representation ironically euphemizes global relations of exploitation in presenting the North as dependent on "being supported" by the South, and the South enacting "voluntarily" its self-exploitation—in a globalized World Bank regime. Activating the sexualized imagery of the SM-constellation, Doujak's piece invites reflections on voluntariness in relations of domination, thus hinting at the fact that the neoliberal globalized economy is a paradox in itself: Gains in power and pleasure won from participation in the economic regime depend on a hegemonic consensus that demands self-exploitation and submission to the regime's rules. Rhetorically, the paradox also results from combining the incongruous strategies of inversion and ironic euphemism, thus mimicking on the aesthetic level what is also a question of political strategy: Does one better change global relations of domination by occupying available roles of the hegemonic order and claiming its power, or by depriviliging or decentering dominant positions and undermining the principles of identity and categorical differentiation that underlie these positions? In not answering but rather raising this question, the image may also provoke considerations on the

role of paradoxes in upholding relations of power and domination. Do paradoxes support and reproduce global injustice by suggesting that incoherence can be sustained and even made economically productive?

Doujak's work becomes productive as a critique of relations of power and domination exactly by working from within neoliberalism's logic—specifically by seizing on the neoliberal affinity to paradoxes. In upholding the paradox rather than turning it into an antagonism or cutting its agonistic character by translating it into ambiguity, *Drag Feeding* effects a situation where the beholder is forced to act on the paradox in order to make sense of the representation. In experiencing the paradox, that is, in realizing that any interpretation is build on a provisional fixing of meaning that remains questionable and that cannot rely on any definite point of reference, one finds oneself confronted with the poststructuralist understanding of the political. In this understanding, politics is making decisions under conditions of undecidability, without any grounding in political or epistemic truth (Laclau & Mouffe, 1985; Derrida, 1992; Butler, Laclau, & Žižek, 2000). Or, to put it another way, it is exactly because there is no safe grounding of truth that defines and rationalizes the decisions, but only relative and contextual power/knowledge, that there is the political.

In raising questions but withholding definite criteria for the answer, *Drag Feeding* simultaneously collaborates with the neoliberal paradigm and also opens up the possibility that decisions could disrupt relations of domination in general, as well as particular norms, normalizations, hierarchies, subordinations, exploitations, dominations, and privileges. Thus, it is the beholder of the image, who can foreground its continuously changing meaning or who can let one side of the paradox (either the pleasure or the coercion), define the situation, or who interprets the paradoxes as made up from structural global inequalities. But it is the formal set-up of the image, its aesthetic and rhetorical strategies, which sustains the paradox and upholds the undecidability—thus pushing the experience of the political.

If Doujak's collage subverts simple antagonisms and totalizing political answers, how does it also avoid a relativistic position or the neutralization of power relations? This question can be answered on both a thematic and rhetorical level. On the one hand, it avoids relativism by taking up a stance in unfolding the processes of how relations of domination develop. For example, it invites readers to ask how gendered, racialized, and sexualized ambiguities evolve by presenting socio-historical constructions of difference as the results of singular or intimate power relations.

In realizing that one cannot exchange the roles of the two figures without turning it into a racist and sexist constellation, the workings of structured and structuring processes of domination are disclosed. On the other hand, the image avoids neutrality in not only quoting many different kinds of socio-historical relations of domination, but also in activating the destabilizing function of paradoxes in order to intervene in these discursive constructions. Here, a difference between ambiguities and paradoxes is made productive: while ambiguities indicate a permanent shift in meaning, an unfixability and impossibility of closure, the paradox is an agonistic figure, which points out what is irreconcilable but reconciles them anyway. Even if paradoxes never can be fixed, thanks to the contradictory simultaneity of "neither/nor" and "as well as," there are nevertheless definable elements. Therefore, the paradox pushes the strategy of equivocation, which destabilizes normative identity constructions and binaries into an agonistic struggle. Practically, this manifests itself in the fact that Doujak's collage is also displayed by the artist as part of an installation that criticizes biopiracy, that is, the patenting and commercialization of life by the agricultural and pharmaceutical industries, the exploitation of natural resources and the appropriation of indigenous knowledge.[15]

I conclude by suggesting that Doujak's collage provides an idea of what I call "queer politics of paradox." Politics of paradox are interesting from a queer perspective for two reasons. First, they open up space for representations of difference that do not follow the identity principle and are often claimed to be unintelligible. Second, the logical figure of the paradox allows us to illustrate agonistic dimensions in politics. Queer politics of paradox make use of the pleasure in paradoxes and parasitically inhabit neoliberal appellations of individualized difference and processes of projective integration. But, in destabilizing rigid identity constructions and binary oppositions, they also make use of the fact that the paradox is a logical, rhetorical and aesthetic figure that is not only anti-identity, but also thoroughly agonistic. Thus from a queer perspective, paradoxes do not have to be read as symptoms of depoliticization. Rather than striving to overcome paradoxes by translating them into "proper antagonisms" or by harmonizing them into coherence, a queer politics of paradox turns the neoliberal deployment of paradoxes against itself.

ACKNOWLEDGMENTS

I would like to thank Renate Lorenz and Jessica Dorrance for valuable comments and support in finalizing the manuscript as well as the *Institute for Cultural Inquiry* (ICI-Berlin) for providing intellectual inspiration and the resources to write this text. Thank you also to David J. Prickett, Kevin S. Amidon, and Tom Haakenson for their supportive feedback to an earlier version of the text.

NOTES

1. I am referring to developments in northern and western Europe; "Western," though, is not so much a geopolitical location as an attitude of cultural dominance that builds upon historical traditions and is reflected in international institutions.

2. Gabriele Dietze (2010) suggests using the term "occidentalist" in order to capture recent transformations of racism in Europe and North America after September 11, 2001. Her feminist version of the critique of occidentalism points out the interplay of anti-Muslim racism, polarizing gender discourses, and homonationalism in hegemonic regulations of migrant populations. Using the term coined by Fernando

Coronil (1996) and Walter Mignolo (2000), Dietze agrees with the shift from the critique of orientalism to the critique of occidentalism that highlights Christian values, enlightenment discourses, and capitalist economy, as central moments of Western dominance in the globalized world In contrast to "eurocentrism," the term captures the fact that occidentalism is promoted not only by the European, the Northern American, and Australian as well as Western educated middle- and upper- class constituencies in Southern countries. It also avoids overwriting the fact that many people living in Europe do not subscribe to occidentalist world views.

3. Queer politics, as I understand the term, is built upon a critique of identity politics, and it shifts attention towards mechanisms of exclusion within emancipatory movements or sexual politics. Therefore, I neither use queer as an umbrella term for LGBTI (lesbian, gay, bisexual, transgender/transsexual, intersex) nor do I refer to queer as an identity category. In employing a skeptical attitude towards categorization and demands for the coherence and stability of sex, gender, and sexuality, I prefer to understand queer in a verbal sense, namely as a process of queering normative, normalizing, hierarchizing, or exclusionary regimes. Not only (hetero-)sexism and homophobia, but also discriminations pertaining to the rigid binary gender order as well as racist discriminations are issues of importance to queer politics.

4. Yet, I suppose that celebrating diversity is typical only for those segments of society whose lifestyle is defined by consumption, maybe, even brand-name consumption. One may find such segments in the metropoles of Eastern and Southern nations, whereas not all members of Northern or Western societies can be characterized like this. While neoliberalism is a worldwide development, it has to be considered as a differentiated and differentiating process and a global and local movement.

5. In my book *Wider die Eindeutigkeit* (2002), I coined the neologism *VerUneindeutigung*. It has later been translated variously as equivocation or un-disambiguation. See also endnote 12.

6. For my argument, I refer to theories of hegemony, particularly to Ernesto Laclau and Chantal Mouffe (1986) that explain how relations of domination may depend as much on repression as on forms of discursive and habitual consensus production. Processes of identity constitution and alliance building accomplished by means of "articulation" make people agree to hegemonic forms of rule that may not be to their advantage. The edited volume *Hegemony and Heteronormativity* (Castro Varela, Dhawan, & Engel, 2011) provides queer perspectives on theories of hegemony and reflects on intersections and mutual inspirations of the two concepts.

7. In order to elucidate processes of projective integration, the book offers nine close readings of commercial advertisements and art works that visually intertwine sexuality and economy. I analyze how heteronormative and capitalist hegemony is supported through the interplay of neoliberal and queer discourses, yet also how queering provides for disruptions and incites socioeconomic change.

8. For example, the installation "Follow the Leader/Seguid vuestro chefe" (2004), consists of 10 plexiglass model boats and 50 ostrich eggs, and reenacts Herman Melville's story titled *Benito Cereno*, of a rebellion on a slave ship. Doujak draws connections to postcolonial imperialism through her depiction of the boats as contemporary Navy ships carrying safari trophies (ostrich eggs) symbolizing romanticism, yet, simultaneously, uses these objects as carrier material for photographs and drawings that narrate various historical liberation struggles. The binary logic of power and resistance is undermined by a multiplicity of revolutionary forces. For more information on Doujak's work see: http://de.wikipedia.org/wiki/Ines_ Doujak (retrieved August 29, 2011).

9. Michel Foucault's notion of governmentality points out that modern forms of ruling rely on the active participation of individuals. Subjectivity and relations of domination are not divided between the personal and the state, but are in fact deeply intertwined. The term "government," in Foucault's sense, focuses on how people conduct their lives and how they condition the agency of others, and it indicates how certain forms of subjectivity are constituted within rather than repressed by relations of domination—the regulation of populations rather than state sovereignty (Foucault, 1982, 1991).

10. The term "racialization" here stands in for the constructed binaries of white and black as well as North and South, which only go together because a racist cultural imaginary blends racial anthropology and colonial history into a universal hierarchy of the unmarked norm and its other. Concerning modernized forms of racism and neocolonialism, one has to consider how diversified "ethnicizations" and "economic developmental stages" provide the material for more elaborate hierarchizations.

11. Though many scholars have fervidly argued that this is rarely the case. For example, Cohen (2005) and Erel, Haritaworn, Gutiérrez Rodríguez, and Klesse (2008) point out that even when, on an abstract level,

a general critique of relations of domination is claimed, the concrete effects of racism, antisemitism, transphobia, and ablesim are mostly ignored. Contradictions and tensions that arise from the complex simultaneity of various processes of categorization, hierarchization and normalizing power relations are not acknowledged but subsumed to a (queer) master narrative.

12. "Un-disambiguating" might be the more pointed translation, recently suggested by artist and cultural theorist Renate Lorenz, because it underlines the fact that previously, a process of disambiguation has taken place and that homogeneity and coherence are not natural givens but the product of socio-historical power relations.

13. Norms in the plural acknowledges that, for example, some social contexts might be organized by homonormativity rather than heteronormativity, or that racialized, heterosexualized and classed norms may need to be challenged in their complex interplay.

14. By "agonistic," I mean in a very broad sense the ongoing conflicts and struggles between incompatible perspectives, which do not have to be understood as distinct, consistent and unambigious positions in themselves. In the use of this term, I want to stress the ambiguity of all positions even more than Laclau and Mouffe (1985), who underline that "antagonism" does not imply an opposition between fixed entities—but instead the conflicts and contradictions that result from the impossibility of closure—but Laclau and Mouffe still ultimately opt for provisional identities in their argumentation.

15. The installation, also called *Victory Gardens* (2007) presents the 70 motives of the series on oversized seed packages assembled on a 17m elevated flower bed. The backsides of the seed packages inform viewers about neocolonial exploitation and the commercialization of life; the cover images ironically quote the discourse on biodiversity by appropriating it to visually represent a multiplicity of genders and sexualities. The title refers to the colonial occupation of native and communal territories into the "victory gardens" of the colonizer's world. See Doujak (2008).

REFERENCES

Butler, J. (2004). *Undoing gender.* New York, NY: Routledge.

Butler, J., Laclau, E., & Žižek, S. (2000). *Contingency, hegemony, universality: Contemporary dialogues on the left.* London, UK: Verso.

Castro Varela, M., Dhawan, N., & Engel, A. (Eds.). (2011). *Hegemony and heteronormativity: Revisiting "The political" in queer politics.* Aldershot, UK: Ashgate.

Cohen, C. J. (2005). Punks, bulldaggers, and welfare queens: The radical potential of queer politics? In P. E. Johnson & M. G. Henderson (Eds.), *Black queer studies: A critical anthology* (pp. 21–51). Durham, NC: Duke University Press.

Coronil, F. (1996). Beyond occidentalism: Toward nonimperial geohistorical categories. *Cultural Anthropology, 11*(1), 51–87.

Derrida, J. (1992). Force of law. In D. Cornell, M. Rosenfeld, & D. G. Carlson (Eds.), *Deconstruction and the possibility of justice* (pp. 3–67). New York, NY: Routledge.

Dietze, G. (2010). The critique of occidentalism. In H. Brunkhorst & G. Grözinger (Eds.), *The study of Europe* (pp. 87–116). Baden-Baden, DE: Nomos.

Doujak, I. (2008). *Siegesgärten/Victory gardens,* Vienna, AT: Schleebrügge.

Duggan, L. (2003). *The twilight of equality?: Neoliberalism, cultural politics, and the attack on democracy.* Boston, MA: Beacon Press.

Engel, A. (2002). *Wider die Eindeutigkeit: Sexualität und Geschlecht im Fokus queerer Politik der Repräsentation.* Frankfurt, DE: Campus Verlag.

Engel, A. (2006). A queer strategy of equivocation. The destabilisation of normative heterosexuality and the rigid binary gender order. *Interalia, 1.* Retrieved August 29, 2011 from http://interalia.org.pl/pl/artykuly/2006_1/02_a_queer_strategy_of_equivocation.htm.

Engel, A. (2007a). Loud & lusty lesbian queers. In N. Giffney & K. O'Donnell (Eds.), *Twenty-first century lesbian studies* (pp. 265–273). Harrington, UK: Harrington Park Press/an imprint of the Haworth Press.

Engel, A. (2007b). No sex, no crime, no shame. Privatized care and the seduction into responsibility. *Nora: Nordic Journal of Women's Studies, 15* (3), 114–132.

Engel, A. (2009a). *Bilder von Sexualität und Ökonomie. Queere kulturelle Politiken im Neoliberalismus.* Bielefeld, DE: Transcript.

Engel, A. (2009b). How to queer things with images: On the lack of fantasy in performativity and the imaginativeness of desire. In B. Paul & J. Schaffer (Eds.), *Mehr(wert) queer: Queer added (value)—Visual culture, art, and gender politics* (pp. 119–131). Bielefeld, DE: Transcript.

Engel, A. (2011). Tender tensions – antagonistic struggles – becoming bird: Queer political interventions into neoliberal hegemony. In M. d. M. Castro Varela, N. Dhawan, & A. Engel (Eds.), *Hegemony and heteronormativity: Revisiting "the political" in queer politics* (pp. 63–90). Farnham, UK: Ashgate.

Erel, U., Haritaworn, J., Gutiérrez Rodríguez, E., & Klesse, C. (2008). On the depoliticisation of intersectionality-talk. Conceptualising multiple oppressions in critical sexuality studies. In A. Kuntsman & E. Mikaye (Eds.), *Out of place: Interrogating silences in queerness/raciality* (pp. 265–292). York, UK: Raw Nerve Books.

Foucault, M. (1982). The subject and power. In H. L. Dreyfus & P. Rabinow (Eds.), *Michel Foucault: Beyond structuralism and hermeneutics* (pp. 208–226). Chicago, IL: University of Chicago Press.

Foucault, M. (1991). Governmentality. In G. Burchell & C. Gordon (Eds.), *The Foucault effect: Studies in gouvernmentality. With two lectures by and an interview with Michel Foucault.* Chicago, IL: University of Chicago Press.

Hennessy, R. (2000). *Profit and pleasure: Sexual identities in late capitalism.* New York, NY: Routledge.

Holzhey, C. (2001). *Paradoxical pleasures in aesthetics: Masophobia, sexual difference, and E. T. A. Hoffmann's Kater Murr.* Unpublished Ph.D. dissertation, Graduate School of Arts and Sciences, Columbia University, New York, NY.

Laclau, E., & Mouffe, C. (1985). *Hegemony and socialist strategy: Towards a radical democratic politics.* London, UK: Verso.

Mignolo, W. D. (2000). *Local histories/global designs: Coloniality, subaltern knowledges, and border thinking.* Princeton, NJ: Princeton University Press.

SECTION 4

GENDER

13

POSITIONING THE
VEILED WOMAN

*An Analysis of Austrian Press
Photographs in the Context of the
European Headscarf Debates*

RICARDA DRÜEKE, SUSANNE KIRCHHOFF, AND ELISABETH KLAUS

INTRODUCTION

In this chapter, we examine how identities are being constructed in the current headscarf debate in the Austrian media. In media discourse, images of veiled women or women wearing headscarves are often utilized as a means to redefine cultural and geographical constructs—West and East, Occident and Orient, Christianity and Islam,[1] national or European affiliation and non-affiliation—and to position social subjects within these constructs in specific ways. The headscarf debates in various European countries have made it clear just how vehemently Western European societies are grappling with the significance of headscarves. We understand media as providing the symbolic spaces in which identities are (re)produced, contested, and modified.

Within the different national and media contexts, the debate about *hijabs* ("proper dressing," usually applied to headscarves), *chadors* (the Iranian body and head cover), *niqabs* (face veils), *burqas* (the Afghan full body and face covering), and other forms of veiling serve to raise questions of gender equality, secularism, integration, and citizenship (cf. Berghahn & Rostock, 2009). This chapter addresses the headscarf debate in Austria and focuses on the positioning of veiled women in press photography. The discussion is theoretically grounded in theories of space, which—as in other social sciences—have led to a spatial turn in communication studies.

The media infiltrate our everyday lives with images of various places and spatial orders. Hence the politics of media images cannot be separated from the politics of space. The dialectical sense of belonging and alienation, self and system, is an integral part of the experience of media spaces (cf. Couldry & McCarthy, 2004, p. 3). In a society dominated by mass media, communication is both an engine and an actor in the processes of self-making and being-made by space. Accordingly ("all forms of communication occur *in space*, and all spaces are produced *through representation,* which occurs *by means of communication'*) (Falkheimer & Jansson, 2006, p. 9, original emphasis). New spatial orders such as globalization and the emergence of new information and communication technologies reinforce these changes.

(The construction of space in the media—especially if linked to issues of identity and migration—is often connected with the demarcation of external and internal boundaries, which define a national identity and determine who does and who does not belong) Saskia Sassen (2006) stresses the fact that contemporary identities are always at least partially constituted by whom they exclude. Seyla Benhabib (2004), discussing the terms of political membership, argues that the boundaries established by nation states are no longer an adequate basis for determining the rules of belonging. Nevertheless, Austria and other Western European countries seem obsessed with exactly this task of constructing boundaries that distinguish legitimate inhabitants from the Others, from foreigners and migrants.

Establishing European borders and in particular a European culture with common religious norms is by no means accomplished by reference to value-neutral categories. Edward Said (1978) analyzed the construction of the Orient as an imaginary space in European history by exploring the historical formation and the emergence of Western perceptions of the Orient. He dismantled taken-for-granted mental mappings as constructions that are strongly connected to categories of race, class, and gender. (The symbolic geography and the imaginative space called Orient is thus a Western European product that is based on differentiations referring to territorial, religious, social, sexual, moral, and cultural issues.)

Mass media are centrally involved in the production, reproduction, and modification of those differentiations that lead to the construction of mostly symbolic and imaginary spaces. As a consequence, they play an influential role in the decision of which subjects belong to the spaces designated as Europe or Austria. The concept of media-constructed spaces of identity helps us to analyze the complex interconnectedness of markers of belonging in the media's coverage of migration. The media theorist, Brigitte Hipfl (2004) defines the media itself as a social space that enables the formation of identity (Media create spaces of identity in which identities are positioned and cultural markers are located; they negotiate the boundaries of a symbolic community and determine boundaries that exclude or include identities in the imaginative space designated as Austria) Our differentiation of three types of media spaces is based on Hipfl's conceptualization (2004) among others:

1) The media devise *geo/political (geographical and political)[2] spaces*. They apply boundaries to territories, position nations, and identify landscapes in which particular identities find their place.

2) The media content provides *spaces for identification* in which people can position themselves, or let themselves be positioned, as Europeans, women, Austrians, Catholics, and so forth.

3) *Spaces of in-between* are not so much media-constructed as mediated. They emerge within the circuit of meaning production, especially through the interaction of audiences with the media. These processes may run counter to hegemonic identity discourses.

We elaborate further on these three types of spaces that guided our qualitative analysis later in the presentation of the findings from our study. They prove helpful in analyzing the role of media and communication in the construction of nation-states and communities of belonging. This is evidenced by the headscarf debates in Europe.

In subsequent sections we briefly focus on spatial theory, which serves to contextualize our own findings theoretically. We then explore the social and political background of the issues we address, namely the Austrian headscarf debate and its European context. In addition, we present findings from our study of pictures of veiled woman published in three major Austrian newspapers. Importantly, we combine a content analysis of key factors–such as the manner of veiling—with a qualitative analysis of the staging strategies of the photographs, based on our distinction of media-constructed spaces. Finally, we summarize some of our main results.

MEDIA-CONSTRUCTED SPACES OF IDENTITY

Concepts of space and place have a long philosophical tradition that has been developed in a variety of disciplines, such as philosophy, geography, sociology, literature, and communication sciences. For much of social science research, the existence of a physical space, a defined place or specific location, was the central assumption: social structures and societal processes were examined in specific locations, while the spaces themselves were taken for granted. The emergence of postmodern and poststructuralist approaches, however, has changed the conceptualization of space. Nowadays, it is seen not as a specific place, but as a product of social and cultural practices. Taking the nation-state and the European Union as an example, it rapidly becomes clear that the idea of fixed borders has mostly been viewed as a pre-given, while at the same time, wars were fought over neighboring territories, making it quite obvious that the idea of a nation was not a natural, self-evident category, but was based on a specific construct. In the European Union, a fierce debate has arisen about whether Turkey should be accepted as one of its members. Depending on the criteria used (geographical borders, religion, historical time periods, human rights issues, etc.) Turkey will be considered either as belonging to or being very different from a—however defined—"Western Europe." The debate is a prime example for the importance of the shift in paradigms from space as something given and natural to space as a social and cultural construction. Edward Said's "Orientalism" exemplifies the importance of seeing space as something that is defined and constructed by differentiating it from another imaginary place. "Europe" emerged as a space by creating another space called the "Orient."

Since the mid-1990s, the social sciences and humanities have developed an orientation toward spatiality, understood broadly as the "spatial turn." In accordance with social geography, theoretical approaches are now often based on concepts of space, time, and place in such a way that space is assumed to be socially and culturally constructed. Spaces are understood as a product of different histories and seen as relevant for the understanding of societal practices. For instance, the huge Habsburg Empire and its territory were very different from the small state that evolved after 1918, although both are labeled "Austria." The concept of space is also exemplified by many social problems which have been defined on the basis of territories, although they are not grounded in spatiality, for example social movements or religions. By assigning them to a specific country or region, these places were in turn constructed and defined.

Henri Lefebvre (1992) was the first theorist who focused on the production of space not as materially given, but as a socially constructed space embedded in the social relations of production. Power thus is implicated in the way space is represented and conceived. Building on Lefebvre's work, Edward Soja (1989) introduced the concept of a "Thirdspace," that we will draw on in our analysis. Soja argues that the effects of a changing culture ought to be viewed as creating "Thirdspaces," or hybrid spaces of transition emerging from transitions between localities and across time. The concept of a "Thirdspace" undermines the dualistic construction of spaces that place ideas, people, or products either as being inside or outside a space. Thus, attention is drawn to the intimate linkages and the interrelationship of such constructions as "we" and the "other," the "insider" and the "outsider," the "legitimate citizen" and the "migrant." Using the veil as an example, we can trace the history of veiling in Europe to the Christian tradition of nuns wearing the headcloth or to the rural tradition of women wearing headscarves, which is still quite common today. We also can trace the history of full-body veiling in some of the Arab states to the colonial rule, when women covered their bodies as a protection against the sexual violence by colonial soldiers. When observing people on a busy street in any European metropolis, a whole array of different styles of clothing, of covering and uncovering of the body can be seen, showing that the distinction between those who cover their hair and body and those who don't is in constant flux. The "Thirdspace," thus, is a concept that alters the perspective and overcomes the dual notions of including or excluding people from "Western" societies by their style of clothing. This in turn changes the concept of what constitutes a place called "Western society" and opens venues for new conceptions.

Doreen Massey (1994) enhanced the concept of spaces by observing that spaces have multiple identities and are processes within time: "Space is not static, nor time spaceless. We need to conceptualize space as constructed from interrelations, as the simultaneous coexistence of social interrelations and interactions at all spatial scales" (p. 264). Studies of space thus allow observations of various interactions, and all kinds of communication, in particular.

Following up such reconceptualizations of space, communication research investigates how spaces enable communication. As early as 1951, the media theorist Harold Innis (1986) proposed to look at power structures with regard to those historically specific areas in which media are produced and consumed. He was interested in the possibilities for developing new and alternative spaces for media and communication. Innis's analysis focused on the distinction between time-biased and space-biased media as well as

their role in the use of different means of communication within the contexts of different political systems and diverse power structures.

The book *Spaces of Identity* by David Morley and Kevin Robins (1995) is regarded as a milestone for the "spatial turn" in communications research. Morley and Robins argue that today, it is not so much physical limitations but rather symbolic constraints that function as boundaries for cultural communities. They show that in Europe the media primarily offer an ethnic white identity, leaving only marginal spaces for other social groups (e.g., migrants, diasporic communities). Benedict Anderson (1993) in his book on the *Imagined Communities* perceives cultural systems such as nation-states as identity spaces in which identity positions are predefined. In this view, the nation is an "imagined community" that differentiates itself from other communities, and whose members assume the existence of certain norms, values, and attributes that bind them together. For example, the imagined community of Europe is based on its self-description as a space in which democracy, human rights, and liberty have been realized as paramount goods.

THE AUSTRIAN HEADSCARF DEBATE IN ITS EUROPEAN CONTEXT

Muslim women's veiling has come under close scrutiny in many European countries. While Muslim men and unveiled women may go unnoticed in everyday life, veiled women are highly visible, signifying both Islam and the foreign (cf. Blosat, 2005, p. 111). This reaction has intensified in the decade after September 11th, although Hafez (2002, pp. 230–232) shows that already after the Iranian revolution of 1979, headscarves and chadors have become symbols in the German press for Islamic fundamentalism. However, during the 1980s and 1990s, the Austrian media primarily constructed the headscarf as a symbol of a cultural and economic threat rather than as a religious or political threat. In a number of European countries, suspicions of cultural

"*Überfremdung*"[3] and a steep rise in unemployment figures lay at the heart of these discourses. More recently, the fear of terrorist attacks has been added to the discourse spurring debates about migration, integration, national security, and gender equality (for the German debates, cf., Berghahn & Rostock, 2009; Farrokzhad, 2006; Schiffer, 2007; and Röder, 2007).

Freedom of belief, equal treatment of religions, and laicism (the separation of state and church) are important issues in the political-judicial realm. Yet, media debates generally revolve around migration laws and the wearing of headscarves in public institutions and/or by public servants, focusing in particular on teachers and students. This is especially important since national and cultural conceptions of self and other are to a large extent constructed by the media. In the media, hegemonic meanings of veiling and the social positions of Muslim women are constantly reaffirmed, negotiated, and contested.

Despite their differences in national discourses, in Great Britain, Germany, and Denmark studies on the media's portrayal of Islam in general and the veiling of women in particular reveal a number of similarities: news about Islam is event oriented, and the number of reports has increased over the last decade. On the average, Islam gets more public attention today than any other religion, especially when compared to the number of believers. However, the reporting tends to be negative and oversimplistic, using emotional language, which serves to raise fears and suspicions in both Muslim and non-Muslim communities (cf. Quraishy, 2001, p. 717 for the Danish press; Greater London Authority, 2007, p. xiv for the British press; Hafez & Richter, 2008, p. 10 for the German public broadcasting service). Accordingly, the findings suggest that the media reporting about Islam is best described in terms of homogenization, stereotyping, and polarization.

Homogenization: Islam is often viewed as a homogenous religion with a unified church, ignoring its variety of religious traditions and practices (Hafez & Richter, 2008). Likewise, the different reasons that women cover themselves are seldom reported in the media. For instance, the French media see veiling as a symbol of oppression and as an indicator of the lack of integration into society. They distinguish between the "*jeune fille voilée*" and the unveiled "*beurette*" who strives for emancipation and integration, disregarding the women's values and living conditions (Schumann, 2002, p. 343; Tévanian, 2005; Deltombe, 2005).

Stereotyping: This homogenous view of Muslims and Islam leads to the stereotype of veiled Muslim women as being universally oppressed, backward, and/or extremist—which then contributes to their social marginalization. The stereotype interplays with other forms of exclusion. For example the public debate in France portrays veiling as being a phenomenon of the *banlieues*, the suburbs with a large migrant population, which signify the Other of the Grande Nation (Hancock, 2008, p. 173). In Turkey, the headscarf is often associated with a countryside background and/or lack of education (Schumann, 2002, p. 343). In Germany, the debate focuses on women from the lower social strata (Amanuel, 1996, p. 99). Thus media representations of veiling combine religious and cultural stereotypes with stereotypes of social class. In Austria, where the debate has been less fierce, the political right tries to reframe the issue of veiling from one of religious freedom of choice to a fundamental cultural difference (Gresch, Hadj-Abdou, Rosenberger, & Sauer, 2008).

Polarization: Homogenizing discourses and cultural stereotypes obviously fall short of a differentiated analysis and ignore the variety of ideas and positions of people in both European and non-European countries. The media tend to present Islam as a threat to Western values and lifestyles, and its followers appear unwilling to integrate themselves into European societies. A collision between seemingly incompatible cultures is then often seen as the inevitable consequence (Poole, 2000, pp. 162–164).

Media studies from different European countries support the claim that the meaning attached to the headscarf must be viewed in relation to the ongoing national debates (Kiliç, Sakarso, &

Sauer, 2008; McGoldrick, 2006). Thus, legislation on veiling policies across Europe varies considerably. Hege Skjeie (2007, p. 130) has identified three different models of regulation: a prohibitive approach, selective prohibition, and a nonrestrictive, tolerant approach. Different models of regulation are grounded in and express the diverse historical-political contexts of the respective countries. Kiliç et al. (2008) suggest that the following key factors explain the differences and similarities between regulatory policies: citizenship regimes and integration policies, the relations between church and state and the recognition of religious communities, gender equality and antidiscrimination policies, and finally strategies of framing.

Countries following a *prohibitive approach* usually practice a strict laicism, banning all religious symbols from public institutions. The most notable cases are France, home of Europe's largest Muslim migrant community and Turkey, Europe's only country with a Muslim majority (McGoldrick, 2006, pp. 34–36, 132–134).[4] In Germany, which does not practice state secularism, the decision lies with the federal states. Some of them have passed restrictive laws, while others are more tolerant (cf. Oestreich, 2004; Rottmann & Marx Ferree, 2008, p. 491).

In the *selective prohibition model* only some forms of body covering, such as *niqab* and *burqa* are banned from public institutions. This is practiced in countries such as the Netherlands, Finland, and Sweden (Kiliç et al., 2008, p. 398). The *nonrestrictive, tolerant approach* model does not restrict head and body coverings in any way. One example is Great Britain, where despite widespread criticism the government upholds nonregulation. A majority of the British citizens view the ideal of a multicultural society as a failure, ignoring ongoing processes of integration and instead focusing on the so-called migrant ghettos overstressing the fact that large migrant ghettos have emerged (Kiliç, 2008; McGoldrick, 2006, pp. 173–204; Atkinson, 2010).

Austria is another country with a tolerant stance toward veiling, but the sociopolitical context is somewhat different. Gresch et al. (2008)

argue that one might expect Austria to follow a more rigid course, given the fact that the country upholds the ideal of an ethnically and culturally homogeneous community, has highly restrictive migration laws and a lax antidiscrimination policy that yields little effect. Thus, citizenship regimes and antidiscrimination policies can be discounted as explanatory factors for adhering to a tolerant approach in Austria. Here the state-church relationship can be seen as the prime reason for adopting the current legislation (ibid., p. 412). Indeed, Austria practices religious pluralism within a form of institutionalized corporatism between the state and religious communities. Those religions that are officially recognized by the state are granted far-ranging autonomy. Their representatives are heard whenever legal or political decisions concern religious matters. Islam was recognized as an official religion in 1912 and as a religious community in 1979, with the Islamic Religious Community of Austria as its representative in dealings with the state (Islamische Glaubensgemeinschaft Österreich [IGGÖ], 2003).

In recent years, however, the nonrestrictive approach has been challenged in several ways. First, since roughly 66% of Austrians are members of the Catholic Church (Juriatti, 2010) and the country does not practice laicism, crucifixes are often displayed in courtrooms, classrooms, and other public buildings (Gresch et al., 2008, p. 417). Second, the debate on religious pluralism and the Islamic faith has so far focused mainly on headscarves (ibid., p. 421). But, in 2008 the issue of veiling gained a new dimension when a woman accused of a terrorist conspiracy was excluded from the court proceedings because she refused to take off her *niqab*. The court viewed this as "improper behavior" (Seeh, 2008). In 2010, the Medical University of Graz decided to ban students who wear a face veil from class on the grounds that, in European tradition, the face is an important transmitter of nonverbal communication and essential to the contact between doctors and patients. In addition, students need to identify themselves when taking examinations (Brickner, 2010). Third, liberal legal practices have long been under attack from right-wing parties, reframing the issue as one of cultural values rather than religious freedom (Gresch et al., 2008, p. 424). In one recent example, the FPÖ's (Freedom Party of Austria) election campaign featured an advertisement bearing the slogan: "We protect free women. The SPÖ (Social Democratic Party of Austria) protects the compulsion to wear a headscarf." The poster appeared in the communal elections in Vienna, which has the largest Muslim community in Austria. But it can be argued that because it reproduces widespread stereotypes about gender relations in Islam (cf. Jäger & Jäger, 2007, p. 110), the advertisement was mainly addressed at non-Muslim voters.

Until now, restrictions on wearing headscarves, face-veils, or body-coverings have been limited to public institutions such as class- and courtrooms, but in the last five years the debate has spread to other domains. Currently, a general ban on *burqas* is being discussed in many European countries. In 2010, several governments have either banned *burqas* from all public places or are planning to do so. Belgium and Spain were the first countries to pass respective laws. France and the Netherlands are likely to follow. In Austria, Germany, Switzerland, and other countries, the discussion has so far lead to some political initiative, mostly by right-wing parties, but has not yet resulted in legal action (Wöhrle, 2010).

The heated debate on the different forms of veiling in general and on the *burqa* in particular is interspersed with discourses on gender equality and women's rights, state-church relations, migration, and national or European identity. Most arguments in the debate ignore the long Christian tradition of religious veiling in European countries (von Braun & Matthes, 2007, p. 52), and the involvement of European colonialism in the issue. Instead veiling is invariably attributed to the concept of the Orient (cf. Said, 1978). Furthermore, it becomes quite obvious that the *burqa* is a symbolic token in this debate, if one considers the actual number of women who practice full body veiling. For instance, in France with the largest Muslim community in Europe (more than 5 million members) the numbers of women who practice full body veiling is estimated to range between 350 and 2000. In Denmark, experts speak of 100 to 200 women wearing a *niqab* and three wearing a *burqa* in a Muslim population of about 275,000 (Gabizon, 2009; Brandt, Evers, von Mittelstaedt, von Rohr, & Sandberg, 2009; Wöhrle, 2010).

In sum, despite the obvious differences between national discourses, headscarf debates are used to constantly redefine policies of citizenship and belonging. They can be viewed as a part of the process of negotiating identities (Who are *We*? Who belongs to *Us*?) in which the concept of space plays a prominent role in two ways. First, many of the debates evolve around the construction of actual physical space, most notably class- and courtrooms, and more recently public places such as streets or museums. The question of designated public spaces, of who is allowed or denied access to those places is thus posed in a very literal sense. Second, the debates assign spaces of identity to veiled Muslim women, thereby excluding them from the majority society. Berghahn and Rostock state that

> in the European headscarf debates specific norms and values are exploited as 'floating signifiers' in order to define affiliation or disaffiliation with to the respective national state. In most countries the discourse draws on the normative concepts of 'gender equality,' 'secularism' and 'integration' to legitimize or defy the ban on headscarves or defend the women who wear them (2009, p. 12).

These norms are treated as if they have already been realized in the countries mentioned above, but are now threatened by Islam and undermined by women wearing headscarves or body veils (ibid.). Where concepts such as gender equality, secularism, and integration are used as markers of the (national) self, the identity position reserved for the veiled woman is that of the oppressed and/or religiously fanatic other, who refuses to be integrated into the majority society or is prevented from doing so. The following chapters take a closer look at the spaces of identity the media provide for the veiled woman.

Images of Veiled Women in the Austrian Press

Our study examines identities that are produced, reproduced, modified, or rejected in the current debate on veiled women in Austrian newspapers. For this purpose, we selected all pictures of veiled women published in three major daily newspapers between October 2008 and March 2009. The sample includes a total of 122 photographs—43 from the quality paper *Der Standard*, 46 from the regional newspaper *Salzburger Nachrichten*, and 33 from the tabloid *Kronen Zeitung*. In a first step, we compiled a content analysis of key aspects such as the newspaper section and size of the picture, relationship of picture and text, number of people in the picture, subject of the article as well as the type of veiling.[5] Subsequently, the staging strategies of the photographs were subjected to a qualitative analysis based on the distinction of three media-constructed spaces of identity introduced earlier: geo/political spaces, spaces for identification, and spaces of in-between.

The interpretation of media photographs is usually influenced by the topic of the accompanying article. In the first step of the quantitative analysis, we looked at the different thematic contexts in which pictures of veiled women appear in our sample. Among the home-related stories, the terrorist trial of Mona S. features most prominently (16%, for further detail see the following section). Stories about migration make up 12% of our sample. Another major subject covered in our sample is the Israel/Palestine conflict, which accounts for 16%. The sample includes both foreign correspondence and home stories, which deal with the situation in the Near East as well as with political demonstrations in Vienna. Foreign correspondence stories about Muslim countries

such as Iran, Iraq, Afghanistan, and Turkey also play an important role in our study with a total of 18% covering this category.

In a second step, we examined the different types of veiling as well as the women's positioning in each photograph. Veiled women most frequently appear as the only person in the picture (36%), as members of a group of veiled persons (15%), or as members of a group that also contains men and unveiled women but in which the focus is placed on the veiled women (14%). Thus a total of 65% of the pictures emphasize veiled women. In comparison, only 25% of the pictures capture veiled women together with unveiled people without putting an emphasis on them. Therefore, one can argue that the newspapers tend to focus on the veiled image as a device with primarily illustrative or symbolic functions to draw interest and attention.

Among the different types of veiling, the headscarf figures most prominently in our sample (43%). Other forms such as *chadors*, *niqabs*, and *burqas* in portrait shots are shown less often. If combined, however, these three types are as frequent as pictures of women wearing a headscarf (45%). Considering the fact that the number of women who practice full-body veiling in Austria and Europe is negligible, this enhances the argument for the token character of the veil as a marker of Otherness and invisibility. All in all, headscarves are rarely displayed as a taken-for-granted element in the everyday life of Austrian society. Instead, pictures tend to emphasize this piece of cloth. At the same time, full body veiling—which is an uncommon sight in Austria—figures comparatively often in the pictures and is in most cases used for illustrative reasons.

Based on the symbolic nature of many pictures and their implications as markers of the Other, our qualitative analysis was guided by the question: how do press photographs locate the veiled woman, as an individual or a symbolic entity, within the center or the margins of a community? Which spaces are attributed to her and from which is she excluded? We will use the distinction between geo/political spaces,

spaces for identification, and spaces of in-between as an organizing principle and select relevant examples from our sample of photographs in order to reveal the respective placing strategies. The reader should be aware that the separation of geo/political spaces, spaces for identification, and spaces of in-between and the attribution of specific pictures to one of these spaces are done solely for analytical purposes. In fact all three spaces intersect, overlap, and refer to each other.

THE VEILED WOMAN AS A FOREIGN COUNTRY: GEO/POLITICAL SPACES

The media make geo/political spaces accessible through their specific selection on which world events to report and the manner in which they report on them. This includes processes such as setting people in conjunction with cultural practices and in comparison with other territories or places. In this way, an imagined geography is created with images of landscapes and people who populate them. Such constructions lead to a positioning of people in specific regions. Locating the Other is always paralleled by an assessment of one's own sociocultural identity and supports the construction of a national identity by showing what does not belong to and is foreign to "Us," the imagined communities of Austria or Europe.

In Said's (1978) famous analysis of *Orientalism*, the Orient serves as the counterpart to the Occident and is instrumental in the construction of a common European identity.[6] Under the colonial perspective, the women of this region are imagined as gentle, passive, and sexually available. Studio shots played on this fantasy by depicting women with bare breasts beneath a lifted veil or gazing seductively at the spectator from behind a face veil (cf. Graham-Brown, 1988; Volkening, 2001). In our sample, the echo of these once popular motifs can be found in Figure 13.1, which is taken from an article advertizing a tourist trip to the East. The headline

Figure 13.1

Source: Salzburger Nachrichten (Jan. 17, 2009). Orient pur auf Schienen, p. XVI. (Copyright: Geo Reisen)

reads: "Pure Orient on the Rails—The famous Persian poets, Saadi and Hafis have carried the enchanting mysticism of the Orient into the world. Experience the many facets of the mysterious Orient with GEO Travels and Austrian Airlines" (*Salzburger Nachrichten,* Jan. 17, 2009, p. XVI).

The cartoon Figure 13.2 is a rebus or picture puzzle that plays on harem fantasies in the form of caricature (*Kronen Zeitung,* Jan. 14, 2009, p. 47). Both pictures refer to the erotic connotations of veiling in the Orientalist tradition. In the first illustration, the women's eyes make contact with the viewer. Her seductive gaze can therefore be read as an invitation to the "mysteries" of the Orient, as the headline suggests, promising sexual adventures. The caricature highlights another aspect of the topic. Here a man, who is accompanied by six women (presumably his wives), stares longingly at a seventh passing in the other direction. Within the Orientalist frame, the picture suggests not only an erotic attraction and availability of the veiled women, but also sexual insatiability on the man's part.

Few pictures in our sample are so directly related to Orientalist iconography. It is in fact only one string of the media discourse on veiling, alongside numerous others currently in existence.

Figure 13.2

Source: Kronen Zeitung (Jan. 14, 2009). Unser Doppelbild-Rätsel, p. 47. (Copyright: Kronen Zeitung)

Afghanistan—a Burqa-Wearing Woman

Photographs accompanying articles about Afghanistan can further illustrate the creation of geo/political spaces by the media. Various studies have shown that images of *burqa*-clad women figure prominently in reports on the country's numerous problems, for the most part serving as purely illustrative or symbolic functions (e.g., Fahmy, 2004). Although Afghanistan was not one of the prime topics in our sample, several pictures belong to this group. A picture published in the *Standard* (Oct. 8, 2008, p. 5) combines a map of Afghanistan with an image of a woman wearing a *burqa*, a soldier at her side, who is either protecting or guarding her. By explicitly linking the map, the soldier and the woman the picture supports the creation of an imagined geography, locating the wearer of a *burqa* firmly within it. The picture invokes a standardized Western portrayal of Afghanistan under the rule of the Taliban, when the rights of women were severely violated (cf. Klaus/Kassel 2005). The demand for women's rights was a prime argument in generating support for the NATO's war against Afghanistan, and the presence of both the woman and the soldier refers to this topic.

A similar connection between the *burqa* and Afghanistan was made in a picture published by the *Salzburger Nachrichten* (Jan. 20, 2009, p. 5). It combines a photograph of a presumably female head dressed in a *burqa* with a text referring to the political process in Afghanistan under the headline "To Build a Nation," thus positioning the woman in that country. The veil is used for a geo/political representation in connection with concepts of identity. Moreover, it is correlated to the failure to build this nation, as the accompanying article makes quite clear. Thus, the image of the veiled woman at the same time serves as a signifier of Afghanistan and is, in turn, signified by the political chaos in that country. In contrast to the previous picture, this illustration refers more generally to the backwardness of a country that is unable to organize the process of nation-building. The nations in Western Europe signify the beginning of a new era where civil rights and democratic procedures are granted—a stage of development that Afghanistan obviously failed to achieve as is symbolized by the prevalence of the *burqa*.

The veil in these illustrations is an instance of gendering politics and includes references to religion, sex, and power. The postcolonial perspective on veiled women relegates her to the position of the Other. Although it is not visible, this iconography clearly marks the West as the place of reference, as a sphere where democratic procedures, safety, legality, and human rights prevail. The pictures then construct an antagonism between the two regions, in which the colonial and neocolonial involvement of the West in the history of Afghanistan are ignored and masked. We find this confrontation between West and East, Orient and Occident in many of the pictures in our sample.

Locating Anti-American Sentiments and Islam

In his thorough study of foreign correspondence, the communication scholar Hafez (2002) has shown that in German media the veil is very strongly associated with Islamic countries and often represents Islam in general. In our Austrian sample, several pictures confirm this close link. They are highly symbolical and construct a tension between the veiled women portrayed in the foreground and a background containing a political message in the form of posters, graffiti, slogans, and so forth. Typically, such pictures accompany political reports on Turkey, Iraq, Iran, or other Islamic countries.

Figure 13.3, published in the *Salzburger Nachrichten* on January 28, 2009 (p. 1), depicts a mural that voices strong anti-American and anti-Semite feelings. On top of the Washington Capitol an Israeli flag is waving, while the ripped American flag has a spreading hole in its middle. A woman dressed in a black *chador* is passing in front of this mural creating a strong link between her and the painting. She is not looking at it, thus making it appear to be a normal part of her place of residence. In this way, the veiled woman comes to personify anti-Americanism, it is almost written on her body. The line underneath the photograph reads "President Obama wants a dialogue with Islam," a peaceful gesture, but the intention seems misplaced in view of the antagonist painting and the unsmiling, detached person passing in front of it. The black *chador* signifies the cultural gap between the American president and the people to whom his peace offer is addressed. The dress seems to prevent its bearer from entering into communication and dialogue so that the hateful message on the wall cannot be transformed by a cultural exchange. We don't know where the picture was taken, but it doesn't seem to matter since it makes the general claim that all Islamic countries are appropriately characterized by this illustration. Islam does not appear not as a religion with followers worldwide, including in the United States. Instead, it serves as a bond binding a conglomerate of different countries together, creating a region far removed from the United States and its civil and diplomatic offer of dialogue.

The symbolic value of the composition is strengthened by its appearance in similar contexts.

Figure 13.3

Source: Salzburger Nachrichten (Jan. 28, 2009). US-Präsident Obama will Dialog mit Islam, p. 1. (Copyright: Abedin Taherkenareh/EPA/picturedesk.com)

For instance, *Der Standard* (Jan. 30, 2009, p. 4) also published a picture with two veiled women passing in front of a mural with references to the United States. The headline again links the women to anti-American feelings, this time locating them explicitly in Iran.

In these media representations, the veil signifies a specific geo/political space and at the same time expresses identity positions, since the veiled women is seen as belonging to a cultural and religious entity different from the West.

SPACES FOR IDENTIFICATION

Media content constructs spaces for identification where identities are formed and delineated along dimensions that include gender, class, race, culture and religion. Conceptualizing media content as media spaces for identification raises questions such as: Which identities occur in the media? Which identities are conceivable in what contexts? How is the membership in imaginary communities determined? What differentiations occur and which forms of exclusion are practiced in these spaces? Discussing examples from our sample, we ponder the media's role in setting boundaries that distinguish the veil-bearer from other citizens and inhabitants in Austria by either excluding her from the national community or attributing to her a low social status at the margins of society.

The Veiled Woman as a Symbol of Terrorism

During the migration wave of the 1960s and 1970s, veiled women were usually represented as oppressed, poor, and uneducated wives of "guest workers" (Farrokhzad, 2006; Lutz, 1989). While the backward headscarf wearer was the subject of pity and often remains so, September 11th and the public debates on migration led to the construction of a new image—that of the well-educated but potentially harmful woman (Farrokhzad, 2006, p. 74). In this context, the headscarf and especially the fully veiled body have become powerful symbols of the threat to so-called Western values and are viewed as emanating from a fundamentalist, extremist, and violence-prone Islam, which operates "under cover"—in both a literal and metaphorical sense.

The trial of Mona S. was widely publicized and provides a rich example for analyzing the significance of the veil, as very similar photographs as that of Mona S. in a black *niqab* comprise 16% of our sample. The story that accompanies these images regards Mohammed M., who was accused of being engaged in propaganda for Al Qaeda and his wife, Mona S., an Austrian citizen, who allegedly translated his writings—this charge resulted in an unusually long pretrial containment for her. Since the issue involved terrorist activities, the media took a great interest in the case. Public interest was further sparked when Mona S. refused to remove the *niqab*. As a consequence, the judge excluded her from the entire court proceedings. This was a controversial decision because the presence of the accused at the trial is a fundamental democratic right that cannot be overruled by a preference for a certain piece of clothing. For the newspaper readers, Mona S. nevertheless remained visually present because her photograph frequently illustrated reports on the trial.

Following the example set by the tabloid *Kronen Zeitung*, articles featuring her case referred to her as "Die Schleierfrau" ("The Veil-Woman") and the significance of the veil was directly addressed in the Austrian media during the pretrial investigation. Figure 13.4 (*Salzburger Nachrichten,* Nov. 13, 2008, p. 12) shows a typical press photo of Mona S. that contrasts sharply with Orientalist images of veiled women. For example, the earlier Figure 13.1 shows the head of a woman dressed in a bright orange garment. Wearing heavy makeup she directly looks at the observer. The perky look stimulates colonial sexist fantasies of unveiling her and disclosing her body under the colorful veiling. The photograph of Mona S. does not rouse such feelings. Her painted eyes under the veil are reminiscent of the

Figure 13.4

Source: Salzburger Nachrichten (Nov. 13, 2008). Hitzige Debatte um Schleier, p. 12. (Copyright: Roland Schlager/ APA/picturedesk.com)

Orientalist tradition, but unlike the woman in Figure 13.1, Mona S. does not look directly into the camera, her eyes are cast down instead. The picture is an example of a strong visual "othering," it presumably shows us a person unwilling to look at us and thus refusing to speak to the viewer. There is no communication with the observer; this perception together with being dressed in the black robe disturbs established viewing patterns, making her appear undecipherable, foreign, and potentially dangerous.

From the outset, the reporting on Mona S. takes on a strong symbolical character. Implicitly as well as explicitly, a link is made between her veiling and her presumed terrorist activities. The full veil becomes her core attribute; she is presented as being devoid of personality traits. As a veiled woman, she loses her individual traits and is symbolically stripped of her citizenship rights. This line of reasoning is explicitly voiced in a letter to the editor published in the *Kronen Zeitung*:

> What does this woman expect? One can assume that as the wearer of this garb she is not gainfully employed and therefore dependent on her husband. If he's unemployed, she's living off money derived from our taxes. The advantages of our social welfare institutions and our health insurance are taken for granted. Such people do not want to be integrated. They should be stripped of their Austrian citizenship and sent off to the land of their grandparents. Racism? No, but there's a limit when it comes to these people! (Nov. 18, 2008, p. 26).

In the Austrian tabloid, the veil symbolically designates Mona S. as an unworthy member of society. In the reader's letter, the veil is tied to notions of citizenship, migration, national affiliation, religion, social standing, and the relationship between the sexes in order to symbolically exclude her from the Austrian nation. Interestingly enough, Mona S. refrained from wearing the *niqab* in 2010 and this fact was not mentioned in the great majority of papers; rather it appeared only as a side remark in an article about the banning of the full body veils at Graz Medical University mentioned earlier in our paper (Brickner, 2010, p. 10). The "veil woman" is a symbol that denies the woman's capacity to act. Behind the veil, no social actor that can redefine her religious association and change her style of clothing is visible. In other words, Mona S. without a veil is not conceivable and thus does not become a worthy news item.

Migrants in Everyday Life

Since the headscarf can be seen quite frequently on the streets of all Western-European countries, it comes as no surprise that articles with Austria-related topics cover a range of issues in the context of migration, in which veiled women often seem to be captured by chance. These include a photograph of fugitives, but also snapshots of people waiting for buses in front of the Salzburg main station. There are little commonalities in this group of photographs, but a strong link between the veil, migration, and social class emerges that reflects the precarious position of veiled migrant women in the Austrian society.

A snapshot published in *Der Standard* (Mar. 05, 2009, p. U8) is an especially striking example of this intersectional link that unconsciously expresses a stereotypical positioning of the veiled woman in the discourse on migration, class and gender. The photograph was accompanied a story about the rising number of students at Austrian universities. It shows a cleaning woman in the front and a throng of students in the back pushing at the door to enter. The composition of the photograph generates a tension between the headscarf-wearing cleaning woman and the female students. Although they inhabit one and the same workplace, there is a distinct and very visible separation. The headscarf serves as a clear marker of the boundary between the manual laborer and the academic learners. It is a headdress that is primarily worn by migrant women and women of Islamic belief. At the same time it designates class differences and educational barriers. In this way, the migrant woman is set apart from the female students, who are waiting for her to finish the cleaning job so that they may enter the university and continue with their studies which open career opportunities and signify a middle-class lifestyle. On a broader socio-cultural level the picture evokes associations with "new housemaid-debate" (Lutz, 2007): Emancipation, which has improved the professional opportunities for middle-class and upper-class women— as exemplified by the mostly female students in the picture—has at the same time (re)established firm class boundaries among women. While middle-class women have entered the universities and subsequently gained better paid jobs, the gendered division regarding the distribution of housework and responsibilities of reproduction has only marginally changed. Therefore migrant women and women from lower social classes fill in as housekeepers and nannies.

The significance of the veil intersects with other categories such as class, race/ethnicity, gender, and religion. Thus women wearing the veil are allocated to specific places that include a marginal positioning within the Western European societies and an attribution to Islamic countries and terrorist movements. At the same time, it is important to note that the meaning of the veil is not fixed by colonialist iconography or neocolonialist tendencies, but remains a variable, negotiated, and sometimes contested terrain. This constant mediation of meaning and the accompanying ambiguities are precisely the grounds that open up spaces for alternative signification practices and a different positioning of the veil-wearer.

SPACES OF IN-BETWEEN

Geo/political spaces and spaces for identification are not unequivocally defined and therefore not free of ambivalence and contradictions. There is a long-standing tradition in cultural and social theory supporting the idea that hegemonically defined spaces are never totally closed but leave room for redefinitions. Also, the dominant positionings of members of imagined communities

and the self-positioning of individuals are not always identical. In the German-speaking countries, the notion of spaces of in-between ("*Zwischenräume*") can be traced back to the unconventional scholar, Aby Warburg, who applied the term in the 1920s to his analysis of cultures in order to grasp the mixing, the discontinuities, and the transfer of cultural artifacts and signs (cf. Haustein, 2008; Warburg, 2010, p. 630). It is closely linked to his idea of "*Denkräume*" (thinking spaces), that allow for the reflection and analysis of the meaning of cultural artifacts originating from quite different cultures. The novelist Heinrich Böll, who was also concerned with changes in society, used the same term "*Zwischenraum*" in his Nobel Prize speech in 1973, referring to a space of hope, "a remaining space, in which poetry and resistance grow." No country in the world could suppress and prohibit the existence of such a space of in-between, "this relic, which we may call irony, which we may call poetry, which we may call god, fiction or resistance" (Böll, 1973). Böll's phrasing surpasses a narrow attribution of the idea of spaces of in-between to arts and culture, and allows its extension to language, media, and the public sphere. In public sphere theory, we find a concern with the question how alternative publics and oppositional movements can develop counter-hegemonic practices and make their voices heard. An interest in breaking out of the prison of a unifying cultural description appears in Homi Bhabha's concept of a third space characterized by hybridity (Rutherford, 1990; see also Soja's concept of a "Thirdspace") and also in Chantal Mouffe's (2005, p. 145) idea of public spaces as being always, and at the same time, "striped and hegemonically structured." For example, while the public sphere on the one hand is defined by dominant meaning production and peopled by the elite, there always remain possibilities for counter-hegemonic interventions (Mouffe, 2005, p. 147; see also Hofmann, Lazaris, & Sennewald, n.d.). Thus, we use the term "spaces of in-between" in a broad sense, including all notions of Other, alternative, counter-hegemonic, third, striped, or hybrid spaces.

With regard to communication studies, spaces of in-between that run counter to hegemonic positioning practices emerge primarily in processes of reception and interaction with media texts that allow for their unconventional and partial appropriation. New and previously unintended spaces can be constructed by audiences, "in which specific identities of users are (re-) constituted" (Hipfl, 2004, p. 17). The "in-between" indicates that recipients do not simply arrange themselves in the spaces allotted by the media. The construction of new spaces and identity positions becomes possible due to the fact that the spaces of identity constructed by the media are not static and fixed for all time, but are polysemic in nature.

In our study, spaces of in-between are rare since mass media are usually not the site where nonhegemonic meanings and alternative positionings are created. However, two newspapers, *Kronen Zeitung* (Jan. 22, 2009, p. 45) and *Salzburger Nachrichten* (Jan. 20, 2009, p. 11) each reproduced the same picture taken from a photography project by the Persian-American artist Shirin Neshat informing the readers about an exhibition of her work in Vienna. In the photo, a woman can be seen dressed in a black veil covering almost her whole body but leaving her arms and hands exposed. Her head is tilted toward the floor and she is covering her face with both hands, thus again unable to make contact with the viewer. But unlike Mona S., her gesture suggests despair rather than refusal. Her body language as well as her black clothing reveals her as a victim of a crime or a person in mourning. The meaning of the picture remains ambiguous, the traditional Persian symbols that cover her hands and arms, might either suggest that Iran, with its policies and religious rules is the source of her misery, or it might mean that her religion is an essential part of her being for which she has to suffer. The picture is part of a series titled "Women of Allah" where Neshat deals with fundamentalism in Iran. While the women in these photos are all clothed in the *chador* and seem very still and passive, they are diversified in other aspects. On some photographs, the women

carry lines of poetry by feminist Persian authors engraved on bared areas of their bodies. Some carry arms. The images are disturbing because they do not fit into conventional patterns of expression or interpretation. They pose questions as to who is actually hiding behind the veil. In the tension created between the veil and the bared body parts, the veil is robbed of any clear-cut meaning. The artist herself views the photographs as an answer to a personal crisis triggered by her migration from Iran to the United States:

> Leaving has offered me incredible personal development, a sense of independence that I don't think I would have had otherwise. But there's also a great sense of isolation. And I've permanently lost a complete sense of center. I can never call any place home. I will forever be in a state of in-between (Neshat, 2004).

In her series, Neshat gives an ambiguous message that undermines the cliché of the veiled and militant woman exactly because she exposes it in her pictures. Whether the viewer disentangles this ambiguity in the direction of a hegemonic reading—feeling pity for the suppressed objectified woman or seeing her as a threat—or rejects the one-dimensional readings in favor of the agency and subjectivity of the veil bearer, is to a large extent due to his or her interpretative frame (cf. von Rosen, 2005).

Both newspapers selected one photograph from Neshat's whole series that when viewed alone can very easily be adjusted to the construct of the poor, passive, and subordinated veiled woman.[7] Without its context, the illustration is largely robbed of the ambiguity that characterizes the series as a whole. In this case, we can conclude that mass media transmit the material for creating spaces of in-between, but also limit their unfolding.

Reinterpretations of various types of veiling are no longer uncommon. It is mainly the work of (female) artists, in which multifaceted, disturbing counterconventional interpretations are offered, but such reworkings have entered pop culture as well. Spaces of in-between are primarily produced by those women for whom the hegemonic discourse reserves only precarious spaces for their identification and affiliation with society. The positioning of mainly migrant women in the "state of in-between," as Neshat calls it, obviates identification with the dominant associations attributed to the veil. The resulting effect among many women with a migratory background is the search for other, new meanings that pen up possibilities for the creation of spaces of in-between with regard to national affiliation or migration.

CONCLUSIONS

The media construct spaces of identity in which people are positioned; with some ease, readers can position themselves as Europeans, women, Austrians, Catholics, and so forth. The headscarf debates of Austria and various European countries show how manifest physical spaces and spaces for identification are constructed, from which veiled women are excluded. On the one hand, legislation in a number of countries prohibits veiled women from entering public places such as classrooms and courtrooms with reference to "floating signifiers," to presumably national traditions and values. The current debate on the ban of the *burqa* in all public places is a case in point. On the other hand, the veiled woman is constructed as the Other of an imagined, homogenous national community from which she is symbolically excluded. In this discourse, Islamic veiling serves as a token of perceived religious, moral, and cultural differences. Such a view, however, neglects the underlying economic and social conflicts in Western European nation-states, which are based on dramatic changes in their welfare policies as well as on a fundamental restructuring of their labor markets and their educational systems (Berghahn & Rostock, 2009, p. 10).

Our analysis of press photographs also highlights the symbolic function of the veil as an important part of media discourse. We used the concept of three types of media-constructed spaces of identity in order to reveal how veiling

is used as a marker for geo/political spaces and for spaces for identification, and to ponder the question of how spaces of in-between can be opened using the very media material that helps to exclude the veiled woman from the imagined community of Austria. Orientalism is still directly reflected in some of the illustrations, but in recent years the full-body veil has become a less colorful token, signifying not so much sexual fantasies, but a terrorist threat. In our sample, there are powerful iconographic images that position the veiled woman outside of Austria and Europe. This, in turn reinforces the precarious status of women wearing headscarves or full-body veils within these imagined communities. Where the veiled woman appears in an Austrian context, the headscarf serves as a marker of a low social status, thus relegating her to the margins of society. Only by the creation of spaces of in-between can she gain a voice and acquire agency. Spaces of in-between allow for the participation in the ongoing social discourse establishing the meaning of the veiled woman in Austria and Europe. This, in turn is the precondition for the inclusion of the women deciding to wear veils into these imagined communities.

NOTES

1. We view "the West," "the Orient," "Europe," and so forth as constructs of geo/political and cultural spaces rather than as fixed entities. However, we refrain from putting such terms in quotes to make the text more readable. Likewise, when we write about "the Other," "Us," or "We" we are referring to constructs that distinguish those who are included in an imagined community from those that are excluded from it.

2. We do not speak of "geopolitics," because the word carries negative connotations linked to its misuse by the imperialistic 'Third Reich.' Instead, we use the term "geo/political" to underline the assumption that such spaces are not fixed physical entities but always emerge as the product of specific discourses.

3. This is a term that conveys the idea that regional or national cultures are destroyed by a high number of foreigners who do not assimilate and instead elect to uphold their own culture.

4. In Turkey, restrictions on wearing a headscarf are a constant source of political tensions (McGoldrick, 2006, p. 171). In 2008, the Turkish Parliament passed a bill to lift the ban on wearing headscarves at universities, but this was invalidated by the Constitutional Court. However, in 2010 the Government University Board ruled that the wearing of headscarves, while still counting as a violation of existing law, would no longer result in exclusion from classes (Güsten, 2010).

5. In this article we focus on the last three, which due to the limited space are the most important for our argumentation.

6. Edward Said, however, largely ignores both the involvement of women in the construction of the "Orient" and the sexual implications of "Orientalism" (for further discussion cf. Lewis, 1996; Yegenoglu, 1998).

7. The photograph is available at http://www.iranian.com/Arts/Dec97/Neshat/p9.html.

REFERENCES

Amanuel, S. (1996). Frauenfeind Islam? Wie die Frauenzeitschrift, Brigitte an Klischees weiterstrickt. In B. Röben & C. Wilß (Eds.), *Verwaschen und verschwommen. Fremde Frauenwelten in den Medien* (pp. 95–108). Frankfurt/Main, DE: Brandes and Apsel.

Anderson, B. (1993). *Imagined communities: Reflections on the origin and spread of nationalism.* London, UK: Verso.

Atkinson, Z. (2010, July 21). *Burqa ban—YouGov.* [Opinion Poll]. Retrieved December 21, 2010 from http://today.yougov.co.uk/life/burqa-ban.

Benhabib, S. (2004). *The rights of others: Aliens, residents and citizens.* New York, NY: Cambridge University Press.

Berghahn, S., & Rostock, P. (2009). Der Stoff, aus dem die Kopftuch-Konflikte sind. In S. Berghahn & P. Rostock (Eds.), *Debatten um das Kopftuch in Deutschland, Österreich und der Schweiz* (pp. 9–29). Bielefeld, DE: Transcript.

Blosat, L. (2005). Zoff um den Stoff. Über die Kopftuchkontroverse in Deutschland. *Ethnoscripts, 7*(2), 109–127.

Böll, H. (1973, May 2). *An Essay on the Reason of Poetry.* Nobel Lecture delivered on receipt of Nobel Prize in Literature. Retrieved June 1, 2012 from http://www.nobelprize.org/nobel_prizes/literature/laureates/1972/boll-lecture.html.

Brandt, A., Evers, M., von Mittelstaedt, J., von Rohr, M., & Sandberg, B. (2009). Angst vor Eurabien. *Der Spiegel, 50*(7), 112–117.

Brickner, I. (2010, September 30). Schleierverbot bei Prüfungen bekräftigt. *Der Standard*, p. 10.

Couldry, N., & McCarthy, A. (2004). *MediaSpace: Place, scale, and culture in a media age.* London, UK: Routledge.

Das große Rennen um billigen Sport. (2009, Mar. 5). *Der Standard*, p. U8.

Deltombe, T. (2005). *L'Islam imaginaire. La construction médiatique de l'Islamophobie en France 1975–2005.* Paris, FR: La découverte.

Die Schnörkel kommen wieder. (2009, Jan. 22). *Kronen Zeitung*, p. 45.

Eine Nation aufbauen. (2009, Jan. 20). *Salzburger Nachrichten*, p. 5.

Exitstrategie aus Afghanistan gesucht. (2008, Oct. 08). *Der Standard*, p. 5.

Fahmy, S. (2004). Picturing Afghan women. A content analysis of AP wire photographs during the Taliban regime and after the fall of the Taliban regime. *Gazette. The International Journal for Communication Studies, 66*(2), 91–112.

Falkheimer, J., & Jansson, A. (Eds.). (2006). *Geographies of communication: The spatial turn in media studies.* Gothenburg, SE: Nordicom.

Farrokhzad, S. (2006). Exotin, Unterdrückte und Fundamentalistin—Konstruktionen der "fremden Frau" in deutschen Medien. In C. Butterwegge & G. Hentges (Eds.), *Massenmedien, Migration, Integration* (pp. 55–86). Wiesbaden, DE: VS-Verlag.

Gabizon, C. (2009, September 9). Deux mille femmes portent la burqa en France. *Le Figaro.* Retrieved December 22, 2010 from http://www.lefigaro.fr/actualite-france/2009/09/09/01016-20090909ART-FIG00040-deux-mille-femmes-portent-la-burqa-en-france-.php.

Graham-Brown, S. (1988). *Images of women. The portrayal of women in photography of the Middle East 1860–1950.* New York, NY: Columbia University Press.

Greater London Authority (Ed.). (2007). *The search for common ground. Muslims, non-Muslims and the UK media.* A report commissioned by the Mayor of London. Retrieved April 10, 2009 from http://www.london.gov.uk/mayor/equalities/docs/commonground_report.pdf.

Gresch, N., Hadj-Abdou, L., Rosenberger, S., & Sauer, B. (2008). Tu felix Austria? The headscarf and the politics of "non-issues." *Social Politics, 15*(4), 411–432.

Güsten, S. (2010, December 22). Kopftuch bleibt verboten, wird aber nicht mehr bestraft. *Der Tagesspiegel*. Retrieved from http://www.tagesspiegel.de/politik/kopftuch-bleibt-verboten-wird-aber-nicht-mehr-bestraft/1949726.html.

Hafez, K. (2002). *Die politische Dimension der Auslandsberichterstattung*. Baden-Baden, DE: Nomos.

Hafez, K., & Richter, C. (2008). Das Islambild von ARD und ZDF. Themenstrukturen einer Negativagenda. *Fachjournalist*, *3*, 10–13. Retrieved on July 13, 2009 from http://www.dfjv.de/uploads/tx_eleonartikel/Hafez-Richter_Islambild_ARD_ZDF.pdf.

Hancock, C. (2008). Spatialities of the secular: Geographies of the veil in France and Turkey. *European Journal of Women's Studies*, *15*, 165–179.

Haustein, L. (2008). *Global Icons. Globale Bildinszenierung und kulturelle Identität*. Göttingen, DE: Wallstein.

Hipfl, B. (2004). Mediale Identitätsräume. Skizzen zu einem "spatial turn" in der Medien- und Kommunikationswissenschaft. In B. Hipfl, E. Klaus, & U. Scheer (Eds.), *Identitätsräume. Nation, Körper und Geschlecht in den Medien* (pp. 16–50). Bielefeld, DE: Transcript.

Hofmann, F., Lazaris, S., & Sennewald, J. E. (n.d.). *ZWISCHEN RÄUMEN. Vorüberlegungen zur Erkundung dynamischer Räumlichkeit*. Retrieved December 21, 2010 from http://www.transcript-verlag.de/ts251/ts251_1.pdf.

Innis, H. A. (1986). *Empire & communications*. Victoria, BC: Press Porcépic (Originally published in French in 1951).

Islamische Glaubensgemeinschaft Österreich [IGGÖ]. (2003). *Die Islamische Glaubensgemeinschaft in Österreich stellt sich vor. Geschichte, Struktur und Arbeitsfelder*. Retrieved December 21, 2010 from http://www.derislam.at/islam.php?name=Themen&pa=showpage&pid=3.

Jäger, M., & Jäger, S. (2007). *Deutungskämpfe: Theorie und Praxis kritischer Diskursanalyse*. Wiesbaden, DE: VS Verlag für Sozialwissenschaften.

Juriatti, R. (2010). *Kirchenstatistik Österreich: Katholikenzahlen 2009 leicht rückläufig*. Retrieved December 21, 2010 from http://www.kath-kirche-vorarlberg.at/organisation/pressebuero/artikel/kirchenstatistik-katholikenzahlen-2009-leicht-ruecklaeufig.

Kilić, S. (2008). The British Veil Wars. *Social Politics*, *15*(4), 433–454.

Kilić, S., Sakarso, S., & Sauer, B. (2008). Introduction. The veil—Debating citizenship, gender and religious diversity. *Social Politics*, *15*(4), 397–410.

Klaus, E., & Kassel, S. (2005). The veil as a means of legitimization. An analysis of the interconnectedness of gender, media and war. *Journalism*, *6*(3), 335–355.

Lefebvre, H. (1992). *The production of space*. Oxford, UK: Blackwell (Originally published in French in 1974).

Lewis, R. (1996). *Gendering orientalism: Race, femininity and representation*. London, UK: Routledge.

Lutz, H. (1989). Unsichtbare Schatten? Die "orientalische" Frau in westlichen Diskursen - Zur Konzeptualisierung einer Opferfigur. *Peripherie*, *37*, 51–65.

Lutz, H. (2007). *Vom Weltmarkt in den Privathaushalt. Die neuen Dienstmädchen im Zeitalter der Globalisierung. Unter Mitarbeit von Susanne Schwalgin*. Leverkusen-Opladen, DE: Barbara-Budrich.

Massey, D. (1994). *Space, place and gender*. Minneapolis: University of Minnesota Press.

McGoldrick, D. (2006). *Human rights and religion: The Islamic headscarf debate in Europe*. Oxford, UK: Hart.

Morley, D., & Robins, K. (Eds.). (1995). *Spaces of identity: Global media, electronic landscapes and cultural boundaries*. London, UK: Routledge.

Mouffe, C. (2005). Aktionskunst und agonistische Räume. In R. Dempf, S. Mattl, & C. Steinbrener (Eds.), *Delete! Die Entschriftung des öffentlichen Raums* (pp. 141–148). Vienna, AT: Orange Press.

Neshat, S. (2004, April). An interview with Shirin Neshat. *Erudition*, *4*. Retrieved October 15, 2010 from http://www.eruditiononline.com/04.04/shirin_neshat_interview.htm.

Oestreich, H. (2004). *Der Kopftuchstreich: Das Abendland und ein Quadratmeter Islam*. Frankfurt/Main, DE: Brandes und Apsel.

Orient pur auf Schienen. (2009, Jan. 17). *Salzburger Nachrichten*, p. XVI.

Ornament ist oftmals Politik. (2009, Jan. 20). *Salzburger Nachrichten*, p. 11.

Poole, E. (2000). Framing Islam: An analysis of newspaper coverage of Islam in the British press. In K. Hafez (Ed.), *Islam and the West in the mass media. Fragmented images in a globalizing world* (pp. 157–179). Cresskill, NJ: Hampton Press.

Quraishy, B. (2001). Islam and Muslim minorities in the Western media. After the World Trade Center attack. *Nord-Süd Aktuell, 15*(4), 714–722.

Röder, M. (2007). *Haremsdame, Opfer oder Extremistin? Muslimische Frauen im Nachrichtenmagazin Der Spiegel*. Berlin, DE: Frank und Timme.

Rottmann, S. B., & Marx Ferree, M. (2008). Citizenship and intersectionality—German feminist debates about headscarf and antidiscrimination laws. *Social Politics, 15*(4), 481–513.

Rutherford, J. (1990). The Third Space. Interview with Homi Bhabha. In J. Rutherford (Ed.), *Identity: Community, culture, difference* (pp. 207–221). London, UK: Lawrence and Wishart.

Said, E. W. (1978). *Orientalism: Western conceptions of the Orient*. London, UK: Penguin.

Sassen, S. (2006). *Territory, authority, rights: From medieval to global assemblages*. Princeton, NJ: Princeton University Press.

Schiffer, S. (2007). Die Verfestigung des Islambildes in den deutschen Medien. In S. Jäger & D. Halm (Eds.), *Mediale Barrieren. Rassismus als Integrationshindernis* (pp.167–200). Duisburg, DE: Edition DISS.

Schumann, A. (2002). *Zwischen Eigenwahrnehmung und Fremdwahrnehmung: Die beurs, Kinder der maghrebinischen Immigration in Frankreich*. Frankfurt/Main, DE: IKO Verlag für Interkulturelle Kommunikation.

Seeh, Manfred (2008, November 14). Mona S.: "Bin unschuldig, kann es beweisen." *Die Presse*. Retrieved December 21, 2010 from http://diepresse.com/home/panorama/oesterreich/430169/Mona-S_Bin-unschuldig-kann-es-beweisen.

Skjeie, H. (2007). Headscarves in schools: European comparisons. In J. Goldschmidt & M. L. T. Loenen (Eds.), *Religious pluralism and human rights in Europe. Where to draw the line* (pp. 129–146). Antwerp, BE: Intersentia.

Soja, E. (1989). *Postmodern Geographies: The reassertion of space in critical social theory*. London, UK: Verso Press.

Szenen eines Konflikts, Antiamerikanismus in Teheran. (2009, Mar. 21). *Der Standard*, p. 4.

Terrorprozess. (2008, Nov. 18). *Kronen Zeitung*, p. 26.

Tévanian, P. (2005). *Le voile médiatique. Un faux débat: "L'affaire du foulard islamique."* Paris, FR: Raisons d'agir.

Unser Doppelbild-Rätsel. (2009, Jan. 14). *Kronen Zeitung*, p. 47.

US-Präsident Obama will Dialog mit Islam. (2009, Jan. 28). *Salzburger Nachrichten*, p. 1.

Volkening, H. (2001). Den Schleier schreiben. In H. Beressem, D. Buchwald, & H. Volkening (Eds.), *Grenzüberschreitungen. "Feminismus" und "Cultural Studies"* (pp. 239–259). Bielefeld, DE: Aisthesis.

Von Braun, C., & Mathes, B. (2007). *Verschleierte Wirklichkeit: Die Frau, der Islam und der Westen*. Berlin, DE: Aufbau.

Von Rosen, V. (2005). Verschleierungen. Frauen im Tschador in Shririn Neshats. In J. Endres, B. Wittmann & G. Wolf (Eds.), *Ikonologie des Zwischenraums. Der Schleier als Medium und Metapher* (pp.75–93). Munich, DE: Wilhelm Fink.

Warburg, A. (2010). *Werke in einem Band*. Frankfurt/Main, DE: Suhrkamp.

Wöhrle, C. (2010, February/March). Europa—Diskussion um Burkaverbot. In *Migration und Bevölkerung*. Retrieved December 21, 2010 from http://www.bpb.de/files/I8OKFW.pdf.

Yegenoglu, M. (1998). *Colonial phantasies: Towards a feminist reading of Orientalism*. Cambridge, UK: Cambridge University Press.

14

Constructing and Being the "Other"

Young Men's Talk on Ethnic and Racist Violence

Kjerstin Andersson

Introduction

The Swedish population is perceived to be ethnically homogeneous, both in Sweden and elsewhere in the world. Sweden is also believed to have relatively few problems with racism and conflicts between ethnic groups. However, Sweden has a rather complex ethnic landscape; for the past 50 years, large groups of people have immigrated to Sweden from all over the world. This is especially apparent when considering the demographics of youth in Sweden. Today, 25% of all children under the age of 17 who were born in Sweden have at least one parent who was born outside of Sweden (Bernhardt, Goldscheider, Goldscheider, & Bjerén, 2007). In 2008, Statistics Sweden, a government agency that produces statistics reported that 2.3 million people out of a total population of 9.4 million are either non-Swedish born, or have at least one parent born outside Sweden (www.scb.se, 2011). This is particularly significant since in Sweden, there is a discursive difference between being considered a "Swede" and being considered an "immigrant" (*invandrare*). The term "immigrant" refers not only to someone who recently immigrated to the country, but also to any non-Western European–looking person, irrespective of how well integrated the person is in Swedish society. In addition, "immigrant" is broadly understood as a derogatory term and is rarely used in public or political discourse. Refugee, migrant, or "new-Swede" are preferred terms.

Although Sweden today is a multiethnic society, the public debate still associates ethnicity with tradition-bound "foreign" cultures, and persons of minority status, and there is a "widespread assumption that ethnicity does not refer to the dominant group" (Ålund, 2002, p. 3). Rather, ethnicity is largely attributed to minority groups, which makes them vulnerable to racism and prejudice by the majority group. In most of the Western world, racism refers to "white racism," which includes negative discourses held by white people against members of other racial groups as well as corresponding violence, prejudice, power abuse, and social inequalities (van Dijk, 1993). However, "white racism" renders other types of racism invisible in addition to veiling the ethnicity of the majority group. Rather, Aleksandra Ålund (2002) argues that ethnicity and racism should be understood as being constructed by both minority and majority groups in society. Depending on how identity is constructed, racism can be used as legitimating grounds for using or being the target of ethnic violence. In Sweden, the term "race" is most commonly associated with organizations that are openly racist or xenophobic; it is avoided or used in inverted commas in the public debate (e.g., 'race'). On the other hand, ethnicity is often used in the public and academic debate. The two terms, albeit defined differently, are here both understood to be part of the same discourse constructing difference and otherness based on physical appearance.[1]

This chapter is part of a larger study on young men's identity construction in talks about violence (Andersson, 2008). In the study, young men with a documented history of violence were interviewed about their own use of violence. In some of the interviews, the young men construed violence in relation to a specific ethnic or racist identity. Mary Bucholtz (1999, p. 446) argues that "fight stories serve as resources for the construction of masculinity as well as racial [or ethnic] identity in a public, for-the-record telling of personal experiences to an outside researcher." In the following analysis, fight stories are the basis for investigating how ethnicity and racism are constructed. I analyze two interviews with two young men who construct ethnic and racist identities, albeit from

different positions and toward different interactional objectives.

DISCOURSES OF VIOLENCE, ETHNICITY, AND RACISM

Talking about one's own use of violence is potentially troublesome to one's self-presentation. Although Stanko (2003) argues that violence is not condemned, disapproved of, or punished in all situations, one may risk becoming the target of condemnation in a conversation about one's own use of violence. Therefore, it may be seen as imperative to attempt to achieve *normality* and to reinstate a "proper way of being" (Edley & Wetherell, 1997, p. 210) in any talk about violence. Language is seen here as a resource for achieving normality as well as for understanding and knowing the world around us. A central component to language is discourse. By discourse I do not only mean talk *about* different subject matters. Rather, I am referring to the preconditions of talk, *that which makes it possible to talk about* the matter. Simplified, this could be called language rules, for example enabling us to talk about men and women as being opposed to each other. At the same time, it prevents us from using "illogical" categories such as "mach-girl," or referring to a middle-aged businessman as a rape victim. Our discursive understanding of the power relations between sexes, age categories, and so on steer our interpretation to more easily seeing the girl as a victim of rape and the businessman as a perpetrator than vice versa. These unwritten language rules or discourses and the categorization that follows not only affect our way of speaking but also how we understand the world around us (Andersson, 2008).

According to Wendy Hollway (1984/2001), discourses make available different positions for people to assume, in relation to other people. However, discourses do not exist independently of their reproduction; rather they are continuously negotiated, reiterated, challenged, and reworked, by the very subjects that they produce (Hollway, 1984/2001; Brickell, 2005).

Bamberg (1997) advocates using a positioning analysis in order to get at the sense-making of narratives. Here, positioning is understood as a discursive practice. People position themselves in relation to each other in conversations, and in so doing they are "producing" one another and themselves as social beings: "even in the most fleeting of interactional moves, speakers position themselves and others as particular kinds of people" (Bucholtz & Hall, 2005, p. 595; see also Aronsson, 1998).

Positioning one's self is a discursive process of locating selves in conversation as "observably and subjectively coherent participants" in collectively produced narratives (Davies & Harré, 1990/2001, p. 264). In conversation I have the opportunity to present myself as a coherent and unified self; this is achieved together with present and absent interlocutors. I have the possibility to present myself in a preferred way, depending on the situation and the context of the conversation. In one conversation, I can choose to position myself as a man, in another as a father, or son, or teacher, or student all depending on the preconditions surrounding the conversation and what I want to achieve in the conversation. The approach to understanding positioning and identity entails a critical approach to the idea of "self-as-entity," conveying a shift in analytical focus to the construction of the self. In this construction of self, language is central as selves are constructed using "socially available meanings and discourses" as interactional resources (Brickell, 2005, p. 37). Groups as well as individuals project images of themselves "that are not independent of and do not pre-exist the social practices in which they are displayed and negotiated" (De Fina, 2007, p. 372).

In contemporary sociolinguistic research, social categories such as race, class, and gender are understood to be constructed in interaction rather than as fixed ready-to-use entities (Bucholtz, 1999). Such categories are "potentially omnirelevant to social life, individuals inhabit many different identities, and these may be stressed or muted, depending on the situation" (West & Fenstermaker, 1995, p. 30). Goodman and Speer (2007, p. 167) argue that the social categories used in any particular instance "will be driven in some way by the social action that is being accomplished." This can be exemplified by Harvey Sacks's (1992) classic example, *The baby cried. The mommy picked it up.* The categories used in the example, baby and mommy, infer not only family ties but also a moral relationship based on unequal dependency. The behaviors are understood in a commonsensical way to be normal and natural to each category (babies cry and mothers pick them up). Centrally important is the fact that the categories and phrasing used in these statements lead listeners to infer that the mommy who picked up the baby is the mother of the child—not the mommy of some other child.

Drawing on Michael Billig's (1995) understanding of nationalism as a mundane activity in which ordinary people engage, I understand ethnicity and racism as the outcomes of everyday social interactions. West and Fenstermaker (1995) argue that categories such as gender, class, and race are ongoing accomplishments and their relevance cannot be determined apart from the context in which they are accomplished. They must be located in social situations "rather than within the individual or some vaguely defined set of role expectations" (West & Fenstermaker, 1995, p. 25). Hence, ethnicity and racism cannot be understood separate from social and discursive practices.

To analyze the production of ethnic categories, I draw together elements from Membership Categorisation Analyses (MCA) (for an introduction see Schegloff, 2007; Silverman, 1998; Weatherall, 2002), positioning theory, and narrative analysis (de Fina, 2007; Georgakopoulou, 2005). My research is also informed by critical discursive psychology (Edley, 2001; Goodman & Speer, 2007; Wetherell, 1998; Wetherell & Edley, 1999), which orients my analysis toward "the action orientation of talk and attitudes" (Goodman & Speer, 2007, p. 169). Discursive psychology offers a framework for understanding attitudes as well as interactions.

CATEGORIZING THE OTHER

A commonsense attitude leads people to believe that social categories have fundamental essences (Verkuyten, 2003) as social realities. They are talked about and referred to as natural, inevitable, and unchangeable.[2] Essentialist categorizations attempt to fix social groups and individuals; such categorizations are then used as resources to achieve interactional tasks (Verkuyten, 2003). Cultural essentialism presents people as personifications of an ethnic group, and implies a form of social control in which people of a particular ethnic group (for instance, white Europeans) should and do act in manners particular to that group, divergent from other ethnic groups. Nick Lynn and Susan Lea (2003) argue that ascribing importance to ethnic origin develops a particular sense of self, which in turn cultivates an awareness of difference or "the Other"; it encourages a sense of "us" and "them." Designating someone as "the Other" creates a position from which it is possible to act (Staunæs, 2005). In one sense, it is productive and necessary to create an understanding of Other(s) in order to position oneself in relation to a societal and cultural context. This is the process of *racialization*; the social process whereby 'the Other' is created—consciously or implicitly—in terms that are both explicit and veiled (Ålund, 2002). Also, otherness can work as a constructive position for oneself in particular circumstances, which is discussed later in this chapter.

Society is racialized and/or ethicized when both "we" and "the Others" are constructed as biologically self-reproducing social collectives with distinct histories, and unique, distinguishing characteristics (Ålund, 2002). In constructing an understanding of one's own ethnic adherence (be it to a majority or minority group in society), this construction becomes not only a filter in interpreting one's own positioning but also useful in interpreting others as either part of the same grouping or part of "the Others." Consequently, ethnic and racial features are understood as given by nature, and they assume the function of designated difference. Thus both "we" and "the Others" appear to possess certain organic marks that distinguish us in ways that may not be visible or measurable (Ålund, 2002).

Anoop Nayak (2006) argued that even though there is no such thing as biological race or ethnicity, the impact of the concepts on social organization is no less strong. Discourses of race and ethnicity influence how societies are organized, how people live their lives, how they construct their identities, and how they relate to other people. According to Caroline Howarth (2006, p. 442), race "may inform social spaces, linguistic styles, and fashion"; however, it is "primarily linked to the body, or more particular to the skin." Similarly, West and Fenstermaker (1995, p. 23) note that "appearances are treated as if they were indicative of some underlying state," meaning that physical appearance becomes the basis for evaluating and making judgements about a person; the character of the person; my position in relation to the person; and how I can and should react to the person.

MARKED AND UNMARKED CATEGORIES

An important aspect of racist talk, in general, and in the interviews analyzed here, in particular, regards how categories are marked or unmarked in interaction. The most common unmarked racial category in Western societies is whiteness. In Sweden, "Swedish" is an unmarked ethnic and whiteness category. "Swedish" is per se understood to be white, while "new-Swede" is a marked ethnic non-white category. Unmarked categories are not explicitly mentioned in talk; rather it is the not-talked-about parameter that other categories use as a relational measurement. It informs how people in conversations construct their identity, and how they position themselves in relation to these categories. By not mentioning whiteness as a social category in talk, it is assumed to be the natural background against which the presence of people who are "not white" becomes marked; whiteness functions as the norm and thereby a resource that can be used in interaction for identity performances (Kiesling, 2001). In this sense, in Western societies whiteness should be understood as a racialized, and in Sweden, as an ethnicized position that is enacted in people's everyday lives irrespective of race or ethnicity. In much the same way, masculinity can be understood as an unmarked category and a resource in conversations that is not always mentioned in talk, but which forms a backdrop of norms and expectations. According to Kiesling (2005), people generally assume that the majority of men in society should act, talk, and feel in specific ways, in order to be regarded as "normal men." These assumptions are usually silenced in interaction, yet they regulate and organize talk, as well as, the positions that are possible for participants to take. Neither masculinity nor whiteness should be seen as monolithic; their local varieties respond to and use dominant ideologies rather than just reflecting them (Bucholtz, 1999, p. 444).

Bucholtz (1999) points to the fact that both whiteness and masculinity are terms that connect identity and ideology, "while most males can be said to project some form of masculinity in at least some contexts (that is, as identity), only a certain subset of possible or actual masculinities are culturally acceptable (that is, as ideology)" (p. 444). Physical power and the use of violence can successfully be linked ideologically to masculinity (Bucholtz, 1999), albeit under legitimizing circumstances (Andersson, 2008). There are instances when the use of violence is regarded as demasculinizing, for instance, rape or pedophilia are often viewed by other men as cowardice, thereby resulting in a weakened masculine position (cf. Hearn & Whitehead, 2006; Andersson, 2008, 2012).

THE STUDY

For this article, I studied young men who were temporarily detained for assessment at a youth detention home. The young men are described by the detention home as having serious psychosocial problems, including past and ongoing criminality

and drug abuse. During my stay at the ward, the group was made up of about 50% ethnic Swedes, that is, people born in Sweden by Swedish-born parents, and 50% young men with immigrant backgrounds (i.e., people born outside of Sweden or with non-Swedish born parents). This distribution reflects the demographics of the social youth care system in Sweden. In 2002, 32% of the young people within the residential care system had parents born in countries outside Sweden, and this group was composed of more young men than young women (Hedman-Lindgren, 2004). In total, I interviewed three ethnic Swedes, three young men with immigrant backgrounds and one non-European adoptee. Their social backgrounds varied, coming from academic as well as working class families, and their living situations varied from rural to urban areas in Sweden. All of the young men in my data have a documented history of violence; and the majority of them had been charged with or were facing charges of assault.

To some extent, in most of the interviews the youth anchored their talk about violence to issues of race and ethnicity; however, I have chosen to focus on two interviews: one with Jakob and another with Roger (pseudonyms).[3] I chose these two interviews for this analysis because of their explicit use of ethnic categories and because of descriptions of relationships between what they present as different ethnic groups. Both young men use the same categorizing terms, such as black, but from two different positions and to accomplish divergent interactional projects. Both young men can be seen to negotiate and renegotiate their previous ethnic and social identities and are in the process of deconstructing their association to specific categories. The examples chosen are illustrative in that they problematize a normative understanding of racist violence and the function of ethnic categorizations.

At the time of the interview, it had been 12 years since Jakob arrived from Kosovo with his mother. He lived in a midsize town, about two hours from Stockholm. Jakob talks with an easily recognizable "broken" Swedish or "immigrant" accent.[4] In the beginning of the interview, Jakob also makes a point to not choose a Swedish-sounding pseudonym for himself. The name he chose, Jakob, works in many ethnic and racial contexts as it is used in Christian, Islamic, and Jewish societies. Jakob explained in the interview that he was involved in drugs, assault, extortion, and other "stupid stuff." Jakob used several ethnic epithets in the interview, and categorized people as Swedes, Turks, blacks, or neo-Nazis, and so forth. Roger, on the other hand, was born in Sweden of Swedish parents. He tells me that one of the main reasons he is detained at the youth detention home is because of his connection to the Swedish National Socialist Party (National Socialistisk Front), commonly known as a neo-Nazi organization.[5] However, Roger also acknowledges he has problems with alcohol and violence. Roger and Jakob both make self-presentations based on ethnicity and subsequently position themselves in relationship to ethnic and racial categories in their narratives.

I locate excerpts in the interview data where the young men explicitly mention ethnic categories or orient toward racists relations. Then, I analyze how they use these categories *to position themselves* in the conversation. I use excerpts to illustrate the young men's style of speech, but also as grounds for the analysis and to allow the reader to validate the analysis. However, information that is relevant to the analysis—but not included in the excerpts—is also used to enhance understanding of the young men's statements.[6] The following questions guide the analysis: How are ethnic and racial categories used in talk? How do these categories intersect with other organizing categorizations such as age and masculinity? Finally, how are the categories used in specific relation to talk on violence?

Black

The first categorization focused on in the analysis is the term "black" (*svart*), which both Jakob and Roger use to describe people in situations when they have used violence. Both Jakob and Roger position themselves as inflictors of violence against the target: "the black person." However, black functions as a discursive resource in different ways for Jakob and Roger.

Jakob tells me in the interview that he always wants to fight when he is drunk, so I ask him if he has ever been in a fight while sober, whereupon he recounts an instance in which he and a friend visited the local bathhouse. After narrating the story, he comments that he had been drunk at that time after all, "'cause, it's fun to swim when you're drunk," as Jakob puts it.

		Jakob 1[4]			
1	Jakob	ah:: /	1	Jakob	yeah:: /
2		vi var på badhuset en gång /	2		we were at the bath house once /
3		så var det en svart kille som håll på /	3		so it was a black guy that messed /
4		du vet /	4		you know /
5		med en polare till mig /	5		with a friend of mine /
6		(0.5) så sköt han i /	6		(0.5) so he shoved /
7		öm han /	7		um he /
8		den svarta killen /	8		the black guy /
9		kasta i min polare i vattnet /	9		threw my friend in the water /
10		du vet /	10		you know /
11		så gick han upp å:: /	11		so he got up an:: /
12		putta till (.) negern /	12		shoved (.) the negro /
13		å han den svarta killen slog till min polare så käken /	13		and he the black guy hit my friend so his jaw /
14		du vet /	14		you know /

15		det vart nånting knas där /	15		there was something wacky there /
16		[asså /	16		[like /
17	Kjerstin	[uhum	17	Kjerstin	[uhum /
18	Jakob	å så kom jag bakifrån å /	18	Jakob	and so I came from behind and /
19		å ha- han vänder om /	19		and he- he turned around /
20		så slår jag till han en gång /	20		so I hit him once /
21		å han fick huvet i golvet där /	21		and he gets [sic] his head in the floor there /
22		så där vart /	22		so it got /
23		där /	23		got /
24		det var det äckligaste jag sett /	24		it was the grossest thing I've seen
25		°han bloda överallt° asså /	25		°he got blood everywhere° like/
		((borttagna rader))			((omitted lines))
37	Jakob	ah han anmälde mig efter jag hade slagit han /	37	Jakob	yeah he pressed charges after I had hit him/
38		men han var 23 år också /	38		but he was 23 years old also /
39		det var det som var grejen /	39		that was the thing really /
40		efter jag slog till han /	40		after I hit him /
41		aldrig (jag trodde) han skulle anmäla mig då så /	41		he never (I thought) would press charges then like /
42		(1.0) men han var flintis också /	42		(1.0) but he was bald too /
43		så det syntes asså/	43		so it showed like /

In narrative, Jakob does not ascribe much importance to the fact that the man is black. The color of the man's skin is not the reason why Jakob engages in a fight with him. However, both black and Negro can be seen as racial descriptions drawing on a particular type of discourse concerning black masculinity. However, in a Swedish cultural context, the term *Negro* does not have the same symbolic value as it does in an American context. Negro is most certainly a derogatory term, but here, in a Swedish context, the term specifically refers to a person of African descent, and also indicates a particular type of masculinity. According to Bucholtz (1999), a discourse of "the dangerous black man" associates hyperphysicality (including physical strength, hyper(hetero) sexuality, and physical violence) with blackness, which in turn is ideologically linked more to men than to women. By referring to the man in the narrative as "the negro" and "the black guy," Jakob is constructing a particular image of the man, which could allude to the discourse of an inherent dangerousness related to the man due to his blackness. In the narration, the black man starts the fight by "messing" with Jakob's friend, then after being hit, shoves or throws Jakob's friend in the pool. After he hits Jakob's friend in the jaw, Jakob has legitimate reasons for joining the fight and attacking the man. In narration, the characterizations of fighting an older man and defending your friends are used to legitimize violence and increase your position as a man, which Jakob also can be seen to be doing here (cf., Andersson, 2007). Jakob's description of the man as black and Negro indicates that Jakob categorizes himself as something other than black or Negro. Earlier in the interview, Jakob also made the point that he was non-Swedish. Here the dichotomous terms black and white do not really apply, but rather black and non-black. However, I would argue that the term "black" here is an essentialistic category, giving essence to the positioning of the man. As such, race is made relevant in Jakob's narrative. Importantly, though, Jakob does not use the racialized description of the man as black and Negro to motivate the violence in the narrative. Rather, the

man's actions, shoving and throwing Jakob's friend in the water are the motive for Jakob's use of violence

Now, consider how Roger uses the same term *black* and the significance it has in relation to violence. Recall that Roger had told me in the interview that he recently had applied to become a member of the neo-Nazi party, the National Socialistisk Front (NSF). When I asked him to tell me about some incident when fighting had occurred, he provided the following narrative.

Roger 1

1	Roger	va vi ute på stan /	1	Roger	we was out on town /
2		hade druckit öl /	2		had been drinking beer /
3		hade vart på puben /	3		had been to the pub /
4		hade dragit i mig *heh* 15, 18 bärs *heh* ungefär *heh heh* /	4		I had downed *heh* 15, 18 brewskies about *heh heh* /
5	Kjerstin	um /	5	Kjerstin	um /
6	Roger	var dyngrak /	6	Roger	was smashed /
7		vet du /	7		you see /
8		sen går man där med polarna /	8		then you're walking there with your friends /
9		alla liksom /	9		all together like /
10		förstår du /	10		you know /
11		sen kommer det en svart människa på andra sidan gatan /	11		then a black person walks down the other side of the street /
12	Kjerstin	um /	12	Kjerstin	um /
13	Roger	det ba går över liksom /	13	Roger	it just flows over kind of /
14		du- du liksom /	14		you- you like /
15		förstår du /	15		you know /
16		du- du /	16		you- you /
17		vad fan heter det /	17		what the fuck's it called /
18		(1.0) "du ska inte vara här" /	18		(1.0) "you're not supposed to be here" /
19		förstår du /	19		you know /
20	Kjerstin	um /	20	Kjerstin	um /
21	Roger	det här är liksom ett svenskt land /	21	Roger	this is like a Swedish country /
22		förstår du /	22		you know /
23		det är ett ariskt ursprung /	23		there's an Aryan heritage /
24		förstår du /	24		you know /
25		"pang pang" /	25		"bang bang " /
26		låg han liksom /	26		he lay there /
27		springa därifrån /	27		run away /
28		förstår du *heh heh heh* /	28		you know *heh heh heh* /

Roger begins his narrative by stating that he and his friends had been out on the town, they had been drinking and had been to the pub. Roger includes himself in a group of friends, using the general Swedish pronoun '*man*' (line 8), which means both you and *man*, but is used by both men and women when referring to oneself. Drinking and walking in town with a group of like-minded, neo-Nazi friends works to set a stage for potential violence. Indeed, in light of his neo-Nazi sympathies, Roger constructs a narrative that prescribes violence by adding a black person to the narrative. Roger can be heard to draw on a discourse of natural, inherent, and uncontrollable masculine aggression (cf. Hearn, 1998) in describing how "it just flows over" (line 13) when a black person walks down the other side of the street (line 11).

In the narrative, Roger marks the racial category—black—but not the gender category. The unmarked category of masculinity reproduces masculinity as the social/discursive norm. "The person" is therefore understood to be a man.[7] In this context, if the person had been a woman, gender would have been marked. The person becomes a target for violence because he is categorized by Roger and his friends as black. Moreover, Roger justifies the use of violence by stating that this is a Swedish country (line 21) with an Aryan heritage (line 23), telling the man in his narration, that "you should not be here" (line 18). Roger draws on a national discourse of ethnic and racial "purity"; a Sweden without "black" people. For Roger, *blackness* is a sufficient justification for inflicting violence. In this narrative, the term *black* is used as a factor to explain why Roger and his friends engage in violence. Nothing the black man does or says is constructed as the reason for the attack. This is further backed up by Roger's argument about Sweden being an Aryan country and his previously stated connection to the NSF. The violence and its effects are not specified in detail by Roger, just "bang, bang/he lay there kind of" (lines 25, 26), meaning that the man was hit to the ground; obfuscating the type of violence used and what role Roger played in the violence.

In both cases described above, Jakob and Roger are describing themselves as inflictors of violence against black men. However, *black* as an interactional resource is used to achieve divergent identity constructions. Jakob uses the epithet to construct a non-black position, and as a justification for violence. Roger, on the other hand, constructs a more explicit racist position by using *black* as the only motive for using violence.

On a speculative note, it can be argued that Roger feels safe in the group, being one of several inflictors of violence. However, in the following excerpt, he is on his own and becomes the target of violence because of his connections to neo-Nazism.

Alone Against Many

Next, both Jakob and Roger describe situations in which they have found themselves alone and identified as "the Other," due to ethnic or racist categorizations. Both young men describe themselves as being subordinated. Jakob describes himself as the target of violence and bullying by Swedes in a new school, while Roger describes himself as the target of violence because he is recognized as a neo-Nazi.

Immediately following the earlier excerpt regarding drinking with friends, I ask Roger if he has ever been in a fight on his own. In response, he told me a story of when he met a group of Afa sympathizers. Afa is the abbreviation for Anti-Fascistisk Aktion, an extra-parliamentary militant network of loosely connecting groups on the extreme left that explicitly use violence and counterdemonstrations to fight neo-Nazism, as well as using violence against representatives of the Swedish government and civil society.[8] Afa is not related to any specific ethnic or racial grouping, but is seen here as an unmarked racial category, working to counteract "white racism" and actively showing solidarity with immigrants.[9] In the narrative, Roger becomes the target of violence because he is identified as a neo-Nazi.

Roger 2

1	Kjerstin	har du varit i slagsmål själv nån gång då /	1	Kjerstin	have you been in a fight on your own at any time then /
2		har du varit [ensam /	2		have you been [alone /
3	Roger	[ensam /	3	Roger	[alone /
4	Kjerstin	ja /	4	Kjerstin	yes /
5	Roger	ah jag har varit en gång /	5	Roger	yeah I have been once
6		jag gick i mina kläder som vanligt /	6		I went in my usual clothes
7		var i Tredjestad /	7		was in Thirdville
8		polarna hade gått hem *heh* /	8		my buddies had gone home *heh*
9	Kjerstin	um /	9	Kjerstin	um
10	Roger	jag skulle ta bussen hem /	10	Roger	I was taking the bus home
11		gick jag in så här /	11		I went in to like
12		vad fan heter det /	12		what the fuck's it called
13		så här fritidsgård typ /	13		like a youth center kind of
14		((borttagna rader))	14		((omitted lines))
15	Roger	sen gick jag ner /	15	Roger	then I went down /
16		kommer *heh* det fem tio killar som är lite äldre än mig /	16		five, ten guys come *heh* that are a bit older than me /
17		förstår du /	17		you know /
18	Kjerstin	um /	18	Kjerstin	um /
19	Roger	liksom med Afa-sympatier /	19	Roger	kind of Afa sympathies
		((borttagna rader))			((omitted lines))
26	Roger	kommer sånna liksom /	26	Roger	those kind are coming like /
27		förstår du /	27		you know /
28		man står där /	28		one's standing there /
29		ja hum /	29		yes hum /
30		"um kommer man åka på rejält med däng du" /	30		"um you're in for a proper beating, aren't you"/
31	Kjerstin	ja ok /	31	Kjerstin	yes ok /
32	Roger	*heh heh* /	32	Roger	*heh heh* /
33		ja det gjorde jag ju också /	33		yes I did too didn't I /
34		förstår du /	34		you know /
35	Kjerstin	ja /	35	Kjerstin	yes /
36	Roger	det är ju inte så jävla enkelt å försvara sig /	36	Roger	it's not that bloody easy to defend yourself /
37		förstår du /	37		you know /
38	Kjerstin	nä /	38	Kjerstin	na /
39	Roger	det är ju bara att stå där /	39	Roger	you just have to stand there /
40		förstår du /	40		you know /
41		å försöka prata sig ur det (eller) liksom /	41		and try to talk your way out of it (or) kind of /
42		slå tills man ligger ner /	42		hit till you're lying down
43		förstår du /	43		you know /
44	Kjerstin	ja /	44	Kjerstin	yes/

45		så du åkte på rejält styrk där? /	45		so you got a proper beating there? /
46	Roger	ja /	46	Roger	yes /
47		jag dela ju ut två tre smällar /	47		I gave a punch or two /
48		men sen hann man ju inte mer /	48		that's all you can manage /
49		förstår du /	49		you know /
50	Kjerstin	nä /	50	Kjerstin	na /
51	Roger	sen liksom var det ju kört *heh heh* /	51	Roger	then I was screwed *heh heh* /
52	Kjerstin	ja /	52	Kjerstin	yes /
53	Roger	man fick högen över sig /	53	Roger	you got the pile on top of you/
54		visst om det skulle vart två visst /	54		sure if it had been two sure /
55		men tio liksom /	55		but ten, you know /

In organizing the narrative, Roger constructs a situation in which it is possible to talk about getting beaten, or losing a fight, and still remain in a position that does not challenge his masculine identification. Roger orients toward this identification in his reply to my question asking whether he got "a proper beating" (line 26), by saying that he managed to give "a punch or two" (line 28) before he was overpowered. He goes on to estimate that with two rather than ten, he would have been able to defend himself. Also, he distances himself from the beating by using the generalizing "you"—"hit until you're lying down" (line 42). In the narrative situation, it can be argued that I both affirm the story he is telling and challenge his masculine position. Also, my initial question (line 1) can be heard as potentially challenging Roger's position as a man, but given the context of the fighting situation, Roger's masculinity can remain intact, even though he was beaten up. This is achieved using particular discursive resources in the narrative. According to Roger, he is on his own, and is wearing clothing representing his ideological affiliation with neo-Nazism ("my usual clothes," line 2; the clothes are further described in a subsequent excerpt).

Another discursive resource in fight stories is to position yourself as inferior or subordinate in the situation. For example, Roger describes entering the youth center, at which point a group of 5 to 10 slightly older guys arrive, which can be heard as creating an inferior position. You are not expected to win over older men or a large group of men. Roger identifies these men as connected to Afa and immediately recognizes the fact that he is in for a beating. According to Roger, the Afa members attack him because they identify him as a neo-Nazi, which is sufficient to motivate violence. Roger constructs the same legitimizing reasons for being attacked as he did when he argued for using violence against the "black person" in the previous excerpt. His positioning as overtly racist, in the narrative, is constructed as the reason why he is exposed to violence rather than because of something he says or does. In the same way, in the narrative labeled as Roger 1, the black person is exposed to violence simply due to his blackness. The Afa category and the neo-Nazi category within which Roger positions himself are used as self-explanatory concepts. Roger does not explain why the group is attacking him, and there is nothing to indicate that the violence is instigated by anything other than the fact that they are Afa sympathizers and he is identified as a neo-Nazi. In the narrative,

Roger can be seen to construct a position of being the Other in the eyes of the Afa group, and therefore the target of violence.

Similar to Roger, Jakob describes becoming the target of violence due to being identified as "the Other." In the following excerpt, Jakob can be seen to draw on an understanding of Swedish as a particular category of whiteness. In a Swedish context, the terms *black* and *white* are rarely used in conversation, particularly the term *white*. Swedish can therefore be understood as an unmarked and implied whiteness category. In the following narrative, Jakob is relating his experience of the relationship between Swedes and immigrants in a specific situation. Jacob tells me about moving from his hometown to a larger city in the south of Sweden and starting a new school.

Jakob 2

1	Jakob	men jag bodde nere i X-land ett tag också i K-stad där /	1	Jakob	but I lived down in X-county for a while in K-ville /
3		då gick jag i nian /	3		then I was in ninth grade /
4		å i den skolan där jag gick/	4		and in that school I was in /
5		du vet /	5		you know /
6		det va ba typ svenskar /	6		there were like only Swedes /
7		du vet /	7		you know /
8	Kjerstin	um /	8	Kjerstin	um /
9	Jakob	så varje gång jag kom till skolan /	9	Jakob	so every time I came to the school /
10		jag kände ingen /	10		I didn't know anybody /
11		du vet så där /	11		you know like /
12		så allt- jag hamna alltid i bråk /	12		so alw- I always got in trouble /
13		du vet /	13		you know /
14		folk håller på å puttas /	14		people kept shoving /
15		så /	15		so /
16		man va tvungen å slåss asså /	16		you had to fight like /
17		å det va ba svenskar /	17		and there were like only Swedes /
18		så /	18		so /
19		asså jag är inte rädd /	19		like I'm not afraid /
20		asså det betyder inte att jag är rädd för nån asså /	20		it doesn't mean that I'm afraid of anybody like /
21		jag var inte rädd för dom där idioterna / men asså /	21		I wasn't afraid of those idiots / but like /
22		dom var fem, sex styckna mot mig /	22		there were five, six people against me /
23		det var så <u>där</u> du vet /	23		it was like you know /
24		å då var man tvungen å slåss asså / då /	24		and then you had to fight like /

25		det fanns inget alternativ /	25		there was no option /
26		antingen får du spö /	26		either you get a beating /
27		du vet /	27		you know /
28		eller så får du slåss asså /	28		or you have to fight like /
29		(0.5)	29		(0.5)
30		men jag klara mig ganska bra /	30		but I did pretty good /
31		men sen sket jag i det /	31		but then I didn't give a damn /
32		asså jag sket i fyra månader /	32		like I didn't give a damn for four months /
33		jag palla inte gå dit du vet /	33		I couldn't stand going there you know /
34	Kjerstin	um /	34	Kjerstin	um /
35	Jakob	(2.0) ah det var en tråkig stad asså /	35	Jakob	(2.0) yeah it was a boring town really /
36		bara, bara svenskar du vet /	36		only, only Swedes you know /
37		det var några invandrare som asså /	37		there were a few immigrants that like /
38		dom våga knappt röra på sig /	38		they hardly dare to move around /
39		dom va rädda /	39		they were afraid /
40		du vet /	40		you know /
41		svenska(rna) /	41		(the) Swedes /
42		dom hade tagit över riktigt rejält asså /	42		they had really taken over the place like /
43	Kjerstin	um /	43	Kjerstin	um /
44	Jakob	(1.5) så jag trivdes inte i den skolan /	44	Jakob	(1.5) so I didn't like it in that school /
45		den var inge kul /	45		it was no fun /
46		(2.0) det var ingen bra skola det /	46		(2.0) it wasn't a good school that one /

Jakob begins the narrative by describing the school he attended, in the south of Sweden, as consisting of "only" Swedes (lines 6, 17). It is inferred, in the narrative that Jakob gets into trouble because he is not included in the category of Swede, and conversely, that the "people" who are doing the "shoving" (line 14) are. Jakob uses the impersonal pronoun *man*, arguing that he "had to fight" (line 16) and so would anybody in his situation. Swedes are, however, constructed as non-frightening. Three times, Jakob states that he was not afraid of the Swedes (lines 19, 20, 21),

but rather argues that they were "idiots" (line 21). Moreover, the number of opponents is used as the reason why Jakob had to fight (lines 24, 28) or he would get a beating.

As can be seen, this narrative mirrors how Roger previously organized his narrative about meeting the Afa sympathizers. Jakob is also left without any option (line 25), alone against a group of people, he is categorized as "the Other," and therefore the target of violence. Jakob's positioning as non-Swede, in turn, is contrasted to the immigrant category (line 37).

Jakob categorizes the immigrants according to their fear of the Swedes: "they hardly dared to move around" (line 38).

According to Bucholtz and Hall (2005, p. 595), positioning can be achieved by evaluation: "I evaluate something and thereby position myself, and align [or dis-align] with you." Jakob can be heard to position himself in opposition to the Swede category in his evaluation of the school: "(1.5) so I didn't like it in that school / it was no fun / (2.0) it wasn't a good school that one/" (lines 44, 45, 46). Jakob constructs two, mutually exclusive categories, "Swedes" and "immigrants," however, he does not include himself in either of the two categories. Jakob can be heard to mark Swedes as a particular ethnic category, but also to "minoritize" them (Staunæs, 2005). In his narrative, Swedes are not described as a taken-for-granted majority; indeed neither group appears to be a majority in this narrative. Interestingly, Jakob describes Swedes as intruders: "(the) Swedes/ they had really taken over the

place, like" (lines 41, 42). Jakob constructs the category of Swede as consisting of bullies, both in relation to himself and in relation to immigrants: people kept shoving (line 14), taking over the school (line 42), forcing Jakob to fight (lines 12, 16, 24, 26, 28), and finally forcing Jakob to quit school (line, 31, 32, 33). In the next excerpt, Jakob constructs Swedes as a category of whiteness quite differently.

The Neo-Nazi Boots

In the following section, I examine how both young men draw on a discursive understanding of the symbolic meaning of the boots worn by neo-Nazi adherents. Jakob constructs neo-Nazis as dangerous and something one can (and perhaps should) fear. A few minutes after the previously excerpted narrative, Jakob tells me about how he accidentally ended up at a party with neo-Nazis outside his hometown.

Jakob 3

1	Jakob	så var jag med en turk /	1	Jakob	so I was with a Turk /
2		så drar vi på en fest /	2		so we're going to a party /
3		å den festen visa att det var bara nassar där inne /	3		and that party turned out that there were only neo-Nazis there /
4		så var det typ 20 pers / ((borttagna rader))	4		so there were like 20 people / ((omitted lines))
8		så kommer dom där tjugo typ:femton /	8		so they're coming 20 like 15 /
9		dom var femton pers /	9		there were 15 people /
10		då var jag riktigt skraj asså /	10		then I got really scared /
11		då kan vi snacka om å va rädd asså /	11		then you can talk about getting scared like /
12	Kjerstin	um /	12	Kjerstin	um /
13	Jakob	då jag våga inte röra mig ur fläcken / ((borttagna rader))	13	Jakob	I didn't dare move an inch then / ((omitted lines))
14		då kommer det en snubbe som jag känner/	14		then a guy comes that I know /
15		en ah /	15		a eh /
16		han är den största av dom alla /	16		he is the biggest of them all /
17		han är 34 år /	17		he's 34 years old/

18	du vet /	18	you know /
19	en nasse asså /	19	a neo-Nazis you know /
20	en /	20	a /
21	han är överschysst /	21	he's super decent /
22	asså mot mig /	22	to me like /
	((borttagna rader))		((omitted lines))
33	så drog vi iväg asså /	33	and we left like /
34	jag hade tur där asså /	34	I was lucky there like /
35	sen därifrån har jag tagit det lugnt asså /	35	since after that I've been playing it cool like /
36	det fan /	36	It's damn /
37	den rädslan jag hade där (har jag aldrig) haft asså /	37	that fear I had there (I have never) had like /
38	den var för mycket folk där asså /	38	there were too much people there like /
39	emot mig där asså /	39	against me there like /
40	alla hade kängor /	40	everybody had boots /
41	det vill man inte ha i ansiktet asså /	41	you don't want that in your face like /
42	jag hade tur asså /	42	I was lucky like /

Telling the story, Jakob marks the situation ethnically by saying that he was with a Turk (line 1). This is cast in contrast to the party, which Jakob describes as made up of neo-Nazis only (line 3). Here, neo-Nazi can be understood as a particular category of whiteness representing a type of dangerous masculinity. The neo-Nazi is associated with, not only physical strength and physical violence, but with racist-induced and deadly violence. The neo-Nazis can be understood here to be men, just in Roger's narrative about the Afa. The lethalness of the neo-Nazis is symbolized by their boots (line 40), and this detail enables Jakob to produce a narrative in which it becomes apparent that he and his friend potentially risked their lives by going to the party.

Expressing fear could potentially be demasculinizing, which Jakob manages to avoid by drawing on a discourse of the dangerous neo-Nazis and being outnumbered, enabling him to describe his paralyzing fear, "I didn't dare move an inch then" (line 13). Constructing the neo-Nazis as dangerous allows Jakob the possibility to state that he was scared (lines 10, 11), and that

he had never have been so afraid before (line 37), without compromising his masculinity. Ordinarily fear and masculinity are incompatible concepts (cf. Burcar, 2005), such that fear is only reconcilable with masculinity under highly particular circumstances.

In the narrative, however, the category of neo-Nazi is produced in two different ways. The first is constructed in an essentialist way in that the neo-Nazis are dangerous per se; second, the neo-Nazi category is de-essentialized by the description of "the biggest of them all" (line 16), the 34-year-old man (line 17), saving Jakob from the situation. Despite being a neo-Nazi, the man is evaluated as being "super decent" (line 21). Here, age is used as an interactional resource, a factor explaining why it is possible for the man to stop the fight from starting. In this instance, "the biggest of them all" can be understood both as being physically large and as being older than any of the others, indicating that the man is at the top of a hierarchical order. Jakob constructs a narrative setting within which he is not able to avoid the imminent violence—just as Roger did. However, in Jakob's case, he is rescued by a man—potentially, a troublesome position for masculinity. Yet by drawing on the dangerous neo-Nazi discourse, it is possible for Jakob to be rescued while not becoming demasculinized.

Jakob can be seen to position himself in an unmarked non-white category, as immigrant or minority, when he describes his encounter with the neo-Nazis and being the target of violence because he is identified as non-white—the Other—in the eyes of the neo-Nazis. Here, Jakob and his friend are the targets of potential violence because they are categorized as non-Swedish, in a similar way as the black person in Roger's previous narrative (Roger 1). By constructing themselves as the Other, both Jakob and Roger are able to narrate fight stories in which they are the target of violence and maintain a masculine position. Both narratives can be seen as fight stories that position them according to gendered and ethnic orders (Bucholtz, 1999) as well as age. Age is a position that enables Jakob and Roger to construct preferred fight stories, indicating an inferior or underdog position offering them the possibility to come across as competent fighters, able to fight an older man (as seen in the Jakob 1 narrative), or being exposed to violence without being demaculinized. It can be argued that the symbols of the neo-Nazis, the boots (line 40),

are more intimidating to Jakob than the bullying by the Swedes that he was exposed to in ninth grade (Jakob 2 narrative). Subsequently, it would not be possible for Jakob to articulate fear in relation to the Swede category and maintain his preferred masculine position; this is something, however, that is possible for him to do in relation to the neo-Nazi category. Jakob does not construct whiteness as a homogeneous category; rather it is composed of two distinctly different categories: Swedes and neo-Nazis. Jakob also excludes himself from a third category he constructs: the immigrant who is afraid of Swedes.

Roger also uses the symbolic power of the neo-Nazi boots as a narrative resource. In previous excerpts, Roger can be seen to create a narrative past, talking about how things used to be. In the following excerpt, he positions himself in relation to this narrative past and it becomes apparent that the neo-Nazi position is problematic in Roger's narrative present. Early on in the interview, he presents reasons why the neo-Nazi position is problematic or even an imposition for him now—a position that he also returns to at the end of the interview. The following excerpt comes from the first part of the interview, shortly after Roger had told me that he had applied to become a member of the NSF party, and I ask him if he is still involved in these things.

		Roger 3			
1	Kjerstin	um /	1	Kjerstin	um /
2		men håller du på med det fortfarande /	2		but are you still doing that /
3		eller har du kvar dom /	3		or do you still have those /
4	Roger	ähj fan /	4	Roger	na hell /
5		det där har jag lagt ner /	5		I've stopped /
6		(rätt) så mycket faktiskt /	6		(pretty) much really /
7	Kjerstin	ok /	7	Kjerstin	ok /
8	Roger	men visst /	8	Roger	but sure /
9		det finns alltid kvar /	9		it's always there /
10		förstår du /	10		you know /
11	Kjerstin	ah /	11	Kjerstin	yeah /
12	Roger	det går inte å släppat så här /	12	Roger	you can't just let it go like that /

13		förstår du /	13		you know /
		liksom jag börja smått när jag kom till mitt andra hem ((HVB-hem)) /			I kind of started when I came to my second home ((residential care home))
14		jag hängde upp Bomberjackan /	14		I hung the Flight jacket up
15		jag hängde upp kängerna på väggen /	15		I hung the boots on the wall
16		förstår du /	16		you know
17	Kjerstin	um/	17	Kjerstin	um
18	Roger	liksom sen när jag kom hit liksom /	18	Roger	kind of when I came here kind of
19		vad fan kan jag göra liksom /	19		what the hell can I do like
20		jag kan inte ha dom /	20		I can't have them
21		förstår du /	21		you know
22	Kjerstin	nä /	22	Kjerstin	na
	Roger	för jag vet /		Roger	cause I know
23		min tid kommer gå mycket långsammare /	23		my time will go so much slower
24		förstår du /	24		you know
25		[jag kommer inte kunna umgås med nån /	25		[I can't hang out with anybody
26	Kjerstin	[um /	26	Kjerstin	[um
27	Roger	förstår du /	27	Roger	you know
28		kommer inte å funka /	28		won't work
29	Kjerstin	nä /	29	Kjerstin	na
30	Roger	så liksom jag har lagt ner det så länge i alla fall /	30	Roger	so I've kind of like stopped that for now at least

Like Jakob, Roger affords special significance to the boots as a symbol for the neo-Nazi ideology. Upon arriving at his second residential care home, Roger made the decision to stop wearing the clothes symbolizing neo-Nazism, the flight jacket and the boots (lines 2, 3). Hanging the boots and the jacket on the wall is produced as a symbol for his decreasing involvement in the neo-Nazi organization, albeit these items are kept as memorabilia. Roger describes a situation in which he has no choice but to let go of his neo-Nazi sympathies (lines 19, 20). Upon arriving at the present detention home, Roger positions himself as not having any other choice but to take this action. Expressing neo-Nazi sympathies compromises his ability to have a social life, and the time spent at the home would pass much more slowly. Roger also risks being cast as "the Other" by the young men at the ward. According to Roger, his neo-Nazi affiliation would be a liability rather than a social resource. So in the narrative present, at the ward, he is opting out of the neo-Nazi position. This is also something he has expressed to the staff members at the current detention home. According to them, Roger was afraid that at the ward it would become publicly known that he used to be a neo-Nazi. In treatment sessions, he never mentioned anything that could have been interpreted as neo-Nazi. Rather, Roger preferred a different masculine position; that of devoted boyfriend, often referring to his girlfriend of the past nineteen months. In the interview, he sees the fact that she does not have the same sympathies as an improvement and as something good in his life.

DISCUSSION

In this article, I have shown how two young men use ethnic and racial categorizations in talking about violence from two rather different positions; Jakob as non-Swedish but at the same time as non-black, while Roger takes an explicitly racist position. Both positions draw on essentialist and racist categorisations. Moreover, the analyses show how ethnic positions are impossible to disentangle from age and gender. The perception of youth allows the men to take up particular masculine positions and construct preferred fight stories: such as an inferior fighting position, which results in either coming across as a very competent fighter or enables the young men to be beaten down and lose the fight without the loss of their masculine position. Further, in constructing fighting opponents as particular kinds of Others, both Roger and Jakob are able to draw on discourses of nationalism (ethnically pure Swede) or racism (the dangerous neo-Nazi) in their identity construction.

Importantly, both Roger and Jakob use racist discourse differently in talking about violence, and they present different types of talk on what is constructed as a legitimate reason to engage in violence. In Roger's case, violence is directly linked to a racist discourse, where the color of someone's skin is sufficient motivation for an attack. By contrast, Swedes are not marked as a unified and discriminated category; they are divided into different categories of whiteness that can be as different as neo-Nazis and Afa sympathizers. Therefore, being a Swede becomes a troubled category for Roger— particularly since the possibility of positioning himself a as neo-Nazi, is greatly reduced. He is forced to establish a new subject position (as devoted boyfriend), which is easier for him because of the privilege of whiteness.

Jakob more closely relates violence to an unmarked masculine position, and cannot be seen to engage in violence based on any simple ethnic or racist categorization of his opponents. The argument is not that Jakob is less racist than Roger, but that the racist discourse Roger uses is not available to Jakob. Jakob's decision to not include himself in any particular category can also be seen as a strategic discursive choice. Rather, he interactively excludes himself from potentially problematic categories such as Swedish and immigrant.

Close analyses demonstrate how, to some extent, two young men with different backgrounds and ideological affiliations use the same ethnic and racial categories, narrative organization, and symbolic representations when talking about violence. However, the discursive resources are used to achieve different positions in interaction. The chapter also shows that racist can be a troublesome position that might expose an individual to violence.

NOTES

1. In the text, I use race and ethnicity at times as synonyms or make a distinction interpreting expressions such as *black* and *white* as race, and expressions such as Turkish or Swedish as ethnicity.

2. In a study on how ethnic Dutch and ethnic minority people define and use essentialist notions about ethnic groups, Maykel Verkuyten (2003) found that the use of essentializing categorizations in conversation can be related to making claims or justifications. Also essentialist categories "can be used in various ways and with various ideological effects . . . as a flexible conversational resource which is variously defined and deployed, depending on the interactional task at hand" (Verkuyten, 2003, p. 374).

3. All the young men interviewed were given the opportunity to choose their own pseudonyms.

4. The accent is employed to create a distance from national Swedish and the majority society. It is used predominantly by youth born in Sweden with an immigrant background or by youth from a Swedish background growing up in segregated suburbs. One example of this accent use is the adoptee I interviewed at the detention home. He grew up with his Swedish adoptive parents, both academics, who code-switched (Cromdal, 2000, p. 223) between national Swedish and "immigrant" Swedish.

5. Here, I use the term neo-Nazi when referring to Roger's connection to NSF, although he himself does

not use the term. It could be argued that being a member of NSF does not automatically mean adherence to a neo-Nazi ideology, but the party is categorized as such by the Swedish authorities, and the party does not hide their close connection to paraphernalia and dates stemming from the Nazi period. For instance, the party has its annual party meeting on Adolf Hitler's birthday, which is celebrated with cakes decorated in swastikas.

6. I made a verbatim transcription of the Swedish interviews and ART recordings. The original analyses were based on the Swedish transcriptions and repeated viewings. In order to increase readability and to represent the young men's style of speaking, I organized the transcription in lines representing "idea units" (Gee, 1991).

Transcription symbols

word	conversation
word	English word used in the Swedish original conversation
"word"	reported speech
(word)	uncertain transcription
(xxx)	inaudible
(5.0)	pause, in seconds
((altered voice))	explanation to non-verbal activities or specification of vocal pitch
[word	overlapping speech
WORD	loud speech
wo:::rd	elongated vowel
wo-	abrupted word
heh heh	laughter
/	end of line

7. Also, the discourse regulating young men's violence against girls makes a girl a highly marked category, and as such, a target for violence (for a discussion, see Andersson, 2008).

8. Very little is written in Sweden on Afa, see the Swedish Security Service website, www.sakerhetspolisen.se. Magnus Sandelin (2007), a free-lance journalist, has also written about political violence and Afa in Sweden.

9. This is according to the network's own website www.antifa.se.

REFERENCES

Ålund, Alexandra (2002). *The spectre of ethnicity.* Department of Ethnic Studies. Linköping, SE: Linköping University.

Andersson, Kjerstin (2007). To slap a *"Kraxelhora"*: Violence as category-bound activity in young men's talk. *NORMA, 2,* 144–162.

Andersson, Kjerstin (2008a). Constructing young masculinity: A case study of heroic discourse on violence. *Discourse and Society, 19,* 139–161.

Andersson, Kjerstin (2008b). *Talking violence, constructing identities: Young men in institutional care.* Linköping Studies in Arts and Science, 444 (Doctoral Dissertation). Linköpings Universitet, SE: Tema Barn.

Andersson, Kjerstin (2012). Gola aldrig! Pedofilen som undantag. In L. Gottzén & R. Jonsson (Eds.), *Andra män. Maskulinitet, normskapande och jämställdhet.* Malmö, SE: Gleerups.

Aronsson, Karin (1998). Identity-in-interaction and social choreography. *Research on Language and Social Interaction, 31,* 75–89.

Bamberg, Michael (1997). Positioning between structure and performance. *Journal of Narrative and Life History, 7,* 335–342.

Bernhardt, Eva, Goldscheider, Calvin, Goldscheider, Frances, & Bjerén, Gunilla (2007). *Immigration, gender, and family transitions to adulthood in Sweden.* Lanham, MD: University Press of America.

Billig, Michael (1995). *Banal nationalism.* London, UK: Sage.

Brickell, Chris (2005). Masculinities, performativity, and subversion: A sociological reappraisal. *Men and Masculinities, 8*(1), 24–43.

Bucholtz, Mary (1999). You da man: Narrating the racial other in the production of white masculinity. *Journal of Sociolinguistics, 3,* 443–460.

Bucholtz, Mary, & Hall, Kyra (2005). Identity and interaction: A sociocultural linguistic approach. *Discourse and Society, 7,* 585–614.

Burcar, Veronika (2005). *Gestaltningar av offererfarenheter. Samtal med unga män som utsatts för brott* (Doctoral Dissertation in Sociology). Lund, SE: Lund University.

Cromdal, Jakob (2000). *Code-switching for all practical purposes: Bilingual organization of children's play* (Doctoral Dissertation). Linköping Studies in Arts and Science 223, Linköping, Sweden.

Davies, Bronwyn, & Harré, Rom (1990/2001). Positioning: The discursive production of selves. In M. Wetherell, S. Taylor, & S. Yates (Eds.), *Discourse theory and practice.* London, UK: Sage.

De Fina, Anna (2007). Code-switching and the construction of ethnic identity in a community of practice. *Language in Society, 36,* 371–392.

Edley, Nigel (2001). Analysing masculinity: Inter-pretative repertoires, ideological dilemmas and subject positions. In M. Wetherell, S. Taylor, & S. Yates (Eds.), *Discourse theory and practice.* London, UK: Sage.

Edley, Nigel, & Wetherell, Margaret (1997). Jockeying for a position: The construction of masculine identities. *Discourse & Society, 8,* 203–217.

Fowler, Roger (1991). *Language in the news: Discourse and ideology in the press.* London, UK: Routledge.

Gee, James Paul (1991). A linguistic approach to nar-rative. *Journal of Narrative and Life History, 1,* 15–39.

Georgakopoulou, Alexandra (2005). Styling men and masculinities: Interactional and identity aspects at work. *Language in Society, 34*(2), 163–184.

Goodman, Simon, & Speer, Susan A. (2007). Category use in construction of asylum seekers. *Critical Discourse Studies, 4,*165–185.

Hearn, Jeff (1998). *The violences of men. How men talk about and how agencies respond to men's violence to women.* London, UK: Sage.

Hearn, Jeff, & Whitehead, Antony (2006). Collateral damage: Men's "domestic" violence to women seen through men's relations with men. *Probation Journal, 53,* 55–74.

Hedman-Lindgren, Birgitta (2004). Rikedom av kul-turer blir trygghet på Sirius. *SiStone, 4,* 3–6.

Hollway, Wendy (1984/2001). Gender difference and the production of subjectivity. In M. Wetherell, S. Taylor, & S.J. Yates (Eds.), *Discourse theory and practice.* London: Sage.

Howarth, Caroline (2006). Race as stigma: Positioning the stigmatized as agents, not objects. *Journal of Community and Applied Social Psychology, 16,* 442–451.

Kiesling, Scott Fabius (2001). Stances of whiteness and hegemony in fraternity men's discourse. *Journal of Linguistic Anthropology, 11,* 101–115.

Kiesling, Scott Fabius (2005). Homosocial desire in men's talk: Balancing and re-creating cultural discourses of masculinity. *Language in Society, 34,* 695–723.

Lynn, Nick, & Lea, Susan (2003). "A phantom men-ace and the new apartheid": The social construc-tion of asylum-seekers in the United Kingdom. *Discourse and Society, 14,* 425–452.

Nayak, Anoop (2006). After race: Ethnicity, race and post-race theory. *Ethnicity and Racial Studies, 29,* 411–430.

Potter, Jonathan, & Wetherell, Margaret (1987). *Discourse and social psychology. Beyond atti-tudes and behaviour.* London, UK: Sage.

Sacks, Harvey (1992). *Lectures on conversation.* Oxford, UK: Blackwell Publishers,

Sandelin, Magnus (2007). *Extremister. En berättelse om politiska våldsverkare i Sverige.* Stockholm, SE: Bokförlaget DN.

Schegloff, Emanuel A. (2007). A tutorial on member-ship categorization. *Journal of Pragmatics, 39*(3), 462–482.

Stanko, Elizabeth A. (Ed.). (2003). *The meanings of violence.* London: Routledge.

Statistics Sweden. (2011). Retrieved March 26, 2011 from www.scb.se.

Staunæs, Dorthe (2005). From culturally avant-garde to sexually promiscuous: Troubling subjectivities and intersections in the social transition from childhood into youth. *Feminism and Psychology, 15,* 149–167.

van Dijk, Teun (1993). Stories and racism. In D. Mumby (Ed.), *Narrative and social control.* Newbury Park, CA: Sage.

Verkuyten, Maykel (2003). Discourses about ethnic group (de-)essentialism: Oppressive and progres-sive aspects. *British Journal of Social Psychology, 42,* 371–391.

West, Candace, & Fenstermaker, Sarah (1995). Doing difference. *Gender and Society, 9,* 8–37.

Wetherell, Margaret (1998). Positioning and interpre-tative repertoires: Conversation analysis and post-structuralism in dialogue. *Discourse and Society, 9,* 387–412.

Wetherell, Margaret, & Edley, Nigel (1999). Negotiating hegemonic masculinity: Imaginary positions and psycho-discursive practices. *Feminism and Psychology, 9,* 335–356.

15

Language as a Means of "Civilizing" the Kurdish Women in Turkey

Ebru Sungun

Introduction

Within the Ottoman Empire, minority uprisings to demand nationhood in the nineteenth century contributed in important ways to the disintegration of the Empire, which had long accommodated a range of minorities and their languages. The early Turkish policymakers reversed the Empire's model of diversity and in the name of "national unity and indivisibility" officially adopted monolingualism. There was a widespread fear that linguistic diversity would constitute a threat to the formation of a national identity. Consequently, reform-minded Republican bureaucrats and ideologues introduced a set of Western reforms within the young nation-state—most particularly that of the adoption of the Latin alphabet over the Arabic one in 1928. Just as the Ottoman caliphate—an institution that had been recognized as the highest authority in the Islamic world—vanished overnight (March 3, 1924), these state-sponsored practices estranged people from their own cultures. Overnight people became illiterate. The reform of the Turkish alphabet cut off the entire nation from its own cultural practices, indeed its own past— the nation experienced a collective amnesia. These changes had particular consequences for Kurdish people living in what had become the Turkish nation.

My aim in this chapter is to point out a set of arguments in current sociological, political, and linguistic research that can be read as investigations of the links among nationalism, cultural-ethnical genocide, language as a tool of domination, and the formation of power through hegomonic discursive practices. I also try to show how the discourse of development and progress can contribute to the annihilation of a nation and the constitution of gendered insecurity in the context of the state of exception. Rather than accepting a limited concept of language as simply a "tool" that reflects or describes a preexisting reality, I draw from Michel Foucault's (1972) notion of language as composed of *discourses* that *produce meaning*. In this sense, discourse is *a social and political entity, the means by which what we know of the world can be created (rather than simply represented)* (McHoul & Grace, 1993, p.13, original emphasis). In this sense, discourses are central both to what we know and what we don't know. As French historian Rénan noted "[f]orgetting is an essential element in the creation of a nation" (Rénan, 1997). Before turning to my analysis, I outline briefly some of the historical and political contexts for this research.

TRANSFORMATION OF A HETEROGENEOUS EMPIRE INTO A HOMOGENEOUS NATION-STATE

During the collapse of the Ottoman Empire, Kurds fought together with Turks in what was known as the War of Independence (May 19, 1919—July 24, 1923). However, the "Kurdish-Turkish brotherhood" was a limited concept. In the Treaty of Sèvres, which was signed on August 20, 1920, the Kurds were promised a homeland. But the Allies, under the leadership of Great Britain and France, were aware that the realization of this treaty required military enforcement in a difficult country and were unwilling to make this commitment.[1] In January 1923, Mustafa Kemal was still seeking local autonomy for Kurdish-inhabited areas.[2] When the Treaty of Lausanne, was signed on July 24, 1923 declaring the creation of the Republic of Turkey and defining its borders, the Kurds were never mentioned. Under the treaty of Lausanne, the Kurds were not even regarded as a minority group (McDowall, 1997, p. 33). In the treaty, references to minorities were limited to non-Muslims, when dealing with a religious reference, although Article 39 appeared to give all linguistic minorities, both Muslims and non-Muslims, the right to use their own language in commerce, religion, the press and publications, and at public meetings (Helsinki Watch, 1990).

Today, Turkish officials continue to claim that the Turkish government's policy on minorities is strictly based on the requirements of the Treaty of Lausanne. According to the current Turkish government, all citizens of Turkey enjoy equal rights and there are no minorities (either ethnic or national) other than religious minorities. Beşikçi (1990, p.11) argues that the Turkish state interpreted the Lausanne Treaty as a signal that they were free to start a genocidal campaign against the Kurds. The government perceived the signing of the Treaty as an international guarantee and approval of a continuation of its policies. With the signing of the Lausanne Treaty, Kurdistan became an interstate colony (Beşikçi, 1990). As it's often argued, the formation of the republic was not a victory but a defeat of the Ottoman Empire. According to Gerger:

> The Turkish psyche is almost enslaved by the spectre of the long, painful and humiliating dissolution of the Ottoman Empire. Turkish nationalism was born in the lost territories. . . . Coupled with the traumatic disintegration of the Empire, these developments engraved the following on the Turkish psyche and nationalism: fear, a reflexive aggressiveness against the outside world, an almost impulsive urge to violence to survival, a bellicosity stemming from a strange interaction of inferiority and superiority complexes and a xenophobic exclusiveness, a reclusive rigidity that reinforces reactionary traits (Gerger, 1997, p.2).

At the onset of the 1920s, the Turkish government believed modernization required a complete civilizational shift from the Ottoman Empire's "backward" and "traditional" social order. The principle that defined the basic characteristics of the new Republic of Turkey became known as Kemalism and the Kemalist project of "westernizing" the newly created nation aspired to transform the formerly heterogeneous and religious Empire into a secular homogeneous nation-state with a single language.

Yet relationships between social, geographic, and linguistic boundaries are complex and often problematic. Fishman (1977, p. 25) refers to language as "the symbol of ethnicity." According to Fishman, ethnicity is an aspect of a collectivity's self-recognition and an aspect of its recognition in the eyes of outsiders. It is an avenue by which individuals are linked to society, that is, to social norms and social values (p.16). When we think about ethnicity as a collective consciousness, we notice that it doesn't automatically follow in a predetermined way. Instead, there is a need for sense of a shared history and a common destiny—the feeling of "us" and "them." Yet ethnic identities are not always internally motivated. To some extent, ethnicity is a relationship between those who have the power to define others and those who have been defined; in this sense, ethnicity is not an inherent characteristic of any group (Skutnabb-Kangas, 2000c, p.176). In this context, nationalism can be seen as an outcome of the interruption of traditional life and the annihilation of tribal, ethnic, and linguistic relations. Nationalism provides a redefinition of personal and collective identity when the previous identification has been rendered inoperative as a result of social change (Fishman 1988, pp.114, 139, 286). A national identity occurs in parallel with the formation of a nation-state and, as a result of the nation-building process, the consciousness of the people becomes more politicized. For this reason, Fishman describes nationalism as conscious or organized ethnocultural solidarity that is directed outside of its initial sphere toward political, economic, and religious goals.

When the Ottoman Empire became the Republic of Turkey, the politicizing of one ethnic identity and the annihilation of other ethnic and religious groups became more obvious. The new Republic implemented hegemonic policies in an attempt to dissolve Islamic and traditional identities of the Empire, to provide control, and to strengthen the "Turkish nationality" and "nationalism." What was once a land of Muslims inhabited by various nations, emerged as the territory of a single Turkish nation as imagined by Turkish rulers. The diversity of various nations became incorporated as a multiethnic society within a modern state. Practices of genocide and deportation were among the most severe political tools used to construct Turkish nationalism. Populations that had lived with great harmony within the Empire, such as the Kurds and Armenians, now were considered to be unassimilable

to such an extent that they were targeted for annihilation or deportation. This process ended in the massacre of the Armenians in 1915 and with the deaths of more than one and a half million Armenians that occurred due to mass deportations, death marches, and killings.[3]

TURKIFICATION: THE KEMALIST FALSIFICATION OF HISTORY

Ziya Gökalp, a sociologist who was inspired by Durkheim's theories, played an important role in developing the dominant ideology used to "Turkify" nations that lived within the Empire (such as Kurds, Armenian, Albanians, Arabs, Greeks, Bosniak, Pomaks, etc.) and to justify a secular, centralized power to the new republic. According to Gökalp—ironically, he was Kurdish—a nation is not a racial, ethnic, or a political group but rather a group of individuals, who share a common language, religion, and morality (Gökalp, 2006). During the turkification period, some mythical "theories," such as the Turkish Historical Thesis (*Türk Tarih Tezi*) and the Sun Language Theory (*Güneş Dil Teorisi*) were developed by Institute of Turkish History to reinforce this new paradigm. According to the Turkish Historical Thesis, ancestors of Turks who lost their direction in Ergenekon Valley in Central Asia were guided and rescued by a wolf called "Börteçine." The Sun Language Theory (*Güneş Dil Teorisi*) complemented the Turkish Historical Thesis by arguing that the Turkish language is the source of all the existing languages in the world, and that it was the first spoken language in the development of mankind. Gerger calls this process of theorizing on the basis of false assumptions "the Kemalist falsification of history" (Gerger, 1997, p.17).

Ramón Grosfoguel argued that the nation's foundational myths are crucial in how cultural racism is articulated. Indeed the concept of nation is central to the understanding of citizenship, identity, and the sociopolitical modes of incorporation. In order to talk about the rights (civil, political, social) and the obligations that citizenship implies, we need to understand the foundational myths, invented traditions (Hobsbawn, 1990), and imagined communities (Anderson, 1991) constructed by states, dominant elites, dominant classes, and/or dominant racial/ethnic groups. From the multiethnic Ottoman Empire to the homogenous national state, the Turkish Republic's formation of a mythical "one state, one nation, one flag, and one language" symbolizes the forced assimilation and annihilation of minorities and formation of the cultural racism.

The creation of an official language can be seen as one of the consequences of cultural racism. Language is the most important thing that gathers people as a nation; it has been foundational to the notion of a state or a common destiny. In order to eradicate an ethnic group within the state, the state must first kill its language. The Turkish ruling elite demanded that the Kurds sever ties with their own language and this oppression resulted in a strong reaction and resistance.

Since the 1920s, the official ideology of the Turkish Republic has been to deny the existence of Kurdish people in Turkey. The purpose of this policy was to convert the Kurds through assimilation into Turks politically, culturally, and socially. Mustafa Kemal's successor, Ismet Inönü, declared in 1930: "Only the Turkish nation is entitled to claim ethnic and national rights in this country. No other element has any such right" (White, 2000, p. 78).

One of the first activities of the Turkish nation-building project was to ban the diverse number of languages spoken within the republic. This is evident in the execution of a series of Constitutional articles. For example, Article 88 of the 1924 Constitution stated: "Everyone in Turkey is called a Turk without discrimination on the basis of religion or race." In March 1924, according to the Turkification policies, Article 66 of the Turkish Constitution confirmed this by stating, "Everyone linked to the Turkish state through the bond of citizenship is a Turk." And "Turkish" is declared as the unique and official language of the new Turkish Republic. The official language of a state is a symbol of who is included within national policy. Cultural racism rooted in the constitutive ideology of the Turkish Republic produced restricted language rights, limited access to education in native languages, impeded socioeconomic mobility, and ultimately, for specific populations, a forced assimilation into the Turkish nationality.

Language has been and remains a mechanism of ideological control of Kurdish society within Turkey and a major factor in the exercise of power through hegemony. The National Assembly passed a government decree that prohibited the use of the Kurdish language in both public and private spheres and, immediately after, the name Kurdistan (which had been the name of the region since the 12th century) was banned and replaced with "Eastern Anotolia." These policies went hand in hand with state-sponsored scientific research. In 1934, the state enacted a new law that allowed the relocation of non-Turkish speakers into Turkish-speaking regions; in 1938, the Kurds were renamed "mountain Turks" and the Kurdish names of over 20,000 settlements were replaced with Turkish names.

The authorities have not registered Kurdish names and parents have been forced to give their children Turkish names. Many Kurds have been forced to take a name that is not only Turkish but also means "Türk," such as the surname *Öztürk* (which means "pure Türk"). Hypocritically reflective of a similar situation, the Turkish state protested in the 1980s when Bulgaria followed a policy forcing the Turks living in Bulgaria to change their names to Bulgarian names.

The denial of a name causes deep effects at the individual and collective levels. For the individual, it is a way of denying his/her own identity and for the group it has a meaning as a disruption of the groups' identity. But at both levels, it threatens the existence of the human being and its entities. Being a Kurd and speaking Kurdish in the Republic of Turkey was outlawed in a provision of the Law to Combat Terrorism; Gerger calls this renunciation process "moral genocide" (Gerger, 1997, pp. 1–2, 9).

Linguistic Human Rights

Language is a system of beliefs, values, and interpretations expressing a certain culture. It is an identity-maker and the heart of a person's belonging to a particular community. Language and identity are related to self-determination—to take away a society's language is to colonize the consciousness of people in order to maintain oppressive structures (Skutnabb-Kangas & Toukomaa, 1976, pp. 7, 37–38). Language becomes the main means of domination and the modern version of domination is increasingly colonizing the minds and consciousness of the dominated (Skutnabb-Kangas, 1996, pp. 124–126).[4]

Education in one's mother tongue and the use of one's mother language in social and official contexts is a birthright—indeed it is referred to as linguistic human rights. According to Skutnabb-Kangas, linguistic human rights accord the possibility that people can become bilingual according to their own choice in their mother tongue(s) and another official language, and require that any change of mother tongue is voluntary, not imposed (Skutnabb-Kangas & Phillipson, 1994, p. 361). Linguistic human rights accord minority groups the right to speak and develop their own languages and to maintain their education. All human beings have the right to realize their culture, religion, and education and social affairs in their own languages.

If linguistic majorities—as speakers of the majority language—have the right to enjoy all these linguistic human rights then minorities must have the same rights. They must be able to provide continuity of language between generations and acquire the cultural heritage of preceding generations. Minorities can achieve the status, which majorities take for granted, only when they are able to use their own languages and run their own schools (Skutnabb-Kangas & Phillipson, 1994, p. 78).

When linguistic rights are not guaranteed and people are not allowed to use and identify with their own languages, deep and hard consequences result: alienation from their history, heritage, and culture; eradication of their identity; increased stress and anxiety; and resulting social problems, for example, school failures (Burnham et al., 1987, pp. 105–130). This is what is called killing a language: *linguicide.*

According to Skutnabb-Kangas (2000b), *linguicism* is one of the ideologies, structures, and practices, which are used to legitimate, effectuate, regulate, and reproduce an unequal division of power and resources (both material and immaterial) between groups (p. 369). The media and the educational systems are the most important direct agents in the process of killing a language (Skutnabb-Kangas, 2000a).

ABSENCE OF DEMOCRACY AND CULTURAL GENOCIDE

In 1948, the United Nations General Assembly adopted the Universal Declaration of Human Rights and recognized the individual's right to a cultural existence. In response to the deprivation of those rights, the Polish jurist, Raphaël Lemkin penned an original conception of genocide:

> Generally speaking, genocide does not necessarily mean the immediate destruction of a nation. . . . It is intended . . . to signify a coordinated plan of different actions aiming at the destruction of essential foundations of the life of national groups, with the aim of annihilating the groups themselves. The objectives of such a plan would be disintegration of the political and social institutions, of culture, language, national feelings, religion, and the economic existence of national groups, and the destruction of the personal security, liberty, health, dignity, and even the lives of the individuals belonging to such groups. Genocide is directed against the national group as an entity, and the actions involved are directed against individuals, not in their individual capacity, but as members of the national group (Lemkin, 1994, p. 75).

A group can survive physically but its collective identity and social entity will be destroyed by this coordinated path. Cultural genocide seeks to eliminate a group's wider institutions. This can be realized in a variety of ways, and often includes the abolition of a group's language, restrictions on its traditional practices, and ways and attacks on its academics and intellectuals. Cultural genocide has two aspects: the destruction of the national pattern of the target group and the replacement of it by the national pattern of the oppressing group (Lemkin, 1944, p. 79). The process requires the absence of democracy. Consequently, cultural genocide often occurs during or following deep-reaching revolutions, which paralyzed old power structures but have not yet created new ones (Bauman, 1989, p. 111).

Similar to Lemkin, Bauman (1989, p. 119) argues that genocide is rarely aimed at the total annihilation of the group; rather, the purpose of the violence is to destroy the targeted group as a viable community capable of self-perpetuation and defense of its self-identity. Indeed, the difference between genocide and other forms of destruction, such as a natural disaster, random killings, warfare, and symbolic or cultural assaults is that genocide is used to "punish" people for being part of some particular group, tribe, race, or religion (Horowitz, 1987, p. 68; Horowitz, 1997, pp. 27–28). We see this cultural genocide as a synchronized attack on the Kurdish people that included:

1. In the political field: Kurdish self-government systems were destroyed in the 1920s and 1930s by deporting local leaders to western Turkey.

2. In the social field: The social cohesion of Kurdish society was broken and its normal development hindered by killing and removing important groups such as intellectuals and religious and political leaders. After some quiet decades since the 1950s, these operations have again intensified in the 1990s.

3. In the cultural field: Kurdish schools, associations, publications, and religious fraternities were closed in 1924, and the use of the Kurdish language in public places was banned.

4. In the economic field: While western Turkey is being developed toward a modern economy, production in the Kurdish provinces is still based on feudal land ownership and the same farming methods are being used that were used during the middle ages. There is almost no industry; the Kurdish area is treated as a colony, which produces raw materials and a labor force for western Turkey.

5. In the biological field: The Turkish state has implemented its policy of depopulation on a massive scale. This practice has intensified during the 1990s.

6. In the field of physical existence: During the 1990s, morbidity and mortality increased among the displaced Kurds, but the Turkish government is still denying permission to international humanitarian organizations to deliver food and medicine (Lemkin 1944, pp. 11–12 as cited in Koivunnen, 2002).

As reflected in Gyan Prakash's (1999) words, there is a "deep awareness of the unbridgeable gap between State and the people" (p. 157), particularly as seen in the Kurdish example, which has been deeply rooted since the 1920s and the founding of the republic, and which still continues to define the parameters of Turkish politics and culture toward the Kurds.[5]

A tragic example of this gap is evidenced by the treatment of Kurdish political prisoners (especially in the Diyarbakir Penitentiary): both during and after the coup d'état in 1980 and even up to today, the prisoners are required to speak in Turkish with their families during weekly meetings. The reality is that many of their mothers don't know even a simple word in Turkish, so this is a striking example of the hard sociological and psychological ramifications of this policy. While speaking Kurdish was strictly forbidden in prisons and elsewhere in the country (and doing so could result in severe punishment), there was a big sign in Diyarbakir Penitentiary that said, "Speak Turkish, talk a lot."

According to the Kurdish journalist Erdem Can, there is an ongoing discussion by Turkish policymakers about the potential use of the Kurdish language, such as limiting it to a minor module in schools instead of accepting it as a native language (Can, 2010). Although the foundational myth of republic, "one nation, one language, one flag" excluded Kurds from the

Figure 15.1 "Türkçe konuş çok konuş," photo of Ramazan Öztürk.

Note: Special thanks to Ramazan Öztürk.

representation of Turkish life and politics, it didn't succeed in "turning Kurds into modern Turkish citizens"—this is a dominant motto of the Kemalist ideology. None of the deported Kurds have been assimilated. Through the deportation, the problems of the east have been shifted to the west. Instead of being assimilated into the Turkish society the deported Kurds have turned urban areas into Kurdish villages.

REMAKING WOMEN

In the formation of the Turkish Republic, women's rights and reforms toward gender equality were a primary way of exerting a new national identity that was in opposition to the Ottoman Empire and its Islamic identity (Kogacioglu, 2004). The unveiled, educated, and "modern" woman of the Republic was the marker of this transition from an imagined "backward" and "traditional" past to a fresh and "modern" future (Göle, 1996). The ideal modern woman is unveiled and secular (Göle, 1996, p. 96), freed from her barbaric, repressive Islamic past and encouraged to participate in a modernizing Turkish national identity.

Although the dominant Kemalist ideology[6] was unsuccessful in turning Kurds into "civilized" Turkish citizens, they particularly targeted Kurdish women to keep them in a subordinated position by reproducing "culturally racist" discourses. In this framework, the gendered power relations are constructed through the idea that "native women" first of all need to be saved from their "primitive" native language (Kurdish). She has to be educated to the values of the west in the schools and in the official language of the Turkish state. The Kemalist intent was that all of women's existence and actions must be in the Turkish language, which validates and symbolizes the "modernity" of the Republic.

Within "The Reform Plan for the East" (*Şark Islahat Planı*), which was prepared by the government immediately after the Sheikh Said Rebellion[7] in 1925, the 14th article said that "all manner of self-sacrifice should be set to establish the girls' schools . . ." (Simsir, 2007, p. 302). Here, the founding of girls' schools was one of the noteworthy politics of the young republic to prevent the Kurdish rebellion. Kurdish women, because they were presumed to be the porters of the culture, traditions, and the Kurdish native language had to be removed from their protected homes and places of reproduction. Through this controlled education, the process of a "cultural, traditional, and linguistic interruption" was designed to start with very young girls. The existence of "Turkishness" was to be reconstructed by the destruction of the Kurdish identity with the help of the Kurdish women. A very striking example of this policy is the story of a Kurdish woman called Sabiha Gökçen, who was the adopted child of Mustafa Kemal. She grew up to become a military officer and the first female combat pilot in the world. Ironically, Sabiha Gökçen was the pilot responsible for the bombing of the Kurdish city of Dersim in 1938.[8] Sabiha Gökçen's education—to become Turkish—her adoption by the founder of the Turkish Republic, and her progress as a military officer transformed the ideology of the state into identities of national subjects, especially if the subjects are Kurdish.

This historical context is especially important for understanding the effects of a recent education project called *Haydi Kizlar Okula* (Let's Go to School, Girls). Through this program, the Turkish state disciplines the daily lives of the Kurdish women using the same justification as the very first days of the republic, that this is a "civilizing mission." This official girls' education campaign launched as *Haydi Kızlar Okula!* (Let's Go to School, Girls!) and is led by the Turkish Ministry of National Education and UNICEF, The United Nations Children's Fund. This massive intersectoral campaign mobilizes various organizations, agencies, and individuals in a drive to increase enrollment rates for girls and to achieve gender parity in primary education attendance by 2005. In order to achieve this, the program focused on the 53 Turkish provinces with the lowest enrollment rates for girls.[9] At the beginning of the campaign, it was ascertained that 273,447 girls of school age were enrolled in school. But at the end of the campaign, there were only 6,239 girls who had earned passing grades. The remainder of the girls did not maintain passing grades.

A primary objective of girls' education, as stated by the program coordinators was to reduce the influence of the Kurdistan Labour Party (*Partiya Karkerên Kurdistan or PKK*). This is evidenced by the expressed desire: "to stop the PKK terror by this way," "these girls will teach Mustafa Kemal to their children," "they won't let their children go to the mountains to participate in the PKK."[10] (These statements are not from a written program or manifesto but were the major aims of the Project and a well-known state propaganda about the Kurdish question.) During the ongoing war between the PKK and the Turkish state, among the very first reasons that Turks offered to explain the conflict was the "uneducatedness" of the Kurds. Consequently, the idea of progress through education was seen as a very important solution in any resolution of the Kurdish war. Unquestionably, the language of all education would be Turkish. Projects such as the Let's Go to School, Girls program were seen as

a very important step in institutionalizing Turkish education in Kurdish cities. But the rate of a "successful" Turkish educational transition by the Kurdish girls (6,239 out of 273,447) gives a clue about the outcome of the campaign. This campaign was started in 2003 and with the support of the "West" (UNICEF), the goal was to reach gender parity by 2005. However, according to the Kemalists, the program was aimed at assimilating Kurdish women and "reaching the contemporary level of civilization." The binary oppositions such as developed-underdeveloped, ignorant-educated, consistency-continuity are all rooted from the very beginning of the Republic and the Turk's belief in their "obligation to civilize."

CAPACITY OF RESISTANCE

The invisibility of the Kurdish language[11] in public spaces has disabled the possibility of its translation into structural power and a resource. The disproportionate access to resources as well as to a political future, and the denial of basic human rights for Kurds plays a major role in the current Kurdish problem in Turkey. Indeed, this denial of Kurdish language rights contains within it the seeds of a cycle of resistance and repression. Hegemonic policies make compromise increasingly difficult and polarization increasingly extreme. The resulting struggle is not "ethnic conflict" grounded in linguistic or cultural differences, but rather a conflict over power and policy resulting from the effort of one group to establish hegemony over others (Tollefson, 1991, pp. 197,198).

Further, the hegemonic policies embodied within the polarized consequences of the general elections of June 12, 2011 reveal of the depth of problems accumulated over the last 30 years and became a striking example of increased controversy. The Labor, Democracy, and Freedom bloc, which is supported by the pro-Kurdish Peace and Democracy Party (BDP, earlier known as DEP) won 36 seats in parliament, but the Supreme Election Board (YSK) unanimously voted to strip Hatip Dicle's[12] member of parliament (MP) status on June 21, 2011. Hatip Dicle's candidacy was denied because of a speech he gave to the ANKA news agency that caused his conviction for "disseminating propaganda of terrorism" in 2009 by the Ankara 11th Criminal Court. After the quashing of his MP status, Oya Eronat, ironically a Kurdish woman from the governing party (Justice and Development Party (AKP), who came in second to Dicle in the voting, took his parliamentary seat.

Dicle's right to enter the parliament as an independent candidate who had received the highest number of votes in the June 12 elections was revoked. In reaction to this decision, the Labor, Democracy and Freedom bloc in the parliament declared Dicle as their "red line" and immediately boycotted the parliament and began preparing a declaration for democratic autonomy in the Kurdish cities of Turkey. Once again a Kurdish woman—this time MP Oya Eronat—positioned herself with the Turkish government—calling Sabiha Gökçen to mind for many. One can see by these two examples of prominent Kurdish women that efforts to assimilate Kurdish women include rewards for women who turn against their own Kurdish culture.

The formal educational system in Turkey continues to reproduce unequal power relationships between Kurdish-speaking Kurds and others. The political elite continue to present the Turkish language as better adapted to meet the needs of a modern and civilized world. Yet, when we talk about representation in Turkish politics there is a paradox between being modern or civilized and gender equality. Turkish women were first elected to the national parliament in 1935. However since then, the percent of women in the Turkish Parliament has never been higher than 5%. It has only been since 2007 that the first Kurdish independents were allowed to become MPs in the parliament. However, the percentage of Kurdish women who are MPs is the highest, at about 33%, within all of the political parties in the Turkish parliament.

The unequal relations of power exist not only through the enforcement of the Turkish language

in schools but also through militarism and gender inequality within the curriculum. For instance, there is a mandatory lecture called National Security in high schools that was taught by a ranking soldier in full uniform. As is true in the military, just before the soldier lecturer enters the classroom, a student gives the command and the others stand to attention. Even though women are not required to participate in military service in Turkey, they are exposed to militarization at a very early age.

The gendered dimension of secularism is also a fundamental feature of male-centered modernization. For example, a headscarf ban in schools has become one of the main problems in Turkey. The Turkish "laïcité" (secularism, as inspired from the French) view the headscarf as a contradiction to the modern way of life. As a result, a Muslim woman's access to higher education has been denied. However, women wearing a headscarf who sought access to secular education wanted to be "modern" and "Muslim" at the same time—which is possible. The headscarf ban is contrary to the premise of equal access to higher education as a democratic right, and has resulted in thousands of women being denied educational access, including Hayrunisa Gül, the wife of the current president, Abdullah Gül.

Development projects, such as the "Let's Go to School, Girls" program are believed to further education and development. The Turkish government believed that with the establishment of progress and development—particularly through the education of women—both Kurdish traditions and "terrorism" would disappear. A very concrete demonstration of this assimilative attempt is the government's use of a Kurdish woman, Elif Bölük, who was educated in this program and currently used as a symbol of militarism in Turkey. She acted in the video of a campaign as *Kardelen Ayşe*—Kardelen is a flower that grows in the snow and the video is intended to signify women growing up in difficult conditions. As a Kurdish woman married to a sergeant who was killed in a bomb

Figure 15.2 Mehmet Çağlar Bölük Funeral Ceremony

Source: From Milliyet.com. Used by permission. Special thanks to Turaç Top.

attack by the PKK on June 23, 2010, she is used to represent the Republic's goals for the program: Kurdish education and patriotism. During the funeral ceremony for her husband (Figure 15.2), she petitioned the Chief of the Turkish General Staff to be able to teach at the military school; her request was accepted.

Through the assimilation of Kurdish women, such as Kardelen Ayşe, militarism is reproduced, while masculine domination and assimilation politics are institutionalized in every day practices and discourses. With the reproduction of Turkish militarist ideology inherited from her husband and her personal requests to the Turkish General Staff, Kardelen Ayşe demonstrated both strong and voluntary links to militarism and state ideology.

When discussing the necessity of civilizing Kurds, again a boundary is drawn between those who belong to and those who are excluded from the representations of the nation. Here it is useful to consider the postcolonial perspective advanced by Partha Chatterjee:

> Nationalism . . . seeks to represent itself in the image of the Enlightenment and fails to do so. For Enlightenment itself, to assert its sovereignty as the universal ideal, needs its 'Other'; if it could ever actualize itself in the real world as the truly universal, it would in fact destroy itself (1986, p.17).

CONCLUSION

The process of nation formation, the destruction of the Kurdish language and the remaking of Kurdish women has relied on "forgetting and forbidding" in order to legitimize existing power relations in Turkey. As a result, we see a growing double stigma: Not only do Kurdish women emerge in official discourse as ethnolinguistic aliens, they are also deemed "insufficiently civilized."

Johan Galtung once wrote: "The amateur who wants to dominate uses guns, the professional uses social structure" (1969, p.181). Indeed, we see this in the new Republic of Turkey, which through their process of reforms cut off the entire nation from its own past and imposed on them a new social structure. Still, the reforms did not succeed in either transforming Kurds into Turkish citizens or Kurdish women into "civilized" Turkish women. Efforts to destroy the language, the social fabric of a group, instead produced more subtle—and apparently civilized ways—for Kurdish women's resistance.

Foucault (1972, 1980) argued that power does not exist where there is no capacity for resistance. Importantly, Foucault links knowledge and power (he writes *power/knowledge* as one word). A very striking example of the continued resistance of women and girls is the story of a 10-year-old Kurdish girl named Medya Örnek who was living in the Sur district of the Kurdish Diyarbakir province. For one year, she had been giving Kurdish lessons to a group of 10 pupils in one of the rooms of her house. Both Örnek and her parents had been interrogated by the Sur Police Department. However, when speaking to a journalist Örmek said she would testify to prosecutors in Kurdish that she cannot speak Turkish.[13] The worldwide French fashion magazine *Elle* decided to pick up her story and listed her as one of ten women to make the headlines of the week.[14]

NOTES

1. Relatedly, during the peace negotiations after the victory of the Allies in World War I, U.S. president Woodrow Wilson discussed the principle of self-determination for the people formerly living in the Ottoman Empire.

2. Mustafa Kemal, founder and president of the Turkish Republic was born in the Ottoman city of Saloniki in 1881 (modern Thessaloniki, Greece). He was an Ottoman military officer; and his father was Albanian and his mother was of Macedonian origin. He was given the name Atatürk (father of the Turks) by the Grand National Assembly of Turkey in 1934.

3. Nobel laureate, Orhan Pamuk was quoted in a Swiss paper (*Das Magazin*, February 2005) as saying that only he had dared to say that Turkey had killed 30,000 Kurds and a million Armenians. Also see Marc Nichanian, *The Historiographic Perversion* (2009) from Columbia University Press.

4. It is important for the rulers that the dominated understand the language of the rulers. Otherwise, they cannot be ruled with their own consent.

5. For a broader understanding of the "unbridgeable gap" between the Turkish state and the Kurdish people, I use the true example of a 12-year-old, Ceylan Önkol, who died in the city of Diyarbakir, Turkey, as a result of an explosion caused by a mortar fired from a nearby military base. On September 28, 2009, Ceylan Önkol went out to tend the family sheep and an explosion occurred. Shortly thereafter, Ceylan was found dead with her midsection shredded. Body parts were scattered over 150 meters with some landing in the branches of nearby trees. Despite the massive damage to her midsection, examination reports said her legs and feet as well as her arms, hands, and head were relatively uninjured. After the explosion, security forces did not arrive. After six hours of waiting, the family was informed that the doctor and prosecutor would not be coming because they feared for their "safety." The village Imam was instructed to take photographs of the scene and the family was asked to gather the girl's remains and bring them to the police station in the city of Bingöl where an autopsy could be performed. According to local protocol, prosecutors should have conducted the autopsy at the site of the explosion. The results of the official investigation were released one week later and denied the claim that Ceylan was hit by a mortar round. The investigation concluded that she detonated an unexploded object that had been left in the area from a previous time. The family has questioned the results of this investigation because of the initial lack of response, the unorthodox autopsy, and the pattern of injuries. The family publicly stated:

Due to the Forensic Examination Record, Ceylan Önkol was not badly injured at her head, her arms or her legs. The problem is; if she stepped on a mine or another explosive, she had to have bad injuries of the legs, either if she found an explosive object and played with it she had to have serious injuries of the arms. Ultimately the striking point is, the place where the explosion happened is situated at the intersection of the 3 police stations, and it is under full control of military. With these speculative answers the family of Ceylan Onkol asks whether Ceylan has been targeted by military forces. (Reference http://bianet.org/bianet/insan-haklari/117378-ceylan-onkol-licede-hedef-gozetilerek-mi-olduruldu).

6. Kemalist ideology is a political thought and belief whose incontrovertible maxims are the rejection of the Ottoman Empire and the traditional way of life. Kemalists fanatically defend a specific version of secularism—understood as the separation of religion from political rule. But the Turkish Republic still has a religion supported through the Religious Affairs Directorate (a Sunni institution that doesn't recognize Alevism—(a religious community, primarily in Turkey, constituting about 15 million people), a "modern"/Western identity and lifestyle and an imposing cultural homogeneity and territorial unity of the nation.

7. The most significant Kurdish rebellion, before the PKK against the Turkish regime in the early years of the Republic, started in February 1925 and was led by Sheikh Said of Piran. The Turkish government deployed more than 50,000 soldiers against him. After the rebellion was crushed, Sheikh Said and 52 of his followers were given the death penalty in a military court. They were hung in the town of Amed on September 4, 1925.

8. The Dersim genocide was committed by the Turkish Government in 1937–1938 in the Kurdish district of Dersim. By the mid-1930s, it is estimated that between 65,000 to 70,000 people were killed. See Martin van Bruinessen, *Genocide in Kurdistan? The suppression of the Dersim rebellion in Turkey (1937–38)* and the chemical war against the Iraqi Kurds (1988). In: George J. Andreopoulos (1994). (Ed.), *Conceptual and historical dimensions of genocide* (pp. 141–170). University of Pennsylvania Press.

9. See http://www.unicef.org/turkey/pr/ge6.html.
10. The Kurdistan Labor Party (*Partiya Karkerên Kurdistan,* PKK) was founded in 1978 by Abdullah Öcalan, a student at the Faculty of Political Science at Ankara University. The PKK has been accepted by the majority of Kurdish people as an organization that has brought a Kurdish identity back to the Kurds that had been annihilated for years by the assimilation and oppression of the Turkish state. After the military coup d'état, up to today, the PKK is the most important opposition movement in Turkey.

11. The Kurdish language (Kurdi or Kurmanji) is recognized in Iraq as an official language and one of the two State languages and it is used in instruction at all levels of education. In spite of this example in neighboring Iraq, Kurdish is still not recognized as a language in its own right in Turkey.

12. Dicle was one of six (Orhan Doğan, Leyla Zana, Ahmet Türk, Sırrı Sakık, and Mahmut Alınak) DEP (Party of Democracy) MPs, who in 1991 were taken from Turkish Parliament, arrested, and sentenced to 15 years in prison. Leyla Zana was the first Kurdish woman to win a seat in the Turkish Parliament in 1991. Her decision to give the Parliamentary Oath in Kurdish led to immediate calls for her arrest. This was the first time Kurdish had been spoken in the Turkish Parliament. But speaking Kurdish in a public space was a criminal offense and she was sentenced to 15 years in prison.

13. Refer to http://www.todayszaman.com/news-185633-10-year-old-faces-probe-for-teaching-kurdish-to-youngsters.html.

14. *Elle* magazine coverage at http://www.elle.fr/elle/Societe/Les-enquetes/Les-femmes-de-la-semaine-09-10-2009/Medya-Ormek/%28gid%29/1000728.

REFERENCES

Anderson, Benedict R. (1991). *Imagined communities: Reflections of the origin and spread of nationalism.* London, UK: Verso.

Bauman, Zygmunt. (1989). *Modernity and the holocaust.* Ithaca, NY: Cornell University Press.

Beşikçi, İsmail. (1990). *Devletlerarası sömürge Kürdistan (Kurdistan, an international colony).* Istanbul, TR: Alan.

Burnam, M. A., Telles, C. A., Karno, M., Hough, R. L., & Escobar, J. I. (1987). Measurement of acculturation in a community population of Mexican Americans. *Hispanic Journal of Behavioral Sciences, 9*(2), 105–130.

Can, Erdem. (2010, December 11). (Kürtçe) Savaşma (Türkçe) Konuş (Don't fight in Kurdish, talk

Turkish). *ANF Ajansa Nûçeyan a Firatê [News Agency]*. Retrieved from http://firatnews.org/index.php?rupel=nuce&nuceID=37267.

Chatterjee, P. (1986). *Nationalist thought and the colonial world: A derivative discourse*. London, UK: Zed.

Destroying ethnic identity: The Kurds of Turkey. (1990, September). *Helsinki Watch Report*. New York, NY: Human Rights Watch.

Durkheim, Émile. (1895). *The rules of sociological method* (8th ed.). (Sarah A. Solovay & John M. Mueller, Trans.). Edited by George E. G. Catlin (1938, 1964). Paris, FR: Felix Alcan.

Galtung, Johan. (1969). Violence, peace, and peace research. *Journal of Peace Research*, *6*(3), pp. 167–191.

Fishman, Joshua A. (1977). Language and ethnicity. In Howard Giles (Ed.), *Language, ethnicity and intergroup relations* (pp. 15–57). London, UK: Academic Press.

Fishman, Joshua A. (1988). *Language and ethnicity in minority sociolinguistic perspective*. Clevedon, UK: Multilingual Matters Ltd.

Foucault, M. (1972). *The archaeology of knowledge*. London, UK: Tavistock.

Foucault, M. (1980). *Power/Knowledge: Selected interviews and other writings 1972–1977*. London, UK: Harvester Press.

Gerger, Haluk. (1997, December). Crisis in Turkey. Occasional Paper No. 28. *Middle East Research Associates*.

Gökalp Ziya. (2006). *Türkçülüğün Esasları (Principles of Turkism. The Ministry of Culture)*. Ankara, TR: Elips Kitap.

Göle, Nilüfer. (1996). *The forbidden modern: Civilization and veiling (Critical perspectives on women & gender)*. Ann Arbor: University of Michigan Press.

Grosfoguel, Ramon. (2003). *Colonial subjects: Puerto Rican subjects in a global perspective*. Berkeley: University of California Press.

Hobsbawm, E. J. (1990). *Nations and nationalism since 1780: Programme, myth, reality*. Cambridge, UK: Cambridge University Press.

Horowitz, Irving Louis. (1987). Genocide and the reconstruction of social theory: Observations on the exclusivity of collective death. In Isidor Wallimann & Michael N. Dobkowski (Eds.), *Genocide and the modern age: Etiology and case studies of mass death* (pp. 61–80). Westport, CT: Greenwood Press.

Horowitz, Irving Louis. (1997). *Taking lives: Genocide and state power* (4th ed. expanded and revised). New Brunswick, NJ: Transaction.

Kogacioglu, Dicle. (2004). The tradition effect: Framing honor crimes in Turkey. *Differences: A Journal of Feminist Cultural Studies*, *15*(2), 119–151.

Koivunen, Kristiina. (2002). *The invisible war in north Kurdistan*. (Doctoral Dissertation). Department of Social Policy, University of Helsinki. Helsinki, FI.

Lemkin, Raphaël. (1944). *Axis rule in occupied Europe*. Washington, DC: Carnegie Endowment for International Peace, Division of International Law.

McDowall, D. (1997). *A modern history of the Kurds*. London, UK: I. B. Tauris.

McHoul, A., & Grace, W. (1993). *The Foucault primer: Discourse, power and the subject*. Melbourne, AU: Melbourne University Press.

Prakash, Gyan. (1999). *Another reason: Science and imagination of modern India*. Princeton, NJ: Princeton University Press.

Rénan, Ernest. (1997). *Qu'est-ce qu'une nation*. Paris, FR: Mille et une nuits.

Right to Life. (2009, Oct. 1). *Bianet* [Independent Communications network]. Retrieved from http://bianet.org/bianet/insan-haklari/117378-ceylan-onkol-licede-hedef-gozetilerek-mi-olduruldu.

Simsir, Bilal. (2007). *Kürtçülük, 1787–1923* (Vol. 2). Ankara, TR: Bilgi yayinevi.

Skutnabb-Kangas, Tove. (1996). Language and self-determination. In Donald Clark & Robert Williamson (Eds.), *Self-determination: International perspectives* (pp. 124–140). London, UK: Macmillan Press.

Skutnabb-Kangas, Tove. (2000a, May 26–27). *Global diversity or not: The role of linguistic human rights in education*. A paper presented at the 25th anniversary of the Seminar on Languages and Education. University of Barcelona, Institute of Educational Sciences, Barcelona, Spain.

Skutnabb-Kangas, Tove. (2000b). *Linguistic genocide in education or worldwide diversity and human rights?*. Mahwah, NJ: Lawrence Erlbaum.

Skutnabb-Kangas, T., & Phillipson, R. (1994). Linguistic human rights, past and present. In Tove Skutnabb-Kangas & Robert Phillipson (Eds., in collaboration with Mart Rannut),

Linguistic human rights. Overcoming linguistic discrimination (pp. 71–110). Berlin, DE: Mouton de Gruyter.

Skutnabb-Kangas, T., & Toukomaa, P. (1976). *Teaching migrant children's mother tongue and learning the language of the host country in the context of the socio-cultural situation of the migrant family*. Research Report 15/1976. University of Tampere, Department of Sociology and Social Psychology, Tampere, Finland.

Tollefson, J. (1991). *Planning language, planning inequality: Language policy in the community*. London, UK: Longman.

Turkey: New restrictive anti-terror law. (1991, June 10). *Helsinki Watch Report*. New York, NY: Human Rights Watch.

van Bruinessen, Martin. (1994). Genocide in Kurdistan? The suppression of the Dersim rebellion in Turkey (1937–1938) and the chemical war against the Iraqi Kurds (1988). In George J. Andreopoulos (Ed.), *Conceptual and historical dimensions of genocide* (pp. 141–170). Philadelphia: University of Pennsylvania Press.

White, Paul. (2000). *Primitive rebels or revolutionary modernizers?: The Kurdish national movement in Turkey*. London, UK: Zed Books.

16

CONTESTED IDENTITY

Transgendered People in Malaysia

CAESAR DEALWIS, MAYA KHEMLANI DAVID,
AND FRANCISCO PERLAS DUMANIG

INTRODUCTION

The nation-state of Malaysia comprises a number of geographical entities, including 11 states of the former Federation of Malaya in the peninsula of Malaya, referred to as Peninsular Malaysia or West Malaysia, and the states of Sabah and Sarawak, which are referred to as East Malaysia (Nair-Venugopal, 2000). Land borders are shared with Thailand, Indonesia, and Brunei; maritime borders are shared with Singapore, Indonesia, Vietnam, and the Philippines. Under the Constitution, the official religion is Islam but other religions such as Buddhism, Christianity, and Hinduism are also practiced in the country.

Malaysia is a multiracial, multiethnic, and multilingual nation of 28.2 million people. According to the Sarawak Department of Statistics (2010), the population is made up of Malays (65%), Chinese (23%), Indians (7%), and a variety of smaller ethnic groups, who make up the remaining balance of 5%. These groups are not homogenous and subethnic groups exist (David, 2001). There are 140 languages and dialects spoken in Malaysia but the national and official language is Bahasa Malaysia or Malay, which is used in all official domains of communication. However, the status of English is listed as "an important second language" (New Education Policy, 1971). Varieties of Malay are used in different regions. For instance, the Sarawak Malay and Sabah Malay dialects are widely used by non-Malays in interethnic communication in the Borneo states of Sarawak and Sabah, respectively.

The *Maknyah* of Malaysia

In Malaysia, transgendered people are often referred to in Malay as *pondan, bapok, or maknyah*, all of which are negative terms. Other countries have their own local terms for transgender communities, for example, they are known as *hijras* in India, *kathoeys* in Thailand, *warias* in Indonesia, and *occult* in Myanmar (Veloso, 2000, p. 513). In Malaysia, the term *maknyah* refers only to men who present themselves in society as women—not to women who present themselves as men. According to Sulastri

Ariffin (2011) in *Star*, a Malaysian newspaper, there are 10,000 *maknyahs* in Malaysia but this figure only includes those who are registered with the only *maknyah* association that is approved by the government, namely the *Persatuan Maknyah Wilayah*. Many of these men are employed in the private and public sectors on the condition that they wear male attire and observe male practices in the workplace. Although there are *maknyahs* of all races in Malaysia, the Malay *maknyahs* are more noticeable largely because they are often seen in groups cross-dressing in public places, often in areas where large crowds make it difficult for the authorities to recognize them.

Increasing Islamization and *Maknyah's* Identity

The public perception of *maknyah* has been aggravated by the Islamization of the country. Islam is the official religion in Malaysia as enshrined in the Federal Constitution (Government of Malaysia, 1971). In 1983, the Conference of Rulers in Malaysia decided that a *fatwa* (legal pronouncement in Islam) prohibiting sex-change operations should be imposed on all Muslims, with the exception of the *khunsa,* or hermaphrodites. In addition, Islam forbids males from behaving like females in terms of cross-dressing, wearing makeup, injecting hormones to enlarge their breasts, and undergoing sex-change operations. Thus, the *maknyah* are considered to be in violation of the tenets of Islam, and consequently are nonentities in Malaysian Muslim society. They can be charged under the Syariah Court for this offense.

The impact of Islam on the *maknyah* is inescapable. According to Teh (2007, pp. 101–114) even though two-thirds of his respondents in Malaysia said they accept their penis, it is also true that 78 % said they would have a sex-change operation if their religion permitted them to do so. Many of the Muslim *maknyah* in Teh's study had promised their parents (especially their mothers who had accepted them as *maknyah*), that

they would not have the sex-change operation done. They made this promise because a sex-change operation would pose a problem in terms of Muslim burial rites. For example, the Muslim burial rules state that only a woman can bathe the body of another woman (which does not include *maknyah*, even if they have undergone a sex-change operation). Yet *maknyah*, who have undergone a sex-change operation, also cannot be bathed by a man. Some *maknyah* even believe that their souls will float aimlessly when they die if they undergo sex-change operations as their bodies are not what God had originally given to them. Their beliefs are reinforced by the religious edicts of the Islamic authorities in Malaysia.

In the face of the increasing Islamization of the country, the media is quick to report the arrests and penalties imposed on the *maknyah*. The *Star* newspaper on April 22, 2010 reported that four *maknyah* were given a one-week jail sentence by a Malaysian Islamic court for dressing as women. Lokman Nazri in *New Straits Times* newspaper dated May 12, 2008, reported that Islamic officials detained 16 maknyah who were competing in the "Miss Universe Asia 2008" contest at a beach resort hotel. This occurred in the northeastern state of Kelantan, which is ruled by a fundamentalist Islamic party. Most of the *maknyah* who took part in the pageant were from professional backgrounds and included teachers and bank staff. Action was taken against them for dressing and acting as women under Section 7 of the Kelantan Syariah Offences dated 1985. They were fined up to RM1,000 (RM–Ringgit Malaysia, the official currency) and jailed for six months (*New Straits Times*, May 12, 2008).

AIM AND THEORETICAL FRAMEWORK

The goal of this study is to describe how the Malay *maknyah* community deals with the negative perceptions of them by the larger society and with their marginalization. How do they contest this negatively constructed identity that is imposed on them by the larger society? This study is anchored on the Self-Categorization Theory (SCT), which asserts that identity is constructed or formed through the process of self-categorization. SCT aims to describe and explain the specific nature of relationships between the self, social norms, and the social context (Stets & Burke, 2000). The theory originated from Social Identity Theory (SIT), which explains that social identity refers to a person's understanding of the group or social category where he or she belongs (Stets & Burke, 2000). It also postulates that individuals can categorize themselves as group members and consequently they act similarly with other members with a common identity, group orientation, and behavior (Turner, 1991, p. 155; Turner & Onorato, 1999). This means that social influence contributes to the process of self-categorization because the way that individuals categorize themselves is based on their social and group membership. According to Turner and Onorato (1999, p. 20), the process of self-categorization results in self-stereotyping. In self-categorization, an individual's identity is accentuated by emphasizing the self and group differences. This is why people of the same group affiliation are able to specifically identify who they are and how they differ from other members.

An individual's social and personal identities represent various levels of self-categorization in which the personal identity is directly dependent on one's social identity (Turner & Onorato, 1999; Mummendey & Otten, 2002). This means that the personal level of self-categorization occurs by emphasizing intragroup similarities and differences. Consequently, through the common group orientations, personal and individual differences are achieved and evaluated. Similarly, social identity is also influenced by the personal and individual distinctiveness because they are the product of various intergroup and interpersonal differences (Turner & Oakes, 1989).

At the social level, self-categorization accentuates the similarities and differences within the in-group as well as the out-group. As a result, the social group comparison may lead to stereotyping of the out-group by the in-group and vice versa. When social identity becomes more apparent

than that of personal identity, this process in known as depersonalization of the self. Depersonalization is described as perceiving oneself more as the representative of a social category and less as a unique personality defined by one's personal differences from other in-group members (Turner & Oakes, 1989, p. 245). Consequently, self-categorization of the social self enhances group behavior due to the commonalities of their collective self-concept, which is transformed into collective self-interests (Mummendey & Otten, 2002; Turner & Onorato, 1999; Turner, 1991). In general, self-categorization is believed to provide the primary source for people's social orientation toward others.

This study adopts self-categorization theory to examine how *maknyahs* in Malaysia categorize themselves both individually and as a group. Being perceived by the society as a marginalized group, the *maknyahs* construct their identity to contest peoples' negative perceptions of who they are. Consequently, this study also examines the mismatches of identity between gender and behavior and given the context of the applicability of Islamic law how this has affected both *maknyahs'* feelings and those of their families. In addition, this study investigates the new language variety created and used by the *maknyahs* to construct their identity. In particular, we are interested in a special language, the *Bahasa Seteng* or *Bahasa Setengah* (half language), which *maknyah* have developed. The language has been created by using the first syllables in a word to form an utterance with the intent that the speech cannot be understood by outsiders. In a country with 140 languages and dialects, the creation of *Bahasa Seteng* or *Bahasa Setengah* gives the *maknyah* a linguistic identity of their own.

METHODOLOGY

With the aim of studying how the community contests the identity imposed on them by others, we interviewed a total of 57 *maknyahs* in Malaysia. They are all Malay Muslims and

23 were from Sarawak, 10 from Sabah, and 24 from West Malaysia. Their names and contacts were made available to us by a 20-year-old *maknyah* named Fasha Nadera (a pseudonym), who is an undergraduate in Sarawak (throughout this chapter, pseudonyms or nicknames are used to identify the interviewees). Fasha introduced other people to us who are his friends on Facebook. Through Skype (video calling) and with the assistance of Fasha, open-ended interviews were conducted over a period of three months. In addition to interviews, we recorded *maknyah* conversations to analyze how the *maknyah* in Sarawak have created a new code called *Bahasa Seteng*, which literally means half language. Since, identity is created through language, communities can create networks through a common language and in this way exclude others who have marginalized them. The new language in the community empowers them and is a way of contesting the negative identity imposed on them by the larger society.

Data was obtained from naturally occurring conversations of the *maknyahs,* for example, small talk among friends. Recordings of the conversations were made with the permission of the respondents and the transcripts analyzed. In addition, the data from the interviews were analyzed and categorized into various identity themes as discussed in the findings.

DISCUSSION OF FINDINGS

Malaysian Perception
Toward *Maknyah*

Generally, Malaysian society perceives the *maknyah* community negatively and refers to them as people in *dua alam* (two worlds). According to the *maknyah* we interviewed, they are generally not tolerated or even accepted by the larger community. Among Muslims, *maknyahs* are perceived to be immoral. In general, Malaysians believe that *maknyah* bring shame to their families.

This situation has changed from bad to worse over the years and today the government authorities regard *maknyah* as immoral people who negatively influence the society (Nini, 47 years old).

In light of prevalent negative attitudes, *maknyah* face discrimination and marginalization. Ten of the people we interviewed were university undergraduates and reported that in schools and public universities, the security officials monitored their activities closely. The Islamic Council at the university often monitored their behavior on campus and questioned them frequently about their activities. In addition, they were forced to participate in "rough" activities such as jungle trekking and survival skills in order to make them more masculine.

All of the people we interviewed complained that the Malaysian media, which is largely government controlled, portray them negatively and news stories about them are generally accompanied by photographs aimed at ridiculing them. For instance, Zakaria Manaf, in *Utusan Malaysia*, a Malay daily newspaper reported on March 22, 2009, that the *maknyah* in Malaysia use contraceptive pills to become effeminate. Joan Lee, in the *Star* newpaper (August 19, 2009) in a front page story reported that several *maknyah* were taking contraceptive pills as they heard that it would "give them breasts, softer skin, and a feminine voice." The article also said that "They are willing to carry out 'medical experiments' and even risked their health just to realize their dreams of becoming women." Malaysian-made movies also portray the *maknyah* negatively. For instance, the latest movie released in June of 2011, *Dua Alam* (Two Worlds) discriminated against the *maknyah*. In our interview Fizzy, discussing the movie says:

> Many *maknyah* were not happy with the storyline in *Dua Alam*. They said the film looked down on the *maknyah*. This is because the way they are depicted in the film is as if they are the garbage of society (Fizzy, 32 years old).

The degraded status of the *maknyah*, as earlier stated, is largely due to the increasing Islamization in Malaysia. In the late 1960s, there was a resurgence of Islam in the country and groups such as Dakwah, Darul Arqam, and Angkatan Belia Islam Malaysia were formed. These are extreme Islamic groups whose members are Muslim Malays. Sixteen people in this study complained that many of the officials from these groups constantly harass them in ways that have affected their livelihood. This is in strong contrast to the situation in the colonial days where the *maknyah* had a better quality of life (Teh, 2002, p. 147). The people we interviewed, who are all Muslims, have a hard time convincing the religious authorities that they are decent people who need to earn a living. In this study, Neza, said:

> They (The Islamic officials) are trying to play God. This has affected my customers who come here for my massaging business. I'm trained in foot reflexology and I need to earn a living. These raids by the officials have cost me and my coworkers who are also *maknyah* dearly (Neza, 34 years old).

Six of the people we interviewed said that they were questioned by officers from the Jabatan Agama Islam Sabah (JAIS–Sabah State Islamic Department) for merely waiting at bus stops and taxi stands. They were even accused of indulging in immoral activities and waiting for male clients. Interviewees explained they always avoided contact with Islamic religious officials and those looking like them because of the fear of being arrested for behaving effeminately. If officials catch *maknyah*, they often send them to boot camps in order to toughen them up. Twelve of the people in this study have had the experience of being sent to various boot camps.

Generally all the interviewees said that they were born effeminate and feel like women trapped in the bodies of men. They would not change just because they have been subjected to rough and tough activities. Suzieana summarized this view:

> I was effeminate as a child. I would dress in my mother's clothes, wear a bra and stuff it with sponges and put on makeup. But I was also *lasak* (tough). As I played football, swam in the river, climbed trees and was like any other child my age. Those activities didn't change me at all. I still feel like a woman inside (Suzieana, 21 years old).

Data from the interviews reveal that the religious nonacceptance and stigmatization of the *maknyah* has increased discrimination against them. The *fatwa* that was decreed by the Conference of Rulers in 1983 changed society's perceptions toward the *maknyah* from bad to worse. Muslim *maknyah*, except for *khunsas* (hermaphrodites), are banned from having sex-change operations. Muslim *maknyah* who violate these laws are considered violators of Islamic teachings, and regarded as more immoral than those who do not undergo a sex-change.

CONTESTING THE NEGATIVE *MAKNYAH* IDENTITY

Despite intense marginalization, we found in our interviews that *maknyahs* do not hide from the general public. As long as they wear masculine clothing, they know that they will not get arrested. However, if they were to wear feminine clothing, they could be arrested for cross-dressing. Thus, they are subject to arrest if they cross-dress when appearing in entertainment outlets or committing other acts the government considers illegal. Although the 57 *maknyahs* do not have any barriers restricting them from interacting with others, society at large shuns them. Consequently, they actively try to construct an identity that might possibly alter public perceptions of them. Such identity construction manifests itself in the workplace, at home, and in online social networking.

Identity in the Workplace

In interviews, all 57 *maknyah* talked about feeling feminine and choosing to be feminine. They realized that they were different from their male siblings and cousins at a young age. Although they wear male attire as adults, all of them have given themselves female names and have female mannerisms. *Maknyahs* are expected to dress as males in the workplace and their feminine behavior is viewed by coworkers as not projecting a healthy image. Therefore, they are still marginalized because of their mannerisms. Although everyone had been hurt by male coworkers who tease them insensitively at the workplace for behaving femininely, they talked about having learned to accept this.

Importantly, maknyahs constructed their identities and communities through female mannerisms, ways of speaking, and also through their female names. This transgender construction is their way of asserting their identity despite the negative attitudes of employers and other employees about them. Such construction and categorization of the social self enhances group behavior due to the commonalities of their collective self-concept, which is transformed into collective self-interests (Mummendey & Otten, 2002; Turner & Onorato, 1999; Turner, 1991).

The *maknyah* we interviewed held the view that many of them are talented individuals who are warm, loving human beings, and respectful toward others. They were determined to show the larger society that they can succeed and have much to contribute to society. Rozina, 33 years old, said: "We are not *manusia dua alam* (people in two worlds) but blessed by having the best of both worlds." They believe that society should allow them to legally form a *Maknyah* association so that they can contribute more and handle their own problems by supporting each other. Tiara said:

> Forming our own association does not mean that we will organise immoral activities. Society has to change. We can contribute tremendously in politics, social and business, if we could have a strong association of our own. It's time to realize that we are different from males and females. We are not a curse that should be abused and rejected by society. We have human rights too. If you allow us to vote, that means we are equal citizens and should be

treated as such. Organizing beauty pageants, becoming makeup artists are things which people associate with *maknyah*. Nowadays, educated *maknyah* own beauty parlors, cosmetic companies, and restaurants (Tiara, 24 years old).

At the social level, self-categorization accentuates the similarities and differences within the in-group as well as the out-group. The *maknyahs* strive to be experts in their own fields and feel morally encouraged when one of them becomes famous and is accepted by society. Consequently, when one with the same gender identity succeeds, they are proud about the recognition given to people like them who excel in various fields.

Identity in the Home Domain

All the interviewees said that they feel more loved by their mothers than by their fathers and male siblings, who often abused them verbally and physically when they were younger. It is evident from our interviews that the *maknyahs'* adherence to a feminine identity is largely supported by their mothers. Their mothers did not discourage them from doing household chores and knew that they were more sensitive than their male siblings. Such support from a young age empowers them to exhibit their identity in society.

Zeena, 21 years old, said, "My *maknyah* friends often joked by saying that our mothers are often supportive of us because we help them to do the housework; they show more love and care than the males in the family." In sharp contrast, when talking about the men in her family, Phila said:

> When I was small, my father and brothers kicked and hit me a lot. They were embarrassed of me because I was not like them. I did not play football with the other boys. My brothers were only loud, but were not good in their studies. My father was a laborer, a bully . . . (Phila, 26 years old).

According to Islam, as it is being practiced in Malaysia, Muslim men are expected to marry and often the *maknyahs* will be matched with women arranged by their mothers. Many of them lead ordinary heterosexual family lives and have children, although some marriages culminate in divorce largely due to the unrealistic expectations by the wives about being able to change their spouses. Lizzie, 16 years old, said:

> My eldest brother is a *maknyah* like me and he got married. My mother matched him with one of the village girls. She is not so educated but my brother is a dentist. You see . . . she always asks him to wear this shirt, that shirt, smoke cigarettes, go for body-building and many other stupid things which she thinks men do. She does not allow him to cook and cooking is his passion. After five years, they divorced and he keeps the 2 children. She is now happier, I guess, as she is married to an Indonesian construction worker with bigger biceps.

Identity in School and University

Social influence contributes significantly to the process of self-categorization because the way that individuals categorize themselves is based on their social and group membership. In self-categorization, individuals accentuate their own identities by emphasizing the self and group differences. For example, most of the younger *maknyahs* whom we interviewed carry mini lipsticks, combs, skin lotion, tissues, and other cosmetics in their bags. They smoked light cigarettes and considered this as being modern and feminine. However, they do not consume alcohol because they are Muslims.

Most of the younger *maknyahs* wanted to have breasts like women and they frequently adjusted and readjusted their blouses to make it appear as if they had them. Further, they reported that in their sexual fantasies, they imagine themselves as women and they all wanted to have steady male companions. Seven people we interviewed were university undergraduates who enjoyed the fine arts, dance, and drama and participated in those type of activities regularly on campus. All the interviewees said that they feel themselves becoming more feminine each day as they get support from

other *maknyah* through social media, specifically Facebook. They want society to accept them as human beings with brains, talents, and skills and to stop ridiculing and denigrating them. Mohniza said:

> People always see us as sex maniacs. Well, perhaps some are but not me, and not many of my *maknyah* friends. Some girls feel disgusted when I buy blouses in the ladies department. Something is terribly wrong with those silly girls. It's my money. Others feel amused that I should have a female name. So what, I have the right to be who I want to be. I'm not disturbing anybody. I'm still using the name which my parents gave me for official matters. It's against the law to change my name. Otherwise, I would rather be called Liza on my birth certificate (Mohniza, 23 years old).

Generally, as *maknyah* students their freedom is constrained. Even their rooms in the university hostel are often invaded by guards to ensure that they have not brought sex toys to the campus. The university is a place for them to study but the authorities do not tolerate *maknyahs* who do not conform to the university's expected social behavior and dress code. At the workplace too, there are rules and guidelines for employees to adhere to in terms of dress code and image. During job interviews at graduation time, potential employers expect the *maknyahs* to dress and behave like other men.

Identity in an Online Social Network

Maknyahs in Malaysia are not large in number and forming an official group remains impossible due to religious constraints. However, they have managed to silently organize a group for themselves without it being officially known or registered. With the emergence of technology and the Internet, they are able to communicate with one another frequently through Facebook and other social networking sites. Social media enables them to make new *maknyah* friends and to feel that they are not facing these difficult circumstances alone.

In addition, social media have helped to establish a rapport with a larger network of a in-closet *maknyah*, that is people with issues similar to those of the *maknyah* but who hide their identity. Through online networks *maknyah* have developed the strength to ask for recognition by society and to petition for equal rights. However, the people we talked with complained that some of the websites created by the *maknyahs* were not accessible at the university due to university policy, which denied access to such websites to its students and staff. The Islamic Council or JAIS (Jabatan Agama Islam) religiously monitors all such on-line activities and reports them to the relevant authorities. Mamar says:

> I was once questioned by the security guard in campus when he saw me reading something from the *maknyah* association website. He was rude and reported me to one of the lecturers. I know I dress like a boy with effeminate qualities but that does not mean I cannot read or talk about the association. What's wrong? They think they can control our existence (Mamar, 29 years old).

Maknyah's Linguistic Identity

Our research shows that the *maknyahs* have created a language that they use to identify themselves as unique and also as a linguistic tool to communicate privately. Out of the 57 respondents, 23 were from Sarawak in East Malaysia, where Sarawak Malay is widely used for communication. When compared to other dialects and languages in Sarawak, Sarawak Malay has the most number of speakers and is spoken widely without feelings of embarrassment in informal domains (Johari, 1988, p. 45). Generally, Malay *maknyah* in Malaysia speak Bahasa Malaysia or the official language. However, we found that the *maknyah* in Sarawak can be identified through a particular language that they alone speak. The *maknyah* created *Bahasa Seteng* or *Bahasa Setengah* (half language), which gives the *maknyah* in Sarawak a linguistic identity of their own. *Bahasa Seteng* is spoken by taking the first syllable in a word to

form an utterance and is spoken very rapidly. Using their own language helps them to keep their secrets and to talk openly—they feel confident that outsiders cannot understand them when they use *Bahasa Seteng*. Consequently, they feel free to talk in public about personal matters, sex, men and to just generally gossip. The use of their own language gives them the freedom to express themselves. They are able to openly, yet privately, discuss issues, subjects, and feelings. Having a language that is understood only by the group members enhances the *maknyah's* power and authority to discuss various issues and topics in public. The sentences in Table 1 were frequently used and are illustrations of their talk. Table 16.1 shows some examples of *Bahasa Seteng*.

Bahasa Seteng is used to gossip. Since it is only their own group who can understand the language, this gives the *maknyah* the freedom to express their disapproval of those who perceive them negatively. They are able to express their grievances toward others—particularly those who really do not like them (see Extract 1).

Extract 1

B: **Ben kam nang Nis** ia **ju**, tang **nge gil** ngan **muk** nya nok **ked muk pan** ia. **Ab lak** nak di **god n**ya. **Muk ibl** ia. **B kam** pun **ma** nya **ju**.

I hate to see Nisah, she is showing off and her face is very ugly. She wants to attract all the boys. She has an evil face. Even my boyfriend is one of her targets.

C: **Em jal ked** ia. Mak nya **sunl ju** bah, apa **ag** nya. Sik **lam**a **ag bas** nya **kel**.

For a slut like her, it is common. Her mother is a slut, too and she'll be worse. Soon she'll be stale.

Key: Times New Roman Bold–Bahasa Seteng; Times New Roman–Sarawak

Table 16.1   Bahasa Seteng

Sarawak Malay	Bahasa Seteng	English
Suka kamek nangar rambut nya. *(Transcription 5)*	Suk kam nang ram nya.	I like to see his/her hair.
Kacak muka orang laki ya. *(Transcription 1)*	Kac muk or lak ya eh.	The boy is handsome.
Kamek rasa nak makan nasik. *(Transcription 7)*	Kam ras nak mak nas.	I feel like eating rice.
Bencik aku diat perempuan ya!*(Transcription 3)*	Benc ak di perem ya!	I hate to see that woman!
Jom, mencuci mata dekat pasar! *(Transcription 2)*	Jom, mencuc mat dek pas!	Come, let's go to town!
Nak pergi siney kitak orang ya? Sik embak kamek kah?*(Transcription 9)*	Nak per sin kit or ya? Sik emb kam kah?	Where are you guys going? Not bringing us along?
Sik ada kerja lain kah? Nak ngaco orang jak! *(Transcription 8)*	Sik ad kej lai kah? Nak mengac or jak!	Don't you have anything else to do? You just like to disturb!
Apa diat-diat? Ada utangkah?*(Transcription 13)*	Ap di-di? Ad ut kah?	What are you looking at? Do I owe you anything?
Berbau sekali jak mulut orang laki ya eh! *(Transcription 15)*	Bebau sekal jak mul or lak ya eh!	That man has a smelly mouth!
Kau ku tampa kelak! Kurang ajar!*(Transcription 11)*	Ko ku tam ku lak! Kur aj!	I'll slap you for being rude!

According to the interviewees, gossip is one way the *maknyahs* release their anger about their marginalization by society. One way of expressing their anger is to talk about other people and make fun of them (see Extract 2).

Extract 2

G: **Mem**ang **kam**ek maok ny**akit hat**i nya. **Buk**an **mai**n **ag**ik. **Mul**utnya ia sik **pan**de ny**im**an **rah**sia. **Kel**ak aku **gas**ak nya

I want to hurt him this time. He is too much. His mouth is bad and can't keep secrets. I'll do it this time.

H: **Sukatipompun. Ga**sak **aj**ak kelak **takgin** maok **molah ag**ik.

It's up to you. Just hurt him, otherwise he'll do again.

Key: Times New Roman Bold–Bahasa Seteng; Times New Roman–Sarawak

Creating an argument can be intimidating. However for *maknyahs,* when they argue with one another, the use of their own language minimizes the seriousness of the talk. According to the interviewees, even if they make derogatory statements the use of the *maknyah* language reduces the intensity of the impact.

The use of their own language allows them to have control of their own feelings and expressions (see Extract 3).

Extract 3

D: **Make bar**ang **kam**ek sik **beri ba**lit. **Mu**ka **jer**wat sik ada **laki ma**ok ko.

You used my things without returning. With your kind of pimples on your face, boys won't get attracted to you.

E: **Mu**ka **puc**at **ceri**dak ko ia, **ma**ke **ce**lak pun sik **pan**de nak **ngan**ok **ur**ang.

You're scolding me but you don't realize that you have a garbage face and still unable to wear a lipstick.

Key: Times New Roman Bold–Bahasa Seteng; Times New Roman–Sarawak Malay

---

As mentioned, *maknyahs* use Bahasa Seteng because it makes them feel freer when they are in public and want to talk about personal matters, sex, men, and generally just to gossip. However, when they are talking about other matters such as political situations, work, and school, they would use the Sarawak Malay dialect.

CONCLUSION

This study investigates how the *maknyahs* in Malaysia manage their identity. From the perspective of Malaysian society, they do not fit into the dichotomous gender system because of their gender display. For Muslims in Malaysia, the presence of transgender people violates the teachings of the Holy Quran. Muslims believe that in the past, Prophet Mohammed tried to help them by guiding them onto the right path, but the *Quran* emphatically states that men should not dress as women. Thus, it is the duty of the Islamic religious associations to monitor and arrest men who cross-dress. Their behavior is considered unlawful and is punishable under Syariah Law. The *maknyah* community contests this marginalization in a number of ways. Through social online networks, they have been able to create a network of relationships with fellow *maknyahs*. Maintaining female names and mannerisms while wearing male attire is another strategy. Asserting their capability and talent and ability to earn a livelihood in specific professions where they are respected for their expertise and talent is yet another strategy. The community has even created a language of their own that has many functions and which helps them strengthen their solidarity. Finally, obtaining a tertiary education often makes the *maknyah* more acceptable to family members and society. In families, where the other siblings are less educated, the *maknyahs'* parents turn to them to support them in their old age. Consequently, once parents understand the academic (and economic) potential of their *maknyah* children, they quite often accept them and stop their other children from making fun of their *maknyah* siblings. Nevertheless, it appears that with increasing Islamization in the country, the *maknyah* must continue to assert the value of their identity and attempt to contest and reconstruct the identity imposed on them by the larger society.

REFERENCES

David, Maya. (2001). *The Sindhis of Malaysia: A sociolinguistic account.* London, UK: Asean.

Johari, Madzhi. (1988). *Fonologi dialek Melayu Kuching.* Kuala Lumpur, MY: Dewan Bahasa dan Pustaka.

Lee, Joan. (2009, August 19). Prejudice in modern society. *Star* [Newspaper]. Kuala Lumpur, MY, p. 12.

Mummendey, Amélie, & Otten, Sabine. (2002). Theorien intergruppalen Verhaltens. In D. Frey & M. Irle (Eds.), *Theorien der Sozialpsychologie, Band II* (pp. 95–199). Bern, CH: Hans Huber.

Nair-Venugopal, S. (2000). *Language choice and communication in Malaysian business.* Bangi, MY: University Kebangsaan Press.

Nazri, Lokman. (2008, May 12). "Maknyah arrested in raid." *New Straits Times* newspaper. Kuala Lumpur, MY, p. 7.

New Education Policy. (1971). *Federal Constitution of Malaysia.* Kuala Lumpur, MY: National Printing.

Sacks, Harvey. (1995). *Lectures in conversation.* Oxford, UK: Blackwell.

Sarawak Department of Statistics. (2010). *Department of Statistics, Malaysia.* Kuching, MY: Lee Ming Press.

Stets, Jan, & Burke, Peter. (2000). Identity theory and social identity theory. *Social Psychology Quarterly, 63,* 224–237.

Sulastri Ariffin. (2011, April 27). Born this way. *Star* [Newspaper] p. 21.

Teh, Y. K. (2002). *The mak nyahs: Male to female transsexuals in Malaysia.* Singapore: Eastern Universities Press.

Teh, Y. K. (2007). Male to female transsexuals (mak nyah) in Malaysia. In K. L Puah (Ed.), *Malaysia public policy and marginalized groups.* Kuala Lumpur, MY: Ninlin Press.

Turner, John. (1991). *Social influence.* Buckingham, UK: Open University Press.

Turner, John, & Oakes, Penelope. (1989). Self-categorization and social influence. In P. B. Paulus (Ed.), *The psychology of group influence* (2nd ed.) (pp 233–275). Hillsdale, NJ: Erlbaum.

Turner, John, & Onorato, Rina. (1999). Social identity, personality and the self-concept: A self-categorization perspective. In T. R. Tyler, R. Kramer, & O. John (Eds.), *The psychology of the social self* (pp. 11–46). Mahwah, NJ: Lawrence Erlbaum.

Veloso, Sandra. (2000). Mak nyah community in Kuching. In *Borneo 2000, Printed Proceedings of the Sixth Biennial Borneo Research Conference* (Malaysia: Connections, 2000).

Zakaria, Manaf. (2009, March 22). Siapakah yang patut dipersalahkan? (Who's to be blamed?). *Utusan Malaysia* [Newspaper], p. 15.

SECTION 5

NATION

17

LANGUAGE AND IDENTITY

Turkish Soap Operas and Language Policy in the Bulgarian Mediascape

NADEZHDA GEORGIEVA-STANKOVA

"What are these Turkish soaps and news in Turkish on the national television? Is there another country, where a foreign language is being imposed to such an extent? What Bulgarians are we, if we don't remember our history?"

(A chat-room participant)

"I watched Binbir Gece. People keep talking about it, so I decided to see why they are so impressed. I liked it. It has brought me back to my childhood years, when old people were of this kind: good, humane, and wise. There were good manners of addressing family members, using 'kako' (elder sister), 'batko' (elder brother), aunt and uncle. People showed respect for each other in the streets and shops. Perhaps in the Ottoman empire

Bulgarians and Turks became one people, our customs are almost the same and many of the words in Bulgarian are of Turkish origins."

(A chat-room participant)

INTRODUCTION

Bulgaria's past has been intimately related to that of Turkey—not only because it shares a southeast boundary with Turkey. The two countries also share a common historical and cultural fate that affects contemporary politics, cultural practices, and modes of communication. Bulgaria and Turkey were both part of the Ottoman Empire between the 14th and 19th centuries. Today, in Bulgaria cultural and political elites—each in line with their dominant ideological state nationalism—define this period of Ottoman rule differently. For some, Ottoman rule is recalled as "oppression" and "yoke," while others have attempted to define it as a "Turkish presence" in the Bulgarian lands. This milder definition emerged in the late 1980s. Such ideological debates continue both in Bulgarian historiography and in public discourses with competing arguments of either forced Islamization and suffering or more in-depth analysis of strategies of economic adaptability and peaceful ethnic coexistence (Georgieva, 2007, pp. 21–38). Despite the lack of shared agreement on the meaning of this time, what should be acknowledged is that the five centuries of imperial dependence and the subsequent processes of nation-state formation led to significant migrations and mixing of the Bulgarian and Turkish populations. This, in turn, led to greater linguistic and cultural proximity, to border crossings and exchanges of cultural traits, as well as to unique examples of fusions of particular customs and traditions. These are all important facts that remained muted and forgotten by the nationalistic policies that direct hostility toward Turkey and the numerous ethnic Turkish populations in Bulgaria. Skillfully manipulated by Bulgarian politicians waving a nationalistic flag, the image of Turkey and the Turk as the ultimate Other and Bulgaria's "archenemy" is now well established.

In this context, it is then quite surprising that Turkish soap operas broadcast on private Bulgarian television channels have become a booming media phenomenon in the last few years. Their presence has highlighted the contested terrain of national identity, dividing the nation into ardent Turkish soap fans and strong "patriotic" opponents. The Turkish soap bubble, however, has not remained restricted to popular discourse alone. It has also added fuel to the flames of the much heated debate on Bulgarian-Turkish relations, which is primarily associated with the strong presence of the Turkish MRF (Movement for Rights and Freedoms) party in Bulgarian political and economic life. In addition, this debate has contributed to demands to limit the language rights of the Turkish minority in the media, an issue that nationalists demanded and that may be decided by means of a national referendum. Nevertheless, the

fairytale dramas of the modern Cinderellas of Scheherazade in *Binbir Gece (Arabian Nights),*[1] of *Gumus (Pearl)* in the soap opera of the same name, of Lamia in *Dudaktan Kalbe (Melody of the Heart)*, and numerous other Turkish heroines draw audiences from all walks of life with different age, gender, or ethnic profiles and they virtually empty streets at the appointed broadcasting hours. Viewers readily get involved in the fates of the characters, empathizing with the trials and tribulations of the heroines, nostalgically gazing into a world of family customs and values that have been lost in Bulgarian society, and dwelling on mutually shared cultural and linguistic traditions.

The simple and original formula of the Turkish soap-opera scripts, combined with an extremely successful marketing campaign, have turned the genre into a hit phenomenon in the Middle East as well. Notwithstanding, the Turkish soap operas have been strongly criticized in conservative Muslim circles for promoting an extremely liberal version of Islam. It is an irony that while their success in the Arab world derives from modernizing powers and questioning traditions, for Bulgarians, the Turkish soap operas have become synonymous with lost patriarchal customs and traditions. The soap operas remind Bulgarians of life in a pre-modern era with the centrality, warmth, respect, and security of a big extended family, and the simple values of love, honesty, and dignity.

In general, Turkish soap operas present a different picture of Turkish life, culture, language and traditions that contradict viewers' previous knowledge and expectations. The initial curiosity among Bulgarians about the assumed cultural differences between the two nations has helped audiences to realize the extent of both the cultural and linguistic proximity shared by Bulgarians and Turks and the constructed nature of existing nationalistic ideologies. For audiences, Turkish soap operas became the terrain for opening debates on important normative issues within Bulgarian society. For example, the fall of communism denounced certain preexisting collectivist values, which gave rise to a stronger individualism—coupled with growing aggression and anomic processes. Family life was affected by this individualistic mind-set, resulting in a growing number of single-parent households, divorces, and a decline in marriage rates in general. Further, the nature of the relations between parents and children changed. On one hand, the younger generation acquired greater freedom. However, on the other hand, changing relationships between parents and children also have contributed to numerous instances of parental neglect, growing aggression, and underage criminality. Intergenerational relations have additionally been affected. The elderly are now regarded with less care and respect. In some instances they have become major victims of this economic and social transformation. In this context, Turkish soap operas nostalgically remind Bulgarian viewers of something missing—a past way of life that was organized mainly around the family and the small neighborhood. It is a way of life that had stronger communal ties and greater social cohesion.

What does the debate around such a popular media phenomenon tell us about the Bulgarian national identity in this contemporary context? What meanings do audiences create in the process of viewing and communication? How is it possible to transform a centuries-long hostility toward the Turkish "arch-enemy" into the lost image of the *komşu* (neighbor) with all the warmth and emotional coloring implied in both languages, eroding ethnic boundaries, and creating an ever-increasing awareness of shared cultural values and sameness of a particular way of life?

In order to answer such questions, I examine how traditional hostile attitudes toward the Turkish Other are sustained and the ways in which social actors use the terrain of popular culture as a medium for questioning and reconsidering traditional perceptions.

This chapter examines the ways in which language turns into a symbolic battlefield of identity in Bulgaria. It then demonstrates how ethnic boundaries are erected and dismantled by linguistic means. And, finally the chapter traces the important changes in audience attitudes of Turkish soap operas and analyzes their significance.

I begin with discussion of key theoretical premises that concern the role of culture in social transformation. I then establish a close link between nationalism, religion, and linguistic policy in order to analyze the nature of Bulgarian nationalism and the assimilation of ethnic Turks. Finally, by analyzing data from a case study of several soap-opera chat rooms, I conclude by considering the extent and nature of changes in audience attitudes.

THEORETICAL PREMISES

Culture plays a significant role in attitude change and processes of social transformation, helping actors to devise particular action strategies that may lead to important changes in social structure. For Ann Swidler (1986), culture functions like a "toolkit" which provides an important repertoire of instruments for social action. Media culture creates a world in miniature, which although imaginary and fictional, helps viewers to reflect back on their own lives and position in society. This is not an innocent world, but one that consists of different discursive positions established in the process of meaning-making. While engaged in viewing, audiences become equipped with particular resources and the whole gamut of "habits, skills and styles" (Swidler, p. 273) necessary for constructing strategies of action. Such strategies may involve creating a better picture of themselves and reality, their relationship with the Other, and the place they occupy in the contemporary world, if presented on a broader plane.

Through media, audiences get involved in particular signifying practices, further restructuring their reality and making it more meaningful and intelligible. Common symbolic experiences and ritual practices can involve a reevaluation of current social situations and the creation of new forms of social bonds (Swidler, p. 284). More particularly, Turkish soap operas provide viewers with a terrain for contesting nationalistic ideological constructs as well as a terrain for reflecting on important issues regarding national identity, interethnic contacts, family relations, gender, and intergenerational problems. For Zigmunt Bauman (1999, p. 96), culture is exactly this specific form of human praxis, which has an ordering capacity, structuring a chaotic world into meaningful experiences. In this sense, discussions of Turkish soap operas, can be considered a meaningful exercise for people, which helps them and their neighbours to make sense of their particular situation and their place in the global village, as well as to overcome a range of boundaries and distances not only spatially, but also in the normative and moral landscape.

Given that nationally situated media function in a global framework as cultural, ideological, and economic institutions, it is important to analyze how audiences create meanings and strategize actions. Arjun Appadurai's theory of the social imaginary and the five dimensions of the global cultural flow (1996) is a useful theoretical framework for understanding the role of the media. For Appadurai, globalization accelerates the chaotic spread of different resource flows, called *scapes* that function in a disjunctive order (as cited in Featherstone, 1995, p. 118). Appadurai (1996, pp. 33–36) identifies five possible *scapes*, which do not fall into any centre-periphery or multiple-centres and peripheries models. These are *ethnoscapes* (involving flows of people, such as tourists, migrants and refugees), *technoscapes* (flows of technology produced on national and multinational level), *financescapes* (flows of money in the stock exchange and the currency markets), *mediascapes* (flows of media-produced images and information), and *ideoscapes* (flows of Western Enlightenment ideas of democracy, freedom, welfare, etc.).

Such flows of images, people, finance, and ideas exist at a global level and nation-states can (to a varying degree) only direct or exert control on them. What is more, the nation-states are seen as forced to stay open by consumerism, new media technology, and increased mobility (Featherstone, 1995, p. 305). By such means,

global flows create new imaginaries and organize people into other possible communities, that exist both above and below the level of nationhood. The Turkish soap opera phenomenon is a good illustration of the way such flows or *scapes* manage to elude the control of national ideologies and create new imagined communities. The *mediascape* that the soap operas represent plays a significant role in negotiating local and global identities. It provides the "building blocks" of certain "imagined worlds," capable of connecting people in different historical and geographical settings (Appadurai, 2006, p. 589). The work of imagination, in this sense, is considered of primary significance, as a proper fuel for action (Appadurai, 1996, p. 7). In the words of Arjun Appadurai:

> It is the imagination in its collective forms that creates ideas of neighbourhood and nationhood, of moral economies and unjust rule, of higher wages and foreign labour prospects. The imagination is today a staging ground for action and not only for escape (1996, p. 7).

New global *media-, finance-, techno-, ethno-,* and *ideoscapes* enter into a complex relationship with traditional national ideologies. The strategies applied by existing nationalistic discourses can be seen as imagining the world in terms of binary oppositions, of dividing it into Self/Same vs. Other, of suppressing difference, imposing sameness and drawing strict boundaries between "we" and "they" groups. Such differences are presented as natural and biologically given, relying on the primordialities of blood, kinship, language, and religion.

Nationalism invents the image of the Other as necessary for erecting ethnic boundaries and creating bonds of solidarity. The nation, as a product of social imagination, provided new forms of legitimacy through the common values of solidarity and comradeship that concealed existing forms of inequality (Anderson, 1983, pp. 5–7). The process of imagining community was facilitated by the combination of capitalism and print technology (Anderson, 1983). Today, mass media and the culture industries can be seen as playing a more ambivalent role in promoting difference and imposing sameness as part of more complicated multidirectional global flows. Moreover, new *media-, finance-,* and *ideoscapes* can be seen as affecting or even challenging the homogenizing strategies of the nation-state. If in the modern era culture could be "managed" or 'administered' space," the nation-state can no longer impose monopoly over such processes (Bauman, 1999, p. 26). The nation remains an important actor in constructing identities and defining loyalties, but its primacy no longer remains uncontested.

In the history of Bulgarian nationalism, Turkey and the image of the Turk have served to reinforce national loyalties and to organize particular sentiments of "Bulgarianness" and nationhood. Although performing the function of an "ultimate Other," the image of the Turk has remained quite ambivalent, simultaneously representing an omnipresent "internal Other."[2] The latter has provoked even greater anxiety as a threat to the territorial and religious integrity of the country. The "inside-outsider" challenges the imagined homogeneity and clarity of all "we"—"they" distinctions (Bauman, 1999, p. 104).What is more; it challenges the entire logic that nationalist ideology creates. This chapter examines how new media technologies, driven by globalizing processes, have helped to transgress both the image of the Other (represented by the Turk) and the boundaries of the imagined community of Bulgarians. It considers how this transgression ultimately created a national crisis by demolishing the distinctions on which the construction and legitimization of nationhood relied.

BULGARIAN NATIONALISM, MINORITY LANGUAGE POLICY, AND ETHNICITY

The central markers of national identity include a common historical territory, myths and historical memories, mass and public culture, legal rights and responsibilities of all members (Smith, 1991, p. 40). Traditional classifications of "Western" nationalism present legal equality as centrally important while in "Eastern" types of nationalism national culture, vernacular language, customs and traditions can be seen as bearing vital importance. Although we must acknowledge both Western "civic" and Eastern "ethnic" types of nationalism are ideal types—elements of each are contained in any nationalistic form (Smith, 1991, p. 13). In Bulgaria, beginning with the Revival period, it is possible to trace how Bulgarian national elites mobilized language, customs, common origins, traditions, and religion. For example, language and the alphabet have been used as essential elements in nation-building processes. Religion also has helped to sustain Bulgarianness throughout history. For instance, Orthodox Christianity adopted in the 9th century, as a homogenizing element for both Slavs and proto-Bulgarians, also helped to sustain Bulgarian identity later under Ottoman rule. The Orthodox Church was an important factor in preserving historical knowledge, language, and traditions. It is considered to have performed important consolidating and defensive functions for the nation (Stoyanov, 2009, p. 227).

Bulgarian scholar Luchezar Stoyanov (2009, p. 227) argues that the nature of Bulgarian nationalism is predominantly of a compensatory and defensive nature, because it had to defend itself from the aggressive national doctrines of its neighbors. This defensiveness defines Bulgaria's self-contained character, based solely on the Bulgarian ethnic Orthodox element and the exclusion of other ethnic and religious groups (Stoyanov, 2009, p. 227). The emphasis within Bulgaria, on the ethnic and linguistic markers of identity, was the central to nation-building and the "mythological" or "myth-servicing," discourses that accompanied national development (Aretov, 2006, p. 42). According to the author, the "myth-servicing" role of such scholarly discourses, which were present to varying degrees in textbooks, academic publications, and the public sphere was to justify the claims of the nationalistic mythology (Aretov, 2006, p. 42).

Nationalistic policies toward the Turkish minority in Bulgaria illustrate the defensive nature of Bulgarian nationalism, which enforced both cultural and linguistic homogenizing strategies. Starting as early as the 1950s, the government attempted to create a kind of scholarship that aimed to prove the Bulgarian origins of the Muslim population living in Bulgaria, to introduce the Bulgarian language as the language of school instruction in the ethnic Turkish regions, and finally, to assimilate the Turks completely by changing their Turkic-Arabic names to Bulgarian ones. A distinguished scholar of the Ottoman past, Tzvetana Georgieva, concluded that the communist government's main strategy for assimilating ethnic minorities included the invention of historical and linguistic facts, the rewriting of history, and turning science into a political servant (Georgieva, 2009, p. 23).

After 1989 and the fall of communism, Bulgaria adopted a number of constitutional changes, decrees, legislation and European Union policies to acknowledge the rights of ethnic minorities in Bulgaria, including their linguistic rights. Nevertheless, hostile Bulgarian nationalistic discourses against Turkey in the disguise of patriotism have continued to function quite successfully.

THE ECONOMIC MEDIA CONTEXT

Part of the success of Turkish soap operas can be traced to the economic media context that includes the nature of the broadcast channels, their program policies, and the successful marketing of the series as media products. Turkish soap operas broadcast in Bulgaria are the result of the private-media program policies that are held by two national broadcast televisions networks: Murdoch's *bTV* and the former Greek channel, *Nova* TV. After the initial enormous success of *Binbir Gece (Arabian Nights)*, *Gumus (Pearl)*, and *Yaprak Dokumu (Leaf Fall)*, these soaps went on to break all of the ratings records for expensive reality shows, football matches, and New Year's programs ever shown on *Bulgarian National Television (BNT)*, the former television leader. The increased ratings developed serious competition between the two media rivals. A "media war" continued for more than a year, during which Turkish soap operas were used as audience magnets to ensure *bTV's* leading position. The success of the Turkish serials has been unprecedented in terms of ratings, market share, and audiences.[3]

By adjusting programming formats to reflect particular local settings and expectations, such as with soap operas, global media tend to apply "glocal" strategies to draw larger audiences.[4] Turkish soap operas present dramas in a particular narrative structure—and within a particular cultural framework—that is readily accessible to audiences. Turkish soap operas are most popular in countries in the Middle East, the Balkans, and Eastern Europe, which can be explained not only by their geographical proximity, but also by similar cultural and historical experiences. Despite existing cultural similarities, audiences use different decoding or meaning-making strategies. As a consequence, Turkish soap operas have challenged the existing *ideoscapes* in the countries where they are broadcast. At the same time, the different ways that audiences decode media messages has guaranteed the economic success of the Turkish series, especially in wider international markets. For example, *Gumus (Pearl)* was a flop in Turkey, yet it took the Arab world and Bulgaria by storm. Consequently, this media success led to substantial increases in tourism to Turkey by Saudi and other international tourists, ensuring substantial economic gains in times of an economic downturn.

Having met initial success abroad, Turkish soap operas evolved into a big industry. In 2009, they were shown in more than 39 countries in the world, mainly in the Middle East, the Balkans, and Ukraine; they provided a living for more than 150,000 people and brought in profits of half a billion Euros (Suleiman, 2009). Bulgaria—with 29 scheduled programs—has the second largest number of imported Turkish soap operas in the world; it follows Kazakhstan, which imports 42 soap operas and precedes Azerbaijan (23), Macedonia (17), and Greece (8) (*Vesti.bg*, 2011). In 2008 alone, Turkish television channels showed 63 Turkish soap operas that included 150 TV directors (ibid.). Meanwhile, actors who star in the soaps have turned into real media stars, both in terms of popularity and earnings, which can be about to 10,000 Euros per episode (ibid.). Advertisers naturally seem to be satisfied; for an 80-minute prime-time episode, 30 minutes are allocated to commercials, which bring in profits between 170,000 and 450,000 Euros, and provide about 80% of the total TV revenue (ibid.). Advertising sponsorship is also a big source of money for the TV channels, as rates for showing a sponsor's logo at the end of the episode vary between 5,000 and 35,000 Euros (ibid.). This media success is multiplied several times and results in an indirect effect on other businesses, such as tourism, real estate, the music industry, and trade, which is also calibrated (ibid.). However, the pursuit of economic success within the *mediascape* has led to unexpected results in the flow of ideas and ethnic images.

TURKISH SOAP OPERAS AND THEIR POLITICAL IMPLICATIONS

Wherever the soap opera series has been shown, it has provoked political debates. The Islamic world reacted strongly to the new forms of gender, family relations, and values that were introduced by the genre. Islamic political and institutional organizations moved to restrain the media that they believed were contributing to growing divorce rates, increased violence, and declining sexual morals. In addition, despite the series contribution to improved diplomatic relations, cultural exchanges, and tourism between Turkey and other Islamic countries, such as Saudi Arabia, Morocco, and Jordan (Mihova, 2009), there also were waves of indignation and institutional reactions in Turkey in response to the more liberal forms of family and gender relations (Hristova, 2009).[5]

In Bulgaria, debates provoked by the Turkish series became extremely politicized in the context of the approaching Parliamentary Elections in June 2009. Public reactions ran the gamut: from the extreme hostility of traditional nationalistic parties, such as *Ataka*, to media and public discussions registering warming diplomatic, cultural, and economic relations between the two neighboring countries. The Turkish minority party, MRF (MRF is no longer in Parliament) had a strong parliamentary presence in the former parliament, and was the primary political opposition for Bulgaria's two leading political powers, GERB and Ataka (Attack). Given that the rise of the Turkish soap operas corresponded with the electoral period, the shows were often decried as a deliberate strategy of the MRF to raise its popularity and win votes. As a consequence, the MRF remained at the centre of public attention throughout the whole electoral period. While a growing number of Turkish soap-opera fans were experiencing warm neighborly sentiments, anti-Turkish feelings emerged among a growing population that attempted to use the soap operas to diminish the popularity of the MRF and to distract public attention from the major economic and political problems in the country.

A number of subsequent political events followed the election season that strengthened anti-Turkish attitudes and culminated in Ataka's decision to petition for a national referendum to shut down a 10-minute Turkish-language news bulletin that was (the broadcast is still on TV) broadcast in the afternoon on the *Bulgarian National Television* (*BNT*). In December 2009, the leader of the political party Ataka, Volen Siderov, approached the Premier, Boyko Borisov, with a proposal to hold a national referendum to ban the Turkish-language newscast. He argued that according to the Constitution of the Republic of Bulgaria, only the Bulgarian language should be used on national broadcast channels.[6] Although Siderov gained support from another nationalist organization and was able to garner the necessary signatures, the President of the Republic considered the proposal unconstitutional. However the attempt to ban the Turkish-language on national broadcast channels provoked ethnic tensions.

The Director of the *BNT*, Ulyana Pramova, also declared the idea unconstitutional arguing that it contradicted the Framework Convention on National Minorities, which was signed by Bulgaria, as well as the Law on Radio and Television. A sociological agency was commissioned to conduct research on the need to use Turkish on the *BNT* and to establish the size of the audience that viewed that specific news bulletin. The final decision recognized that the newscast in Turkish is important for providing information to the Turkish-speaking population in Bulgaria and for preserving their constitutional right to such information. The referendum debate is a good illustration of the way language can be turned into symbolic terrain for drawing ethnic boundaries, which can easily be manipulated by politicians to create ethnic divisions and draw political dividends.

SOAP-OPERA CHAT ROOMS: A CASE STUDY

Methodology

The primary goal of my research is to provide insight into the way global media flows can challenge traditional national mythologies contained within the nation space. By analyzing discussions in several online chat rooms, I examine audience perceptions and viewing practices regarding Turkish soap operas. The Internet is largely a supplementary medium for watching episodes of Turkish soap operas. It provides a place to find out information, to express opinions on viewed episodes and character relations, as well as to establish a community to discuss relevant issues of interest, exchange information, and look for emotional support. The nature of the debates about the soap operas and the sensitive issues regarding language, ethnicity, and national identity seemed to demand an examination of chat room discussions in order to gain access to information that conventional interviews would not

reveal. Chat-room discussions also allow people from different ethnic and cultural backgrounds, as well as ones living in different countries, to exchange ideas and establish close relationships online that would be much more difficult in face-to-face communication. I chose four chat rooms[7] based on the criterion of a continuity of existence from the period May 2009, when the soap-opera phenomenon started to draw public attention, until May 2010. I selected those four chat rooms that were in Bulgarian but which discussed key aspects of the Turkish soap operas. I was particularly interested in discussions of this genre and not of other fictional forms. My choice was also dictated by the increasing number of regular participants and their engagement with new titles, as well as by the structuring of fan groups of particular Turkish series. The dates of the establishing forums were of particular significance as I wanted to trace how opinions evolved through time, since the early broadcasting of the first Turkish titles on Bulgarian TV.

Conceptualizing Soap Operas as a Genre

Historically soap operas have been considered to be an entirely female genre. As such, they were usually considered by men to be "low" forms of "women's" culture (Terry Lovell as cited in Brundson, 2000, p. 133). This sexist valorization of certain genres as "good" and degradation of others as worthless meant that audiences watched soap operas with a mixture of pleasure and guilt (Brundson, 2000, p. 2). Further, soaps have been blamed for infusing a lot of patriarchal ideas and imposing patriarchal values on women, keeping them "down," according to some feminist critics in the 1970s (Brundson, 2000, p. 138). Nevertheless, a new analytical treatment of soap operas focuses on audience reception, meaning-making strategies, decoding texts, and social agency. Although related to leisure activities, soap-opera viewing and reception have a lot to do with power and control within the household as well as in public and national discourses.

Today as a genre, soap operas can be very broad and versatile, containing mostly elements of romance, but also drama, comedy, suspense, and even realistic features, thus appealing to a wide range of audiences that increasingly includes men (Geraghty, 1991, p. 4). Audiences regularly get involved with particular problems, which usually do not reach an easy resolution—a fact that allows for the continuation or serialization of the shows. Discussing the popularity of *Dallas*, Stuart Hall makes the following comment:

> At a certain point, the program attracted a type of popularity that was not popularity in terms of figures and ratings. I mean it had a repercussion on culture as a whole. The viewers' involvement became something different. You couldn't help talking about the popularity of Dallas, because people were starting to refer to categories taken from the serial and interpreting their own experience (as cited in Geraghty, 1991, p. 5).

Notably soap operas have the capacity to initiate a public debate, to be both self-reflexive and also reflect back on the social structure. This is made possible by a genre-specific strategy of that mixes the pleasure of viewing with an involvement in particular value systems and norms represented by the themes and the debates they provoke (Geraghty, 1991, p. 5).

While romance and lifestyle are important to soap operas, they are not central elements of the genre. For a substantial numbers of audience members, Turkish soap operas are a form of escapism that is related to the appeal of the actors, the tourist sights of Istanbul, the rich houses of the middle class, and their lifestyle. Nevertheless, there is much hidden beneath the seemingly obvious surface of viewing preferences. We need to acknowledge that pleasure-seeking is goal-oriented, as viewers rationally and actively select media content that best suits their needs (McQuail, 2000, pp. 387–388). On the one hand, such a form of escapism may be deemed a reaction against dominant media discourses[8] in the Bulgarian media that deal with crime, corruption and catastrophic events. On the

other hand, it may further fulfill particular personal and relationship needs, as well as serve as a source of information, value reinforcement, and identity building (ibid.).[9]

Chat rooms participation provides an important basis for comparing viewer responses and a starting point for understanding public discussion on important issues that are often missing in public discourse—such as national identity, gender, and interethnic relations. Using the Turkish series as templates for imagining a desired identity, modes of communication, and a way of life familiar from the past, audiences actively engage in processes of (re)constructing community life and social ties they perceive most beneficial in the future.

Audience Characteristics

Turkish soap operas differ structurally from others, since many of them are based on classic Turkish novels, which depict life in a more realistic manner. They do not seek simple formulaic resolutions or a happy ending, and generally do not target only women as potential viewers.[10] My research demonstrates that although the majority of participants in chat rooms are women within a very wide age span (from teenagers to elderly women), there are quite a lot of men joining online conversations. The national and ethnic characteristics of chat-room participants also vary, with the majority consisting of people living in Bulgaria, of ethnic Bulgarian origins, but also including participants of ethnic Turkish origin who speak Turkish. There are also Bulgarians living abroad, who provide valuable information for comparison with other parts of the world on some of the considered topics.

Viewers can be also categorized according to the degree of their emotional involvement, realistic treatment of the plot, or the demonstration of ironic distance. The strongest opponents of the genre—those who according to Ien Ang, can be defined as soap opera "haters"—simultaneously derive pleasure in perceiving themselves as more cultivated, treating soap "lovers" as stupid and naive (Ang, 1995, p. 525). In her early work, Ang makes the following more detailed categorization of viewers (Ang, 1985): *dismissive*, those for whom "soap operas are rubbish and a waste of time"; *fanatic*, those who won't miss any opportunity to watch soaps and are addicted to them; *ironic*, those people who watch them frequently, but ironically remark on their low quality and formulaic nature; and the *non-committed* who watch only occasionally. In terms of their emotional involvement, the *Fanatic* and *Ironic* viewers are strongly attached, whereas *Dismissive* and *Non-committed* viewers show less attachment (ibid.).

In my research, both male and female audiences fall into the categories delineated by Ang. Although existing literature documents that male viewers usually show more negative, dismissive, or ironic views, such gender distinctions are not clearly displayed in Turkish soap-opera chat rooms. In my data, many women presented negative or dismissive views, while men demonstrated strong involvement and commitment. Therefore, what can be argued is that dismissiveness is neither gender-specific, nor related to a particular social status or level of education. Rather, there is a correlation between dismissiveness, strong anti-Turkish sentiments, and nationalistic prejudices. However, evincing emotional involvement was not necessarily correlated to a lack in objectivity and critical judgment.

Language as a Form of Capital

As already discussed, the Turkish soap-opera phenomenon developed in a specific political and cultural context. A central issue in soap opera chat-room discussions is language, particularly concerning the use of Turkish language in the *Bulgarian National Television* (*BNT*) and in the Turkish series shown on the two private channels. For viewers, language is considered to be a part of the sacred territory of Bulgarianness, yet it is also experienced as a unique form of social, cultural, and symbolic capital. For this reason, language competence is highly valued by chat-room participants. A good command of both the Turkish and Bulgarian languages provides a symbolic position of prestige and respect for participants.

Curious to follow the development of soap operas, fans view many of the episodes online in advance of the televised broadcasts—even though they usually find them in the original Turkish language. The music and lyrics of the songs in the soaps are also of particular interest for this participant group, and in many cases a translators' help is required and valued. Translators in soap-opera chat rooms are considered unique guides not only for understanding the Turkish language, but also for insight into Turkish culture and traditions. Such chat rooms create the opportunity for viewers with different ethnic backgrounds to meet online—something hardly possible to happen in other circumstances. Many sincere friendships are formed with them, based on shared viewing preferences. In such discussions, the linguistic similarity between the Bulgarian and Turkish languages is frequently observed. Keen interest in the richness and beauty of the Turkish language is commonly expressed. Often participants comment on its "melodiousness," especially in songs (Online forum comment by Kitty, June 30, 2009, *Slusham.com Forum*). For example, this is how Eli[11] expresses her special gratitude to Sami for her translation:

> Sami, you are so nice and kind. I like your postings so much and I'm happy to read them all. You are rich with your knowledge of the language and your experience as a translator. And we can be rich only with our dreams (On-line forum comment, June 2, 2009, *Slusham.com Forum*).

Other viewers are interested to know more about the precise translation of titles, the pronunciation and spelling of characters' names and meanings of words. They feel unhappy about bad translations, accept the ones proposed by unofficial chat-room translators and strictly follow their guidance in language. Still others are even more creative, inserting Turkish words and sentences in their comments. New media, as evident from chat-room discussions, have made participants aware that the Balkan languages have more in common than originally claimed by nationalistic ideologies. With the advent of Turkish soap operas, this conviction has been strengthened. This has given rise to a new phenomenon—a growing linguistic passion among participants for using Turkish words and whole expressions in chat rooms, and in other media formats that make specific references to the soap series.

Nevertheless, in traditional media, strong nationalistic sentiments are still in full swing as far as language policy is concerned. The public and political debates around the proposed referendum on the Turkish language newscast find a substantial voice in soap-opera forums. For a male *Dismissive* viewer, for example, the reason for his disapproval of the genre is linguistic and ("patriotic.") Litrek writes the following:

> Don't get me wrong, but this is already over the top. As if it's not enough to have a newscast in Turkish-language on BNT, but now these [Turkish] series. (It's over the top! Some people must have forgotten their history!) On-line forum comment, Sept. 22, 2009, *ABV.bg Forum*).

To this Daisy replies:

> Oh, give me a break with this nonsense. What if the series were Latin American, not Turkish? I'm also against the news in Turkish and think that they should be banned by law, but what do they have to do with the soap operas? (On-line forum comment, Sept. 22, 2009, *ABV.bg Forum*).

(Language is perceived as a sacred symbol of national identity by Litrek, especially when spoken on national television channels, both in newscasts and entertainment genres) For Daisy, soaps as a form of entertainment, have nothing to do with identity and politics. On the other hand, she views news programs as obligated to represent the Bulgarian identity, which in her opinion does not include the language of ethnic minorities. Kim joins in this debate by making

the following concession: "I have nothing against the Turks [. . .], but do they broadcast news in Bulgarian on the national television in Turkey? Do they show news in Spanish in the USA?" (On-line forum comment, Sept. 30, 2009, *ABV.bg Forum*).

To this Nicole, a Bulgarian living in Chicago, explains that in the United States Mexican channels do exist and broadcast in Spanish (On-line forum comment, Oct. 1, 2009, *ABV.bg Forum*). Although, later, she agrees with Tony (a male dismissive viewer) that news bulletins should exist in the Turkish language only on private Turkish channels (On-line forum comment, Oct. 2, 2009, *ABV.bg Forum*). Obviously, for the soap opera viewers national broadcasting airtime is a sacred space representing the Bulgarian nationhood and identity, and which can be represented solely by the official language of the country.

What can be concluded is that some of the traditional lines of hostility organized around the Turkish language and culture remain intact. Media airtime is perceived as a national territory that needs to be defended from an assumed foreign invasion—in this case, an invasion in linguistic terms. Nevertheless, there is a trend toward more unbiased and less emotional handling of this problem, facilitated on the one hand by the socializing role played by the Turkish soap genre and on the other, by establishing real contacts of sympathy with other ethnic Turkish participants.

IMAGES OF TRADITION, FAMILY, AND GENDER ROLES

Soap operas are also spatially and temporarily bound. Turkish society—represented in them, as well as in chat-room discussions—is based on the scale of *tradition vs. modernity, backwardness vs. Europeanization*. The majority of opinions expressed in the forums range between dichotomous extremes regarding social, gender, and family values that are embedded in the social relations among characters, both in the soap operas and in the chat rooms. Nevertheless, there are significant signs evidenced in chat-room discussions that preexisting stereotypes and prejudices are deteriorating.

In Turkish soap operas, the family, and not the state, is the moral and normative regulatory institution, with the oldest man in the family standing as its lead. The main male hero in each of these series is also in a position of power, due to the social standing of his family, his professional qualifications (usually a successful businessman), and his moral principles and sound judgment. To male audiences, much of the appeal of this genre lies exactly in this constructed image (reminiscent of the Bulgarian patriarchal family of the 19th-century Revival period). It is not a coincidence that many of the forum participants emphasize the role of the patriarch of the family in all the series. The tragic character of Ali Riza in *Yaprak Dokumu* (*Leaf Fall*) is such an example of wisdom, responsibility, and moral integrity. The male head of the family is admired as its pillar, and similar to the idealized elements portrayed by the female heroines, is the epitome of moral integrity and wisdom.

The maintenance of tradition and the nostalgia felt for a bygone past, where such family and gender roles existed, is particularly visible in some chat-room postings. As one participant comments, soaps present for him a familiar picture of his childhood past:

> They have brought me back to my childhood years, when old people were of this kind: good, humane, wise. There were good manners of addressing family members, using 'kako' (elder sister), 'batko' (elder brother), aunt, and uncle. People showed respect for each other. It's quite possible that in the Ottoman Empire, Bulgarians and Turks became one people, our customs are almost the same and many of the words in Bulgarian are of Turkish origins (On-line forum comment by Pavel, Aug. 29, 2009, *1001 Nights Forum*).

For this participant as well as for others, Turkish soaps stand for something positive in human relations, which is found missing in contemporary Bulgarian society, such as respect, kindness, and the special place of the elderly as figures of moral control and wisdom. This nostalgia for a patriarchal past carries a positive connotation, signifying order and stability, whereas the present is interpreted as chaotic, criminal, lacking in moral standards and subverting traditional hierarchies once responsible for maintaining social order.

There is a strong sense of loss of tradition that chat-room participants express, when dwelling on similar problems in Bulgarian society. For instance, Lora comments nostalgically: "I like the fact that in Turkish society there still exist some values, which we have forgotten a bit, although I may sound sentimental" (June 15, 2009, *Slusham.com Forum*). Mary also adds how much she liked *Gumus (Pearl)*, as people never used rude or vulgar language in this Turkish series, and unlike Bulgarian media, it did not popularize the values of mafia thugs that prevail in Bulgarian society (Oct. 2, 2009, *ALL.bg Forum*). Viewers like the humanity, warmth, wisdom, and respect shown in the series, which they remember from their childhood. For Tanya, the series and television as a whole give the viewer patterns of behavior to follow, and this is what she considers valuable (May 22, 2010, *ABV.bg Forum*). Following their customs and traditions, Turkish people are seen as maintaining a national identity and cultural individuality, which makes them happier and more deserving to be EU citizens (Archer, Sept. 26, 2009, *ALL.bg Forum*). Moreover, the handing down of traditions is considered a bridge between generations— Hera even paraphrases the words of one of the actors starring in *Binbir Gece* (*Arabian Nights*) in an interview—when she says that a vital thread is seen as broken in Bulgarian society (June 19, 2009, *All.bg Forum*).

Images of Turkish life and culture are not uncritically accepted, however. The warm and cordial relations within the family and neighborhood are positively evaluated, while there is criticism expressed on the lack of privacy in such families and on the position of women in certain cases. For example, I. K. dislikes the model shown in the series *Gumus* (*Pearl*) where adults are presented as still living with elderly family members, obliged to follow the wishes of their fathers, grandfathers, or numerous relatives in the extended family (July 13, 2009, *Slusham. com Forum*). Nevertheless, the Western model in which children leave the family early in their lives and break contacts with their parents is also not perceived as a good option (ibid.). What is preferred as optimal is living separately from one's parents, but still being close to them (ibid.).[12] Even if the Turkish series present people living an affluent life in big houses, individual freedom and privacy are still considered as restricted within the pattern of the extended family (*Ema*, July 8, 2009, *Slusham.com Forum*).[13] Although these shows are nostalgically perceived, they are not seen by viewers as a desire to return to older traditions in family life. Rather in chat-rooms people write about seeking an in-between situation of greater individualism and personal freedom, but still with the opportunity to maintain close relations with parents and family members. In this sense, chat-room discussions reconfirm existing patterns of family life in Bulgaria, but also show a desire to reform modes of communication, which they see as well-preserved in Turkish series and typified by previous generations.

How do perceptions of gender roles in patriarchal families in Turkish soap operas fit in with audience expectations in Bulgaria? Images of women shown in different titles present a mixture of traditional positive qualities, such as the combination of modesty and beauty, both in moral and physical terms. Again in accordance with the rules of the genre, female heroines have to work hard and suffer a lot to achieve something in life and to fulfill their dreams. Nevertheless, they aren't portrayed as blind victims to fate, but instead demonstrate their own will, determination, and self-confidence, seeking to escape the fetters of patriarchy. They are shown as struggling to be treated equally as family partners and good professionals, making

successful careers in business, art, architecture, and so forth. For example, Gumus (*Gumus*) and Lamia (*Dudaktan Kalbe*) manage to build careers as business women, although they both have humble origins and come from small rural areas. Gumus succeeds as an independent business professional in gaining her husband's respect as well as that of his rich family. Scheherazade (*Binbir Gece*), the epitome of traditional virtues, such as beauty and modesty is a single mother and the most successful female architect in Turkey. She works hard to survive and is capable of enormous self-sacrifice to save the life of her child.

Successful careers give these heroines not only financial, but also personal independence and self-confidence, as well as a better choice in life. For example, they can file for a divorce, if the family restricts their sense of freedom and personal happiness. Although love and romance are usually central to the plot, the female characters are portrayed as not ready to give up everything for family life. What is more, they even succeed in changing the attitude of their male partners toward gender stereotypes and traditional family roles. The victory of these female characters is their ability to make men realize that the true virtue of women lies equally in the family and in their professional careers.

Such images correspond with the experience of Bulgarian female audiences. Women's emancipation in Bulgaria is a fact. Nevertheless, despite effective policies under communism to emancipate women, Bulgarian women still internalize some patriarchal patterns and suffer from the consequences of late modernization and the remains of patriarchal relations within the family. The emancipation of women continues to be accepted ambivalently in Bulgarian society; a fact which is also reflected in chat-room discussions. On the one hand, this emancipation is viewed as something positive when comparing the status of Bulgarian women to Arabic women. On the other, it is assumed that emancipation should exist within certain limits and not at the expense of sacrificing family life and obligations. Comparing their lives to those of the Turkish soap-opera characters, Bulgarian chat-room participants discuss both patriarchy and gender relations. For example, one participant wrote that Turkey still differs considerably from Bulgaria and other European countries, as it "demonstrates strong patriarchal relations" (on-line forum comment by *Asen,* Aug, 29, 2008, *ABV.bg Forum*). The existence of arranged marriages in the 21st century, as in *Gumus (Pearl),* is interpreted as another sign of backwardness, although with an expressed sense of empathy for women (On-line forum comment by Hera, June 15, 2009, *All.bg Forum*).

On the other hand, female characters are admired not for being "too good," "too modest," or "too ready" to sacrifice their happiness for others—e.g., Lamia in *Dudatkan Kalbe (Melody of the Heart)*—but also for showing generosity, humanity, perseverance, and determination in the business world, as represented by Leila and the Steal Princess in *Dudatkan Kalbe (Melody of the Heart)* (on-line forum comment by Hera, June 15, 2009, *All.bg Forum*). Nevertheless, delicacy, good nature, and manners are positively evaluated as rare features in contemporary female heroines, such as Zeynep in *Elveda Derken (Tears above the Bosphorous),* although they may be the source of a lot of suffering (on-line forum comment by Ema, June 10, 2009, *All.bg Forum*). Dignity is another feature that viewers admire, as evidenced in the situation where Lamia from *Dudatkan Kalbe (Melody of the Heart)* leaves home, because she is not respected (on-line forum comment by Hera, July 4, 2009, *All.bg Forum*). Lale in *Elveda Derken (Tears above the Bosphorus)* is admired for her strength and moral responsibility, although she may go to extremes interfering in other people's lives (on-line forum comments by Dani and Ema, June 15, 2009, *All.bg Forum*). In many cases, female chat-participants don't seem to like characters who are either too sensitive, and therefore less inclined to fight for their happiness, or characters who are "too emancipated" and determined

to succeed, such as Sabiha in *Son Biha (Borrowed Love)* who therefore sacrifices love (on-line forum comment by Sami, May 21, 2010, *1001 Nights Forum*).

Turkish society, as presented in the soap operas, shows contrasting examples of traditional and modern gender roles, while mostly giving prominence to images of emancipated women, who are equally successful in business and family affairs. Based on chat-room discussions it seems that for Bulgarian viewers, the Turkish soap operas neither present a desire to return to traditional gender roles and family patterns within the patriarchal family, nor do they urge women to seek alternative routes of emancipation. Rather, in the minds of viewers what is established as positive in Turkish culture are the communal ties and the evidence of greater warmth, care, and respect in communications with family members and neighbors. It is exactly the loss of such family and community ties that audiences regret and nostalgically recognize as something positive, which is perceived as missing in contemporary Bulgarian society. On the other hand, traditional patterns of patriarchal gender roles (whenever present) are perceived as dated, while the striving for greater freedom of women both in the family and in the workplace is not treated as exceptional, but as simply taken for granted. In its reformed version, the family (or the ideals that the main female characters pursue) appear central to the plots, with attention paid equally to these ideals by both the series' authors and their Bulgarian viewers. The innovative family pattern presented in the Turkish series makes a significant step forward from traditional patriarchal modes, even when coexisting with them. There is a space of greater equality, partnership, and independence presented that the female heroines are striving after. Bulgarian viewers, however, tend to interpret selectively such family patterns. Comparing the examination of greater women's emancipation in the job market with a significant crisis in the contemporary Bulgarian family, the portrayals place the higher value on improved family relations and communication. This also explains why, even if emancipation is highly valued, viewers won't accept it as a sacrifice, at the expense of love and family life. Viewing soap operas is a situational practice, which depends on the context. Equally situational are the interpretations made by audiences, who elaborate a strategy of selectively highlighting particular elements, while leaving others in the background, depending on which elements best suit their particular needs and their own interpretations of the world.

NATIONAL IDENTITY REVISITED

A lot of the comments in the chat rooms, are actually a self-reflective exercise in defining what Bulgarian national identity should be based on, how it should be maintained, and to what extent it can "borrow" from the Turkish example. Some viewers openly express their negative attitudes to the genre. Their comments are similar to other *Dismissive* viewers, although their negation always goes hand in hand with nationalistic sentiments. For one viewer, for example, watching Turkish soap operas is a sign of "national degradation" (on-line comment by Dani, Jan. 15, 2010, *1001 Nights Forum*). "How is it possible to show such soaps in prime time?!" she exclaims. "I decided to watch one episode to understand why they discuss them even in the news. This is something disastrous! Our nation is dying!" (ibid.) However for Anonymous, the Turkish soap operas cause culture shock as it contradicts conventional hostile nationalistic perceptions. Consequently the reasons people like them appear to be inexplicable.

> I've started asking myself different questions, since these Turkish soaps started "spreading" on our TV channels. [. . .] Weren't the Turks supposed to be stupid, backward, and ugly creatures? From what I can see, it all contradicts my preconceptions. For goodness sake, what's going on? Can somebody explain this to me? (On-line forum comment, July 23, 2009, *Slusham.com Forum*)

Negative comments, however, are often presented with analytical criticism by chat members. An article published in the on-line television news source, *Klassa.bg* and posted in the forums, titled "The Art of the Fake Pearls" (Plamenov, 2010), criticizes Turkish soap operas as "Orientalizing" Bulgarian culture, depriving Bulgarian TV viewers of choice and giving them "circuses" instead of "bread." Roman, a chat participant makes the following response to the article:

> The above article reveals the undisguised envy and spite toward the Turks, just because the soaps are good and popular. Yes, we are well aware that we are envious as a tribe and that we also have other similar "positive" qualities. But every time our pervert [sic] prejudices, sustained for more than 100 years, that the Turks are backward Orientals and think only about conquering other countries, clash with reality, the nationalists, the chauvinists, the xenophobes in our country get extremely active again, and become excessively arrogant and brutal, and start attacking others, because the image of the Devil they'd been constructing for decades has collapsed. The time has come for our prejudices to bang us on our empty heads, because we have invented nothing to impress other nations, but just boast and vilify the foreign. Thus, our cultural infertility becomes obvious. It's our entire fault. The fake pearls are not the successes of others but our own prejudices (On-line forum comment by Roman, Jan 10, 2010, *ABV.bg Forum*).

I find this to be a good example of the self-reflexivity and attitude change that a better acquaintance with Turkish culture has brought forth in the soap-opera viewers. Chat-room discussions introduce a new vision of Turkish society—one that is more progressive, modernizing, and capable of maintaining the traditions and values that they prize. What is more, Bulgarian culture is identified as deficient in certain moral aspects and as maintaining a false picture of its true worth to foreigners. Traditionally stereotypical perceptions still exist, however, and these represent Turkey as "backward," "uncivilized," and "Oriental," whereas Bulgaria is viewed as "less Oriental," more "civilized" and deserving to be part of Europe) Nevertheless, as witnessed in the chat-room discussions, there is a gradual erosion of such negative binarisms, possibly leading to their collapse and a growing awareness of their constructed nature. Moreover, we can even speak of a reversal of stereotypes evident from some chat-room comments, in which a previous negative stereotype of Turkey has been inverted. In such cases, Turkish soap operas have helped viewers to realize the unreasonable nature of long-sustained negative prejudices toward the neighbor and of unjustified instances of self-glorification.

FICTION VERSUS REALITY

The popularity of the Turkish soap opera genre has inevitably been linked to ongoing political debates and to the role of the Turkish *MRF* in the context of the Parliamentary elections in July of 2009. Some chat participants quite explicitly accused the *MRF* of a conspiracy—specifically of purchasing the Turkish series in large quantities in the attempt to affect voting behavior by creating particular culture "sympathies" with the Turkish neighbor (on-line forum comments by White Chief, July 4, 2009, *All.bg Forum*; Rick, July 1, 2009, *Slusham.com Forum*; Metal Man, Sept. 9, 2009, *ABV.bg*). Others even extend the "conspiracy theory," with the claim that while showing Turkish soaps on the Bulgarian channels, the Turkish channels officially announced the departure times for buses with Bulgarian Turks organized en masse to vote for the *MRF* in the Bulgarian elections (on-line forum comment by Joan, July 6, 2009, *All.bg Forum*). Still, other viewers found such claims ridiculous, as they did not expect the soaps to affect significantly the voting behaviors of people (on-line forum comment by Barbara, July 1, 2009, *ABV.bg Forum*). For such viewers, it was necessary for people to be able to make a clear distinction between media and reality (ibid.). Therefore, the channels' program policy was seen to have a purely economic reasoning, solely aimed at raising their

ratings (ibid.). A similar distinction between the soap operas and politics was made by another Anonymous participant who argued that one may enjoy watching Turkish soaps and at the same time continue to vote for the nationalists (on-line forum comment, July 1, 2009, *ABV.bg*).

While no direct link has been found between buying Turkish soap operas and the political activity of the *MRF*, a strong connection has been established between Turkish soap operas, the increased rate of tourism to Turkey, and other forms of economic activity (on-line forum comment by Metal Man, Sept. 29, 2009, *All.bg Forum*). This becomes obvious both from official statistics on tourist exchanges between Turkey and Bulgaria, as well as from the personal experiences shared by forum participants. Many of them describe in beautiful poetic language their travels to Istanbul and other places; they even exchange pictures, post video clips in *YouTube* or give recommendations to others what places to visit and what things to buy. For Eli, for example, the magic of the Turkish genre is not so much found in the romantic plots, as in the images of the beautiful scenery, the Bosphorus and its coastline (on-line forum comment, May 30, 2009, *ABV.bg Forum*).

Another indicator of the indirect effect of Turkish soap operas on Bulgarian-Turkish relations can be found in the increased number of cultural exchanges. Some chat participants comment on the artistic activities of the Turkish Theatre, "Kadrie Lyatifova" in the Bulgarian town of Kardzahli, where the Turkish actress and soap-opera star Fadik Sevin Atasoy took part in *Carmen*, a Prosper Mérimée play. Kitty, a chat member, writes to another participant, named Kardzhali, the following:

> Good for you, Kardzhali! Had there been better promotion of the performance in Sofia in 2004, we would have been proud now of being able to applaud the live performance of Carmen-Atasoy. Yet, we join in your pride. This is another reason to stick another nail in the improvised panel of culture and education tonight on Battenberg Square (On-line forum comment, June 23, 2009, *Slusham.com Forum*).

Kitty refers to a performance aimed at dealing with the crisis, the problems, and the fears experienced by contemporary Bulgarians (Details, 2009). What can be perceived as a promising sign is that for her, and hopefully for her generation, Turkey and Turkish culture no longer provoke such fears, as she has learned a new language—that of communication between cultures.

CONCLUSION

This chapter shows the discursive construction of identity of two neighboring peoples—the Bulgarians and Turks, in which language and language polices have played a significant role for centuries. The popular medium of Turkish soap operas became the terrain for contesting prior stereotypes and ethnic prejudices. Research on audience chat rooms registered a particular tendency for expressing an increasing number of culture sympathies with Turkey, based on common historical, cultural, and linguistic experiences and facilitated by the important role played by the new global media. Points of cultural convergence between Bulgarians and Turks were registered as a result, contradicting well-established nationalistic ideologies. This may be a promising indicator that the shared Ottoman past is being reconsidered in a more positive way, as a period of mutual exchange and enrichment. This reconstruction of the past emphasizes the nodal points of commonality rather than difference and hostility and potentially leads to a new post-national treatment of both ethnicity and nationhood.

The overall implication is that the mass media and new technologies have started to play an increasing role in processes of value change and identity transformation. This does not directly result from particular ideological interests, or as an effect of economic or political gamesmanship. Rather it is a result of the influence of global and local configurations that involve the continuous flow of money, people, and ideas in complex combinations and multiple directions. The case of Turkish soap operas in Bulgaria can be used to exemplify such changes, and especially the role of culture in resolving normative dilemmas—ones related to particular national spaces and their historical contingencies, but also going beyond concepts of nation through novel global frames. National hostilities, as part of the homogenizing and dividing efforts, will continue to exist. Nevertheless, more hope can be placed in the acts of people who when armed with the instruments of global culture will succeed in creating new imagined communities and will learn new languages to be able to exist in the "in-between" spaces of the global landscape.

NOTES

1. The title in brackets is the one translated into Bulgarian and under which the series became popular.

2. According to the latest census in 2011, the population of ethnic Turks in Bulgaria is 588,318, which is 8.8% of the total population.

3. Some data reveal that from their initial launching in Bulgaria in late 2008, the popularity of Turkish soap operas grew considerably achieving very high ratings (ranging from 8.68% to 23.68%), market share (52.25–58.18% MS), and audiences with a constantly increasing number of viewers (Telemaniac Media Group, May 2010). These statistics reflect the highest figures for the period from December 2008 to June 2010, with a unique record for *Yaprak Dokumu* (*Leaf Fall*), leading the top 50 chart for months and providing *bTV's* highest audience share. As a result, the media war between the two private broadcast channels was won by *bTV*, with the help of the Turkish soap operas.

4. As Robertson explains, the term "glocalization" emphasises the unity of the global and the local (as cited in Featherstone, 1995, p. 118). The concept is two-dimensional: on the one hand, being modeled on the Japanese term *dochaku* used in farming and agriculture, it reflects global business maneuvers seeking to adapt their produce to local market conditions (Robertson as cited in Featherstone, 1995, p.118). On the other, it is viewed as the democratic practice of local actors who are enabled to select, interpret, and modify creatively global elements (Cohen & Kennedy, 2000, p. 377).

5. The Turkish authorities, represented by the Office for Social Services and Families objected to the growing number of divorces, extramarital affairs, and homosexual relations, which they interpreted as the result of the wide popularity of the Turkish series and which they perceived was seriously affecting social morals with its explicit sexual scenes and violence (Hristova, 2009).

6. Additionally, Volen Siderov claimed that the news bulletin was viewed only by a limited number of people. Initially, he received support from the Premier, who promised to consult MPs on their opinion. If the petition for a national referendum received the necessary 20,000 signatures, they believed the President of the Republic would have to issue a special decree for setting up the national referendum. The national referendum was also supported by another nationalist party—the Internal Macedonian Revolutionary Organisation (VMRO).

7. Researched chat rooms are the following: *1001 Nights Forum* at http://1001noshti.com/forum/21; *Forum ABV. bg* at http://forum.abv.bg/index.php?showtopic=90242&pid=1336516&mode=threaded&show=&st=#entry1336516; *Slusham.com Forum* at http://www.slusham.com/category/komentari; and *All.Bg Forum* at http://forum.all.bg/showflat.php/Cat/0/Number/2411625/an/0/page/0.

8. I define discourse according to MacDonnel (1986) as a "particular area of language use, [which] may be identified by the institutions to which it relates, by the positions from which it comes and which it marks out for the speaker" (p. 3).

9. Such comments are developed by the "Uses and Gratification" theory in media effects studies, which are applied by media scholars of popular genres, including soap operas. The "Uses and Gratification" theory focuses on the needs and personal satisfaction of audiences, perceived as active agents in the communication processes. The particular uses were grouped into four categories, namely: diversion, personal relationships, personal identity and information (Watson & Hill, 1993, p. 197)

10. Explicit statistical data on the audience profile of Turkish soap operas is unavailable and exists only in the ratings data of viewers in the category All 4+ (target audience consists of all people over the age of 4).

11. The profile names of participants have been changed for ethical reasons.

12. This is the model that prevails in Bulgaria, since young families rely on help from elderly family members, especially in child rearing.

13. The extended-family model is recent for Bulgarians only going back one or two generations, and which still exists mainly in some rural or ethnic communities.

REFERENCES

Anderson, B. (1983). *Imagined communities*. London, UK: Verso.

Ang, I. (1985). *Watching* Dallas: *Soap opera and the melodramatic imagination*. London, UK: Methuen.

Ang, I. (1995). *Dallas* and the ideology of mass culture. In D. Boyd-Barrett & C. Newbold (Eds.), *Approaches to media: A reader* (pp. 525–530). London, UK: Edward Arnold.

Appadurai, A. (1996). *Modernity at large*. Minneapolis: University of Minnesota Press.

Appadurai, A. (2006). Disjuncture and difference in the global economy. In G. D. Meenakshi & D. Kellner (Eds.), *Media and cultural studies: Key works* (rev. ed.) (pp. 584–603). Oxford, UK: Blackwell.

Aretov, N. (2006). *National mythology and national literature*. Sofia, BG: Queen Mab Publishers.

Bauman, Z. (1999). *Culture as praxis* (2nd ed.). London, UK: Sage.

Brundson, C. (2000). *The feminist, the housewife and the soap opera*. Oxford, UK: Oxford University Press.

Cohen, P., & Kennedy, P. M. (2000). *Global sociology*. London, UK: Macmillan.

Details. (2009). 900 nails in the crisis—interactive art installation [Web Blog post]. *WorldPress.com*. Retrieved June 15, 2010 from http://allmera.wordpress.com/2009/06/18/900pirona /

Featherstone, M. (1995). *Undoing culture: Globalization, postmodernism and identity*. London, UK: Sage.

Georgieva, Tz. (2009). The Ottoman studies in contemporary Bulgarian historiography. In R. Genov, Tz. Cholova, & L. Stoyanov (Eds.), *Ethnic groups, culture and politics in South-East Europe* (pp. 21–38). Sofia: New Bulgarian University.

Geraghty, C. (1991). *Women and soap opera: A study of prime time soaps*. Cambridge, UK: Polity Press.

Hristova, Z. (2009). The Turkish series—successful business or a political means. *E-vestnik.bg*

[Newspaper]. Retrieved Feb. 01, 2010 from http://e-vestnik.bg/7868.

MacDonnel, D. (1986). *Theories of discourse: An introduction*. Oxford, UK: Blackwell.

McQuail, D. (2000). *McQuail's mass communication theory* (4th ed.). London, UK: Sage.

Mihova, M. (2009, August 18). "Gumus" gets Turkey out of the crisis. *Maritza* [Newspaper]. Retrieved Aug. 4, 2011, from http://marica.bg/show.php?id=10170.

Plamenov, P. (2010, January 7). The art of the false pearls. *Klassa.bg.* [Television news source website] Retrieved from http://www.klassa.bg/news/Read/article/55589.

Smith, A. D. (1991). *National identity*. London, UK: Penguin Books.

Stoyanov, L. (2009). On our nation's destiny: Elites and national psychology. In R. Genov, Ts. Cholova, & L. Stoyanov (Eds.), *Ethnic groups, culture and politics in South-East Europe* (pp. 222–236). Sofia: New Bulgarian University.

Suleiman, B. (2009, August 24). Turkish series bring half a billion Euro profits. *Bulgaria Zaman* [Newspaper], Retrieved June 17, 2010 from http://bg.zaman.com.tr/bg/detaylar.do?load=detay&link=2380.

Swidler, A. (1986). Culture in action: Symbols and strategies. *American Sociological Review, 51,* 273–286.

Telemaniac Media Group. (2010). Online Statistics. *Telemaniac* [online news source]. Retrieved June 6, 2010 from http://www.telemaniac.com/ratings-april2010.

Watson, J., & Hill, A. (1993). *A dictionary of communication and media studies*. London, UK: Arnold.

We are second in buying Turkish series. (2011, Feb. 9). *Vesti.bg* [BTA –the Bulgarian Telegraphic Agency]. Retrieved Aug. 4, 2011 from http://www.vesti.bg/index.phtml?tid=40&oid=3602171.

18

TINY NETIZENS MOCKING THE GREAT FIREWALL

Discourse, Power, and the Politics of Representation in China, 2005 to 2010

WEIZHUN MAO

INTRODUCTION

Discourse analysis[1] is an important tool for analyzing the relationship between politics, power, and new media. This chapter draws from discourse analysis to explore how the Internet and the related "Information Era" shape the current political and social structure in the world. How do "netizens"[2] perceive the changes and construct their own identities in the Internet era? Given that netizens are both a community and the key actors in Internet space, how do their discourses frame the political and social power structures? How are discourse and knowledge implicated in power imbalances and inequalities?

In this chapter, I explore these issues by examining Internet information censorship in China, through the theoretical framework of "Politics of representation." The "Politics of representation"

refers to "the competition over meaning among groups" (Holquist, 1983; Shapiro, 1988; Wenden, 2005, p. 90). This paper assumes netizens construct a space of free expression through Internet languages, within the prevailing structure of the Chinese Internet censorship. Their discourse demonstrates the mechanisms through which netizens interact with the state powers in China. How do the netizens struggle for equal rights and construct their own discursive power? How can netizens deconstruct the discourse of state authority as they justify their own discourse about greater rights and stronger power in expression and speech?

This research is based on a data set that includes 80 independent phrases, 200 typical sentences, and 50 pictures collected from Chinese Internet sources from 2005 to 2010.[3] All the data regard political issues or have political meaning related to hot Internet issues and events that arose over the last six years. They come from a variety of Internet spaces in China, including Internet forums, news comments at web portals, chat software groups, Bulletin Board Systems (BBS), blogs and microblogs (*weibo*), and social networking services (SNS) websites, and so forth. In addition, this research draws from the *Analysis of Internet Public Discourse*, 2007–2010 (Zhu, Hu, & Sun, 2008; Zhu, Shan, & Hu, 2008, 2009, 2011) and the *Statistical Report of China Internet Development* (1997–2010), published by the China Internet Network Information Center (CNNIC, 1997–2010).

The chapter is organized as follows: the next section presents the basic introduction of Internet development, netizens' brief conditions, and the Internet censorship systems. The third section discusses the tools, features, and composition of netizens' discourse. It analyzes the strategies, mechanism, and skills that netizen's use to challenge the incumbent power structure. The fourth section explores representation practices regarding power struggles in virtual space. Finally, the conclusion sums up the arguments, indications, and examines the implications for a balance of power and equality of rights.

New Media, New Actors, and the Politics of Representation in China: Background

Internet as a Kind of New Media in China

This chapter focuses on the struggle between the government and ordinary people who used the Internet in China between 2005 and 2010. This struggle has roots in 1978, when Chinese development started to become globally significant in both economic and political arenas. Accordingly, the Chinese domestic structure changed a lot in the last thirty years. With the influence of Western cultures and the subsequent clashes between Sino-Western civilizations, many people within China have raised the awareness of citizen rights. In spite

of the reluctance of authority, new changes in economics and knowledge have created a series of "domino effects" in China. Following the introduction of the Internet, struggles over freedom of speech and greater social and political power intensified as technology introduced changes, with respect to the formerly isolated nation-state and also with respect to individual values and lifestyles. Most importantly, the popular use of the Internet and home computers has undermined the information monopoly of traditional government media. Internet space has quickly become a kind of frontier in which common people freely interact and communicate. It is the first time that the masses have been able to present opinions through a public medium. However, the government is still reluctant to recognize the existence of such a public space. Even so, at present, there are 2.79 million websites in China and there are more than 11.21 million domains in 2010 according to official statistics. And the international bandwidth is 998,217 Mbps, which shows the measured capacity of China to connect with the international websites (CNNIC, 1997–2010).

As a new medium, the Internet is a site of struggle over the politics of representation. Most importantly, Chinese Internet discourses have different features from those in other countries, because they are produced within the broader context of a state that limits free expression. Consequently, the netizens' reactions to strict regulation and control—namely Internet censorship—is an important consideration as they struggle with political actors who seek to limit freedom on the Internet in order to maximize their own power and interests.

Netizens: Identity and Features

According to Michael Hauben,

Netizen represents positive activity and no adjective need be used [. . .] As more and more people join the online community and contribute toward the nurturing of the Net and toward the development of a great shared social wealth, the ideas and values of Netizenship spread (Hauben & Hauben, 1997, pp. x–xi).

In 1997, China began to estimate the number of netizens. According to the CNNIC, the netizen population has risen from 620,000 in 1997 to 4.2 billion in 2010 (CNNIC, 1997–2010). After just over a decade, this growth is amazing.

The increased rate of Internet prevalence in China is also quite rapid compared with other countries. In addition, currently there are more diverse technologies that enable netizens to gain easy access to the Internet, including laptops,

Figure 18.1A

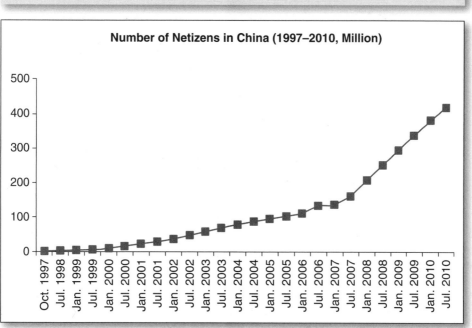

Source: Based on data from Statistical Report of China Internet Development (1997-2010), China Internet Network Information Center.

mobile phones, iPads (tablet computer produced by Apple), and so forth.

The primary demographic of this group of netizens are the young (ages 16 through 30), accounting for at least 50% of all its members.

In particular, students comprise about one-third of all online users since 2000 and the numbers of netizens with higher rates of education continue to increase, despite the Internet's popularity and spread.

Ratios of Student, Youth, and Higher Education Individuals Using the Internet[4]				
	1997–1998	*1997–2002*	*1997–2006*	*1997–2010*
Students	13.9%	26.2%	36.2%	30.7%
Youth (16–30)	76.4% (16–30)	54.1% (18–30)	57.3% (18–30)	28.1% (20–29)[5]
Higher Education	58.9%	31.7%	27.6%	11.3%

Sources: Statistical Report of China Internet Development (1997–2010), China Internet Network Information Center.

Figure 18.1B

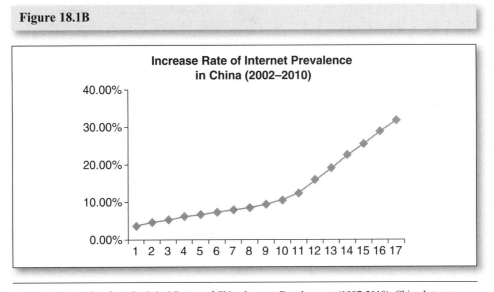

Increase Rate of Internet Prevalence
in China (2002–2010)

Source: Based on data from Statistical Report of China Internet Development (1997-2010), China Internet Network Information Center.

There is a special group considered as the mainstay of those called netizens, who comprise the bulk of the mentioned three categories. This generation is often referred to as the "post-Eighties generation" or "After 1980s" (Zhu, Hu, et al., 2008; Zhu, Shan, et al., 2008; Zhu, Shan, & Hu, 2009, 2011). As younger people, they usually are unsatisfied with the current situation and act as "angry youth" to gain more power and recognition. With advanced education, they are able to identify and analyze the problems in the society; they are mostly idealistic in that they hope to create a perfect world. And most importantly, this group is familiar with the most current technologies and prefer to keep an open mind at all times about technological developments. The worldwide web provides them with wider and freer spaces. At the same time, they also try to both maintain and broaden the Internet space through technology and discourse.

Mr. Han Han might be the most famous netizen in China; he is usually portrayed as a public intellectual searching for democracy, humanism, and freedom (Tatlow, 2010). Han Han is regarded as the representative of the "post-Eighties generation," and his blog[6] has received about 490 million hits since 2006. The Sina Blog (a Chinese portal) that contains millions of blogs of analysts, commentators, entrepreneurs, scholars, and actors, ranks Han Han's blog at seventh in accordance with the extent of popularity measured by the click rate and Internet flow (Sina, 2011). In 2010, the *News Statesman* recognized Mr. Han as number 48th in a list of the 50 most important people (Statesman, 2010).

Given the enormous and diverse population of netizens, there are frictions and competing ideas within the group and within this "imagined community" that often collide. However, netizens all regard themselves as having an alternative identity—that of netizen—which, on the one hand articulates their membership among Internet users, and on the other hand, their sense of social responsibility as Chinese citizens. Chinese netizens carry a burden of responsibility as the literati and as the pioneers who have a great interest in social concerns. Despite their diverse backgrounds, most netizens try to act as a kind of social conscience.

Among netizens, there is another group known satirically as "Internet commentators" (*wangpingyuan*) who are mostly employed by the government to advance propaganda for government policies and to reject negative information against the government. Because they are rumored to be paid 50 cents for every article they post online, most netizens refer to them as the Party of "Half a Dollar" or the "50-Cent Party" (Bristow, 2008). It is difficult to estimate the number of Internet commentators, but propaganda departments at every level hire many of them to monitor public opinion and to object to the negative information presented in the main Chinese Internet forum. However, netizens prefer to regard the so-called Internet commentators as simply one part of the state powers rather than as real netizens.

STATE POWER AND INTERNET CENSORSHIP IN CHINA

The Worries of State Power Toward the Internet

Setting limitations against the encroachment of government power is a constant issue since people in positions of power have an impulse to expand and maximize their interests. Consequently, two quotes have become very popular among people in China. The first is one from William Pitt's speech delivered in 1763: "*It may be frail—its roof may shake—the wind may blow through it—the storm may enter—the rain may enter—but the King of England cannot enter*" (cited in Heffernan, 2002, pp. 14–15). The other, comes from Thomas Paine's Common Sense, published in 1776: "*Society in every state is a blessing, but government, even in its best state, is but a necessary evil; in its worst state an intolerable one*" (cited in Paine, 1966, p. 54). In democratic countries, the mechanisms that keep power in balance can help to avoid the worst state. However, without democracy the people lack sufficient mechanisms to keep power in balance. This situation is complicated in China by the increasing "securitization" over Internet space.[7]

From a constructivist approach, Buzan, Wæver, and Wilde (1998) argue that securitization points to the processes through which ideas and identities are constructed as security issues. The framework of securitization includes "who securitizes, on what issues (threats), for whom

(referent object), why, with what results, and not least, under what conditions" (1998, p. 82). We must always ask in particular: security for whom? The essence of security depends on the intersubjective understanding of threat. During the securitization of the Internet, government is the securitizing agent, the Internet—in particular government critique—is the threat agent and the reference objective includes the nation/state, vulnerable residents such as children, and the audience as the general population.

The securitization of Internet space can be explained by the case of the Green Dam (*lvba*). Under the guise of preventing youths from accessing bad information, the government enforced a compulsory securitization process regarding the "Green Dam."[8] This caused a mass resistance among netizens who criticized and debated the securitization process. Netizens criticized the government's real intent, which they believed was surveillance of computer use. Eventually, the government had to withdraw some steps and give up the compulsory regulation (Jacobs, 2009; Yoshikazu, 2009). Since then, a majority of netizens have continued to resist compulsory regulation and the government has continued to attempt to exercise surveillance and control.[9]

As the Internet expands, the Chinese government is concerned especially with issues of government ideology and legitimacy. In face of the free flow of information, the ruling group fears the Internet may damage their information control system and subsequently hurt the ruling ideology; this in turn may ruin its legitimacy in China and lead to the eventual loss of the current government's ability to remain in power. At the same time, they also want to make good use of the advantages of the Internet in order to maintain their ideology and legitimacy and finally to stay as the ruling power.

Consider the significant effects of an article on the Internet that appeared in the (*Renmin Ribao*), the official newspaper of the Central Committee of the Communist Party of China (CCCPC) and the most influential and authoritative newspaper in China. In January 23, 1996, they ran an article titled "Thousands of Families Access the

Internet" that stressed the Chinese government's initial focus on the Internet and netizens and introduced a comparison of Internet use in key countries at that time (*People's Daily* Editorial, 1996, p. 7). From that point forward, the government began to be sensitive to the effects of the Internet, especially the potentially negative impacts. The first Internet regulation law was enacted in February, 1996 by the State Council, which is quite cautious about national security (State Council, 1996). Further, they then introduced international regulations such as "Internet Category Regulations" (S. Wang, 1996). In April 2000, the Communist Party of China (CPC) officially connected the threats of the Internet with government ideology after several Falun Gong incidents.[10] According to an article titled, "A Clear Sense of Frontier," the leaders of the CPC see the Internet as "a sense of frontier" that needs to be regulated for ideas, culture, and so forth, while also hoping to use the Internet and information technology to promote CPC ideology (*People's Daily*, April 23, 2000, p. 1). Gradually, the priority of Internet regulation rose from the back page to the most important place on the front page of the government agenda. In 2002, the 16th National Congress of CPC claimed "Internet websites should serve as important fronts for spreading advanced culture" (Jiang, 2002), and the 17th National Congress in 2007 was required to "strengthen efforts to develop and manage Internet culture and foster a good cyber environment" (Hu, 2007).

In addition, the collapse of the Soviet Union made a deep impression on the CPC. The government fears repeating the apparently disastrous road taken by the Soviet Union and other Eastern European communist countries. According to the perception of the CPC and its think tanks, one of the most troubling factors in the Soviet lesson is "the uncontrolled media," and subsequently the "public opinions out of control" (Zhao, 2010, p. 57).

Clearly, the Chinese government has connected Internet use with political stability as they continue to use security priorities to advance a political agenda. The Internet has brought many challenges to governments and vested interest groups in China, specifically to those who belong primarily to the current ruling system and who enjoy most of the rights. Through the Internet, netizens can discover social injustice and inequality, deter corruption, and monitor bad behaviors of governmental organizations and staffs.[11] For these reasons, the Internet has been accused by the government of facilitating protest activities in effective ways and providing a new protest strategy, that of online protests. The government sees the link-up (*chuanlian*) mobilization of netizens as a big threat to the regime (Yang, 2003, p. 475). Some officials in the CPC propaganda sector even said: "It was better before when Internet didn't exist; people just dare to say what we order them to say" (Zheng, 2008, p. 33). The recent event known as, "My Father Is Li Gang," also demonstrated that the Internet enables people to monitor officials' behaviors at least in the level of speech, which has been a deterrence against the crude abuse of public power for private interests (Wines, 2010).

However, there is a great contrast between the attitudes of officials and the general public regarding the Internet. The *People's Daily* conducted research through questionnaires, interviews, and an Internet online poll and found that 70% of the people in their research think that the Internet monitors are a sign of fear among officials (Xu & Li, 2010). At the same time, research has found that 87.9% of netizens pay great attention to Internet monitoring corruption; and 93.3% of them prefer to use the Internet for exposure when they detect unjust issues (Xiao & You, 2009).

Internet Regulation in China

The government has designed a strict Internet regulation system, including technology, laws and rules, and institutional structures. It is believed that the government sustains this "great firewall" through four primary methods: DNS cache poisoning, blocking unwanted domain names and IP addresses, deploying key word and HTTPS filtering, and cracking proxy software. Charles R. Smith first described Internet censorship and surveillance as the "Great Firewall of China" (GFW, *Guojia Fanghuoqiang*) designed to "stem the tide of foreign ideas from invading the authoritarian one-party state" (Smith, 2002). Gradually the concept of a Great Firewall has gained wide acceptance and popularity, however the Chinese government has never admitted its existence. The Chinese government officially admits to a project of Internet censorship and surveillance that they call the "Golden Shield Project" (*Jindun Gongcheng*), which indeed has the identical meaning and functions (Zhang & Niu, 2000).[12]

By whatever name, the project to filter and censor the Internet has prompted hot debates. For example, Jack Goldsmith and Tim Wu (2006) demonstrate how the Chinese government uses its powers of Internet censorship and filtering both to block dissent and to create a form of nationalism. A few Chinese scholars, like Yonggang Li, examine the legitimacy of GFW or the "Golden Shield" in China from the political perspective. Li tries to underline the various logics that motivate the desire to control the Internet, both within the central government and local governments. He asserts that the regulation system is affected by the law and rules, the power comparison, and the traditions or cultures (Li, 2008, 2009). All actors involved in the issue of Internet censorship have different logics or core values. For example, the central government holds its ruling status as a core value; the relevant sectors and local authorities regard economic interest and increased power as the core value; the operating agencies see profit maximization as the key point; and the Internet users prefer a calm cyber life in the tensions between their own identity and some other factors, such as democratization (X. Wang, 2009).[13]

Importantly, the government sets both horizontal and vertical structures that extend from the central government to the local governments. The central government establishes special agencies

at different levels of government to regulate the Internet within its own authority. For example, The Bureau of Internet Security Safeguard, The Ministry of Public Security, The Bureau of Internet Propaganda Management, and the State Council Information Office. And in different sectors such as education, there are also complete top-to-bottom Internet regulatory agencies in universities and schools. The relevant government sectors also hire many part-time workers, called "Internet commentators," to monitor the public opinion in the Internet, to promote propaganda for some policies, and reject others.

In addition, the government intervenes by deleting specific types of Internet sites. It is difficult to get the exact number of national websites that have been deleted. However, some netizens have developed an estimate based on the official numbers by an article from *People's Daily* that claims the Chinese have full freedom of speech and press. It says the "number of Netizens reached 420 million . . . people post articles more than 3 million per day . . . 66% of Netizens usually post articles on the Internet. . . " (Ren, 2010). Based on this estimation of the official number of netizens and Internet articles, there should be about 270 million netizens usually posting articles on the Internet. However, using those statistics reveals that there is an inherent contradiction. Then, by those statistics if active netizens post one article on the Internet per day, this would mean that 95.5% of articles are deleted; if they post one article every 10 days, then 85.2% of the articles are deleted; and if active netizens post one article per month, then that equates to 55.6% of the articles are being deleted (X. Zhu, 2010).

In 2009, some netizens[14] drew an illustration called "Netizens Anti-Assault," in order to indicate the difficult situation of netizens who have to confront powerful attacks by the state authorities from all directions.

In sum, the government has established a strict, comprehensive, and powerful Internet censorship system. Yonggang Li (2008) vividly describes the situation that the Chinese government confronts:

Figure 18.2 Netizens Anti-Assault (*wangluo fanweijiao xingshitu*)

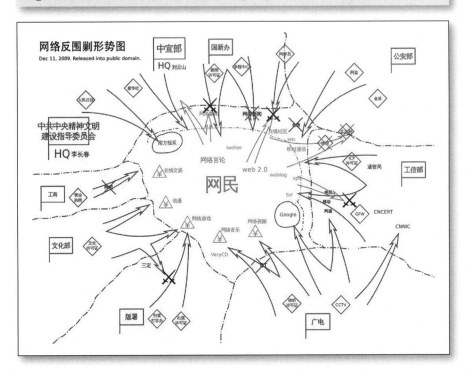

they seek to capture each step of information technology development, while avoiding political dissent voiced through new technology; they seek to improve their public service through the Internet, however at the same time, they have to restrict the free expression of people and any ensuing angry sentiment.

STRATEGIES AND SKILLS OF NETIZENS IN "THE WAR WITHOUT GUNSMOKE"

In face of a strong hegemonic government power, deconstruction is one of the most effective weapons of the weak (Scott, 1985). In the virtual space, netizens still need to follow general rules similar to the everyday behaviors of normal people, but they don't need prior coordination or resistance. Through the shared understanding of the informal Internet, people help themselves and each other and avoid directly confronting authority. In this asymmetric conflict, netizens collectively hold a strategy of nonviolent resistance and noncooperation with respect to the government. This is the most reasonable and rational approach among the alternatives—that is, direct challenge, disobedience, mischief, and an open struggle with government. Nonviolent resistance and noncooperation bring maximal progress with relatively minimal cost. Some scholars have named the approach, Guerrilla War in the era of the Internet (Bandurski, 2008). Netizens apply a primarily nonorganizational approach in order to counter the organization and power of Internet censorship.

This part of the chapter examines the mobilization approach and action tactics of netizens in the struggle for an equal society. It is important to note that netizens are not fighting alone, even though millions of netizens don't have a fixed or recognizable way to mobilize themselves. They are primarily issue-oriented, which means that if there is a hot issue in an interactive forum, they post comments to express their attitudes and to share the issue in other forums (such as blogs, bulletin boards (BBS), social network sites (SNS) and microblogs) in order to circulate this information among their peers. Therefore, the message dissemination grows bigger and bigger just like a snowball. In a very short period of time, most main Internet forums, bulletin boards, and microblogs are then filled with the current issue information.[15]

Netizens have applied a diverse range of technologies, skills, and tactics to counter the speech control by the government power. For example, in order to deal with Internet filtering of politically "sensitive words" (*Mingan Zi*), netizens created unique methods that split the Chinese characters into two or more parts to avoid the filtering. In addition, they use Chinese Pinyin, traditional Chinese characters, to avoid filtering. Netizens even applied a kind of "Mars language" (*Huoxing Wen*) to avoid the censorship. This Mars language is composed of a series of symbols from many languages, including Chinese, English, and Japanese. Subsequently a lot of relevant software is in development to help write and translate this Mars language.

In general, netizens prefer to use a few specific skills to update Internet languages and combat censorship; for example, they rely on harmonic tone, transformation, metaphor, metonymy, analog, interchangeability, ideographs, splitting words and letters, and a recombination of characters. Almost every classic Internet language contains satirical or sarcastic expressions. In accordance with the diverse language features—there are no regular rules in these language grammars—this indicates that netizens look toward a freer world. In addition, netizens usually use pictures, cartoons, jokes, songs, videos, or/and "performance arts" to express opinions that must bypass the restrictions of Internet censorship.

The most controversial strategy applied by netizens is the human-powered search (*Renrou Sousuo*). This technology is based on hundreds of netizens from different backgrounds and their information hunting skills. As a "double-edged sword," a human-powered search in China can be used to publish private information about a person who committed some unjust or bad actions on the one hand; however, this action can also damage the privacy of innocent people and become one form of "Internet violence."

DISCOURSE AND THE LANDSCAPE OF POWER AND POLITICS

Internet languages have a close relation with power and politics in China, which can represent and reflect the rising groups, the power structure, and political change. First, with the increase in netizens, the sphere of free expression is relatively decreasing. As an expression, Internet language can indicate some tensions among the process of two competing trends, for example, the expansion versus the contraction of free expression. Second, Internet language is developed within the current power system, which may reflect the features of the existing power structure. Finally, the bulk of netizen groups, the "After 1980's generation" usually have much more independent ideas, critical spirits, and rebelling discourses, which would reflect the power change and deconstruct the existing power structure.

Key Focuses of Netizens

I examined 60 "hot issues" on the Internet during 2007–2009 (Zhu, Hu, et al., 2008; Zhu, Shan, et al., 2008; Zhu, Shan, & Hu, 2009). As seen in the table, we can conclude that the subjects of "government capacity and credibility" and "abuses of public power" accounted for more than 56%.[16]

Netizens Issues, 2007–2009		
Categories of Hot Events	Frequency of Hot Events	Percent
Government Capacity and Credibility	26	40.6%
Abuse of Public Power and Privilege	10	15.6%
Rights Inequality	9	14.1%
Nationalism	7	10.9%
Corruption and Collusion of Officials	6	9.4%
Social Moral, Disaster Response, Gap between Rich and Poor	6	9.4%
Total	64	100.0%

Netizens were mostly attracted by, or engaged in, discussions of the decline of government capacity and credibility, abuse of public power and privilege, and the issues of rights inequality, which accounted for more than 70% of the issues.

Rather than directly criticize the government, netizens use a variety of step by step approaches to deliberately demonstrate their opinions and deconstruct the existing power while avoiding direct challenges to the force and power of local, regional, and state governments. They have successfully created revolutionary rhetoric and discourse models within Internet censorship, filtering, and some other political taboos, such as the discussion about the Tiananmen Square incident in 1989.[17]

From Word to Sentence: The First Step to Deconstruct and Represent

Any discussion of this special netizen rhetoric and discourse begins with the words. The selection of representative words examined here originated in Japan and then came to Mainland China in 2006. These words were chosen to indicate the overall situation and the feelings of ordinary people. Word selection is a voluntary activity; anyone can provide a suggestion on the most representative Chinese characters.

The netizens construct their own discourse from these Chinese characters—and even these single words can embarrass the government in some ways. From 2006 to 2009, five characters were used to indicate the netizens' perceptions on the country's development, their feelings on their livelihood, and their confidence in the future. Generally the characters stand for discontent or grievance in the overall situation and generally reflect a politically weaker group. The representative characters over the years have been *Chao (炒)*, *Zhang (涨)*, *He (和)*, *Bei (被)*, and *Huang (慌)*. These are mostly normal words in Chinese characters and literally have less political sensitivity.

In addition to annual characters, netizens use a different way to construct their discourse system, such as using "Saint Animals" in China, which is a vivid communication method. According to Chinese tradition, Saint Animals can bring happiness and fortune to people. However, netizens use them to express opinions, mostly grievances about Internet censorship or to describe a famous Internet event. Most animals are fabricated through the pronunciation of some inelegant and rude words.

The most famous example is that of grassmud-horse; when written in Chinese the symbol is similar to the meaning of "Fuck You." It is commonly used as "a dirty pun" (Wines, 2009a, 2009b) to express anger toward Internet surveillance and Internet filtering established by the "National Campaign against Vulgar Websites"[19] in 2009. The animals are named by very strange Chinese characters that demonstrate the thoroughly rebellious attitude of netizens toward the political system.

The netizens also created a few words in English. Their goal is not to internationalize

"Annual Word" in China, 2006–2010		
Year	Annual Word	Explanation/Interpretation
2006	Chao (炒)	Used as a speculative word about various products, including stock, house, commodities, and even reputations.
2007	Zhang (涨)	Used to reflect the inflation of overall prices.
2008	He (和)	A source from the CPC's future ruling target, i.e., "He Xie," means harmony in English however, netizens changed the property of the word.[18]
2009	Bei (被)	A word between a preposition and a verb, somebody passively acting out a role, like somebody has "been represented" to do something or "been suicide."
2010	Huang (慌)	Similar to the word "scare," people began to be nervous and frightened because of the social instability, growing prices, and other phenomena.

Note: All the words are from the Internet. The copyright should belong to all of the netizens in China.

Examples of the Saint Animals in the Internet of China			
Animals	Species	Pron.	Meaning
草泥马	Horse	Cao Ni Ma	Reads as fuck your mother.
法克鱿	Squid	Fa Ke You	Reads as fuck you.
河蟹	Crab	He Xie	Signifies harmony.
朵猫猫	Cat	Duo Mao Mao	Used when a man was beaten to death in prison; but the authorities lie and say the dead person committed suicide while he was playing the "hide-and-seek game."
打浆鼬	Weasel	Da Jiang You	A person has no business with something and indicates this indifference with social affairs.
伏卧蛏	Razor Clam	Fu Wo Cheng	A girl is suspected of being killed by a governor's son in Weng'an, Guizhou; however, the suspect claims he was exercising when the girl committed suicide. His arguments were accepted by the local police.
公务猿	Ape	Gong Wu Yuan	Refers to government officials and servants.
菊豹	Leopard	Ju Bao	Used to report a censorship offence on the Internet.
荡猿	Ape	Dang Yuan	Refers to members of the Communist Party of China.

(Continued)

(Continued)

叁鹿	Deer	San Lu	A famous brand of a poisonous powdered milk that the government supported.
璀狸猿	Ape	Guan Li Yuan	The manager of an Internet forum or BBS, SNS, etc. who can delete Internet posts.
骋鳍	Ochetobibus Elongatus	Cheng Guan	The inspectors in urban areas who often rudely and violently attack the people.
央虫	Louse	Yang Shi	Refers to Central China TV, seen as a purely propaganda media, typified by its fake news.
古鸽	Dove	Gu Ge	Used to represent Google, the search engine that was almost blocked by the Chinese government in January 2010.
鞑癫痢马	Horse	Dalai Lama	Represents the Dalai Lama, a Nobel Laureate in peace, who is listed as a taboo person in China.
甘鲸	Whale	Gan Jing	Refers to policemen who have lost the trust of the netizens.
症懈萎猿	Ape	Zheng Xie Wei Yuan	Represents member(s) of the National Committee of the Chinese People's Political Consultative Conference.
鲤冈鲃	Carp Barbel	Li Gang Ba	From the case of "My Father Is Li Gang"; when the second generations of governors commit crimes, they avoid any punishment because of the power of their parents.
毒豺	Jackal	Du Chai	Refers to a dictatorship.
欺实马	Horse	Qi Shi Ma	Used when a rich youth was speeding in his car and caused a person's death. The local police said his speed was only 70 miles per hour in order to reduce his legal obligation because the youth had a rich and powerful background.
亚克蜥	Lizard	Ya Ke Xi	It has the meaning of "great" in Uighur, which is intended to be ironic. It is from an Uighur festival game "Party's Policy Is Great (ياخشى)," after severe conflicts in Xinjiang in July 2009.

Note: All the words are from Internet. The copyright should belong to all the netizens in China.

Internet discourse but to express their anger and dissatisfaction through a different and interesting way that can demonstrate privileges, inequalities, and marginalized groups, such as the poor.

Dictionary of Contemporary Netizen Vocabulary in English			
New Words	*Pronunciation*	*Meanings*	*Explanations*
Shitizen	屁民, Pi Min	Shit-like Citizen	The weak status of citizens, from an official's speech to the ordinary people, "you are a shit!"
Antizen	蚁民, Yi Min	Ant-like Citizen	The poverty-stricken situation of people, mostly the young in the urban areas.
Halfyuan	五毛, Wu Mao	Fifty cents	The jobs as Internet commenters employed by governments.
Departyment	有关部门, Youguan Bumen	The Responsible department	When some events occur, the spokesman or leader usually says: "Youguan Bumen," "we'll deal with it" and won't tell you what department it is.
Jokarlist	记者, Ji Zhe	Journalist	The news written by journalist is usually faked like a joke.
Innernet	互联网, Hu Liang Wang	Internet	The Internet is gradually blocked from the overseas Internet because of the GFW–Great Firewall.
Freedamn	自由, Zi You	Free+damn, Freedom	The government perceives freedom as a damn issue.
Democrazy	痴心妄想, Chixin Wangxiang	Democracy is crazy.	It is perceived to be crazy to petition for democracy.
Harmany	河蟹, He Xie	River Crab, Harmony	The official aim is to be a harmonious society with the pronunciation of river crab.
Canclensor	审查, Shen Cha	Cancel and Censorship	The rude action, i.e., cancel or delete everything when operating a censorship.
Humant	人肉搜索, Renrou Sousuo	Human-Powered Search	A skill by netizens to hunt a person's private information.
Suihide	躲猫猫, Duo Maomao	Suicide+Hide	A man is beaten to death in prison; the authorities lie and say that the dead person committed suicide when he played the "hide-and-seek game." It is a satire about the government and their ignorance about human life. (Same as Cat, above.)
Z-turn	折腾, Zhe Teng	Drastic movements	Usually used as no Z-turn; to avoid drastic movements in development from Hu Jintao, the Chinese president.
Yakshit	亚克西, Ya Ke Xi	Yak+Shit; Great in Uighur	It is a pronunciation of "great" in Uighur, which has an ironic meaning. It is from a Uighur festival game "Party's Policy is Great (ىشخاي)," after severe conflicts in Xinjiang in July 2009. (Same as Lizard, above.)

(Continued)

(Continued)

Breastplit	开胸验肺, Kaixiong Yanfei	Split the Breast to Test Lung	To operate on a migrant worker just to prove his occupational lung disease; used to describe the irresponsibility of a hospital, factory, and government.
Emotionormal	情绪稳定, Qingxu Wending	Peaceful emotion	A most useful phase by the government when an accident happens, i.e., "The families of the dead are in peaceful emotion"; used to mean irresponsible and indifferent.

Note: All the words are from Internet. The copyright should belong to all the netizens in China.

FROM EVENT TO STRUCTURE: THE SECOND STEP IS TO DECONSTRUCT AND REPRESENT

In addition to specific linguistic and discursive constructions, netizens also attempt to deconstruct relations of power by analytically connecting individual events to broader structural factors as a means of criticizing the dominant ruling model of the government. They attempt to analyze a broad range of events in order to understand the fundamental essences of the behaviors associated with state power.

Netizens attempt to counter the public authority by critically analyzing the government's credibility over the long term, specifically the bad records of central and local governments. These governments usually control relevant information to ordinary people and even release false information in order to pursue social stability and the real benefits of information manipulation. The collapse of the stock market[20] in 2007 and the earthquake forecasts[21] in 2008 provide two clear examples of this behavior. For instance, once there are a few rumors about earthquakes, the government will refute every rumor. Netizens ask, why can't you foresee *when* an earthquake will happen, if you can foresee when it *won't* happen? The government engages in cycles of seeking and denying rumors because they are afraid that the rumors will start chaos and damage the country's stability. Ironically, some netizens even regard any official denial of a rumor as the proof that the rumor might be true.

In addition, netizens openly doubt official statistics and published data. Many numbers are fabricated and official data are far from reflecting people's feelings or experience. An interesting example of statistical fabrication is the number 87.53%. Netizens call it "the most magic number in the earth," because it is used so often by the Bureaus of Statistics and local governments (Guo, 2009).

Meanwhile, netizens strongly criticize many key public statistics such as housing prices, the Consumer Price Index, and crime rates. Different interest groups and government departments will publish different and even controversial data in order to protect or enlarge their own interests. The lack of public confidence in these "public" statistics leads to a vicious circle in which official statistics undermine the most important legitimacy of the CPC.

After government credibility, the second key point of netizen analysis is the institutional inefficiency that adversely affects the state and the people. According to the current perception of netizens, the governments and state-owned monopolies are trying to avoid their own duties or responsibilities and to gain more benefits through the propaganda change between "Chinese Characteristic" (*Zhongguo Tese*) and "International Standard" (*Guoji Biaozhun*). These two phrases have been abstracted as the key behavior model of state power. When governments don't want to take responsibility for programs such as a nationwide social protection system or other human livelihood issues, they cite *Chinese Character* as their excuse, which means that China has a population of billions and doesn't have the financial capacity to deal with that particular duty. However, when the government and state-owned monopoly want to increase the tax rate, increase the price of necessary goods (like gas and oil), raise the service fees, or even get rid of some certain public duties (like privatization), they claim the need to "be geared to international standards" (Xun, 2006).

In order to demonstrate just how big the gap is between earned income and the increasing cost of living, netizens assert that for the average person, their salaries are in line with those in Africa, while prices are geared to those in America and Europe. "Tax burdens are similar to those in Europe, housing costs are almost equal to the United States and the United Kingdom, while the level of welfare is close to that in Antarctica" (Xinhua article on netizens, 2010). As a result, netizens often ask: Is it the socialism we have been pursuing? Similarly, when China asserts the efficiency of the nation's disaster response system, netizens are highly critical of the claim. Netizens bolster their analyses by deconstructing

Figure 18.3

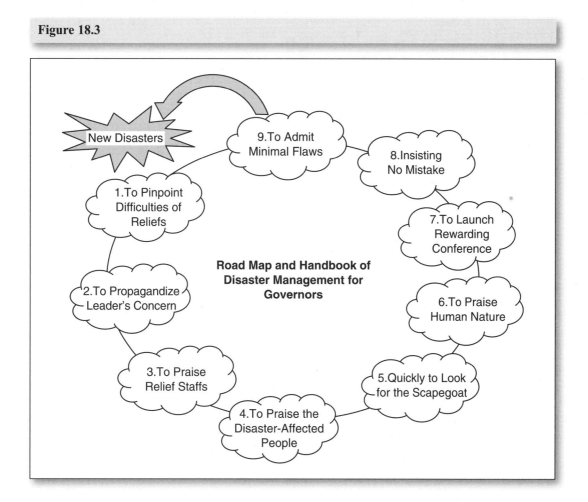

New Disasters

9. To Admit Minimal Flaws

8. Insisting No Mistake

1. To Pinpoint Difficulties of Reliefs

7. To Launch Rewarding Conference

Road Map and Handbook of Disaster Management for Governors

2. To Propagandize Leader's Concern

6. To Praise Human Nature

3. To Praise Relief Staffs

5. Quickly to Look for the Scapegoat

4. To Praise the Disaster-Affected People

government responses to disasters. In essence, they argue that the government arrives on the scene to transform the tragedy into a national mobilization, which then diminishes the numbers of public accusations that the government had responsibility to prevent the disaster, which then can be seen as contributing to increased government power. In response to this process, some netizens developed a "road map" to illustrate and criticize government response to human-made disasters (Bingdouxiaobao, 2010).

Online, some netizens assert that "*our government can only cope with the aftermath of a disaster*" or they are good at "*transforming the bereavement into a wedding.*" In many human-made accidents, the migrant workers or temporary workers are often accused and arrested by the government as the responsible parties; rarely is any official held responsible for these accidents.[22] Ironically, the officials are often promoted or rewarded on the basis of their own relief efforts!

The third area of government distrust among netizens concerns the public powers' treatment of marginalized groups in urban areas. For netizens, the urban inspectors, who often rudely and violently attack people are a primary focus of discussion. They have almost become the "Public Enemy" of netizens—particularly because of the forced demolition and relocation that has caused deaths. When these kind of events take place, netizens post the photos and articles around the Internet to attract the sympathy for the poor and to incite anger toward the public authorities.[23] In addition, netizens target urban inspectors because of their practices that disadvantage the poor people and their belief in that it reflects a possible collaboration between the housing industries and the local governments.

REPRESENTATION:
DECONSTRUCTION AND CONSTRUCTION

In the face of a strong state power to produce hegemonic discourse, netizens find ways to resist—despite their own relatively weak position. Their most effective tool is their ability to use diverse methods to deconstruct the mechanisms and rules of the official discourse, which are connected with the ruling pillars of the incumbent.

First, netizens try to challenge the official ideology-dominated state history in order to undermine the historical legitimacy of the CPC in China. One of the most popular methods of doing this is to circulate newspaper articles and commentary by the CPC dated before 1949, when the organization was still struggling with Kuomingtang (KMT), the former ruling party in China.[24] Netizens usually compare the former ideas with the current ideologies to question the historical promise of the CPC. Their search for a real and nonmainstream history demonstrates that netizens don't believe the current history but seek to write their own histories that will reflect their own realities.

Second, netizens compare the collapsed Soviet Union and Eastern European communist countries with the current Chinese politics and social problems (including the gap between the poor and rich, abuse of power and privilege, and loss of state-owned properties). Netizens also use the current developments in these countries to indicate that the collapse of the above countries could happen in China as well. Additionally, netizens also refer to the current Chinese regime as the "Saint Dynasty" (*Tian Chao*), which conveys some sense of feudalism.

Third, netizens pay close attention to economic achievements, which construct the most important pillar of the CPC legitimacy in China. Their criticisms include: local officials use over-estimated economic indicators; the development of a richer state yet poorer people; the gap between rich and poor; the damage to the environment, and price inflation. All these criticisms aim to break the myth of CPC's economic development, especially regarding the Gross Domestic Product (GDP), an important statistic to the government. More and more people have begun to criticize the limitation of GDP measurements. For example, the Chinese government's claim that its GDP exceeded that of Britain, Germany, and Japan drew numerous serious reflections and criticism on the Internet. Netizens also point out that there is a relationship between GDP and the destructive behaviors of local governments, such as the problems of forced demolition and relocation (Y. Wang, 2010).

Finally, the netizens' source of power rests not only in the construction of information but significantly in its communication advantages. On the one hand, the Internet has become a quick source of information—particularly when microblogs, bulletin boards, and forums are compared with traditional media. This dynamic interaction facilitates the spread of information—both international news, like the selection of the 2010 Nobel Peace Prize, and national news such as violent incidents occurring in China—that has been blocked by the government.[25] The netizens have constructed a media system to deal with information dissemination that includes microblogs and blogs, bulletin boards (BBS), and discussion forums throughout the censorship and counter-censorship process.

However, there are two new worrying trends: The first is that in addition to rational criticism and humor, there is an increasing presence of radical and irrational emotions that arise, especially in relation to the behaviors of state power. The second is the growing polarization among netizens that may undermine their own power to shape discourse and which may result in trapping netizens in an internally isolated discourse that is estranged from dialogue with people who are not on the Internet.

Concluding Remarks: Discontinuous Politics Within Condensed Structure

The Chinese power structure shapes typical Internet discourse via censorship. Yet, netizens have developed discursive strategies that focus on privileges, rights, and inequality, which undermine the rationales that sustain the credibility and efficiency of government authority. The government now finds that its own monopolized discursive space has been deconstructed. At the same time, the Internet struggles completely embody the current Chinese crises—the power struggle in virtual space pits an arrogant state power against the powerless whose lack of institutionalized channels of expression results in an unequal structure.

With great pressure from the public (especially via the Internet), the Chinese government during the last decade has changed a few rules and policies related to this unequal structure in order to reduce the degree of inequality. In this regard, the most significant example of the government's abandonment of the *Policies on Detention and Repatriation* that violated the Chinese constitution and endangered human rights was the Sun Zhigang incident.[26] In addition, the netizens' focus on privilege and power abuse have, at least, deterred some government activities. This was evident both in the Zhou Jiugeng corruption case and the recent Chinese Red Cross Society Scandal.[27]

Given the structural ability to block free communication, government power becomes more arrogant and rude. When a new communication channel, even in the virtual space, is greatly restrained then mass resistance will be inevitable. At the same time, China is typical of a strong state-weak society; its immature civil society is not strong enough to act as the buffer zone to avoid conflicts at the same time the authorities in power seem reluctant to allow the occurrence of a strong civil society. Therefore, the tension between the state powers and other groups like the netizens will be easier to ignite. If the situation worsens then the instabilities will probably move from the virtual spaces to reality.[28]

As Lucian W. Pye pointed out in *Aspects of Political Development*, that there generally are six crises in political development and state building of any given country: the Identity Crisis, the Legitimacy Crisis, the Penetration Crisis, the Participation Crisis, the Integration Crisis, and the Distribution Crisis. In an ideal design, these crises should take place one by one, however it is also possible several crises may happen at the same time (Pye, 1966, pp. 62–67). This situation can be much more serious when a developing country like China tries to catch up to the pace of developed nations within a short period of time. A lot of unstable factors that were condensed in the structure are released with the rapid change. The radical transformations within this limited time frame surely make the various crises more complex.

The polarized dominance of vested interest groups finally leads to a structure of rights imbalance, which is the "Logic of a Fractured Society" (Sun, 2003, 2004).[29] Elites prevail too much while the marginalized groups have a diminished ability to speak. Political struggles are discontinuous, because the ideology, institutions, and behaviors are discontinuous as evidenced by the presence of six crises.

All these discontinuities can be found in the Internet discourses and the netizens' interactions with the public powers. Importantly, the government has not yet become accustomed to or found an adequate approach to the Internet dialogue. The linear approach of government power has proven useless in a fluid and multidimensional space.

NOTES

1. In this chapter, discourse analysis as a qualitative method is mainly applied to investigate the meanings embedded in the written or spoken languages, such as the social perspectives and cultural identities, etc. It tries to resolve ways to make certain things significant, to enact activities and the relationship with others, to communicate social goods, and so on. It should also be noted that the term "discourse" is seen as a rather flexible word according in the context of this chapter. It includes both the meaning of "beyond the sentence," and the meaning of the language alone (Gee, 2005, pp.1–13; Schiffrin, Tannen, & Hamilton, 2001, pp. 1–10).

2. This term was created by Michael Hauben (1973–2001), an Internet pioneer based at Columbia University. The term *Netizen* is the combination of the two words, "Net Citizen" and is used to mean "people who care about Usenet and the bigger Net and work toward building the cooperative and collective nature, which benefits the larger world" (Hauben & Hauben, 1997, p. x).

3. It should be noted that this research only focuses on the political language or the discourse consisting of political meaning. It will not describe complete discourses about other issues.

4. The three categories in this table are not mutually exclusive. The data of students are sourced from the survey on vocation types; the youth data are from the survey on different ages; and the data on higher education are composed of people holding bachelor, master or Ph.D. degrees (CNNIC, 1997–2010).

5. Netizens from ages 10 to 39 account for 80.8% of this named group according to the reports in July 2010: respectfully, 29.9% for ages 10 to 19; 28.1% for ages 20 to 29; and 22.8% for ages 30 to 39 (CNNIC, 2010, pp. 13–14).

6. You can read Han Han's blog at China's biggest web portal, SINA, http://blog.sina.com.cn/u/1191258123.

7. For a brief timeline of Chinese censorship of the Internet, refer to Branigan (2010).

8. The full name of Green Dam (*lvba*) is "Green Dam Youth Escort" (*lvba huaji huhang*), which is a content-control software for Windows used in China with the publicly stated intent of protecting children from harmful Internet content and promoting a healthy Internet environment. Green Dam was originally to be installed on the computers in primary and middle schools according to a government notification of April, 2009 (Ministry of Education, Ministry of Finance, Ministry of Industry and Information Technology, State Council Information Office, 2009). Afterwards, it was ordered that the software was to be preinstalled compulsorily on all the new computers after July 1, 2009 (Ministry of Industry and Information Technology, 2009). Because of a huge overall boycott, the government gave up the compulsory installation of the Green Dam system in August 2009 (Taylor, 2009).

9. Google encountered a great challenge in 2010 when they tried to resist censorship and filtering requirements mandated by China, by insisting that they were self-censored. Because netizens can search relevant key words through Google and read and see some politically sensitive information and pictures, Google was regarded as a threat to the national security and an ideological challenge to the government. The Chinese government thought that Google was illegal and wouldn't provide a new permit. With few exceptions, the netizens sympathize with Google (See BBC article on Google, 2006; *New York Times* article on Google, 2010).

10. Falun Gong was good at using the Internet as one kind of communication technique. Even before

Falun Gong was defined as a "cult" by the Chinese government, they were accused of using the Internet to promote propaganda and mobilize people against the government. After being labeled a cult, Falun Gong accelerated the pace of their Internet usage and expanded their struggle against the Chinese government via the Internet and other techniques, such as hijacking satellites to transmit TV signals. since 1999, Falun Gong has built a few Internet websites, such as "*Falun Dafa Clearwisdom.net.*" Since then, the Chinese government has gradually become more aware of this kind of conflict in the Internet space. The government began to call for more Internet usage in order to maintain Internet security and keep their discourse power (see National Computer Network & Information Security Administration Center, 1999).

11. There are some successful examples where netizens have helped the anti-corruption sectors target and investigate corrupt officials, for example, the Zhou Jiugeng case (see Macartney, 2009).

12. The "Golden Shield" first occurred in the *People's Daily* in 2000, when Luo Gan, one of the seven members of the Politburo Standing Committee of the CPC Central Committee, went to inspect the Beijing Municipal Public Security Bureau (see Zhang & Niu, 2000).

13. For similar literature that discusses the Internet development and censorship in China and its subsequent impacts on political factors like democratization, etc. please refer to X. Wang, (2009).

14. This picture is anonymous. The Square Flags around the margin of the picture stand for authorities of the CPC and ministries of the Chinese government, including The Propaganda Department of the CPC; State Council Information Office; Ministry of Public Security; Ministry of Industry and Information Technology; The State Administration of Radio, Film, and Television; General Administration of Press and Publication; Ministry of Culture; State Administration for Industry and Commerce; and CPC Steering Commission of Spiritual Civilization Development, etc. The bigger flag indicates a larger power to regulate the Internet. The diamond stands for the methods that the ministries use to control the Internet, including the special agencies, licenses, and the block technology and software.

15. For example, when the case of "My Father Is Li Gang" was reported by the *New York Times* on November 18, 2010, the discussion on this report immediately was posted by the user at www.huaren. us, and immediately most Chinese main forums and

BBS had republished this news within two days. Once an event is regarded as an unjust one, little chips can light great fires through the Internet.

16. The reports provide the 20 hottest events every year from 2007–2009, which includes the most postings from the three to five largest Internet forums. After we deleted the pure sport news, entertainment news, and health news, then 53 events are left that can be interpreted as political. Considering that one event can have more than one meanings, each event can be classed into multiple categories. And there are 64 categories for the 60 "hot events." For example, the *Deng Yujiao* incident in 2009 had 25,133 posts in five forums, which was defined as one "hot event" and counted as one time when listed in the category of "Abuse of public power and privilege."

17. Whenever netizens discuss the Tiananmen Incident that occurred on June 4, 1989, they will indirectly use the code of "8×8" that is 64, or "eight four" etc. to refer to a given context. With the advent of strict censorship, the netizens learned to develop methods to avoid the censorship.

18. When the word *He* becomes *harmonize*, it changes the former meaning and is used to indicate that somebody or some issues are harmonized, which means that somebody is being controlled, kept in silence, or even imprisoned. Another meaning is that some public articles or speeches on the Internet or in the paper-based media h deleted.

19. The "National Campaign against Vulgar Websites" (*zhengzhi hulianwang disu zhifeng zhuanxiang xingdong*) is a nationwide campaign since 2009 with the stated intent to avoid the spread of pornography, to protect the public morality, and the mental health of the young people. However, this campaign is greatly criticized and perceived as a plan to block political information of the foreign media (*China Daily*, 2009; Hille, 2009a, 2009b).

20. On May 29, 2007, the State Administration of Taxation denied the so-called rumor that the stamp tax would be increased; however, after five hours, the Ministry of Finance increased the stamp tax effective on May 30, which caused a storm in the stock market in China. This type of government denial also happened several more times, specifically concerning the regulation of oil prices and electricity prices.

21. Take earthquakes as an example. Before May 12, 2008, the people near Wenchuan county noticed unusual phenomena concerning the behaviors of their animals, which they believed foretold an earthquake. However, the Aba government refuted this

rumor on May 9, 2008; an earthquake occurred three days later with thousands of lives lost.

22. For example, there were several incidents where "temporary workers" were blamed for incidents that occurred when City Inspectors attacked citizens in Zhengzhou and Wuhan during 2009 and 2010. A similar story also happened in Shanghai in November of 2010 when, after there was a large fire, some migrant workers were detained and accused of starting the fire with by their poor workmanship.

23. When on November 30, 2010, we input *Cheng Guan Da Ren* in Chinese (*The City Inspectors attack citizens*) Google retrieved 17.4 million results within 0.20 seconds including videos, news, and pictures on incidents involving attacks on citizens.

24. The methods are in fact from XiaoShu, who edited a book, including famous articles from the CPC's party newspaper that indicated the CPC were looking for democracy and freedom and disagreed with the party-state system and one-party system before 1949 (Xiao Shu, 1999).

25. On May 7, 2009, an accident occurred involving a wealthy "second generation" (family has powerful connections for two generations) and the main media silenced the story. However, the local Internet forum reported the news and 14,000 comments regarding the incident were posted that night. See the "Qi Shi Ma" description in the examples listed of the netizen's use of "Saint Animals" (see H. Zhu et al., 2009).

26. One of the significant events was the Sun Zhigang incident. On March 17, 2003 in Guangzhou, Sun Zhigang, 27 years old, was beaten to death after he was detained because he forgot to carry a valid residency permit. This event resulted in a huge popular outcry and finally resulted in the termination of the Custody and Repatriation System that had existed for several decades. Furthermore, this incident was widely debated, and many people called for some form of constitutional review in order to address and avoid any problems with legislation seen as violating basic human rights. This incident also played an important role in the current and forthcoming "rights protection movement" (weiquan yundong). For further discussion, see Hand, 2006; Human Rights Watch, 2008; and Pils, 2006.

27. The scandal of the Chinese Red Cross was triggered by a woman, Guo Meimei, who claimed to be a manager on staff with the Chinese Red Cross. On her microblog, she flaunted her wealth by writing about her famous cars and luxury handbags. With the poor records of the Chinese Red Cross Society, the public didn't trust the explanation of Red Cross Society and tried to look for possible corruption within the society. Some netizens called for a boycott against the Chinese Red Cross Society because of their lack of transparency and accountability. This event is still ongoing and the Red Cross Society has promised to be more transparent (BBC article on Businessman, 2011).

28. Recently, the attacks against the government have turned more and more violent, and bombings have occurred. It is hard to say that the Internet has increased the level of violence, but it is certain that the Internet plays a role in the information spread. The most recent incident was the Fuzhou suicide bombing in May 2011, see Yan & Gao (2010).

REFERENCES

A clear sense of frontier: The 3rd discussion of party's ideological and political problem in new situations (yige qingxing de zhendi yishi: san lun zhuajin xin xingshixia dang de sixiang zhengzhi gongzuo). (2000, April 23). Commentator. *People's Daily (Renmin Ribao)*, p. 1.

Bandurski, D. (2008). China's guerrilla war for the web. *Far Eastern Economic Review, 171*(6), 41–44.

Bingdouxiaobao. (2010). For the dream of freedom (weile na ziyou de lixiang). Retrieved from *izaobao.com*(807). [Special Note: This Internet address has been blocked by the government since 2011.]

Branigan, T. (2010, January 14). Internet censorship in China. *The Guardian*. Retrieved December 10, 2010, from http://www.guardian.co.uk/world/2010/jan/14/internet-censorship-china.

Bristow, M. (2008). China's Internet 'spin doctors.' *BBC News*. Retrieved from http://news.bbc.co.uk/2/hi/7783640.stm.

Businessman quits amid China Red Cross scandal. (2011). *BBC News. Asia-Pacific*. Retrieved July 20, 2011, from http://www.bbc.co.uk/news/world-asia-pacific-14026592.

Buzan, B., Wæver, O., & de Wilde, J. (1998). *Security: A new framework for analysis*. Boulder, CO: Lynne Rienner.

China campaigns to clean up vulgar websites. (2009, January 5). *China Daily*. Retrieved December 24, 2010, from http://www.chinadaily.com.cn/china/2009-01/05/content_7367249.htm.

China Internet Network Information Center (CNNIC). (1997–2010). *Statistical report of China Internet development (zhongguo hulianwangluo fazhan zhuangkuang tongji baogao).* Beijing: (CNNIC).

Fang, H. (2002). Falungong and the Internet (falungong yu hulianwang). *Journalism and Communication, 9*(2), 2–12.

50 people that matter 2010: 48. Han Han. (2010). *New Statesman.* Retrieved from http://www.newstatesman.com/2010/09/han-china-matter-taken-200.

Gee, J. P. (2005). *An introduction to discourse analysis: Theory and method* (2nd ed.). New York, NY: Routledge.

Goldsmith, J., & Wu, T. (2006). *Who controls the Internet? Illusions of a borderless world.* Oxford, UK: Oxford University Press.

Google censors itself for China. (2006, January 25). *BBC News.* Retrieved December 10, 2010, from http://news.bbc.co.uk/2/hi/technology/4645596.stm.

Google or China: Who has more to lose?. (2010, March 23). Editors. *New York Times.* Retrieved December 15, 2010, from http://roomfordebate.blogs.nytimes.com/2010/03/23/google-or-china-who-has-more-to-lose/.

Guo, J. (2009, December 12). Magic 87.53 (shenqi 87.53 zhege shuzi jingran zouhong). *Chengdu Business Newspaper (Chengdu Shangbao),* p. 6.

Hand, K. J. (2006). Using law for a righteous purpose: The Sun Zhigang incident and evolving forms of citizen action in the People's Republic of China. *Columbia Journal of Transnational Law, 45*(1), 114–195.

Hauben, M., & Hauben, R. (1997). *Netizens: On the history and impact of Usenet and the Internet.* Los Alamitos, CA: IEEE Computer Society Press.

Heffernan, W. C. (2002). Fourth Amendment privacy interests. *The Journal of Criminal Law and Criminology, 92*(1/2), 1–126.

Hille, K. (2009a, January 5). China bolsters Internet censors' scrutiny. *Financial Times.* Retrieved December 19, 2010, from http://www.ft.com/intl/cms/s/0/f858f9aa-dac8-11dd-8c28-000077b07658.html#axzz1SdQhUikq.

Hille, K. (2009b, January 5). China cracks down on Internet content. *Financial Times.* Retrieved December 20, 2010, from http://www.ft.com/intl/cms/s/0/dd9c3a30-daf7-11dd-be53-000077b07658.html.

Holquist, M. (1983). The politics of representation. *The Quarterly Newsletter of the Laboratory of Comparative Human Cognitions, 5*(1), 2–9.

Hu, J. (2007). Full text of Hu Jintao's report at 17th Party Congress. *Xinhua News Agency.* Retrieved from http://news.xinhuanet.com/english/2007-10/24/content_6938749.htm.

Jacobs, A. (2009, June 11). China faces criticism over new software censor. *International Herald Tribune,* p. A8. Retrieved from http://www.nytimes.com/2009/06/11/world/asia/11censor.html.

Jiang, Z. (2002). Full text of Jiang Zemin's Report at 16th Party Congress. *Xinhua News Agency.* Retrieved from http://news.xinhuanet.com/english/2002-11/18/content_633685.htm.

Li, Y. (2008). National GFW: The Regulation Logic of Chinese Internet (guojia fanghuoqiang: zhongguo hulianwang de jianguan luoji). *The 21st Century (21 shiji)*(106), 79–87.

Li, Y. (2009). *Our great firewall: Expression and governance in the era of the Internet (women de fanghuoqiang: wangluo shidai de biaoda yu jianguan.* Guilin, CN: Guangxi Normal University Press.

Macartney, J. (2009). China jails corrupt government official Zhou Jiugeng. *The Times.* Retrieved from http://www.timesonline.co.uk/tol/news/world/asia/article6869806.ece.

Ministry of Education, Ministry of Finance, Ministry of Industry and Information Technology, State Council Information Office. (2009). *Notification of installing green Internet filtering software in middle and primary schools (guanyu zuohao zhongxiaoxue xiaoyuan wangluo lvse shangwang guolv ruanjian anzhuang shiyong gongzuo de tongzhi).* Beijing, CN: Government Printing Office.

Ministry of Industry and Information Technology. (2009). *Notification regarding requirements for pre-installing green filtering software on computers(guanyu jisuanji yuzhuang lvse shangwang guolv ruanjian de tongzhi.* Beijing, CN: Government Printing Office.

National Computer Network & Information Security Administration Center. (1999, August 9). Rapid Internet Development, Heavy Internet Security (wangluo fazhan tufei mengjin xinxi anquan renzhong daoyuan). *People's Daily (Renmin Ribao),* p. 12.

Netizens' suggestion on "the 12th Five-Year Plan": Income should increase with the price (wangyou jianyan shi'erwu: shouru zengzhang yingyu wujia shuiping tongbu). (2010, December 27). *Xinhua*

News Agency. Retrieved from http://news.xinhua net.com/fortune/2010-12/27/c_12887161.htm.

Paine, T. (1966). Common Sense. In N. F. Adkins (Ed.), *Common sense and other writings* (pp. 53–101). New York, NY: Pyramid Books.

Pils, E. (2006). Asking the tiger for his skin: Rights activism in China. *Fordham International Law Journal, 30*(4), 1209–1287.

Pye, L. W. (1966). *Aspects of political development: An analytic study*. Boston, MA: Little, Brown.

Ranking of Sina blog total flow. (2011). *Sina.* [The largest Chinese-language infotainment web portal]. Retrieved July 20, 2011, from http://blog .sina.com.cn/lm/top/rank/.

Ren, W. (2010, October 26). People have the freedom of speech and press is an indisputable fact (woguo gongmin xiangyou yanlun chuban ziyou shi buzheng de shishi). *People's Daily (Renmin Ribao),* p. 7.

Scott, J. (1985). *Weapons of the weak: Everyday forms of peasant resistance*. New Haven, CT: Yale University Press.

Shapiro, M. J. (1988). *The politics of representation: Writing practices in biography, photography, and policy analysis*. Madison: University of Wisconsin Press.

Schiffrin, D., Tannen, D., & Hamilton, H. E. (2001). Introduction. In D. Schiffrin, D. Tannen, & H. E. Hamilton (Eds.), *The handbook of discourse analysis* (pp. 1–10). Malden, MA: Blackwell.

Smith, C. R. (2002). The great firewall of China. *Newsmax.* Retrieved from http://archive.newsmax .com/archives/articles/2002/5/17/25858.shtml.

State Council of the People's Republic of China. (1996). *Temporary Regulations on the International Internet of Computer Information System in P.R.China (zhonghua renmin gongheguo jisuanji xinxi wangluo guoji lianwang guanli zanxing guiding)*. Beijing, CN: Government Printing Office.

Sun, L. (2003). *Cleavage: Chinese society since 1990s (duanlie: 20 shiji 90niandai yilai de zhongguo shehui)*. Beijing, CN: Social Sciences Academic Press.

Sun, L. (2004). *Imbalance: The logic of a fractured society (shiheng: duanlie shehhui de yunzuo luoji)*. Beijing, CN: Social Sciences Academic Press.

Tatlow, D. K. (2010, May 14). In search of a modern humanism in China. *International Herald Tribune*. Retrieved from http://www.nytimes.com/ 2010/05/14/world/asia/14iht-letter.html?_r=1.

Taylor, M. (2009, August 13). China drops Green Dam web filtering system. *The Guardian*. Retrieved December 10, 2010, from http://www.guardian .co.uk/technology/2009/aug/13/china-drops-web-censorship.

Thousands of families access to Internet (qianjia wanhu zoujin hulian wangluo). (1996, January 23). Editorial. *People's Daily (Renmin Ribao),* p. 7.

Walking on thin ice: Control, intimidation and harassment of lawyers in China. (2008). *Human Rights Watch*. New York, NY: HRW.

Wang, S. (1996, April 16). Introduction of Internet category regulations (hulianwang fenlei guanlizhi). *People's Daily (Renmin Ribao),* p. 7.

Wang, X. (2009). *Behind the great firewall: The Internet and democratization in China*. Ann Arbor: The University of Michigan Press.

Wang, Y. (2010). Special indicators lead to achievements lie (feichang zhibiao biding huangbao zhanji). *Guang Ming*. Retrieved from http://guan cha.gmw.cn/content/2010-05/22/content_ 1128802.htm.

Wenden, A. L. (2005). The politics of representation: A critical discourse analysis of an Aljazeera special report. *International Journal of Peace Studies, 10*(2), 89–112.

Wines, M. (2009a, March 12). A dirty pun tweaks China's online censors. *The New York Times,* p. A1. Retrieved from http://www.nytimes.com/ 2009/03/12/world/asia/12beast.html.

Wines, M. (2009b, March 20). China: Censors bar mythical creature. *The New York Times,* p. A8. Retrieved from http://www.nytimes.com/ 2009/03/20/world/asia/20briefs-CENSORS BARMY_BRF.html.

Wines, M. (2010, November 17). China's censors misfire in abuse-of-power case. *International Herald Tribune*. Retrieved from http://www .nytimes.com/2010/11/18/world/asia/18li.html.

Xiao, J., & You, H. (2009, February 3). Analysis of Internet monitor in people's online (benban yu reminwang wangluojiandu lianhe diaocha jieguo fenxi). *People's Daily (Renmin Ribao),* p. 8.

Xiao Shu (Ed.). (1999). *The voice of pioneers in history: The great promises before half a century (lishi de xiansheng: bange shiji qian de zhuangyan chengnuo)*: Guangdong, CN: Shantou University Press.

Xu, J., & Li, Z. (2010, May 18). Internet fear (wangluo kongju). *People's Daily (Renmin Ribao),* p. 17.

Xun, J. (2006, October 22). Focus on China: Be geared to international standards. *BBC Chinese*.

Retrieved December 10, 2010, from http://news .bbc.co.uk/chinese/simp/hi/newsid_6070000/ newsid_6075500/6075590.stm.

Yan, J., & Gao, C. (2010, May 27). Fuzhou blasts kill two, destroy vehicles. *China Daily,* p. 3.

Yang, G. (2003). The Internet and civil society in China: A preliminary assessment. *Journal of Contemporary China, 12*(36), 543–475.

Yoshikazu, K. (2009). Debates on Green Dam (lvba zhi zheng). *FT Chinese.* Retrieved from http:// www.ftchinese.com/story/001027084.

Zhang, L., & Niu, A. (2000, August 5). Luo Gan require police technology in capital should keep ahead in China (Luogan zai beijingshi gong'anju kaocha shi yaoqiu shoudu keji qiangjing ying zouzai quanguo qianmian). *People's Daily (Renmin Ribao),* p. 2.

Zhao, Q. (2010). Uncontrolled public opinion: The catalyst of Soviet Union collapse (yulun shikong: sulian jieti de cuihuaji). *Qiu Shi, 21,* 57–58.

Zheng, T. (2008). When the school president meet county governor (dang xiaozhang yushang xianzhang). *Southern People Weekly (Nanfang Renwu Zhoukan),* (3), 31–33.

Zhu, H., Hu, J., & Sun, W. (2008). Analysis of the public sentiment in China's Internet 2007 (2007 nian zhongguo hulianwang yuqing fenxi baogao). In X. Ru, X. Lu, & P. Li (Eds.), *Society of China analysis and forecast 2008 (zhongguo shehui xingshi fenxi yu yuce 2008),* (pp. 234–253). Beijing, CN: Social Sciences Academic Press.

Zhu, H., Shan, X., & Hu, J. (2008). Analysis of Internet public discourse 2008 (2008 zhongguo hulianwang yuqing fenxi baogao). In X. Ru, X. Lu, & P. Li (Eds.), *Society of China analysis and forecast 2009 (zhongguo shehui xingshi fenxi yu yuce 2009)* (pp. 280–299). Beijing, CN: Social Sciences Academic Press.

Zhu, H., Shan, X., & Hu, J. (2009). Analysis of Internet public discourse 2009 (zhongguo hulianwang yuqing fenxi baogao 2009). In X. Ru, X. Lu, & P. Li (Eds.), *Society of China analysis and forecast 2010 (zhongguo shehui xingshi fenxi yu yuce 2010)* (pp. 246–262). Beijing, CN: Social Sciences Academic Press.

Zhu, H., Shan, X., & Hu, J. (2011). Analysis of Internet public discourse 2010 (2010 zhongguo hulianwang yuqing fenxi baogao). In X. Ru, X. Lu, & P. Li (Eds.), *Society of China analysis and forecast 2011 (zhongguo shehui xingshi fenxi yu yuce 2011)* (pp. 187–207). Beijing, CN: Social Sciences Academic Press.

Zhu, X. (2010, October 26). Comments on people have the freedom of speech and press is an indisputable fact (*woguo gongmin xiangyou yanlun chuban ziyou shi buzheng de shishi*), [Web blog post]. Retrieved December 10, 2010, from http:// xizhizhu.blogspot.com/2010/10/blog-post.html.

19

FRAMING EXTREME VIOLENCE

The Collective Memory-Making of Argentina's Dirty War

ROBERTA VILLALÓN

INTRODUCTION

Thirty-five years ago, one of the bloodiest phases in Argentine history began. On March 24, 1976, the *Junta de Comandantes en Jefe* led by militarists Rafael Videla, Emilio Eduardo Massera, and Orlando Ramón Agosti, assumed governmental power with an explicit mission: to restore order and regain the state monopoly of the legitimate use of force by eliminating "subversive" activists and organizations. In the historical context of the Cold War, military governments fighting leftist groups were not breaking, but rather conforming to this pattern. As was the case in many other countries, this type of political action resulted in tens of thousands of deaths (Romero, 1994).

In Argentina, the casualties of seven years of military rule—of this so-called *Guerra Sucia* (Dirty War)—are still in the process of being found and counted: at least 10,000 people were considered "detained/disappeared" (that is,

kidnapped, apprehended, tortured, murdered and buried, or eliminated without keeping public record of the person's identity), and 2,422 people were killed (with a public record of their identities) by the security forces of the state. It is reported that the total number of direct victims of this repression is estimated at 30,000 people. Of the people who were detained/disappeared, 70% were men and 30% were women, and of those women, 10% were pregnant. The majority of the people who were detained/disappeared were between 16 and 35 years old, and they were mostly blue-collar workers (30.2%), students (21%), secondary sector employees (17.9%) and professionals (10.7%) (CONADEP, 1984). This information was compiled and published in the *Nunca Más* report by the *Comisión Nacional sobre la Desaparición de Personas* (National Commission on the Disappearance of People) or CONADEP, which was created by the democratic government that took over power in 1983 in order to clarify "events relating to the disappearances of persons in Argentina and investigate their fate or whereabouts" (CONADEP, 1986, p. 428). The investigation that CONADEP completed served as complementary evidence for the trials of the military and paramilitary in charge of the systemic repression, most of whom were condemned by the courts in 1985. However, these trials did not close "the horrible chapter" of Argentinean history (Solá, 2005). To this day, the process of seeking justice and healing remains open. On the one hand, two Argentinean laws, *Punto Final* (Full Stop) enacted in 1986, and *Obediencia Debida* (Due Obedience) in 1987, limited the extent of possible accusations and trials. Furthermore, presidential decrees in 1989 and 1990 pardoned military and civilians condemned for their participation in the *Guerra Sucia*. On the other hand, in 2003 the National Congress nullified those laws (*Punto Final* and *Obediencia Debida*) and they were declared unconstitutional by the Supreme Court of Justice in 2005, and then in 2007, a federal court overturned the presidentially decreed pardons. Since then, and at the time of this writing, several trials of the military have been reopened and are in process.[1]

Throughout the last 28 years of democracy, the complex sociopolitical process of understanding the *who*, the *what*, the *how*, and the *why* of this political time has been ongoing. A number of human rights organizations, grassroots, and political groups are mobilizing to raise levels of public awareness and to reach justice. In turn, many scholars and researchers are (re)thinking these issues in order to keep the process of remembering and comprehending, alive and growing. Divergent interpretations of "a past 'that does not pass'" have emerged (Jelin, 2003, p. 101), as history, "a continuous recomposition of the past in the present," continues to be rewritten (Chizuko & Sand, 1999, p. 137). Through this contentious politics of representation and collective memory-making, people and groups with various ideologies and capitals have striven "to affirm the legitimacy of 'their' truth" (Jelin, 2003, p. 26), while hierarchies of knowledge and power have been socially (re)organized

(Bietti, 2009). In this chapter, I identify hegemonic and counter-hegemonic frames that have been used to create meanings and organize experiences of the Dirty War. I propose alternative frames (an intersectional frame and an emotions-conscious frame) with the aim of contributing to the collective efforts to understand this phase of history. By looking into the report prepared by CONADEP, which included hundreds of testimonies by survivors of torture and their acquaintances, and taking it as an open source for furthering the still ongoing process of (re)framing the past, I discuss how the *Nunca Más* became a hegemonic narrative from which subsequent interpretations (including counter-hegemonic readings) of the Dirty War emerged.

At the core of the CONADEP report were the testimonies offered by the survivors of torture, and the victims' relatives and acquaintances. The inclusion of these personal stories as part of the new official narrative of history was a radical change from the past, not only in historiographic terms (Phelps, 2004), but also in contrast with the obliteration of all the voices that were not considered to be "in tune" with hegemonic ideals of the nation during the military regime. The testimonies of those who had been forced to become "voiceless" (Jelin, 2003, p. 68) require of their readers "the capacity to identify their own identities, expectations, and values with those of another" (Beverley, 2005, p. 550). Testimonies "might be seen as a kind of speech act that sets up special ethical and epistemological demands" (Beverley, 2005, p. 550), allowing for a transition to democracy that included the respectful listening to these testimonies by a citizenry that had been politically polarized, as well as subjected to extreme levels of fear and repression. It is believed that testimonies allowed direct and indirect victims of violence to recover their lost sense of self and provided a new ground for Argentineans to rebuild a dignified collective identity as a people in a democratic context where all voices are in principle worthy to be heard (Phelps, 2004; Jelin, 2003; Rey Tristán, 2007; Kaplan, 2007).

The role of testimonies, however, has been problematized. Are testimonies trustworthy sources? Can testimonies be taken at face value? What is left out? Is it even possible to express the pain of violence through language? Who is able to speak up? Can testimonies be collective? Who is to pay attention to which testimonies? Do testimonies reify violence and generate yet another opportunity for a voyeuristic, and thus abusive, attitude on those who did not experience the violence and/or those who perpetrated it (Hartman, 2004; Jelin, 2003; Scarry, 1985; Franco, 1987)? Far from deterring activists and scholars from using testimonies, enthusiasts have included critical analyses of the way in which testimonies are collected and shared, as well as an analysis of their content and implications (Marín, 1991; Yúdice, 1991; Mallon, 1994; Chizuko and Sand, 1999; Brison, 1999; Memoria Abierta, 2005; Assmann, 2006). Despite debates, the report with its testimonies became the dominant source—or *master frame*—from which to develop historic understandings and alternative explanations of what had happened during the dark years of the military regime.

Therefore, I take *Nunca Más* as an open source for furthering our understanding of what I believe is one of the densest and most dividing phases of Argentine history. My study of the report, while focusing on the testimonies, intends to contribute to the still ongoing, collective process of (re)framing the past, and re-membering a conflicted society (Phelps, 2004, p. 50). So, instead of judging whether the report was partial or impartial, inclusive or exclusive, official or subaltern, I try to understand how it presented events in particular ways. I want to comprehend which voices were included, how they were included and organized, and ultimately, how one can continue to learn about the *Guerra Sucia*, Argentina, and about political violence, torture, and the process of overcoming such traumatic experiences. By reading scholarly analyses on this matter, and analyzing testimonies published in other venues, I identify various primary frames that have been utilized to comprehend the hidden and atrocious occurrences during the military regime and, by articulating alternative frames, provide yet another round of interpretation.

I draw from Goffman's (1986) frame analysis theory to understand the complexities and nuances of processes of collective memory-making, particularly in regard to historical periods of acute abuses of power. While this use of frame analysis may be considered "unorthodox" (König, 2004, p. 1) since scholars do not generally impose a frame on a document—by doing so, I intend to demonstrate the power of framing and reframing as tools to animate what existing frames may be masking and thus to reach deeper levels of subject comprehension. By looking into the politics of "framing public memory" (Philips, 2004, p. 1), I hope to contribute to the ongoing "process of (re)construction of individual and collective identities in societies emerging from periods of violence and trauma" (Jelin, 2003, pp. 17–18). The politics of framing public memories can be thought of as a long-term dialogue between parties with diverse views and power, yet all struggling for legitimacy and recognition of their version of the past, and thus, their expectations for the future (Weine, 2006; Jelin, 2003; Cohen, 2001). This kind of politics is thus a process of contestation that continues to develop over time and space where a set of diverse and changing social actors become involved (Roniger & Sznajder, 1999; Jelin, 2003). The various (re)framings are necessarily multilayered and reflective of psychological, sociological, political, cultural, and ideological intersections that may allow for certain aspects to be brought forth or put back, to be connected in particular ways, and hence, to yield new understandings.

In my analysis of the politics of (re)framing public memory of the traumatic experiences of Argentina's *Guerra Sucia*, I highlight the power of framing and suggest that an intersectional and an emotions-conscious reframing may further elucidate what occurred during the years of extreme violence. First, I find that certain structures of power—along intersecting gender, sexual, racial/ethnic, religious, and class lines—pervade the way in which repression was instrumented during the Dirty War. Second, I find richness in including the space that feelings occupied in the process of surviving violence by noting the rift between emotional and nonemotional testimonies published in *Nunca Más* and in the book *Pájaros sin luz* (Ciollaro, 1999).

In what follows, I expand on frame analysis and collective-memory studies. Then, I focus on the way in which the CONADEP report was structured and consequently how it provided a particular interpretation about the *Guerra Sucia*, which became the master or hegemonic frame. Next, I propose an intersectional, counter-hegemonic reading that may further the analysis of Argentina's *Guerra Sucia* by including portions of testimonies published in the report as well as in other venues. After that, I discuss how an emotions-conscious frame may contribute to understanding the central role played by feelings during the repression. Also, by presenting illustrative portions of testimonies of survivors of torture, I discuss the process of collective memory-making and personal/social healing. Finally, I share concluding thoughts about how the continuous, contentious, and complicated processes of (re)framing help in reaching deeper levels of historical comprehension.

FRAME ANALYSIS
AND COLLECTIVE MEMORY

In my work, I put frame analysis in dialogue with collective memory studies; a dialogue that I believe can bear fruitful results, particularly when interjected with ideas coming from the literature on subaltern studies and the role that testimonies have played in processes of democratization and social struggles for justice and equality. Indeed, the long-lasting process of collective memory-making of the years of the last regime in Argentina emerged and has been maintained by groups of people who had been considered subaltern, who had been silenced and pushed further into the margins of society by the military. These groups (including survivors of repression, relatives of the disappeared, and

numerous political activists for human rights) have explicitly and collectively worked to recover the voices of the detained/disappeared, to uncover the hidden abuses of power on the part of the military (and, to a lesser extent, of the paramilitary forces), and to legitimize a collective memory that defied official histories. They have accomplished this by locating the subaltern, their experiences, and their testimonies at the core of the alternatively created narrative of the *Guerra Sucia*. I propose to think about the labor of collective memory-making by these subaltern groups and its fruits (which include the CONADEP report *Nunca Más*) as processes of framing—that is, of understanding and organizing the experiences and events of the *Guerra Sucia*. Moreover, I suggest looking into how these initial processes of framing motivated further reframing given the concealed, extreme, tortuous, and complex character of the deeds by the military and paramilitary forces, and the complex and long-term nature of historical comprehension and collective healing.

According to Goffman,

> when individuals attend to any current situation, they face the question: "What is it that's going on here?" Whether asked explicitly, as in times of confusion and doubt, or tacitly, during occasions of usual certitude, the question is put and the answer to it is presumed by the way the individuals then proceed to get on with the affairs at hand (Goffman, 1986, p. 8).

Individuals use "basic frameworks of understanding available in [their] society for making sense out of events and to analyze the special vulnerabilities to which these frames of reference are subject" (Goffman, 1986, p. 10). Frames are social principles of organization that govern events and the subjective involvement of people in them. Frames organize experiences and when analyzing these frames, one can comprehend the "structure of experience individuals have at any moment in their social lives" (Goffman, 1986, p. 13).

Primary frameworks or schemata of interpretation render "what would otherwise be a meaningless aspect of the scene into something that is meaningful" (Goffman, 1986, p. 21).[2] Primary frameworks and particularly "framework of frameworks" reveal central aspects of the culture of social groups and societies, which tend to prefer order, organization, and stability over change, disorganization, and instability (Goffman, 1986, p. 27). In regard to this tendency, Goffman makes reference to how stories about extraordinary events are told: he notices that people use conventional frames as a means to

> cope with the bizarre potentials of social life, the furthest reaches of experience. What appears then to be a threat to our way of making sense of the world turns out to be an ingeniously selected defense of it. We press these stories to the wind; they keep the world from unsettling us (Goffman, 1986, p. 15).

Hence, the application of primary frameworks not only provides meaning, but concomitantly organizes experience, maintains a sense of stability, and allows individuals (and groups) to form "conjectures as to what occurred before and expectations of what is likely to happen now" (Goffman, 1986, p. 38).

By applying these concepts to the case of the *Guerra Sucia*, I find that (a) people who were detained/disappeared and those who survived used primary frames to make sense of the exceptional situation in which they found themselves during (and after, if they survived); (b) members of the CONADEP who collected survivors' testimonies and organized them in the report also utilized primary frames in order to comprehend the past and contribute to the process of collective memory-making; (c) scholars and activists who interpreted the report and its testimonies, and/or collected new testimonies after the publication of the report not only used primary frameworks, but also built on the master frame resulting from the report itself and created (partially) new frames of understanding; and (d) the employment of these various frames by all of these individuals and groups in different circumstances have not only organized the extreme characteristics of the *Guerra Sucia* (and thus restored a sense of collective order and social

stability) but also shaped the development of our knowledge about it.

In this chapter, I analyze the mounting layers of frames in the CONADEP report, the testimonies in the report, exemplar scholarly analyses of the report and the *Guerra Sucia,* and testimonies published in alternative venues. These texts have become open, living sources where generations on generations have looked for answers to remaining and new questions about the past. Since "texts are not just effects of linguistic structures and orders of discourse, they are also effects of other social structures, and of social practices in all their aspects" (Fairclough, 2003, p. 25), I believe that a sociological reading of a selection of key texts can lead to a deeper understanding of the dynamics beneath the collective processes of memory-making. Moreover, I claim that this use of frame analysis can help in furthering the process of collective memory-making of the *Guerra Sucia* in Argentina because of the central role that framing has in these kind of processes in general. Individually and collectively, simultaneously and consecutively, people try to make sense of the events that affect them, by directly or indirectly applying various frames of interpretation that work as "principles of selection, emphasis, and presentation composed of little tacit theories about what exists, what happens, and what matters" (Gitlin, 1980, p. 6). Thus, when making use of primary frames, people prioritize certain aspects while minimizing, dismissing, or ignoring other aspects that indeed may have been important; when framing, individuals tend to simplify for the sake of reaching at least some understanding of the situation—an understanding that usually is appropriated as control over past and current circumstances.

While subjects make use of these frames in all and every "normal" situation, it is particularly revealing to pay attention to how people frame extraordinary events (like being detained and tortured, and having a repressive government implementing such techniques systematically and secretly) both during times of repression and after these extreme circumstances occur. Argentina's *Guerra Sucia* is a case that has triggered very deliberate efforts to better comprehend what happened, to whom, and why, given both the hidden and atrocious nature of its events. Each round of interpretation has built on previous frames; each round of reframing has brought further depth and complexity into the process of understanding this chapter of Argentina's past.

The *Nunca Más* Report as the Hegemonic Frame of the *Guerra Sucia*

Much has been written about the *Comisión Nacional sobre la Desaparición de Personas,* CONADEP (National Commission on the Disappearance of People) and its report *Nunca Más* that has been "recognized as the first serious attempt to use a truth commission to reckon with the past" (Phelps, 2004, p. 82), "considered successful" (Phelps, 2004, p. 84) and celebrated both in Argentina and across the world. In the report, one finds only a fraction of the 50,000 pages of documents and evidence gathered by members of the CONADEP, who went around the country and abroad to collect declarations of people who were kidnapped, tortured, and liberated, and about people who were killed and disappeared. The report also identified secret detention centers, and documented irregularities in hospitals, clinics, morgues, cemeteries, police headquarters, and other institutions that may have been involved in the system of disappearances.

The *Nunca Más,* almost 500 pages long, includes a prologue written by the chair of the Commission, Ernesto Sabato. The prologue makes the tone and logics of the report explicit and describes the six sections of the document that is structured to try to make sense of Argentina's recent, obscure past: (1) The Repression, (2) The Victims, (3) The Judiciary during the Repression, (4) Creation and Organization of the National Commission on the Disappeared, (5) The Doctrine behind the Repression, and (6) Recommendations/Conclusions. The prologue and the report itself reflect the Commission's politics of framing the *Guerra Sucia*—it is a politics shaped both by the official (hegemonic)

and alternative (counter-hegemonic) histories of these years of dictatorship and great political activism and violence.

In the prologue, the Commission makes clear that it did not have the power or intention to judge those responsible for the excesses that took place during the regime of the *Junta de Comandantes en Jefe* (that was the task of the judicial branch of power). Yet, the Commission's investigations led its members to assert that "the recent military dictatorship brought about the greatest and most savage tragedy in the history of Argentina" (CONADEP, 1986, p. 1) and to claim that

> we cannot remain silent in the face of all that we have heard, read, and recorded. This went far beyond what might be considered criminal offences, and takes us to the shadowy realm of crimes against humanity (CONADEP, 1986, pp. 1–2).

Given that, in a systematic fashion "human rights were violated at all levels by the Argentine state during the repression carried out by the armed forces," the Commission dismisses those who may claim that the events were the result of "individual excesses" or that they were "inevitable in a dirty war," and argues that the calculated kidnappings, tortures, killings, and disappearances were conducted by military officers "who were carrying out orders" of senior officers (CONADEP, 1986, p. 2).

In the prologue, the Commission also makes explicit that its "arduous" task was filled with "sadness and sorrow" as well as insults and threats, and that the Commission's members were only able "to piece together a shadowy jigsaw, years after the events had taken place, when all the clues had been deliberately destroyed, all documentary evidence burned, and buildings demolished" (CONADEP, 1986, p. 5). They offered appreciation of those who provided "the statements made by relatives and by those who managed to escape from this Hell or even the testimonies of people who were involved in the repression but who, for whatever obscure motives, approached us to tell us what they knew" (CONADEP, 1986, p. 5).

The CONADEP adopted a perspective that I label a *humanistic frame*: it portrayed all victims as equal in their condition as abused human beings and it included selections of their testimonies as evidentiary material while reaffirming their human worth. Most testimonies in *Nunca Más* included names, last names, or initials, gender, and age; there were graphics indicating professions and occupations of the detained and/or disappeared. In the section titled "Victims," there were eight subsection categories: "Children and pregnant women who disappeared," "Adolescents," "The family as a victim," "The repression did not respect the sick or disabled," "Members of the clergy and religious orders," "Conscripts," "Journalists," and "Trade Unionists." In the section titled "The Judiciary during the repression," there was a subsection devoted to the "Disappearance of lawyers."

As presented in the report, the victims not only included adult men and women, but also minors and pregnant women. The victims were not individuals alone, but also entire families. The victims who were disabled or had some sort of ailment were not treated differently but further victimized. Moreover, victims who were actively involved in professions or occupations usually associated with free speech, critical thinking, and social justice—such as journalists, union leaders, lawyers, human rights activists, and members of religious organizations "who were committed to helping the less fortunate, or who denounced the violation of human rights" (CONADEP, 1986, p. 337), were especially targeted.

It is important to note that these groupings qualified the universalized victim: yes, they were all humans, and their human rights were unfairly abused; but there were certain attributes of these people that pointed to the moral unacceptability as well as the strategic planning by the military in their implemented system of abduction, torture, and disappearance. Thus, the humanistic frame under the human rights umbrella did not preclude the CONADEP from pointing to the particularistic way in which the Dirty War developed, as well as indicating the Commission's worldview.

Therefore, the *Nunca Más* report provides *a* frame—a frame that soon became the hegemonic text or metanarrative of the *Guerra Sucia*—through which the reader can make sense of how the system of repression and killing came to pass, as well as learn about the actual experiences of "pain and horror" based on the hundreds of first-person testimonies included in the text (CONADEP, 1986, p. 9). However, the Commission warns the readers that the cases included in the report comprise a selection made "in order to substantiate and illustrate our main arguments" and accepts responsibility for possible errors and points out the fact that other cases may have been more adequate to justify their points (CONADEP, 1986, p. 7). This warning, together with the prologue, can be read as disclaimers through which the Commission showed that it was cognizant of its own ideological, political, and thus, particular and potentially controversial position regarding what they found out about the *Guerra Sucia*. Indeed, as researchers Dworkin (1986), Nino (1998), Roniger and Sznajder (1999), Jelin (2003), Phelps (2004), and Crenzel (2008a, 2008b) among others pointed out, the report was bound to reflect certain politics of representation and memory. To be aware of this politics does not erase the value of the report, but rather allows for more nuanced readings of what became "Argentina's biggest bestseller" (Phelps, 2004, p. 84).

The report became "the canonical narrative about the disappearances [that] occurred in Argentina" (Crenzel, 2008a, p. 48). At the same time, this "master narrative" (Jelin, 2003, p. 27) became a fundamental open source to learn, think, and (re)write about that very critical portion of this country's history. The *Nunca Más* generated diverse reactions (Camacho, 2008) and further investigations that allowed for alternative and presumably better understandings of these traumatic years of history. For instance, Phelps (2004) emphasizes the central role that storytelling has had in the process of individual and national healing, and argues that the new democratic state should make the effort to include divergent voices into the new national narrative.

Crenzel critically analyzes the reasons and effects of CONADEP's strategy to depoliticize the persona of victims and survivors. He points out that the limitations of the *Nunca Más* cannot be attributed solely to the state (represented by the Commission), but also to the difficulties that Argentinean society has had to "think in complex terms about the past of violence that ripped it apart" (Crenzel, 2008a, p. 59).

Jelin (2003) explores the complexities of memories and collective memory-making and argues that all memories are bound to highlight something while leaving other things in the shade—both metanarratives and their alternative narratives are inevitably partial. Roniger and Sznajder (1999) and Rey Tristán (2007) critique the report for failing to offer a subsection devoted to the experiences of political exiles, despite their large quantity and important role in the struggle for democracy. Kaufman (1989), Graziano (1992), Braylan, Feierstein, Galante, and Jmelnizky (2000), and Navarro (2011) all examine the problematic way in which religious and ethnic issues were presented in, or excluded from, the report. Several authors offer a gendered reading of the *Guerra Sucia,* pointing to the role that the mothers and the grandmothers of *Plaza de Mayo* had in bringing the dictatorship to an end (Taylor, 1997; Waylen, 2000; Bejarano, 2002; Navarro, 1989), addressing the role of sexual violence (Franco, 1987; Taylor, 1997; Kaplan, 2007), and uncovering the silenced issues around sexual orientation (Bazan, 2004; Oviedo, 2010).

These various alternative readings of the CONADEP report and the *Guerra Sucia* can be analyzed as part of the long, contentious, and complex process of collective memory-making. In my view, the *Nunca Más* and the following reinterpretations of what happened should not be simply read as a conflict between history written from above (official history) and histories written from below (subaltern histories) (Mallon, 1994; Beverley, 2005). I argue that this report breaks this dichotomous view of history making: the official/subaltern (hegemonic/counter-hegemonic) binary opposition is challenged by the combination of (a) the sociopolitical conjuncture when the report was written, together with the central role that testimonies occupy in the elaboration of the report and the text itself, as well as the Commission's recognition of its own subjectivity, and (b) the fact that indeed further readings and writings were developed and published later on. In particular circumstances, history has been (re)written as a result of a (more or less contentious) dialogue within and between members of the official or dominant groups of power and those of subaltern or subordinate groups of power. However, these groups are never unified, homogeneous entities. These are heterogeneous groupings with members who have diverse interests, various degrees of power, and therefore, disparate levels of influence.

For example, in the case of Argentina's narrative of the *Guerra Sucia*'s history, the groups that may be identified as hegemonic and counter-hegemonic were indeed very heterogeneous and replete with debates about the recent events as well as the political future of the country (Roniger & Sznajder, 1999; Jelin, 2003; Rey Tristán, 2007; Crenzel, 2008b). Moreover, the group that authored the new official narrative of the *Guerra Sucia*, the CONADEP, built its version of the events in collaboration with many human rights and other grassroots organizations of civil society, and on the basis of the testimonies provided by survivors of political violence and acquaintances. These various organizations and individuals had been considered the subaltern, the other, and subversive—not only by the military but also by significant sectors of the population who considered their activism as marginal and insubordinate. As Roniger and Sznajder (1999) claim, "For the first time in the history of violence and turmoil of Argentina, the story told by victims and from the perspective of the victims was published with an official seal" (p. 194). However, while it is true that the *Nunca Más* report "officialized" the histories of those who had been labeled and punished as "the subaltern" during the military regime, I believe that standing hegemonic/counter-hegemonic divides were displaced by the more complex realities of each of these groups, and by the processes of interaction involved as these heterogeneous forces rewrote a collective memory/history.

Intersectional Reframing of the *Guerra Sucia*

By paying attention to the way in which the CONADEP framed the occurrences of the Dirty War, how the *Nunca Más* report became the hegemonic text, and then, how this master frame emphasized certain aspects over others, I point to the strength of using frame analysis and identifying subsequent framing or interpretations of the metanarrative. At the same time, the identification of subsequent alternative readings (reinterpretations that emphasize, for example, the depolitization of the report, the missing perspective of exiles, or the gendered and sexualized aspects of the military regime) furthers the understanding of the various processes at play during the Dirty War. However, as one learns from intersectional theory, each of these social dimensions do not work alone, but overlap in particular ways configuring unique forms of oppression (Hill Collins, 1986). Thus, I propose to apply an intersectional frame of analysis with the goal of comprehending how violence and repression interacted with factors such as class, gender, sexuality, sexual identity, race/ethnicity, religion, and politics. I believe that an *intersectional reframing* will contribute to further develop counter-hegemonic readings of the *Nunca Más* given one of the main characteristics of such epistemology: the unmasking of how latent or hidden sociological factors overlap with manifest ones and configure specific forms of oppression.

An intersectional reframing demonstrates how sexual violence was not only intrinsic to the way in which repression was implemented by the military but also intersected with gender dimensions, religion, race/ethnicity, and social class. For example, from the testimonies in *Nunca Más* one learns that rape and other forms of sexual abuse were systematically used by the military to humiliate and subjugate detainees. The way in

which sexual violence was implemented against women and men, regardless of their age or health conditions, showed that this kind of aggression worked as a way to strengthen the hypermasculine gender structure of the military. On the one hand, military male officers belittled women by treating them like worthless objects that were to be used and abused sexually and violently. The rape of women in groups with several officers watching and cheering as if the violations were "collective feasts" (CONADEP, 1984, p. 52) also worked to reaffirm the hegemonic masculinity of the military officers who showed to others their uncontrollable sexual desire and power, and the "pleasure" that these sexual manifestations generated (CONADEP, 1984, p. 37). On the other hand, military officers belittled subversive men by demeaning their potency through sexual molestation and by having military women introducing "burning chemical liquids" through their penis (CONADEP, 1984, p. 48).

The use of sexual violence fed not only hypermasculine gender regimes, but also a certain racial/ethnic order that prioritized white Catholics (an order that implied a particular social class hierarchy with the idea that this racial/ethnic group was worthy of higher socioeconomic status). The testimony of Mónica, who was a Jewish pregnant woman, illustrates this point,

> I was taken to the torture room by some men who began to hit me because I refused to get undressed. Then, one of them tears off my shirt and they throw me to a metal table in which they tied me by my hands and feet. I tell them that I was two-months pregnant and the 'Turco Julián' replies: 'If so-and-so could endure the (torture) machine being six months pregnant, you can stand it, and be raped too.' Then the torturers became more and more incensed with me, for two reasons: because I belonged to a Jewish family, and because I did not cry, which exasperated them (CONADEP, 1984, p. 346).

The testimonies of Jewish survivors and other victims who were addressed in racial terms illustrate how an intersectional reframing allows one to expose dimensions of repression that would otherwise remain opaque. In other words, if the frame utilized was exclusively focusing on sexual violence, the fact that the religion of the victim affected the way in which violence was implemented would be ignored or dismissed as unimportant. However, with an intersectional framework in mind, one is prone to identify the various degrees and complexities of violence with multiple intervening factors. For example, Daniel testified

> that the Jewish were punished only for the fact of being Jewish [. . .] and were subjects of all types of tortures, but principally one that was extremely sadist and cruel: 'the rectoscope' that consisted of a tube that was introduced in the anus of the victim, or the vagina of the women, and inside the tube a rat was inserted. The rat would look for an exit and tried to enter by biting the internal organs of the victims (CONADEP, 1984, pp. 74–75).

The case of Rubén Schell shows the intersection of race/ethnicity and religion. Rubén, who was of German descent, ended up receiving "better treatment" because of his "Aryan" looks. He declared that "after a long session of torture, 'Coco' or 'the Colonel' said to me: 'Listen, *Flaco* (Man), what are you doing amongst these niggers? With your looks, you should be an S.S.'" Then, the Colonel showed him "a swastika he had tattooed on his arm," giving orders that from then on, Schell had to be well fed. "From that day on I was not longer tortured," added Rubén (CONADEP, 1986, p. 68).

The intersection of race with social class, politics, and sexuality is illustrated in the testimony of D.N.C. who shared that after being raped, the officer who raped her told her that the irony was "that he was a *cabecita negra*[3] who wanted to be with a blonde woman but did not realize that she was actually a guerrilla warrior (*guerrillera*)" (CONADEP, 1984, p. 155). In this case, one sees the use of sexual violence to transgress racial/ethnic and class social divides that separated Argentineans of European descent (people with a lighter phenotype, identified as whites, usually middle-class, and predominantly

of the Radical Party) from Argentineans of indigenous or African descent (with a darker phenotype, mostly *mestizos*, but catalogued as *negros*, usually lower-class, and predominantly of the Peronist Party).

By using an intersectional frame to read the testimonies, one finds a more intricate equation of power and its abuses during the military regime. For example, it was not only the gender of the victim that shaped the ways in which he or she was treated (a conclusion that one could come up with by reading the *Nunca Más* report with its special subsections devoted to pregnant women, for example), but also the victim's social class, race/ethnicity, religion, (assumed) political affiliation, and sexual orientation. These nuances are apparent in testimonies published in other venues, such as in the book *Pájaros sin luz: Testimonios de mujeres de desaparecidos* (Ciollaro, 1999). This book is not an official government account but rather offers accounts of lived experiences by wives and partners of men who disappeared, as well as the experiences of many women in that group who were themselves kidnapped and tortured. While Ciollaro's focus is intentionally directed to women, and thus her book allows for a gendered analysis of trauma and survival of political violence, the testimonies included in her book become valuable data that can be interpreted intersectionally.

For instance, Eva's declaration shows the overlapping of social class and gender. She observed,

> the workers were the ones that disappeared the most, they were always putting their bodies in all the struggles, in the strikes, against the coups, however they are the least recognized. And if these men are not recognized, how would we, the women, be recognized? (Ciollaro, 1999, p. 263)

Read with intersectional lenses, one learns about the class distinctions but also how these were affected by gender as well: low-income men were particularly targeted but minimally acknowledged in their struggles; low-income women also were distinctively attacked, but because they were women, they were ignored and silenced even more.

When looked at from an intersectional perspective, María del Socorro's account reveals the interplay between the issues of gender, social status, and the underpinning weight of the ideals of motherhood maintained by the military and that were socially hegemonic at that point in time in Argentina. She addressed the issue of how to deal with the social suspicion about women who were activists together with their husbands or partners, but who ended up not being killed:

> the malicious question of 'how is it that you are alive and he is not?' made many women walk away in a lot of pain, some left politics for ever, while others did what they could, maintaining their activism, supporting, collaborating, but always with a low profile. . . . Ironically, these women are most of the mothers of the sons and daughters of the disappeared . . . those who had to fight alone, with those kids. . . including the fact of being looked down upon as an irresponsible mother and questioned because you were an activist while having kids (Ciollaro, 1999, p. 285).

The links between ideals of motherhood and citizenship, and how these reflect social hierarchies along intersecting gender, sexual, racial/ethnic, religious, class, and political lines can also be seen in the testimonies from and about pregnant women and their children. Captured women delivered their babies in the infirmaries of the clandestine centers of detention, in their jails, or in military hospitals, sometimes with medical assistance, at times without any, but always under surveillance, most of the times tied to their beds and blindfolded, which prevented them from seeing their babies and where they were detained. In the *Nunca Más* report, one finds Adriana's declarations about the experience of Inés,

> after twelve hours of contractions, (the officers) took Inés to the kitchen of the jail and put her on a dirty table, blindfolded, and in front of many other officers, she had her baby with the assistance of presumably a doctor, who only shouted at her

while the rest of the officers laughed loudly. She had a boy called Leonardo. After 4 or 5 days of having him with her in the cell, the officers took him away (CONADEP, 1984, p. 305).

The "kids of the subversive women," as a gynecologist of a military hospital called them (CONADEP, 1984, p. 312), were to be permanently separated from their mothers, in order to save them from their subversive parents and to make them "good" citizens. In addition to taking away babies at birth, the security forces kidnapped kids when they removed "subversive" parents from their homes (CONADEP, 1986, p. 14). The CONADEP and Grandmothers of Plaza de Mayo estimated that between 170 and 200 kids were kidnapped by these two methods (CONADEP, 1984, p. 299).

By adopting an intersectional framework of analysis, I find that the strategy of the military regime to eliminate "subversive" mothers, to separate the children from their "subversive" families and to assign them to "good" families reflected a particular politics of motherhood. This kind of politics determined that women's citizenship was defined by their biological differential characteristic from men (the possibility of childbirth) and consequently, their political duty as citizens was limited to the private spheres of rearing good citizens. The conservative, heteropatriarchal, and moral issues behind these politics took extremely violent forms during the years of the military regime by emphasizing the selective aspect of "good" motherhood. Ideally, "good" mothers were politically conservative, Catholic, middle-or upper-class women who followed the hegemonic path of femininity and did not take action against the politics enforced by the military regime. Conversely, "bad" mothers were "subversive" women who were suspected of being politically active and having liberal/progressive ideas, or simply women who did not fit the traditional profile because of other reasons (such as believing in sexual freedom or gender equality). This type of action violated not only women's reproductive privacy (Roberts, 1995), but also reinforced the heterosexual conceptualization of a woman's body as a reproductive (and disposable) machine (Briggs, 1998). What emerges is a moral doctrine: women were considered reproductive moral machines who were to be destroyed, if they did not fulfill both of those functions.

As a whole, an intersectional reframing allows for a more nuanced understanding of what happened. Narratives are always more than factual accounts, simply by virtue of the fact that they must always be situated in particular contexts, perspectives, and interests. In other words, the collection and presentation of testimonies always expresses certain politics of framing (be it by the governmental institution gathering the declarations, the researcher doing the interviews, the human rights activists calling for the documentation of abuses, etc.). An analysis of framing does not invalidate the legitimacy of the accounts, but reveals the circulation of knowledge and power that give accounts particular kinds of value (Taylor, 1997). In particular, an intersectional reading of the politics of framing of the *Nunca Más* goes against the grain of the document itself and can make it possible to identify how overlapping systems of oppression rendered the experiences of certain victims more important than others by emphasizing specific traits while submerging and/or omitting others.

Emotions-Conscious Reframing of the *Guerra Sucia*

While the hundreds of accounts of abduction and torture in *Nunca Más* most certainly mobilize the readers' feelings, I found that the testimonies of repression in the report appeared to be robustly factual yet lacking in emotional content. An example is Adriana's declaration,

> After 3 or 4 hours of being on the floor with continuous contractions, and thanks to the shouting of my mates, (the officers) took me to a police car with two men in the front and a woman in the back (who was called Lucrecia and who participated in the tortures). We left toward Buenos Aires, but my little girl could not wait [. . .] and they stopped the car in the side of the road, where Teresa was born.

Thanks to those things of nature, the delivery was normal. The only attention that I got was that with a dirty piece of cloth, Lucrecia tied the umbilical cord that had Teresa together with me because they did not have anything to cut it with. In less than five minutes, we continued our way to the theoretical 'hospital.' I still had my eyes blindfolded and my baby cried in the seat [. . .]. [After arriving to a detention center, a] doctor [. . .] made me undress and in front of an officer, I had to clean the bed, the floor, my dress, the placenta, and, ultimately, they let me wash my baby, all in between curses and threats (CONADEP, 1984, p. 305).

Adriana's matter-of-fact testimony is moving, and readers may assume that these traumatic experiences were highly emotional for the victims, even if feelings are not mentioned at all. Indeed, one may wonder whether the overt inclusion of emotions in the testimonies is at all necessary given the fact that most appreciations of the *Nunca Más* report point to its harrowing quality. Dworkin (1986) calls it "a report from Hell" (p. xi) and Crenzel (2008a) acknowledges its "high emotional density" (p. 55). I believe like Jaggar (1997, p. 386) that "emotions may be helpful and even necessary rather than inimical to the construction of knowledge" about the politics of violence, death, and survival of Argentina's *Guerra Sucia*. The way in which emotions are included, submerged, or omitted speaks to "how intricately the problem of pain is bound up with the problem of power" (Scarry, 1985, pp. 11–12) and with the politics of representation.

The lack of emotion in the testimonies in *Nunca Más* should not be attributed to a faulty performance on the part of the CONADEP or on a disguise purposely put forth by the victims when they shared their experiences. Instead, the omission of emotions is fairly typical in the narration of violence and trauma. The fact that emotions themselves are missing in the testimonies points to how "the atrocities committed defy language and representation" (Taylor, 1997, p. 139). Extreme "physical pain does not simply resist language but actively destroys it" (Scarry, 1985, p. 4). "Even where it is virtually the only content in a given environment, it will be possible to describe that environment as though the pain were not there" (Scarry, 1985, p. 12). However, pain as well as other emotions such as anger, rage, despair, anguish, sadness, and love are fundamental aspects of the politics of violence and survival.

Based on her personal experience, Ciollaro (1999) wrote about the paralyzing effects of the dictatorship and the system of disappearances. Her book, *Pájaros sin luz: Testimonios de mujeres de desaparecidos* emerges as a project that came out from the "darkness" of silence and pain she endured when her husband was abducted in front of her and her children (Ciollaro, 1999, p. 32). Twenty years after his abduction and disappearance, her recollection was triggered by one of the many crises her children went through. At that point she writes that she began to "talk with many other women who had gone through similar experiences in order to see myself, to feel myself, to know what happened to me" (Ciollaro, 1999, p. 32). In an effort to remember and recover, to "feel that it is important to be alive" (Ciollaro, 1999, p. 32), she made a deliberate effort not to deny the role of emotions. Consequently in her book, her interviews with women include significant expressions of feelings. Ciollaro's book is a great example of how an emotions-conscious frame can lead to even more of an understanding of the events of the *Guerra Sucia* and its aftermath.

In *Pájaros sin luz*—the title references the lyrics of the tango song "Naranjo en flor" by Homero and Virgilio Expósito, and points to the impeding effects of a traumatic past that puts people in a state of fright like "birds without light" (*pájaros sin luz*)—several women talked about how this sentiment permeated their experiences. Marta made reference to the impossibility of talking given her suffering; she said "it was very difficult to talk . . . I cried and cried; I could only cry, I could not do anything else, there was nothing else" (Ciollaro, 1999, p. 205). Delia linked pain, anguish, and silence, "it was difficult to raise the issue of the disappearance of the father because the family did not talk about it;

did not talk about it because of pain, not to generate more anguish" (Ciollaro, 1999, p. 44). Ada spoke of fear and its paralyzing and long-lasting effects,

> inside, I had fear, and if there is something that I have not lost, it is fear. The person that does not know fear is able to do whatever they please, but when one knows fear, one is partially broken (Ciollaro, 1999, p. 215).

María explained her surprise about the emotional aspects of repression, and also talked about silence, denial, and the long-lasting effects of experiencing violence:

> I was ready for all the political aspects, including torture. The truth is, my emotional shock, which I believe I still have, was not to be ready for the other. For the disparaging, for watching (the torturers) spend a whole night raping a minor and killing him after [. . .] Things that normally are not talked about, but [. . .] In order to survive and move on, live a normal, correct life, one had to hide all these in some part of one's brain, and then, it is very difficult to think that after going through all of that, one would be able to believe in something [. . .] Nothing surprises me anymore (Ciollaro, 1999, pp. 272–273).

Eva talked about anger and pain,

> I have a lot of anger. It is terrible the anger that I have. I see other people that have had worse experiences than I did, but they can manage things in a better way. And me, no, I have a horrible anger. And what do I do with this anger? Lately, what I do is to feel bad, because I see that justice is getting worse and worse. Justice has been sold. I see the assassins free, in the streets, the torturers, the thieves of kids, relaxed, everywhere. I thought that there was going to be justice. But the way things are gives me pain and anger. It doesn't let me live (Ciollaro, 1999, p. 259).

María del Socorro shared her pain and rage after losing her baby following repeated torture, and how she tried to be hopeful again:

they gave me a shot with a drug, Cristerona Forte, to which I did not resist because I thought that it was to save my pregnancy, afterwards I found out that it was an abortive. Two days later, I discharged something bloody looking, black. It was only then that I realized that . . . well, that there was nothing that could remain, that I did not have anything else . . . nothing. I kept what I discharged in a little bag. Next morning, when the officers were counting us, I smashed it in the face of one of the officers. That is all that was left from my son. Later on, I would try to feel better by thinking that eventually I would be able to be back again with Guille and that we would have a dozen of children (Ciollaro, 1999, pp. 274–275).

In her testimony, María del Socorro also included the letters that her partner, Guillermo, wrote for her in captivity, pointing to the role that love plays in keeping people alive and enduring torture,

I feel strange writing this letter to you without knowing how I am going to send it away, but at the same time, it is painful not having been able to tell you how much you helped me in the most difficult moments. When at night the handcuffs were hurting me, when the cold made me as stiff as wood or the wounds became unbearable, thinking about you, remembering all the minutes we had had together, took me out of that world and brought back the strength that they were trying to take away from me. I also remember your screams and my desperation when I heard them and my constant insomnia in order to distinguish which ones were yours in the loud screaming nights [. . . .] And I want you to know that the memory of yours was the most resistant shell that I had and will have, and that I deeply wish to be together with you and tell you things with my eyes, with my hands, with my mouth and heal all that is there to be healed, and laugh without knowing what we are laughing about, and make love until we fall asleep and keep loving each other in a dream that lasts a thousand years (Ciollaro, 1999, pp. 286–287).

As all of these excerpts illustrate, testimonies that are framed in terms of an emotional content provide a more comprehensive (and more painful) portrayal of how victims experienced torture in particular, and the military regime in general. Emotions, however, may be perceived as a complication of what seemed to be an orderly (and thus more manageable) description of the events as presented in the *Nunca Más* report. By telling what happened without emotion, victims, investigators and readers are able to frame a chaotic and extreme history of violence into what is commonly associated with rationality. Emotions may jeopardize this apparent order, which may be a reason why the testimonies included in the CONADEP report avoided presenting feelings as a constitutive element of the events of the *Guerra Sucia*.

CONADEP's rational, nonemotional framing of traumatic, systematic repression implemented during the military regime offers a comprehensible narrative that is uncomplicated by feelings. It is plausible that the addition of emotions in the testimonies could have become too incendiary in a time when the democratic government was trying to leave behind a phase of extremely high and violent political activism that had "ripped [the country] apart" (Crenzel, 2008a, p. 59). However, it cannot be denied that emotions were a fundamental element in how people experienced violence, managed to survive, dealt with losses, and kept politically active to fight for democracy and claim for "memory, truth and justice" to this day.[4] Their central role deserves the attention of researchers, particularly of those who are willing and able to deal with the uncertainties raised when looking at social issues in all of their complexity.

CONCLUDING THOUGHTS

The *Nunca Más* report, in particular the testimonies of repression, is an open source that continues to generate analyses that contribute to the development of a more complete comprehension of Argentina's *Guerra Sucia*. The politics of representation that are implicated in the process of collective memory-making include highly contentious and intricate processes in which heterogeneous groups of changing social actors struggle to present their version of the truth. The diverse framing and reframing of what happened in the past lead to diverse understandings of the future. These highly dynamic processes reflect as well as challenge existing structures of power that are continuously changing yet constantly oppressive at some level.

In this chapter, I maintain that a critical frame analysis of the report and testimonies provides a more complete and complicated version of the *Guerra Sucia*. In addition, it offers insight into how processes of analysis and interpretation have been affected by competing political forces and intersecting social structures of inequality. By looking into the structure of the report and the content of the testimonies included, one can begin to understand the politics of framing in Argentina's construction of a public memory of the military regime. The *Nunca Más* report, which became the celebrated hegemonic narrative of the dictatorship, reflects a social order that is not as oppressive as the one enforced by the military *Junta*, however it still represents a certain normative hierarchy that prioritizes certain groups of people and events over others. For example, subsequent critical analyses of the report offer counter-hegemonic interpretations that complicate the dynamics of repression instrumented by the military by examining the omission of politics, gender, and sexuality as structuring dimensions of the Dirty War. My own analysis contributes an intersectional reframing of events that points to the overlapping of gender, sexuality, race/ethnicity, religion, class and political affiliation.

In addition, my analysis highlights the role that emotions played in the politics of repression and survival. While the emotional experiences of the people who were detained and disappeared can be inferred from the factual testimonies in the master report, there is a need to look for alternative sources (like Ciollaro's book) where more complete accounts are compiled. Arguably, including emotions in the reports and in the analyses of them, challenges state efforts to order or organize the chaotic and horrific events of the *Guerra Sucia*. The passage of time has allowed for more and different analyses of the period to be written. It also has allowed for increased analytical complexity—a complexity that may be enriched by incorporating the potentially disturbing power of emotions.

These research strategies—that is, to read between the lines of and beyond the limits of the *Nunca Más* report, to analyze the frames and consecutive reframing of the report, and to develop counter-hegemonic readings—are only feasible because of the intrinsic wealth of the report, its testimonies and the rich growth of literature on the topic. All of this work is the result of the enduring efforts of many people and organizations involved in one way or another with the process of re-membering (Phelps, 2004) and comprehending what happened in Argentina (Jelin, 2003).

In the same month that the *Junta* took power, I was born to parents who were catalogued as "subversive" and "threatening to the nation" because of their occupations and ideologies. We were among the fortunate; we were not detained or disappeared. Now I hope my work contributes to the long-lasting, collective processes of history-making. I hope it adds to the ongoing process of imagining alternative futures—futures that Sjoberg, Gill, and Cain (2003) describe as not trapped in an unresolved past, an unfair present and a given order, but that instead grow out of processes of understanding, elaboration, and contestation. A frame analysis of collective memory-making can certainly help us move forward in this direction.

NOTES

1. See, for example, the article by Alejandra Dandan (2011) on the status of the trials on crimes against humanity, which was published together with the March 24, 2011 special section of the *Página 12* newspaper commemorating the 35 years since the Junta coup (http://www.pagina12.com.ar/diario/especiales/index.html). See also the article on the still

ongoing work of forensic anthropologists in La Nación (http://www.lanacion.com.ar/1352743), as well as the piece on the acts that will be held to commemorate the coup, including the several organizations that continue to be active in their human rights claims (http://www.lanacion.com.ar/1359821-marchas-y-actos-a-35-anos-del-golpe).

2. Natural primary frameworks "identify occurrences seen as undirected, unoriented, unanimated, unguided [. . .] due totally, from start to finish, to "natural" determinants" (Goffman, 1986, p. 22). That is to say that these frames attribute events to so-called natural forces. Social primary frameworks "provide background understanding for events that incorporate the will, aim, and controlling effort of an intelligence, a live agency, the chief one being the human being" (Goffman, 1986, p. 22). Socially and natural primary frameworks are mutually related, particularly because socially guided acting "cannot be accomplished effectively without entrance into the natural order" (Goffman, 1986, p. 23). At the same time, it is important to note that Goffman's binary distinction is not comprehensive of all meaning-making processes, which are now understood to be more complicated than what can be captured by the natural/social primary frames.

3. "*Cabecita negra*" (literally "little black head") is a term that has been used in Argentina to indicate a person with darker skin color, usually dark hair, who has a lower socioeconomic status and little (if any) formal education. The term has been used politically in various ways, and is certainly derogatory and discriminatory. "*Cabecitas negras*" were assumed to be affiliated with the Peronist Party—and the military regime was openly against this political force.

4. See the events planned for the 35th anniversary of the coup at http://encuentromvyj.wordpress.com/ and http://www.pagina12.com.ar/diario/ultimas/20-164831 -2011-03-24.html.

REFERENCES

Assmann, A. (2006). History, memory, and the genre of testimony. *Poetics Today, 27*(2), 261–273.

Bazan, O. (2004). *Historia de la homosexualidad en Argentina: De la conquista de América al siglo XXI*. Buenos Aires, AG: Editorial Marea.

Bejarano, C. (2002). Las super madres de Latino America: Transforming motherhood and house-skirts by challenging violence in Juárez, México, Argentina and El Salvador. *Frontier: A Journal of Women Studies, 23*(1), 126–150.

Beverley, J. (2005). Testimonio, subalternity, and narrative authority. In N. Denzin, & Y. Lincoln (Eds.), *The SAGE Handbook of Qualitative Research* (3rd ed.) (pp. 547–557). Thousand Oaks, CA: Sage.

Bietti, L. (2009). Entre la cognición política y la cognición social: El discurso de la memoria colectiva en Argentina. *Discurso & Sociedad, 3*(1), 44–89.

Braylan, M., Feierstein, D., Galante, M., & Jmelnizky, A. (2000). *Report of the situation of the Jewish detainees-disappeared during the genocide perpetrated in Argentina*. Buenos Aires, AG: Social Research Center of DAIA.

Briggs, L. (1998). Discourses of 'forced sterilization' in Puerto Rico: The problem with the speaking subaltern. *differences: A Journal of Feminist Cultural Studies, 10*(2), 30–66.

Brison, S. (1999). The uses of narrative in the aftermath of violence. In C. Card (Ed.), *On feminist ethics and politics* (pp. 200–225). Lawrence: University Press of Kansas.

Camacho, F. (2008). Memorias enfrentadas: Las reacciones a los informes *Nunca Más* de Argentina y Chile. *Persona y Sociedad, 22*(2), 67–99.

Chizuko, U., & Sand, J. (1999). The politics of memory: Nation, individual and self. *History and Memory, 11*(2), 129–152.

Ciollaro, N. (1999). *Pájaros sin luz: Testimonios de mujeres de desaparecidos*. Buenos Aires, AG: Planeta.

Cohen, S. (2001). *States of denial: Knowing about atrocities and suffering*. Oxford, UK: Polity Press.

CONADEP, The National Commission on the Disappeared. (1984). *Nunca Más: Informe de la Comisión Nacional sobre la desaparición de personas*. Buenos Aires, AG: Eudeba.

CONADEP, The National Commission on the Disappeared. (1986). *Nunca Más: The report of the National Commission on the disappeared*. New York, NY: Farrar Straus and Giroux.

Crenzel, E. (2008a). El relato canónico de las desapariciones en Argentina: El informe "Nunca Más." *CONfines, 4*(8), 47–61.

Crenzel, E. (2008b). *La historia política del* Nunca Más: *La memoria de las desapariciones en la Argentina*. Buenos Aires, AG: Siglo Veintiuno Editores.

Dandan, A. (2011). Los juicios en números. *Página 12* [Newspaper]. Accessed at http://www.pagina12 .com.ar/diario/elpais/subnotas/164806-52717-2011-03-24.html.

Dworkin, R. (1986). Introduction. In CONADEP, *Nunca Más: The report of the National Commission on the disappeared* (pp. 11–28). New York, NY: Farrar Straus and Giroux.

Entman, R. (2007). Framing bias: Media in the distribution of power. *Journal of Communication, 57,* 163–173.

Fairclough, N. (2003). *Analysing discourse: Textual analysis for social research.* London, UK: Routledge.

Franco, J. (1987). Gender, death and resistance: Facing the ethical vacuum. *Chicago Review, 35*(4), 59–79.

Gitlin, T. (1980). *The whole world is watching: Mass media in the making and unmaking of the new left.* Berkeley: University of California Press.

Goffman, E. (1986). *Frame analysis: An essay on the organization of experience.* Boston, MA: Northeastern University Press. (Original work published 1974)

Graziano, F. (1992). *Divine violence: Spectacle, psychosexuality & radical Christianity in the Argentine "Dirty War."* Boulder, CO: Westview Press.

Hartman, G. (2004). Public memory and its discontents. In H. Bloom (Ed.), *Literature of the Holocaust* (pp. 205–222). Philadelphia, PA: Chelsea House.

Hill Collins, P. (1986). Learning from the outsider within: The sociological significance of black feminist thought. *Social Problems, 33*(6), S14–S32.

Jacobs, S., & Johnson, K. (2007). Media, social movements, and the state: Competing images of HIV/AIDS in South Africa. *African Studies Quarterly, 9*(4), 127–151.

Jaggar, A. (1997). Love and knowledge: Emotion in feminist epistemology. In D. Meyers (Ed.), *Feminist social thought: A reader* (pp. 384–405). New York, NY: Routledge.

Jelin, E. (2003). *State repression and the labors of memory.* Minneapolis: University of Minnesota Press.

Kaplan, B. (2007). *Género y violencia en la narrativa del cono sur 1954–2003.* Woodbridge, UK: Tamesis.

Kaufman, E. (1989). Jewish victims of repression in Argentina under military rule (1976–1983). *Holocaust and Genocide Studies, 4*(4), 479–499.

König, T. (2004). *Reframing frame analysis: Systematizing the empirical identification of frames using qualitative data analysis software.* Paper presented at the American Sociological Association (ASA). Annual Meeting, San Francisco, CA, August 14–17.

Mallon, F. (1994). The promise and dilemma of subaltern studies: Perspectives from Latin American history. *The American Historical Review, 99*(5), 1491–1515.

Marín, L. (1991). Speaking out together: Testimonials of Latin American women. *Latin American Perspectives, 18*(3), 51–68.

Memoria Abierta. (2005*). La representación de experiencias traumáticas a través de archivos de testimonios y de la reconstrucción de espacios de represión.* Paper presented at Encuentro Internacional, El arte: Representación de la memoria del terror, November 1–4, Buenos Aires, Argentina.

Navarro, M. (1989). The personal is political: Las madres de Plaza de Mayo. In S. Eckstein (Ed.), *Power and popular protest: Latin American social movements* (pp. 241–258). Los Angeles: University of California Press.

Navarro, V. (2011). Discriminación y reconciliación: Comunidad Judeo-Argentina y su relación con el régimen militar Argentino (1976–1989). *Estudios Judaicos, Cuadernos.* Accessed at http://www.estudiosjudaicos.cl/cuadernos/node/41.

Nino, C. (1998). *Radical evil on trial.* New Haven, CT: Yale University Press.

Oviedo, G. (2010). Argentina: La comunidad LGBTTI espera su Nunca Más con sus 400 desaparecidxs en la dictadura. *Crítica Digital.* Accessed at http://www.insurrectasypunto.org/index.php?option=com_content&view=article&id=3489:argentina-la-comunidad-lgbtti-espera-su-nunca-mas-con-sus-400-desaparecidos-en-la-dictadura&catid=3:notas&Itemid=3.

Phelps, T. (2004). *Shattered voices: Language, violence, and the work of truth commissions.* Philadelphia: University of Pennsylvania Press.

Philips, K. (Ed.). (2004). *Framing public memory.* Tuscaloosa: The University of Alabama Press.

Rey Tristán, E. (2007). *Memorias de la violencia en Uruguay y Argentina: Golpes, dictaduras, exilios (1973–2006).* Santiago de Compostela, ES: Universidade, Servizo de Publicacións e Intercambio Científico.

Roberts, D. (1995). Punishing drug addicts who have babies: Women of color, equality, and the right of privacy. In K. Crenshaw, **N.** Gotanda, G. Peller,

& K. Thomas (Eds.), *Critical race theory: The key writings that formed the movement* (pp. 384–425). New York: The New Press.

Romero, L. A. (1994). *Breve historia contemporánea de la Argentina.* Buenos Aires, AG: Fondo de Cultura Económica.

Roniger, L., & Sznajder, M. (1999). *The legacy of human rights in the Southern Cone: Argentina, Chile and Uruguay.* New York, NY: Oxford University Press.

Scarry, E. (1985). *The body in pain: The making and unmaking of the world.* New York, NY: Oxford University Press.

Sjoberg, G., Gill, E., & Cain, L. (2003). Countersystem analysis and the construction of alternative futures. *Sociological Theory, 21*(3), 210–235.

Solá, J. M. (2005). Una etapa que nunca había sido cerrada. *La Nación* [Newspaper]. Accessed at http://www.lanacion.com.ar/713045-una-etapa-que-nunca-habia-sido-cerrada.

Taylor, D. (1997). *Disappearing acts: Spectacles of gender and nationalism in Argentina's "Dirty War."* Durham, NC: Duke University Press.

Waylen, G. (2000). Gender and democratic politics: A comparative analysis of consolidation in Argentina and Chile. *Journal of Latin American Studies, 32*(3), 765–793.

Weine, S. (2006). *Testimony after catastrophe: Narrating the traumas of political violence.* Evanston, IL: Northwestern University Press.

Yúdice, G. (1991). Testimonio and postmodernism. *Latin American Perspectives, 18*(3), 15–31.

20

THE CHANGING DYNAMICS OF POLITICAL DISCOURSE ABOUT ORPHANS IN SOVIET AND POST-SOVIET PERIODS

MARGARITA ASTOYANTS

INTRODUCTION

Orphanhood in Russia cannot be called a new social phenomenon; it has always existed and will probably always exist. Observing the dynamics of this phenomenon, one can notice how more or less stable periods in history were followed by rapid increases in the numbers of orphaned children during the hard times of revolutionary and war years. As one might expect, the numbers of orphaned, neglected, and homeless children have grown the most in the years when there were political, economic, and social changes.

A record of the first orphanages in Russia dates back to the first half of the 17th century. These orphanages were created under the auspices of the monasteries and churches. In the second half of the 18th century, the system of orphanages, both state and private, was formed in Russia. According to experts and scholars, by the

year 1917 there were more than 170 institutions for orphaned children in Russia (Bayeva, 1977, p. 142), institutions experienced manifold increases and by the beginning of 1919, there were 1,279 institutions of childhood protection that housed 75,574 children in 36 provinces of Soviet Russia (Bayeva, 1977, p. 143). By 1922, there were more than 540,000 children in orphanages, and the amount of neglected and homeless children numbered about 7 million people (Dorokhova, 2005, p. 401). During the Great Patriotic War (1941–1945) and the postwar years, there was yet another booming increase of the number of orphaned children. In Soviet Russia by the end of the 1940s, there were 6,543 functioning orphanages housing 636,000 children.

During the Perestroika (restructuring) period in the 1990s, the problem of orphaned children worsened considerably because of the economic and spiritual crisis in Russian society. The numbers of orphans grew so rapidly, that the existing system of childhood support ceased to function satisfactorily. Consequently, the state created institutions with different orientations toward childhood support: social asylums, centers of family and children support, social rehabilitation centers, centers of psychological and pedagogical help, and so forth.

Statistics from the Public Chamber's (2010) report indicate that there are about 750,000 orphaned children in Russia, and this number is increasing every year. It should be noted that during the last 15 years, the total number of children in Russia decreased from 40 to 29 million people, while the number of orphaned children within that same period increased by 20%. Further, the same report shows that more than 100,000 children are left without parental care (guardianship), and the majority of this group are described as "social" orphans. This term refers both to children whose parents lost their parental rights by order of the court because they did not fulfill their parental duties, and to children who are neglected or left at the institutions by their parents for different reasons. Significantly, 114,715 children were registered as having been left without parental care in 2009— this means that on average 314 children were abandoned daily; of these children 50,323 were officially proclaimed as orphans by the court and their parents were deprived of their parental rights (Statistics from the Public Chamber's report, 2010).

With the absence of any efficient rehabilitation techniques for the biological family and no effective search for adoptive families, the childhood protection agents are left with few options. As a result, they resort to depriving parents of their parental rights and sending children to the state institutions, thereby remanding all responsibility for these children to the state. Yet state orphanages contribute to children's deprivation, and their chances of further adoption are extremely low.

In recent years, the transition in Russia from a mainly collective system of values to a system that recognizes individualism and the priority of individual rights, produced gradual changes in orphan care that correspond more closely to the child's self-interests. The most popular model for adoption and adaptation is a trusteeship and/or guardianship (more than half of all the orphaned children are handled under this format), and another one-third of the orphaned children are placed in state institutions. Today, other models are gradually developing to deal with these children, such as systems for adoptive families and family orphanages.

The ideology behind the state social policy plays a leading role in solving the problem of orphaned children. Thus, only after 2002, amidst public outcry, the neglect of children and their homelessness began to be defined as a social problem. Consequently, a program was formulated and advanced to state officials by the President, V. V. Putin. As noted earlier, in modern Russia orphaned children are one of the most burning social problems and constantly under discussion by both ordinary citizens and high-ranking officials. Mass media pay considerable attention to this problem as well. This is why an analysis of the dynamics of the political discourse about orphaned children is so important—it can identify trends or tendencies of the social policy and practice relating to these specific groups. Social problems generally, and the problem of orphans in particular, are the result of collective meanings and processes. To a considerable extent, how a society defines the social *meaning* of orphans (or relatedly the social *problem* of orphans) will determine society's strategy concerning orphans—for example, the collective aspiration for social integration or social exclusion.[1]

Language plays a particularly important role in regulating and creating social reality. That is why the analysis of discourses about orphans and orphanhood is an important method of research. According to Foucault (1996), discourses systematically form the objects that they name. In this case, exclusion or inclusion is understood as the consequence of certain forms of knowledge that are produced and circulated via mass media. By contrast, in my research I use critical discourse analysis and understand discourse as a form of social practice, which creates the world and at the same time is created by other social practices.

In particular, analyzing how political discourse forms practices of integration (or exclusion) of orphaned children, I take into consideration that discursive influences are connected with a social reality that does not have a discourse character. For example, in the structure of the social institutions of childhood support there are federal and municipal influences, which (as we will see further) will produce different types of discourse.

I chose critical discourse analysis as it particularly focuses on investigating changes and it gives great significance both to the active role of discourse in social creation of the world and also takes into consideration the fact that discourse itself is the product of other nondiscourse activities (Jorgensen & Phillips, 2002). Following N. Fairclough, I believe

> that the formation of the society with the help of discourse takes place not because people freely play with ideas. It is the consequence of their social practice, which is deeply planted in their life and oriented to the real, material social structures (Fairclough, 1992, p. 102).

Yet, Foucault's ideas are also important for my research since I analyze the dynamics of political discourse about orphaned children in the corresponding sociohistorical and sociocultural context by considering discourse as "the fragment of history" (Foucault, 1996, p. 30).

Every discourse has its own definite semantic content that is filled with judgments. For example, political discourse (a discourse of authority) is built as a dialogical opposition between "one's own" (correct) viewpoint and "someone else's" (erroneous) viewpoint. In a totalitarian state, any statement within the authority's discourse is given the status of an absolute truth, and any other point of view is interpreted as erroneous or as a conscious lie. However, political discourse, even in a totalitarian state, is not homogeneous. One can distinguish discourses that can appear rather stable and others that can change over the course of time.

In all of the discourses about orphans in Russia, orphans are constructed as having a collective character with definite features. Thus, in different ways each discourse produces the essence of orphans as a problem and suggests different measures to solve this problem. Therefore, every discourse presupposes that certain actions are necessary to solve the problem of orphans—which can promote social inclusion or lead to exclusion. For that reason, discourse appears to be a key factor launching the cultural mechanisms of exclusion/inclusion.

To examine discourses about orphans and orphanhood during critical moments of Russian history in the 20th and 21st centuries, we must begin with three primary points in time that historically have been considered the hardest periods for Russia. These are the October Revolution and Civil War period (1920–1926), the years of the Great Patriotic War (1941–1945),[2] and "Perestroika" and the period following it (2002–2005; 2008–2009). During these periods, the numbers of orphans increased; consequently, they are always mentioned in literature and in disputes of social policy regarding orphans.

All three of these periods of Russian history can be characterized as times of crisis in which there was a disintegration of society, anomie appeared and the dysfunction of social institutions increased. A common characteristic of these periods was the mass impoverishment of people, which especially affected children and the poor. However, a significant difference is that during the October Revolution, the Civil War, Perestroika and the post-Perestroika periods, society was characterized by a systemic spiritual crisis that entailed the loss of life-meaning and the destruction of guiding values, both for the individual and the broader society. By contrast, the Great Patriotic War (1941–1945) united the Soviet people in the struggle against the common enemy and strengthened the system of values and solidarity in the society. Consequently, although the scale of orphanhood considerably increased in each of these periods, the sociocultural context influenced the discourses about orphans in very different ways. To understand discourses about orphans during these periods, I examined materials of the State Archives of the Rostov Region and mass media (newspaper publications and radio programs). My ability to reference additional texts was conditioned by their availability and the purposes of the study. The data is described in detail in subsequent sections.

DISCOURSES ABOUT ORPHANED CHILDREN DURING THE OCTOBER REVOLUTION AND CIVIL WAR (1920–1926)

To investigate political discourse about orphans and orphanhood during 1920 to 1926, I analyzed materials on this topic from four archive departments of the State Archive of Rostov Region (SARR), which contains 4,224 documents. In order to analyze the documents, I systematized them and stored them in a database. Every document in the database was coded according to several categories: (a) number of the document, (b) archive information (archive department, inventory, document's number, page), (c) date of the document's origin, (d) categories that define the image of the orphans/children, (e) categories identifying behavioral characteristics of the orphans/children, (f) ways of solving the problem of orphanhood suggested by the author and, (g) discursive frame or type. Altogether I analyzed 81 documents for this period and found a pattern of four stable political discourses: social danger, social sympathy, social responsibility, and social utility. Notably, each discourse is related to consequences that range from exclusion to integration of orphans into society. The subsequent sections elaborate on each discourse.

Discourse of Social Danger

Discourses that construct orphans as a present danger for the rest of the society generate the greatest degree of alienation. This danger can be constructed in relation to an alien, criminal element (increased crime) or in relation to an epidemic threat to society (hygiene morbidity, dirt, chaos). The consequences of discourses that construct orphans as a danger to society range from social exclusion to physical isolation.

The discourse of an alien, criminal element emphasizes both a criminal past and present of orphans by relying on characterizations such as "vagrant element," "juvenile delinquents," and "criminal elements" when referencing orphans (SARR. Dep. 97, Inv. 1, Doc. 581, p. 29; Doc. 1817, Inv. 2, Doc. 84, p. 3; Dep. 97, Inv. 1, Doc. 581, p. 210; Dep. 1817, Inv. 1, Doc. 75, p. 105). The discourses make clear that orphans are alien to most communist societies since "they increase crime and theft," and "hooliganism, stealing, and other outrages flourish" (SARR. Dep. 1817, Inv. 1, Doc. 75, p. 105; Dep. 97, Inv. 1, Doc. 581, p. 48; Dep. 1817, Inv. 1, Doc. 74, pp. 13–14; Dep. 1798, Inv. 1, Doc. 295, p. 20; Dep. 97, Inv. 1, Doc. 581, p. 36). Within this discourse, there is a presumption that a tough attitude toward such a hostile element will prevent the increase of orphans and of associated crime. Therefore, suggestions are made to take the strictest measures possible: "to punish by people's courts," "to fight, to send guard, to call to account," "to isolate, to keep locked" (SARR. Dep. 97, Inv. 1, Doc. 581, pp. 29, 48, 36; Dep. 1817, Inv. 1, Doc. 75, p. 105). When orphans are constructed as a criminal element, they are lumped into the same category as criminals and others who infringe on society. All orphans, regardless of age, are treated the same way—homeless children and homeless adults. In the official documents, those who do not fall within the category of "our people" become "aliens" and consequently often are united by the general notion of belonging to the same "element."

By contrast, the discourse of an epidemic threat to society referred to orphans as "mass of orphans," "neglected mass," and "homeless mass" (SARR. Dep. 97, Inv. 1, Doc. 1013, p. 7; Dep. 97, Inv. 1, Doc. 1013, p. 6; Dep. 97, Inv. 1, Doc. 581, pp. 14–20; Dep. 1817, Inv. 1, Doc. 75, p. 105).

It is difficult even to imagine that this discourse refers to children; rather, it sounds like a reference to a dull mass devoid of human faces. The mass is featureless, but as dangerous as a natural disaster. Indeed the origin of this faceless mass appears to be natural rather than social. Orphans are referred to as a "mass influx," and "their movement becomes disastrous threatening the city" (SARR. Dep. 97, Inv. 1, Doc. 1013, p. 7; Dep. 97, Inv. 1, Doc. 1013, p. 6; Dep. 97, Inv. 1, Doc. 581, p. 14–20). In this discourse, it seems that this "mass" will gush across society, flooding everything around.

This discourse also constructed orphans as the source of infection. The masses of orphans "are dangerous as epidemic spreaders," and they "concentrate at railway stations, move chaotically without destination" (SARR. Dep. 97, Inv. 1, Doc. 581, pp. 210, 207). In this discourse, railways particularly suffer from the presence of orphans; documents characterize orphans as homeless children dirtying railway stations, as "causing dirtying trains" and even "sowing epidemics on the railway tracks" (SARR. Dep. 1798, Inv. 1, Doc. 237, p. 32).

What is the suggested public response to orphans in this discourse? As one might expect: "Not to admit," "to take measures," "to stop," "to clean railway stations and streets," "to get rid of," "to remove from the railway station," "to stop unorganized transportation, not to allow independent travel," and to "send away to the town of Novocherkassk."[3] According to the officials of the Don Committee of Fighting the Consequences of Famine,[4] homeless children were indeed sent to Novocherkassk as a means of cleaning Rostov streets and railway stations. In Soviet times, there was a practice to send the so-called "unreliable" citizens from big capital cities to smaller towns. For example, homeless children were removed from Rostov-on-Don, the capital city of the Don Region, to the small town of Novocherkassk. The intent of this practice was to conceal any elements that could spoil a decent picture of a well-to-do Soviet city. Discourses that construct orphans as a criminal and epidemic threat often interlace subsequent measures of exclusion and alienation. Yet, along with demands to take almost military measures, some perplexity is evident. It is as if officials understand that it is next to impossible to stop a natural disaster, and it is not always clear what exactly should be done or who should do it.

Discourse of Social Sympathy

The focus of a sympathetic discourse is the social inadequacy of children, either as physically or morally defective. In this discourse, the difficult situation in which orphans find themselves arouses pity and sympathy, but it is rarely supported by concrete measures to solve the problems. Rather, the conceptual characteristics deployed in this discourse arouse pity but not action. This discourse constructs orphaned children as "neglected, hungry and homeless," as "having no clothes and shoes," as "sick," or as "defective"(SARR. Dep. 97, Inv. 1, Doc. 427, p. 25; Dep. 1817, Inv. 2, Doc. 84, p. 3, 23). These are children who "lost their parents, wander in the open air or in stinking basements, and catch tuberculosis." Their "feet and legs are swelled up and covered with wounds, their nutrition is under any standards, they sleep on the floor on the straw," "they are freezing" (SARR. Dep. 1798, Inv. 1, Doc. 237, pp. 109, 137).

The authors of documents that use this particular discourse type suggest actions that should be directed to satisfy the primary needs of these children. For example, children must "be medically treated," one must "eliminate trading them," one should "help, promote, improve their life" (SARR. Dep. 1817, Inv. 2, Doc. 84, p. 30; Dep. 97, Inv. 1, Doc. 581, p. 203; Dep. 1798, Inv. 1, Doc. 237, p. 109). However, it is not always clear how these measures can fundamentally improve children's lives when the overarching conditions are so dire.

Discourse of Social Responsibility

This discourse can be regarded as a step toward the social inclusion of orphans. The discourse constructs the need to help orphans; yet even here, the discourse does not recognize the child as an active subject, but rather as an object of social assistance and help. The meaning of "orphans" is formulated as "neglected children," "children who abandoned native land," or "unattended children" (SARR. Dep. 97, Inv. 1,

Doc. 581, p. 20; Dep. 97, Inv. 1, Doc. 1013, p. 6; Dep. 97, Inv. 1, Doc. 427, pp. 43, 67).

This discourse reveals very little about the children themselves since they are not produced as active subjects. All the action in this discourse is performed by adults in relation to the orphaned children: they "are caught, directed, not accepted" or alternatively "they are accepted" and "picked from the street" (SARR. Dep. 97, Inv. 1, Doc. 581, p. 176; Dep. 1798, Inv. 1, Doc. 237, p. 20). Children are referred to as objects of some grown-up influence. This discourse expresses the businesslike and official language of functionaries who make decisions concerning the national objective—a struggle against orphanhood and the neglect of children turns into a struggle with neglected children themselves. The discourse has a nearly complete absence of any children's activity; the only active figure here is the adult who is preoccupied with the organizational and financial aspects of working with neglected children.

Recommended responses to orphans suggested by this discourse type are quite diverse. Some have a prohibitive or restrictive character: "to send away, to prohibit entrance," "to evacuate," "to stop sending in, to take out," "to withdraw, to distribute to orphanages" (SARR. Dep. 97, Inv. 1, Doc. 87, p. 21; Doc. 581, p. 82; Dep. 1817, Inv. 2, Doc. 84, p. 29, 30). Others suggest the need to organize work with children properly: "to watch at railway stations, pick up children," "to transfer, to remove, to take, to direct, to move to their domicile, to pick up, to attend" (SARR. Dep. 1817, Inv. 2, Doc. 84, p. 21, 30). The discourse gives an important role to the orphanages, communes, and other similar institutions to solve the larger problem of unattended children.

In this discourse there is a constant concern about financing measures to fight orphanhood. It is necessary "to give money to fight orphanhood," "to assign means," "to allocate, to distribute money," "to find means," or "to get means" (SARR. Dep. 97, Inv. 1, Doc. 427, p. 43, 67; Dep. 1817, Inv. 1, Doc. 74, P. 12, 13, 14). Financial

matters are raised in almost all of the documents that use this particular discourse. It seems likely that this discourse—which characterizes orphans as objects in need of social assistance—would produce more effective solutions for the plight of orphans than the previous ones. However, it is important to note that children themselves are reduced to objects of external action.

Discourse of Social Utility

This discourse characterizes orphaned children as a kind of social resource—future adults who can and must be useful to society. Consequently, rendering assistance to children is a social investment in the future development of the society. The concept of social utility promotes problem-solving by means of social integration and active participation in social life. Orphaned children in this discourse are referred to as "boys, girls," or "children, teenagers" (SARR. Dep. 1798, Inv. 1, Doc. 295, p. 49; Dep. 1798, Inv. 1, Doc. 342, p. 7; Dep. 1817, Inv. 1, Doc. 74, p. 61). Indeed they are represented as behaving as ordinary children: they "study, go to school, get professional training, are involved in some work, develop proletarian psychology." They are "admitted to orphanages, leave orphanages, make their way in life" (SARR. Dep. 1798, Inv. 1, Doc. 342, p. 7). There are some problems as well: orphan-children "cannot use money rationally, have poor diet, cannot keep house" (SARR. Dep. 1798, Inv. 1, Doc. 295. p. 49). The discourse is aimed at creating useful members of society.

In this discourse the highly constructive potential of children is evident—not only in the concern about the conditions of their lives, but also in concern for their futures and for the public benefit in general. In official documents, this discourse type is perceived as turning to a new stage in solving the problems of orphaned children.

In general the post-revolution period is characterized by a strong discourse of alienation/exclusion that peaks in the earlier years of this period. For example, the years 1920 to 1922 are

Table 20.1 Discourses About Orphaned Children, 1920 to 1926

Discourse types	Attitude toward orphans	Image of orphans	Characteristic features of orphans	Ways to solve problems
Social danger discourse	Exclusion and alienation	Vagrant element, juvenile delinquents, criminal elements, people with criminal past	Contribute to crime, get their food exclusively by committing offenses; hooliganism and stealing flourishes among them	To punish by people's courts, to detain, to call to account, to isolate, to keep locked
		Children's stream, neglected mass, homeless and unattended mass	They are dangerous as epidemic spreaders, cause dirtying of railway stations, threaten development of diseases	To clear railway stations and streets, to pick from the station, stop disorganized transportation, not to allow independent travel
Discourse of sympathy	Recognition of defectiveness and pity	Hungry and homeless, having no clothes and shoes, sick, defective	Lost their parents, wander in the open air, catch tuberculosis, their feet and legs are swelled up and covered with wounds, nutrition is below standards, sleep on the floor, they are freezing	To treat medically, eliminate trading them, to help, to promote, to improve their life
Discourse of social responsibility	Orphan-children as an object of assistance	Neglected children, children who abandoned native land, unattended children	They are caught, directed, not accepted, or accepted, picked from the street	To send, to evacuate, to distribute into orphanages, to pick children, to remove, to resettle them to their places of residence, to attend them, to develop the network of orphanages
Discourse of social utility	Social integration of orphans	Boys and girls, children, teenagers, inmates of orphanages	Study, go to school, get professional training, are involved in some work, develop proletarian psychology, make their way in life	To teach profession, train qualified labor force for enterprises, to distribute among enterprises, to involve into active work and komsomol (Russian communist youth organization)

characterized by the greatest degree of exclusion; beginning from 1923, the discourses regarding orphans become more diverse; and by 1926, a more inclusive discourse begins to increase. However, even during this period, the early discourses of exclusion do not disappear completely as the discourse of social utility appears. In official documents, the greatest attention to the problem of orphaned children appears in 1923 when the discourses broaden and, accordingly, public attitudes toward orphaned children move in the direction of greater inclusion and acceptance as members of the society.

DISCOURSES ABOUT ORPHANED CHILDREN DURING THE GREAT PATRIOTIC WAR (1941–1945)

In this section, I examine political discourse about orphanhood during the Great Patriotic War. My analysis is based on articles appearing in two wartime newspapers (the newspaper *Izvestiya* (began as the *News of the Petrograd Soviet of Workers Deputies*), during the years 1942 to 1948 and the central newspaper of the Rostov Region *Molot*, in 1944). The choice of mass media as a source of research material was dictated largely by the lack of availability and incompleteness of archival documents for this particular historical period (archive documents from SARR for the occupation period in Rostov-on-Don are absent and parts of the documents are still closed for research).

With that said, newspaper material can be especially valuable, since mass media in a totalitarian society completely reflect the views of government authority and the directives of the ruling ideology. In all, I analyzed 41 newspaper publications during the Great Patriotic War and found only one discourse regarding orphaned children, which is why this period can be called monodiscursive. This is quite logical since beginning in the 1930s, the very possibility of ideological and political pluralism was practically excluded.

Discourse about orphans during the Great Patriotic War was an integral part of a wider political discourse aimed at uniting the Soviet people in an aspiration to defeat the enemy. During the war, the authoritative discourse produced the notion of orphaned children as "our children," children of the whole Soviet people. In this sense, the monodiscourse of the war period can be characterized as the discourse of social unity.

News articles described orphans in relationship to parents—and it is in their relationship to parents that orphans find their most socially significant role—that of defender of the Motherland. For example, newspapers describe orphans as belonging to "one's own people," and as "the nearest and dearest," to the whole Soviet people—proved by the fact that they are "soldiers' children" (*Molot*, April 7, 1944, p. 2). In addition orphans are referred to as "children of glorious Motherland defenders" (*Molot*, April 21, 1944, p. 2) and as "children whose fathers and mothers, brothers and sisters fight in the fronts of the Patriotic War" (*Izvestiya*, April 11, 1943, p. 3). The discourse emphasizes that these children's parents were killed fighting for their Motherland. For example, "these children's mothers died and their fathers are in the Red Army" (*Molot*, April 8, 1944, p. 2), "parents were killed by fascist invaders" (*Molot*, April 21, 1944, p. 2), and "whose fathers perished in the fronts of the Patriotic War" (*Izvestiya*, October 7, 1943, p. 2). The fact that their parents are defenders of the Motherland gives them a special status and special rights.

Not only does this discourse unite orphans with the people but also with the common torment that Soviets suffered and the hardships everyone had to go through. In this discourse, orphaned children are recognized as having endured much woe: they are described as "exhausted children" "plucked from the fascist hell" (*Izvestiya*, August 21, 1943, p. 2), and as "Soviet children, plucked from the hands of fascist barbarians" (*Izvestiya*, October 13, 1943, p. 3). Most importantly, this wretchedness is known and shared by everyone. Portraits of war time orphans are drawn with warmth and at the same time with a heavy heart because of the children's suffering. So, on the pages of the national newspaper *Izvestiya* readers read about "a grey-eyed tot, Alik by name," who "forgot how to smile, did not tell anything about himself and often and disconsolately wept lying prone on the bed"; a girl Masha by name who "treated everything absolutely indifferently and did not say a word," and "kindness and toys gave access to her soul" (*Izvestiya*, August 21, 1943, p. 2). When characterizing orphaned children of the war period, mass media used particular children's images, and stories that were easily understandable to everyone. In this discourse about orphaned children's sufferings, the answer to the main question "What must we do?" is answered: "We all will help 'our' children."

In this discourse, children were not divided into "our own" and "someone else's." Consequently, aid to orphaned children acquired deep parental meaning: to save "our" children (while their parents are defending us) for a future peaceful life. Orphanages then become necessary for the "defenders of Motherland, who will find here their children safe and sound, having recovered from the sufferings, and they will be sincerely grateful to those who created the orphanage" (Kavskaya, 1943). The same discourse leads to adoption of the children since they are not "someone else's" but "our own."

The discourse about orphans during the war period did not directly address the fact that the state was weakened by the war and unable to take care of the orphans without public help, but such ideas were implied. Care about orphans was defined as "a patriotic matter" (Abdurakhmanov, 1943), as the "everyday affair of Soviet patriots" (*Izvestiya*, April 28, 1944, p. 3), and as "all people's sacred business" (*Izvestiya*, October 30, 1943, p. 3). In the official discourse, measures of helping orphaned children were diverse, and what is important is that they were formulated not as "something that will be done," but as "something that has already been done and is being done now." It is possible that in many

cases, initiatives to help children in the provinces occurred in advance of instructions from the authorities. Yet the political task remains the same—"to raise healthy, civilized people devoted to their Motherland of Soviet citizens" (*Izvestiya*, October 30, 1943, p. 3). Consequently, the official discourse about orphanhood during war time can be characterized as a discourse of social unity that considers orphan-children as "our own"—as children of the whole Soviet people. Therefore, helping orphaned children was seen as a significant patriotic matter—a duty not only before their parents, but also before their Motherland. All the social groups were encouraged to fulfill numerous assistance measures without relying on state assistance. The ultimate aim was to prepare children for a future peaceful life as competent citizens of the Soviet State. This discourse undoubtedly can be referred to as integrating, promoting a swift conquering of the social exclusion of orphaned children.

However, the logic that underpinned this discourse—an attentive attitude to children in response to heroism and self-sacrifice of their parents justified during the hardships of war—also led to sad consequences in peaceful times. By the end of 1946, any mention of orphans had become increasingly rare in political discourse. And in 1948 to the 1950s, at a time when orphanages were filled with more and more children of single mothers and prisoners (one consequence of postwar repressions), any mention of orphans disappeared from all official sources. Children of those parents who did not correspond to the idea of the Soviet state citizen could not claim the state's attention and care.

DISCOURSES ABOUT ORPHANED CHILDREN BEGINNING IN PERESTROIKA (2002–2005; 2008–2009)

I analyzed modern political discourse by examining several types of official mass media publications over two time periods: 2002 to 2005 and 2008 to 2009. I began with articles on orphaned

Table 20.2   Discourses About Orphaned Children During the Great Patriotic War

Discourse type	Attitude toward orphans	Image of orphans	Characteristic features of orphans	Ways to solve problems
Discourse of social unity	The Soviet people are one family, orphans are the children of the whole people	Soldiers' children, children of the soldiers of Red Army, children of glorious Motherland defenders, children whose parents, brothers and sisters are fighting in the fronts of the Great Patriotic War	Parents were killed by fascist invader; parents defend Motherland; stirred up children who have been pulled out from a fascist hell; the Soviet children who have been pulled out from hands of fascist barbarians	To involve the population in accepting orphans under patronage or guardianship; workers and employees collect money, clothes, food for the orphanages; to impart to children labor skills, to prepare for labor activity

children that were published between 2002 and 2005 in the national paper *Rossiyskaya Gazeta* and stories that were aired on a weekly radio program called "People and Authority" (radio station *Mayak*).[5] With these two sources combined, I researched a total of 44 documents. For the period 2008 to 2009, I examined articles published in the national paper *Rossiyskaya Gazeta* (78 articles) and those published in the regional newspapers, *Nashe Vremya* and *Vecherniy Rostov* (64 articles combined). In addition, I analyzed a variety of materials, documents, and social advertisements about orphaned children (84 pieces in all). Modern political discourse proved to be quite heterogeneous but I distinguished four main discourses: (a) danger, (b) social self-justification, (c) social responsibility, and (d) social partnership.

Discourse of Social Danger

The image of orphaned children in this discourse is paradoxically similar to the discourse of social danger in the 1920s. Orphaned children are referred to as "vagabonds," "juvenile beggars," "thieves" (Fedorinov, Domcheva, Ruzanova, Dobrynina, & Krivoshapko, 2005), "a million

strong army of little social outcasts," "homeless juvenile part of the society" (Fridinskiy, 2005), "neglected pupils," "pedagogical and social defect," "deviated children," and "wolf-cubs" (Stepura, 2008). They are characterized as being "under the influence of drugs" (Melikhova, 2008) and as committing crimes without any remorse. In short, the discourse asserts that because they under the influence of alcohol and drugs their "moral-ethic values have been washed away" (Melikhova, 2008). Consequently, a corresponding response to their undesirability is suggested. For example "underage children are threatened with imprisonment" (Melikhova, 2008), and "the final decision must be made by the court" (Olenev, 2009).

When the official discourse constructs orphaned children as a dangerous menace to the social order, it implies particular consequences in modern Russia similar to those that were imagined in the 1920s. As feelings of deadlock and pessimism grow in Russia, it is important to note that the recurrence of the discourse of orphans as a social danger is not accidental. It is much easier to toughen punishment of offenders on the bottom strata of the society than to improve their living conditions. Thus, orphaned children—even before they commit any offense—appear to be stamped twice: first as orphans, and second as potential criminals.

The pathos of condemnation and aversion in discourses that emerged in 2002 to 2005, considerably lessened in data from the period 2008 to 2009. In this second set of data, official discourse focused on solving the problems of orphaned children by suggesting it was necessary for bodies of law and order to "reduce the influx," to "catch," to "fight," and "turn to the right way." (Fedorinov, Domcheva, Ruzanova, Dobrynina & Krivoshapko, 2005) More and more often discourses on orphaned children focused on the professional level of specialists working in orphanages. Cruelty and aggressive behavior in children is explained by the fact that adults who are supposed to help and support these children are instead treating them badly. Consequently, adults were held accountable. For example:

in 2007 in the Khabarovsk region, 44 people were convicted according to article 156 of the Criminal Code of the Russian Federation" (non-fulfillment of duties connected with bringing up of the underage); among these people there are both parents and professional educational specialists. Of these cases, 11 people were sentenced to correctional work, 20 people were fined and given a suspended sentence (Stepura, 2008).

On one hand, there is a clear decrease in the circulation and use of the discourse of social danger in mass media; on the other hand, the change of the focus within the discourse itself now suggests surveillance and punitive measures in relation to adults in charge of the children and the orphanage specialists.

Discourse of Social Self-Justification

Perhaps the most common discourse in modern Russia regarding orphans is that of social self-justification. This discourse constructs orphaned children as a serious problem and then searches for the guilty parties. Most often problem families are blamed. I refer to this discourse as one of "self-justification," since blaming supposedly careless parents allows officials to avoid, displace, or remove their own partial responsibility for any inefficient measures regarding the orphans.

This discourse emphasizes either the problematic character of the family or the parents' poor treatment of their children. Orphans appear as "children from problem families" (Dmitrieva, 2005), or as "unattended children, that is orphans with parents alive" (Fridinskiy, 2005). By focusing on the nonfulfillment or inadequate fulfillment of parental roles, the presence of orphans is made to appear as the consequence of their parents' personal problems—not as expressions of any broader social problems. Most often this discourse concerns alcoholism, laziness, or an unwillingness to work. Importantly, poor parents also find themselves placed in the same category as careless parents. In official discourse, there is no mention of the reasons that lead to hard drinking, unemployment, or poverty. As a consequence, the discourse constructs parents as careless, and emphasizes the need to strengthen social control. However, the only effective response to the problems of the parents seems to be the removal of parental rights, which in most cases means separating the child from the family.

At the same time, this discourse does have a constructive component since it is able to initiate preventive work with families where children are at risk of being neglected. But one cannot be completely certain that these preventive measures won't take the form of social support that will lead to toughening social controls and thereby become a form of marginalization or exclusion of the families.

The discourse of self-justification is more dominant in the Russian national mass media than in regional media. Russians hear it more often from government officials than from other subjects that shape the public discursive space (such as journalists and public figures). According to our data, received during expert interviewing (Astoyants, 2009), those who are closer to the problems of broken families understand the hopelessness of accusation and try to find more fruitful ways of solving the problems of orphanhood.

Discourse of Social Responsibility

While this discourse was prominent in the 1920s, it disappeared from the mass media reporting until around 2008. Between 2008 and 2009, every fifth article about orphans in both the Russian national and regional newspapers contains the discourse of social responsibility that constructs orphaned children as the object of social assistance and help. This discourse refers to "orphanage leavers," "orphan's unsettled state" (Kulikov, 2009), "orphans," "nobody's children" (Tkachyova, 2008), and "graduates of orphanages" (Masyukevich, 2009). Orphaned children face many problems both in the orphanage and after they leave it. As in the 1920s, this modern version of this discourse almost completely lacks any mention of children's activity; the only actors in this discourse are adults who are concerned about organizational and financial aspects of the issue. Consequently, the response to orphans is constructed in similar terms. "Reducing the number of orphanages and increasing the number of adoptive families" are measures to solve the orphanhood problem, as is the "the protection of lodging and property rights" (Golubnichy, 2008).

In modern mass media, this discourse does not demonstrate a maximum level of inclusion, but it is a positive step in this direction as it occupies the place in public discourse that once belonged to discourses of social danger and social self-justification. The transition from accusations to constructive actions offers a real opportunity to improve the situation with orphaned children.

Discourse of Social Partnership

While my research conducted between 2002 and 2005 demonstrated the emergence of this type of discourse, it was very rare. However, between 2008 and 2009, a social partnership discourse became much more prevalent and appeared in about 40% of the articles in the Russian national mass media and in more than 50% of the articles in the regional media.

This discourse constructs orphans as the consequence of social inequality—therefore; the problem of orphans belongs to the whole society. It is "the problem of whole Russia" (State Duma Parliamentary Report, 2002). Orphans and "children from problem families" are represented not as the object of social assistance, but rather as independent subjects: these are "little compatriots" (Bryntseva, 2009) or "young people." (Bitkina, 2009). This discourse leads to corresponding solutions that involve some collective action and presuppose the integration of social forces and the state. For example, a specific suggestion to prevent orphaned children is to turn to public organizations and associations as important structures of civil society. Through public organizations, volunteers provide children with assistance in difficult situations, or children can get help in the form of adoptive or patronage families.

This discourse emphasizes the importance of the cooperation among all parties involved and the important role of social partnerships, both in creating social programs and in providing people with social service. The authorities are given the responsibility of coordinating and directing the joint efforts: "Social partnership among the government authority and social organizations allows for the effective solution of critical social problems that arise from the insufficiency of one's own resources" (Syryamkina, 2005). Social partnership among authorities, public and religious organizations, as well as mass media enables effective solutions to the urgent social problems of orphaned children and promotes inclusion of the children into society.

In examining the development of discourses about orphaned children in Russian mass media in recent years, one should mention a comforting tendency that the discourse on social danger (expressing ideas of social exclusion and alienation of orphan-children) is declining while discourses of social integration (reflecting ideas of social inclusion) have become considerably stronger.

Table 20.3 Discourses About Orphaned Children in Perestroika Years (2002–2005; 2008–2009)

Discourse types	Attitude toward orphans	Image of orphans	Characteristic features of orphans	Ways to solve problems
Discourse of social danger	Exclusion and alienation	Juvenile beggars, thieves, street ragamuffin, neglected anarchy, million strong army of little social outcasts	Threaten society, take in the ideology of the social bottom, take part in grown-ups' crimes	Reduce influx, catch, fight, speed up the adoption of the Federal Law, introduce amendments into criminal code
Discourse of self-justification	Search for the guilty	Children from problem families, children of illegal immigrants, neglected children, abandoned and unattended children	Suffer, are subject to violence on the part of their parents or guardians, suffer from their parents' carelessness	Establish strict police in relation to families, conduct pedagogical work with parents, deprive of parental rights, raise parents' responsibility
Discourse of social responsibility	Orphan-children as an object of assistance	Orphanage leavers, orphan's unsettled state, nobody's children, graduates of orphanages	Face many problems both in the orphanage and after they leave it	Reducing the number of orphanages and increasing the number of adoptive families, the protection of lodging and property rights
Discourse of social partnership	Social integration in solving problems of orphan-children	Orphans are children from problem families	Father and mother are busy looking for food, children work with peers and grown-ups, acquire skills of business communication, creative mutual aid, and responsibility	At institutions there appear public associations; work in partnership with the nongovernmental organizations, social partnership of the authority with public organizations

Although the Russian national and regional mass media have approximately identical structures, the discourses within each differ to some extent. While the prominence of the discourse of social danger is equal both in national and regional mass media, the regional mass media include a greater variety of other discourses. For example, the occurrence of the discourse of social partnership is considerably larger in regional media (52%) than in national mass media (44%) while the prominence of the discourses of social responsibility and social self-justification is less. And this is not accidental. My research demonstrated that a discourse of social partnership (2002 to 2005) was constructed primarily by municipal officials for whom solving the problems of orphan-children occupied a considerable place in their daily routine—unlike federal officials. Municipal officials in the provinces have been concerned with the issues of collective action involving the integration of different public and state forces. This initiative in the provinces displays the sound potential of civil society.

The professional journalists, authorities, representatives of public organizations, and citizens who shape public discourse in mass media produced a dominant discourse of social self-justification (43%). The discourse of social partnership (33%) turned out to be predominant among those that presented the authorities' viewpoint. By contrast, journalists' utilized both a discourse of social partnership (45%) and a discourse of social self-justification (25%). Journalists relied on discourses that displayed a higher level of inclusion in comparison with state authorities who more and more often were inclined to blame parents instead of cooperating with the society and trying to solve the orphans' problems.

CONCLUSION

Throughout this chapter I have demonstrated how the discursive construction of orphaned children has changed in relationship to different attitudes, times, and political discourses. The characteristics attributed to orphaned children changed depending on the politics of the time. Thus, the discourse of social danger characterized them as being juvenile delinquents, defective, and a criminal element, while discourse of social sympathy focused on their being unattended, hungry and homeless, and as having no clothes and shoes. The discourse of social utility invoked the common qualities of children, teenagers, boys and girls, and guys. Depending on the discourse, the same children acquire different characteristics. Accordingly, every discourse type contributes, in its own way, to measures the authorities should take to solve the problem of orphaned children. For instance, the discourse of social danger prescribes these actions: to call to account, to punish by people's courts, to detain, to send to militia (police) stations, and to isolate. The discourse of social self-justification suggests imposing a strict policy in relation to the families

where children do not get the necessary development, bringing up parents with the help of administrative measures, and deprivation of parental rights. By examining the changing discourses over time, we see how the opportunities for the orphans' integration into society change as well.

The discourse of social danger turned out to be fairly stable—both in its use and in its consequence of socially excluding orphans by representing them as a menace to social stability, law, and order. The discourse of social danger in the 1920s is virtually the same as the one in the early 21st century; it presupposes not only state power but also legislative measures to solve the problem.

Three very different discourses turned out to be the most positive ones from the point of view of social integration of orphan-children: in the social utility discourse of 1920 to 1926, there was the idea that orphaned children must be included into society as they can become its useful members; the social unity discourse of 1941 to 1946 considered assistance and help to orphaned children to be a meaningful and patriotic business, a duty not only before their parents, but before the Motherland as well; finally, the social partnership discourse of 2003 to 2005 considered the role of orphaned children to be a very important starting point for the integration of the whole Russian society. During the Great Patriotic War (1941–1945) the only discourse supported by the state promoted the social integration of orphaned children, but during both the postrevolution and modern periods, the discursive space of mass media appeared to be much more diverse. However, in this case it turned out that monodiscoursiveness was not all bad and greater diversity of discourses does not mean that they all will promote social integration of orphaned children. Today, the discourse of social partnership has great possibilities. Incorporating a wider discourse of civil society, it initiates development of institutions in the process of solving a particular social problem (the problem of orphaned children) and may help orphans to become part of a national discourse that is able to unite Russians.

Table 20.4 Political Discourses About Orphaned Children, 1920–2006

1920–1926		1941–1946		2003–2006	
Types of discourse	*Attitude toward orphans*	*Types of discourse*	*Attitude toward orphans*	*Types of discourse*	*Attitude toward orphans*
Discourse of social danger	Exclusion and alienation			Discourse of social risk (danger)	Exclusion and alienation
Discourse of social sympathy	Recognition of defectiveness			Discourse of self-justification	Search for the guilty
Discourse of social responsibility	Orphans as an object of rendering assistance and help			Discourse of social responsibility	Orphans as an object of rendering assistance and help
Discourse of social utility	Social integration of orphans	Discourse of social unity	The Soviet people is a common family also orphans are the children of all soviet people	Discourse of social partnership	Integration of the society in solving the problems of orphans

(Right margin arrows: **Exclusion** ↑ / **Inclusion** ↓)

Notes

1. I define social exclusion to mean the multidimensional cumulative process which breaks social connections of individuals or groups and which hinders them from participating in social life, and the state of estrangement of individuals or groups which appears as a result of this process.

2. This is the period of the Soviet Union involvement in World War II.

3. Novocherkassk is a city in Rostov Oblast, Russia, the nearest small town to Rostov-on-Don.

4. The years 1921 to 1922 are known in the history of Russia as a period of terrible famine, which caused serious consequences for the young Soviet Republic. About 5 million people became victims of this famine. In 1921, the Bolsheviks' government created the Central Committee of Aid to the Starving People to fight famine. This committee was dissolved in 1922 and it was reorganized into the Central Committee of Fighting the Consequences of Famine. The Don Committee of Fighting the Consequences of Famine was a regional branch of the central committee, specifically in the Don Region.

5. Mayak is a radio broadcasting company in Russia, which broadcasts news, talk shows, and popular music and is also responsible for the youth music channel.

References

Abdurakhmanov, A. (1943, April 11). Our care and attention to the families of our Motherland defenders. *Izvestiya [Newspaper]*.

Astoyants, M. (2009). The prevention of neglect: Is it still in the emergency regime? (Based on the data of the Rostov region). *The Journal of Social Policy Studies, 7*(2), 175–196.

Bayeva, L. K. (1977). *Social policy of October Revolution. (Oct. 1917–end of 1918).* Moscow, RU: Politizdat.

Bitkina S. (2009, January 27). New home out of turn. *Rossiyskaya Gazeta.*

Bryntseva G. (2009, March 25). Orphan across the ocean. *Rossiyskaya Gazeta.*

Dmitrieva V. (2005). Creation of conditions for joint solution of the problems. *Social orphanhood is on the agenda: "Children of the streets" on the pages of regional newspapers.* Retrieved from http://www.tolerance.ru/biblio/siroti/0-2_dmitrieva.html.

Dorokhova, T. (2005). Formation of the system of social upbringing in Russia in the 20s of the 20th century. In P.V. Romanov & E. R. Yarskaya-Smirnova (Eds.), *Need and order: History of social work in Russia, 20th Century* (pp. 397–411). Saratov, RU: Naychnaya kniga.

Editorial Information. (1943, April 11). *Izvestiya.*

Editorial Information. (1943, August 21). *Izvestiya.*

Editorial Information. (1943, October 7). *Izvestiya.*

Editorial Information. (1943, October 13). *Izvestiya.*

Editorial Information. (1943, October 30). *Izvestiya.*

Editorial Information. (1944, April 7). *Molot.*

Editorial Information. (1944, April 8). *Molot.*

Editorial Information. (1944, April 21). *Molot.*

Editorial Information. (1944, April 28). *Izvestiya*

Fairclough, N. (1992). *Discourse and social change.* Cambridge, UK: Polity Press.

Fedorinov, E., Domcheva, E., Ruzanova, H., Dobrynina, C., & Krivoshapko, Y. (2005, September 6). Past school: Thousands of children in the capitol did not go to school on the 1st of September. *Rossiyskaya Gazeta* [Government newspaper].

Foucault, M. (1996). *Archeology of knowledge.* Kiev, UA: Nika-center.

Fridinskiy, S. (2005, April 12). Criminal age: Head office of public prosecutor suggests creating federal service and network of working schools to eliminate orphanhood. *Rossiyskaya Gazeta.*

Golubnichiy, A. (2008, April 15). There will be more adoptive families. *Gazeta Nashe Vremya.*

Jorgensen, M., & Phillips, L. (2002). *Discourse analysis as theory and method.* London, UK: SAGE.

Kavskaya, N. (1943, August 21). Returned childhood. *Izvestiya.*

Kulikov, V. (2009, January 15). A flat from general prosecutor. *Rossiyskaya Gazeta.*

Maksyukevich, O. (2009, October 7). Orphans will be looked after. *Rossiyskaya Gazeta.*

Melikhova, E. (2008, December 10). Mummy treated Lyuba with pills for sclerosis almost to death. *Gazeta Vecherniy Rostov.*

Olenev, A. (2009, October 26). In technical school an orphan killed a PE teacher deliberately and in cold blood. *Gazeta Vecherniy Rostov.*

One shouldn't infringe upon orphans' rights. (2008, September 3). *Gazeta Vecherniy Rostov.*

Public Chamber of the Russian Federation. (2010, December 30). *Report on the condition of the civil society in the Russian Federation for 2010.* Retrieved May 30, 2011, from http://www.oprk.ru/news/462.

Sidibe P. (2008, April 2). All together. *Rossiyskaya Gazeta.*

State Duma discusses state measures to support orphan children. (2002, October 7). *Report of Parliamentary Hearings of the State Duma.* Radio Station *Mayak* [On air broadcast]. Retrieved from http://www.radiomayak.ru.

Stepura, I. (2008, April 15). Wolf cubs syndrome. *Rossiyskaya Gazeta.*

Syryamkina, E. (2005). Social partnership of authorities and public organizations in solving the problem of preventive measures against orphanhood. *Social Orphanhood is on the Agenda: "children of the streets" on the Pages of Regional Newspapers.* Retrieved from http://www.tolerance.ru/biblio/siroti/0-2_sirymkina.html.

Tkachyova, T. (2008, December 11). Kindness reflex. *Rossiyskaya Gazeta.*

ABOUT THE EDITOR

Celine-Marie Pascale is an associate professor in the Department of Sociology at American University, Washington, D.C., where she teaches courses on language and inequality. Her primary scholarly interest is in exploring the (re)production of culture, knowledge, and power through sociological analyses of language and representation. Her scholarship is informed by expertise in qualitative methodologies and contemporary theory.

Professor Pascale received the 2008 Distinguished Contribution to Scholarship Book Award from the American Sociological Association Section on Race, Gender, and Class for her first book, *Making Sense of Race, Gender and Class: Commonsense, Power and Privilege in the United States* (Routledge, 2007). In 2012, Professor Pascale received the Distinguished Contribution to Qualitative Inquiry book award from the International Congress of Qualitative Inquiry for her second book, *Cartographies of Knowledge: Exploring Qualitative Epistemologies* (Sage in 2010). Dr. Pascale's scholarship also is published in numerous national and international peer-reviewed journals.

Professor Pascale serves as president of the Research Committee on Language and Society for the International Sociological Association and is a former Research & Media Fellow of the Center for Social Media at American University.

ABOUT THE CONTRIBUTORS

Kjerstin Andersson is Assistant Professor at the Department of Child Studies at Linköping University. In 2008, she defended her dissertation, *Talking violence, constructing identity: Young but in institutional care*. Her research interests include identity, masculinity, and violence. She can be contacted at k.b.a.andersson@gmail.com.

Margarita S. Astoyants is a Professor of Sociology and Head of the Applied Sociology Department and a member of the Faculty of Sociology and Political Science in the South Federal University, Russian Federation. She graduated from the Rostov State Pedagogical University in the field of social work. She has worked as a social worker at a shelter for orphans for 8 years. Her professional interests are social orphanhood and problems of social exclusion. She has published more than 70 scientific articles, including four monographs: *Universe of orphanhood in Soviet and Postsoviet Russia* (2007); *Social exclusion in contemporary Russian society: Sociocultural analysis* (2007); *Social orphanhood: Strategies, dynamics, & mechanisms of social exclusion* (2009); and *Social orphanhood: Problems & outlooks of inclusion* (2010). She won the American Council of Learned Societies' short-term grant in the humanities. Research topics included, *The social exclusion of orphans in Russian society: Ideological and practical analysis (Soviet and Postsoviet period)* and the President of Russian Federation's grant for state supporting of young scientists, *Social orphanhood: Problems & outlooks of inclusion*. She can be contacted at AstoyancMS@yandex.ru.

Nataša Simeunović Bajić holds a Ph.D. and is an Assistant Professor teaching Cultural Politics and Communication History at the Faculty of Culture and Media at the Megatrend University in Belgrade, Serbia. Professor Simeunović Bajić's background in Media Studies, Cultural Studies, and Political Science has shaped her interest in cultural politics, social analysis, ethnic minorities, and media representations. She has published several significant works in national and international scientific journals and presented several conference papers in Serbia and abroad. Currently, she is involved in two research projects for the Ministry of Education and Science of the Republic of Serbia. She can be contacted at vasariste@gmail.com or nsimeunovic@megatrend.edu.rs.

Shiao-Yun Chiang holds a Ph.D. in Communication and Sociology at the State University of New York at Albany and is on the faculty of the Department of Communication Arts of the State University of New York at Oneonta, New York. His recent research interests include social semiotics, intercultural pragmatics, interethnic relations, and instructional interaction. He has produced a large number of publications in international journals regarding language and social interaction within and across cultural boundaries. He teaches courses in intercultural communication and interpersonal communication at SUNY. He can be contacted at John.Chiang@oneonta.edu.

Hae Yeon Choo is an Assistant Professor of Sociology at the University of Toronto, Canada. Her research centers on the intersections of gender, sexuality, transnational migration, and citizenship for understanding the changing dynamics of complex inequalities. Her interest in using intersectional analysis empirically informs her articles in *Sociological Theory* and *Gender & Society.* She is working on her book manuscript, *Contentious Citizenship: Gender, Migration, and the Practice of Rights in South Korea,* a comparative ethnographic analysis of gendered migrant incorporation regarding migrant factory workers, marriage migrants, and military camptown bar hostesses. Her second research project, "Cartographies of Gender: The Dynamics of Global Stratification in Gender-Related Refugee Case Law," examines the shifting dynamics of global stratification that emerge from the encounter between women refugee claimants and adjudicators at the site of refugee case law in Canada. She can be contacted at hy.choo@utoronto.ca.

Dr. Maya Khemlani David is a professor on the Faculty of Languages and Linguistics at the University of Malaya. She received the Linguapax Award in 2007 and is an Honorary Fellow of the Chartered Institute of Linguists, United Kingdom and an Honorary Member of the Foundation of Endangered Languages. As a sociolinguist, Dr. David has a special interest in discourse analysis, languages in Malaysian minority communities, and the role of language in establishing and maintaining national unity within and across cultures. She can be contacted at mayadavid@ yahoo.com.

Dr. Caesar DeAlwis is a senior lecturer at MARA University of Technology (UiTM) in Sarawak, Malaysia. His research interests focus on the identity of minority groups, language choices, marriage, and migration in East Malaysia. As a sociolinguist, he has a special interest in

identity and assimilation of children from mixed marriages in Malaysia. He can be contacted at caesardealwis@gmail.com.

Dr. Francisco Perlas Dumanig is a Senior Lecturer at the Faculty of Languages and Linguistics, University of Malaya, Kuala Lumpur, Malaysia. He has published and presented a number of research articles in the Philippines, United States, Australia, Japan, Malaysia, Singapore, Indonesia, and Thailand. His research interests are in language teaching, cross-cultural communication, world Englishes, and discourse analysis. He can be contacted at fdumanig@yahoo.com.

Dr. Eoin Devereux is Senior Lecturer and Head of Department at the Department of Sociology at University of Limerick, Ireland. A media sociologist, he is the author of *Understanding The Media,* 2nd edition (2007) and the editor of *Media Studies: Key Issues and Debates* (2007) both published by Sage. Eoin's book, *Devils and Angels: Television, Ideology, and the Coverage of Poverty* (1998, John Libbey) examined how Irish public service broadcasting explained poverty. A fan of the singer Morrissey, Eoin coedited a book (with Aileen Dillane and Martin J. Power), *Morrissey: Fandom, Representations and Identities* (2011, Intellect Books). His essay "Heaven Knows We'll Soon Be Dust, The Smiths, Catholicism, and Fan Devotion" was published in *Why Pamper Life's Complexities?* (2010, Manchester University Press) edited by Colin Coulter and Sean Campbell. He can be contacted at eoin.devereux@ul.ie.

Dr. Ricarda Drüeke is a senior scientist in the Department of Communication Studies at the University of Salzburg, Austria. She holds a Ph.D. from the Department of Communication Studies at the University of Salzburg and an MA in Political Sciences and Sociology from the University of Hamburg, Germany. Her research interests are political communication, online communication, and theories of the public sphere. She is also involved in a study researching the interconnections between culture, ethnicity, gender, and class in the representations of migrants in the mass media. She can be contacted at ricarda.drueeke@sbg.

Antke Engel is director of the Institute for Queer Theory in Berlin, a site where academic debate meets up with political activism and artistic/cultural practices. She received her Ph.D. in Philosophy at Potsdam University and works as independent scholar in the fields of queer, feminist, and poststructuralist theory, political philosophy, and cultural politics. She held visiting professorships at Hamburg University (2003 & 2005) and at Vienna University (2011), and was a research fellow at the Institute for Cultural Inquiry (ICI/Berlin, 2007 to 2009). She has published two monographies: *Wider die Eindeutigkeit* (*Against Unambiguousness*) (2002, Antke Engel) and *Bilder von Sexualität und Ökonomie* (Images of Sexuality and Economy) (2009, Antke Engel) and is coeditor of *Hegemony and Heteronormativity* (2011, Ashgate). She can be contacted at www.queer-institut.de and mail@queer-institut.de.

Myra Marx Ferree is the Alice H. Cook Professor of Sociology at the University of Wisconsin-Madison and Director of the European Union Center of Excellence. She is a long-time student of women's movements, especially in the United States, Germany, and the European Union. Her latest book is *Varieties of Feminism: German Gender Politics in Global Perspective* (2012, Stanford University Press). In politics Politics & Society, Social Politics, Gender & Society, and the American Sociological Review. Her previous books include *Shaping Abortion Discourse: Democracy and the Public Sphere in Germany and the U.S.* (2002) and *Global Feminism: Women's Activism, Organizing and Human Rights* (2006) and she is coediting a collection on new gender perspectives on human security issues. She can be contacted at mferree@ssc.wisc.edu.

Nadezhda Georgieva-Stankova is an MA graduate of the University of Veliko Turnovo, Bulgaria in English Philology and British Cultural Studies (1998) and the Sociology Department of the Central European University (CEU)

of Warsaw (2002). She defended her Ph.D. dissertation at the Graduate School for Social Research (GSSR), Institute of Philosophy and Sociology (IFiS) at the Polish Academy of Sciences (PAN) in 2006 on the topic *Reconfiguring Ethnic Identity: Romani Ethnogenesis and Cultural Emancipation in the Contemporary Context of Bulgarian Society*. She has taught English language, Cultural Studies, and Mass Media as Assistant Professor at the University of Veliko Turnovo and Warsaw University. Currently she is Chief Assistant Professor at Trakia University (Stara Zagora, Bulgaria) and teaches Economic Sociology and Mass Media at the Economics Faculty. Dr. Georgieva-Stankova is also coeditor with S. Eliaeson of the book, *New Europe: Growth to Limits?* (2010, Bardwell). Her main interests include nationalism, race, ethnicity, identity construction, and mass media. She can be contacted at nadyageorgieva@yahoo.com.

Dr. Amanda Haynes is a lecturer in Sociology at the University of Limerick. Amanda's research interests center on the analysis of discursive constructions as processes of exclusion and strategies for inclusion. Amanda's publications include "At the Edge: Media Constructions of a Stigmatised Irish Housing Estate" (with E. Devereux and M. J. Power), in the *Journal of Housing and The Built Environment* (26:2); "Behind The Headlines: Media Coverage of Social Exclusion in Limerick City—The Case of Moyross" (with E. Devereux and M. J. Power) in *Understanding Limerick,* Cork University Press; *How Politicians Construct Transnational EU Migrants* (with M. J. Power and E. Devereux), Limerick: Doras Luimní; and "Mass Media Re-Presentations of the Social World: Ethnicity and 'Race'" in E. Devereux (Ed.), *Media Studies: Key Issues and Debates,* London: Sage. She can be contacted at Amanda.haynes@ul.ie.

Dr. Susanne Kirchhoff is a postdoctoral assistant in the Department of Communication Studies at the University of Salzburg, Austria. She graduated from the University of Göttingen, Germany with a master's degree in German and American Literature, and in Communication Studies. Her main areas of research and teaching are journalism studies, media and war, discourse analysis, and gender studies. She is currently involved in a study on changes in the field of professional journalism. Recent publications include work on legitimization strategies in the media after September 11th, journalistic careers in Austria, and media representations of female soldiers. She can be contacted at susanne.kirchhoff@sbg.ac.at.

Dr. Elisabeth Klaus is professor and chair of the Department of Communication at the University of Salzburg, Austria. Her focus in research and in her teachings is feminist media studies, popular culture, and theories of the public sphere. She is involved in a study researching the interconnections between culture, ethnicity, gender, and class in the representations of migrants in the mass media. Her numerous publications include: *Kommunikationswissenschaftliche Geschlechterforschung. Zur Bedeutung der Frauen in den Massenmedien und im Journalismus (Media Gender Studies. On the Importance of Women in Mass Media and Journalism)* (2005, Halem Verlag); *Media Industry, Journalism Culture and Communication Policies in Europe* (coeditor, 2007, Lit Verlag); *Identität und Inklusion im europäischen Sozialraum (Identity and Inclusion in the European Social Space)* (coeditor, 2010, VS Verlag). She can be contacted at elisabeth.klaus@sbg.ac.at.

Laura García Landa is a full-time professor at the Center of Foreign Languages (CELE) at the National Autonomous University of Mexico. She teaches Sociolinguistics and Language Policy and Planning in the undergraduate and postgraduate programs in Applied Linguistics at CELE. She leads the project "Language Diversity: The Uses and Functions of Language by the University Community at UNAM" and participated in the project "Vitality of Indigenous Languages in Mexico: A Study in Three Contexts"

granted by PAPITT, Programa de Apoyo a Proyectos de Investigación e Innovación Tecnológica (Supporting Program for Research and Technology Innovation Projects). Her areas of interest are Sociolinguistics, and Language in Education Policy and Planning. She coedited with Roland Terborg the book, *Los retos de la planificación del lenguaje en el siglo XXI* (The Challenges of Language Policy in the 21st Century) (2006, UNAM) and *Muerte y vitalidad de las lenguas indígenas y las presiones sobre sus hablantes* (Death and Vitality of Indigenous Languages and the Pressures on their Speakers) (2011, UNAM), She can be contacted at laura.garcia@cele.unam.mx.

Dr. Jackie Jia Lou is an assistant professor in the Department of English, City University of Hong Kong. Her primary research interest lies in the discursive and semiotic construction of place and the ways in which cultural, economic, and political forces underpin such constructions. She is also engaged in projects that investigate the kinds of creative language use mediated by new communication technologies, particularly in the contexts of globalization. In both strands of research, her work combines a variety of methodologies, including ethnographic fieldwork, qualitative discourse analysis, quantitative variation analysis, and visual semiotic analysis. She can be contacted at jialou@cityu.edu.hk.

Weizhun Mao is a doctoral student at the Department of Political and Public Administration, University of Konstanz, Germany. He is interested in Chinese Studies, Conflict Studies, Global Governance, and Political Methodology. He has published several papers in Chinese journals (e.g., *World Economics and Politics* and *Quarterly Journal of International Politics*) and at a few international conferences (such as the European Political Science Association Annual Conference). Prior to the doctorate program at University of Konstanz, he received his Ph.D. in International Relations (2012) from Renmin University of China; his master's degree in International Humanitarian Actions (2007) from

Ruhr University in Bochum, Germany; a master's degree in International Politics (2006) from Nankai University, China; and his bachelor's degree in Political Studies (2004) from Nanjing University, China. He can be contacted at Department of Politics and Public Administration, University of Konstanz, Universitätsstr. 10, 78457, Konstanz, Germany and maoweizhun@gmail.com.

Sanya Osha currently works as a research fellow for South African Research Chairs Initiative (SARChI) at the Institute for Economic Research on Innovation (IERI) at Tshwane University of Technology in South Africa. His previous work has appeared in *Transition, Research in African Literatures, African Review of Books,* and the *Blackwell Encyclopedia of Twentieth Century Fiction*. In 2010, the *Oxford Encyclopedia of African Thought* published a series of his articles on knowledge. His latest book is *Postethnophilosophy* (2011, Rodopi). He can be contacted at babaosha@yahoo.com.

Valentina Pagliai is currently an Adjunct Assistant Professor at CUNY Queens College, Queens, New York. She received her Ph.D. from University of California, Los Angeles (UCLA) in 2000 in Linguistic Anthropology. Her main areas of research are racial formation processes in discourse, gender, and sexuality, and argumentative language. She recently guest edited an issue for the *Journal of Linguistic Anthropology* (2010, June) titled "Performing Disputes: Cooperation and Conflict in Argumentative Language." Other recent publications include "Unmarked Racializing Discourse, Facework, and Identity in Talk about Immigrants in Italy" (*Journal of Linguistic Anthropology*, August 2011). She is collaborating on a project coordinated by Luca Greco (Sorbonne, Paris III), *La présentation de soi genrée dans la parole, les textes et les conduites corporelles en interaction. Interactions, corps et culture (Gendered self-presentation in speech, text, and lines in bodily interaction. Interactions, body, and culture)*. She can be contacted at valentina.pagliai@qc.cuny.edu.

Dr. Martin J. Power is a Lecturer in Sociology at the University of Limerick, with a specific focus on the sociology of urban regeneration. His research interests include social class, inequality and social exclusion, and Neoliberalism and the retraction of the Welfare State. His most recent publications include, "Tarring everyone with the same shorthand? Journalists, stigmatization & social exclusion," in *Journalism: Theory, Practice & Criticism,* (2012, 13:4, 500–517), and "At the Edge: Media Constructions of a Stigmatised Irish Housing Estate," in the *Journal of Housing and the Built Environment,* (2011, *26*:2, 123–142) (both with E. Devereux & A. Haynes). In 2011, Martin coedited *Morrissey: Fandom, Representations, and Identities* (with E. Devereux & A. Dillane) published by Intellect Books, and *Marxist Perspectives on Irish Society* (with M. Flynn, O. Clarke, & P. Hayes) published by Cambridge Scholars. He can be contacted at martin.j.power@ul.ie.

Viviane Ramalho has a Ph.D. in Linguistics (Language and Society). She is a Professor of the Linguistics Graduate Program at the University of Brasília (UnB) and assistant coordinator of the Language and Society Research Center (NELiS/CEAM). She develops research on communication in health and education, with a focus on Critical Discourse Analysis. Dr. Ramalho has published the following books: *Análise de discurso (para a) crítica: O texto como material de pesquisa (Critical discourse analysis: Texts as research material,* Ramalho, V. & Resende, V. M. (2011, Pontes)); *Análise de discurso crítica da publicidade: Um estudo sobre a promoção de medicamentos no Brasil (Critical discourse analysis of advertising: A study on endorsement of medication in Brazil* (2010, LabCom)); and *Análise de Discurso Crítica (Critical discourse analysis,* Resende, V. M. & Ramalho, V. (2006, Contexto). She can be contacted at vivi@unb.br.

Viviane de Melo Resende received her Ph.D. in Linguistics (Language and Society) from the

University of Brasília (UnB), Brazil. Professor of the Linguistics Graduate Program and Coordinator of the Núcleo de Estudos de Linguagem e Sociedade (NELiS—Language and Society Research Center) at the University of Brasília, she is also a member of the Red latinoamericana de estudios del discurso de las personas sin techo o en situación de extrema pobreza (REDLAD—Latin American Network of discourse studies on homeless and extreme poverty). Author of several books and papers on critical discourse analysis, her main research interests are social movement theory, critical realism, discourse, ethnography, poverty, and social mobilization. She can be contacted at viviane.melo.resende@gmail.com.

Hemant Shah is a professor in the School of Journalism and Mass Communication at the University of Wisconsin-Madison, where he is also affiliated with the Asian American Studies Program and the Global Studies Program. His research and teaching focus is on the intersection of race/ethnicity, and nation and global flows of culture. Dr. Shah is the author of *The Production of Modernization: Daniel Lerner, Mass Media and the Passing of Traditional Society* (2011, Temple University Press), *Newspaper Coverage of Interethnic Conflict: Competing Visions of America* (2004, Sage), and coeditor of *Re-Orienting Global Communication: Indian and Chinese Media Beyond Borders* (2010, University of Illinois Press). He can be contacted at hgshah@wisc.edu.

Ebru Sungun is a Ph.D. candidate at the Department of Sociology, Ecole des Hautes Etudes en Sciences Sociales, EHESS, Paris. The title of her research is "The perils of the proactive security policies after 9/11 in France and Britain and the Islam; the Enemy within." Her areas of scholarly interest include feminist theory, postcolonial theory, ethnography of the state, political sociology, and gender politics in the everyday life of Turkey. Her recent publication is "The French Ban on Headscarf: Rendering Racism Respectable," coauthored with Professor Erzsébet Barát from University of Szeged, Hungary. This publication will be used as teaching material by the ATGEN-DER (The European Association for Gender Research, Education and Documentation) series, "Teaching with Gender" in the volume, *Teaching Race with a Gendered Edge*. She can be contacted at ebrusungun@gmail.com.

Roland Terborg is Associate Professor in the Department of Applied Linguistics, Center of Foreign Languages in the National Autonomous University of Mexico. He teaches in the master's degree program in Applied Linguistics. His research interests are in sociolinguistics, especially language shift. He spent over two years working on language death in the Mayan region in Yucatan, Mexico. He has taught at the Free University in Berlin, the University of Sonora, the University of Veracruz, the Autonomous Metropolitan University, and the Autonomous University of the State of Mexico. He is coeditor of the collections *Language: Issues of Inequality* (2003, UNAM); *Los retos de la planificación del lenguaje en el siglo XXI (The Challenges of Language Policy in the 21st Century)* (2006, UNAM); and *Muerte y vitalidad de las lenguas indígenas y las presiones sobre sus hablantes (Death and Vitality of Indigenous Languages and the Pressures on Their Speakers)* (2011, UNAM). He can be contacted at rterborg@unam.mx.

Roberta Villalón is an Associate Professor at Saint John's University in New York City. Originally from Argentina, her background in political science and international relations, together with her expertise in Latin America, Latin American immigrants, and feminist theory and praxis, has distinctively shaped her sociological perspective. Her publications all illustrate her global feminist politics: *Violence against Latina Immigrants: Citizenship, Inequality and Community* (2010, NYU Press), articles like "Feminist Activist Research and Strategies from within the Battered Immigrant Women's Movement," in *Interface: A Journal for and about Social Movements* (2011, 3, 2)), "Neoliberalism, Corruption and Legacies of Contention: Argentina's Social Movements, 1993–2006," in *Latin American Perspectives* (2007, *34*, 2), and her chapter "Accounts of Violence against Women: The Potential of Realistic Fiction," in *Men Who Hate Women and Women Who Kick Their Asses!: Stieg Larsson's Millennium Trilogy in Feminist Perspective* (edited by King and Smith, 2012, Vanderbilt University Press). Roberta is currently writing an article that analyzes the effects of the recent economic crisis and anti-immigration environment in the battered women's movement in the United States (forthcoming in the *Journal of Civil Rights and Economic Development*), and editing a Special Issue on the politics of collective memory-making in Latin American democracies for the journal *Latin American Perspectives*. Visit *https://sites .google.com/site/robertavillalonphd/home* for updates, and contact her at villalor@stjohns .edu.

Kevin Whitehead is a Senior Lecturer at the University of the Witwatersrand, Johannesburg, South Africa. He obtained his Ph.D. in Sociology, with an interdisciplinary emphasis in Language, Interaction, and Social Organization from the University of California, Santa Barbara. His research focuses on the development of an ethnomethodological, conversation analytic approach to studying race and other categorical forms of social organization and inequality. In particular, he is interested in the ways in which racial and other social categories are used, resisted, and reproduced in talk-in-interaction. He can be contacted at kevin.whitehead@wits .ac.za.

⑤SAGE research**methods**

The essential online tool for researchers from the world's leading methods publisher

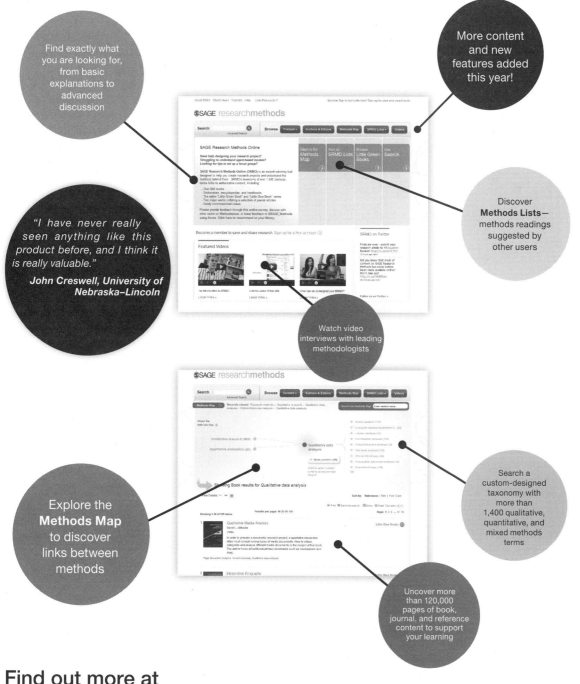

Find exactly what you are looking for, from basic explanations to advanced discussion

More content and new features added this year!

"I have never really seen anything like this product before, and I think it is really valuable."

John Creswell, University of Nebraska–Lincoln

Discover **Methods Lists**— methods readings suggested by other users

Watch video interviews with leading methodologists

Explore the **Methods Map** to discover links between methods

Search a custom-designed taxonomy with more than 1,400 qualitative, quantitative, and mixed methods terms

Uncover more than 120,000 pages of book, journal, and reference content to support your learning

Find out more at
www.sageresearchmethods.com